Contesting Copyright

Leipzig Studies on the History and Culture of East Central Europe

Volume 8

Series editors: Christian Lübke and Maren Röger

Published in the Series:

Dietmar Müller and Stefan Troebst, eds., *Philanthropy, Conflict Management, and International Law: The 1914 Carnegie Reporton the Balkan Wars of 1912/1913* (2022)

Alfrun Kliems, *Underground Modernity: Urban Poetics in East-Central Europe, Pre- and Post-1989* (2021)

Oksana Myshlovska and Ulrich Schmid, eds., *Regionalism without Regions: Reconceptualizing Ukraine's Heterogeneity* (2019)

Hannes Siegrist and Augusta Dimou, eds., *Expanding Intellectual Property: Copyrights and Patents in Twentieth-Century Europe and Beyond* (2017)

Jérôme Bazin, Pascal Dubourg Glatigny, and Piotr Piotrowski, eds., *Art beyond Borders: Artistic Exchange in Communist Europe (1945–1989)* (2016)

Agnieszka Halemba, *Negotiating Marian Apparitions: The Politics of Religion in Transcarpathian Ukraine* (2015)

Maria Todorova, Augusta Dimou, and Stefan Troebst, eds., *Remembering Communism: Private and Public Recollections of Lived Experience in Southeast Europe* (2014)

Contesting Copyright

A History of Intellectual Property in East Central Europe and the Balkans

Augusta Dimou

CEU PRESS

Published in 2025 by
Central European University Press
an imprint of Amsterdam University Press
E-mail: ceupress@press.ceu.edu
Website: www.ceupress.com

ISBN 978-963-386-614-6 (hardcover)
ISBN 978-963-386-615-3 (ebook)
ISSN 2416-1160

Library of Congress Cataloging-in-Publication Data

Names: Dimou, Augusta author
http://id.loc.gov/authorities/names/n2009008057
http://id.loc.gov/rwo/agents/n2009008057
Title: Contesting copyright : a history of intellectual property in East Central Europe and the Balkans / Augusta Dimou.
Description: New York : Central European University Press, 2025.
Series: Leipzig studies on the history and culture of East-Central Europe, 2416-1160 | Includes bibliographical references and index.
Identifiers: LCCN 2025010123 (print) | LCCN 2025010124 (ebook)
ISBN 9789633866146 hardback | ISBN 9789633866153 adobe pdf
Subjects: LCSH: Copyright—Europe, Eastern—History | Copyright—Europe, Central—History | Copyright--Balkan Peninsula—History | Intellectual property—Europe, Eastern—History | Intellectual property—Europe, Central—History | Intellectual property—Balkan Peninsula—History
Classification: LCC KJC2655.D56 2025 (print) | LCC KJC2655 (ebook)
DDC 346.404/82--dc23/eng/20250424
LC record available at https://lccn.loc.gov/2025010123
LC ebook record available at https://lccn.loc.gov/2025010124

For Product Safety Concerns and Information please contact our EU representative:
GPSR@taylorandfrancis.com
Taylor & Francis
Verlag GmbH, Kaufingerstraße 24, 80331 München, Germany

Dedicated with Gratitude and Affection
to *Elpida Psalidas*

Who Showed Me
the "Value" of Culture

Elpida in Greek
Means
Hope!

Table of Contents

Acronyms and Abbreviations xi

Preface xiii

Acknowledgements xvii

Introduction 1

Problematique 2
Historical Background 5
Historiography 6
Methodology 9
Structure and Outline 12
Rethinking the Berne Union 17

Where It All Started: Translation 25

The Old Regime 28
A Business Model: Translations Authorized by the Author 32
Counter Positions 41
From the Printing to the Original-Copy Paradigm 45
Translation as a Cultural World System 50
Taming Difference 53
Creating Law, Modelling Literature 56
The Economy of Translation 62

The Empires of East and Southeast Europe 69

The Habsburg Empire 71
The Russian Empire 81
The Contexts of Copyright Debates 83
The 1911 Copyright Law 94
The Ottoman Empire 101
The 1910 Copyright Law 109

The Expansion of Copyright in Eastern Europe: Preconditions of Development and European Comparisons 115
Legacies of Empire 115
Publishing 117
Reading Revolutions 120
The Author 125
Modernity 129
Regulation before Copyright 130
Historical Time and Temporalities of Copyright 133

Comparisons: Europe and Beyond 135
East–West Europe 135
Empires 139
Strategies of Expansion of Intellectual Property Regimes in Europe and around the World 146
Bilateralism vs. Multilateralism 149
China 153

Orchestrated Globalization: The Expansion of Intellectual Property Rights in Southeast and East Central Europe in the Context of World War I 159
The European Book Trade and Its Models 159
The First World War and the Versailles System 171
Conclusion 184

Interwar Bulgaria 187
Before Copyright 187
The 1921 Copyright Law 191
Professionalization Processes in Culture 199
Copyright as Practice 205
Copyright and Culture in the 1930s 211
Law and Territory: The Space of the Union 217
Who Gets to Profit? 222

Interwar Yugoslavia 225
Labile Professionalization 227
Cultural Professions, Professionalization and Higher Education 234
The Social Status of the Creative Intelligentsia 238

Enter Entertainment 239
Associations and the State: Professionalization, Protectionism, Ideology 241
Theatre 246
Actors 247
The 1929 Copyright Law 252
The Dawn of a New Era: From Print to Audiovisual Media 258
Applying the Law, Interpreting the Law 260
Moral Rights 266
Applying the Law: Organizational Structures, Social Agents and Practice 269
Nationalization as a Defense Strategy 281

Interwar Czechoslovakia 289
Introduction 289
Authors Get Organized: Syndicalism and Lobbyism in Tandem 293
The Law on the Publishing Contract 298
Debating Copyright 307
The 1926 Copyright Law 313
Debating the Effect of the Berne Convention 316
A Closely Knit Network of Actors 320
Amendment of the Copyright Law in 1936 327
OSA: The Association for the Protection of Composers, Writers and Publishers of Musical Works 329
The Protectorate 332
Broad Contours of the Czechoslovak Copyright Regime before Communism 334

Comparative Perspectives on National, Regional, International and Transnational Trajectories up to and Including the Interwar Period 337
Governance Strategies of the Berne Union 337
Legacies of Empire in the Conception of Copyright Law 342
The Interwar Context and the Rise of New Media 344
Copyright in Southeast and East Central Europe 346
Actors 361
Broader Social Trends of the Interwar Period 364
Collecting Societies 366
Other Actors: Intermediaries 368
Copyright, Creative Elites and Avant-Garde Practices in the Interwar Period 370

Communist Copyright 377
Copyright in Communist Bulgaria 382
Comparative Overview of Copyright Law Development 383
JUSAUTOR: The Bulgarian Copyright Agency 389
Creative Funds 390
Contextualizing the Propertization Trend of the 1970s 392
Copyright in Communist Yugoslavia 394
Renegotiating Key Notions of Socialism 396
Precarious Balancing between Market and Ideology 399
Yugoslav Copyright Legislation: From State Governance to Self-Management to Liberal Propertization 404
Yugoslavia in the Cold War 410
Copyright in Communist Czechoslovakia 411
Some Theoretical Innovations 412
The Evolution of Copyright Legislation 414

Conclusions: COPYRIGHT IN EAST CENTRAL AND SOUTHEAST EUROPE—A LONG-TERM PERSPECTIVE 423

Sources and Bibliography 445

Index 469

Acronyms and Abbreviations

AKM	Gesellschaft der Autoren, Komponisten und Musikverleger (Austrian collecting society)
ALAI	Association Littéraire et Artistique Internationale (French authors' society)
AfmA	Anstalt für musikalisches Aufführungsrecht (forerunner of GEMA)
BC	Berne Convention for the Protection of Literary and Artistic Works
BIEM	Bureau International de l'Edition Mécanique (international collecting society for mechanical rights)
BIPRI	Bureaux Internationaux réunis pour la protection de la propriété industrielle, littéraire et artistique (forerunner of WIPO)
BU	Berne Union (i.e. Union constituted by the member states of the Berne Convention)
BUMA	Het Bureau voor Muziek-Auteursrecht (Dutch collecting society)
CISAC	Confédération Internationale des Sociétés d'Auteurs et Compositeurs (international collecting society for music rights)
CMO	Collective Management Organization (Collective Rights Management)
CP	Communist party
ČSR	Československá republika (Czechoslovak Republic)
ČSSR	Československá socialistická republika (Czechoslovak Socialist Republic)
DILIA	Divadelní, literární, audiovizuální agentura, z.s (Czech collecting society)
EDIFO	Édition phonographique et cinématographique
ΕΕΘΣ	Εταιρεία Ελλήνων Θεατρικών Συγγραφέων (Greek Company of Theatrical Authors)
GATT	General Agreement on Tariffs and Trade
GDT	Genossenschaft Deutscher Tonträger
GEMA	Gesellschaft für musikalische Aufführungs- und mechanische Vervielfältigungsrechte (German collecting society)
ICCI	International Commission of Intellectual Cooperation

ICIC	International Committee on Intellectual Cooperation
IIIC	International Institute of Intellectual Cooperation
ILO	International Labor Organization
IP	Intellectual Property
IPRs	Intellectual Property Rights
KNIK	Komitet za Nauka, Izkustvo i Kultura (Science, Art and Culture Committee, Bulgaria)
LITA	Slovenská literárna agentúra (Slovak collecting society)
OSA	Ochranný svaz autorský (Czech collecting society)
p.m.a.	post mortem auctoris
SACD	Société des Auteurs et Compositeurs Dramatiques (French playwrights' society)
SACEM	Société des Auteurs, Compositeurs et Éditeurs de Musique (French collecting society)
SOZA	Slovenský ochranný zväz autorský pre práva k hudobným dielam (Slovak collecting society for music)
STAGMA	Staatlich genehmigte Gesellschaft zur Verwertung musikalischer Urheberrechte (forerunner of GEMA)
TRIPS	Agreement on Trade-Related Aspects of Intellectual Property Rights
UFA	Universum-Film AG (German film society)
UJDA	Udruženje jugoslovenskih dramskih autora (Association of Yugoslav Theatrical Authors)
UJMA	Udruženje jugoslovenskih musičkih autora (Association of Yugoslav Music Authors)
UNESCO	United Nations Educational, Scientific and Cultural Organization
WIPO	World Intellectual Property Organization
ZAIKS	Związek Autorów i Kompozytorów Scenicznych (Polish authors' society)

Preface

There are many ways to think about culture, its purpose, function, economy and organization and the multiple actors involved in its production. The present book offers one such approach by exploring from a long-term perspective the copyright history of East and Southeast Europe. Do we need such a history? I hope the current monograph will convince you that we do.

Oddly enough, in the popular mind, copyright and culture are strange and distant bedfellows; the first is a tedious and arcane instrument of legal experts, the second the site where marvels of creativity and the imagination are born. Allegedly, they barely impinge on one another save for transgressions, and moreover, the second (i.e. culture) is infinitely more significant than the first. I likewise adhered to such a view before embarking on this project. With time, I got used to the puzzled looks I encountered every time I elaborated on my research topic during conversations: What is there to say about this? And is there any depth behind the history of copyright?

Copyright designates a legal institution, a time-limited monopoly granting creators an exclusive right to dispose of their intellectual products in the way they deem best. It is commonly associated with notions like protection, ownership, property, propriety, autonomy and often imagined through these qualities as well.

Most importantly, however, copyright is also a way of talking about culture, a means of communicating, relating and coming to an understanding on the meaning and value of creative labor and the arts for society. Against this backdrop, copyright constitutes more than the plain administration of legal rules and norms. It simultaneously encompasses presumptions about the particulars of human creativity, like its very nature and scope; culture's social significance, economic function, organization, management and supervision; questions of access, proprietorship and distribution; together with the beliefs, intentions and roles of the stakeholders involved. In this regard, the historical evolution of copyright resembles more a black box than a limpid directory of action. Copyright is constituted at the nexus between law, politics, economy, society, creativity and technological change and was at different periods variably affected and shaped by those factors in a synergistic manner or separately. For that reason, copyright history is also an elusive history; it tells the story of a perpetually mutating institution. Copyright is influenced by technological innovation, political systems, corporate interests, aesthetical, legal and economic theories, ethical prescripts and assumptions about human nature, about economy and the market. Moreover, it is negotiated between actors operating on national, transnational and international levels; through collective organizations, interest groups and/or individual stakeholders; corporate, public and/or private interests participating at national, international and supranational discussions, institutions and fora. The complicity and entanglement between all these levels and actors is where (international) copyright law usually comes into being. Part of this book is about opening up the black box, by making these processes visible.

This multiplicity of factors is the reason why the history of copyright, or intellectual property (IP), cannot be narrated from a single, consistent and valid-for-all perspective, and certainly not from a sole official and rightful standpoint. In that respect, copyright and IP history will always remain a contested and multi-perspective history, also because—fortunately—human inventiveness cannot be easily made to fit in the box. Though IP history primarily focuses on the norm-creating capacity of copyright, at times it was in fact the trespassing of rules that paved the way for new models in the dissemination and commercialization of culture. For exactly the same reasons, copyright cannot be tackled sufficiently from a purely theoretical, constantly universalistic perspective, let alone by one discipline. Culture depends heavily on practices, and throughout their history humans have always been incredibly resourceful in devising, combining, altering, adapting, optimizing, circumventing and desecrating practices. This is all the more true when the media that carry cultural and intellectual goods are perpetually transformed and, moreover, when technological transformations are supplanting each other at an accelerated pace.

This is precisely the condition we are currently in, a completely new phase both in the history of humanity and IP history. The unprecedented technoeconomic transformation that was inaugurated in the 1970s is currently picking up speed as analogue technology is largely displaced through the digital revolution and artificial intelligence transforming economies and societies globally; and there is much more to come. This epoch-making change, relying greatly on human–machine interaction, touches in multiple ways on the very foundations of IP: should machine-created works be considered original on a par with human creativity? Can or should they be copyrighted? Should prompts be considered a form of creativity? What constitutes a copy? What determines value and how is it created? What constitutes the nature and limits of authorship? What is the content and nature of originality? What ought to be protected and what not? What are the ethical boundaries in human–machine interaction and how does IP relate to them? Should creativity and innovation in this new age be regulated through IP or does it represent an obsolete instrument of regulation? And if so, what should replace it? Opinions on how to tackle these all-important questions that will determine the future of the twenty-first century are divided.

Digitalization is a double-edged sword; it can lead to a gigantic concentration and monopolization of intangible resources but equally has the capacity to democratize information and knowledge. Neither of the two are self-propelled processes. As a consequence, for the first time in the roughly 200-year history of IP, publics —as producers and end users—are called to play a significant role in shaping the governance of intangible resources. This chance should not be gambled away, should not fall victim to populist promises of easy solutions or be entrusted solely to big corporations, governments and politicians. Citizens ought to have an informed opinion about the capabilities and perils of IP and data regulation, and play an active role in securing a constructive and propitious direction in the production and dissemination of knowledge and culture. The current monograph on the history of copyright in East and Southeast Europe deliberates the past, while thinking about the future that is already here.

Finally, a note on terminology and translation. The author is conscious that the terms "author's rights," "authors' rights," "copyright," "copyrights," "Intellectual Property (IP)," "Intellectual Property Rights (IPRs)" can and do signify different things, or at least contain fine semantic/philosophical differences in various expert legal cultures of the world. In the context of the current work, they are, however used neutrally and interchangeably to signify the equivalent of *droit d'auteur/Urheberrecht* without any predilection or prejudice for any one legal tradition and/or school.

All translations from all languages were conducted by the author, who carries the sole responsibility for them.

Acknowledgements

The current monograph is a revised version of my habilitation, completed in 2022 at the Institute for the Study of Culture of the University of Leipzig. I would like to express my gratitude and appreciation to the numerous institutions, friends and colleagues that helped me carry out this work and contributed in countless ways to the materialization of this publication. My research was initiated within the collaborative project "Legal and Cultural Influences in Modern East Central Europe" (Rechtskulturelle Prägungen in Ostmitteleuropa in der Moderne), at the Leibniz Institute for the History and Culture of Eastern Europe (GWZO) and between 2010 and 2012 was sponsored by the German Federal Ministry for Education and Research (BMBF). During that initial phase, which laid the groundwork for the current monograph, I conducted a large part of my research in archives and libraries. Coming full circle, the final publication was completed likewise with generous GWZO support, which included the funding for the final copyediting and proofreading of the manuscript, as well as the incorporation of the book into the institute's own book series, "Leipzig Studies on the History and Culture of East-Central Europe" with CEU Press. Additional scholarships, grants and academic sojourns provided by the Freiburg Institute of Advanced Study (FRIAS), the Gerda Henkel Foundation, the German Historical Institute in Paris (DHI) and the New Europe College, Bucharest (NEC) helped me complete diverse sections of the manuscript at different stages of the project.

I would have never entered the universe of intellectual property, nor ever dreamt of delving into such a convoluted and expert subject matter, were it not for the felicitous encounter with Hannes Siegrist at the University of Leipzig. IP is his pet subject and I developed a liking for the topic by learning to see it through his eyes. Coming from an exquisite school of comparative history, Hannes had his own particular take on the history of IP with strong influences from social and cultural history as well as sociology, and he quickly taught me to respect, but not let myself get intimidated by the legal and highly technical IP jargon, to see it for what it was: a norm-creating process with a multifaceted yet often invisible history, an institution at the intersection between creativity, society and the economy with busy actors negotiating their particularistic interests, a process situated at the heart of society and not only in the academic back rooms of legal experts. This work owes a lot to him. Our numerous and genuinely exciting discussions helped me crystallize my research questions, my thoughts and eventually my arguments. He took the time to read and helped me recover my balance whenever I seemed to get stuck or lose an important thread of inquiry. He gave generously from his own arsenal of experience, thoughts and writings.

A comparative endeavour of such a scale as this book can never be accomplished by one person alone. I had the fortune to work with and receive valuable practical support from some very competent young researchers, often themselves historians, who either helped me quickly orient myself in local contexts, and/or assisted with the collection and systematization of materials from libraries and archives. In this regard, I am deeply indebted to Jelena Rafailović in Belgrade, who was the most resourceful, effective and assiduous researcher one could ever wish for. Karin Rolle did a wonderful job helping me get an initial grasp of Czech materials. Dimitar Kalogerov was a precious source of assistance in Sofia, as was Johanna Bichlmaier at FRIAS. Several colleagues provided me with important counselling regarding archival depositories and facilitated my access to them and/or to local expertise. I would like to thank Juří Kocian, Jan Mervart and Frank Hadler regarding research in the Czech Republic. Pavel Janáček took the time to answer questions and queries, and so did Michal Kopeček.

The precarious times for academics (and not only academics) in which we currently live could not but leave their mark on this book as well. I was able to complete the very last section of my habilitation with unemployment benefit support, and though it bruised my ego badly, it was a life-saving measure, at least for this book. Though grateful for that temporary assistance, it presages nothing good for the future of academic workers. I would like to express many thanks to the members of my habilitation and expert review committee for engaging with my work and helping to bring this undertaking to a successful conclusion, particularly Maren Möhring, Hannes Siegrist, Louis Pahlow and Hannes Grandits. Equally, I would like to thank the two anonymous reviewers of CEU Press for their time and comments. The final manuscript owes a lot to the skills and tenacity of Charlotte Mosedale, who proved to be a most attentive, resourceful and diligent language editor.

Finally, special credit goes to my companion, Andreas Krauss, for going through this challenge with me. Without his undiminished support and patience, this project would never have been completed. He put me back on my feet every time I stumbled, he brought me down to earth every time I became unrealistic in my goals and ambitions, he tended to my wounds every time I lost a battle, he consoled me in my darkest hours of self-doubt and confusion. All along he ensured I got a sufficient dose of culture, fresh air, Peking duck and wine in order to endure to the end. In the final stretch, as we raced against time and all odds in order to pull off my defence on time, and while I was completely out of breath, he took charge of all bureaucratic concerns regarding the submission of my habilitation, and yet he still likes me. I cannot thank him enough for this journey.

Somewhere along the academic trail, and though I had never meant it to be this way, it became a sort of pattern to dedicate my monographs to people that have impacted me and my worldview in profound ways, and who, for this reason, I have come to deeply cherish. Most of them are no longer with us, and I missed many occasions to spend more quality time with them as I had repeatedly promised, and let them know just how much they meant to me; there was always something more urgent (usually academic stuff) to tend to. As a result, almost intuitively, my guilty conscience has chosen this arrangement in order to compensate for my failure: every time a book is born, it is dedicated to my beloved dead. It is probably this pledge that motivates me to get it finished in the first place, as if publication, almost like a shamanic rite, could bring them back to life. Admittedly, it does not work this way in the real world but it does work out in my little subjective universe.

The current monograph is dedicated to Elpida Psalidas. Elpida was a bosom friend and confidant of my mother's, though significantly older. They got acquainted while working for the Avgerinos Co., a retailer of electric appliances in Athens of the post-WWII years. Even more significantly, they resided in the same neighbourhood, the district of Nikaia, until 1940 also known as Nea Kokkinia, one of the newly-built suburbs of Piraeus created especially for the settlement of the Asia Minor refugees after 1922. Our family dwelled at the intersection of Moudanion and Costantinoupoleos streets, Elpida at the intersection of Moudanion and Ellispondou. Readers acquainted with Greek history most likely already conjecture our life itinerary and identity, frame of mind and daily rituals, all that, which formed out of our comparatively modest, working and lower middle class, "red" and quite single-minded neighborhoods, a community of destiny and solidarity.

It was wonderful growing up there, amidst homes with gardens and courtyards where the smells of fresh laundry, oriental cooking, lemon tree blossoms and jasmine intermingled. Our neighborhood was more like an extended family; I was surrounded by a group of strong-willed, audacious, energetic and resourceful women that made any theoretical feminism redundant. I simply learned by following them. I developed my own relationship with Elpida during my adolescence, when little by little, and due to the absenteeism of my real godparents, she became a surrogate godmother and eventually a good friend. As I matured and developed my own personality, our communication grew more substantial and I became a better interlocutor for her. Our language of communication was culture. Elpida was a theatre and arts enthusiast and her passion was contagious. She passed her favorite books on to me and in that delicate age, full of bittersweet aporias and universal questions, I came to read such gems as Rilke's *Briefe an einen jungen Dichter* and Kazantzakis' *Askitiki*. Above all, she delighted in theatre, and under her guidance and in her company I saw some emblematic plays and performances: Ellie Lambeti, in her last role ever in Medoff's *Children of a Lesser God*; a ferocious Tzeni Karezi in Edward Albee's *Who's Afraid of Virginia Woolf?*; the duo Moschidis and Michalakopoulos in Charles Dyer's *Staircase* and innumerable other performances. Inconspicuously, she sowed that tiny seed of magic, which with time grew into a mystical inner garden that would carry me for life, providing consolation and protection through the transformative power of culture. When I departed for studies abroad, Elpida eagerly awaited my return, and during my short sojourns in Athens she continued to feed me selflessly with cultural delicacies: audio cassettes and CDs, recorded radio emissions, newspaper clippings with interviews and reviews of important cultural events, new book releases in original or translation. Our dialogue was ongoing and as a rule took place as soon as I returned, when I paid her a visit for our time-honoured afternoon Turkish coffee. This ritual went on for years.

The socially controlled petty bourgeois environment in which we lived was both kind-hearted and generous, but equally merciless. Elpida floated in it like a fly in milk but she did not care much. Though appreciated by her surroundings, people struggled with her straightforward manner and her strange predilections for classical music and serious literature. A spinster both by choice and by destiny, she defied expectations of female roles and duties. She acted as a watchdog for her family, and had swift and eloquent ripostes at hand to counter mindless and unkind comments. She let very few people glimpse her loneliness; she had an amazing resilience and dignity. She drew much of that strength from culture. Elpida did not consume culture, she essentially lived for culture and through it. Culture in the sense of Bourdieu's social distinction, that is, as a pose befitting a certain social class or status, was completely foreign to her. Quite the contrary, she experienced culture as something as fundamentally and existentially essential as oxygen, as a form of liberation. Through culture she created her own worlds, where she breathed and lived freely. That was the conception of culture that Elpida bequeathed to me: no postures, no self-fashioning, no strings attached, only freedom.

I have carried this therapeutic dimension of culture with me as a treasure trove all along, and just like Elpida, I have repeatedly drawn strength and inspiration from its supernatural garden. During one of our last discussions, not long before she would depart forever, and in a moment of rare candidness, she confided to me, not without a tinge of sadness, how she bemoaned having missed the chance to "touch" (a direct translation of the Greek word "αγγίζω," which in a figurative sense means to have an impact on) someone in this life. This book is all about proving her wrong: Thank you, Elpida!

Chapter 1

Introduction

Since the late eighteenth century, intellectual property (IP) has developed into a major institution regulating the national, international and transnational traffic and exchange of material and immaterial goods. Now consolidated as an indispensable regulating mechanism of modern knowledge and free-market society, the historical evolution and worldwide expansion of intellectual property has been neither unilinear nor synchronic. Framed as the intersection between private and public interests, the development of intellectual property rights (IPRs) reflects the diachronic wrangling that occurs in order to balance and regulate access to, and distribution of, knowledge between creative labor, commercial interests and the common good. The consolidation and expansion of intellectual property rights followed on the heels of major social, economic, cultural and technological transformations that helped reconfigure the structures of modern European societies. These profound changes demarcated the passage from the mercantilist to the liberal economy, from manufacture to industrial production, from the dynastic to the democratic state, and finally from estate-based society to that defined by modern class. Intellectual property—among other institutions—has played a decisive role in regulating the dynamism and transformational capacity of modern societies and cultures.

Despite its ostensible institutional robustness, intellectual property has repeatedly been called into question. What ought to be the purpose and scope of knowledge, whether it should be owned just as any other form of property, and finally how it ought to be applied or exploited, are the issues that have provoked and still provoke passionate debates on a global scale. This recurrent flaring of passions is caused, on the one hand, by the speed at which technological change in particular causes major modifications to the means by which we transport, and by extension also disseminate and commercialize knowledge, a truism with diachronic validity from Gutenberg to Bill Gates. On the other hand, there is a growing awareness of humanity moving towards a knowledge-based society, where the source of economic growth and value-adding activities—so goes the argument—will increasingly rely on knowledge.[1]

---

1 See UNESCO, *Towards Knowledge Societies* (Paris: UNESCO Publishing, 2005); Nico Stehr, *Knowledge Societies* (London: Sage, 1994); Dan Schiller, *Digital Capitalism: Networking the Global Market System* (Cambridge, Mass.: MIT Press, 1999).

Along with trademarks, patents, design, trade secrets, integrated circuits and geographical indications of source, copyright forms part of general IP law. It designates a legal right, granting authors and creators of original works the exclusive prerogative to determine the use and distribution of their intellectual labor.[2] While permitting authors and creators ownership or property rights in order to protect their material interests, at the same time copyright law needs to take account of end users' and society's need for access to knowledge and information. In order to maintain a fair balance between those diverse interests, copyright protection is subject to a number of exceptions and limitations. Such restrictions include a time-limited term of protection after the expiration of which works wander into the public domain and the provision of fair uses for educational and other purposes. As a legal instrument, therefore, copyright fulfils multifarious tasks: it protects the individual output of authors; provides for predictable relationships between creators and third parties; legitimizes specific group interests in culture and the cultural industries; and finally helps govern and operate complex cultural, social, economic and political interests.[3] The institution of IP is the principal mechanism via which intangible goods enter the market of commodity exchange. Finally, copyrights are territorial rights; they come into being inexorably linked to the nationality of a work, or that of its creator and/or rights owner. International copyright law is therefore the mechanism that guarantees the exterritorialization of territorial rights and allows them literally, but also metaphorically, "to travel."

Problematique

The present work deals with the introduction of intellectual property/copyright/authors' rights in the societies of East and Southeast Europe in the course of the late nineteenth and twentieth centuries, covering to a varying extent an approximate

2 For a general orientation see Manfred Rehbinder, *Urheberrecht*, 15th ed. (Munich: C. H. Beck, 2008); Eugen Ulmer and Gerhard Schricker, eds., *International Encyclopedia of Comparative Law*, vol. XIV: Copyright (Tübingen: Mohr Siebeck, 2007); UNESCO Culture Sector, *The ABC of Copyright* (Paris: UNESCO, 2010); Jeanette Hofmann, ed., *Wissen und Eigentum: Geschichte, Recht und Ökonomie stoffloser Güter* (Bonn: Bundeszentrale für politische Bildung, 2006); Lionel Bently et al., *Intellectual Property Law*, 6th ed. (Oxford: Oxford University Press, 2022).

3 See Hannes Siegrist, "Strategien und Prozesse der 'Propretisierung' kultureller Beziehungen. Die Rolle von Urheber- und geistigen Eigentumsrechten in der Institutionalisierung moderner europäischer Kulturen (18.–20. Jh.)," in *Wissen – Märkte – geistiges Eigentum*, ed. Stefan Leible et al. (Tübingen: Mohr Siebeck, 2010), 3–11.

time span from the late imperial to the late communist period. Its core consists of a three-case interregional comparison, examining the significance and function of copyrights in Bulgaria, Yugoslavia and Czechoslovakia in the period 1918–1989. The comparative parameters are, however, on every occasion extended to include international, global and transregional comparisons that help situate East and Southeast Europe historically in a world context. Based methodologically on a broad interdisciplinary approach combining social, cultural, legal, political, literary and media history, the current book analyses the role and development of intellectual property rights in the institutionalization, development and regulation of modern culture in East Central Europe during the various phases and diverse political regimes of the late nineteenth and twentieth centuries. Particular attention is paid to the issue of continuities and/or discontinuities regarding structures and processes, tensions and conflicts of the twentieth century.

With an analytical focus on the multifarious relationships between creators (authors), commercializers, media, state authorities and the public on the one hand, and between states and international organizations on the other, the present research seeks to answer the following questions: (1) The equalization of intellectual labor to intellectual property was introduced comparatively late in parts of Eastern and South Eastern Europe and followed, moreover, varying patterns. What are the factors that account for this delay and variation in experience? (2) Were there European, national or regional principles, norms or patterns that influenced the transfer but also the configuration of the social and legal organization of culture in the examined areas? (3) Did intellectual property rights play a role, and if so to what effect, in stabilizing and/or promoting cultural processes? (4) Is there a distinction (and disparity) between the rhetoric and the practice of copyright?

Having emanated from Western Europe in the context of a specific historical constellation, IP was eventually established as a universal instrument regulating the exchange of intellectual and cultural commodities. How and why did this expansion take place? By seeking to understand the regional, international and global extension of IP, the book focuses on diverse forms, strategies, mechanisms and patterns of IP expansion and is concerned with the following generic questions: (1) How do institutions expand at the interface between national, international, transnational and global constellations of interest? (2) What forms does this expansion take? (3) Who are the actors/protagonists in this process? (4) How are national and international stakeholders brought to endorse, promote, modify or resist such developments? (5) How do authors' rights affect the relationship between private and public interests but also the interaction between the "self" and the "other"?

A precise classification of the nature of intellectual labor and production, and by consequence of the rights that emanate from it, has rather formed part of the problem than shown the pathway to its solution. This "discomfort" is reflected also in the terminological surplus surrounding our object of study. Defined at times as "authors' rights," "intellectual property rights," "copyrights," "immaterial property," "personal rights," "moral rights," "intellectual property" and so on, the multiplicity of terms denotes more than simple differences of a formal and/or philosophical nature in diverse national legal traditions. It testifies at the same time to the uneasiness surrounding the legal status of intellectual production and the extent to which it can be framed in terms of a property language equivalent to that of material commodities.

The notion of "property" has been central to this research, not because it forms the common noun behind the adjective "intellectual" in the concept of IP. Rather, in the inverse manner, my work asks the question why social and cultural relations are perceived, constructed, arranged or regulated by reference to the institution (and the ideology) of property and/or non-property,[4] and what kind of dynamic this correlation acquires in the regions of East and Southeast Europe. Why is property such a seminal concept when conceptualizing and ordering the world and society? Is IP the state of knowledge and culture, a convention, or a specific epistemological choice? What is the relationship between (intellectual) property, law, market and expansion?

Consequently, a multifunctional and polyvalent definition of IP is employed throughout this work, where intellectual property rights are thought to stand for an institution, a set of collective rules of operation, a symbolic order, a legal instrument, a power, a commercial and legal regime, but also for a metaphor and a narrative of social and cultural order.[5]

---

4 The scholarship on property and property relations is vast; see exemplarily Hannes Siegrist, ed., "Entgrenzung des Eigentums in modernen Gesellschaften und Rechtskulturen." Special issue, *Comparativ* 16, no. 5/6 (2006); Hannes Siegrist and David Sugarman, eds., *Eigentum im internationalen Vergleich, 18.–20. Jh.* (Göttingen: Vandenhoeck & Ruprecht, 2000); Katharina Pistor and Olivier de Schutter, eds., *Governing Access to Essential Resources* (New York: Columbia University Press, 2016); Chris Hann, "Property: Anthropological Aspects," in *International Encyclopedia of the Social and Behavioral Sciences*, 2nd edition, ed. James D. Wright, vol. 19 (Oxford: Elsevier, 2015), 153–59; Peter Häberle, "Vielfalt der Property Rights und der verfassungsrechtliche Eigentumsbegriff," *Archiv des öffentliche Rechts* 109, no. 1 (1984): 36–76; Margaret Davies, *Property: Meanings, Histories, Theories* (Abingdon: Routledge, 2007). See also the multiple publications of the interdisciplinary research project on cultural property at the University of Göttingen (DFG-Forschungsgruppe 772).

5 Hannes Siegrist and Augusta Dimou, eds., *Expanding Intellectual Property: Copyrights and Patents in Twentieth-Century Europe and Beyond* (Budapest: CEU Press, 2017), 3.

Historical Background

Though the idea of intellectual property had been brewing since the early modern period, it was only in the late eighteenth, and essentially in the nineteenth century that the demand for effective regulation of the trade in intellectual products arose beyond the longstanding customary distribution of privileges. The quest for regulation arose from the extension of capitalist relations and as a result of the combined effects of the industrial revolution, the intensification of transportation, commerce and exchange, the professionalization of new liberal professions (author, scientist, engineer etc.), coupled with the call for an effective protection of creativity and investments. It was the same "globalization" of the late nineteenth century that energized the claim for multilateral regulation of the same trade beyond the habitual form of bilateral treaties. The second half of the nineteenth century was indeed the birth hour of the international system of intellectual property management that is still in place today. The *Paris Convention for the Protection of Industrial Property* (1883) and the *Berne Convention for the Protection of Literary and Artistic Works* (1886, BC), along with their revision and/or supplementary treaties,[6] constructed the foundation of the current global system of intellectual property protection.

The creation of the Berne Union (BU)[7] was neither a simple nor evident task;[8] nonetheless, its constitution signified a breakthrough in the international and transnational governance of IPRs through the establishment of a uniform and comprehensive legal framework of regulation.[9] The BU's legal regime was based on two fundamental principles that have endured to this day: (1) the *principle of national (domestic) treatment* obliging every Union member country to confer on authors of other Union member states the same rights that it confers on its own nationals;

6 The Berne Convention was amended at Berlin in 1908, at Rome in 1928, at Brussels in 1948, at Stockholm in 1967 and at Paris in 1971. The nation states that have signed and ratified the various versions of the Berne Convention (BC) form the Berne Union (BU), a treaty alliance of countries that are bound to each other via the principle of national treatment, a legal principle that designates a particular form of "automatic" reciprocity. Due to their close association, the terms Berne Convention and Berne Union are often used interchangeably in this book.

7 On the Berne Convention see Sam Ricketson, *The Berne Convention for the Protection of Literary and Artistic Works: 1886–1986* (London: Centre for Commercial Law Studies, Queen Mary College, 1987); Sam Ricketson and Jane C. Ginsburg, *International Copyright and Neighboring Rights: The Berne Convention and Beyond*, 2nd ed., 2 vols. (Oxford: Oxford University Press, 2006).

8 See György Boytha, "Urheber- und Verlegerinteressen im Entstehungsprozess des internationalen Urheberrechts," *Archiv für Urheber-, Film- und Theaterrecht/UFITA* 85 (1979): 1–37.

9 With time the BU also developed relevant administrative structures, such as an international office (the Berne Bureau) set up to act as a coordinating centre and clearing house for information pertaining to copyright issues in the different member states.

(2) the *principle of minimum protection* requiring each Union member state to offer the rights specially granted by the Berne Convention to authors of all Union countries, excluding its own. In other words, the minimum standards of protection that are contained in the Berne Convention apply to authors from other Berne Union member states but no Berne member is obliged to accord this protection to its own authors.[10] In practice, these regulations translate into a legal regime providing for: (1) automated reciprocity and legal symmetry between all Union member states;[11] whereas (2) the minimum protection stipulation contains the potential of *ex iure conventionis*, whereby the protection accorded under unionist law can override and surpass the level of protection offered by local/national copyright legislation. This in turn can place states with lower protection standards and their nationals at a disadvantage in relation to foreign authors. In order to avoid such side effects, this last mechanism "motivates" and/or "compels" (the choice of verb is contingent on the perspective and/or the constellation) states to regularly "upgrade" and harmonize their national legislation with international law and standards.

Historiography

The research focus on Eastern Europe was motivated by intellectual curiosity and my own area studies specialization, but also by a significant gap in IP historiography. Whereas the history of IP has received increased scholarly attention since the 1990s, both the literature and critical assessments of its historical evolution show a tendency to concentrate on the history of the institution's pioneering actors, which as a rule overlaps with the history of the big European cultural nations (England, France, Germany) and later the history of the USA.[12] In fact, they—and perhaps

---

10 Tanya Aplin and Jennifer Davis, *Intellectual Property Law: Text, Cases and Materials*, 3rd ed. (Oxford: Oxford University Press, 2013), 66.

11 The initial Berne Convention (until its revision by the Berlin Act in 1908) provided states with the option of joining the Convention by retaining particular reservations, a circumstance that allowed for a certain flexibility and freedom of action. Reciprocity remained, but legal symmetry was still adjustable. This option was cancelled after 1908.

12 Literature on copyright for the mentioned cases is vast; here I list only some exemplary publications. For a good survey of the existing literature, various focal points and takes on copyright history until approximately 2013 see, among others, Meredith L. McGill, "Copyright and Intellectual Property: The State of the Discipline," *Book History* 16 (2013): 387–427; Ronan Deazley et al., *Privilege and Property: Essays on the History of Copyright* (Cambridge: Open Book Publishers, 2010); Ronan Deazley, *On the Origin of the Right to Copy: Charting the Movement of Copyright Law in Eighteenth-Century Britain* (Oxford: Hart, 2004); Mark Allen Rose, *Authors and Owners: The Invention*

rightfully so, at least in historical terms—still form the matrix of the core narration of IP history, which is indeed a history of expansion of this modern institution from its Northwest European cradle into the world. Within the European area, Scandinavia and Spain have been recently added to the list of studied cases. Contemporary impulses stemming from global history have directed attention to the history of international organizations such as the Berne Union and the World Intellectual Property Organization (WIPO), the effect of international trade agreements such as the Trade Related Aspects of Intellectual Property Rights treaty (TRIPS) and the General Agreement on Tariffs and Trade treaty (GATT), as well as the role of intellectual property rights in the context of colonial history, and the cultural, commercial and political relationships between center and peripheries within the metropolitan realm. When dealing with the twentieth century, there is a strong overall emphasis on very recent history (from approximately the 1980s) though works dealing with colonial copyright do cover variously greater or lesser parts of the twentieth century. China, for obvious reasons (i.e. its spectacular economic development in the late twentieth and early twenty-first centuries and its passion for counterfeiting), has also drawn academic attention lately; so have some additional regions (India, Africa) of the "Global South."

East and Southeast Europe are almost totally absent from this endeavor to narrate a world history of IP,[13] or even to narrate a regional history of IP to this end. Interest flared up situationally in the 1990s, after the collapse of the Eastern Bloc and in conjunction with developments and trends regarding legal harmonization in the context of the European enlargement process, albeit within a predominantly presentist agenda and with little historical depth. Legal historians furnished ambivalent assessments

of Copyright (Cambridge, Mass.: Harvard University Press, 1993); Isabella Alexander and H. Tomás Gómez-Arostegui, eds., *Research Handbook on the History of Copyright Law* (Cheltenham: Edward Elgar, 2016); Brad Sherman and Lionel Bentley, *The Making of Modern Intellectual Property Law: The British Experience, 1760–1911* (Cambridge: Cambridge University Press, 1999); Catherine Seville, *Literary Copyright Reform in Early Victorian England: The Framing of the 1842 Copyright Act* (Cambridge: Cambridge University Press, 2003); Oren Bracha, *Owning Ideas: The Intellectual Origins of American Intellectual Property, 1790–1909* (New York: Cambridge University Press, 2016); Ludwig Gieseke, *Vom Privileg zum Urheberrecht: Die Entstehung des Urheberrechts in Deutschland bis 1845* (Baden-Baden: Nomos, 1998); Elmar Wadle, ed., *Historische Studien zum Urheberrecht in Europa: Entwicklungslinien und Grundlagen* (Berlin: Duncker und Humblot, 1993); idem., *Geistiges Eigentum: Bausteine zur Rechtsgeschichte*, 2 vols., (Munich: Beck, 1996–2003) a.o.

13 For the most recent publication on the region combining historical and contemporary analyses, see Mira T. Sundara Rajan, ed., *The Cambridge Handbook of Intellectual Property in Central and Eastern Europe* (Cambridge: Cambridge University Press, 2019). For the most recent publication on patent history to include elaborate contributions on Southeast, Central and Eastern Europe, see Graeme Gooday and Steven Wilf, eds., *Patent Cultures: Diversity and Harmonization in Historical Perspective* (Cambridge: Cambridge University Press, 2020).

of communist copyright. Following broader interpretative frameworks in historical scholarship after the end of the Cold War, post-World War II copyright in Eastern Europe was elucidated as a deviation from regular IP development and as a "break" with the European IP tradition, though its European roots were readily acknowledged.[14] The strong interest in the Soviet Union during the Cold War resulted in the production of a voluminous and important (Western) legal scholarship (1960s–1980s), which however pertains to both categories, as much to that of legal scholarship as to that of contemporary sources.[15] An additional complication is the apparent idealization of IP in the region. Motivated predominantly by the desire to eschew the stigma of a "pirate," local analysts, in an act of self-orientalization,[16] often tend to internalize IP's

14 See for example the assessment by Silke von Lewinski that although "those laws and their respective amendments were based on the continental European system, they contained a number of distinguishing common features *that set them apart from the continental European regime* on which they rest. The result was a unique socialist legal system" [emphasis added]. In other words, communist copyright was not understood as a variation of the European legal tradition but as a system apart. See Silke von Lewinski, "Copyright in Central and Eastern Europe: An Intellectual Property Metamorphosis," *Fordham Intellectual Property, Media and Entertainment Law Journal* 8, no. 1 (1997): 41 ff. By contrast, newer research is questioning such neat dichotomies that tend to replicate the chronology of political history. Rudolf Leška, for example, argues against a historiographic canonization of copyright history along the lines of an East-West division, identical and overlapping with the geography of the Iron Curtain, which would ostensibly exorcise East Central European copyright developments from the European norm. See Rudolf Leška, "Performers' Rights: A Central European Export," in *The Cambridge Handbook of Intellectual Property in Central and Eastern Europe*, ed. Mira T. Sundara Rajan (Cambridge: Cambridge University Press, 2019), 223.

15 Serge L. Levitsky, *Introduction to Soviet Copyright Law* (Leiden: A. W. Sijthoff, 1964); Levitsky, "Grundzüge des sowjetischen Urheberrechts," in *Urheberrecht Russlands und der UdSSR*, eds. Serge L. Levitsky and W. B. Simmons (Vienna: Manz, 1985), 29–61; Konstantin Katsarov, *Gewerblicher Rechtsschutz und Urheberrecht der UdSSR und der Volksdemokratien Europas* (Weinheim: Chemie, 1960); M. A. Newcity, *Copyright Law in the Soviet Union* (New York: Praeger Publishers, 1978); D. A. Loeber, *Urheberrecht in der Sowjetunion: Einführung und Quellen* (Frankfurt am Main: Alfred Metzner, 1981); Karel Knap, "Grundzüge der persönlichkeitsrechtlichen Theorie im sozialistischen Urheberrecht," in *Benvenuto Samson zum 90. Geburtstag*, ed. Georg Roeber et al. (Berlin: De Gruyter, 1978), 99–122; Yolanda Eminescu, "Aktuelle Probleme des Urheberrechts der europäischen sozialistischen Länder," in *Gewerblicher Rechtschutz und Urheberrecht*, Internationaler Teil (GRUR Int.) 7 (1980), 387–396; Mihály Ficsor, "The Past, Present and Future of Copyright in the European Socialist Countries," *Revue Internationale du Droit d'Auteur* 118 (1983): 32–107; György Boytha, "The Berne Convention and the Socialist Countries with Particular Reference to Hungary," *Columbia VLA Journal of Law and the Arts* 11 (1986): 57–72; Adolf Dietz, "Transformation of Authors' Rights: Change of Paradigm," *Revue Internationale du Droit d'Auteur* 138 (1988): 38–42; Dietz, "Trends in the Development of Copyright Law in the Countries of Central and Eastern Europe," *Revue Internationale du Droit d'Auteur* 162 (1994): 121–226; Dietz, "Intellectual Property and Desocialization in Eastern Europe," *International Review of Industrial Property and Copyright Law* 26, no. 8 (1995): 851–72; Dietz, *Protection of Intellectual Property in Central and Eastern European Countries: The Legal Situation in Bulgaria, CSFR, Hungary, Poland and Romania* (Paris: OECD, 1995).

16 By "self-orientalization" I refer to a concept (and a process) similar to what Alexander Kiossev has appropriately described as "self-colonization." See Kiossev, *The Self-Colonizing Metaphor*, Atlas of Transformation, http://monumenttotransformation.org/atlas-of-transformation/html/s/self-colonization/the-self-colonizing-metaphor-alexander-kiossev.html.

civilizational rhetoric and indiscriminately postulate the introduction of IP *a priori* as a major step towards modernization and progress, pre-empting thereby its importance and benevolent effect on the lives of local creators/authors.

Methodology

The venture builds on the strengths of comparative and transfer history alike. Transfer processes seek to elucidate the dynamic interplay between international processes and local appropriations and reflex reactions, by analysing how international norms and institutions are transported, adapted and legitimized in local settings and by pointing at the specificity of adaptation processes, articulated through specific or distinct legal orders and practices. The three case studies (Bulgaria, Yugoslavia and Czechoslovakia) are related to each other by means of synchronic comparison and were chosen for their capacity to provide for both variation and contrast. Though all three cases share similar typological traits to begin with (belated nation state building, a limited number of cultural consumers due to the limited territorial extension of the spoken idiom, i.e. small nations, chronologically simultaneous inclusion into international copyright structures etc.), their historical development contains sufficient variation to allow both for a typologically similar as well as for a contrasting comparative approach (central states vs. federative states, experience with copyright within the context of the Habsburg Empire vs. no experience whatsoever, variance in the organization of political power and political economy of communist regimes and in their surveillance systems etc.).

While the interplay between different contexts, levels of interaction, decision-making echelons and perspectives (national-international, interregional, bilateral and multilateral etc.) formed part of the research design from the start, the work had no intentions (and also no pretensions) to narrate a global story. This angle arose (and ultimately offered itself) as a perspective through the sources, that is, by default rather than by design. It was, in fact, the main actors' own perspective (reconstructed through their publications), the firm conviction and undiminished zeal of the Berne Union architects and lobbyists, who sought to apply copyright with global and universal validity, the way they ordered the world into regions, and the way they devised expansion policies and strategies with distinct conceptions of world regions in mind that compelled me to ruminate on the inclusion of East and Southeast Europe into the international copyright regime, in correlation to other areas of the world. Moreover, the geography of copyright's expansion interrelated and intersected more often than not with colonial trajectories and also with market and commercial routes, already existing or targeted ones. I was therefore literally compelled by the nature and the perspective of my materials to enlarge my viewpoint. Instead of focusing exclusively on the intraregional comparison between the three case studies, as had been my initial intention, I extended the horizon to include multiple and varying scales of comparison that placed East and Southeast Europe into perspective with broader Europe and other world regions. It must be emphasized in advance, however, that I am not narrating the history of the Berne Union (though its presence had a significant impact on developments to which I regularly refer); to a certain extent, it could be argued that I am narrating the story from the reverse side, that is, not top-down (from the perspective of the BU) but rather bottom-up (from the standpoint of the diverse local actors).

The work noticeably subscribes to the view of the historian William St. Clair that it is impossible to tell the story of copyright as the story of the development of legal doctrine.[17] As a consequence, it has been a main concern of the present analysis to relate law and practice to each other and as far as possible to maintain a methodological perspective that capitalizes on the dialectic between the two. For this reason, and where possible, social practice is dialogically embedded in extensive explanatory contexts related to the development of trade, the evolution of ideas about aesthetics, changing epistemologies of knowledge, geopolitical power struggles, book history, media development and diffusion, but also changing practices of commercialization, communication, consumption, language use and so on. Nevertheless, analysis of the various copyright legislations, changing legal doctrines and the contents of specific legal regimes are taken seriously and presented in detail in several sections. Though incorporating the interaction between copyright and social practice, the current analysis does not present any litigation cases and does not include court practice for two reasons: firstly, because I did not consider the category of court records in my archival research; such an overstretch would have made a comparative endeavour impossible. Secondly, because I did not stumble upon any litigation cases in my other archival venues and resources. In the case of historical events where litigation could be presumed (in the case of interwar Yugoslavia, for example), it is doubtful that court records would have altered the picture I was able to reconstruct through other archival materials.

17 William St. Clair, "Metaphors of Intellectual Property," in Deazley et al., *Privilege and Property*, 370.

In agreement with Michael Birnhack, I contend that no matter what kind of viewpoint one adopts on copyright, whether it is considered a natural or a positive right, the fact is that copyright law has practical implications; it regulates the cultural field and establishes—in part—the rules of the game.[18] Copyright law denotes in a concise and condensed manner a society's viewpoint on creativity, culture and the production of information and knowledge. Therefore, "the rules that compose the *copyright regime* within a jurisdiction reflect (and also construct) the social values about the creative process."[19] Along with other instruments, copyright law mirrors a "socially constructed space that reflects a society's decisions about power, access to knowledge, distribution of cultural resources, perhaps fairness, and much more."[20]

As a consequence, demonstrating and analyzing how legal rights and legal doctrine mesh with relations of power has been just as important and relevant for this research. In more than one instance, the current analysis demonstrates how international copyright legislation legitimized specific commercial practices, serving particularistic corporate interests, but also how IP regimes did not simply regulate, but were also designed to structure and streamline world markets of cultural goods.

With a view to analyzing property relations and for the heuristic purposes of this analysis, the notions of "propertization" and "de-propertization" are employed in order to denote strategies of incapacitating (limiting) and/or capacitating access to cultural goods by means of erecting, negotiating, controlling or dissolving property boundaries but also through the employment of the language and rhetoric of property, both literally and metaphorically.[21]

Finally, the work takes a long-term, *longue durée* perspective upon the history of copyright development in East and Southeast Europe, covering chronologically approximately a century. Just as the "global" scale offered itself inadvertently, so too did the expanded time horizon offer itself fortuitously. The initial research design was intended to start with the end of World War I, which witnessed the simultaneous introduction of copyright legislation in all three case studies under analysis and offered therefore an ideal, synchronized kick-off moment for comparison. The need, however, to place my case studies into historical perspective relegated me backwards in historical time to the imperial era, whose analysis disclosed certain contours and patterns which I then became inclined to follow as a possible orientation compass.

18 Michael D. Birnhack, *Colonial Copyright: Intellectual Property in Mandate Palestine* (Oxford: Oxford University Press, 2012), 4.

19 Birnhack, *Colonial Copyright*, 5.

20 Birnhack, *Colonial Copyright*, 5.

21 See Hannes Siegrist, "Die Propertisierung von Gesellschaft und Kultur," *Comparativ* 16, no. 5/6 (2006): esp. 31–39.

Even more significantly, and as I came to realize on the way, copyright/intellectual property is precisely the kind of institution that offers itself to structural, long-term analyses. Copyright is a convoluted and potent legal instrument, regulating and endowing rights and entitlements that structure revenues and cash flows from the use of arts and culture. Remaining largely (and purposely) invisible, it engineers itself at culture's deep junctures and performs best when it is predicated on mass consumption and can shape economies of scale; those qualities *ipso facto* predestine it for a *longue durée* analysis.

Structure and Outline

Chapter two focuses on the regulation of translation as a milestone in the setup of the international copyright regime. The transnational management of translation represented the inaugural act of media transformation and intermedial transmission that set the machine of international copyright in motion, and played a seminal role in the expansion and solidification of the "authorial paradigm." The chapter reconstructs the old translation regime and traces its gradual transformation in the context of the Berne Union's establishment. The ensuing standardization, which subsumed translation rights under the author's reproduction rights, signified both a way of disciplining the production and circulation of texts predominantly for commercial purposes (since culturally, hermeneutically and subjectively, texts are anyway appropriated in far more erratic ways) and also a way of taming space and difference in the context of expanding industrial modernity. International attitudes towards translation transformed around the mid-nineteenth century, at a precise moment in time when multiple sweeping changes regarding the organization of the book trade and book markets, the status of languages, the relationship between language and territory, the expansion of readers and tastes but also changes in philosophical and aesthetical doctrines related to the concept of "originality" dynamically converged. Further, this chapter takes a closer look at the official argumentation of the main actors, the metaphors and frames of signification they applied when discussing translation but also the inherent contradictions and the underlying world views that their discourses conveyed. Finally, relying on newer approaches to translation studies, which have redirected interest from source to receptor culture, the analysis takes a close look at the function of translation in the Ottoman Empire and underscores its role as innovator of literary genres and a medium for the construction of modern languages and identities.

With a view to understanding the *longue durée* of regional development, chapter three analyses the copyright regimes of the three East European empires (Habsburg, Ottoman and Romanov) in the late nineteenth and early twentieth centuries until approximately the outbreak of World War I, which inaugurated a different chapter both in European history and in copyright development in the region. The starting point of the analysis is the reluctance of all three East European empires to join the international BU regime. Though they adopted copyright legislation with temporal discrepancies and were governed by different IP regimes, the three empires nevertheless shared some common characteristics that conditioned the reception and perception of copyright's role in this part of Europe, such as the multiethnic, plurilingual and multilingual human fabric of empire, as well as the "soft" translation regimes that all three states adopted, independently of each other. Apart from commonalities, this chapter also points to certain specificities of each case study, such as the self-perception of intelligentsia in the Russian case, the particular relationship of Austria-Hungary to the German Reich, and the distinct role played by calligraphy in the case of Ottoman book production.

Chapter four discusses comparatively the multifarious factors that affected the degree of readiness to conceptualize and apply copyright in the regions of East and Southeast Europe. This chapter deliberates on some of those general preconditions by examining an array of topics covering broadly the period from the second half of the nineteenth century to the outbreak of World War I. The thematic clusters include the legacies of empire, embedding copyright in a local history of publishing and reading, the images and strategies of the author figure, alternative modes of regulation, significations of modernity, as well as the relationship between historical time and the temporalities of copyright.

Contrasting aspects of copyright development between East and West Europe, but also with and between extra-European regions, are at the center of analysis in chapter five. The central question here is why copyright became entangled with identity discourses of peoples seeking self-determination in the case of the British colonial realm but did not do so in the case of the East European empires. In order to approach this issue, the chapter takes a closer look at the governance of copyright in the British and French empires, how it related to colonial policies and administration but also to the expansion of their respective publishing industries. International copyright both complicated and facilitated the expansion of the two empires' cultural industries. Whereas Britain tried to stir and balance those contradictions for its own benefit, France purposely kept its colonies out of the BU until 1930, aiming precisely at avoiding those same complications. The French position is then explained with reference to the French book trade and the vital role that francophone colonies came to play around 1900 for the entire French publishing industry. This chapter focuses further on strategies of expansion and presents a systematic reflection on the means and instruments applied to help expand the international copyright regime globally in the late nineteenth and early twentieth centuries. By discussing different models and regions, rather than creating a typology, the analysis aims predominantly at outlining the diversity of means and strategies of expansion. It thereby seeks to situate developments in Eastern Europe within a global context and discusses them in analogy to developments in other regions like Ibero-America and Asia. It is the contention of this chapter that the global expansion of IP rested not on a singular and homogeneous strategy to be applied uniformly, but remained flexible and was adjusted to suit political circumstances, short- and long-term objectives, historical legacies, the status of certain regions or countries, opportunities offered by specific situational constellations, as well as the positionality of other actors, be it allies or contenders, all factors that determined in each case the specific logic and choice of action. In addition, the chapter takes a critical look at the correlation between bilateralism and multilateralism in the historical development of copyright, and questions narratives predicated on progress that assume multilateralism to be the natural and evolutionary successor of bilateralism. Subsequently, the two forms of association are shown to have functioned practically as supplementary rather than antithetical forums. Finally, this chapter turns its attention to the case of China at the turn of the century, where a thick web of bilateral treaties constructed a fictive terrain of intervention serving the needs of European and non-European powers. The Chinese case exemplifies well both the concept of expansion and the capacity of international copyright law to construct new spheres of influence by simultaneously assembling and dismantling territorial entities through territorial jurisdiction.

Chapter six deals in detail with the expansion of the BU's international copyright regime in East and Southeast Europe in the context of World War I. In the late nineteenth and early twentieth centuries, the Eastern European empires had been reluctant to join the newly created international structures for the protection of intellectual property. World War I diametrically changed this constellation as both existing and newly created nation states of East Central and Southeast Europe were ordained into the BU via clauses inserted into the postwar peace settlement. As the chapter's title "Orchestrated Globalization" suggests, this section embeds the "prescribed accessions" of the East European states into multiple (geo)political, economic, social, technological and cultural contexts. Further, the chapter elucidates the positionality of various states and their cultural industries before and after

World War I, which goes some way towards explaining the logic of the "prescribed accessions" and the keen interest in the regions of East Central and Southeast Europe. The Paris Peace Conference offered a window of opportunity and the moment was expediently used in order to advance the Union's agenda and enlarge its membership and territorial reach at a—for various reasons—critical juncture for the international copyright regime. The analysis makes a strong argument for the capacity of international copyright to structure politico-cultural-commercial relations, an aspect that had always formed part of copyright interactions but was particularly buttressed through the postwar settlement and the subsequent institutional linkage of the Berne Convention with the League of Nations. This association meant a significant upgrading of the BC as it linked an essentially European with a rising global player. Though we retrospectively know that the League of Nations was not an assertive actor, associating copyright with a major modern institution of international law helped IP gain in significance, legitimacy and respectability. The analysis shows that there were different designs and alternatives regarding the inclusion of Eastern Europe into the Union and explains why a specific option ultimately prevailed. On their part, old and new European states, though diversely predisposed towards the BU, well understood the political clout included in the accession process and calculated their own cost-benefit ratios. Finally, World War I represented an important transition in one additional way. Until the turn of the century, the book (and consequently also translations) represented the most significant trade item relevant to copyright. The spectacular success of the novel, the first blockbuster of modern times, is a testimony to the supremacy of print. This chapter also explores European book trade models and underscores the growing predominance of the German commercial regime in the regions of East Central and Southeast Europe. Starting with the Belle Époque and intensifying in the period around World War I, the audiovisual revolution and the internationalization of new media and cultural goods opened up a novel chapter in the history of communications. A series of innovations (cinema, gramophone recording and radio) signalled the ascent of a new technology-led cultural industry, which multiplied options of intermediality and the number of copyright stakeholders, since it permitted the mechanical reproduction of culture, and most importantly the rise of a new phenomenon, that of mass entertainment.

Chapters seven, eight and nine deal with the three case studies (Bulgaria, Yugoslavia and Czechoslovakia) that form the core of the comparative endeavor of the book. To the degree possible, they are structured along similar organizing principles and focal points: a short account of the period before World War I, expounding on existing local conditions and traditions upon which copyright (law) was predicated;

analysis of the copyright laws that were introduced after World War I (BG = 1921, YUGO = 1929, CZ = 1927), their main tendencies and characteristics, the intellectual and legal traditions and influences from which they emanated, as well as the elements that single them out as legal acts; analysis of the professionalization processes of stakeholder groups such as authors' and publishers' unions as well as the diverse dynamics among actors; copyright in practice; analysis of the political context to the degree that it is conducive for putting copyright developments and cultural politics in perspective; state policy towards culture in connection to copyright; foreign interventions; and subsequent amendments of copyright laws in the 1930s and their rationale. In many ways, the interwar period represented a change of setting. While rapidly developing new technologies broke through, new handling problems and allocation battles, technical and legal issues concerning performing, broadcasting, mechanical and moral rights and compulsory licenses were raised, and new actors such as national and international collective management organizations (CMOs) and performers as a category made their appearance on the scene and/or made their presence felt.

Chapter ten brings the strings of the three case studies together in a comparative synthetic overview, drawing conclusions and discussing similarities and differences. Among the many themes upon which this chapter touches are: the Berne Union, and its actors, motives and strategies; the ways in which the legacies of empire impacted on copyright; the rise of new media; formal copyright regarded from above but also from below, by zooming in on the social actors; broader social and cultural trends in interwar Europe such as the introduction of social security for cultural professions and the role of the interventionist state; the rise of collecting societies and other intermediaries; the ideological standpoints of creative elites and avantgardes; the transnationalization of media and genres but also the transgression and creative blurring of boundaries between genres in the interwar period.

Concludingly, in an effort to present a *longue durée* perspective of copyright development in East and Southeast Europe, chapter eleven takes a cursory look at the copyright regimes of the communist period. With no pretentions to an exhaustive analysis, this chapter merely examines in parallel the copyright legislation of the three countries under analysis, its subsequent mutations and amendments in the second half of the twentieth century, and where possible it associates copyright with communist policy.

Finally, chapter twelve brings together in an epigrammatic manner some concise remarks, theses and conclusions that outline the trajectory of copyright in East Central and Southeast Europe in the late nineteenth and twentieth centuries.

Rethinking the Berne Union

Habitually, historical narratives expounding on the creation of the BU build on arguments that underline the two aspects of innovation and continuity. On the one hand, the innovative accomplishment of the Union's masterminds and pioneers is stressed. With much effort and perseverance, they conceptualized and promoted international cooperation in the field of intellectual property rights. At a time when such cooperation was by no means self-evident, driven by a vision to consolidate respect for intellectual production and to honor and protect the labor of authors and curb the injurious activities of pirates on an international level, the pioneers' efforts kept pace with internationalization efforts in several other spheres of commerce and human activity that came to be regulated by international law in the late nineteenth century. Changing social, economic, technological and cultural conditions unleashed by the industrial revolution and the initial globalization of the second half of the nineteenth century—both processes that effectuated an increased traffic in cultural commodities—required new rules of international and transnational conduct and regulation.

In this exegesis, the BU is embedded in the foundation hype that propelled the creation of numerous international organizations in the second half of the nineteenth century (among others, the Universal Postal Union in 1874, the International Telegraph Union in 1865, the International Bureau of Weights and Measures in 1875), as part of the larger drive to regulate an ever-growing exchange of information, knowledge and cultural goods.[22] The creation of the BU features almost as a "necessary" outcome of the dynamics of globalization, an effort to reach standardization and maintain security in an increasingly complex and interconnected environment. Concurring with this stance are the perceived "insufficiencies" of the previous condition: the insufficiency, and often inefficiency, of bilateral agreements, the incompatibility

22 The present work does not engage with the emergence of international organizations *per se*, which is a broad field and a convoluted topic in itself, represented moreover by a voluminous literature. It touches upon the history of the Berne Union to the degree that it is relevant for the analysis of its actual subject of inquiry, that is, the development of copyright in East and Southeast Europe. A good overview of the different historiographical viewpoints related to the initiation of international organizations in the nineteenth century can be found in Klaas Dykmann, *Internationale Organisationen und ihre Zivilisierungsbestrebungen: Die Geschichte der Weltgesundheitsorganisation* (Vienna: Lit, 2017), 20–21. For a proficient, helpful and succinct history of international organizations with good overviews, useful chronological ordering and strong theses see, among others, Madelein Herren, *Internationale Organisationen seit 1865: Eine Globalgeschichte der internationalen Ordnung* (Darmstadt: Wissenschaftliche Buchgesellschaft, 2009); Akira Iriye, *Global Community: The Role of International Organizations in the Making of the Contemporary World* (Berkeley: University of California Press, 2002); Craig N. Murphy, *International Organization and Industrial Change: Global Governance since 1850* (Cambridge: Polity Press, 1994).

of conflicting national regulations and the existence of cumbersome formalities that hampered the smooth circulation of commodities. The popular nineteenth-century faith in progress undergirds the narrative composition of the history of the BU in the accounts of its contemporaries, but has also outlived this period.[23]

The above emphasis on innovation is complemented by a narrative stressing both continuity and evolution. The BU was constructed on already existing diplomatic models; bilateral treaties as well as copyright settlements included in commercial treaties had proliferated in the nineteenth century, but had increasingly proven inadequate for tackling the dynamics of modern exchange. This circumstance dictated the need for more complex governance instruments, leading plausibly from outdated bilateral to modern multilateral solutions. In this narrative, the BU appears both as a natural outcome of the dynamics of globalization and as an effort to come to terms with its consequences. The development from "unsophisticated" bilateralism to complex multilateralism is portrayed as the result of a "rational" evolution from simple to compound structures, understood as more "adequate" and more contemporary forms of organization. Some of the fundamental BU principles, such as the concept of "domestic treatment" (colloquially known as "national treatment"), had already been applied and tested in the framework of bilateral arrangements. As a result, the BU appears both as a consequence of global growth and as an effort to regulate the same.

Having a vantage point in international relations and occupying a more reflective, intermediary position are narratives expounding on the BU as a form of global governance. The BU's formation signified the creation of a supranational, intergovernmental forum capable of assembling and voicing the multifarious and complex stances of diverse stakeholders and agents with diverse interests (authors, publishers, diplomats, lawyers, entrepreneurs, states etc.) and helping them to engage in multilevel cooperation.[24]

A different group of researchers, originating, interestingly, predominantly from countries that had—in historical terms—been sceptical and reserved towards the creation of the BU, like the USA, Great Britain and Spain but also Scandinavia, emphasize correctively the limited enthusiasm for the BU that prevailed in their countries, and provide historical accounts explaining the different motivations behind their countries' eventual change of heart. In their accounts, the creation of the

[23] See for example Jean Cavalli, *La genèse de la Convention de Berne pour la protection des œuvres littéraires et artistiques du 9 novembre 1886* (Lucerne: Imprimeries réunies, 1986).

[24] See for example Isabella Lohr, *Die Globalisierung geistiger Eigentumsrechte: Neue Strukturen internationaler Zusammenarbeit 1886–1952* (Göttingen: Vanderhoeck & Ruprecht, 2010).

multilateral treaty was the result of contingency, and nothing had preordained this course of development. Moreover, from a legal history perspective, there was no European, commonly shared legal tradition of authors' rights that inescapably led to this course of events, that is, the unification and internationalization of copyright law.[25]

Taking this line of thought further, it is possible to argue that the creation of the Berne Union in 1886, instead of an evolutionary development, represented rather a kind of "paradigm shift," that is, a fundamental change in approach concerning the management of cultural goods. The main objective in the administration of publishing rights during the period of printing privileges, covering chronologically what we broadly refer to as the early modern period, had been territorial regulation. Printing privileges were valid for a specific period of time and for a specific geographical area independent of any national considerations. Such had been the rule in a period when book trade was still of a manageable volume, addressed predominantly the limited cohort of the learned of the universal republic of letters, when the majority of books were printed in Latin and four or five other vernacular languages, and finally when language was not necessarily congruent with territory. The granting of publishing patents designated a right that was valid only within a certain territorial jurisdiction and had no effect beyond it. In order to have one's work protected, let's say, in what could be considered the broader German-speaking world, one needed to collect permissions from the more than 300 individual German states, a feat only ever accomplished by one author, Johann Wolfgang von Goethe.

In addition, the system of bilateral treaties that was applied in the nineteenth century, and provided for reciprocal protection of works in trade relations between states, was based on the territorial principle. It concerned all works "exchanged" between those two (territorially defined) signatory states. References to "nationality" or to "nationals" implied territory, not ethnicity. Characteristically, the first such bilateral treaty, the Austrian-Sardinian Copyright Treaty of 1840, carried the title "Vertrag zwischen Österreich und Sardinien zur Sicherstellung der Eigenthumsrechte hinsichtlich der in Ihren beyderseitigen Staaten erscheinenden litterarischen und artistischen Werke."[26] As suggested by the title, the location (territory) of publishing mattered; the nationality of the works and the authors was insignificant.[27]

25 See for example Jose Bellido, "Colonial Copyright Extensions: Spain at the Berne Convention (1883–1899)," *Journal of the Copyright Society of the U.S.A.* 58 (2011): 501–522; Eva Hemmungs Wirtén, *Cosmopolitan Copyright: Law and Language in the Translation Zone* (Uppsala: Uppsala Universitet, 2011).

26 Treaty between Austria and Sardinia to ensure property rights with regard to literary and artistic works published in their respective states.

27 Several relevant treaties for various parts of the world, moreover accompanied by helpful historical

Research on copyright history has somehow neglected to make visible the conceptual passage from pure territorial rights to copyrights as territorial rights relying on the nationality of the work or the author or the rights holder. Why, when and how is nationality grafted into the copyright regime as an indispensable attribute? What were the underlying historical processes that helped "naturalize" the relationship between territory and nationality in copyright? As is often the case, the "national" in the "international" is taken for granted. The pioneering countries and leading case studies when it comes to developing a chronological-analytical scheme of history for copyright are the "usual" West European suspects (Britain, France), that is, dynastic states with developed conceptions of state sovereignty, clearly discernible cultural and linguistic profiles, and, finally, continuity in written culture as well as in the political and cultural elite personnel of the early modern period. Furthermore, they were the trailblazers of industrialization and media development, notwithstanding a certain chronological discrepancy between them. In other words, they hold the kind of privileged historical pedigree that cannot be applied to the largest part of the globe in the nineteenth century.

Before addressing the international, it is therefore necessary to stress the degree to which preceding processes of nationalization (of markets, readerships, literatures, creators) played a role in helping bring about a notion of copyright akin to and congruent with ethnic nationality. Posing the question in those terms may help us to understand why this model was not necessarily attractive or applicable to all world regions, states, populations or relations in the field of creativity.[28] It reveals, moreover, how closely a legal institution like copyright partook, directly and indirectly, in the greater socioeconomic, political and cultural transformations of the late eighteenth and nineteenth centuries that shaped the modern world, pointedly brought together by Eric Hobsbawm as the triadic age of revolution, capital and empire. It reveals, finally, the cognate nature of the institutions of modern copyright and the modern nation state and identifies them as strategic governance mechanisms in the entanglement and regulation of human, material and immaterial capital.

A tentative answer to the entanglement between copyright and the nation may involve the correlation between authors' rights and a country's vested interests in promoting primarily its national culture and education. Such a "national" viewpoint was reinforced, for example in the British case, by the belief that copyright laws, just

introductions and/or commentaries, can be found in the (very useful) digital archive *Primary Sources on Copyright (1450–1900)*, eds. L. Bently and M. Kretschmer, http://www.copyrighthistory.org/.

28 The question has also been addressed by Birnhack, *Colonial Copyright*, 12–14.

as literature, were supposed to reflect national character.[29] Copyright is moreover preoccupied with the regulation of regimes and systems of knowledge such as those of national education and national literature, and has to make a choice about which works deserve to be protected, for how long, for and from whom. Such questions often represent controversial issues in the national context, and even more so on an international level.[30] It can probably be assumed with a certain degree of confidence that the progressive modelling of copyrights as strong, absolute subjective rights of the author over his/her creation was a defining moment for the syncretism between territory and nationality. In other words, the figure of the "romantic" author defending his/her property denoted not only the "romantic individualistic" but also the "romantic national" author. Did authorial identity automatically imply nationality, or did the law superimpose the national over authorial identity? Or did they simply feed reciprocally on each other? Did the expansion of national commerce simply absorb and streamline cultural commodities as one additional national export product? Did the creation of literary canons, but also the success and exportability of national, to-be-international, bestsellers promote such syncretism?

It is not within the scope of this work to provide definitive answers to all these questions, but the intention rather is to raise the issue and provide some food for thought. It is intriguing to think about what the outcome might have been had the German proposal succeeded, to construct unionist protection on the grounds of one uniform legislation, common and binding for all member countries, instead of the French proposal which ultimately prevailed, and which defended the concept of protection on the basis of domestic/national treatment. Copyright required that foreign works were legally equalled to domestic/national ones, a fact that only underscored their difference; had they been truly similar, they would not need to be assimilated. They had to be assimilated because they were "foreign." Even if they were similar (in terms of language, genre, style etc.), their processes of commodification and commercialization required that they were different, because by such means the legal status and the commercial dimension of copyright acquired a unified, congruent identity. In order for the above mechanism (i.e. the congruence of law, commerce and identity) to become functional, it was necessary to absorb the "Other" into the "Self," that is, the "Other" merely simulated resemblance, it was not authentically identical but only a "simulacrum." The "Other" was always "Another."

29 Sherman and Bently, *The Making of Modern Intellectual Property Law*, 111–15.

30 See Catherine Seville, *The Internationalization of Copyright Law: Books, Buccaneers and the Black Flag in the Nineteenth Century* (Cambridge: Cambridge University Press, 2006), 10–11.

The national had to be invoked in order to activate the international in the law. In fact, such a conception is inherent to international law, which concerns the law between states, that is, the rules of how states relate to each other. Thereby, "nationality" was irreversibly stamped onto the DNA of copyright. It was the very mechanics of the law (i.e. ascribing nationality inevitably) that institutionalized this interplay between sameness and difference, and which automatically, even today, perpetrates and recycles "value" and "meaning" in the cultural market. In fact, the nationality of a work is—ontologically speaking—largely irrelevant, unless the issues of ownership and trade are raised.

The German proposal surely fitted better the interests of the German commercial regime and the largely networked character of its book trade. The French proposal surely made acceptance of the BU as a supranational organization easier for nation states and was most likely predicated on the experience of the capacity of French culture to assimilate foreignness. Moreover, the juridification of cultural commodities on a par with nationality had the double effect of rendering them both more stable and more mobile. On the one hand, it stabilized them as recognizable national export goods and linked them to national territory/identity/culture/economy even in their most remote or immaterial "voyages." Cultural goods remained (or were made to remain or it was claimed that they remained) stable even if they traversed a thousand seas and cultures. On the other hand, the concept of domestic/national treatment followed the mobility of subjects and objects, and through this elasticity it kept producing out of these novel trajectories of movement new fictional and functional territorialities: sometimes fixed, sometimes relational, floating, flexible, overlapping, intersecting, superimposed and so on. By definition, copyright is an institution that axiomatically nationalizes works. In the copyright universe, there are no hybrid, ambivalent, creole or mestizo works. Every work and every author has a passport, and moreover a national passport to this end, no matter how intricate, cosmopolitan or unorthodox an author's subjective identity might be. By such means, copyright contributed to the circulation of a concept of reified and objectified culture on a par with modern nationalism.

Most certainly, it was no coincidence that modern copyright was internationalized in the late second half of the nineteenth century. In that sense, the law was a fine seismograph of the times, as it chronicled (and systemized) the passage to new formalized notions of codified belonging, designating broadly the passage from imperial to national subjects. Belonging (i.e. nationality/ethnicity, identity, individuality) was no longer about how one (subjectively) felt, but was now standardized according to fixed categories and criteria (citizenship, passports, the residence of publishers etc.). At the turn of the century, therefore, several processes concurred simultaneously: a revolution in technologies and communication, the dynamic of industrial capitalism and the reorganization of the international (political) order. Copyright development is related to all these processes simultaneously and cannot be affixed to just one.

No matter what the answers are to the above questions, what needs to be stressed is how historically bound, culturally determined and context dependent national and international copyright rules and solutions—even the concept of IP itself—have been diachronically. Embedding copyright, from the vantage point of Southeast and East Central Europe, into those multifarious contexts, situated between empire and nation state, between the local, regional and global, between norm creation, transfer and practice, but also between law, culture, technology, trade, cultural professions and cultural politics, is what this work is all about.

Chapter 2

Where It All Started: Translation

If there was one topic that dominated the agenda of copyright in the late nineteenth century and exemplified like no other the multiple radical transformations of that period, it was undoubtedly the issue of translation, the "international literary question"[1] *par excellence*. The creation of the Berne Union (BU) was instrumental in helping bring about a lasting revision in the handling of translation, and solidified a new legal regime that can be properly understood as a fundamental change of approach. Translation represented the first act of "transmittance" or "relay" that set the machine of international copyright in motion. Though it would be an exaggeration to claim that the BU was primarily created in order to regulate translation, it is certainly accurate to claim that translation was a top priority in the late nineteenth and early twentieth centuries, and dominated the agenda both of the *Association Littéraire et Artistique Internationale* (ALAI) and the BU until the final settlement of this question at the Berlin BC revision conference in 1908.

By means of its equivocal and unsettled nature, translation questions in more than one way an unambiguous concept of authorship, the "very nature of the work,"[2] as well as the "dichotomy between original and copy,"[3] and by consequence also that of a tidy theoretical distinction between content and form, the formula that lies at the heart of modern copyright. The solution that was finally adopted in Berlin awarded "translations, adaptations, arrangement of musical and other reproductions in an altered form of a literary or artistic work as well as collections of different works" an original right of protection, "without prejudice to the copyright of the original work."[4] While on the one hand the translator was granted an original right

---

1 *Association Littéraire et Artistique Internationale (ALAI), Son histoire – ses travaux 1878–1889* (Paris: Bibliothèque Chacognac, 1889), 54.

2 Eva Hemmungs Wirtén, "A Diplomatic Salto Mortale: Translation Trouble in Berne, 1884–1886," *Book History* 14, no. 1 (2011): 89.

3 Hemmungs Wirtén, "A Diplomatic Salto Mortale," 102.

4 *Berne Convention Centenary 1886–1986*, The Berne Convention for the Protection of Literary and Artistic Works from 1886–1986 (Geneva: BIPRI, 1986), 229.

distinct from that of the original author, on the other, translation was considered a derivative work. The settlement on translation legislated indeed a "paradox": though it classified translation among the reproduction rights of the author, at the same time it allowed translation to emerge as a separate and original work.[5] Copyright protection was granted to translations as to originals; however, legally, translation was categorized as a reproduction (i.e. a copy, replica, duplicate) and was thus classified under the author's reproduction rights. And though modern copyright adopted the originality of form as its most distinctive trait, translation into another language, which embodies a major change in form, is classified under the category of a "copy."[6]

The regulation of translation was conceivably one of the most significant stepping stones in the establishment of the inviolability of the authorial paradigm in the long run. Translation confirms the author as the alpha and omega of the text, precisely at the moment when the text is set in motion. The codification of translation as a reproduction right thereby stabilizes and solidifies even further the sanctioning authority of the author in transnational relations and naturalizes a process of propertization in copyright relations.

Long before the issue of translation was officially taken up as a topic in BU conventions, it was an issue of debate, perhaps even the centerpiece, at the various ALAI conferences that took place from the foundation of the organization in 1878 in various European cities and capitals. The ALAI was an assembly point for diverse interest groups, representing authors, publishers, diplomats and lawyers and pursuing an ambitious practical, but no less ideological, agenda concerning intellectual property. The ALAI represented an alliance of interests for actors, who though possessing conflicting goals, closed ranks in the face of the big challenges related to the internationalization and expansion of trade in cultural goods. Artists and publishers exploited the legal expertise of jurists in favor of their interests, while on the other side lawyers developed a doctrinal thought, which perpetuated in the international context the presuppositions and major guidelines of the philosophy of authors' rights in the national context.[7] The ALAI's declared practical goals were to define and affirm the rights of literary property, specify the nature of those rights, study the problem of intellectual property protection in international relations, examine the

5 Hemmungs Wirtén, "A Diplomatic Salto Mortale," 101.

6 Hemmungs Wirtén, "A Diplomatic Salto Mortale," 101; and Salah Basalamah, "Translation Rights and the Philosophy of Translation: Remembering the Debts of the Original," in *In Translation: Reflections, Refractions, Transformations*, eds. Paul St-Pierre and Prafulla C. Kar (Amsterdam: John Benjamins, 2007), 122.

7 Salah Basalamah, *Le droit de traduire: Une politique culturelle pour la mondialisation* (Ottawa: Les Presses de l'Université d'Ottawa, 2009), 226.

contemporary situation of authors in different countries and deliberate on measures in order to ameliorate their universal condition.[8] The organization presented itself as a champion and guardian of such lofty ideals as the universal solidarity of spirit, whose intention was to unite all world literatures and authors through the establishment of fraternal relationships among them. In doctrinal terms, the ALAI held on to a natural rights justification, which it zealously sought to universalize; authors' rights were not legal concessions but a form of property that the legislator had to acknowledge and guarantee.[9] The ALAI presented itself as a modest player, who, though engaging with international affairs, had no intentions to intervene in the activity or encroach on the competences of nation states and various national authors' societies. Rather, it aimed at the creation of permanent and regular relations among the literary societies and authors of all countries, with the purpose of diffusing literary works and safeguarding authors' interests regarding international property and translation.[10] The proclaimed profile, however, did not correspond to the organization's actual role, which in reality was to be the agenda-setter and trendsetter of the BC conferences. In fact, the ALAI's role rather resembled that of an "éminence grise"; no practical/doctrinal/theoretical issue was ever discussed in the BU that had not previously been approved by the ALAI. Equally or perhaps even more important was the ALAI's role as an indefatigable networker in international relations. The organization worked assiduously to set up national branches of its association in different countries, which were usually manned by the same categories of people (lawyers, diplomats, authors, publishers) and functioned as transmission belts for its agenda. Thereby, it ensured that its doctrinal positions as well as favorable personnel circulated between the national and international levels, and moreover that the organization could secure some leverage in the respective political and cultural national contexts.

In the modern period and until the ALAI was founded, there had been no unambiguous doctrine or practice regarding translation. Freedom of translation was largely assumed and practiced; where it did exist, regulation tended to take into account, broadly speaking, two directives: (1) the obligation of the author to make a translation of his work within a specific—usually very short—timeframe, while providing for a much shorter protection term than in the case of the original; (2) the assimilation of the right of translation to the right of reproduction, as was developed rather early in France and consequently practiced in its bilateral trade

8 *ALAI, Son histoire*, 2.

9 *ALAI, Son histoire*, 2.

10 *ALAI, Son histoire*, 7.

relations with other countries.[11] The ALAI's second congress in 1879 in London was influential in turning the tables on this loose translation regime. During the deliberations, translation was transformed from an open issue treated in variable ways into a target defined predominantly through a negative objective, that is, how to achieve the prohibition of translation without authorization (and no longer how to regulate translation). The numerous ALAI congresses that followed developed a line of argumentation which effectively forged into consciousness two presuppositions: (1) in terms of genre, the assimilation of translation to reproduction; and (2) the equation between counterfeit and (unauthorized) translation. (Unauthorized) translation and the reprinting of books were equalized.[12]

The Old Regime

Initially, under the old regime, the authorization of translation was considered to exist *ipso facto*, and resulted from the mere fact of a work's publication. Quite contrary to what came to prevail later as the dominant doctrine, in order to reserve the right of translation, an author had to expressly prohibit the translation of his work. In other words, there was no such entitlement existing in its own right, but rather it had to be created by the author as a kind of exception to the rule. Since the specific prerogative was conditional, that is, it was created only on the condition that a "defense of translation" was inscribed into the work, evidently the right of translation was not conceptualized as a property right. What is more, this prohibition did not constitute law, but only for a limited period of time, during which the author was obliged to translate the work himself or have it translated, otherwise the right expired.[13]

Protection of translation was conferred conditionally and different states applied varying standards. Portugal, Belgium and Switzerland demanded that translation begin within one year of publication in the original language and be completed within a period of three years. In Britain the term was five years. In the cases of Austria and Italy, if a translation was published within one year, the right of the original author was unlimited. In Russia, all works could be translated freely, save scientific works (i.e. works that required extensive research) for which an exclusive

11 Basalamah, *Le droit de traduire*, 250.

12 Basalamah, *Le droit de traduire*, 264.

13 *ALAI, Son histoire*, 17.

right of translation could be reserved, on condition that such a reservation was stated in the first publication, and the right of translation applied within two years from the day the sale of the original work was authorized.

Likewise, the German law of June 11, 1870 put few, selective restrictions upon the freedom of translation. An unauthorized translation was considered a counterfeit only in the following three instances: (1) if an original work written in a dead language was translated into a living language; (2) if a work published simultaneously in several languages was translated in one of those languages; and (3) if the author had reserved the right of translation on the title page of the work, provided that the reserved translation appeared within one year of the year of publication. For dramatic works the term of protection was even shorter: it was reduced to six months, starting from the day of appearance of the original. The beginning and completion of the translation were subject to registration, in the absence of which the author was deprived of his right of translation.[14]

France and Spain (law of January 12, 1879) were the only countries that acknowledged an exclusive author's right that encompassed all literary forms and their corollaries; the rest of the existing legislations placed various obstacles on the implementation of an exclusive author's translation right. Belgian legislation required that the author's consent be sought only when a work had reached its second edition (law of September 23, 1814). Norway (June 8, 1876) and Sweden (August 10, 1877) restricted free translation only in the following instances: (1) when it involved a translation from one dialect into another of the same language; (2) in the case of yet unpublished works; and (3) if it concerned a work published initially in a dead language. Considered to be dialects of the same language, Swedish, Danish and Norwegian authors enjoyed protection from unauthorized translations for five years in the Scandinavian countries if the translation appeared within two years of the original publication. Italian legislation (June 25, 1865) allowed for an exclusive right of translation, which was, however, of limited duration. The author retained the exclusive right of translation for ten years, starting from the year of the work's publication; during that period nobody could translate a work without the author's consent. After the term of protection expired, the author's right ceased to exist and the work passed into the public domain. Mexican copyright (civil code of March 1, 1871, article 1269ff.) required that the author reserve the right of translation through an explicit reservation in the work itself, and moreover stipulate whether the reservation applied for a specific, or for all languages. In the absence of such reservations, works could be translated freely.

---

14 *ALAI, Son histoire*, 18–19.

Other legislations were even more liberal: they demanded that the author not only state a reservation but also imposed a time limit within which the author had to translate his work. The examples of the Austrian, German and Russian legislation have already been mentioned; Danish copyright law (February 23, 1866) followed the same principle and granted a two-year period for accomplishing the translation, provided that the translating activity had effectively started nine months after the work's deposit. Six months to one year was the customary time frame granted to authors in order for them to translate, or have their work translated for the purpose of securing the right of translation.[15]

As can be deduced from the above-mentioned examples, the deadlines for initiating translations were short, and failure to comply with them signified loss of the right of translation by the author. This approach to the early regulation of translation leads to certain conclusions being drawn. The first and most important one concerns the value and ownership of knowledge. The practice of short deadlines for translations suggests that the main idea was to make knowledge and/or works move quickly between cultural worlds. It hints at a quick sharing of ideas and works and, moreover, the author himself was often made responsible for assuring the speedy implementation of this process. The author became entitled to an exclusive right of translation (no matter how short that was) only when he ensured circulation, not when he impeded it. Moreover, the world of knowledge was a shared world; though political obstacles like censorship might have restricted its internal flow, the ontological status of knowledge was that of belonging to the commons.[16] Apparently, as long as the means of knowledge transfer and the modes of transport were fairly slow, it was imperative to have knowledge and information move quickly; with the acceleration and multiplication of both the means of transfer and transport, speed became self-evident and discretionary. Knowledge transmission could now be adjusted to different cadences, and in order to be able to determine and control those flows (i.e. how much knowledge in how much time), it had to be locked in or compartmentalized.

---

15 *ALAI, Son histoire*, 59–60.

16 The early modern world was not completely anarchic and unregulated, nor were all works in the public domain. There were customary practices of exchange, ethical responsibility towards the original work and its author, tacit modes of conduct concerning appropriations, attributions, particular ways of communicating to the public what the prototype is and what an imitation of the prototype is, ways of receiving artistic or creative licences and so on. They constituted some of the codes, idioms and registers that authors applied in creative labor. See here Matthew H. Birkhold, *Characters before Copyright: The Rise and Regulation of Fun Fiction in Eighteenth-Century Germany* (Oxford: Oxford University Press, 2019). See also Monica F. Cohen, *Pirating Fictions: Ownership and Creativity in Nineteenth-Century Popular Culture* (Charlottesville: University of Virginia Press, 2017).

The regulation of translation also gives indications about the nature and extent of the book markets. It points in the first place at a controlled market and a hierarchy of languages; dead languages (Latin, etc.) were obviously still highly valued and prominent in the world of knowledge, which is why translations from dead languages into living ones (vernaculars) were considered encroachments. There is also an indication that the status of vernacular languages, far from being settled, was still exploratory and in motion, as suggested by the case of the Scandinavian legislations, which restricted the otherwise normal practice of free translation only in the case of works that were translated from one dialect into another of the same language. Almost certainly, such measures reflect ongoing processes (and uncertainties) related to linguistic canonization among the various Scandinavian languages. Finally, the modality of regulation of translation also signals that the publishers had little interest in regulating translation, the spheres of their operation being focused primarily on confined markets of the same linguistic group or on limited and dispersed groups of educated cosmopolitan multilingual readers. Their efforts concentrated rather on curbing the reprinting of books, that is, unauthorized reproductions in the same language as the original work. The boundaries of copyright protection were congruous with the intended area of distribution of the original work.

In the second half of the nineteenth century, the issue of translation was included in bilateral treaties on trade granting reciprocal treatment. They were, however, of limited duration and effect. France was the indisputable champion of the bilateral universe, having completed 23 treaties for the reciprocal protection of authors' rights during the decade 1852–1862.[17]

In the world view of the early eighteenth century, neither translations nor abridgements were considered a transgression of the law or a violation of the original. A translation was not considered an illegitimate copy but a different (new) book.[18] The crucial criterion in this early phase of copyright development was the absence of the notion of an "original" copy, or otherwise stated, the absence of the later dominant dichotomy in copyright ontology between a singular original and multiple derivative copies.[19] Analogous was the situation with abridgements, which were evaluated by reference to whether they were "real and fair" and were appreciated as "an act of understanding" that saved readers time.[20] Before the emergence of originality as an aesthetic category

17 Stephen P. Ladas, *The International Protection of Literary and Artistic Property*, vol. 1, International Copyright and Inter-American Copyright (New York: The Macmillan Company, 1938), 27–28.

18 Stina Teilmann-Lock, *The Object of Copyright: A Conceptual History of Originals and Copies in Literature, Art and Design* (London: Routledge, 2016), esp. 27–32.

19 Teilmann-Lock, *The Object of Copyright*, 50.

20 Simon Stern, "Copyright, Originality, and the Public Domain in Eighteenth-Century England," preprint version, SSRN, 9–10, available at https://papers.ssrn.com/sol3/papers.cfm?abstract_

in the late eighteenth century, imitation was valued as part of literary production. In other words, there existed no incompatibility between "originality" and "imitation."[21] As emphasized by Simon Stern, the eighteenth-century marketplace included all kinds of forms of copying, imitation and revision, while there was little reference to originality and plenty of references to authorial labor.[22]

This approach changed with the increasing economic and commercial significance of translation literature, a process that started at the end of the eighteenth century but reached its climax in the middle of the nineteenth century. As observed by Martin Vogel, the belated restriction of the freedom of translation—or otherwise stated, the late but then unlimited international recognition of the right of translation—has to be credited to the growing reciprocity and unanimity in the economic interests of the various national publishing industries in securing supranational and transborder protection for such a right, and also, most likely, to the growing insight into the nature of copyright, which next to form, also protects, to a certain degree, the contents of a work.[23] As stated in the following excerpt, by the ALAI's general secretary Jules Lermina, in a far more pragmatic tone than the habitual grandiloquence, exalting civilization and the fraternization of peoples and literatures, translation "is the truly international literary question and [...] could be summarized in two words: export and import."[24]

A Business Model: Translations Authorized by the Author

How closely the adopted copyright regime on the legal regulation of translation correlated with specific publishing models and publishers' business choices, as well as specific prerequisites of industrial capitalistic publishing, is best demonstrated in the case of France, which also pioneered this legal viewpoint. Research on the

id=1299302, otherwise published in Reginald McGinnis, ed., *Originality and Intellectual Property in the French and English Enlightenment* (New York: Routledge, 2008), 69–101.

21 Stern, "Copyright," 13–14.

22 Stern, "Copyright," 17–20.

23 Martin Vogel, "Die Entfaltung des Übersetzungsrechts im deutschen Urheberrecht des 19. Jahrhunderts," in *Die Notwendigkeit des Urheberrechtsschutzes im Lichte seiner Geschichte* (ÖSGRUM vol. 9), ed. Robert Dittrich (Vienna: Manzsche Verlags- und Universtitätsbuchhandlung, 1991), 203.

24 *ALAI, Son histoire*, 54.

strategies of French publishers in the second half of the nineteenth century in connection to the development of copyright on translations tends to confirm the instrumental role played by publishers like Hachette and the Levy Brothers in enforcing a specific conception of the relationship between authors' rights and translation. They championed the equation of translation with reproduction and further promoted the internationalization of this model.[25]

As in other places, the role and effect of translation in French publishing and literature was nonlinear. In the second half of the eighteenth century and beginning of the nineteenth, foreign (German, English, Italian) fiction was assiduously translated, making up approximately one-third of Parisian publications. Starting with the globalizing decade of the 1760s, this period represented a moment of intense, largely reciprocal circulation that tallied with the unprecedented acceleration of transnational mobility and the progressive commodification and liberalization of the world of print and writing. The industrial revolution also affected the urban centers of the Atlantic space, which became wealthier, progressively more literate and educated. Aiming to reverse stagnation, starting in the 1830s, publishers abandoned the old publishing regime, thereby inducing a sharp decline in translation. The new strategy corroborated a nationalization of French literary life in close connection with a revolution in publishing.[26] The publishers' new approach followed the logic of offer and demand and was carried by innovations such as the roman-feuilleton and the "format-Charpentier," a low-priced pocket book in octodecimo format, which permitted the organization of works in "collections" and made them accessible to a mass audience. The basic idea was to diminish production costs for books by radically augmenting the size of the edition. Industrialization and national structuring of the market were thereby closely linked.[27]

In its turn, the industrialization of the book had a massive effect on the translation of foreign literature. International copyright regulation, under way in Europe around 1840, and in France particularly since 1852, allowed some French publishers to relaunch a dynamic around literary translation, which stimulated the expansion of capitalistic publishing. Such was the case with publishers like Louis Hachette and the Levy Brothers, who from the 1850s built up their enterprises by relying on a massive and highly supervised translation operation, framed by international

25 This section draws largely on the work of Blaise Wilfert-Portal, "Traduction Littéraire: Approche Bibliométrique," in *Histoire des traductions en langue française, XIXe siècle 1815–1914*, eds. Yves Chevrel, Lieven D'Hulst and Christine Lombez (Lagrasse: Verdier, 2012), 255–344.

26 Wilfert-Portal, "Traduction Littéraire," 337–38.

27 Wilfert-Portal, "Traduction Littéraire," 289–91.

copyright law and involving a complex organization and division of work between publisher, coordinator and affiliated translators.[28]

Hachette's vested interest in translation was a corollary of a large and particularly ambitious contract he concluded with Charles Dickens for the translation of several of his works into French in the 1850s. In order to achieve this, Hachette made huge efforts to rationalize translation activity: his multiple translators were under the supervision and control of one chief editor; there was a system of hierarchization, division of tasks, centralization, controlling procedures, coordination of the operation through its various stages, and promotional strategies that authenticated the translation. In other words, it was an activity that became industrialized, rationalized and standardized; it placed translation at the heart of the publisher's strategy and represented a rupture with previous practices.[29] Hachette launched his "Library of the Best Foreign Novels" in 1857, which after only eight years consisted of 150 titles, all distributed in rail station libraries.

Hachette's investment in Dickens' work represented a transformation of the publishing world. He instigated not only a change towards industrially produced literature but also towards capitalistic publishing. Moreover, he was able to reposition himself within the field, moving into the area of general literature rather than his previous domain of textbooks. Finally, it represented a diversification strategy with respect to publications, which went far beyond books.[30]

Hachette acquired a monopoly of works by renowned authors and associated his name and the name of his collection with them. With this enterprising step, he participated in the invention of the collection, consisting of a lineup of authors and a system of reciprocal accumulation of symbolic capital for both authors and publisher. It was a particularly successful model and it is therefore no surprise that it was eagerly copied by the majority of publishers in the European peripheries. They also predicated their respective "local" forms of capitalistic publishing on collections of the best foreign novels (though preferably without paying copyright fees).

In order for his investments to pay off, Hachette needed a time advantage, and this in turn required the complete or partial resolution of the issue of international copyright. Hachette fought, therefore, on both the national and international fronts. Participating in his capacity as president of the French Publishers' Union (*Circle de la Librairie*) at the 1858 literary congress on IP in Brussels, he advocated for the universal adoption of an international copyright system fashioned on the French

28 Wilfert-Portal, "Traduction Littéraire," 339.

29 Wilfert-Portal, "Traduction Littéraire," 295–96.

30 Wilfert-Portal, "Traduction Littéraire," 297.

model. Ever since the law-decree of March 28, 1852, foreign authors had enjoyed the same protection in France as French authors without formalities. Moreover, in a decision of that same year, the Court of Paris had passed a judgement claiming the full assimilation of translation to reproduction. The original author and the publisher as copyright owner were declared owners of the translation rights. Hachette and other publishers were in favor of this development and as a result put pressure on various French governments to unilaterally impose a radical and altruistic solution to the question of nonauthorized reproductions. Instead of the traditional and endless bickering between states, the French state should take the initiative and promote the assimilation of the rights of foreigners to the rights of nationals, and then convince foreign states to follow suit. Accordingly, Hachette advocated a concept of copyright founded on the purest notion of property, that is, perpetual property, which conferred to the author the absolute and unlimited right of reproduction and further allowed him to bequeath it to his heirs.[31]

Hachette was conscious that his investment in Dickens and the "collection" was long term, and that in the absence of a pertinent legal framework, the profit-earning capacity of his product would soon evaporate. His policy thus differed significantly from the logic of the old regime of translation, which had been exacerbated by the flood of industrially produced literature and the drastic sinking of book prices. Hachette opted instead for a sustainable strategy, comprising an expensive investment, team labor, the construction of a planned and consistent collection and accumulation of literary capital, meaning that his translations were authorized by the author in the book's preface, and were to a certain degree cared for, edited and verified by an agent, distancing themselves thereby from inferior products.[32]

As maintained by Blaise Wilfert-Portal, the invention of capitalistic publishing was directly linked to the import of foreign novels in translation at the end of the 1850s and the beginning of the 1860s. It was foreign novels framed by national and international copyright that allowed the development of a risky, but in certain ways also very efficient strategy, permitting the growth of publishing houses that quickly became pivotal for the entire publishing sector, and which was firmly based on strong capitalization. This strategy also gave rise to a new publisher logic with respect to translation, one that, in contrast to the previous practices of popular editions and translations on the fly, sought to construct an intermediate regime, that of the translation "authorized by the author."[33]

---

31 Wilfert-Portal, "Traduction Littéraire," 298–99.

32 Wilfert-Portal, "Traduction Littéraire," 300–301.

33 Wilfert-Portal, "Traduction Littéraire," 301–302.

The publisher could now acquire a monopoly of the translated work, purchased according to terms regulated by international law. For the first time it was possible to secure a right of exploitation over a work and to conform to a publisher's right to a French work, for the lifetime of the author and several decades after his death. The principles of international IP that were applied in France aimed not at protecting the content of the translated works, but rather the French publishers and translators. Obtaining an imprimatur allowed the publisher to forego competition in the legal sphere and authenticate the translation a priori.[34] Protection against other concurrent and simultaneous translations allowed the publisher to transform the role of translation in the publishing world. The "authorized translation" was certainly an expensive investment but a profitable one as well, moreover one promising both financial and symbolic gains. For publishers with a solid economic foundation, and only those, translation could become a particularly effective medium-term investment, allowing them to quickly assemble an entire literature collection by importing a large number of titles by the same author all at once, keeping ahead of weaker competitors who were unable to replicate investments of a similar scale.[35]

This gradual paradigm shift radically transformed the old translation regime and turned its basic presuppositions on its head. The author was no longer responsible for the circulation of texts, but almost paradoxically for the exact opposite, that is, he acquired the right to prohibit the circulation of his texts in translation without his prior authorization. The circulation of texts was significantly slowed down and texts were locked in through the gradual extension of the right of translation to the author's lifetime plus additional years post mortem auctoris (p.m.a.).[36] Instead of being one link in the chain of circulation, the author was transformed into an absolute source, the beginning and the end of a text; the right of translation was transformed from an exception to the norm as it became naturalized and eventually assimilated to the author's right of reproduction. Moreover, the improvised, volatile and unstructured paths via which texts circulated and were reproduced and the hybrid forms of transmission were disciplined and subjected to control and supervision. Ironically, just as additional hurdles were built into the international system of textual circulation, the agenda aiming to establish the author's exclusive right of translation proclaimed its goal as "removing the multiple obstacles that still hinder our literary liberty."[37]

---

34 Wilfert-Portal, "Traduction Littéraire," 336.

35 Wilfert-Portal, "Traduction Littéraire," 339.

36 Post mortem auctoris (p.m.a.) is the legal term used in copyright to designate the period of protection after the author's death.

37 *ALAI, Son histoire*, 20.

The enforcement of the right of translation as an exclusive right of the author, and moreover the establishment of this legal interpretation as the international standard, was slow and not without resistance. By the time translation came to be debated in the Berne Union, the various ALAI congresses of the late nineteenth century had already paved the way towards a specific perception and interpretation of the problem by forging into consciousness the equation between counterfeit and unauthorized translation. The justification followed the French legal solution, which regarded translation as part of the author's reproduction rights without any formalities. The figure that secured the lawfulness and validity of this conceptual step was the author; the legal institution that secured his prerogative was property. This point was emphasized by the lawyer Eugène Pouillet: "[...] from the point of view of pure law, that is, from the standpoint of property law, which is born uncontestably to the author of every new creation, it is surprising that the right of translation should be discussed at all [i.e. it is evident]. [...] [S]een therefore from a purely rational standpoint, the best legislation regarding translation is to avoid any specific regimentation, which formulates exceptions but rather let the author be absolute master of his work, free to dispose of his work as he likes, that is, a true proprietor of his property [c'est-à-dire un véritable propriétaire de sa propriété]."[38]

The language of property purported various notions and shades of the liberal political economy of the nineteenth century.[39] In the following metaphor applied in order to underscore the necessity of removing all reservations regarding translation, property is a natural, absolute and self-evident right of ownership, commensurate to material property: "there is no need to place on houses a banner claiming the defense of theft. Why should it be different for literary property?"[40]

A different liberal version was expressed by Numa Droz, the Swiss statesman who headed several of the international negotiation meetings that led to the creation of the BC. He justified IP on the one hand on the grounds of labor, while on the other he struck a political tone, portraying it as a kind of barrier against anxieties of social upheaval: "in the current moment, when even the foundations of material property are contested, it is a most remarkable phenomenon to see philosophers, jurists and diplomats unite in order to affirm the legality of property in the intellectual sphere. Devoting attention to the fruits of intellectual labor, isn't it analogous to reciprocally recognizing thought in the material world? Is there a more beautiful and more significant work of *social conservation*, of individual and collective

38 *ALAI, Son histoire*, 57–58.

39 Basalamah, *Le droit de traduire*, 220.

40 *ALAI, Son histoire*, 65.

progress, a work *that can best counter anarchism*, a labor that deserves more the support of governments than that of manual and intellectual workers?"[41]

The above quotation is interesting, because it is unusual. Analogies of this kind, where IP is directly correlated to the sociopolitical order, are rare. Ideological battles over IP were (and still are) habitually fought on economic, legal, philosophical, practical and moral grounds, rarely on explicitly political ones. Droz's quote implicitly suggests that the organization of knowledge, its production and division of labor are political issues, intricately linked to politics, the political imaginary and the prevailing or desired sociopolitical order. Such an interesting and explicit correlation between IP regimes and conceptions of social and political order we will encounter again only in the discussion of communist copyright. Finally, Droz's reference to anarchism here could have multiple origins: it could be an allusion to the movement of political anarchism, widespread among watchmakers in his home canton of Neuenburg in the second half of the nineteenth century,[42] or it could be an allusion to the challenge posed by P.-J. Proudhon in his *Les majorats littéraires*, in which, while arguing against the utilitarian and liberal French economists of the mid-nineteenth century, Proudhon rejected the property theory regarding authors' rights.[43]

The 1879 ALAI congress in London defended the position that the exclusive right of translation belongs to the author of the original work for the same term of protection as the right of reproduction with the sole reservation that the authorized translation had to be published in its entirety within five years of publication of the original. The five-year term became the basis for further developments.[44] The 1880 ALAI congress in Lisbon pushed the margins of argumentation a step further. Among its resolutions were: (1) the right of translation formed part of the exclusive rights of the author; (2) the development of one uniform legislation concerning translations; diplomatic treaties would have to conform to this standard; (3) distinctions should no longer be made between literary and dramatic works; (4) the deadline imposed upon the author to conduct the translation was extended from five to ten years; and (5) the need to state a reservation of the right of translation in the original work was dropped altogether.[45]

41 *ALAI, Son histoire*, 269. Emphases added.

42 On anarchist watchmakers in Switzerland see Pierre Maillard, "Anarchists and Watchmakers," https://www.europastar.com/the-watch-files/archives-heritage/1004113260-anarchists-and-watchmakers.html. I am grateful to Hannes Siegrist for indicating this connection to me.

43 See here Dominique Sagot-Duvauroux, "La propriété intellectuelle, c'est le vol ! Le débat sur le droit d'auteur au milieu du XIXe siècle," *L'économie politique* 2004/2, no. 22 (2004): 34–52.

44 *ALAI, Son histoire*, 21.

45 *ALAI, Son histoire*, 65–66.

The diplomatic conferences that took place in Berne in 1884 and 1885 assured the exclusive right of translation a unique duration of ten years. After the expiration of this term, the translation of a work in any language was free. The BC revision conference of 1896 that took place in Paris succeeded in ascertaining the assimilation of the right of translation to the right of reproduction, on condition that a translation was published in the languages in which protection was sought during the first ten years from publication of the original. Beginning with the eleventh year, it was legal to translate works but only into the languages in which no translation had appeared in the course of the first ten years. Supporting the assimilation of the two rights during the Paris conference were Germany, France, Monaco, Luxemburg and Switzerland. Norway and Sweden did not ratify the additional act, adhering to the regulation standards of 1886. Japan, a signatory of the 1886 BC, was among the most vocal challengers of the proposed translation regime and staunchly defended the freedom of translation at the Berlin revision conference of 1908. A reluctant attitude was also adopted by the Dutch and Russian delegations, which supported a transitional regime for the countries that could not immediately adopt the new advanced benchmark for translations. In order to accommodate them, a system of reservations (art. 25) was agreed upon in order to facilitate convergence of opinion.[46] Allowing for regimes of different speeds concerning translation rights was a concession arising from the realization that translation was indeed a major point of discord and also the main reason behind the reluctance of states to join the BU. In the "spirit of reconciliation," the Berlin conference abstained from declaring a final and absolute principle. On the grounds of article 25, it was possible for non-contracting states to approach the BU in two stages, with the final goal fixed by article 8. New members also had the option of adhering to the previous acts of 1886 and 1896, which assigned an exclusive translation right of short duration without reservations or the observation of specific formalities. The right of translation was nothing less than a watershed: "in any case, the recognition of the right of translation remains the *condition sine qua non* for participation in the consortium of the Union."[47]

The degree to which the specific handling of the issue of translation was of French inspiration and design, how vital such a solution was to French interests and how persistently and systematically it was pursued internationally is evidenced by reports in *Le Droit d'auteur*. Reports on the first diplomatic conference in Berne in

46 "Partie non officielle, Études générales, La Convention de Berne révisée du 13 Novembre 1908, Le Droit exclusif de traduction," *Le Droit d'auteur*, year 25, no. 4, April 15, 1912, 45–47.

47 "Partie non officielle, Études générales, La Convention de Berne révisée du 13 Novembre 1908, Le Droit exclusif de traduction (suite et fin)," *Le Droit d'auteur*, year 25, no. 5, May 15, 1912, 67.

1884 claim that "France achieved at least a theoretical victory," so that "wherever possible the tendency towards the complete assimilation of the right of translation to the right of reproduction was to be favored." During the Paris revision conference in 1896, "France resumed the struggle," while the compromise that was achieved (assimilation of the right of translation to the right of reproduction but with a time limit of ten years) was considered only an intermediate step towards a clearly defined and tenaciously pursued end goal, namely the total assimilation of translation to the right of reproduction for the same term of protection as copyright. Memoires reveal the well-calculated and strategic character of various steps in the legislating process: "due to the usual intervention of Mr. de Borchgrave, [the resolution] was given a better editing according to which the principle of assimilation is mentioned in the first line, and the condition [of a time limit] was mentioned only in the second. [...] [O]ur successors—mentioned M. Renault shrewdly in his report—will only have to suppress [i.e. replace] everything that follows this first line of the new paragraph."[48]

According to Jacques Michon, specialist in French-speaking literary and book history, the French vested interest in translation was a result of the competition among the West European publishing industries and the assets specific to each of them, which in turn also determined their capacities and options of expansion:

> At the beginning of the 20th century, having exploited all resources in their own markets and having realized the economic importance of exterior publics, enlarged partially through the help of pirate publishers, the European metropoles embarked upon conquest of the world. London thus opened branch offices in its colonies, India, Australia and Canada; Germany enlarged its zone of influence in the countries of Central and Northern Europe and Italy; Paris, which in the 19th century had had only a limited success in expanding its branches abroad, played the card of translation, of entertainment literature and that of the grand laic culture, the heritage of the Enlightenment.[49]

48 "Partie non officielle, Etudes générales, La Convention de Berne e la révision de Paris, XI. Du Droit exclusive de traduction," *Le Droit d'auteur*, year 16, no. 1, January 15, 1903, 3.

49 Jacques Michon, "Introduction," in *Les mutations du livre et de l'édition dans le monde du XVIIIe siècle a l'an 2000*, eds. Jacques Michon and Jean-Yves Mollier (Québec/Paris: Les presses de l'université Laval/L'Harmattan, 2001), 12.

Counter Positions

The gradual build-up of translation as a rigorous, exclusive and impenetrable author's right was contested from the very beginning, while similar concerns were also aired regarding the practice of adaptations. It was mainly participants from the European and world peripheries that redirected attention from the author's exclusive property rights to the social, cultural and political conditions in their respective homelands and the different role and significance that translations acquired in those contexts. East European participants from Poland and Russia, from the European South, for example from Portugal, as well as Japanese representatives contested the dictum that unauthorized translations and adaptations harmed both the home author and the target literature. During the 1879 ALAI congress in London, the plenipotentiary of Portugal in Paris, Jose da Silva Leal, stressed the significant contribution and the great service of adaptations in the development of various national literatures, especially if they emanated from competent authors such as Shakespeare or Molière.[50] The importance of the practice of translation for Poland was argued by M. Mickiewicz: "Art in Poland is a means and not a goal. Literature is nothing but the servant of national thought. Its particular situation transforms literature into a precious and invincible fortress of the national language. A library is [respected as] the shrine of the Lares deity [...] Poland needs to translate. Unfortunately, it can remunerate foreign authors only imperfectly but literary piracy is rare. As a result of the cult status that literature enjoys in Poland, literary property is respected by everybody."[51] Polish delegates likewise made a strong case for the necessity of easy access to scientific literature, claiming science to be—on a par with literature and culture—a collective and social value, which would be seriously imperilled were it to become dependent on the will of an individual. The author's prerogative to inhibit translation contained the danger that works would remain unknown in other countries; it was therefore imperative to establish temporal limits in order to guarantee the translation of scientific works. It is noteworthy that this preoccupation regarding access to science and scientific knowledge, which we will also encounter in the case of Russia, and which is ultimately a discourse about catch-up modernity, is an exclusive discourse of the European and world peripheries and does not appear in the West European copyright discourse.

---

50 *ALAI, Son histoire*, 25–27.

51 *ALAI, Son histoire*, 76–77.

Intellectuals stressed the contextually dependent role that translation played in different countries. For "importing" countries strategically reliant on foreign intellectual production, translation was a source of revenue for a far greater group of people than in the knowledge-exporting countries, which by nature translated little. Participating in the 1878 ALAI congress, the Russian author Ivan Turgenev underscored the importance of translators for Russia, explaining that they were mostly youngsters living on nothing else but this profession. Adopting a hard line on translation was equal to attacking "this numerous class of people," and would serve very well the intentions of the [authoritarian] Russian government. Answering to Walt Whitman, who labelled [unauthorized] translators "a race of malignant literary bandits," Turgenev explained: "those translators I am referring to are no bandits. In a certain way, they are the pioneers of civilization in our country. You will tell me: it's fine, but this which they introduce at home, they take from us. It is true, but there are also precedents. Had Peter the Great not been such an illustrious bandit, I would not stand here in front of you [...]. I, personally, would probably be the only person to agree with you, since I am honoured to have my books translated. But for me, this here is not a question of principle, it is a national question."[52]

The asymmetries characteristic of uneven world development constituted a potentially explosive topic that surfaced repeatedly in international discussions on copyright. This automatically raises the question of whether such discrepancies were discernible to contemporary actors or whether they were bypassed on the grounds of law's lofty ideals of universalism, and/or the prevalent colonial mindset of the times. Apparently, and as can be deduced from the quotes below, asymmetries were indeed perceptible but were basically ignored in an admixture of universalism and sentiments of colonial superiority. Furthermore, it was clear that IP was a game for strong players: "small states, which do not as yet possess a literature, have insisted upon signing this convention, not out of vanity without a cause, but with the intention of envisioning progress and the future, so as to convey to the great states their wish to be in step with European civilization."[53] A few sentences further on, the same Eugène Pouillet remarked with apparent remorse: "Tunisia, the Republic of Liberia [both BU members at the time, AD] do they have authors? I do admit my ignorance and simultaneously regret it."[54]

If a state was in doubt regarding its ranking on the civilizational ladder, the "great states" made sure to dispel that uncertainty. The Bulgarian publisher Stojan

52 Basalamah, *Le droit de traduire*, 235.

53 Basalamah, *Le droit de traduire*, 262.

54 Basalamah, *Le droit de traduire*, 263.

Atanasov recalled an episode that took place during the post-World War I peace settlement in Versailles. As the Bulgarian state's new borders were settled and consequently communicated to the Bulgarian delegation attending the conference at Neuilly, the latter protested, deploring that the settlement was disadvantageous and arguing that by such means a "small cultural nation" was being deprived of its capacity to develop. In response to the Bulgarian protest, Clemenceau retorted: "You claim to be a cultured nation, well then, bring me evidence in the course of the next 24 hours of any one of your books [that was] ever translated into a foreign language."[55]

Reluctant voices had argued early on that the ALAI was pursuing an agenda exclusively to the benefit of French authors and poets, whose works dominated the universal markets, to the detriment of other literatures.[56] The ALAI went a long way towards dispelling such claims as false perceptions, arguing that the issue of literary property was not about mercantilism, but about the independence of the author and the emancipation of literature from patronage, since the decision-making capacity now lay with the public.[57] French book history, however, has countered this representation, demonstrating on the contrary how closely knit the relationship was between publishers and the French state. In fact, France's pioneering role in promoting the model of bilateral treaties and international IP protection was precisely the result of strong publisher pressure upon their government ever since the beginning of the July Monarchy.[58] The idiosyncrasy of the French position becomes apparent when compared to the mode of legal regulation in other countries. Since 1817, Holland had declared its entire intellectual production to belong to the public domain; the same legislation was applied in Belgium after 1831. The USA refused to ratify international treaties during the whole of the nineteenth century and up until 1909, while the North German Confederation (Norddeutscher Bund) let all works published prior to 1867 fall into the public domain. France, on the contrary, led the movement for the unification of existing national legislations and prepared the path for the Berne Convention. Compared to English legislation, which recognized copyright only during the author's lifetime, and the German one (German Bund/Deutscher Bund) that initially protected IP for the duration of ten years, and after 1837 for 30 years p.m.a.,. France had already by 1866 raised the stakes of protection

55 P. Trumbev, "Krizata v pazarja na pročitnata kniga," *Knižarska Duma*, no. 149 (1939): 5.

56 *ALAI, Son histoire*, 81.

57 *ALAI, Son histoire*, 85–86.

58 Jean-Yves Mollier, "La construction du system éditorial français et son expansion dans le monde du XVIIIe au XXe siècle," in Michon and Mollier, *Les mutations du livre*, 55.

to 50 years, an important concession to the local publishers.[59] As a result, the French model of publishing limited competition by restricting the extension of the public domain, whereas, by contrast, Germany rather acknowledged market completion; it was only through the release of thousands of classics into the public domain that Philipp Reclam was able to build his universal library. The French state protected publishers: it delineated the parameters of their profession, controlled them closely, and placated them by accommodating their wishes in the form of an exchange of favors.[60] It appeared that internal protectionism was coupled with, or rather was the propitious precondition for, external expansion.

There is an additional explanation for the pioneering role that France played in promoting the internationalization of copyright. In contrast to other countries, such as Britain and Germany, authors' rights in France were confirmed and institutionalized in the context of a seminal political event of international magnitude with universalistic overtones: the French Revolution. Moreover, in the case of France, there was significant overlap between the political and intellectual/literary elites, a circumstance that promoted the prominence of authors' rights and moved it upwards on the political agenda. In fact, a series of French men of letters had simultaneously pursued a political career (Chateaubriand, Beaumarchais, Lamartine, Victor Hugo, later Paul Claudel etc.), breeding an admixture of *homme politique* and *homme intellectuel*; some of them, such as Chateaubriand, Beaumarchais and Hugo, were instrumental in promoting the copyright cause. In contrast, therefore, to the British case, where the struggle for copyright maintained a predominantly legalistic profile and evolved largely in the courtroom through litigation cases between contending publishers, and in contrast again to the German case, where the defense of the copyright cause was fought largely on philosophical and legal-philosophical grounds between philosophers/authors, publishers and jurists, the French case was particularly suited to ensuring a prominent connection between literature and politics, of which internationalization was the best example.

59 Mollier, "La construction du system éditorial," 56.

60 Mollier, "La construction du system éditorial," 56.

From the Printing to the Original-Copy Paradigm

The qualities and boundaries of the benchmarks for copyright protection were already being debated in the world of book print and the book trade in the late eighteenth century. They often revolved around norms: which criteria ought to be prioritized and what validated an "original" or the right to a commercial monopoly? While it was initially the procurement of "the original" (i.e. the original physical manuscript) that sanctioned the publishing rights of publishers and printers, later on, with the progressive contouring of the author as "proprietor" of pioneering ideas, the discussion shifted towards the antithesis between the material and immaterial properties of the book, while the problem of "originality" was eventually transposed to the nature of ideas: what ought to be protected, the content of ideas or the specific form in which they were expressed?

The early nineteenth century witnessed yet another transformation of legal doctrine that was to affect the question of what an "original" is. It triggered a further shift away from the initial "printing" paradigm of copyright towards the solidification of what could be termed the "original-copy" paradigm. This shift was heavily influenced by developments in the visual arts.[61]

This transition involved a redefinition of key concepts such as "copy," "work" and "reproduction." The resignification of "reproduction" as duplication or multiplication was related to the emergence of new technologies such as lithography and photography, which changed the perception of art and conceptually intensified the dichotomous relationship between a singular original and multiple derivative copies.[62] The initial "printing" paradigm that developed in the eighteenth century had been constructed upon the dichotomy of authorized versus nonauthorized copies, whereby infringement was assessed on the basis of the production of unauthorized copies. The new paradigm of the nineteenth century totalized the antithetical relationship between an "original work" and the "copy." It was the birth hour of the notion of an "original" as unique, exclusive and inspired, and of its opposite, the copies, understood as multiple, mundane and derivative.[63]

This new valorization of "originality" in the context of new media allowed for an even greater expansion of the system of copyright. It was precisely the above doctrinal revision that facilitated the inclusion of the right of translation into the

61 Teilmann-Lock, *The Object of Copyright*, 96.

62 Teilmann-Lock, *The Object of Copyright*, 50–51.

63 Teilmann-Lock, *The Object of Copyright*, 96.

author's exclusive right of reproduction. Following a paragon line of argumentation, jurists drew parallels between engravings and translations, transposing upon literature the logic of the visual arts (somewhat reversing the previous practice, where the arts had followed the logic of the printing paradigm).

French lawyers vigorously defended the assimilation of translation to reproduction. As elucidated by Eugène Pouillet:

> we decided invariably that the translation was nothing else but a mode of reproduction, [then] that which in a work belongs in the first place to the author, is not the adornment [la parure], nor the clothes [le vêtement] (the language in which a work is written is nothing else but a dress), but the work itself, its composition, the subject matter it deals with. A work does not change by nature when, instead of being written in French, it is written in Italian or Spanish. Translation is to the literary work what an engraving [la gravure] is to a work of art. Would it be tolerated if the author of a painting could not prohibit his work from being engraved without his consent? French courts have never admitted at any time that the right to translate could be considered as detached from the right of reproduction which belongs to the author of the original.[64]

An issue that could be interesting to explore further in this context is whether modifications that took place in printing techniques in the eighteenth and nineteenth centuries, namely the shift from movable type to stereotype, were conducive to creating the analogy between lithography and translation.

No matter how forcibly jurists expounded their arguments in favor of the assimilation of translation to reproduction, they were frequently betrayed by their own language, which registered and preserved the contradictions of their reasoning. The intelligibility of the concept of "reproduction" was challenged as jurists sought to expound on its nature and inevitably paired it with "synonyms," which more often than not contradicted the essence of the term. The following excerpt from *Le Droit d'auteur* nicely captures this persistent hermeneutical and etymological ambiguity:

> In fact, translation is the international form, the most common, of reproduction. In the relationship between peoples of different languages, it is indeed reproduction that puts a work within reach of a new public, speaking another language and for whom the literary work would not exist without that *prior mutation* [...] [T]his is so true that on the one side the interests of this public are often opposed through [...] the right of the author to control *all versions of his works*, and from the other

64 "Partie non officielle, Etudes générales, La Convention de Berne e la révision de Paris, XI. Du droit exclusif de traduction," *Le Droit d'auteur*, year 16, no. 1, January 15, 1903, 2.

side, any restriction in exercising this right is experienced by the authors as one of the most sensitive attacks on literary property.[65]

While in the above quotations "reproduction" is associated with concepts like "mutation" and "version" which point at transformation and difference rather than outright likeness/copying, in the following quote from the same article, "reproduction" and "translation" are discussed not as synonyms but as contrasting concepts. Criticizing the legislation of countries that protected foreign authors against piracy (i.e. reprints) but refused them the right of translation, the author claimed this to be only an appearance of protection, for "*if reproduction is prohibited and translation permitted*, this means that we protect the author by defending a thing that cannot be produced and by permitting the sole possible attack on this right."[66] Even more, the main justification for the assimilation of translation to reproduction, which claimed in a nutshell that "translation is the *international form of reproduction*,"[67] was hardly intelligible. The concept of reproduction related to the mode of production and was indifferent to any geographical specification. Reproduction as the practice of reprinting had been both a "national" and cosmopolitan, international activity. In fact, the efforts to provide justification for the new semantics of "reproduction" in transnational terms point rather to the significance of space, that is, a reshuffling of the notion of space and its relation to the economy than to the act of "reproduction" as such. "International" is intelligible in the above quote only as the antithesis of "national," which is here only implied but ubiquitous. All these semantic tensions point at diverse complex political, social, cultural and economic processes that were taking place in parallel and were influencing the arts, or more accurately stated, the market for the arts and culture. They point simultaneously at a cognitive process so characteristic of modernity: the taming of space and difference.

Though doctrinal revision and the perseverance of the "original-copy" paradigm facilitated the shift towards a new interpretation and consequently towards a new treatment of translation, aesthetic philosophy and theory represented just one dimension of a far more composite phenomenon, being rather the symptoms than the causes of this theoretical revision. The reasons translation became so central—

---

65 "Partie non officielle, Études générales, La Convention de Berne révisée du 13 Novembre 1908, Le droit exclusif de traduction," *Le Droit d'auteur*, year 25, no. 4, April 15, 1912, 45. Emphases added.

66 "Partie non officielle, Études générales, La Convention de Berne révisée du 13 Novembre 1908, Le droit exclusif de traduction," *Le Droit d'auteur*, year 25, no. 4, April 15, 1912, 45. Emphases added.

67 "Partie non officielle, Études générales, La Convention de Berne révisée du 13 Novembre 1908, Le Droit exclusif de traduction (suite et fin)," *Le Droit d'auteur*, year 25, no. 5, May 15, 1912, 67. Emphasis added.

both pragmatically and symbolically—to modern copyright in the late nineteenth century are intricately linked to processes inherent to this age, the age of nationalities, empires and capitalism.

During the initial phase of the "printing" paradigm of copyright, which coincided with the slow process of industrialization, centralization and nationalization of the print industries, protection encompassed the intended area of distribution of the original work. It largely concerned the regulation and domestication of areas of the same linguistic group. This phase was closely linked to the control of reprinting practices, that is, securing larger spaces of commercial activity and overcoming obstacles of sovereign (physical) borders, which, however, did not represent or coincide with linguistic borders. Under the old regime, the number of educated and literate consumers of print was limited, while many scholars and readers were multilingual, at least in the basic languages of the *res publica literaria*.

In the late eighteenth and nineteenth centuries, a series of factors came together, affecting the mindset as well as the legal understanding and development of copyright in Western Europe: technological innovation; the establishment and preponderance of text-based culture; the centralization and uniformity to be found in a regime of regulated printed-book production that was financially and culturally self-reinforcing; the proper commercialization of the book trade and its incorporation into world trade; changes in aesthetic attitudes and doctrines; a rearrangement of the role of world languages and the explosion of new vernaculars; the development of entertainment industries; the second reading revolution; the expansion and democratization of education, print literacy and the reading public; that is to say, a "literal" revolution in media and communications. The proliferation of IP cannot be understood independently of these wide-ranging structural factors, and it was their evolution, their temporal convergence and synergistic effect that helps to explain why IP was able to develop in such a dynamic way in the second half of the nineteenth century.

In fact, in the period under examination, a substantial reorganization of the relationship between language and territory took place, which invariably affected the traffic in texts. It related to the following processes: (1) a reordering of the hierarchy of world languages, and moreover an unprecedented territorial expansion of specific world languages in the context of empire-building and colonization; (2) a change in the geographies related to intermediary or vehicular languages (i.e. languages that act as transport vehicles between cultures) in the context of new regionalisms, affecting both the transfer channels for texts and the loci of printing. Where certain languages established themselves as new authoritative regional players, new balances were created between established world languages and aspiring world and vehicular languages. The geography, propelled by these changes, corresponded roughly to shifts taking place in the European power structure and was associated in one way or another with processes of empire-building, colonization and/or nationalization; and (3) a new territorialization of languages following on from the process of nation state building, leading to an ever-greater congruence between language and territory. The imperative that language and territory had to overlap became the world norm. These processes were coupled with the massification of culture and the multiplication of transfer media.

The strengthening of vernacular culture and the consolidation of the nation state as the authoritative model of governance in the nineteenth century brought about the dissolution of the *res publica literaria*, the transnational, cosmopolitan world of scholars and erudites that had characterized European intellectual development from the sixteenth to the eighteenth century. It was substituted by the creation of national public spheres, whose main vehicle of communication became national language. Following the slow dissolution of this world, a reshaping of the European geography of printing took place, with long-established and cosmopolitan centers of the printing (and reprinting) industry of the early modern and modern period, such as Venice and Amsterdam,[68] progressively losing their commercial and cultural significance. It is therefore no coincidence that prominent centers such as Amsterdam (itself the center of an overseas empire) did not become world leaders in printing in the age of nationalization. As a result of the subsiding of the propitious conditions that in the seventeenth century had transformed the Netherlands into a publishing hub (e.g. the religious wars on the European continent that made the Netherlands a safe haven for religious exiles, and the temporarily weak position of their neighbors), subsequent developments like the demise of Latin and the ensuing ascendance of vernaculars, as well as the far-reaching curbing of reprinting, meant that Dutch printing in the national language had little chance to expand. In other words, it missed the backing of a world language upon which to build an expanding print industry. It therefore contracted to the limited environment of Dutch-speakers.

How printing and industrialization converged to form new geographies and how printing followed the geography of industrialization is demonstrated well in the Italian case, where the longstanding (international) centers of printing like Venice and Naples progressively ceded their leading roles to the industrializing centers

[68] Paul G. Hoftijzer, "The Dutch Republic, Centre of the European Book Trade in the 17th Century," *European History Online (EGO)*, published by the Leibniz Institute of European History (IEG), Mainz, 23 November 2015, http://www.ieg-ego.eu/hoftijzerp-2015-en.

of the north (Milan and Florence). Several international centers of printing such as Vienna, Venice and Trieste declined in significance as they progressively lost, in the course of nationalization and nation state building, their habitual clients, that is, the elites and authors of the various ethnic groups who, lacking their own national state printing industry, had their works printed in these cosmopolitan printing hubs. Such had been the case with Greek printing, where the above-mentioned cities, along with urban centers of Central Europe and the Ottoman Empire, had formed important hubs of Greek publishing before the establishment of the Greek kingdom in the first half of the nineteenth century. With the creation of the Greek state, now functioning as a national center, not only was the printing business in the Greek language moved there, but the Greek state claimed for itself the role of a publishing center with the pretension to supply the significant number of Greek-speakers of the Ottoman Empire with printed matter as well. Nationalization meant, depending on the case, contraction or expansion of a culture and was intricately linked to the existence and continuous recruitment of new groups of vernacular speakers, who could guarantee the consumption of print culture, and thereby the expansion of printing.

Translation as a Cultural World System[69]

It is due to the growing significance of translation studies that translation is nowadays considered to be much more than a simple transfer of texts from one culture and language into another. Whereas the "normative" approach to translation traditionally focused on the relationship to the original text, contemporary "polysystem" theorists, embracing a sociological approach to the study of translations, have shifted scholarly interest from source-text to target-context.[70] Moreover, in conventional conceptions (and perhaps copyright has no small share in the popularization of this conception), translation had long been conceived as an allegedly neutral and symmetric, linear and horizontal transfer, presupposing the existence of equal, self-contained and juxtaposing national languages.[71] Contemporary theory, by contrast, views translation

69 The title of this section was partially borrowed from Johan Heilbron, "Towards a Sociology of Translation: Book Translations as a Cultural World-System," *European Journal of Social Theory* 2, no. 4 (1999): 429–44.

70 Polysystem theory was developed from the 1970s onwards by Israeli scholars of culture, notably Itamar Even-Zohar and Gideon Toury.

71 Pascale Casanova, "Consécration et accumulation de capital littéraire: La traduction comme échange inégal," *Actes de la recherche en sciences sociales* 144 (September 2002): 7.

as a cultural world system, that is, as the expression and result of the relations of power played out in the international literary field, involving a global constellation of language groups and of national and supranational cultures. In other words, "[t]he inequalities and hierarchies, both literary and linguistic, which order the world literary field, demonstrate a different economy of linguistic exchanges: far from being a horizontal exchange or the pacified transfer often described, translation can be understood on the contrary, as an 'unequal exchange' produced in a strongly hierarchized universe."[72] The structure of the world literary field concerns: (1) the unequal distribution of literary capital in the literary universe, which is doubled by an unequal linguistic-literary capital; (2) next to linguistic capital, a linguistic-literary one also attached to each language, the second being relatively independent of the first.[73]

The significance of translations within language groups depends mainly on the position of the language within the international system. The international translation system, though not quite corresponding to Wallerstein's model, is likewise a hierarchical structure consisting of central, semi-peripheral and peripheral languages. The centrality of a language is affirmed when it enjoys a larger share in the total number of translated works worldwide; the total number of translated books worldwide, however, stems from a very limited number of languages and is therefore very unevenly distributed.[74]

A language's degree of centrality in the translation system is not determined by the size of the language group; it is therefore possible that a language like Chinese, which is spoken by a very large number of speakers, can occupy only a peripheral position in the world system of translation. The more central a language in the translation system, the greater its capacity to function as an intermediary or vehicular language, that is, to become a means of communication between language groups, which are themselves peripheral or semi-peripheral.[75] Through their choices of which literature to import, the leading centers of the international system set a precedent for peripheral and semi-peripheral language groups to follow. A considerable part of international communication regarding books takes place in this manner and is therefore dependent on the choices of the leading centers of the international system. "International cultural centers are not only interested in the diffusion of their own goods, they also have a vested interest in transit trade and the benefits it offers. Symbolic and economic *transit profits* are an essential component of the

72 Casanova, "Consécration et accumulation," 7.

73 Casanova, "Consécration et accumulation," 8.

74 Heilbron, "Towards a Sociology of Translation," 432–34.

75 Heilbron, "Towards a Sociology of Translation," 434–38.

working of the international cultural system."[76] Seen from this angle, it is perhaps possible to propose an additional explanation for the single-handed French gesture in 1852 to offer protection unilaterally to all foreign works, regardless of the protection offered in other countries. Usually interpreted as a decision indicating "the imaginative power of the doctrine of *droit d'auteur*, which required that the author's natural property rights should not be restricted by national or geographic boundaries" and representing "a clear attempt to put moral pressure on other nations to recognize this universal truth, and to reciprocate,"[77] the French move can additionally be regarded as a confirmation of the central role, both real and symbolic, that France (and more specifically the city of Paris) as well as the French language and literature played in the cultural world system. It was this centrality that inspired and propelled this gesture of multilateral generosity in all directions.

Fundamentally, the translation system is a historical system, and the period studied in this chapter, the late eighteenth and nineteenth centuries, witnessed significant changes in the position (status) of languages and cultures. The valorization of translation—though also indebted to the already discussed modifications of aesthetical and philosophical doctrine—cannot be considered independently of them.

Among vernacular languages, French was the most central in early modern Europe and would retain this position until the late eighteenth century, when for geopolitical and geocultural reasons it had to retreat from its privileged position. During the late eighteenth and early nineteenth century, the portion of books translated from French declined rapidly, and German in particular was able to profit from this decline.[78] French had played no minor role as a vehicular language; French translations of foreign works had served as the basis for their translation into other languages. Moreover, in the seventeenth century, in order to have classical texts better understood, French scholars had often translated freely by adapting foreign and classical texts to indigenous norms of elegance and clarity; such translations were better known as the "belles infidèles" (the pretty [but] unfaithful). However, retranslation from French translations, which had been common practice during the seventeenth and eighteenth centuries, "fell into disrepute at the end of the old regime, when nationalism became a political and cultural force. German and English literature gained more recognition and translations into French lost their exemplary role."[79]

---

76 Heilbron, "Towards a Sociology of Translation," 437.

77 Catherine Seville, *The Internationalization of Copyright Law: Books, Buccaneers and the Black Flag in the Nineteenth Century* (Cambridge: Cambridge University Press, 2006), 57–58.

78 Heilbron, "Towards a Sociology of Translation," 434–35.

79 Heilbron, "Towards a Sociology of Translation," 435–36.

Taming Difference

Researchers of translation history such as Salah Basalamah have already pointed at the discrepancy between the lofty humanistic principles of equality and universalism that officially motivated the internationalization of IP and the actual reality of global hierarchies, inequalities and colonial authoritarianism.[80] Others, like Eva Hemmungs Wirtén, have emphasized the asymmetries between importing and exporting nations, minor and major languages that produced divergent stances regarding the mode of regulation and the significance attributed to translation.[81]

How strongly, however, the topic of translation correlated to transformation processes in political governance, such as the prevalence of the nation state and/or the expansion of colonial empires, has not been adequately stressed. While the topic of translation as an issue requiring regulation helped to solidify the incontestable authority of the author, the assimilation of translation to reproduction served to obscure the aspect of intermediation, that is, of "difference" in cultural exchange processes. Managing translation was intricately connected to the broader enterprise of governing difference in the modern period, either by erasing or by domesticating it. Cognitively, it was supplemented by an evolutionary world view, firmly committed to "progress," which irrefutably asserted a universal movement from primitive to more sophisticated forms of existence. Such an evolutionary scheme predicated not only the lives of nations and their cultures, but those of institutions such as the BU as well. Along these lines, countries that failed to follow or ratify the newest version of the BC were informally categorized as "remaining stuck in the primitive stage [of the BC] of 1886."[82] In several ways, the suppositions and the epistemology feeding the project of translation corresponded closely to those upholding the colonial project.

Exemplary of the significance of translation for a large part of the world is the discussion on that score triggered by Japan, as well the reactions it sparked. During the 1908 Berlin conference, Japan, a signatory of the initial 1886 BC, asked to be exempted from all relevant obligations with respect to translation, and advocated, following the example of the American-Japanese treaty of November 10, 1905, the liberty of translation for union members' works into Japanese, and reciprocally of Japanese works into European languages.

---

80 Basalamah, *Le droit de traduire*, 226.

81 Hemmungs Wirtén, "A Diplomatic Salto Mortale," 93–94.

82 "La Norvège et la Suède n'avaient pas même ratifie l'acte additionnel de Paris *et s'étaient arrêtées à l'étape primitive de 1886*" [emphasis mine] quoted in "Partie non officielle, Études générales, La Convention de Berne révisée du 13 Novembre 1908, Le droit exclusif de traduction," *Le Droit d'auteur*, year 25, no. 4, April 15, 1912, 46.

Like the Scandinavians before them, the Japanese argued their standpoint largely on the grounds of global asymmetries and difference:

> [a] great etymological difference of form and depth existed between the European languages and Japanese. Due to this intricacy, it was almost impossible to render verbatim into Japanese the signification of terms, which connoisseurs of European languages in Japan would rather read in the original, and those who do not dispose of such knowledge, with the help of a translation. In educated milieus the sale of original books is therefore guaranteed in both cases and the interests of the author and the publisher safeguarded in this country. Consequently, translation is a kind of publicity or advertisement to the benefit of Western editions in order to facilitate their sales.

Moreover, the liberty of translation was dictated by progress, with the superior aim to facilitate contact among Eastern and Western civilizations. In any other case, intellectual relationships suffered, and the translators, "whose work was no reproduction but equivalent to the creation of a new book, essentially different through the expression of ideas, the phrase structure and the value of words," were discouraged.[83]

Answering the Japanese proposal, the German delegate, Albert Osterrieth, defended the right of translation as a measure advantageous to all countries. It ensured that worthy works were selected for translation and guaranteed likewise the quality of the latter. His most striking argument, however, praised not the virtues of international regulation but pointed at the perils lurking behind the prevalence of different regional patois and minor ethnolinguistic groups and identities. The implicit and unstated consequence of his reflection emphasizes the virtues of the standardized national language, that is, the epitome of the nation state. The correlation between language, identity and the monolingual nation state, both as an ideology and as the

[83] "Partie non officielle, Études générales, La Convention de Berne révisée du 13 Novembre 1908, Le droit exclusif de traduction," 46-47. Japanese attitudes towards international copyright regulation, especially regarding the issue of translation, but also Japan's broader attitudes and strategies towards the Berne Union from the late 19th to the 1950s have been studied by Maj Antonie Hartmann, "Towards a Global Copyright Law: Japan's Involvement in the Prewar International Copyright Negotiations," *Japan Forum* 0, no. 0 (2021): 1–23. Hartmann emphasizes the entanglement of state and non-state actors, especially publishers, in the elaboration of Japanese attitudes towards international copyright, and provides an analysis of the diverse stakeholders, their interests and rhetorical justification strategies within the country and abroad. She further underlines Japan's contradictory behavior, contrasting her policy towards the BU with that towards China, which Japan treated as a prospective export market for its own industries and where—in contradistinction—she sought protection for Japanese works translated into Chinese. Hartmann credits Japanese statesmen, jurists and publishers with hindering the international development of translation rights, a somewhat inconclusive argument that overrates the role of Japan in this context, given the multiplicity of international actors and voices opposing excessive terms of protection that encumbered translations. This fact is also testified by the strivings of the majority of "third world" countries in the post-WWII period to secure easier and cheaper access to translations.

legitimate unit of cultural production, could not be clearer. A notion of national culture arises as contained in itself, suppressing its renitent fragments. Finally, by admitting that Japanese was not a very popular world language and therefore posed no real threat, Osterrieth indirectly confirmed the hierarchy of central and peripheral languages in translation practice, discussed earlier in this chapter.

> Japanese language is admittedly less known in the countries of the Union and therefore a translation into Japanese can never really injure the interests of the author and the publisher of the original. But is Japanese the only language for which one could make such a claim? In many Union countries we find languages and patois, whose command is restricted to a relatively small part of the population. Take for example: *le breton, le picard, le romanche dans les Grisons, le basque, le welsch dans le pays de Galles*. If we accept the Japanese proposal, we will undoubtedly be forced, by the logic of things, to grant to these particular languages the same privileges and thereby annihilate even the system of the Berne Convention itself.[84]

The above quotation is a good indicator of the political and sociocultural processes that underlay the development of the international copyright regime. Copyright appeared to represent a legal instrument that best served territorial spaces (nations) that were more or less linguistically and culturally consolidated, that is, nations possessing what Ernest Gellner has called "a single intellectual currency."[85] For IP's pioneering nations, the promotion and defense of the concept of copyright was closely tied to a specific concept of culture that presupposed the proliferation and homogenizing effects of "print capitalism" and its intimate connection to the nation state.[86] As a legal mechanism, it seemed less suited to help address the complex realities and labile equilibriums of multiethnic and plurilingual imperial realms or states-in-the-making, and the multitude, ambivalence, malleability and fluidity of existing identities in such parts of the world.

---

84 "Annexes, Mémoire concernant la protection du droit de traduction, présenté en séance de commission par M. Albert Osterrieth (délégué de l'Allemagne)," *Le Droit d'auteur*, year 22, no. 2, February 15, 1909, 26. Emphasis added.

85 "By the common or single intellectual currency, I mean that all facts are located within a single continuous logical space [...], and so that in principle one single language describes the world and is internally unitary; or on the negative side, that there are no special, privileged, insulated facts or realms, protected from contamination or contradiction by others, and living in insulated independent spaces of their own. Just this was, of course, the most striking trait of pre-modern, pre-rational visions: the coexistence within them of multiple, not properly united, but hierarchically related sub-worlds, and the existence of special privileged facts, sacralized and exempt from ordinary treatment." Ernest Gellner, *Nations and Nationalism* (Ithaca, NY: Cornell University Press, 1983), 21.

86 Benedict Anderson, *Imagined Communities: Reflections on the Origin and Spread of Nationalism* (London: Verso, 1983).

Additional aspects of linguistic communication, particularly metaphors, exemplify the world view and the approach of the actors. Particularly salient is the use of a power language that purports an imaginary of domination, and discusses translation within those parameters. Commenting on the qualities of good translations, the French jurist Eugène Pouillet argued that: "[...] translation [...] is all the more appreciated because she is *both faithful and more servile*. The translator strives to render, in another language, the author's own genius, his thought, and even his expression."[87]

If in the above quotation the image of the "faithful and servile" translation/translator evokes distant associations of "race," such as the image of the "bon négre," who is "good-natured, devoted to his master at the expense of his own self, and without bitterness about his servile state,"[88] the next quotation is explicit in its biological imaginary. Pointedly bringing together the notion of difference and the evolutionary biology of the times, the resolution of the 1880 ALAI congress in Lisbon spoke of "translation, this kind of transfusion of foreign blood into a country's veins [that] has to be practiced with prudence, knowledge and honesty."[89] More than anything else, it is a notion of biopower that is purported through all these images and metaphors, implying through different semantics the subjugation of bodies and the control of populations. While Osterrieth is worried about the corroding effects of ethnic polyphony that threatened to shatter the coherence of the national body, in the last quote on the blending of blood it is exactly the opposite; it is the fear of métissage, of creolization as the careless mixing of genes and cultures, that causes anxieties.

Creating Law, Modelling Literature

The pro or contra debates on translation deserve attention less for their argumentative content than for their function as rhetorical and persuasive campaigns. What is often overlooked in relevant analyses is the degree to which—on a meta level—the discussion on legal regulation also implicitly modelled the field literature.

The question of what happened to a text when crossing into another language created a series of reasonable concerns; anxieties about losing linguistic control over

87 *ALAI, Son histoire*. Emphasis added.

88 Pratima Prasad, *Colonialism, Race, and the French Romantic Imagination* (New York: Routledge, 2009), 17.

89 "Partie non officielle, Études générales, La Convention de Berne révisée du 13 Novembre 1908, Le Droit exclusif de traduction (suite et fin)," *Le Droit d'auteur*, year 25, no. 5, May 15, 1912, 68.

the work or the necessity for a controlled conversion into another language were certainly real worries. Furthermore, "[a]nxieties regarding the stability of the work coalesced in the question of whom translation really 'belonged to': the author or the reader."[90] Adversaries of the assimilation of translation to reproduction argued for the necessity to facilitate translation by all means; liberty of translation was therefore the appropriate instrument in order to promote translation. The proponents of protection argued on the contrary that the exclusive right of translation assured the production of correct versions and the integrity of the original.

Economic arguments played no minor role in the debate. Whereas opponents castigated the expensive procurement of rights and the rise of book prices, proponents argued against the liberty of translation, that is, the complete liberty of competition, on the grounds that it restricted a work's chances of circulation. Publishers were primarily preoccupied with keeping their expenses to a minimum and cared little about the quality of translation. Their main concern was low prices in order to stand competition, while translators usually concentrated on less qualitative works, also known as "Lesefutter." Unlimited freedom of translation therefore incited the impoverishment of national literature as publishers preferred to publish translations instead of local works, and evaded the necessity to remunerate local authors. Furthermore, by translating works from the public domain, they managed to evade all costs.

For these reasons, publishers' rights were best accommodated through the legal exercise of the right of translation, which gave publishing enterprises the necessary stability, eliminating rushed speculations as well as deregulated and ruinous competition. This principle of law served as an efficient moderator of commercial transactions and guaranteed reasonable sale prices. The right of translation for foreign authors therefore established the equality of local and foreign conditions of production and helped national literature regain its independence.

Safeguarding the right of translation, so the argument went, reduced the number of available translations, but due to the inevitable selection process, the results were better. Hence, it was less the ephemeral and futile publications but rather the good, refined, serious and useful works that deserved the honor of translation. By such means, popular education drew a greater profit and "genuine" civilization saw a more normal and vigorous development.[91]

The author was, after all, the best judge of the pecuniary and moral interests emanating from his work. The likelihood that an author might refuse authorization

90 Wirten, "A Diplomatic Salto Mortale", 102.

91 "Partie non officielle, Études générales, La Convention de Berne révisée du 13 Novembre 1908, Le Droit exclusif de traduction (suite et fin)," *Le Droit d'auteur*, year 25, no. 5, May 15, 1912, 67–68.

of translation was only hypothetical, because such a stance ran contrary to the logic of exploitation and expansion of the book. In addition, the author had an interest to safeguard his literary personality, which through hasty and cheap translations could be exposed to great injuries; "a right of proper surveillance" had to be institutionalized in order to prevent disfigurations and mutilations of all works. To this end, the duration of the right to control had to be sufficiently long, since works with less influence and those of long-lasting value penetrated only slowly those countries where different languages were spoken.[92]

The protection of translation had stood its ground, being a system that favored authors, the entire field of literature and even national interests. It allowed the author, who was generally pleased to see his work translated into foreign languages, to choose the best translator and find a publisher willing to take on the costs of a professional edition to be sold at a reasonable price. On the contrary, the liberty of translation and concomitant unlimited competition produced, instead of one single, neat, professional translation, multiple translations, mostly poor, mutilated and badly edited.[93]

The discussion on translation elucidates quite clearly the rhetorical aspects in the construction of copyright. It demonstrates how economic doctrine and legal reasoning varied according to the subject matter or the agenda they were called on to justify. Whereas, for example, the BU's central concept, the principle of national treatment, created equity of conduct between nations and countries and consequently promoted a free trade regime based on market freedom as well as demand and supply, the argumentation in the case of translation is based on exactly the opposite premise. Free trade—that is, competition of translations—is discarded as harmful, while monopolization in the form of one authorized and controlled translation—that is, protectionism—is concocted as beneficial to all actors involved.

These economic postulations were directly correlated to assumptions about the workings of literature and culture, modelling in many ways the field of literature as the harmonious equivalence between literature, economy and the law. In other words, the impression was created that literature, economy and the law were not independent, perhaps at times even contradictory and rivalrous fields, but rather domains whose inclination was to naturally overlap, and moreover that IP regulation was the result of this innate correspondence. It seemed as if law could capture and address the essence and contradictions of art in the form of codifications, while in reality

92 "Partie non officielle, Études générales, La Convention de Berne révisée du 13 Novembre 1908, Le Droit exclusif de traduction (suite et fin)," *Le Droit d'auteur*, year 25, no. 5, May 15, 1912, 67.

93 "Partie non officielle, Etudes générales, La Convention de Berne révisée du 13 Novembre 1908, Le droit exclusif de traduction," *Le Droit d'auteur*, year 25, no. 4, April 15, 1912, 47.

exactly the opposite was happening: law was applied in order to erase the contradictions. The first assumption was based on the construction of "a false prisoner's dilemma,"[94] which presumed that only authorized translations, and translations under authorial control, were good translations, or otherwise stated, the absence of authorial surveillance automatically classified a translation as inadequate. The logical objection that the authors of ancient or early modern classics were long deceased and naturally abstained from overseeing the translation of their works was apparently not disconcerting. Nor was the obvious fact that original authors, in the majority of cases, were unable to control the final result of the translation process due to their lack of relevant linguistic skills. The second assumption presupposed that copyrighted works were worthy works and moreover that authorized translation fostered only valuable works. Such inferences promoted the ostensibly self-evident overlap of the field of literature and its legal regulation, as well as the apparently indisputable overlap of the field of literature and the market for literature. Such tautologies were conceivable by ignoring or levelling out the diverse forms of "capital" (cultural, social, economic) involved in the field of culture, as well as the various transformations and conversions between these interrelated but also independent forms of "capital." As we will see later on, these transactions (transformations and conversions of capital, relocations and revaluations of texts) are all the more important when texts cross linguistic and cultural borders.

The agent that remained conspicuously absent from the discussion on translation was the translator.[95] By postulating authorial surveillance, control and authorization as the prime qualifiers for the endorsement and quality of translation, the copyright discussion at the turn of the century erased a whole series of attributes apposite to the professionalization of the translator, including his/her familiarity with the foreign culture and language, the ethical imperative to live up to the challenges of intercultural work, the skills and professional experience as well as the desire to communicate the author's message. Paradoxically, though invested with increased competences and surveillance authority, the figure of the author was similarly immobilized and depersonalized. Previously disposing of any real decision-making capacity regarding the fate of his/her work (relevant declarations and reservations in the original, mentioning of the languages for which the right of translation was reserved, expiration of the right if

94 Basalamah, *Le droit de traduire*, 220.

95 This aspect has been repeatedly underscored in scholarly translation studies; see here the classic work of Lawrence Venuti, *The Translator's Invisibility: A History of Translation* (London: Routledge, 1995); see also Basalamah, *Le droit de traduire*.

the author did not use it actively, etc.), in the course of norming translation the author was transformed into a function, something like a toll station sanctioning access or exclusion but devoid of any individual or personalized voice.

The author-function[96] is confirmed through one last observation. As already witnessed, the rationale for equating translation to reproduction was based on incessant invocations of the author, appeals to the author's rights and the integrity of the original text, the correspondence and faithfulness of the translation to the original, protection from crude interventions, mutilations and distortions and so on. In essence, the argumentation referred to a whole bundle of rights that are normally subsumed under the generic notion of "moral rights," that is, rights safeguarding the unique personality of the author as it is reflected in and through his work. However, the cudgels in the case of translation were not taken up for the truly cogent concept of moral rights, but rather were subsumed under the obscure notion of reproduction rights. Moral rights had to wait another 40–50 years (roughly 1878–1928) before they became relevant for international codification in the interwar period during the Rom revision of the BC, and in the context of another paradigm, that of the audiovisual revolution. Why? It is rather obvious that the objective was not the protection of the author (whom moral rights would have ideally defended), but unequivocal control over the commodity. Reproduction was handy. It degraded translation into a copy and confirmed the complete sovereignty of the author-function as a toll station; it ensured that nobody else could interfere in the chain of production, even when the production process became dialogical, collaborative, inter-, cross- and transcultural, that is, messy.[97]

---

96 The notion of the "author-function" was initially coined by Michel Foucault in his famous essay "What Is an Author?" in *Aesthetics, Method and Epistemology*, ed. James D. Faubion (New York: The New Press, 1998), 205–222. Here, I am borrowing his concept and use it with a similar logic and intention, that is, the desire to denaturalize the romantic notion of the individual author by asking the question of what function the author figure fulfils in society and the literary system. However, my ideas are far more simplistic than Foucault's elaborate deconstruction of "authentic" authorship.

97 What is more, historical research on the relationship between translated authors and their foreign publishers, even in a country like France, where moral rights arguments were publicly passionately defended, has demonstrated the lack of complaints and/or contestations by foreign authors concerning the translation of their works. Even in proven cases of misappropriation, that is, in cases where texts were actually mistreated or presented in a mode disrespectful of the express will of the author, writers did not protest. In his research on French translations of foreign authors, Blaise Wilfert-Portal lists such examples (Gabriele D'Annunzio, Russian authors) which confirm the operation of translation as an unequal exchange, that is, as a question of the balance of power, which is established in an unequal mode, and above all to the benefit of the publisher. See here Wilfert-Portal, "Traduction Littéraire," 327–35.

Translation was not the only genre in which legal codification and developments in the arts were at odds with one another. Just as jurists were eager to define with greater or lesser precision the types and categories of works to which copyright protection pertained (usually, when drafting laws, it concerned the question of whether the legislator should provide an exhaustive list of the types of works that enjoyed protection or only an exemplary and open-ended catalogue that could be supplemented with additional types of works along the way), artists at the turn of the century programmatically collapsed the borders between art genres. Rejecting dominant classifications, creators sought the ligature of diverse areas of artistic expression, with no clear prioritization among them. On the contrary, specialization in one, self-contained art category (literature, painting, music etc.) was perceived as redundant.[98] Talented authors and poets of the nineteenth century, such as Théophile Gautier and Victor Hugo, oscillated between literature and painting/drawing when confronted with the dilemma of having to choose their primary form of expression, and stand as examples of the rapprochement between literature and the visual arts in the first half of the nineteenth century. A significant foray in this direction took place around 1900, as various avant-gardes applied fluid borders between graphic arts and the art of writing in their publications. Analogous was the cooperation between authors and painters in the context of theatrical staging, as décor became an essential dramaturgic tool and the creation of theatrical posters a flourishing art. Several emblematic creators of the fin de siècle stand testament to the talents of multitasking: August Strindberg was a talented author and painter, while William Morris combined graphic arts, architecture, typography and applied arts with great literary dexterity. The notion of a "Gesamtkunstwerk" was born precisely out of this practice and expressly set syncretism as a goal, that is, the synthesis of different arts and the creation of a new unity out of these diverse means of expression.[99] If the expectation that the intellectual history of the arts and the history of authors' rights protection should be intertwined, or at least ought to moderately converge, were to be considered over-optimistic, then the examples given here show not only that an elementary convergence was not necessarily present, but on the contrary, that intellectual history and IP history can, and at times do, properly contradict one another.

---

98 Jacques Dugast, *La vie culturelle en Europe au tournant des XIXe et XXe siècles* (here in Greek translation by Alexandra Nestoropoulou) (Athens: Gutenberg, 2020), 194.

99 Dugast, *La vie culturelle en Europe,* 195–99.

The Economy of Translation

In order to understand the logic behind the movement for the assimilation of translation to the right of reproduction, it is necessary to shift focus for a moment from the authorial paradigm (the absolute right of the author to control the fate and the reproduction of his work), which was eminently used in the debates of the period in order to legitimate the right of translation, to the economy of intangible goods and its relationship to the economy of book publishing.

The differences in the nature of tangible and intangible goods are well known. Whereas tangibles wear out in the course of time and can thus experience depreciation, the substance and nature of intangibles can remain unaffected. A distinguishing trait of intangible assets is amortization, that is, the spreading of an asset's cost over the asset's useful life span. Translation creates new works out of old ones, as pointedly argued by Eva Hemmungs Wirten.[100] Translation has, in other words, the capacity to prolong the amortization period through its ability to tap into and open up new markets in diverse languages. Cultural and linguistic variations and differences are not collateral qualities, but rather the precondition for this kind of supranational expansion, which feeds on the transformative power of translation as intercultural encounter. It is effectively difference that enables the extension of the market, and it is precisely difference that is suppressed and/or "tamed" in the rhetorical and cognitive constitution of the right of translation.

Translations prolong the life span of national works through the asynchronous, wave-like expansion into different cultures and their respective national markets. Neither the time frame of this life extension nor its value can be precisely estimated in advance, as they are both dependent on a variety of social, cultural, economic, intellectual and contingent factors. As a result, translation creates sameness out of difference by bringing diverse worlds together in terms of dialogical intercultural communication; and conversely, it creates difference out of sameness in terms of value, when by way of translation it transforms the (old) original into a new work.

Though already mentioned earlier in this chapter, it is nevertheless expedient to recall that the international attitude towards translation changed at the precise moment in time when a series of countries recognized in translation a capacity for expansion of their culture and knowledge industries in the context of the changing geopolitical and linguistic world landscape. Political, economic, cultural and by extension linguistic influences therefore fed on and reinforced each other. This process

100 Hemmungs Wirten, "A Diplomatic Salto Mortale," 89.

of transformation included the explosion of new vernaculars, the nationalization of new knowledge markets, the reshuffling of the roles and hierarchies of world, learned, mediating, regional, national and local languages, all coupled with an increased potential in the means of communication, a multiplication of the means of reproduction, the growth of literate publics and a concomitant change in aesthetic and philosophical doctrines. It was their combined force that propelled the preoccupation with the judicial nature of translation, which had not previously been an issue. In other words, the reordering of the geopolitical landscape and the division of labor in the fields of knowledge and culture recast the question of access in commercial, legal, political and symbolic terms.

Germany is a good case study in this respect. It demonstrates clearly the changing attitude and consequently the shifting positionality of actors (i.e. states) in the global division of labor and the global market of knowledge and culture, a mutation that was related to the move from importers to exporters of knowledge. At the beginning of the nineteenth century, Germany was inundated with unauthorized translations of English and French literature, predominantly novels, which often appeared in multiple simultaneous translations.[101] The period between the 1820s and 1850s was the high point of this development, with contemporaries speaking of "translation factories" (*Übersetzungsfabriken*), whose often average production was mostly driven by competition among German publishers for speedy and cheap publications. The absence of international regulation and bilateral treaties, as well as the dispensable obligation to pay remuneration to foreign authors or publishers, apparently played a role in encouraging the publishers' approach. Though the consequent conclusion of bilateral treaties (from approximately the 1840s) evidently contributed to the decline of this phenomenon, it was rather a combination of diverse factors that led to the decrease in translations starting in the 1850s. Such factors included the augmentation of reading publics and the creation of output tailored to their tastes, as well as a stable overall production of German *belles lettres* during a phase when the repertoire of attractive English and French authors was already exhausted. Under these conditions, German publishers promptly turned their attention to the production of German authors. The German experience basically replicated the French experience, that is, an early period that built up the print industry and relied largely on enhanced and often unregulated translation activity, and a later phase characterized by the nationalization and centralization of both literature and the print business.

101 All information here is from Norbert Bachleitner, "'Übersetzungsfabriken'. Das deutsche Übersetzungswesen in der ersten Hälfte des 19. Jahrhunderts," *Internationales Archiv für Sozialgeschichte der deutschen Literatur* 14, no. 1 (1989): 1–49.

What happens with a text in the process of translation is much more than a simple crossover from one language into another. Translation has the capacity to reposition texts within the literary system and the written universe, a process that can affect both the source and the target culture. Translation, for example, can turn canonical texts in the source culture into non-canonical texts in the receiving culture, and vice versa. Translation can affect the positionality of texts and thereby also their range of influence and value. The transformative capacity of translations is enhanced through intermediality, that is, the transportation from one medium to another. In the "transfer" process, texts may be relocated from the periphery to the center, or from the center to the periphery of the literary field. Such relocations or repositionings are promoted by the cultural reshuffling that takes place in the process of translation, that is, the status and the value allocated to the text in the new context.

In several ways, translations in the context of peripheries developed according to a similar scheme and played a role comparable to that in the core West European countries during earlier phases of their intellectual and literary development. In both cases, translation was long understood as creative adaptation and acculturation to local culture,[102] before in Western Europe translation became fixed to a "copy" of an original. Translations were in both cases important vehicles for the transfer of new literary models and ideas or, as in the case of the literary avant-gardes at the turn of the twentieth century, were used subversively in order to challenge the literary status quo and the (commercial) literature produced by established publishers. Such similarities in functional terms are conducive to the conclusion that the immobility and commodification of texts imposed as an international standard in the second half of the nineteenth century by the BU members could be interpreted as a refusal to grant other parts of the world the prerogative to develop at their own pace. In spite of similarities, there were also differences. In peripheries, translations played a far greater role with regard to the broader project of modernization, and as can be demonstrated in the case of the Ottoman Empire, translations had first to create the preconditions for the acceptance of new and largely foreign literary genres before a demand for foreign literature could be generated.

When it came to translations, taming difference was not solely a project of the literature-exporting countries but a venture of the receiving cultures as well. The dominant translation strategy in the second half of the nineteenth century, in the Ottoman Empire and elsewhere, was acculturation. As an approach, it helped enrich the target literary system by bringing in new models (for example new literary

102 See here the memoires of Heinrich Börnstein, *Fünfundsiebzig Jahre in der Alten und Neuen Welt, Memoiren eines Unbedeutenden*, vols. 1 and 2 (New York: Lang, 1986).

genres), new subject matter, and by assisting the development of the native vernacular language and literature.[103] Acculturation was a broad phenomenon, and particularly in the cases where standardized languages were lacking or were only just emerging, translation was identified as an essential contribution to culture. Acculturation included free interpretation and literary revision of the original in order to suit local specificities, but also represented a procedure for transforming newly introduced literary models into national ones.[104]

Characteristic of this period was the development of prose and the introduction of new genres such as the novel and drama from Europe. Adaptations of drama, for example, signified the manipulation of texts in such a way that they became like an "original" in the target systems. The changing of names and insertion of aspects akin to local tastes into the texts were some of the measures used to assimilate texts.[105] Additional changes included omissions and abridgements in order to moderate the foreignness of the source text, but also additions in order to tone down the foreignness of the original and make the target text acceptable to the target system.[106] The acculturation strategy was practiced at different levels. In some cases the translations were presented as original works, with the distinction between translations and original works being hardly distinguishable to audiences. Translators also tried to make works conform to the manners of their native lands, and most European dramatists became popular on the Turkish stage with their translated works in adaptation.[107]

When selecting texts for translation, it was the socio-literary conditions of the receiving context that determined the choice. If certain forms or styles were lacking in the receiving culture, it was lucky that this gap could be filled by translations; this was the case with the development of prose literature in the Ottoman Empire.

Traditionally, the Ottoman literature system was based on a dichotomy between *Divan* (court) and popular (folk) literature. Divan literature was produced by the ruling class and was at the center of literary production, while folk literature occupied the periphery. Divan literature focused on poetry and was long under the influence of Persian literature in terms of form, subject matter, imaginary, vocabulary and construction. In Divan literature, prose narrative maintained a "secondary position," mainly because Ottoman writers identified literature predominantly

---

103 Özlem Berk, "Translation and the Westernization of Turkey (from the 1840s to the 1890s)" (PhD in Translation Studies, Centre for British and Comparative Cultural Studies, University of Warwick, June 1999), 2.

104 Berk, "Translation and the Westernization of Turkey," 3.

105 Berk, "Translation and the Westernization of Turkey," 27.

106 Berk, "Translation and the Westernization of Turkey," 79.

107 Berk, "Translation and the Westernization of Turkey," 95–99.

with poetry. Folk narratives, on the other hand, were mostly oral, based on spoken Turkish and transmitted through minstrels.[108] Framed by this pattern, Ottoman literature suffered from a lack of genres, and whereas the Divan system was unable to produce non-canonized written works, translated literature could fill this gap.[109] As a consequence, the hierarchies of the Ottoman literary polysystem, which prior to the Tanzimat period were impenetrable to European literatures, started to change, enabling translated literature to move from the periphery towards the center of the polysystem, obtaining a primary position and representing innovation.[110]

Translation in the case of the Ottoman Empire was also a way of dealing with the broader and more complex issues of modernization and Westernization. Translation accomplished important sociocultural and political tasks, such as the didactic aim of illuminating and educating the public and the nation by introducing new subject matter and ideas. Serialized translations in journals and magazines encouraged the growth of Turkish vocabulary and the development of simplified prose, facilitating the introduction of new concepts, terms and styles.[111] The novel was among the most translated genres; in fact, "the real innovations in the Ottoman literary polysystem took place in prose narration and it was through the medium of prose that translated literature was able to move from the periphery towards the center of the polysystem and gain a primary position within the system."[112] Translated literature assumed a primary position "in modelling the center of the polysystem" and was an integral part of the forces of innovation. No clear-cut distinction was made between original and translated writings and it was usually prominent writers who produced the most important translations. Translation was a medium utilized to elaborate new emerging literary models. Virtually all writers of late nineteenth-century Ottoman literature began their literary careers by translating,[113] a pattern that can be encountered in most cultures and literatures.

Ottoman translators conceived differences from European literary standards as opportunities to become creative, and consciously exaggerated the notion of translation as a way of exploring new spaces. Moreover, intermingling between oral and print cultures obscured the definition of literary genres. Finally, there was strong communication among the empire's diverse communities and the millets affected

108 Berk, "Translation and the Westernization of Turkey," 58–60.
109 Berk, "Translation and the Westernization of Turkey," 60.
110 Berk, "Translation and the Westernization of Turkey," 58.
111 Berk, "Translation and the Westernization of Turkey," 78.
112 Berk, "Translation and the Westernization of Turkey," 79.
113 Berk, "Translation and the Westernization of Turkey," 101.

each other's choices and tastes in modern translated literature.[114] In fact, the practice of translations cut across linguistic and communal boundaries within the empire, but there was also a collective engagement of various religious and linguistic groups with literary fiction imported from Western Europe, all processes that have prompted literary scholars to speak of a "transcommunal translational community."[115]

The study of translation practices in the Ottoman Empire has received increased attention in recent years and produced some methodologically and theoretically original and sophisticated works. Their common denominator is the perception of Ottoman "translation" as a deeply creative and hybrid, strongly intercultural and polyphonic practice. Marilyn Booth has used the concept of "lateral cosmopolitanisms" to designate the multilingual, multi-sited contexts, venues and channels that generated these texts. Instead of a linear language-to-language advance, this approach emphasizes "languages-to/from-languages" transfer.[116] Saliha Paker has applied the notion of "Ottoman interculture" to define the general Ottoman approach to translation, which allowed all sorts of interventions and relied on a much looser conception of textual transfer, where translators were motivated not by the duty to remain faithful to the source text but by the need to satisfy the expectations of their times and their readers. There thus existed no binary between an "original" and the translated text.[117] In a similar vein, Şehnaz Şişmanoğlu Şimşek proposes to view those processes of textual transfer as "palimpsests," where "the new and the old, the master and the apprentice, translation and the copyright coexist without ever annihilating each other."[118]

The role played by translation in the late Ottoman Empire, as an innovator of literary genres and a medium for the construction of modern languages and identities,

---

[114] Günil Özlem Ayaydın Cebe, "To Translate or Not to Translate? 19th Century Ottoman Communities and Fiction," *Die Welt des Islams* 56 (2016): 187 and 217.

[115] Etienne E. Charrière, "Translating Communities: Reading Foreign Fiction across Communal Boundaries in the Tanzimat Period," in *Ottoman Culture and the Project of Modernity: Reform and Translation in the Tanzimat Novel*, eds. Monica M. Ringer and Etienne E. Charrière (London: I.B. Tauris, 2020), 179–80.

[116] Marilyn Booth, "Introduction," in *Migrating Texts: Circulating Translations around the Ottoman Mediterranean*, ed. Marilyn Booth (Edinburgh: Edinburgh University Press, 2019), 11.

[117] Saliha Paker, "Ottoman Interculture: A Short Interview with Saliha Paker on Her Studies in Ottoman Translation History," in *Borders and the Changing Boundaries of Knowledge*, eds. Inga Brandell, Marie Carlson and Onver A. Cetrez, Transactions, vol. 22 (Stockholm: Swedish Research Institute in Istanbul, 2015), 211 and 214. See also Paker, "Ottoman Conceptions of Translation and Its Practice: The 1897 'Classics Debate' as a Focus for Examining Change," in *Translating Others*, vol. 2, ed. Theo Hermans (London: Routledge, 2012), 325–48.

[118] Şehnaz Şişmanoğlu Şimşek, "The Yeniceriler of Ioannis Gavriilidis: A Palimpsest in Karamanlidika," in *Turkish-Speaking Christians, Jews and Greek-Speaking Muslims and Catholics in the Ottoman Empire*, eds. Evangelia Balta and Mehmet Ölmez (Istanbul: Eren, 2011), 274.

represents a pattern that could be applied to the majority of the belated nation (and nation state) building cases.[119] It is important to bear in mind that in those cases, the significance of practices (and notions) such as "copy" and "imitation" did not stand for infringement or for second-rate derivatives, but, on the contrary, for emancipation and creativity. Enabling access to texts of other cultures was a national feat, an indicator of compatibility and modernity. It is not surprising, therefore, that in these contexts translators were almost as highly esteemed as national authors and were admired for their skills, dexterity and mediating abilities. Their obituaries in literary journals testify to the veneration they enjoyed for enabling intercultural dialogue and the status attributed to them by the literary establishment.[120]

Finally, translation is intricately connected to the differences in the temporalities of global "modernity." The Ottoman literati of the nineteenth century translated and defined as modern the European authors of the seventeenth and eighteenth centuries such as Fénelon, Defoe, Swift and Cervantes. Temporal deferral is a common experience of national literary fields that entered the international competition at different times. In such specific conditions of asymmetry, translation is the only means by which to "catch up" with literary time.[121]

---

119 See for example Anna Lillova, "Bulgarian Tradition," in *Encyclopaedia of Translation Studies*, 2nd edition, eds. Mona Baker and Gabriela Saldanha (London: Routledge, 1998), 354–361.

120 See here for example the rubric "našite prevodači" [our translators] in the Bulgarian literary journal *Literaturen čas*, the examples of Dimităr Hr. Brăzishtov, no. 2 (271), April 17, 1935, 6, and Ivan P. Ivanov, no. 3 (272), April 24, 1935, 6. The biography of Ivan Ivanov is moreover quite exemplary of an intellectual career in the late nineteenth and early twentieth century. Ivanov started working as a civil servant in various ministries, while simultaneously also translating for the publisher Stojan Atanasov. He was then hired as a translator by the *Direkcija na pečata* (Printing Directorate) and transferred to the War Ministry, where he translated foreign press on the war, while still translating for Atanasov. He translated from French, Italian, Greek, Romanian, Serbian, Turkish, Russian and Croatian.

121 Casanova, "Consécration et accumulation de capital littéraire," 11–12.

Chapter 3

The Empires of East and Southeast Europe

A large part of the world, including many of the existing states and empires of the nineteenth century, refrained from taking up any international obligations in regard to the BU. Though attentive observers of international developments, the multiethnic empires of Southeast and East Central Europe abstained from membership in the BU, motivated largely by political, but also by economic, considerations. In the course of the nineteenth century, both the Habsburg and the Romanov Empires developed elementary legal provisions regarding authors' protection. Rather than international copyright regulation, however, their principal concern remained the cultural relationships within their own realms. The continental empires of Eastern Europe were not only multiethnic but also multilingual. As political realms they wavered between different, often contradictory legitimizing projects whose boundaries were continuously negotiated, such as: legitimation based on the traditional dynastic aura but also on modern forms of political participation; the application of censorship and control in the public sphere coupled with periods of political relaxation, including information and press freedom; and the desire and need to provide for mass education (in the spirit of the Enlightenment but also in order to satisfy the claims of rising ethnic groups) and the quest to keep the political project of empire together. These complex sociocultural and sociolinguistic conglomerates constituted multicultural and pluricultural communication spaces,[1] where language, social milieu and identity remained in a perpetually fluid and dialectical relation to one another on the level of everyday communication and exchange. At the same time, they also operated in a state of potential tension and conflict inherent in the structural asymmetry between the usage and the prestige of different languages.[2]

Though opinions on whether to join the BU or abstain from its international regime varied among different stakeholders (publishers, authors, politicians, lawyers),

1 Michaela Wolf, *Die vielsprachige Seele Kakaniens: Übersetzen und Dolmetschen in der Habsburgermonarchie 1848 bis 1918* (Vienna: Böhlau, 2012).

2 Wolf, *Die vielsprachige Seele Kakaniens*, 366–69.

the Eastern empires appeared to pursue a different set of priorities in the late nineteenth century. These can be summarized as follows: (1) the intention to build up and solidify the publishing sector as a branch of the home industry; (2) the maintenance of low copyright protection levels in order to secure broad access to knowledge and know-how, predominantly of West European provenance. This mainly concerned the right of translation and was related to the quest for broad alphabetization and the desire to keep production costs and book prices low; and (3) the intention to facilitate communication and maintain an equilibrium within the imperial plurilingual and multilingual realms. This related on the one hand to the fact that the empires functioned de facto through the operationalization of multiple levels of formal and informal translation activity, and on the other, to their wish to avoid disturbing the balance of power between the different nationalities. The necessity to devise a copyright regime capable of balancing—also politically—interethnic relations remained a distinct and diachronic trait of East and Southeast Europe in the course of the twentieth century, particularly in countries that retained their multiethnic structure such as the Soviet Union, communist Yugoslavia and Czechoslovakia.

The present chapter takes a closer look at the institutionalization of copyright in the three East European empires in the second half of the nineteenth and early twentieth centuries until approximately the outbreak of World War I. Though they often followed different trajectories, the three continental empires of the East also demonstrate related patterns in the way they handled copyright in their multiethnic, pluri- and multilingual realms. The imperial past left a mark on subsequent developments; for example, the copyright legislations of Austria-Hungary and Russia formed legal matrices or orientation points for subsequent national copyright laws. This was not really the case with the Ottoman Empire, where the notion of copyright was introduced quite late, and where native law was barely applied in practice and apparently did not create a lasting legacy. The social and cultural legacies of the empires also had a long-lasting impact, and they provided the structural patterns that influenced in the long term the conceptualization and the dynamic of the relationship between creative elites, the state, the market and the public.

The Habsburg Empire

It would be misleading to interpret the Habsburg Empire's indifference to the structures of international copyright regulation that developed in the second half of the nineteenth century either as a sign of its disinterest in copyright issues or as a symptom of a quaint monarchical state. In fact, the Austrian Empire was the initiator of one of the earliest bilateral copyright treaties (May 22, 1840), namely between the Austrian Empire and the Kingdom of Sardinia, a treaty that effectively provided for the possibility—through the inclusion of an accession clause—for other states to join in, thereby setting a precedent for the development from bilateralism to multilateralism.[3] Austria-Hungary participated in the initial exploratory talks during the 1883 ALAI conference in Berne and the ensuing diplomatic conference convened by the Swiss government the following year. These acts, however, marked the end of the monarchy's involvement in the efforts to create an international treaty, from which it consequentially abstained, favoring instead the conclusion of bilateral treaties.

The Habsburg Empire's first legal act regulating copyright was the imperial patent (Kaiserliches Patent) of October 16, 1846 "zum Schutz des literarischen und artistischen Eigentums gegen unbefugte Veröffentlichung, Nachdruck und Nachbildung."[4] The law had a series of precursors in the German-speaking world, such as the copyright laws of Prussia (1837), Bavaria (1840), Braunschweig (1842), Saxony (1844) and Württemberg (1845).[5] Enacted under the influence of the politics of the German Confederation (Dt. Bund), it reckoned literary and artistic works to be the property of their creator, but it likewise restricted property rights. Literary and artistic works were protected 30 years p.m.a., and performing rights for unpublished works 10 years p.m.a. Translation rights were reserved for one year, after which translation was free.[6] Musical and photographic works were left unprotected.

A new decree issued in 1859 awarded authors of dramatic and musical works the exclusive right to deliver permission for public performances of their works,

---

3 Herbert Hofmeister, "Der österreichisch-sardinische Urheberrechtsvertrag von 1840," in *Die Notwendigkeit des Urheberrechtsschutzes im Lichte seiner Geschichte*, ed. Robert Dittrich (Vienna: Manzsche Verlags- und Universitätsbuchhandlung, 1991), 239.

4 This translates as imperial patent "for the protection of literary and artistic property against unauthorized publications, reprints and reproductions."

5 Murray G. Hall, *Österreichische Verlagsgeschichte 1918-1938*, vol. I Geschichte des österreichischen Verlagswesens (Literatur und Leben, Neue Folge Bd. 28/I) (Vienna: Böhlau Verlag, 1985), 25.

6 Sybille Gerhartl, "'Vogelfrei' – Die österreichische Lösung der Urheberrechtsfrage in der 2. Hälfte des 19 Jhs. oder Warum es Österreich unterließ, seine Autoren zu schützen" (Diplomarbeit, University of Vienna, 1995), 12–13.

even if the works had been published. Protection lasted for the author's lifetime plus 10 years p.m.a., provided the author had explicitly made such a reservation in the cover page of the printed work.[7]

Austria participated actively in the context of the German Confederation for an amendment of the copyright law ("Frankfurt Entwurf"), an effort that ultimately affected Austria little due to the disintegration of the German Bund. A new copyright law ("das Gesetz betreffend das Urheberrecht an Werken der Literatur, Kunst und Photographie"[8]) was issued in 1895, and represented the first copyright law of local making. This new law also retained major trends from the previous legislation: (1) very short terms of protection for translations; and (2) controlled and limited reciprocity in international relations. Consequently, an author retained the right of translation for three years, whereas translations were protected for five years. After eight years, therefore, translation was essentially free in all languages. Foreign works were protected only when, and to the degree, stipulated by official state treaties, while the option of protecting foreign works on the grounds of formal reciprocity statements, as had been provided previously through the patent of 1846, was withdrawn. This impairment was lamented by different authors' and publishers' organizations, and constituted the principal reason for the partial revision of the law in 1907, which in the absence of state treaties, and when the preconditions for reciprocity existed, allowed the Ministry of Justice to issue a relevant decree.[9] The Habsburg Empire's copyright regime of the late nineteenth century opted for a middle path, clearly favoring the public, while paying respect to the monarchy's particular multilingual and plurilingual setting.[10]

The regulation of translation rights diverged significantly from the evolving Bern Union norms. The 1846 patent envisioned protection for one year, and the 1895 law for a maximum of eight years, while the 1886 BC protected the exclusive right of translation for 10 years from the publication of the original; protected were both the original and its translation. The Paris Act of the Berne Convention in 1896 extended the duration of the right of translation, equalizing it with that of the original work, the sole precondition being that a translation had to appear within 10 years of the publication of the original. Finally, the Berlin Act of the BC in 1908 dropped all reservations and fully equated translation rights to the original.

7 Gerhartl, "Vogelfrei," 18.

8 The Law Regarding Copyright in Works of Literature, Art and Photography.

9 Walter Dillenz, "Warum Österreich-Ungarn nie der Berner Übereinkunft beitrat," in *Historische Studien zum Urheberrecht: Entwicklungslinien und Grundfragen*, ed. Elmar Wadle (Berlin: Duncker & Humblot, 1993), 181.

10 Gerhartl, "Vogelfrei," 29–31.

Differences between the two regimes also prevailed concerning the protection of the original: both laws of the Habsburg Empire limited protection to 30 years p.m.a., whereas in the case of the BC, the 50-year term of protection p.m.a. became the union norm after 1908.

The reluctance to provide for higher terms of protection and keep up with BU standards has been attributed to, among other things, the Austrian government's disinterest in copyright issues, a kind of tardy reflex by an inert, slow-moving and antiquated bureaucratic state unable to keep up with the spirit of the age.[11] This interpretation is corroborated by the fact that several professional actors with a stake in culture and copyright, such as the organization of the Austrian-Hungarian Book, Art and Music Retailers (Österreichisch-ungarischer Buch-, Kunst- und Musikalienhändler), were endorsing an amendment of the copyright law and petitioned the government to this end.[12] Several professional organizations, representatives of musicians, the union of Viennese applied crafts, the journalists' and writers' union "Concordia" and others had equally supported the entry of the monarchy into the BU, and so apparently did the music retailers. The late 1890s saw the creation of additional interest groups such as the Society of Authors, Composers and Music Publishers (Gesellschaft der Autoren, Komponisten und Musikverleger) and the German-Austrian Authors' Cooperative (Deutsch-österreichische Schriftstellergenossenschaft), who advocated for the entry of Austria-Hungary into the BC as well as the conclusion of a copyright treaty with the US.[13] Efforts in this direction did not abate, and various corporations of publishers and music dealers returned to the subject frequently, petitioning the Ministry of Justice in favor of Austria's adhesion to the BU. They lamented the enormous revenues lost to Austria, particularly with respect to the Viennese Operetta, a highly successful export of the recent past and present. Their viewpoints also go some way to explaining the propensity of book and music publishers to move to Germany in order to ensure for themselves and their authors unionist protection.[14]

Opinions therefore on whether to join the BU were split and the issue fervently debated among affected stakeholders. Consideration for the educational needs of the non-German nationalities in Austria, and the wish to avoid raising costs for the imports of foreign educational materials, appeared to be the principal reasons for es-

11 Gerhartl, "Vogelfrei," 29–31.

12 Gerhartl, "Vogelfrei," 22–26.

13 Gerhartl, "Vogelfrei," 51–55.

14 "Autriche," *Le Droit d'auteur*, year 24, no. 4, April 15, 1911, 54. See also Gerhartl, "Vogelfrei," 47; Hall, *Österreichische Verlagsgeschichte*, 30–34.

chewing membership of the BU.[15] Moreover, the fact that Hungary was disinclined towards accession to the BU, an attitude heightened by the local inclination towards free translations, played an important role in determining the Austrian attitude on the matter, and further blocked the issue.[16] It was only in 1887 that the Austrian and Hungarian governments signed a treaty which secured for both halves of the monarchy reciprocal protection for works of literature and art.

In order to sound out the expectations of stakeholders in culture and education empire-wide, in 1900 the minister of justice conducted a survey among diverse institutions, including the academies of science and the arts in Vienna, Prague, Cracow and Lemberg, various literature societies, artists' associations and writers' unions inquiring about their opinion on whether the monarchy should join the BU. The ministry received approximately 50 answers, divided into almost three equivalent thirds which expressed a positive, negative or neutral (entry only after modification of the Austrian legislation) stance. Resistance to potential BU membership was strongest in the eastern territories, particularly in Galicia. The academy of sciences in Cracow, for example, feared that Austria-Hungary's entry into the BU would endanger the literary connections between the Austrian and Russian parts of partitioned Poland.[17] Moreover, it could be observed that the warmest advocates of BU membership came predominantly from German-speaking organizations and associations, in spite of the fact that the monarchy represented a multiethnic and polyglot context. Until 1900, among the non-German populations, only the Czech writers' association *Máj* was committed to the same stance.[18]

Consequently, the monarchy's reluctance to join the BU has to be seen in correlation with the question of nationality and the challenges it posed for a state consisting of 11 main ethnic groups, and territories where nine languages were spoken. There were significant divergences between the German and non-German nations, and the government feared that a change of copyright regime might jeopardize "the ideal end goal of all literary and artistic work, that is, its permeation into the broadest population strata."[19]

The philosophy and the mindset of the Austrian legislator deserve closer attention as they reveal the mode of reception of the copyright idea and the basic parameters of the monarchy's copyright philosophy in the late nineteenth century.

15 Dillenz, "Warum Österreich-Ungarn," 179–80.
16 Dillenz, "Warum Österreich-Ungarn," 183; see also *Le Droit d'auteur*, year 24, no. 4, April 15, 1911, 54.
17 Dillenz, "Warum Österreich-Ungarn," 182.
18 Gerhartl, "Vogelfrei," 57.
19 Gerhartl, "Vogelfrei," 61f.

They show an intellectual pattern that would have a long-lasting influence in the region, well into the twentieth century. Deliberating on the new Austrian copyright law of 1895, *Le Droit d'auteur*, the BU's official organ, published a critique of the new legislation, which when read helps to illuminate the points of friction. The article's anonymous author pointed out the following shortcomings of the law: (1) the absence of a clear legal doctrine concerning the nature of copyright law; (2) inadequate consideration of absolute property rights and far too much emphasis on authors' moral/personality rights; (3) the law was too idealistic and not sufficiently commercially oriented; (4) it was driven by the utopian desire to regulate copyright relations by taking into consideration the interests of the author and the public on an equal footing; and (5) it postulated that the interests of the stakeholders (i.e. authors, publishers and the public) were antagonistic and that the law's objective was to anticipate this predicament.[20] Was it possible, asked the anonymous author, to expound on authors' rights without relying on a precise doctrine concerning the nature, indeed the essence, of this right?

The Austrian legislator's justification of the law was apparently far from agnostic or ill-considered, and relied instead on a clear refutation of the time-honored intellectual property theory:

> this principal idea is manifested in the first place through a rejection of the theory based on what is called "intellectual property," a theory which—as is well known—considers an intellectual product (not so much a material object, but rather its future economic exploitation with respect to the public) an object of which the author can dispose in an absolute and perennial manner, which is exactly analogous to material property. This view sanctions [the stance] that the exclusive right encompasses all pecuniary profits, emanating in whatever way from the intellectual product, to belong to the author perennially. Any limitation of this right in space, time etc. is a departure only permissible when dictated by public interest. [...] [A] ccording to this view, the right in question being a commercial object has to be transferable just as any other kind of 'property' and should conserve in the hands of the rightsholder the quality and scope that it possessed when in the hands of the original owner. [...] The government, on the contrary, departs from the position that copyright means first and foremost to legally assure the author protection of his works, which are exclusively personal, and this protection is justified mainly by the necessity to assure a just remuneration for intellectual labor. *However, it should not be forgotten that this guarantee cannot be attributed but at the expense of the public,*

20 "Partie non officielle, Etudes générales, La réforme législative en matière de droit d'auteur en Autriche (examen du projet vote par la Chambre des Seigneurs)," *Le Droit d'auteur*, year 8, no. 1, January 15, 1895, 5.

> and therefore [can only be granted] in the form of an exception to the genuine and real vocation of all intellectual works, that is, to be easily and widely disseminated. In that sense, all authors' rights involve *limiting and hampering the natural expansion of intellectual produce in universal circulation*. But this limitation is legitimate since its unique goal is to reward intellectual production and thus encourage its development on a large scale. The collision of interests between the author and the public is generally resolved equitably since the products of the first are sold to the second, with a reasonable price increase [and] without overvaluation, in order to guarantee the author the remuneration that provides him with the opportunity to produce, and the public with the opportunity to appreciate intellectual products. The difficult mission of legislation is to find a just compromise to this conflict.[21]

The emphasis on moral rights as a foundation of copyright is underscored further:

> In contrast to the theory of literary and artistic property, defended by the largest contingent of French scholars, and that of the German, English and American writers, who consider copyright in isolation [as] involving solemnly the protection of economic exploitation and the reproduction of the work, the project [of the law, AD] departs from the principle that the diverse authors' rights result from a purely personal right [un droit purement personnel], which in this form is not transferable to the editor but only to the heirs of the author. [...] in its essence, the author's right is neither a right of goods [un droit des biens] nor a requisition right but a personal right, not a right from person to person but an absolute personal right, which concerns only the titular person and consists of maintaining the work in his power as an element of his proper personality; this aspect is worth protecting by law, the protection reverting to the author and afterwards to his heirs, [who become] titular of the orphaned work. This power consists in the exclusive right to take care of something. Consequently, copyright would be the exclusive faculty of the author to exercise his concern regarding his intellectual creation; this constitutes in the first place part of his mental activity and therefore of the person, but the reflection is then communicated to others through his will.[22]

A major reason for the rejection of the BC were differences in the range and scope of legislation; the BC was more comprehensive in substantive protection. Entering the BU would require first an amendment of national copyright legislation in order to avoid the consequences of *jure conventionis*, whereby foreign authors would enjoy greater protection in Austria than local authors. There were five main differences:

21 "La réforme législative," *Le Droit d'auteur*, year 8, no. 1, January 15, 1895, 5. Emphasis added.

22 "L'adoption de la nouvelle loi autrichienne sur le droit d'auteur," *Le Droit d'auteur*, year 9, no. 2, February 15, 1896, 25.

(1) the number of protected works was more comprehensive in the BC, whereas Austrian copyright law excluded several categories such as public speeches, lectures, announcements and so on from protection; (2) the right of translation enjoyed a prominent position in BU legislation; (3) with the exception of news on politics and current affairs, the BC protected all other articles in the periodical press and magazines, when such protection was explicitly declared on the journal's front page. It was prohibited to reprint or translate feuilleton novels and novellas without authorization. In general, the Austrian patent of 1846 allowed reprints from political journals provided their length did not exceed one print sheet and the source was indicated. Austrian legislation permitted reprinting when no explicit reservation was made on the article's header, while reservations concerned only scientific, literary and technical articles; (4) the BC prohibited the transformation of a novel into a theatrical play and vice versa as a form of unauthorized reproduction, whereas under the Austrian law it was only necessary that a work demonstrate the quality of an original work; and (5) in cases of infringement, Austrian law prescribed the confiscation and destruction of all sales exemplars, whereas union law extended this right to all infringed copies.[23]

Finally, in view of the political constellation, the Austrian government could not take a different stance to the Hungarian one, as the two halves needed to coordinate their policy on the issue. Whether the Austrian half could enter into the BC without the consent of the Hungarian half was after all a constitutional question. Though the *Ausgleich* had declared the parity of the monarchy's two halves, single-handed action on this issue was rather improbable and certainly not advisable.[24]

In fact, the Hungarian copyright law of 1884 surpassed in protectionist spirit the Austrian one. It excluded from copyright protection all foreign authors, apart from those whose works had been published by Hungarian publishers, or those who had lived continuously for at least two years, and had consistently paid taxes, in Hungary. This last category enjoyed protection even if they did not publish their works in Hungary. With respect to translation rights, Austrian standards—that is, only very short terms of protection—were maintained, complemented, in the case of Hungary, by a non-negligible number of formalities. Foreign authors seeking protection (for example those who enjoyed protection on the basis of bilateral treaties) had to reserve the translation and performance rights for all languages or specific ones; initiate the translation in the same year the original work was published and

23 Gerhartl, "Vogelfrei," 65–66.

24 Dillenz, "Warum Österreich-Ungarn," 174; and Gerhartl, "Vogelfrei," 63 and 75.

conclude it within three years (six months for dramatic works); and moreover record the beginning and end of the translation in a registry of the Hungarian Ministry of Commerce.[25] In the first decade of the twentieth century, both halves of the monarchy were considering amendments to their respective copyright laws, which would bring them closer to BU standards. The main drive behind this, however, was to reform and update their respective national copyright regimes. It is unclear how far they were willing to go with a view to a prospective BU accession.[26]

Overall, the issue of translation remained the decisive criterion regarding access or not to the BU. It affected mainly the non-German nationalities of the monarchy, who had a passive cultural record and were dependent for their cultural development on foreign products. Catching up, from their point of view, was an urgent issue, while the BU's standards for translations appeared to the linguistic minorities as an impairment of their own cultural development. The empire's Slavic populations in particular, with their need for cheap translations, were bound to be affected by the monarchy's accession to the BU. Feeling underprivileged and overlooked as a result of the *Ausgleich* arrangement with Hungary, they insisted all the more strongly on their cultural rights. The *Ausgleich*'s dualism induced the other nationalities to seek equal treatment and triggered the idea of *Trialism*, an equitable and distinct political representation of the monarchy's Slavic population. Cisleithania in particular, where German-speakers made up 36% of the population, as against 23% Czech- and 16% Polish-speakers, had to be taken seriously. As can be judged from the reactions of the Law Societies of Lemberg and Cracow, negative attitudes to BU accession were particularly pronounced in that part of the monarchy. What is more, the issue of authors' rights could easily be politicized in parliament.[27]

It constitutes a great paradox in the history of the Austrian book trade that from the mid-nineteenth century Austrian literature was traditionally published in the German Reich.[28] By way of illustration, until 1918 the Berlin-based "Fischer" publishing house included approximately 35 Austrian authors in its portfolio, resulting in quite a profitable business.[29] Various historical, political, literary and economic factors were decisive in this development. Censorship was among the principal motivations for the relocation of the Austrian publishing trade to the German states,

25 "Etudes générales, Le nouveau traite littéraire conclu entre l'Allemagne et l'Autriche Hongrie," *Le Droit d'auteur*, year 14, no. 6, June 15, 1901, 64–65.

26 Hall, *Österreichische Verlagsgeschichte*, 36.

27 Gerhartl, "Vogelfrei," 68–69.

28 Hall, *Österreichische Verlagsgeschichte*, 11.

29 Hall, *Österreichische Verlagsgeschichte*, 24.

where it literally flourished. While censorship could have a detrimental effect, and potentially ruin Austrian publishers, it affected German publishers only secondarily, depriving them merely of just one segment of their market. It therefore became a tradition for Austrian authors to flee to Germany in order to avoid censorship.

The monarchy's copyright regime guaranteed reciprocal protection only to a limited number of states (France, Britain, Italy and Germany). The only new treaty signed after the enactment of the new 1895 law was with Germany in 1899, which, however, was rather focused on German than Austrian interests, and the main purpose of which was to effect Hungary's cooperation on copyright issues.[30]

The absence of protection hurt authors and publishers alike, with the latter lacking competitiveness in international markets and failing to secure successful authors long-term. Heirs and legal successors of authors also felt the consequences. As a direct result, publishers and authors migrated to Germany, taking an indirect path to BU protection.

But there was more to this story than just calamity. Long-term cultural and historical reasons also factored into this interdependency, due mainly to the fact that German-speaking Austrians felt an affinity towards Germany and nurtured a sense of belonging to the broader German cultural sphere. The fact that Austrian literature was published outside Austria was not necessarily contentious.[31]

Finally, economic reasons linked to Austria's trade regulations played a role. Whereas the city of Vienna had a long tradition as a printing location and publishing hub, it was in fact only with the ascendance of Maria Theresia to the throne that Austrian publishing consolidated into a distinct branch of trade. "Ordnung für die Buchhändler in den kaiserl. Königl. Erblanden vom 28 März 1772" (the Regulation of the Booksellers in Imperial Royal Patrimonial Lands, March 28, 1772) detached the licensing of booksellers from the competences of the University of Vienna, and confirmed the right to authorize the publishing and selling of books only through state licensing ("Konzessionspflicht"), in contrast to the freedom of trade that prevailed in Germany. A new era began with the ascendance of Joseph II to the Austrian throne, whose landmark "Zensurpatent" of June 11, 1781 practically liberalized the press, publishing and the book trade, and resulted in a consequent relaxation of censorship. His liberal approach was soon revoked by his successors Leopold II and Franz, and paradoxically was also opposed by Austrian booksellers who, considering the freedom of trade to be ruinous, were not displeased with the

30 Hall, *Österreichische Verlagsgeschichte*, 30–31.

31 Hall, *Österreichische Verlagsgeschichte*, 34.

licensing requirements. This period, with a small reprieve in 1848, was characterized by censorship and repression.[32] A new trade regulation act ("Gewerbeordnung") was published on December 20, 1859. The publisher's profession ("Verleger") was not explicitly mentioned but was implied, and catalogued among other professions of the licensing trades. The trend was to keep licences exclusive and avoid extension of the profession.[33]

In multiethnic Austria-Hungary, the trade in German books ranked highest among the different book language markets. While forming part of the dual monarchy, the Austrian German book trade also featured as part of the greater German book trade. The formation of the "Verein der österreichischer Buchhändler" (Society of Austrian Booksellers) in 1859 marked the beginning of publishers' professional organization. With few exceptions, the most representative professional type consisted of the bookseller-publisher ("Buchhändler-Verleger/Auch-Verleger"), designating a low degree of professional differentiation. As a direct consequence there were only very few pure publishers ("Nur-Verleger"). The title "Verlagsbuchhändler" could stand for both, but enterprises engaged exclusively in publishing were clearly under-represented. This structure was typical of the Austrian book trade and constituted one of its most enduring traits, lasting well into the twentieth century.

Austria was a significant and growing importer of books. German books constituted no less than 90% of all book imports and this ratio was maintained until the mid-1930s. Between 1851 and 1905, within five decades, book imports increased tenfold. These facts were happily accepted by German-speaking Austrians, many of whom felt a strong affiliation to Germany. As a phenomenon, nationalism was not limited to the empire's Slavs and Hungarians, but had significant support among German-speakers as well. Since the 1866 war, there was a permanent contraction in the size and territory of the market for German books, a phenomenon directly related to the development of national literatures by other nationalities. This led to a sort of division of labor within the book market for German-speakers, with Austrian publishers limiting themselves to the publication of scholarly literature, which sold quite well in Germany as well, whereas the publication of *belles lettres* was confined predominantly to Germany. Austrian retailers ("Sortimentsbuchhändler") considered the "Börsenverein des deutschen Buchhandels" (German Publishers' and Booksellers' Association) to be the center of the entire book trade for German-speakers, and procured their books mainly from Leipzig. This attitude was not necessarily

---

32 Hall, *Österreichische Verlagsgeschichte*, 20–21.

33 Hall, *Österreichische Verlagsgeschichte*, 22.

reciprocated by German retailers, who considered Austrian literary publishing rather provincial. Finally, Austrian publishers' and booksellers' political orientation, that is, their inclination towards the greater German solution ("großdeutsche Lösung"), also played a role in cementing the affinity towards the German Reich. The loss of territories and the prohibition against joining the German Reich as a consequence of World War I did not diminish these aspirations among the Austrian book trade. Rather, Austrian publishers were content to occupy a satellite position and function as a subdivision of the German book trade.[34]

The Russian Empire

Copyright law in Russia, as elsewhere, was closely linked to the development of printing, an industry that developed with noticeable delay in the case of Russia and did not acquire social significance until the early eighteenth century. From the late sixteenth century until Peter the Great's reign in the latter half of the seventeenth century, printing in Russia was almost exclusively reserved for religious books and was, as in Western Europe, strictly controlled by the monarch. The policy of autocratic government had been to obstruct the introduction of foreign works and to limit the production of domestic works. Books retained a strong religious character (of the 483 books printed in Moscow print shops prior to Peter's reign, only seven were not religious works) and printing was subject to censorship.[35] Peter's modernization reforms required extending all areas of knowledge, and he was the first to grant printing privileges for secular books, though he maintained printing as a state monopoly. The import of foreign literature was among the lasting legacies of Russia's opening up to Western influences, though it was only in 1771, long after Peter's death, that Russian printers were permitted to reproduce foreign literature. Under Peter's reign, publishing grew significantly, slowing down appreciably after his death in 1725. By the mid-eighteenth century an average of 23 books a year were printed in Russia.

Catherine's accession to the throne in 1762 signaled a renewed, positive turn in the world of print, leading to a momentous rise in the dissemination of books published both in Russia and abroad, as well as a significant reorientation in subject

34 Hall, *Österreichische Verlagsgeschichte*, 40–43.

35 M.A. Newcity, *Copyright Law in the Soviet Union* (New York: Praeger Publishers, 1978), 4.

matter. Whereas prior to her reign the majority of published books had been religious, 40% of the 8,000 books published in the second half of the eighteenth century were purely secular. The reverberations of the French Revolution, however, brought a new conservative turn, including the repudiation of previous liberal ideas and the restriction of the freedom of publishing. Political reaction accelerated under Paul, Catherine's successor, while his successor, Alexander, enhanced censorship in the wake of the Decembrist uprising of 1825, in spite of his liberal leanings.

The printing prerogatives granted to that point had been rights accorded to publishers, not to authors. By 1825 the private publishing industry had expanded significantly in size and output, challenging the capacity of the censor to maintain control of the production and dissemination of both genuine and pirated works of literature. As a result, the first copyright law was issued in April 1828 aiming to prevent the unauthorized publication and dissemination of works.[36] Under the title "On Authors and Publishers of Books," it consisted of five articles (art. 135 to 139) in a Censorship Code ("ustav o tsenzure") issued by the tsar, which entitled an author or translator to the exclusive right to reproduce, publish and disseminate a work and confirmed his/her right to receive payment for the use and reproduction of that work. Copyright was vested in the author or translator with the creation of the work, and there were no formalities attached. Protection lasted for the author's lifetime plus 25 years p.m.a. The statute postulated the freedom of translation, that is, it guaranteed the translator's right to his translation, while all works were free to be translated by any person without the original author's consent.[37]

The following consequent amendments to the law were introduced. (1) The decree of 1830, which emphasized that authors' rights were proprietary in nature and could be assigned, devised or transferred. If the author's successor in rights published a new edition of the work within five years of the expiration of the original 25-year period of protection, his rights in the work were extended for another 10 years. (2) In 1845, the Council of State extended the protection of copyright law

36 Newcity, *Copyright Law in the Soviet Union,* 5–6. The 1828 law was preceded by the "Statute on the administration of the Imperial Saint-Petersburg Theater," a sort of precursor legislation enacted in November 1827. It contained a smaller sub-statute entitled "Statute on the remuneration of authors and translators of dramatic plays and operas for presentation in Imperial theaters." The statute provided a tiered reward schedule for five classes of work. Though it cannot be qualified as copyright, mainly because it did not confer any kind of moral and/or proprietary rights to either authors or heirs, it did nevertheless recognize authors' rights to remuneration. The statute's main concern was ranking privilege and despite the development of copyright in musical and dramatic works its privileges were retained and renewed in 1871. See Herceg Michael Westren, "The Development and Debate over Copyright in Imperial Russia, 1828–1917," *Russian History* 30, nos. 1–2 (Spring–Summer 2003): 151–52.

37 Newcity, *Copyright Law in the Soviet Union,* 7.

to musical works, and the following year likewise to works of fine art. (3) The most significant modification was the extension of the term of copyright protection in 1857, when the Council of State, acting on behalf of Pushkin's widow, extended the duration of copyright protection to the lifetime of the author plus 50 years p.m.a.[38]

Russian civil legislation was recodified in 1887, and copyright law was separated from the censorship statute for the first time. As legislators deemed copyright law to pertain to property law, they included it in that section of the new code dealing with proprietary rights and relations. Similar to the earlier statute, the 1887 law granted foreign authors whose works were first published abroad no protection and maintained the principle of freedom of translation, introducing just a small exception regarding scholarly works. Only works whose writing required scholarly research were protected from free translation, and only upon the condition that the author had explicitly reserved this right, and indeed published a translation shortly (within two years) after the original publication. All other works by Russian subjects were in the public domain and could be translated freely without authorial permission or the payment of fees.[39]

The realization that the existing copyright regime resembled a patchwork and had become increasingly outdated and insufficient was the major motivation for the passing of a new copyright law in 1911, modelled after the 1901 German equivalent. The 1911 copyright law was a piece of modern and mature legislation incorporating several contemporary trends in copyright law, and also demonstrating a strong tendency to furnish answers to local needs and priorities.

The Contexts of Copyright Debates

Having had a negligent impact for the greatest part of the nineteenth century, the discussion on copyright picked up between 1880 and 1915, for three main reasons: (1) the creation of the Berne Union; (2) Russia's withdrawal from bilateral treaties with France and Belgium; and (3) the incipient process of canonization and nationalization of writers by Russian educated society in approximately the same period.

Debates were fought in essence around identity issues: they voiced, on the one hand, internal concerns such as the contents of Russian identity, and on the other, external preoccupations such as Russia's positionality in the world. When such abstract

38 Newcity, *Copyright Law in the Soviet Union*, 7.

39 Newcity, *Copyright Law in the Soviet Union*, 7–8.

themes were boiled down to concrete topics, they revolved primarily around the issues of translation, the length of the term of protection of authors' rights, and the protection of authors' personal (and potentially embarrassing) writings post mortem.

In the late nineteenth and early twentieth centuries, by progressively distancing itself from tsar and the church, Russian educated society was rearranging its allegiances with the symbols of Russian nationality. It espoused a more abstract notion of Russian culture predicated on the literature of Russian classics and the social values of the intelligentsia, which it sought to inculcate to newer generations thereby integrating them into a unified Russian culture.[40] Copyright debates were fought by invoking the names of great literary figures, and both supporters and opponents framed their positions around those canonized authors and their works. When it came to issues like more or less extensive copyright protection and/or Russia's accession to the BU, the rival sides claimed to be speaking in the interest of Russian society and expressed their concerns within an existing discourse on backwardness, whereby Russia's position in Europe and among world civilizations was at stake.[41]

Analogously to Austria-Hungary, Russia closely followed the movement for international copyright protection but did not participate either in the drafting or the signing of the Berne Convention. Rather, in the second half of the nineteenth century Russia preferred to conclude short-term bilateral treaties with major West European states (France March 25, 1861, Belgium July 18, 1862 etc.), which permitted flexible manoeuvring regarding the use of foreign cultural goods. Resistance to bilateral and multilateral conventions stemmed on the one hand from the limitations they would place upon Russian theatres and their capacity to produce foreign musical and dramatic works that required authorial permission and the payment of royalties, and on the other from the massive consumption of foreign literature in Russia and the financial drain that would accompany the payment of royalties to foreign authors. Nevertheless, it was also not uncommon for Russian institutions to remunerate foreign authors for the use of their works.[42]

As had also been the case with Austria-Hungary, opinions regarding the accession or not of Russia to the BU were split. This confrontation became more passionate as West European countries, whose literature and various cultural artefacts were consumed in Russia, increased pressure in their efforts to move the Russian government and public opinion to subscribe to the regime of international copyright protection. Émile Zola's open letter in the Russian press, in which he publicly

40 Westren, "The Development and Debate over Copyright," 170–71.

41 Westren, "The Development and Debate over Copyright," 171.

42 Newcity, *Copyright Law in the Soviet Union*, 12–13.

condemned unauthorized translations of French works and appealed for the conclusion of a new literary treaty with France, had been one such action. A common strategy was to engage local lobbyists who tried to influence political and cultural elites, and who likewise tried to create a positive predisposition in the press and in various collective professional bodies.[43]

A common objection raised by Russian opponents to international copyright, and a recurrent theme in international debates, was the question of the trade balance between countries. Opponents emphasized the conspicuously asymmetrical relationship between exporting and importing countries, which rendered such reciprocity prohibitive. Statistical surveys by M. J. Ianjoul, economics professor at Moscow University, demonstrated this imbalance quite patently: in 1890 Russia exported a total of 294,160 kg of books for the sum of 548,000 rubles to Europe and Asia, of which France received only 3,024 kg, whereas Russia procured from France 54,064 kg. Equivalent was the exchange with Germany: Russia exported 160,000 kg, whereas it received 800,000 kg of books from Germany, the greatest contingent being scientific literature, which was deemed "indispensable for Russia." As poignantly mentioned by an anonymous author in *Le Droit d'auteur*: "Indeed, Russia gets entertained in France, but is educated in Germany" ("La Russie, en effet, s'amuse en France, mais s'instruit en Allemagne").[44]

The above example is indicative of the construction of the discursive field and the positionality of the actors. Culture- and science-exporting countries like France and Germany underscored their claims for an international IP regime by invoking a register of values such as ethical and honourable behaviour, decency and propriety, respect for the labor of others, and above all by appealing to the imperative of civilization and progress. Rarely, almost never, did their argumentation in the late nineteenth century address practical issues such as trade balances and world asymmetries, though they were more than apparent. The line of argumentation taken by authors like Zola or prominent lawyers was fashioned on purely idealistic motives, where the observance of IP constituted that imaginative border separating civilization, on the one hand, from barbarism and fraudulence on the other. The international codification of copyright relied on such narrative topoi. Subsuming copyrights under the abstract notion of universal rights often obscured the social character of authors' rights, and equivalently, the socioeconomic disparities between different countries and world regions were glossed over in the name of universal civilization. As can be

43 See also Westren, "The Development and Debate over Copyright," 176–78.

44 "Les droits des auteurs étrangers en Russie (A propos de la 'lettre ouverte' de M.E. Zola)," *Le Droit d'auteur*, year 7, no. 2, February 15, 1894, 23.

expected, it was mostly culture-importing countries that expressly underlined the reverse position, arguing first that excessive IP protection undermined their broad popular, national enlightenment projects, and secondly, pointing precisely at the materialistic aspects of international regulation and the "price" of reciprocity. So, while the exporters were often speaking the abstract language of morals and principles, the importers spoke the concrete language of trade and practice.

Part and parcel of this reality and practice were interventions by foreign literary agents, private and/or international collecting societies, a story we will encounter close up in the chapter on interwar Yugoslavia. It was an experience shared by several countries, including Russia. In the last decades of the nineteenth century, taking advantage of the 1861 bilateral treaty with France, diverse collecting societies and agents for foreign authors had become active in Russia. They raised excessive fee claims and apparently abused their advantage in absolute terms, causing a series of legal suits and complaints. To this effect, the booksellers' and publishers' associations petitioned the Russian government to denounce the bilateral treaty when its term expired.[45] Thus, in 1886, upon the insistence of the Russian publishers, the Russian government declined to renew the 1861 literary treaty with France.

Brazil had had a comparable experience, in the wake of which it likewise rejected conclusion of a treaty with France on the same grounds. The author of an anonymous article in *Le Droit d'auteur* claimed that France, behind the reciprocity strategy, was pursuing purely commercial interests. In a telling comparison, it was asserted that the "refined" manners of the internationally active French syndicates for the protection of literary works could only be matched by the polished demeanours of "coachmen's syndicates." On the basis of this experience, the protection of foreign authors in Brazil was further restricted and was made contingent upon a series of preconditions. In order to enjoy protection, foreigners had to be residents of Brazil, be present in person when negotiating the contract, declare the reservation of rights beforehand and meet additional requirements. Finally, the article emphasized the material dimension of the concept of reciprocity, which ought to compel France to likewise make concessions in order to facilitate the export of Brazilian products, by reducing, for example, duties on Brazilian coffee and sugar, such that could counterbalance Brazil's damages.[46]

As regards the right to translation, a cleavage between jurisdiction and political design had become apparent in Russia. Whereas courts, following the legal

45 "Les droits des auteurs étrangers en Russie (A propos de la 'lettre ouverte' de M.E. Zola)," *Le Droit d'auteur*, year 7, no. 2, February 15, 1894, 24–25.

46 *Le Droit d'auteur*, year 8, no. 3, March 15, 1895, 35–37.

understanding of intellectual property, had begun to interpret the law to allow greater protection for authors, the Senate was attempting to arrest or even reverse this same process. In 1891, in a landmark decision, the Senate explicitly reinforced the freedom of translation in the national interest. It reversed decisions of the St. Petersburg circuit court and Civil Chamber Court of Appeals and reaffirmed that the right of the author consisted only in the publication and sale of the original.[47]

As experienced also in Austria-Hungary, opinions on whether to join the BU were split. Though, as demonstrated by global experience, such variance of opinion was nothing unusual, in Russia, resistance to international regulation was surprisingly espoused by that category of actors among which one would have expected to find its more ardent supporters, that is, the Union of Russian Authors. Their oppositional stance was primarily motivated by the desire to maintain the principle of the freedom of translation as it existed in Russia. The union contended that the most meaningful restriction on copyright, and that which distinguished authors' rights from real property, was the territoriality principle; copyright could not extend beyond the territory of the country in whose language the work was originally written and whose citizens had the duty to remunerate authors, on a legally acknowledged basis, for the works created and/or performed. The author was entitled to remuneration only for the original text. Refuting the argument that the freedom of translation produced only bad translations and mutilated texts, the union countered that literary criticism was a mechanism sufficiently developed in order to combat such vices. Finally, the implementation of an exclusive translation right contained the option of inhibiting a translation, which effectively meant depriving the public of access to works, a condition that was deemed impermissible. It was therefore only logical to refuse the exclusive right of translation to national and foreign authors alike, but on the contrary, to recognize for both those categories of authors the right of reproduction of the original. In order to achieve the above, there was no need to enter into international commitments but only to develop autonomous national legislation.[48]

In conclusion, the union emphasized that authors were not impaired by the current state of affairs, and for that reason a restriction of free translation in their name was unnecessary; on the contrary, the conclusion of a literary treaty would seriously hurt the numerous Russian translators and harm most Russian publishers, since only big and financially strong publishing houses would be able to secure licences

47 Westren, "The Development and Debate over Copyright," 174–75.

48 "Russie. L'union des écrivains russes et la protection internationale des droits des auteurs – Traduction libre et contrefaçon," *Le Droit d'auteur*, year 12, no. 4, April 15, 1899, 43–45.

and profit. As a consequence, the price of translated books would rise at the expense of the reading public, making books an elite commodity.

The conclusion of a literary treaty signified for Russia essentially a step backwards on the path of intellectual progress, and would have the immediate and unavoidable effect of limiting the reception of foreign works, but also that of reducing the creation of original Russian works due to the absence of [external] stimulation. Scientific works would be most affected in this respect. Finally, a literary convention was much more profitable for foreign publishers than foreign writers. The conclusion of a treaty would not ameliorate the legal situation of Russian literature with a view to its specific problems, that is, censorship, and was altogether not in harmony with the current state of affairs.

To these multiple causes discouraging the conclusion of a literary treaty, an additional reason was added, namely the rejection of the notion of property: "The protection of an author's right, which is the fundamental idea of such a treaty, does not imply really the exclusive property of literary works. Next to already existing restrictions, this right needs to be complemented by an additional one, namely that the author will receive a compensation only for the original text."[49]

Deliberations in the Civil Law section of the St. Petersburg Society of Jurisconsults, though not unanimous, shared some common ground with the conceptions expressed by the authors' union. Both groups rejected the universalist pretentions of IP, conceptualizing it rather as a statutory right. The main standpoints of the jurists included the following: (1) the exclusive right of translation did not constitute an immutable element of the right of intellectual property; it was rather contingent, and the legislator retained the prerogative to determine the scope and content of this right variably according to circumstances, time and place; (2) due to the liberty of translation, Russia, which was still lagging behind, had the capacity to borrow important literature from Western Europe; any limitations in this regard would have an unfavorable influence on the subsequent development of Russian culture; and (3) piracy (both of foreign originals as well as national works) should be prohibited by law. However, to this end no special treaties were necessary.[50]

There were also splits within the commission charged with the revision of civil legislation around the turn of the century. A section of the commission (notably members Ihrenew and Karnitzky) endorsed from a doctrinal point of view the

49 "Russie. L'union des écrivains russes et la protection internationale des droits des auteurs – Traduction libre et contrefaçon," *Le Droit d'auteur*, year 12, no. 4, April 15, 1899, 43–45.

50 "Russie. L'union des écrivains russes et la protection internationale des droits des auteurs – Traduction libre et contrefaçon," *Le Droit d'auteur*, year 12, no. 4, April 15, 1899, 43–45.

property paradigm and by extension also an exclusive translation right. During the era of privileges, it was dependent upon the will of the government to confer and revoke copyright and the right of translation, but "from the moment the notion of a *right* was adopted, a right acquired alone by the creation of a work and moreover a *property* right, it is impossible to deny it to foreigners. Foreigners in Russia are entitled to the same protection of material things and persons as Russian subjects."[51] They saw it as a calamity that a right was sacrificed for the interests of specific social groups (publishers and translators), noting the demoralizing effect this had on the sense of justice, the perpetuation of the practice of bad translations and the concomitant corruption of literary tastes, and the competition that local authors were exposed to due to the pre-eminence of free translations in journals and newspapers. On the contrary, they countered, it was always possible to acquire authorial authorization, while the translators' material interests remained unaffected; it was after all a right of short duration and there were plenty of works in the public domain.[52]

They were, however, unable to move the majority of the commission, who were clearly against the right of translation. Their argumentation provides an insight into the majoritarian opinion among legal experts. They countered the property theory and stressed the fundamental nature of copyright as a positive right, rebuffing the principle that the exclusive right of translation was a matter of justice. No judicial theory compelled the absolute recognition of the right of translation, for the simple reason that the limits and the scope of copyright itself were by no means incontestable or fixed. To be sure, authors' rights carried the appellation "property," but they corresponded not in the least to ordinary property, given their limited duration and other particularities. Moreover, they were of far more recent origin than all other forms of property and their limits were only fixed by positive law. As a consequence, it was completely legal to consider a translation an independent creative work and therefore possible to deny such a right to foreigners without injuring them; it meant simply to refuse them a favor that was granted to nationals.

Furthermore, the interdiction of free translations would considerably diminish the number of foreign works translated, while, on the contrary, competition among translators had improved the quality of translations. Though it was accurate to claim that the increased number of published translations reduced rewards for national authors, especially the least prominent ones, it was nevertheless legitimate to sacrifice the private interests of authors for the sake of public welfare.

51 "Correspondance, Lettre de Russie," *Le Droit d'auteur*, year 13, no. 9, September 15, 1900, 118.

52 "Correspondance, Lettre de Russie," 119.

The abolition of the freedom of translation would have the most detrimental consequences in the scientific field. Translations of scholarly works played a seminal role in the development of the sciences, and in this domain Russia would long remain dependent on the fruits of European culture. Barely remunerated, scholarly translations represented difficult and ungrateful labor. It was to be assumed that the interdiction of free translations, and the complications accompanying the quest for authorization, would almost completely obliterate these kinds of editions. The committee's majority concluded that the liberty of translation was too important for Russian society, and this fact rendered an amendment of the existing regulation undesirable. After all, Russian language was barely known abroad, original works barely circulated outside the country and the number of translated works was rather insignificant, so there were no grounds for reciprocity with other countries.

In this context, the deliberations of the jurist and statesman Aleksander Ivanovich Lykochine are interesting, not least because of his reflections on the formation of knowledge and the nature of copyright law. He contended that literary conventions should not be examined solely from the standpoint of the authors' material interests. All cultural development depended upon the freedom with which intellectual and artistic works could be borrowed. He supported the prohibition of domestic and foreign reprints, but stressed that such interdictions ought to be the subject of national laws, and not of diplomatic conferences, which enhanced foreign governments' capacity to interfere in the internal affairs of other countries.

Representing an activity requiring intellectual and personal labor, such as the knowledge of at least two languages and a literary education, translation had nothing in common with vulgar reproduction. If translators were required to pay a contribution to foreigners, nobody in Russia would undertake the translation of demanding works. The abolition of the freedom of translation would render the intellectual exchange between Russia and Europe more difficult. Reciprocity was futile since the exchange was unequal; Russia was forced to borrow from abroad, while the reverse was rarely the case. In a telling metaphor: "[...] to conclude a literary convention with France is equivalent to concluding a commercial treaty in which Russia and France declare the reciprocal liberty to import wines, silk and velvet."[53] Furthermore, Russian scholars and authors had a fundamentally different attitude. When asked to translate their works, they rarely demanded a material reward, being essentially honoured to have their works popularized in Europe. Often, they came up themselves with the translators' and publishers' expenses.

---

[53] "Correspondance, Lettre de Russie," 120.

In terms of legal doctrine, Lykochine emphasized the particular social character of authors' rights, which were neither ancient nor the outcome of common law. Rather, they were the creation of the utilitarian considerations of legislators. Copyright's place in the system of law was controversial and its nature undetermined. The argument therefore that Russia appropriated foreign works had to be formulated differently: who could argue against the fact that intellectual development was achieved by tapping into the knowledge of others?

In a statement that clearly captured the spirit of his times and contained an almost prophetic quality, Lykochine claimed that "the age of excessive individualism has passed and we discern on the horizon the dawn of a different era, where the notion of general will [volonté générale] will find its way into all spheres of life. Even material property is losing ground and distances itself more and more from the romantic notion of *dominium*. The British *Homesteads*, German *Strafrecht* testify to this. Authors' rights are even more endangered; they are too recent and too social in their essence to resist modern influences. One should therefore be proud not to resemble the Western states in that respect."[54]

Other jurists again, like Ujakow, emphasized the progressive character of international unions. The BU's essential problem consisted in the fact that its creation was almost entirely left to the discretion of exporting states, whereas importing countries abstained. By this means, exporters secured the legal codification of their interests, and their alliance was facilitated through common economic benefits. According to lofty and abstract principles, the protection of foreign authors should not be more harmful to Russian economic interests than to French or English ones. However, it was impossible for book-importing countries to accept the form of monopoly in which the book-exporting countries had clothed this principle, with the consent of the states that participated in the conferences.[55]

Reflecting on possible courses of further action, the committee deliberated whether to follow a similar course to the US in the Platt-Simonds Act (or Chase Act, 1891), a course that was found to be less beneficial in the case of Russia though it was considered a potential weapon to force Berne Union countries into concessions. The committee showed a preference for the Italian model, under which reproductions of originals were allowed only after authorization and payment of a fee, which would reconcile the interests of both the national industry and foreign authors.

While deliberations on the drafting of a new law were taking place at the beginning of the century, and prior to concluding a new round of bilateral treaties, the

54 "Correspondance, Lettre de Russie," 120.

55 "Correspondance, Lettre de Russie," 121.

Russian government tasked a committee with the examination of the question of whether to continue the pattern of concluding bilateral treaties with isolated countries or to enter the BU, and furthermore, whether it would be reasonable to enter into negotiations before or after the amendment of local legislation.[56] The committee consisted of a representative sample of stakeholders in major educational and cultural institutions such as the ministries of commerce, industry, justice, foreign affairs and public education, academies of sciences and the arts, the Imperial Society for the Encouragement of the Arts, the Russian Geographical Society, the Society of Art and Literature, the St. Petersburg Photographic Society as well as the Society of Publishers, Music Publishers and Printers. During its meetings on April 13 and 14 (26 and 27) 1906, the majority of delegates expressed their approval for Russia's accession to the BU, which appeared more convenient than bilateral treaties. Only four of 28 delegates, representing the Ministry of Justice, the academy of sciences and the geographical society, expressed a different opinion. The majority held that the current state of affairs, where foreigners were deprived of any protection and nationals were only insufficiently protected, menaced moreover by the disproportional competition created through foreign works, was responsible for the degradation of creative work in all areas. They concluded that a change of regime through adherence to the BU would benefit local authors.

As had also been the case with Austria-Hungary, a significant number, if not the majority, of local stakeholders endorsed the concept of international protection, but were nevertheless unable to channel developments in this direction.

The point of the minority was defended by A. I. Lykochine, the representative of the Ministry of Justice, who on previous occasions had also stood up for the freedom of translation in the St. Petersburg Society of Jurisconsults. In his view, "the countries that agreed on international protection were motivated less by moral reasons than practical ones, i.e. in order to protect their own authors. The international consortium is therefore founded on the principle of utility and egotism. It considers it advantageous to impel less civilized countries to enter [its ranks], which for the sake of their own authors are pressured to join. The US and Austria-Hungary, countries that do not benefit from the union, did not accede; nobody will call them less civilized or advanced for this reason. Russia does not expect to solicit the particular esteem of utilitarian Europe, nor fight the legendary armies of the Knight of La Mancha, but rather protect its own interests."[57]

---

56 "Partie non officielle, Etudes générales, Russie, Etat de la réforme législative en matière de droit d'auteur. – Vues divergentes de la commission extraparlementaire ; majorité et minorité. – La Russie et la convention de Berne," *Le Droit d'auteur*, year 20, no. 8, August 15, 1907, 97–99.

57 "Partie non officielle, Etudes générales, Russie, Etat de la réforme législative en matière de droit

The liberty of translation had existed for a long time and was harmful neither to local literature nor the arts. Free competition guaranteed, through the marginalization of bad translations, the prevalence of quality ones. Moreover, it was unlikely that foreign authors would content themselves with modest remunerations, "something indeed doubtful when it comes to French authors."[58] In any case, it was not the authors but rather the publishers-assignees who were the dealmakers in the first place, and they were not at all interested in carefully translated works, being moreover unable to control the outcome of translations due to a lack of linguistic skills. The price of books would become dependent on the calculation of authors' fees and the exigencies of (local, i.e. Russian) monopolist publishers. And who could guarantee that they would be trustworthy and furnish only good works?

It was therefore not only foreign authors and publishers that were mistrusted, but also local publishers with pretensions to monopolize the market in translations. This circumstance brought a double disadvantage, not only for the reading public but also for the numerous translators, ordinary people, students and publishers of journals who survived through inexpensive translations.

Alternatives were also considered. As foreign translations of Russian works slowly increased, it was contemplated whether it would be meaningful to abandon the principle of free translation only in the realm of literature (*belles lettres*), which could be considered a luxury, and retain it for the domain in which it was considered truly indispensable, that is, for scientific and technical literature. Being "comparable to everyday bread," textbooks and foreign manuals were the sole source of public instruction. The problem consisted less in translation and more in the dearth of local experts who could match Western European scholarly levels. Monopolization would seriously impede the popularization of science and technology and would be detrimental to the Russian nation.

Finally, the above factors had an impact on the smaller ethnic groups at the frontiers, such as Lithuanians, Latvians and Estonians, whose literary development depended more than Russia's on the liberty of translation. It was unimaginable to deprive them of this freedom when it came to translating Russian works into their native languages. No matter how legitimate the wish that Russia enter the path of international protection in the future, every concession in the field of translation would be inopportune and antagonistic to the intellectual needs of the Russian and other peoples of the empire.

d'auteur. – Vues divergentes de la commission extraparlementaire ; majorité et minorité. – La Russie et la convention de Berne," *Le Droit d'auteur*, year 20, no. 8, August 15, 1907, 98.

58 "Partie non officielle, Etudes générales, Russie, Etat de la réforme législative en matière de droit d'auteur. – Vues divergentes de la commission extraparlementaire ; majorité et minorité. – La Russie et la convention de Berne," *Le Droit d'auteur*, year 20, no. 8, August 15, 1907, 98.

Withdrawal from the BU after acceding to the convention would be difficult, so it was wiser to stick to specific treaties. In special and individual negotiations, it was easier for Russia to insist on the precarious home conditions prevalent in the scientific and technical fields, to control the interests of other countries and ensure the freedom of translation in those areas. With the aid of experts and in consultation with the courts, it would always be possible to find ways to circumvent foreign claims.[59]

The 1911 Copyright Law

The last copyright law in pre-revolutionary Russia was fashioned after German legislation and the conceptions of the Russian civil law specialists (Spassovich, Annenkof, Scherschenevich and Karnicky). Rejecting the property paradigm, the law defined copyright as an exclusive right, investing the author with the prerogative to publish, circulate and reproduce his work through all possible means.[60] The justification for the new law brought together a series of interesting themes. It emphasized the social role of the author and knowledge, and underscored the importance of moral rights, which featured prominently in the 1911 legislation:

> In that regard, not only pecuniary interests have to be protected as real rights, but [it also needs to be considered that] the author is a social worker, a propagator of ideas, therefore works are the reflection of common aspirations and they emanate from the social milieu upon which they exercise a great influence; the legislator has therefore the task to set the rights of the author in harmony with the interests of society. [...] Next to the material and pecuniary aspects contained in the right to sanction, [the law] will also consider personal elements. And it is permissible to say that the commission has largely safeguarded them in the [law] project by protecting fully all unpublished works against unauthorized publication, by preserving copyright against any enforcement procedure, by abandoning to creditors nothing but the copies published and offered for sale, and finally by clarifying with precision assignments to the publishers and by delineating the publishing contract.[61]

The law was also debated in the St. Petersburg Literary Society. As already witnessed, its majority defended the freedom of translation and spoke against Russia's entry

[59] "Partie non officielle, Etudes générales, Russie, Etat de la réforme législative en matière de droit d'auteur. – Vues divergentes de la commission extraparlementaire ; majorité et minorité. – La Russie et la convention de Berne," *Le Droit d'auteur*, year 20, no. 8, August 15, 1907, 99.

[60] "Partie non officielle, Études générales, Le droit d'auteur en Russie," *Le Droit d'auteur*, year 21, no. 8, August 15, 1908, 93.

[61] "Partie non officielle, Études générales, Le droit d'auteur en Russie," *Le Droit d'auteur*, year 21, no. 8, August 15, 1908, 94.

into the BU. Even more surprisingly, however, the society also pronounced itself against the prolongation of copyright's term of protection p.m.a., and advocated the restriction of authors' rights p.m.a. from the officially valid standard of 50 years to 25 or a maximum of 30 years.[62]

Attempting to explain to West European audiences and the readership of *Le Droit d'auteur* the reasons behind the Russian authors' programmatic positions, E. Semenoff, intellectual, publicist and French lobbyist promoting the copyright cause in Russia, offered the perfect definition of intelligentsia. Such a world view, he contended, was the result of "false" consciousness:

> the very widespread notion according to which unauthorized translation is not a counterfeit, is due to a special mentality, idealistic and at the same time very basic. According to the Russian tradition, the author has to accomplish a holy mission, that is, free propagation of ideas, knowledge, literature, worship of the principle of freedom in the name of civilization and public education. This conception dominated above every other consideration such as fees to be paid when establishing a publication's budget, considerations about food, clothing, shelter, even the remuneration of the author's work itself appeared totally secondary, purely bourgeois and mercantile; the notion that one could call these appropriations [i.e. free translations] theft, piracy, all this appeared incomprehensible.[63]

The 1911 copyright law was based on West European principles of copyright law. It was largely predicated on the 1901 German copyright law and incorporated aspects of the 1901 German *Verlagsrecht* (publishing law), but also included provisions that were homegrown. They related to specific, local concerns with copyright regulation and in some cases, such as the protection of oral culture and folklore, even set a precedent for future developments in international copyright. The law's most distinctive features can be summed up as follows: (1) departure of Russian copyright law from a property-based notion of copyright; (2) departure from a doctrinal justification of copyright based on natural rights, and an implicit justification based on positive law and/or as a *sui generis* right; (3) continuation of Russia's own, idiosyncratic path with respect to translations; (4) strong emphasis on moral rights, including the intention to empower the author in relation to the publisher; and (5) the innovative tendency—pioneering for the times—to grant protection to oral works and musical improvisations, related to Russia's rich heritage of folklore and traditional culture.

62 "Partie non officielle, Études générales, Le droit d'auteur en Russie," *Le Droit d'auteur*, year 21, no. 8, August 15, 1908, 95.

63 "Partie non officielle, Études générales, Le droit d'auteur en Russie," *Le Droit d'auteur*, year 21, no. 8, August 15, 1908, 95.

The 1911 Russian copyright law was an important highlight in the development of authors' rights in Eastern Europe and for this reason will be presented here in greater detail. It was the first self-reliant, comprehensive modern copyright law among the Slavic populations of Eastern Europe. It represented a forerunner regarding the mode of reception of copyright law in the region, and finally, it became itself a model and point of reference for the drafting of other national copyright laws such as the Bulgarian one.

The law did not provide an exhaustive but rather a representative list of the works protected, including literary, written and oral works, discourses, lectures, reports and conferences, musical works including musical improvisations, artistic works, photographic and similar works.[64] Authors' rights were recognized for all works published in Russia by authors and their rightsholders independent of nationality, and for all works published abroad by Russian subjects and their rightsholders independent of their nationality. Protection lasted for the author's lifetime plus 50 p.m.a.; when not otherwise stipulated by the author and in the absence of heirs, copyright expired with the author's death.

The law sought to protect authors from unfair exploitation by postulating limits for contracts concerning future works to a maximum duration of five years (art. 9), even if the contract was issued for a longer period or contained no time specification. The law provided also for an amplitude of free uses: the use of an existing work for the purposes of creating a new, essentially different one did not constitute a violation of authors' rights; nor did the creation of copies as far as they served an exclusively personal use, and did not contain the signature or the monograph of the original work's author (art. 3). It was permitted to copy without authorial authorization works of art procured by churches, royal palaces, governmental institutions and public corporations, provided copying had been authorized by a competent authority (art. 54). Exchanges between genres, like the reproduction of a painting as a sculpture, and vice versa, were not considered a violation of artists' rights. The following constituted no infringement: the reproduction of isolated works of art in an independent scientific study, or in a work destined for pedagogical use, provided that such a reproduction served exclusively to explain the text; the reproduction of public works of art located in streets, squares and other public spaces through an artistic genre different than the one employed in the original; the utilization of separate parts of a work of art for industrial and artisan products (art. 56). Overall, there were generous exceptions from protection for public, scientific and educational uses

64 "Russie, Loi concernant le droit d'auteur du 20 mars 1911," *Le Droit d'auteur*, year 24, no. 7, July 15, 1911, 87–91.

as well as industrial applications; for example, the reproduction of photographic works in their entirety in the case of industrial and artisanal products did not constitute an infringement (art. 62).

The law sought to protect authors against creditors, stipulating that copyright could not become the subject of sequestration without the author's consent during his lifetime and after his death without the consent of his heirs. Publishing rights or other rights pertaining to the author, which had been ceded by the author to a third person in the form of a contract, could be restrained for the author's debts but within the limits of the contract (art. 10).

One truly novel aspect of the 1911 copyright law was its treatment of folk art. Russian legislation was the first in the world to extend copyright protection to popular art and oral traditions, which also testifies to the significance of folklore in the Russian context. This provides for an interesting East–West comparison. The appropriation of traditional stories, poems, songs and so on by the literary and publishing establishment took place in Western Europe as well, but in an earlier period. As convincingly laid out by William St. Clair, this process of enclosure in the case of Great Britain happened in the form of individual appropriation, with the lock-in of popular texts serving diverse models and formats of printing and publishing.[65] Inserted in copyright-protected anthologies, the popular repository was privatized in order to be commercially utilized. Folklore, oral culture and primitive art, codified as archaic forms of collective expression and somehow irrelevant to the modern commercial copyright regime, which was tied to the figure of the individual author, were left completely off the radar of West European copyright. The eastern part of the continent, by contrast, was still involved in a process of nation-building, where stabilization and codification of language and culture were largely ongoing developments, and where the literary canon was only slowly emerging. Here the systematization of popular texts primarily assisted the codification of national culture(s). Consequently, the same process served a different logic and different priorities in East and West. The centrality of culture in the engineering of the nation supported the perception of folklore as the depository of the collective, and for that reason both folklore and oral culture needed to remain broadly accessible as commons and in the form of open access. Therefore, Russian legislation accorded to authors of collections of popular songs, melodies, proverbs, children's tales, stories, popular legends and similar creations of popular/folk poetry, which had been preserved through oral tradition, and to authors of collections of drawings and other products

[65] William St. Clair, *The Reading Nation in the Romantic Period* (Cambridge: Cambridge University Press, 2004), 79–80.

of popular/folk art, 50 years' copyright protection for their compilations from the day of publication. This right, however, did not restrain others from editing and publishing the same works in an original form or collection (art. 13).

Particularly noteworthy in the 1911 copyright legislation was the inclusion of provisions related to moral rights, specifically the rights of paternity, integrity and divulgence. All legally borrowed excerpts had to be accompanied by an indication of the name of the author and the source (art. 19). A prominent position was reserved for the right of integrity, which was supposed to prevent the unauthorized modification of an author's work and contain arbitrary actions by intermediaries (i.e. publishers). The person to whom copyright was assigned was prohibited from introducing changes, additions and/or omissions without the consent of the author or his heirs, apart from those changes that were completely indispensable and which the author himself, in good faith, would not have been able to refuse (art. 20). Violations or injuries of authors' and heirs' rights necessitated compensation for the damage incurred (art. 21). If copyright injury occurred in good faith and through justifiable error, the perpetrator was obligated to compensate the author and his heirs, though only to the limits of the profit incurred.

The right of divulgence was safeguarded in article 27, which prohibited the public reproduction of an unpublished work, or the publication of its contents, without authorial authorization. Similarly interdicted was the transformation of a prose narrative into a dramatic work and vice versa without the authorization of the author and/or his heirs.

The law maintained freedom of translation for foreign works, excluding only cases where bilateral treaties between Russia and foreign countries stipulated otherwise, and even in those cases, foreign citizens could not enjoy more extensive rights than those attributed to Russian subjects through the native copyright law. Further, the law prohibited the reprinting of a foreign work in original form without the rightsholder's authorization. Authoritative here were the laws of the country of first publication, provided that the foreign law's duration of protection did not exceed the term of protection stipulated by Russian law (art. 32).

A minor change was introduced concerning the translation of domestic works. The author of a work published in Russia, as well as a Russian subject having published a work abroad and their heirs, enjoyed an exclusive right of translation of their works into other languages, under the condition that they had reserved this right either on the work's cover or in a preface. The exclusive right of translation belonged to the author for the period of 10 years from the publication of the original, upon condition that he published a translation within five years of the publication of the original (art. 33). A translator retained copyright for his/her translation, but this right did not exclude others from translating the same work independently.

Journals, reviews and periodical publications were allowed to borrow information related to the daily news from other analogous publications. Articles from periodical publications could be reproduced only in the absence of a relevant interdiction by the author. Continuous reproductions from one and the same publication were prohibited (art. 40).

Chapter VII of the law was dedicated to the publishing contract and contained a series of stipulations regulating the relationship between the author and the publisher, mainly to the advantage of the author. Namely: publishers were prohibited from relinquishing conceded copyrights to third persons; authors could terminate contracts if the manuscript was not published within three years of the date of delivery; if no other indication was given, it was mandatory to mention the exact number of exemplars that constituted an edition; the author had the right to make a new edition after five years; the author had the right to publish a complete edition of his works, containing also works whose copyright had been ceded to third persons, provided that a three-year period had elapsed from the initial publication for literary works, and 10 years for musical works; concession of the right to publish a dramatic, musical or dramatic-musical work did not include cession of the right of public performance or that of adaptation of musical works to instruments of mechanical reproduction (art. 65–75).

The legislator's philosophy was reflected even in the language of the law, which perpetrated a concept of authors' rights that was antithetical to the property doctrine. Consciously defying the language of property, the verb "to own" was mentioned but once, and paradoxically enough, in a formulation that related not to individual but to "common property," and was applied to denote the common ownership of rights by heirs.

Both directly and indirectly, the 1911 Russian law became one of the prime channels of legal transfer, and therefore a supplementary transmission pathway for German copyright legislation and copyright doctrine into Eastern Europe at the beginning of the twentieth century. German influence in the field of copyright law was felt even more strongly in the interwar period, where it became a source of inspiration but also a matrix for a series of copyright laws in the region. Several reasons go to explain the preponderance of German influences: (1) the broader impact of German civil law and strong radiation of German philosophy and legal scholarship; (2) the more "paternalistic" character of the German copyright law, which intervened more actively into market-governed relationships and regulated more closely the relationship between author and publisher, and which (3) as a model fit better the needs and tasks of East European societies and their conception of the role and function of copyright within the field of culture. Russian copyright law, representing the inaugural copyright legislation of the Slavic world, probably became authoritative for the codification of expert terminology in the majority of Slavic languages, though this thesis needs to be qualified further through research into the history of concepts. The Russian denomination "avtorskoe pravo," which designates simultaneously both authors' rights and the legal field of copyright law, was conceptually the exact equivalent of the German "Urheberrecht" and French "Droit d'auteur." The majority of Slavic languages barely made use of the term "intellectual property/propriété intellectuelle" that was initially strongly advocated by French legal circles,[66] and which indeed had a strong influence on copyright terminology and the genealogy of laws in several Romance-speaking countries such as Spain.[67]

Multiple motives lay behind the specific way in which copyright was codified in Russia. Predicated upon the particular role played by authors (i.e. the intelligentsia) and their self-perception as the genuine and sole guardians of Russia's cultural heritage, copyright was codified concurrently with efforts to create a unified Russian culture through the canonization of Russian classics. Public and expert opinion were witness to heirs' efforts (see here the appeals of the Pushkin family, debates within the Tolstoy family and others) to control the uses of the literary estate of prominent Russian authors. Such incidents created awareness of the potentially detrimental influence of heirs on literary heritage, who could use their legal monopoly to prohibit the dissemination of works or conclude exclusive deals with publishers that led to massive price increases, thereby making books inaccessible to the larger public. Maintaining the broadest possible access to Russian cultural heritage also motivated the reluctance towards a protracted term of protection post mortem (though in the end the 50-year term prevailed), and the discussion on the appropriate form of copyright protection regarding diaries and other intimate writings not destined for publication, and their alleged public or private nature.[68]

---

66 In fact, the issue of the appropriate terminology and appellation constituted a major point of discord on the way to the creation of the Berne Union.

67 Even today the term "propiedad intellectual" is more in use in the Spanish-speaking world than the term "derecho de autor."

68 Westren, "The Development and Debate over Copyright," 157, 161, 168, 171, 182. See here also the inspiring and insightful discussion by Ekaterina Pravilova, *A Public Empire: Property and the Quest for the Common Good in Imperial Russia* (Princeton: Princeton University Press, 2014), esp. part III., 215–61.

Equally important was the fact that the Russian Publishers' and Booksellers' Union was weak and divided and failed to form a strong pressure group with a coherent strategy when it came to copyright. The union reacted tardily to the drafting of the new law and had no significant influence on the development of copyright legislation.[69]

Several features of the 1911 Russian copyright law were also formative in the case of other copyright legislations of Eastern Europe. Most importantly, the law rejected the idea of property as the justification for copyright protection; copyright was codified as a *sui generis* right and the outcome of positive law. Through the conspicuous presence of moral rights and a clear focus on the person of the author, the 1911 law underscored the importance of authorship for Russian development. Through the restriction of translation rights, the law aimed at "unifying Russia's diverse people through a common literature, as well as the goal of improving literacy. This policy made sense in view of the international status of the Russian language: its use extended throughout the Russian Empire, but did not reach significantly beyond Russia's borders."[70] The translation policy adversely affected not only foreign but also Russian authors and authors writing in the minority languages of the Russian Empire. The 1911 regulation of translation for domestic works tried to accommodate some of these concerns, granting domestic authors some limited rights over translation, while sticking to freedom of translation for foreign works. Most significantly, freedom of translation was not treated as a private interest right, but was elevated to an issue of national-state significance and justified on the grounds of the public good. Limiting the freedom of translation was deemed harmful, even dangerous, to the development of the enlightenment project in Russia.[71]

The Ottoman Empire

Representing the third major multiethnic empire of the East, the Ottoman Empire, though sharing similarities with the Habsburg and the Romanov Empires, also carried distinct traits that set it apart, such as the persistence of manuscript culture and a formal definition of community structured primarily around religion.

69 Westren, "The Development and Debate over Copyright," 200–208.

70 Mira T. Sundara Rajan, *Copyright and Creative Freedom: A Study of Post-Socialist Law Reform* (Oxon: Routledge, 2006), 81.

71 Westren, "The Development and Debate over Copyright," 215–16; see also Rajan, *Copyright and Creative Freedom*, 86.

Printing was introduced in the Ottoman Empire in the late fifteenth/early sixteenth centuries via Jewish refugees from Spain, who transferred their know-how, equipment and practical experience from the Iberian Peninsula to the urban centers of the Ottoman Empire, such as Istanbul and Salonika.[72] Though a limited number of printing presses had been established by minorities and missionaries by the eighteenth century, the press was not used by the Ottomans until 1726, when Ibrahim Müteferrika, a Transylvanian-born Hungarian Unitarian who became an Ottoman subject and later converted to Islam, obtained permission to print books. He received authorization to print books dealing with science, language and history, but was excluded from printing religious texts, which remained at the discretion of the religious establishment.[73] The total output of printed books was modest. J. S. Szyliowicz estimates that in the period 1729–1830 between 180 and 200 titles were published,[74] while J. Strauss gives an estimate of 436 titles up until approximately the 1830s.[75] Around the turn of the twentieth century, with the exception of textbooks and popular stories, print runs rarely exceeded 2,000 copies; an edition of 3,000 or 4,000 copies was practically unknown.[76] Nevertheless, by the end of the eighteenth century, printing had become a permanent technological fixture of the Ottoman Empire, and by the turn of the nineteenth century, printing was appreciated as a tool for the dissemination of education, bureaucratic improvement and the implementation of law.

Printing properly took off in the first half of the nineteenth century, in the context of the Tanzimat reforms and in connection to the state elites' concerted efforts to employ the press strategically as an instrument in the process of imperial modernization. Fostered by the creation of new institutions and a secular educational system, which developed and diversified rapidly, literacy rates grew quickly from 1% in 1800 to approximately 10% in 1914.[77] Reading expanded in the wake of an

---

72 John-Paul Ghobrial, "Printing," in *Encyclopedia of the Ottoman Empire*, eds. Gábor Ágoston and Bruce Masters (New York: Facts on File, 2009), 471.

73 Orlin Sabev, "A Virgin Deserving Paradise or a Whore Deserving Poison: Manuscript Tradition and Printed Books in Ottoman Turkish Society," in *The History of the Book in the Middle East*, ed. Geoffrey Roper (Series: The History of the Book in the East, ed. Peter Kornicki) (Farnham, UK: Ashgate, 2013), 152–153.

74 J.S. Szyliowicz, "Functional Perspectives on Technology: The Case of the Printing Press in the Ottoman Empire," in Roper, *The History of the Book in the Middle East*, 333–334.

75 Johann Strauss, "Les livres et l'imprimerie à Istanbul (1800–1908)," in *Turquie, livres d'hier, livres d'aujourd'hui*, vol. 1, ed. Paul Dumont (Etudes turques – USHS, 1) (Centre de Recherche sur la Civilisation Ottomane et le Domaine Turc Contemporain, Université des Sciences Humaines Strasbourg, 1992), 6.

76 Strauss, "Les livres et l'imprimerie à Istanbul," 5.

77 Szyliowicz, "Functional Perspectives on Technology," 336.

emerging bourgeoisie associated with the needs of a new bureaucracy and the development of modern (liberal) professions, who consumed printed matter for both entertainment and enlightenment purposes.[78]

The same period also saw the spread of new media, particularly newspapers. The creation of the Turkish press both complements and contrasts with the West European experience. Early Turkish newspapers were issued by the governing elite with the purpose of educating the public, helping to shape public opinion and facilitating the implementation of desired state reforms.[79] In its proximity to the realm of politics and its statist understanding of the role of the press, Turkish development is typologically closer to the French and/or German historical experience, both countries in which the press and journalism developed in symbiotic and complementary ways to state and/or party politics. This type contrasts somewhat with the British and US experience, where the press asserted itself via its claim to represent the "4th estate."[80]

The social and political developments taking place in the Ottoman Empire in the nineteenth and twentieth centuries were also reflected in the development of printing. An increased output of printed material, growing diversity among printers and a change in the content of printed materials were characteristic of the new times. As part of the reform strategy of Mehmed Ali of Egypt, a new printing press was established in the Cairo district of Bulaq in the 1820s, and by the beginning of the twentieth century printing in Egypt was carried out by individuals beyond the ruling elite. Whereas early printing in the Ottoman Empire had been practiced by limited groups, the twentieth century witnessed an expansion of both of the number of printers and the types of published materials. Missionary groups, in their desire to make religious content available and convert local groups, had already contributed significantly to the promotion of printing, and moreover in an array of different languages. An important addition to the development of printing came from the rising group of national enlighteners of various nationalities, who brought local literature into print or went to great pains to codify, revive, invent and disseminate it. The printing press became for this group an important tool for propaganda and the spread of nationalism, and was equally adopted by Muslim reformers, who embraced the press as a means to engage in broader modernization debates. A change

---

78 Szyliowicz, "Functional Perspectives on Technology," 337.

79 Szyliowicz, "Functional Perspectives on Technology," 337–38.

80 A good comparative analysis of the development of the press and journalism in Britain, the USA, France and Germany is offered by Jörg Requate, *Journalismus als Beruf: Entstehung und Entwicklung des Journalistenberufs im 19. Jahrhundert; Deutschland im internationalen Vergleich* (Historische Studien zur Geschichtswissenschaft 109) (Göttingen: Vanderhoeck und Ruprecht, 1995).

in the format of the printed matter took place as well; whereas previously multi-volume texts had prevailed, production now shifted to ephemeral periodical literature such as newspapers and pamphlets.

The question of why the Ottomans did not print or did not use print for approximately three centuries (the fifteenth to the eighteenth) has been an issue of heated scholarly debate. Analysts, more often than not, hurried to predicate such temporal asymmetry between Europe and the Middle East on some kind of a priori "traditionalism" (of the ruling elite, the religious establishment, the closed ranks of professional copyists and calligraphers, the sanctity of the Koran, Islamic conservativism etc.), often applying an analytical framework that advanced the idea of a European printing revolution as a yardstick of universal modernity, on account of which the Middle East was found to be lagging behind. Recently, these implicit or explicit assumptions have come under fire by scholars who castigate the Orientalizing and Eurocentric tropes inherent in the blueprints of a "print-induced modernity."[81]

According to J. P. Ghobrial:

> [h]istorians have speculated about the reasons for the ebbs and flows in the use of print in the Ottoman Empire's long history. The difficulty of reading printed texts as opposed to manuscript ones, the existence of an organized and effective system for copying texts, and even the high costs and technical challenges of printing in Arabic script were probably important factors. Still, specific incidents of the use of print are best understood in light of the unique circumstances surrounding them. The experience of printing in other societies—for example, in early modern Europe or Asia—suggests that it is not surprising that scribal production, or the copying of texts by hand, continued to play an important role in Ottoman society centuries after the discovery of Gutenberg's masterful inventions. Similarly, the introduction of the printing press in the Ottoman Empire need not have ushered in a new era of the "print revolution." Rather, printing remained merely one medium for the spread of information in a complex and dynamic communications network, a world in which print interacted with other media such as manuscripts, visual signs, and, perhaps most importantly, the spoken word.[82]

---

[81] See here Dana Sajdi, "Print and Its Discontents: A Case for Pre-Print Journalism and Other Sundry Print Matters," *The Translator* 15, no. 1 (2009): 105–138; Kathryn A. Schwarz, "Did Ottoman Sultans Ban Print?" *Book History* 20 (2017): 1–39; Jonathan Haddad, "People Before Print: Gens de Lettres, the Ottoman Printing Press, and the Search for Turkish Literature," *Mediterranean Studies* 25, no. 2 (2017): 189–228.

[82] Ghobrial, "Printing," 472–73.

Scholars studying the history of the book in the Ottoman Empire emphasize that the process of transition from scribal to print culture was slow, gradual and arduous.[83] Ottoman authorities allowed the trade in Arabic books printed abroad and prints were traded in the Ottoman market, though they were not particularly popular with the wider public. Orlin Sabev maintains that the Ottomans usually adopted foreign patterns when a need for such novelties was felt; the fact that the tradition of hand copying prevailed for so long is most likely because a related change did not correspond to a social necessity. Moreover, the Arabic alphabet posed serious difficulties for printing in movable type. Lithography proved far more adept to replicate the cursive scripts used in the region and was readily adopted; as a printing technology, it could easily draw on the pre-existing proficiency of local calligraphers and scribes. Characteristically, and in an interesting inversion of the West European experience, the holy scriptures of Islam were not printed first but last in the process of print adoption. The first Ottoman prints of the Koran date from the 1870s. Apparently, some early corrupt Western prints of the Koran discredited it as a technology and confirmed manuscript copying as a more reliable and trustworthy method of text replication.[84] Printing had therefore to compete with calligraphy as a supreme Islamic art.[85]

An additional factor explaining the persistence of manuscript production could well be related to the organization of Ottoman script culture. As maintained by Christoph Neumann in his analysis of manuscripts from the seventeenth and eighteenth centuries, there was little difference between authors and copyists in Ottoman culture. Whereas almost all professionals involved in manuscript production, from miniaturists and bookbinders to ink makers and pencil sharpeners, were organized in guilds, neither copyists nor calligraphers had a guild of their own. This allowed book copying to remain accessible and free from monopoly.[86] Moreover, book production was a decentralized process that took place in an individual setting, whereby Ottoman copyists had considerable leeway to actively rearrange the manuscript. It therefore became difficult to determine whether what was described as a Turkish translation "should be considered a translation or a new work in its own right."[87]

"Ottoman" literary production—to the degree that such a generalization can be made—can only be understood when placed in the context of the multiethnic

---

83 Sabev, "A Virgin Deserving Paradise," 149.

84 Sabev, "A Virgin Deserving Paradise," 162–63.

85 Sabev, "A Virgin Deserving Paradise," 160.

86 Christoph K. Neumann, "Three Modes of Reading: Writing and Reading Books in Early Modern Ottoman History," *Lingua Franca, The History of Book in Translation*, Ottoman Print Culture, issue 5 (2019): 9–10, http://www.sharpweb.org/linguafranca/issue-5-2019-ottoman-print-culture/.

87 Neumann, "Three Modes of Reading," 11.

nature of empire. Istanbul became an intellectual center for various groups, which were far less exclusive than is generally assumed.[88] Reading and literary activity in plural Ottoman society were divided along the lines of, among other things, religion, language and script, whereby ethnic language did not always coincide with the written language of the community, which in the Ottoman context was determined by religion. Many more languages were spoken than written or printed until the nineteenth century, the written languages being essentially Ottoman Turkish, Persian, Arabic, Greek, Armenian and Hebrew.

The written or literate languages used did not necessarily overlap with ethnicity. For example, Greek was used from the eighteenth century onwards as the cultural language of educated Bulgarians and Romanians; Persian did not represent an ethnic language but served rather as a language of culture for the educated Ottoman elite. Turkish poets of diverse ethnic backgrounds and mother tongues such as Bosnians and/or Albanians composed their literary works in Persian. Access to literary production depended therefore principally on the training of the prospective readers and their mastery of a "foreign" language.[89]

In the course of the nineteenth century, significant developments in the realm of languages affected reading habits: (1) classical languages were gradually replaced by vernacular versions, for example the decline of classical Armenian (krapar) in favor of modern Armenian and Armeno-Turkish; (2) ethnic languages emancipated themselves from their domination by other languages; (3) new literary languages emerged, for example Bulgarian; (4) a new Western language, French, was introduced, which acquired the status of a semi-official language in the Ottoman Empire and also became the language of communication between the educated strata of the various linguistic, ethnic and religious communities, both Muslim and non-Muslim.[90]

Printing was and remained essentially a polycentric enterprise. It took place partially in an intense exchange with prominent European and other centers of printing, though the geography of printing and its distribution networks were restructured in the nineteenth century. Until the early nineteenth century, printed matter in the various languages of the Ottoman Empire's populations was produced by the printers and publishers of Istanbul and those of the Danubian principalities, but also largely abroad. West European cities such as Vienna, Venice, Amsterdam and Leipzig were important centers of printing for the non-Muslim communities.

88 Johann Strauss, "Who Read What in the Ottoman Empire (19th–20th centuries)," in Roper, *The History of the Book in the Middle East*, 457.

89 Strauss, "Who Read What in the Ottoman Empire," 457.

90 Strauss, "Who Read What in the Ottoman Empire," 457–58.

The Turkish Muslim readership profited enormously from printing presses on the periphery of the empire, as in the case of Egypt. Developments for each community varied; for example, the Jewish community was served predominantly by Salonika printers. Greek books, including books for the Turkish-speaking Orthodox, were printed prior to the Greek revolution in various European centers such as Vienna, Venice and Trieste, whereas Greek printing in the Ottoman capital was barely significant prior to the Tanzimat. After the Greek revolution and the creation of the Greek state, the traditional providers in Western Europe were replaced by printers and publishers in the Greek kingdom, who now produced a large share of the Greek materials consumed by the Greek Orthodox in the Ottoman Empire. The Bulgarians advanced quickly after the Tanzimat and maintained printing presses in Istanbul, Buda and Belgrade, as well as Bucharest and Braila. The Armenian Mekhitarist order was instrumental in the translation of European works, and its Venetian and Viennese branches acted as training grounds for young intellectuals, who in their turn influenced the intellectual and political development of the Ottoman Armenians.[91] Overall, the Armenians had outstanding printers in Istanbul and served diverse communities such as Greeks and Bulgarians as well as Ottoman Turks.[92] Armenian printers contributed significantly to the development of typography in Arabic letters;[93] in fact, it was an Armenian Ottoman typographer, Ohannes Mühendisyan, who finally succeeded in cutting the perfect Arabic typeface in 1866.

Translations played an enormous role in supporting the rise of modern literature, especially for Turkish and Arabic. This movement took off much earlier in the case of the non-Muslim groups.[94] The paths of transmission and dissemination were complex and intertwined, permitting multiple, often unpredictable and hybrid channels of transfer. The anecdotes of Nasreddin Hoca, a work that was also very popular among non-Muslims, represents a good example here. They were initially translated from Turkish into French and from French into the other languages of the empire, such as Greek.[95]

The cosmopolitan character of printing in the Ottoman capital is testified by the extraordinary diversity of languages and alphabets used. Even for Turkish works, at least four different alphabets were applied: Arabic, Greek, Armenian and Cyrillic. The same diversity characterized the professional printers, which included European

91 Strauss, "Who Read What in the Ottoman Empire," 460.

92 Strauss, "Who Read What in the Ottoman Empire," 461.

93 Strauss, "Les livres et l'imprimerie à Istanbul," 18.

94 Strauss, "Who Read What in the Ottoman Empire," 464.

95 Strauss, "Who Read What in the Ottoman Empire," 475–76.

immigrants as well as members of the various minorities, but also Turkish Muslims.[96] A limited number of presses were available at the beginning of the nineteenth century and they tended to serve specific purposes related to the needs of the state and/or the production of textbooks. Private printers were predominantly European migrants.

French books dominated the sector of imported books in Western languages, a phenomenon that was closely related to the reading classes' predilection for French novels, though book imports were, on the whole, under strict political control. In the second half of the nineteenth century, the expansion of education strongly stimulated the publishing business. The first modern bookstores appeared, slowly replacing the traditional trade of colporteurs and mixed merchandise stores, whereas on the contrary, libraries played a rather insignificant role in the expansion of the book market. In 1908 there were approximately 40 libraries in Istanbul, a good part of their inventory still consisting of manuscripts.[97] The consuming public was limited and Turkish books were considered expensive. As had been the case in the early story of printing elsewhere, the publishing sector was characterized by a low division of labor, where printers were usually also publishers. Authors and publishers tried to counter piracy by placing a stamp in the sale copies, a strategy that was apparently not very effective, judging from the number of available unstamped copies. Authorities intervened frequently in order to bar illicit reprinting but were evidently not particularly successful.[98]

Censorship[99] varied according to the dispositions of the respective rulers and was reinforced at the end of the century under the reign of Abdülhamid II. The import of books and the press were closely monitored, as were local printers and even foundrymen responsible for the production of typographic characters. Censorship was, however, far from systematic and paradoxically even had a positive effect on the quality of the publications, prodding typographers to work particularly meticulously.[100]

96 Strauss, "Les livres et l'imprimerie à Istanbul," 7.

97 Strauss, "Les livres et l'imprimerie à Istanbul," 10.

98 Strauss, "Les livres et l'imprimerie à Istanbul," 21.

99 On censorship in the last years of the Ottoman Empire see İpek K. Yosmaoğlu, "Chasing the Printed Word: Press Censorship in the Ottoman Empire 1876–1913," *The Turkish Studies Association Journal* 27, nos. 1–2 (2003): 15–49.

100 Strauss, "Les livres et l'imprimerie à Istanbul," 22–23.

The 1910 Copyright Law

Religious law and a secular legal system coexisted in the Ottoman Empire. A rudimentary notion of copyright was apparently acknowledged by Islamic law, but it designated neither a form of alienable property nor a personal right. It was regarded rather as a moral good, different from physical goods, the main purpose of which was to incentivize science and the arts and secure rightsholders a right to remuneration from the reproduction and sale of their works.[101] It was therefore only after the extensive modernization of the Tanzimat reforms that the purchasability of copyright was acknowledged as it gradually aligned with European models.[102] Copyright was not included in the *Mejelle* (1869–1876), the new code legislation on civil matters, either. The first provisions regarding authors' rights date from 1850 ("Council of Science Act") and were included in the statute of the organization "Encümen-i Daniş," a scientific society with a broad cultural and scientific enlightenment programme. Modelled on the Académie française, the council's purpose was to prepare textbooks in translation or compilation and help develop the Turkish language. The Act confirmed the authors' right to publish and receive revenue from the sale of their works. Protection guaranteed a pecuniary reward and moral recognition for the author's contribution to science and the arts. The fact that some authors were also awarded medals or were immortalized on a special commemorative plate is to be understood against this backdrop. As maintained by Hasan Kadir Yilmaztekin, copyright in this first codification was conceived as a "quasi-moral right of attribution," a form of honor bestowed upon the author rather than an enforceable right.[103]

Regulations included in the "Act on Publication of a Book" (also known as the "Literary Creation Act") in 1857 further liberalized the right to publish books and provided authors with a lifelong monopoly (privilege) on their publications.[104] It was stipulated that the Ministry of Education had to be notified about publishing contracts. The state also reserved for itself the right to publish books on condition that authors were sufficiently remunerated. It was considered a criminal offence to publish more copies of a book than contractually agreed; reprinting was therefore conceived within the confines and the context of the contract. Illicit reproductions

[101] Hasan Kadir Yilmaztekin, "The Legislative Evolution of Copyright in the Late Ottoman Empire," *Journal of Intellectual Law and Practice* 17, no. 1 (2022): 47.

[102] Nadine Güher Erer, "A Short History of Copyright in the West, in the Ottoman Empire and in Turkey," *Türk Kütüphaneciliği* 28, no. 4 (2014): 642.

[103] Yilmaztekin, "The Legislative Evolution of Copyright," 49.

[104] A lifelong monopoly was likewise guaranteed by article 3 of the "Printing Houses Act" of 1857, whereby the right was untransferable and particular to the approved publishing houses only.

were similarly treated as a form of forgery under article 241 of the Criminal Code of 1858. The Act was amended twice. In 1872, changes targeted the term of protection, which was reduced from the author's lifetime to 40 years, and also specified that copyright could be obtained by succession. Modifications introduced in 1876 regulated copyright conditions post mortem.[105]

The concept of copyright was explicitly mentioned in the "Literary Creation and Translation Act" of 1870, which was adopted in order to complement the previous 1857 Act. It provided supplementary rules concerning rewards for authoring and translating textbooks and established that works were remunerated according to their size. The Act determined rules for the selection and accreditation of textbooks and explicitly recognized the right of attribution; whereas rights for commissioned textbooks were transferred to the Ministry of Education, authors retained the right of attribution, that is, the right to be named as the textbooks' authors.[106]

In the late nineteenth century, privileges were extended to protect performances. Agop Vertovyan was granted a 10-year privilege to stage theatrical plays in Istanbul, while in 1876 Dikran Çuhaciyan was given a 10-year privilege for the staging of operas in the same city.

The first Ottoman copyright law was issued in 1910 and was modelled after the continental laws of the mid-nineteenth century. Apparently, the 1910 law was an updated codification of the previous acts of 1850 and 1857. As maintained by Michael Birnhack for the case of Palestine, we lack evidence to show that the law actually enjoyed practical application in the Ottoman period,[107] a fact that can only be ascertained through further research. A closer look at the Ottoman law is nevertheless illuminating for a quite different reason.

How precarious the conceptualization of copyright could be in cultures unaccustomed to the notion of owning ideas is best evidenced in the case of the 1910 Ottoman copyright law.[108] The law is interesting because it unites within the same law contradictory elements that in some ways clash with one another, demonstrating the ambiguity between a proclaimed pure property right (that is, a natural right) and a right existing only through the guarantee of the state (a statutory right). The law unites within the same framework, on the one hand, the intention, to provide protection for intellectual production, and on the other, the intention to maintain

105 Yilmaztekin, "The Legislative Evolution of Copyright," 49–50.

106 Yilmaztekin, "The Legislative Evolution of Copyright," 50.

107 Michael Birnhack, "Hebrew Authors and English Copyright Law in Mandate Palestine," *Theoretical Inquiries in Law* 12, no. 1 (2011): 206.

108 "Turquie, Loi sur le droit d'auteur du 8 Mai 1910," *Le Droit d'auteur*, year 23, no. 10, October 15, 1910, 148–50.

control over this same production. This ambiguity is already evidenced in article 1 of the law, which jumbled together the theory of intellectual property and the theory of authors' rights.

Whereas in previous acts, copyright had been confined to certain kinds of books and was contingent on the approval of relevant state authorities, the 1910 Act was far more encompassing and extended protection to numerous new categories of works: all types of books, works of art such as paintings, drawings, engravings, sculptures, musical works and notes, translations and adaptations, lectures, sermons, plans and maps, performances as well as news articles, photographs and drawings in daily publications.

The 1910 Act required formalities notice, registration and deposit, which had been common practice in other countries as well, but also required, interestingly enough, the issuance of a relevant certificate, which was equivalent to a property title and was purchased against payment (articles 20–22). The property title was valid until proven otherwise.[109] The source of inspiration as well as the purpose of such a legal provision needs to be researched and contextualized further: the acquisition of a property title against payment strongly resembles the regulation of transactions in tangible goods. Was this a rudimentary attempt to conceptualize copyright legally by transforming intangibles into equivalents of tangibles via property entitlements? Is it a mode of reasoning still indebted to the notion of "work" as a physical object (the manuscript)? Or a notion of copyright akin to "privilege," that is, as an entitlement that can be revoked? Could it possibly reflect a discomfort around how to properly classify copyright and the legal relationships it engenders within a civil law system? Or even represent a cumbersome adjustment of provisions borrowed from patent law? Or could it reflect uncertainty and fluidity surrounding the figure of the author or the question of which other figures (for example publishers, printers, copyists, heirs etc.) could possibly function or pass as rightsholders, and how to go about resolving conflicts in cases where the paternity of a work was claimed by different sides? Had the late Ottoman Empire experienced a rise in such conflicts and claims? Only research into the sociocultural context, the legal mindset and the concrete problems arising from the application of copyright can adequately illuminate

109 The certificate "sera délivré par le service de comptabilité de l'Instruction publique, contre paiement d'un quatre de livre turque, *un certificat de droit d'auteur* équivalant *au titre de propriété* et qui fera foi jusqu'à preuve contraire." ["upon payment of one Turkish Lira, the accounting department of Public Education *will issue a copyright certificate, equivalent to an ownership title* and which will be considered valid/authentic until proven otherwise"] "Turquie, Loi sur le droit d'auteur du 8 Mai 1910," 149, emphasis added.

the motivations behind such provisions.[110] Committed at the same time to control print, the law fixed the chain of responsibility that established the actual rightsholder, not motivated by a notion of authorship, but rather with the intention to ascertain accountability, that is, to determine who is ultimately liable and for what.

Moreover, authors, translators or rights agents and their heirs could cede their copyrights to third persons through contract, subject to payment or free of charge. The act of alienation (i.e. the private contract) had to be registered with the Ministry of Public Education in Istanbul and/or the Directorate of Public Education in the provinces. The transmission of rights was taxed half a Turkish Lira, and in cases where this formality was ignored or forgotten, the offender was fined a penalty equivalent to three times the original tax.

Next to these regulations, which clearly treated authors' rights in an almost equivalent manner to property law, articles were included which encompassed aspects of personality rights. Such was the case with article 28, upholding the right of integrity of a work and prohibiting arbitrary changes to a work by a publisher without the author's authorization, and article 34, which enabled the author to control the number of copies published. In the eventuality that a higher number of copies were published than initially agreed, the additional number of copies, or the sum equivalent to the value of sold copies, had to be returned to the "owner."

Also championed was the right of paternity against plagiarism. This right (art. 30), however, received a very soft contouring. It was not defined as an absolute right but was rather dependent on the degree of *propriety* (i.e. decency) in the act of appropriation. What was chastised was not the act of appropriating but the mode of appropriation. It was considered plagiarism to appropriate a text or segments of a musical composition and publish them under one's own name by modifying or arranging them in such a manner that allowed the public (reader, listener) to guess the original underlying work from beginning to end. Articles and drawings published in daily newspapers and periodicals were protected only when "rights reserved" or "all rights of publication and translation reserved" was mentioned. In all other instances, reprinting was free, including news and pieces of information, provided that the initial source was mentioned.

The duration of protection for texts and music lasted 30 years p.m.a.; other genres such as engravings, drawings, maps and so on were protected for 18 years

[110] Kadir Yilmaztekin has a different opinion and identifies nothing opaque or uncertain in these provisions. He maintains that the registration "was not constitutive of copyright. It was only a prerequisite to sue. Subject to the formalities, the copyright commenced upon the publication of the work." See Kadir Yilmaztekin, "The Legislative Evolution of Copyright," 51.

p.m.a. Most importantly, and in a similar vein to that already encountered in the other Eastern empires under study, foreign authors were not protected, while the right of translation was reserved only for works published in the Ottoman Empire. The right of translation (art. 14) lasted for 15 years after the death of the translator, that is, half the duration of the general term of protection.

The Ministry of Education maintained the prerogative to publish works considered beneficial to the public, even if they had not yet been printed or their publication was impaired by factors such as lack of resources or disagreements among heirs. Orphan works by deceased authors who left no heirs could be reprinted, published and translated by anyone who applied to the Ministry of Education for a respective licence. Licences lasted between 10 and 15 years if printing began within a year of the moment of authorization.

Appraising the development of copyright regulation in the Ottoman Empire in the late nineteenth and early twentieth centuries, it is possible to agree with the generic conclusions drawn by Hasan Kadir Yilmaztekin only to a certain extent. Indeed, it appears accurate that most changes introduced during this period were undertaken in the name of authors, and that legislation evolved from privilege and early statutory protection reflecting reward theories towards a set of substantive and rights-based rules as reflected in the 1919 Copyright Act. However, it is hard to agree with him that in the end it was "the centrality of the modern proprietary author" that was the *raison d'être* of the Ottoman copyright regime.[111] Rather, as also observed (but understated) by Kadir Yilmaztekin, IP predominantly served the purpose of advancing public intellectual life and securing the spread of Enlightenment and education. The author was appreciated as a substantial guarantor of this process but was subordinated to this much loftier task. Thus the multiple instances in the law where the state reserved for itself the right to trespass private property and have the last say concerning the validity and legality of copyright transactions. This observation is equally confirmed by the contouring of the author's moral rights. They are not conceived as an absolute and inalienable right emanating from the particular and very personal bond between the author and his work, but rather delineated within the context of the contract, of propriety and of setting up default lines and rules of conduct.

[111] Yilmaztekin, "The Legislative Evolution of Copyright," 52.

Chapter 4

The Expansion of Copyright in Eastern Europe: Preconditions of Development and European Comparisons

Similar to other parts (perhaps even the greatest part) of the world in the nineteenth century, the belated, slow and uneven infiltration of copyright into East and Southeast Europe rested on a combination of socioeconomic, historical and cultural factors: (1) The preconditions for copyright's inception and/or expansion, such as a proper commercialization of cultural production, were weak or missing. (2) The advancement of the field of culture dictated, or rested upon, other priorities. (3) Actors negotiated their antagonistic relationships in the field of cultural production via other mechanisms of social control and customary practices of regulation. (4) Copyright as a monopoly instrument was not conducive to serving the governance rationale of demographically complex state formations such as the multilingual empires of East and Southeast Europe. (5) The actors who usually play the role of protagonist in the expansion of copyright (lawyers, authors, lobbyists, publishers) were either missing, insufficiently organized or inadequately motivated to enforce such an institution. Multifarious factors therefore affected the degree of readiness to conceptualize and apply copyright. This chapter discusses in a general and comparative manner some of those general preconditions for the region of East and Southeast Europe through thematic clusters covering broadly the period from the second half of the nineteenth century to the First World War.

Legacies of Empire

The perseverance of multiethnic and multilingual structures was undeniably the trait that marked the region of East and Southeast Europe in the nineteenth and early twentieth centuries, in contrast to the model of the more or less solidified monolingual nation state that ultimately came to prevail earlier in the western part of the continent. Beyond creating a different context for the governance of culture and the dynamics of communication, the multinational character of the Eastern empires formed a system that was susceptible to different equilibria. Even after the demise of empire, this remained a long-lasting legacy of the region.

Geography, the social and administrative structure, the form of governance, the plurilingual and multiconfessional makeup of the Eastern empires, the dynamics between centers, regions and peripheries, the parallel—partially contradictory, partially complementary—processes of nation- and empire-building, all left their imprint on the way in which educated subjects and ethnic communities were formed. Imperial administrations devised different strategies and balancing acts between sustaining, integrating, absorbing (suppressing), engineering and performing proximity and difference. The partly deterritorialized character of ethnic communities encouraged, for example, the creation of networked societies, where the dissemination of knowledge and information—sometimes also due to the lack of established, longstanding cultural institutions, as for example in the case of the Ottoman Empire—relied heavily upon circulation and informal networks. Forms of imperial organization and governance affected the creation of identities, where qualities and properties such as ethnic origin, mother tongue, choice of alphabet, languages of instruction, communication and administration, social class, professional status and religion did not necessarily overlap, nor were they congruent with an invariable nature or taxonomy of ethnicity. The choice of language could be dictated by issues as diverse as ethnic origin, but also by class, status, profession, situational context or aspiring social mobility.

Conversely, there were certain social properties inscribed in specific languages. Both German and Greek, for example, functioned as vehicles of ascendance to the middle classes in the Habsburg and the Ottoman contexts respectively. In the early nineteenth century, educated elites were plurilingual and cosmopolitan. They not only read but often wrote in several languages, usually the established and reputable literary languages, and quite often not their own "mother tongue."[1] In the course

---

1 On plurilingualism, the social status of various languages and subsequent changes thereof, as well as the significance of language choice as personal strategy in the context of eighteenth-century Bohemia, see Claire Madl, "Pour une étude des choix de langue en milieu plurilingue: representations et practiques en Bohême á l'époque des Lumières," *Revue Historique* 667, no. 3 (2013): 637–659; on similar experiences in the Balkan context, see Evgenia Davidova, *Balkan Transitions to Modernity and Nation-States, through the Eyes of Three Generations of Merchants (1780s–1890s)* (Leiden/Boston: Brill, 2013), 157–58 and more generally chapter 6, "Tropes of Nationalisms: Visible Markets, Invisible Ideologies." Davidova confirms the observation already advanced by several scholars before her that merchants in their interchanges used a "Balkan-Ottoman commercial *koine*," which was based on Greek but was heavily peppered with Turkish, Arab, Persian and Slav words.

of the nineteenth century, as a result of the struggles for ethnic self-determination, language and culture acquired *ipso facto* a political tinge and even functioned "as a surrogate form of politics."[2] Language became a major mark of distinction and the majority of rising nationalisms in East and Southeast Europe were indeed linguistic nationalisms.[3] It was not just identities, languages and alphabets that were in flux, but also blueprints for national projects. National renewal movements often oscillated between different options, broader and narrower conceptions; these were predicated upon political orientation (liberal, conservative, democratic, radical) but also on imaginaries of exclusive and/or inclusive community (pan-Slavism, Trialism in the Habsburg Empire, Helleno-Ottomanism, Yugoslavism, Czechoslovakism etc.).

Publishing

The ethnic, social and linguistic complexity of East and Southeast Europe therefore created a different starting point for book publishing than was the case in the more or less consolidated, and progressively monolingual nation states in Western Europe. Early publishers and printers—the pioneers of printing—were often immigrants, itinerant or cosmopolitan craftsmen, usually belonging to another ethnic group than the one to which they would eventually introduce the art and skills of printing. A Hungarian who had converted to Islam, Italian printers, various religious orders and religious minorities were among the first active printers/publishers in the Ottoman Empire. German printers played a largely pioneering role in different regions of East Central and Southeast Europe including Serbia, Croatia, Hungary, Bohemia and Russia. Czech printers were among the pioneers of printing in Bulgaria.

Before the creation of nation states, the centers of printing were often located outside what were considered to be the core or historical lands of the ethnic group. Publishing and printing activity rather followed the routes of revolutionaries, the commercial activities of diasporic communities, and the formation of cultural and educational centers necessary for their needs before book production was eventually settled geographically within the territory of the nation state.

2 This argument is advanced by Thomas Ort for the Habsburg Empire but could also be extended to the Ottoman and Russian Empires. Thomas Ort, *Art and Life in Modernist Prague: Karel Čapek and his Generation, 1911–1938* (New York: Palgrave, 2013), 40–41.

3 See discussion by Benedict Anderson in "Western Nationalism and Eastern Nationalism: Is There a Difference That Matters?" *New Left Review* 9 (May–June 2001), https://newleftreview.org/issues/II9/articles/benedict-anderson-western-nationalism-and-eastern-nationalism.

Established continental centers of printing such as Paris, Vienna, Pest, Leipzig and so on functioned as "transterritorial" publishing hubs for many intellectuals from East Central and Southeast Europe, whose printed works were subsequently put into circulation eastbound by West European publishers. The book trade networks ran from West Europe eastwards. West, and particularly Central (German) European booksellers constituted the nodes of distribution that structured the networks of circulation. In the course of the nineteenth century, regional centers also began to play an increasingly important role. Bulgarian publishing developed in Istanbul, Izmir, Bucharest, Belgrade and Novi Sad; Greek publishing in Vienna, southern Italy, Leipzig and Paris. Often printers/publishers of ascending ethnic groups needed to emancipate themselves from professionals of different and more dominant (culturally, politically) ethnic groups, before conditions were ripe (i.e. reading publics and rudimentary funding sufficiently secured) for the creation of an elementary market in a new vernacular. Such was the case for both Czech and Croatian publishing, which were initially strongly influenced by, and dependent upon, the German and respectively the Austrian book trade. Such dependency often had a Janus effect upon publishing, playing both a hegemonic and an emancipatory role.

The fact that linguistic codifications took place later in East and Southeast Europe, and many of the nations-to-be had to emancipate their languages, writings and elites from the influence of more developed literary and print cultures, almost *a priori* relativized the purely commercial dimension of publishing and knowledge, investing it—not just rhetorically—with the character of a public good. Put differently, not only were the social preconditions for an elitist, restricted or tiered educational revival missing (as was the case, for example, in nineteenth-century Italy),[4] but nationalizing elites disfavored exclusive, restricted access to knowledge because the "open access" knowledge model was the best guarantee for the attainment of their goal: collective advancement towards "progress," comprehensive and extensive nation-building.[5] In cases such as Poland, the above-described conditions were additionally buttressed by the experience of partition and censorship as well as the petty protection offered by the three different copyright laws applied in the occupied territories, all circumstances that helped to sustain social norms contrary to a proprietary vision of copyright.[6]

4 See Evelina Scaglia, "The 'Invincible Dualism' of the Italian School System: History of a 'Controversial' Relationship from the Casati Law Debate to Gaetano Salvemini's Interventions in the Early 20th Century," *Formazione, lavoro, persona* 38, no. XII (2022): 9–26.

5 Arguing in the same direction, Krassimira Daskalova, *Gramotnost, Knižina, Čitateli, Četene v Bălgarija na prehoda kăm modernoto vreme* (Sofia: Lik, 1999), 38 ff.

6 Katarzyna Gracz, "Opposing the Expansion of Copyright Law: Social Norms in the Quest against

For these reasons, alongside private initiative, publishing in this part of Europe long remained connected with civil society and learned societies' publishing activities, often in reaction to commercial publishing that sometimes promoted trivial literature[7] or literary cultures other than the national one. Such was the case with the *Matica* foundations[8] that proliferated in the philological development of most Slavic revivals and were ardent publishers of materials in their respective vernacular languages. Established by civil society through private donations, they published all kinds of belletristic, philological and scientific studies, promoted language reform, awarded study scholarships, helped to found libraries and erect monuments, and encouraged pan-Slavic connections.[9] Their cultural and scientific work was often supplemented by the activities of their respective academies of science. In nineteenth-century Croatia and Slavonia, for example, the publishing activity of *Matica ilirksa*, the Yugoslav Academy of Sciences and Arts (*Jugoslovenska akademija znanosti i umjetnosti*), the *Društvo Sv. Jeronima* and others was as energetic as that of private publishers and surpassed the latter's influence in promoting the codification of Croatian literature.[10] This significant contribution of civil society to vernacular publishing continued uninterrupted alongside the strengthening of professional publishers also after the creation of nation states.

With the formation of nation states an additional, significant actor became involved in the publishing business. Due to the specific historical context, the state developed enhanced aptitudes that went beyond its customary areas of competence such as the promotion of mass education and material support for educational

ACTA and the 'Commodification of Knowledge and Culture Project'," in *Expanding Intellectual Property: Copyrights and Patents in Twentieth-Century Europe and Beyond*, eds. Hannes Siegrist and Augusta Dimou (Budapest: CEU Press, 2017), 292–93.

7 Ljubinka Trgovčević, for example, mentions reaction to purely commercial publishing as one of the principal reasons behind the creation of the *Srpska književna zadruga* (Serbian Literary Cooperative) in 1892. Its purpose was to enable associated members, despite the existence of other publishing structures, to publish works as an independent organization. Additional reasons were the desire to make the best of foreign classics known to Serbian audiences and thus help to accelerate local literary, cultural and scientific development, as well as the necessity to republish valuable older works by Serbian authors that were out of print or simply not known to a younger audience. Both these motivations aimed at establishing high literary and aesthetical criteria for readers. Ljubinka Trgovčević, *Istorija srpske književne zadruge* (Belgrade: Srpska književna zadruga, 1992), 10.

8 The most significant of these were Matica srpska (1826), Matice česká (founded as the Bohemian Museum in 1818), Matica hrvatska (established as Matica ilirska in 1842), Matica slovenská (1863) and Slovenska Matica (1864).

9 Marcel Cornis-Pope and John Neubauer, eds., *History of the Literary Cultures of East Central Europe: Junctures and Disjunctures in the 19th and 20th Centuries*, vol. III: The Making and Remaking of Literary Institutions (Amsterdam/Philadelphia: John Benjamins Publishing Company, 2007), 41.

10 Aleksandar Stipčecić, *Socijalna povijest knjige u Hrvata: od početka Hrvatskog narodnog preporoda (1835.) do danas*, vol. III (Zagreb: Školska knjiga, 2008), 37.

infrastructure and its institutions. The state assumed, in several cases, the role of guarantor and supervisor of high culture, a function it adopted, on the one hand, in light of the initial absence of longstanding institutions of cultural and literary criticism[11] that could deliver professional benchmarks, and, on the other, in contrast to forms of popular and commercial entertainment. In the 1890s, in order to counter the expansion of pulp fiction in translation, the Bulgarian Ministry of Education undertook efforts to devise a canon of world classics. The Ministry's educational council tried purposefully to stimulate the publication of the most renowned foreign works, relying on lists of books used for the teaching of literature in middle schools and gymnasia.[12] In order to bolster the initiative, the Ministry also organized anonymous competitions for translators, reserved special funds for the commissioned translations, selected and awarded the best among them and subsidized their publication, while their distribution in schools—to the delight and profit of the commissioned publishers—was guaranteed. In a similar vein, the first canon of Bulgarian and world literature was assembled by the Ministry of Defence in the first decades of the twentieth century in the context of the Balkan Wars and World War I. In order to provide soldiers at the front with motivational readings for their leisure time, the Ministry devised a pocket book series of world literature that included for the first time two Bulgarian novels.

Reading Revolutions

The concept of a "reading revolution" is a compound phenomenon of the late eighteenth century.[13] Though it denotes a process most appropriately qualified as an evolution rather than a revolution, it is on account of the momentous and multifarious

11 For an interesting and thought-provoking poststructuralist approach regarding the notion of "absence" in the constitution and canonization of the self, the nation and its literary canon, see Alexander Kiossev, "Lists of the Missing," in *National Heritage – National Canon*, ed. Mihály Szegedy-Maszák (Collegium Budapest Workshop Series No. 11) (Budapest: Collegium Budapest, 2001), 23–36. Kiossev's deconstructivist approach does not necessarily contradict my argument. I recapitulate the actors' own standpoints by answering frontally the question of why they act the way they do. He deconstructs and puts into context the views of the actors, answering rather the question of what the mental frames and predispositions are that make them perceive things in a specific manner, namely as an "absence."

12 Great importance was given to classical literature; the list is indicative: Demosthenes, Aeschylus, Xenophon, Plutarch, Tacitus, Horacio, Montaigne, Moliere, Corneille, Calderon, Lessing, Goethe, four Shakespearean tragedies, Shelling, Burns, Thomas Moore, and from Slavic literatures Pushkin and Mickiewicz. Ani Gergova, *Knižinata i Bălgarite* (Sofia: Izdatelstvo na BAN, 1991), 175.

13 Reinhard Wittmann, "Was There a Reading Revolution at the End of the Eighteenth Century?" in *A History of Reading in the West*, eds. Guglielmo Cavallo and Roger Chartier (Amherst, MA: University of Massachusetts Press, 1999), 284–312.

effects and changes that it brought about that it deserves the attribute of a "revolution." By adopting variably a top-down and/or a bottom-up perspective, this section discusses European trajectories by examining the correlation between education and publishing, and by taking into account such diverse standpoints as democratization, quantitative and qualitative dimensions, market-driven as well as informal changes, state reforms and revolutions.

It can be broadly argued that whereas in Western Europe the democratization of reading resulted from consecutive waves of political democratization and nationalization in conjunction with the publishing industry's market expansion, in Eastern and Southeastern Europe it was more the conscious result of social, political and cultural engineering. The development of education in Western Europe was basically an urban phenomenon, whereas in East and Southeast Europe the spread of education was predominantly a national project, and only secondarily an urban one. In Western Europe, the expansion of reading and the creation of mass society went hand in hand. Furthermore, as Georg Jäger has attested for the case of Germany, the restructuring of book production brought about a secularization process whereby communication via printed media took over the function of the religious verification of meaning and sense of orientation in the world, and in so doing partially replaced the functions of oral transmission.[14] The paragon in this case is France, whose Revolution embodied a lower-case revolution away from oral habits towards written rationality and the law,[15] enabling more and more people to participate in the world of enculturation through reading. Printed matter became a central pillar of the politicization of the masses, representing a potential opening of the market that subsequently formed the basis for a second reading revolution, that of industrial printing.[16] Judging from the cases of Britain, France and Germany, the first reading revolution, which lasted from the late eighteenth century to approximately 1870, was a corollary of the spread of the Enlightenment, the ascendance of the middle classes and the intervention of the state. By initiating the early mass identification of the reading public, it broke the path for the second revolution, that of industrial printing, between 1870 and 1914. Industrial printing and proper entrepreneurial publishing set in later in Southeast and East Central Europe, taking off properly only after World War I. Analysis of the publishing catalogues of Belgrade's most important and prosperous pre-World War II publisher, Geca Kon, confirms the above

14 Georg Jäger et al., eds., *Geschichte des deutschen Buchhandels im 19. und 20. Jahrhundert.* Vol. 1.: *Das Kaiserreich 1870–1918* (Frankfurt am Main: Buchhändler-Vereinigung GmbH, 2001), 17–18.

15 Frédéric Barbier and Catherine Bertho Lavenir, *Histoire des médias: De Diderot à Internet* (Paris: Armand Colin, 1996), 66.

16 Barbier and Lavenir, *Histoire des medias,* 74.

picture. Statistics on his publications for the period 1901–1935 provide the following picture: between 1901 and 1904, he distributed only foreign publications. This picture changed reluctantly from 1905, when he brought out his first own title. From 1905 to 1919, with the exception of the years 1916–1918, when publishing came to a complete standstill, he achieved his best yearly record of own publications in the years 1912 and 1919, when he managed to publish 40 and 41 titles respectively. The average yearly output for that initial period was approximately 15–20 titles, during the good years. This rather mediocre picture changed radically from 1920, when the number of his own publications rose to 118, and reached its apogee in 1932, with 240.[17]

In the case of Southeast and Eastern Europe, the advance of the Enlightenment was restricted to a relatively narrow audience. Though it led to an extension of the reading public beyond the traditional cohorts of clerks, priests, civil servants and the commercial classes, its outcomes were essentially more limited in scope. Effects like the creation of a mass reading public or the transition from oral to print culture were only conditionally present in Southeast Europe in the nineteenth century, so the preconditions for the second reading revolution were relatively weak. Rather mixed forms of access to mass culture continued to coexist, with no one form supplanting the other.[18] Thus, in several Southeast European countries, like the first Yugoslavia or Bulgaria, efforts to expand publishing took place in the absence of both mass society and large-scale development of a bourgeoisie, though a middle-class educated nucleus undeniably played a vital role. A somewhat different picture arises in the case of Czechoslovakia, with a stronger middle-class presence, at least in the urban centers. Circumstances in the Balkans appear comparable to those of the European South, where the book expanded its reach slowly, transforming over time into a socially and symbolically prestigious good (the sacralization of the book), rather than becoming outright an object of running consumption. Countries like Spain promoted access to mass culture through various means, including different forms of sociability.[19] Culture remained largely based on oral transmission and orality was

17 Geca Kon (1873–1941) was the son of a Jewish family from southern Hungary (Csongrád). He worked initially in Novi Sad as an apprentice to the German bookseller and antiquarian Friedrich Breslauer, before eventually moving to Belgrade, where he set up his own business. He and his family vanished tragically in the Holocaust. See *Katalog izdanja 1901–1935 izdavačkog i knjižarskog preduzeća Geca Kon a.d.* (Belgrade: Geca Kon, 1935), xvii.

18 For a discussion on the passage from intensive to extensive reading in the case of Bulgaria, see Daskalova, *Gramotnost, Knižina, Čitateli, Četene,* 155–59.

19 Jean-François Botrel, "Entre imprimé et oralité: L'essor de la culture de masse en Espagne (1833–1936)," in *Culture de masse et culture médiatique en Europe et dans les Amériques 1860–1940*, eds. Jean-Yves Mollier, Jean-François Sirinelli and François Vallotton (Paris: Presses universitaires de

a principal vehicle for participation in mass culture.[20] Bulgarian book history confirms the importance of oral transmission as a substantial channel for the diffusion of information and education, well into the late 1850s. Consequently, an interesting cycle came about: oral works (speeches, stories, lectures etc.) were written down, eventually printed, and then disseminated orally again.[21] The persistence of orality as a distinctive and diachronic feature influencing the formation of written culture is attested also in the case of modern Greece[22] and should be considered relevant for the whole of Southeast Europe.

It should be noted further that in any given territory, not all social groups and ethnic populations accomplished the passage from the first reading revolution to the second—that is, the transition from intensive to extensive reading—simultaneously. Different temporalities characterized the entrance into literacy. Whereas, for example, the German-speaking populations of Western Croatia and Slavonia completed this transition in approximately the same time frame as the rest of East Central Europe, the middle and lower urban strata completed it later, that is, only after modern Serbo-Croatian had established itself as the common language in all spheres of life.[23]

In East Central and Southeast Europe, similarly to the West European experience, the racing horse of publishing was the press. However, in Eastern Europe the primary function of printed materials and media (newspapers, journals, magazines, calendars etc.) in the late eighteenth and a good part of the nineteenth century remained non-commercial for a long time. Rather, media circulation was to serve to transmit the newly codified language, help to develop and refine it, while at the same time popularizing new ideas and identities. Often, the character of the initial media was very short lived. More noteworthy is the fact that even with the progressive commercialization of printing from the early twentieth century, the involvement and contribution of the state and civil society to the economy of printing remained

France, 2006), 148.

20 Botrel, "Entre imprimé et oralité," 155. On the differences between orality and literacy, see Walter J. Ong's classical text, *Orality and Literacy: The Technologizing of the Word* (London/New York: Routledge, 2002).

21 Gergova, *Knižinata i Bălgarite*, 58–61.

22 See Dimitris Tziovas, "Residual Orality and Belated Textuality in Greek Literature and Culture," *Journal of Modern Greek Studies* 7, no. 2 (1989): 321–35.

23 Wolfgang Kessler, *Buchproduktion und Lektüre in Zivilkroatien und Slawonien zwischen Aufklärung und "Nationaler Wiedergeburt" (1767–1848)*, Sonderdruck aus dem Archiv für Geschichte des Buchwesens, vol. XVI (Frankfurt am Main.: Buchhändler Vereinigung, 1976), 493–94. See also Daniel Baric, *Langue allemande, identité croate: Au fondement d'un particularisme culturel (Paris: Armand Colin, 2013).*

conspicuously high.[24] An analogous picture can be observed in the case of Russia. From the second half of the nineteenth century, and particularly with the advanced industrialization in the last decade of the nineteenth and early decades of the twentieth century, publishing shifted progressively from institutional towards private publishing. Private publishers and joint-stock companies gained predominance (Glasunov, Sytin, Marks, Suvorin, Rikker etc.). Nevertheless, institutional publishing—that is, the publications of the Academy of Sciences, the Synod and Moscow University Press—also retained a strong position and constituted approximately one-third of the book market. An additional phenomenon was the self-organization of authors, who banded together and founded joint-stock publishing houses in order to avoid exploitation by commercial publishers.[25]

Finally, it is of note that in cases such as the Bulgarian Kingdom, as well as the Kingdom of Serbia and later interwar Yugoslavia, the most professional, up-to-date printing enterprises—that is, the enterprises that were best equipped with modern technology and thus had the capacity for fast, mass printing—were either the royal or the state printing house. They far exceeded other printing enterprises in terms of technical and technological capacities. They were usually set up by royal initiative (and subsidy), and even if privately managed, they owed their market supremacy to their narrow symbiosis with the state and the palace. It was with their involvement and support that the printing houses could procure modern technologies in the first place and, most importantly, secure permanent and continuous printing commissions in the long run.

24 A 1935 report on the Czechoslovak printing and book trade provides the following interesting, and rather surprising picture: in 1932, a total of 8189 books and prints were published, with the state contributing 18% of the total. The aggregate consisted of 6040 Czech, 789 Slovak, 926 German and 195 Hungarian titles, while the rest was divided between books in Slavic, German and Romance languages. The distribution of production was as follows: 33% by Czech, 2% by Slovak, 3% by German publishing houses, while the remaining approximately 60% were published independently of the commercial book trade (i.e. through the public sector, self-publishing etc.). If these numbers are accurate (more quantitative research needs to be done here), they signal that the proportions of private–public publishing almost kept the balance, this moreover being the case in one of the most commercialized East Central European societies in the interwar period. See *Der Buchhandel der Welt. Aufbau, Verkehrswesen, Anschriften des Buchhandels in Europa und USA. In Selbstdarstellungen aus 25 Ländern*, ed. Alfred Druckenmüller (Stuttgart: C.E. Poeschel o.J., [1935]), 216–25, in Murray G. Hall, *Böhmische Verlagsgeschichte*, http://www.boehmischeverlagsgeschichte.at/ueberblicksdarstellungen/buchhandel-tschechoslowakei/.

25 *Znanie* (knowledge), *Mir* (Peace), *Zadruga* (Commune) and *Knigoizdatel'stvo pisatelei* (Writers' Publishing House) belonged to these types of joint-stock publishing houses, all founded around and after 1900. See here Miranda Beaven Remnek, ed., *Books in Russia and the Soviet Union, Past and Present* (Series: Publishing, Bibliography, Libraries, and Archives in Russia and Eastern Europe edited by Wojciech Zalewski, vol. III) (Wiesbaden: Harrassowitz, 1991), 10–57.

The Author

Publishing in East and Southeast Europe,[26] in contrast to Western Europe, developed not in correlation with the industrial revolution, but rather in close association with the unfolding of national movements and by trailing their demands and priorities. In addition, as the transfer and exchange of ideas intensified in the revolutionary context of the late eighteenth and the nineteenth centuries, ideas travelling eastwards were confronted with, and had to overcome, predominantly political obstacles (for example, censorship) rather than commercial ones. As a result, intellectual elites developed a certain predisposition concerning the "value" and the "nature" of intellectual goods. In East and Southeast Europe, as elsewhere, it took longer for the realization to come about that cultural and intellectual goods can also hold an economic value. Such awareness did not set in until the turn of the twentieth century, and more emphatically around the period before and after World War I. A cognizance and validation of intellectual work as "labor," that is, as job performance meriting a corresponding remuneration, likewise developed slowly, not only among consumers of culture but among producing intellectuals as well.

Whether as a result of the impact of the Enlightenment and the movements for national independence, or on account of the specific social structures from which intellectuals emanated, or owing to their own self-ascription and self-perception as constituting an "intelligentsia" which served a higher purpose, all these factors as singular causes or in combination stalled an early autonomization of the category of "writer" as an individualistic creator. At its core, the Eastern "intelligentsia"[27] model was collectivistic, and bestowed onto the author specific roles. The author/enlightener maintained an unmediated connection to his folk; his "mission" consisted less in the realization of his particularistic individuality, and more in the illumination of the masses in the name of the people and the nation, the codification of language aiming at the end goal of nation-building and/or state independence, and finally the

---

[26] An informative overview of the development of publishing and printing in the region in the nineteenth and twentieth centuries, which also incorporates broader issues and aspects related to literary culture such as censorship, theatre and folklore, is offered in the form of a concise, transnational factual synthesis by Marcel Cornis-Pope and John Neubauer, *History of the Literary Cultures of East Central Europe*, 39–142.

[27] There is plenty of literature both on the concept and the history of "intelligentsia." See, for example, *Dzieje inteligencji polskiej do roku 1918*, vol. 1: Maciej Janowski, ed., *Narodziny inteligencji 1750–1831*; vol. 2: Jerzy Jedlicki, ed., *Błędne koło 1832–1864*; vol. 3: Magdalena Micińska, ed., *Inteligencja na rozdrozach 1864–1918* (Instytut Historii PAN, Warsaw: Neriton, 2008). See also Denis Sdvižkov, *Das Zeitalter der Intelligenz: Zur vergleichenden Geschichte der Gebildeten in Europa bis zum ersten Weltkrieg* (Vandenhoeck und Ruprecht: Göttingen, 2006).

eradication of social injustice via democratization and/or revolution. Ultimately, his labors were geared towards aligning his people with the universalist project of "progress," that is, the need to overcome that which was often, also subjectively, perceived to be national "underdevelopment." All these distinct priorities resulted in a kind of "socialization" of the author function, a conception that was also ideationally buttressed by the fact that Enlightenment and Romantic ideas in East and Southeast Europe did not necessarily supersede, but rather intersected and intertwined with one another. The Eastern intelligentsia model was by no means unique. Research on other cases of belated nation-building tends to confirm the pre-eminence of an author paradigm privileging in the first place the construction of the collective over the individual.[28]

Different contexts generate different justification strategies, social roles and functions as well as prototypes and self-images. In Western Europe, the author figure arose out of the dynamic of enveloping capitalism, the reconfiguration of social relations, the dwindling of traditional patronage and the decline of traditional trade regulations. By turning his back on old-style seigneurial cultural protection, the author figure justified his new role by reference to the language and the values of the ascending bourgeoisie, that is, as the industrious, individualistic genius meriting just reward for his labor. This novel meritocratic definition of authorship also generated the author's legitimate ownership claims. The East European author justified his role rather by reference to his contribution to collective wellbeing and the codification of the nation, which entitled him to a privileged function: to be the "high priest" and interpreter (in view also of weak capitalistic development) of the symbolic and political content of the nation.

Though the necessity to defend authors' rights and claims for proper recognition and remuneration of authors' labor had been called for since the early twentieth century, a combination of sociocultural factors contributed to the fact that copyright in East and Southeast Europe did not develop into a central signifier of authorial identity. One such factor, characterizing particularly the period of national revivals, was the content and signification of "originality," and by extension those of "authenticity" and "attribution." In contrast to the construction of authorship in Western Europe,[29] where since the eighteenth century the earlier Renaissance defi-

---

28 See here Michael Birnhack's excellent exposition on the author paradigm of Hebrew authors in Mandate Palestine: *Colonial Copyright* (Oxford: Oxford University Press, 2012), particularly 12–14, 128–34.

29 There are several important works dealing with the constitution of the authorial paradigm in copyright, for example Martha Woodmansee, "The Genius and the Copyright: Economic and Legal Conditions of the Emergence of the 'Author'," *Eighteenth-Century Studies* 17, no. 4 (1984): 425–48;

nition of the author as craftsman had slowly subsided to the benefit of the author as an inspired producer, that is, as a "genius" creating something new and unique, authors in Southeast and East Europe were initially faced with a different set of tasks. Whether preoccupied with unearthing the concealed historical-cultural wealth of previous eras, or registering the authenticity of the pristine ethnic soul as preserved in folk culture and poetry, or codifying the spoken language of the people, the authorship project of the national revivals was fashioned in terms of a recovery (or discovery) rather than an invention. Though at times employing very creative and modern means and methods, the revival authors had a stake in proving and staging the anciennity of their ethnic groups, in presenting themselves rather as mouthpieces and "awakeners" of collective will and in familiarizing local audiences with something "foreign" that was made to look familiar, and thus intelligible to a local audience. They drew legitimacy therefore not by standing out as inspired mavericks, but rather by performing positivism and objectivity (also valued qualities of Historicism), thereby effacing the visibility and the intermediating role of the author. To be sure, the two types of author slowly converged. Realism and Historicism instituted the literary terrain that became the broader meeting ground for authors in Europe in the late nineteenth century. The essence and strength of Realism/Naturalism (Zola, Hauptmann, Ibsen, Tolstoy etc.) lay in the creation of literature with a social function. Whereas their prototypical author converted experiences from society and social reality into literary fiction, the archetypical author of late nineteenth-century neo-Historicism leaned on the model of the early nineteenth-century romantic-historical author in the vein and style of Sir Walter Scott.

To have a future, any incumbent nation must go through the past, through history. Southeast and East Central Europe were no exception. The more anonymous, untraceable and time-indefinite national sources and traces were, the more authentic and pristine their authorship was deemed to be.[30] Whereas the modelling of liberal authorship in Western Europe was largely conditioned by the liberalization of the trades and the exigencies of the market, the same period in Southeastern and Eastern Europe, which corresponded largely to the period of national revivals, saw the emerging notion of subjective authorship coexist with a notion of authorship

Mark Rose, *Authors and Owners*; Peter Jaszi, "Towards a Theory of Copyright: The Metamorphoses of 'Authorship'," *Duke Law Journal* 40, no. 2 (1991): 455–502.

30 In fact, the criterion of anonymous authorship persisted for a long time, for example in interwar expert discussions on Serbian folk music, an important and indispensable criterion for distinguishing "authentic" folk music. See here, for example, Ivana Vesić, "Radio Belgrade in the Process of Creating Symbolic Boundaries: The Example of the Folk Music Program between the Two World Wars (1929–1940)," *Muzikologija* 14 (2013): 31–55.

that had its source in the anonymous and collective ethnic genius. The positive validation of folklore and its early inclusion in the copyright regimes of certain Eastern European countries (e.g. Russia, Bulgaria) should probably be understood in this context.

Similar to other cases of belated nation state building processes, involving the construction and assertion of a new community, "emerging cultural life was saturated with nationality," and typically all cultural fields (fine arts, photography, theatre, film, music, literature and journalism) were deeply infused with national ideology, and were meant to serve the national cause.[31] Though the primary role of the author as treasurer and creator of the nation's genius is fundamental to any conception of copyright, and inversely, securing copyright is supposed to incentivize the author to render even greater intellectual services to the community, the image of the romantic author as "nation-builder" in East and Southeast Europe varied in its intensity from the image of the romantic author as codified in West European copyright law. In the latter construction, authors were not called upon to create a new culture from scratch, and their existence was not predicated upon their capacity to invent the new man/woman, community or state.[32] This last type, argue György Konrád and Iván Szelényi, was accustomed to operating in terms of teleologies, that is, serving a rationality oriented towards ends and values, and towards fulfilling a moral mission.[33]

Bearing in mind these basic contours of the "intelligentsia" model is also helpful when contemplating certain aspects of socialist copyright. For example, communist copyright regimes applied the category of "usefulness" (i.e. how useful a work was for the community) as a criterion for the remuneration of works. Such a utilitarian approach to creation was neither a communist novelty, nor did it reflect only an ideological instrumentalization of creative labor on the part of the communists. Apart from having formed part of the justification for copyright law in general—that is, the author was offered copyright protection as an incentive in order to create useful works that would encourage learning[34]—it also had its precedents in the util-

---

[31] Michael Birnhack makes the same point concerning the creation of the Hebrew community and the state of Israel: *Colonial Copyright*, 124 and 110.

[32] Birnhack, *Colonial Copyright*, 128–29 and 134–37. The same argument is also advanced by Andrew Baruch Wachtel, *Remaining Relevant after Communism: The Role of the Writer in Eastern Europe* (Chicago: University of Chicago Press, 2005), particularly chapter 1, 12–42.

[33] György Konrád and Iván Szelényi, *The Intellectuals on the Road to Class Power* (Brighton: Harvester Press, 1979); also Katherine Verdery, "Konrád and Szelényi's Model of Socialism, Twenty-Five Years Later, Symposium Rereading *The Intellectuals on the Road to Class Power*," *Theory and Society* 34 (2005): 1–36, here 3.

[34] The full title of the British Statute of Anne (1710), regarded to be the first copyright law in the world, was "An Act for the Encouragement of Learning, by Vesting the Copies of Printed Books in

itarian notion of creation (i.e. works that further the nation) as expounded by the national movements of the nineteenth century in East and Southeast Europe. Communist justification for socialist copyright was therefore constructed upon already existing building blocks and signifiers of both West and East European provenance.

Modernity

Concerns regarding "originality" and "copies" were by no means absent from the intellectual agenda of Southeast and East Central European societies in the nineteenth and twentieth centuries. In fact, the institutionalization of "modernity," which was the main desideratum, consisted of an ongoing intellectual engagement with conceptions of "authenticity" and "originality," the scope and limits of emulation, the purpose and adaptation of transfers, the Self and the Other, and included a wide-ranging pallet of reactions from proper enthusiasm to outright rejection. Such discourses, however, did not target individual works or genres (as in IP discourses), but related rather comprehensively to the issue of national culture and its relationship to Europe and civilization in the broadest sense.[35] Before those essential cultural questions were settled in some elementary way, and cultural production became sufficiently confident and commercialized, copyright remained—for obvious reasons—largely irrelevant.

Even more importantly, at variance with the experience of long-established dynastic states such as Britain, France and Spain, but very similar to the experience of other European peripheries like parts of Scandinavia (e.g. Norway, Finland), the development of national consciousness and the institutionalization of literature were "symbiotically interrelated."[36] In East Central and Southeast Europe, vernacular culture and national philology decisively shaped the emerging nations. Men of letters constructed the identity of their people by creating institutions and texts simultaneously.[37]

the Authors or Purchasers of such Copies, during the Times therein Mentioned."

35 See Diana Mishkova and Roumen Daskalov, "'Forms without Substance': Debates on the Transfer of Western Models in the Balkans," in *Entangled Histories of the Balkans*. Vol. 2 *Transfers of Political Ideologies and Institutions* (Leiden: Brill, 2014), 2–98; see also Balázs Trencsényi et al., *History of Modern Political Thought in East Central Europe*. Vol. 1 *Negotiating Modernity in the 'Long Nineteenth Century'* (Oxford: Oxford University Press, 2016).

36 Cornis-Pope and Neubauer, *History of the Literary Cultures of East Central Europe*, XI.

37 As outlined by Neubauer, modes of social and material construction included: founding of journals

The core of the cultural projects that succeeded the national movements consisted in the transfer and institutionalization of modernity, often condensed in the formula of "catching-up modernity." In this phase, likewise, intellectuals defined their priorities through the prism and the exigencies of a periphery. After the institutionalization of nation states, efforts were directed (1) into creating and sustaining local, home-grown expert institutions of knowledge and critical inquiry that could act as self-perpetuating instruments of professionalization (e.g. journals, salons, societies, associations etc.); (2) into structuring the literary field and creating works that were compatible with the (aesthetic, epistemological etc.) requirements of their times, and which would prove beyond doubt the nation's place in the hierarchy of civilizations.[38] In other words, the home literary field was structured in a constant dialogue (and comparison) with the "champions" of the international literary field; (3) into embracing political and aesthetical projects that targeted holistic transformations of society and would/could accelerate the coming of modernity. In all these endeavours, several of which were akin to the ambitions of the state, authors/intellectuals often allied themselves with state projects. Multiple factors helped to craft this alliance, which should not be sought solely in intellectuals' survival strategies or the existence of limited audiences and markets for cultural products, but quite significantly also in the psychological disposition of being small nations with restricted public spheres and native speakers, and in the needs of states for legitimating agents and representative institutions at home and abroad.

Regulation before Copyright

The absence of copyright by no means signified a complete absence of regulation in the production, distribution and use of culture. Before the introduction of copyright legislation, professional relationships between authors and publishers, but also

and newspapers in the vernacular; establishing publishing houses; founding literary and cultural societies; staging plays in the vernacular; building national theatres and opera houses; establishing national academies and national libraries; establishing university chairs for the vernacular language and literature; including the vernacular language and literature in school curricula. Modes of textual construction included: language revival; translations into the vernacular; writing lyric poetry in the vernacular; collecting and publishing oral poetry; editing and republishing older texts; writing new national epics; writing historical fiction; canonizing national poets; writing national literary histories. Cornis-Pope and Neubauer, *History of the Literary Cultures of East Central Europe*, 3 ff.

38 A good example of such holistic critique of the "deficiencies" of one's own literature as an exercise in constructing institutions of critical inquiry is provided in the works of Hrăstjo Krăstev, *Mladi i stari* (Sofia: Zaharii Stojanov, 2003); see therein for example his essay "Bălgarskata kniga," 265–78.

within intellectual communities, were governed by a combination of literary, social and contractual norms that ensured the functioning and regulation of the cultural-commercial sphere in local contexts.

Surveillance of the "original" character of intellectual creations that would require the application or intervention of copyright law was often redundant, for several reasons. Firstly, literary and artistic groups (as well as their publishers) were usually closely knit intellectual communities, where monitoring was practiced habitually via reciprocal exchange. In such an environment, it was very hard to "plagiarize" the work of colleagues without being noticed. There was therefore no need to set up any explicit formal rule; "the governing norm was originality in the strongest sense,"[39] and all energies were focused on the act of cultural nation-building. Unauthorized translations were not viewed as illicit copies, but as vital vehicles of connection to the outside world. Versatile, skillfully crafted translations (particularly of demanding foreign texts such as canonical philosophical texts) that helped native language to develop, advanced new literary forms and genres, and enlarged the conceptual horizons and the expressive capacities of language were admired and respected as originals. Secondly, the "noble dream" of crafting the nation provided authors with a deep sense of the high level of originality that was expected of them. Those expectations were higher than the notion of originality codified in copyright law, which essentially signifies that the author is the origin of the work.[40] Publishers applied both contractual and communal/social norms when it came to regulating their business. In order to avoid collisions, when publishing translations of foreign works for example, they informed their fellow publishers in advance of their intentions, either through public announcements and advertisements in local newspapers or timely publication of their yearly catalogues. This widespread social practice, termed "courtesy of the trade," was meant to regulate destructive competition by a counter-practice of self-restraint, and functioned as a surrogate for copyright law.[41] In Bulgaria, publishers contractually committed domestic authors to refrain from publishing the same work with another publisher until exhaustion of the current edition, or they contractually obligated them to jointly persecute any publisher who

---

39 Birnhack, *Colonial Copyright*, 146.

40 Birnhack, *Colonial Copyright*, 159.

41 There are very interesting and detailed scholarly works on the practice of the "courtesy of the trade," particularly for the USA, where it developed into an elaborate system of self-regulation for the appropriation of foreign texts. See here the works by Robert Spoo, *Without Copyrights: Piracy, Publishing, and the Public Domain* (Oxford: Oxford University Press, 2013), particularly chapter 1, "The American Public Domain and the Courtesy of the Trade in the Nineteenth Century," 15–63; idem, "Courtesy Paratexts: Informal Publishing Norms and the Copyright Vacuum in Nineteenth-Century America," *Stanford Law Review* 69 (March 2017): 637–710.

reprinted the same work without authorization. In other words, publishers invested more in the interpersonal aspects of their relations by attempting to motivate and commit their authors simultaneously, rather than seeking the impersonal application of copyright law.

It is to be assumed that the institutionalization of these diverse informal literary, social and communal practices was possible because of the controlled, restricted and personalized environment of the cultural communities and the literary field. Even in the interwar period, which is generally recognized as the apogee of entrepreneurial publishing in the countries under scrutiny, and even though statistical data confirm the growth of the publishing sector, the numbers of really robust and profitable, sizeable and durable, entrepreneurially solid and reliable publishers did not exceed, by generous estimates, on average, the fingers of one hand. Seen from the perspective of the authors, it was hardly expedient to alienate these few crucial associates. The languages of these national communities were very specific, and this circumstance *ipso facto* did not allow for the expansion of publishing in geographical breadth, but only in sociocultural terms, that is, by progressively addressing different social groups (e.g. children's literature) and fashions (the novel), but these options were also exhausted after a certain point. From the late nineteenth century until approximately the interwar period, publishers of particularistic languages could hope for extra profit from the reading publics of immigrants to the Americas. Czech publishers were able to tap into this market and temporarily profit from it. It was, however, only a question of time until assimilation to the English language would make this option redundant. If the horizontal expansion of book sales as described above was restrained, so too were the possibilities for vertical expansion of the book market. Eastern Europe's low social differentiation and stratification, with its predominantly agrarian character and small urban and urbanized enclaves, posed limits to the entrepreneurial capacities of publishers to expand by addressing different class audiences. Social differentiation, for example, allowed British publishers to devise variable models of print circulation tailored to social class and market segment, a practice known as "trancing down the price."[42] First an elaborate, expensive edition for the upper classes, later the same work as an affordable book for the middle classes, and finally a paperback for the lower classes. The capacity to incorporate and tap into social class in the calculation of profit margins was not available in the same manner to East and Southeast European publishers.[43]

42 William St. Clair, *The Reading Nation in the Romantic Period* (Cambridge: Cambridge University Press, 2004), 82.

43 Bulgarian researchers and experts on book culture and history have frequently hinted at the small

In East and Southeast Europe, as in other world peripheries, the process of conceptualizing works as intangibles followed the reverse of the path taken in Western Europe. In the latter, copyright was applied initially to the tangible object, the "copy," signifying the physical book. This was so because copyright was born in the realm of commerce. The right to the "copy" (the copyright) applied to the concrete physical manuscript. It was only in the nineteenth century, through a philosophical process of increasing abstraction and as a result of a paradigm shift, that "work" came to signify the intangible object, representing the contents of the work and not the physical entity. In East and Southeast Europe, in contrast, the creation of modern literary cultures was intricately linked to the transfer of ideas, that is, the transfer of intangibles. Being appreciative of physical books as carriers of ideas, it took time and effort for intellectuals to start conceptualizing the book as a tangible object of commerce and pecuniary value.[44]

Finally, requesting authorization and/or acquiring rights to works was not an unknown practice, but was discretionary rather than mandatory. It was more established in the realm of theatre and musical theatre, and concerned performances staged by formal institutions such as state, royal and national theatres.

Historical Time and Temporalities of Copyright

When reflecting on the history of East and Southeast Europe from the late eighteenth to the early twentieth centuries through the prism of copyright on the one hand, and from the standpoint of intellectual transfer on the other, one is faced with a baffling paradox. The enormous transnational intellectual and cultural fermentation that evidently took place in that period occurred not because of copyright but rather *in spite of* copyright; in other words, because intellectual property was systematically ignored. This is likely one of the reasons why the transfer process was so dynamic and successful. Intellectual transfers in the late eighteenth and nineteenth centuries involved diverse processes of textual "corruption" and/or transformation, such as

volume, often appearing in the form of an extended brochure, and the modest size of books in the interwar period. See here various works by Todor Borov, Ani Gergova and Rumen Daskalov.

44 See here Augusta Dimou, "'Wir verwandeln uns in eine Kolonie fremdsprachiger Bücher': Das Buch als Kulturproblem im Jugoslawien der Zwischenkriegszeit," in *Kultur und Beruf in Europa*, eds. Isabella Löhr et al. (Europäische Geschichte in Quellen und Essays, vol. 2) (Stuttgart: Franz Steiner Verlag, 2012), 259–69.

hybridization, borrowing, copying, modifying, amalgamating, reworking, copy-pasting, translation, invention and inversion, syncretism, imitation, adaptation, interpretation, resignification, abridgement and/or expansion of texts, using texts as templates and so on—that is, the whole array of creative processes of intermediation between texts, cultures and media. Were one to carry this syllogism to its logical conclusion, it would mean that the dynamism of historical and intellectual processes by necessity transcends and at the same time implodes the logic of copyright, since intercultural exchange and revolutionary processes advance in a far more entangled, convoluted, messy and unpredictable manner than the sanitized environment and the one-to-one cultural correspondence assumed by copyright. More than a simple discrepancy, there is an outright opposition between historical time and the "carving" of time imposed by copyright. This results from the fact that copyright as an instrument is less concerned with the flow and more with the "arrest" of time, which is the quintessence of any monopoly. Copyright's capacity to slow down the movement of works is already well documented.[45] The incongruity between historical time and the time cadence imposed by copyright becomes all the more obvious during times of revolutionary upheaval, as the parameters of time are shuffled beyond predictability and, as a rule, political concerns are prioritized over commercial ones.

45 See here Debora J. Halbert, *The State of Copyright: The Complex Relationship of Cultural Creation in a Globalized World* (London/New York: Routledge, 2014); St. Clair, *The Reading Nation in the Romantic Period.*

Chapter 5

Comparisons: Europe and Beyond

East–West Europe

There are several historical reasons that can be given for the series of variations in the development of IP between Western and Eastern Europe. Copyright in East and West Europe was launched from different starting points. In the pioneering countries such as Britain and France, modern copyright legislation was introduced in consolidated and already commercialized literary print cultures, with the intention to break up well-established guild monopolies in the production of culture.[1] Such had indeed been the case with the print monopoly of the Stationers' Company in Britain and the preponderance of the Paris Book Guild in France or the performance monopoly over French-language repertory in the case of the Comédie-Française. Such long-established professional groups and deep-rooted monopolies in the sphere of culture did not exist in East and Southeast Europe. By contrast, there was almost a chronological overlap in the emergence of the cultural professions. The author and the publisher began their careers concurrently, while in the early stages of print, in an analogous experience to parts of Western Europe, the functions of author-publisher-printer were at times united in one and the same person. Moreover, due to the priority given to nation-building, both authors and publishers perceived themselves as being involved in a common endeavour that was predominantly defined in patriotic terms. The differentiation therefore between political/cultural tasks and commercial objectives was a much slower and more ambiguous process, and it took some time for the actors involved to realign their positionalities.

It is possible to schematically argue that in the case of the East European empires, the development of copyright remained connected to political and cultural surveillance, that is, to censorship, for a longer period. However, such comparisons ought not to be overrated and contrasts between East and West should not be essentialized as purely antithetical. Such dichotomic thinking is rather the result of

1 See here Tyler T. Ochoa and Mark Rose, "The Antimonopoly Origins of the Patent and Copyright Clause," *Journal of Patent and Trademark Office Society* 84 (2002): 909–940.

an idealized image of copyright, sustained by a romantic appraisal of "moral rights" that has contributed to an understanding of modern copyright as the complete antithesis of censorship. It should not be forgotten that censorship had been a vital mechanism of the early modern system of privileges, and though it is accurate to say that the abolition of privileges and the emancipation of the trades went hand in hand with the withdrawal of state and seigneurial surveillance over print, forms and regimes of censorship remained present in Western Europe as well, even after the institutionalization of modern copyright.

Censorship was abolished in France, for example, only after 1870, whereas modern copyright legislation had already been passed in 1793. Moreover, the case of France clearly demonstrates that censorship and modern copyright can easily coexist, which is instructive when it comes to analysing subsequent legal regimes such as that of communist copyright. Historically, authors' rights grew alongside, and as a spin-off of human rights in the context of the French Revolution. But even in that early phase, the notion of authors' rights (or intellectual property) implied both freedom of expression and freedom of profession/trade. Differences between West and East, then, apart from discrepancies in timing, can perhaps be best understood as different modes of management. Eastern empires continued to apply a more traditional management formula in a piecemeal manner, whereby surveillance and censorship were built into the law and practiced through the institution of copyright, often via the official and mandatory registration of publications. In Western Europe in the nineteenth century, a modern formula was devised, whereby the regimes of censorship (politics) and copyright (trade) were handled as separate issues, and where it was possible to intervene politically and suppress certain publications without necessarily affecting the book trade as a whole.

Last but not least, it must be stressed that at no point in its history did the BU espouse a clear and unequivocal stance towards the freedom of speech, nor did it morally sanction intervention with the purpose of defending the right to the freedom of opinion. Quite the contrary, throughout its long history the BU had usually washed its hands of the issue. Article 13 of the original 1886 Berne Convention[2]

2 The text of the Convention can be viewed at https://wipolex.wipo.int/fr/text/278701. See Article 13: "Il est entendu que les dispositions de la présente Convention ne peuvent porter préjudice, en quoi que ce soit, au droit qui appartient au gouvernement de chacun des pays de l'Union de permettre, de surveiller, d'interdire, par des mesures de législation ou de police intérieure, la circulation, la représentation, l'exposition de tout ouvrage ou production à l'égard desquels l'autorité compétente aurait à exercer ce droit." [It is understood that the provisions of the present convention cannot prejudice in any way the right which belongs to the government of each of the countries of the union to allow, to monitor, to prohibit by legislative measures or through domestic police, the circulation,

explicitly left it to the discretion of each government and its interior disciplining institutions to decide on the fate of materials to be permitted, circulated, surveilled or prohibited. Even more significantly and quite paradoxically, moral rights were integrated and legislated as a component of international copyright during the BC Revision Conference in Rome in 1928. The proposal was submitted and the conference organized by delegates of the fascist Italian government that had already by the early 1920s installed censorship as part of its own polity. Nobody seemed to discern here a contradiction between principles, legal codification and actual practice.

In the case of East and Southeast Europe, as is often the case when institutions are transferred and adopted posteriorly, we do not experience the cross-fertilization and reciprocal influencing between industrial and intellectual property, or between different genres of creative activity, as was frequently the case with IP development in Western Europe. Examples of this cross-fertilization abound: the term of protection adopted by the first ever copyright legislation, the Statute of Anne, was borrowed from patent law; there is an often indiscernible connection between utility models and modern design; copyright regulation of printed texts initially had a significant impact on music copyright as well as on graphic and plastic arts, and so on. This kind of interpenetration and reciprocal inspiration between technology, the arts and legal codification is not typical for the development of IP in East Central and Southeast Europe. It is again historical factors that determined this pattern of transfer. In the first place, local experience that would give patents a time advantage in comparison to copyright was missing. The regions under discussion were neither pioneers of industrialization nor of the relevant legal doctrines. Since the introduction of legislation usually preceded corresponding socioeconomic developments, and laws did not necessarily emanate from the reality at home or from below, legal doctrines were imported and adopted as already compartmentalized areas of knowledge, that is, as independent patent and copyright laws. Legal comparison, which remained an important source of inspiration and innovation, was practiced exclusively by reference to foreign, more advanced examples. Likewise, IP-specific categories (the "work," "author," "reproduction" etc.) were usually taken over as ready-made, "prefabricated" components. Finally, it should be stressed that the impetus (and quite often the pressure) to introduce national IP legislation frequently came from outside.[3]

---

the representation, the exhibition of any work or production with respect to which the competent authority can exercise this right.]

3 The US also represents an interesting case in this respect, as copyright and patent law were deliberately held distinct and were treated separately due to different state and government objectives.

Adopting capitalistic "modernity" in the European peripheries amounted to a conscious act of copying. In such a context, the practice of "copying" was not conceived in pejorative terms. Imitation, borrowing and copying were not deemed to be vices, but on the contrary were seen as necessary preconditions for attaining modernity. A good illustration of this contrasting attitude to the topic of "copy/originality" is provided in a text by the publisher Louis Hachette (grandson of the initial founder of the Hachette publishing imperium). In a text from 1917 in the *Revue des deux mondes* entitled "The Future of the French Book," the author discussed the enormous success of the Leipzig publishers, which had become for the French "an obsession, a haunting image," and wondered what the appropriate remedies against the German commercial preponderance in publishing should look like. The text ends with the following observation, which nicely encapsulates the self-image of the French as intrinsically pioneering: "Should we conclude from this that the sole redemption for us French publishers and booksellers is a flat, servile imitation of Leipzig? Not the least. We have to do French work here, that is, create not imitate" [Nous avons à faire œuvre français, donc à créer et non à imiter].[4]

The notion of the "public," an *a priori* central concept in the history and the deliberations of copyright regulation, acquired in the context of the Eastern multiethnic empires a somewhat more palpable significance, and to an extent went further than the traditional but abstract concept of "common good" and the advance of learning. "Public" in the multiethnic context of the Eastern empires signified both the "civic" and "national" community. As accurately observed by Catherine Seville, preoccupation with the "public" and "public access" emerged in all geographic areas of the debate.[5] However, the particular demographic configuration in East Central and Southeast Europe meant that "public well-being" retained this double meaning, resulting in something more tangible (and more challenging) than the abstract notion of "society." The "public" consisted of multiple publics, whose interaction constituted the respective public sphere. Though perhaps a minor observation, this does help to add shade to the picture.

Schematically speaking, it can be argued that the development of IP in Western Europe from the eighteenth century was intricately linked to the ascendance of bourgeois society and the needs of its professional elites, and was largely based on the equation Property=Autonomy=Culture. Though essentially an instrument

4 Louis Hachette, "L'avenir du livre français," *Revue des deux mondes*, May 1917, 158, https://www.revuedesdeuxmondes.fr/article-revue/mai-1917-2/.

5 Catherine Seville, *The Internationalization of Copyright Law: Books, Buccaneers and the Black Flag in the Nineteenth Century* (Cambridge: Cambridge University Press, 2006), 313.

of publishers, copyright was embraced by authors largely for its symbolic value, in order to legitimize and justify the latter's claim to belong to the high-status groups and bourgeois proprietors. This equation, due to the prevalent socioeconomic conditions, was largely reversed in the case of East and Southeast Europe, to become Culture=Autonomy=Property. Though also central in this case, symbolic capital was redeemed differently here. Due more to the circumstances (that is, the desire for recognition) than an outright rejection of capitalism, symbolic capital retained a greater value than economic capital with the intelligentsias of East and Southeast Europe for the greater part of the nineteenth century. To put it simply, if the translation of French, German or British authors into a foreign language was certainly a form of recognition and a welcome addition to authorial income, the translation of Eastern or Southeastern authors in the reverse direction meant nothing less than being accepted into Europe.[6]

Empires

It would be misleading to present the national question as a particular preoccupation intrinsic only to Eastern European empires. The complexity of "empire" in the unfolding process of globalization posed a corresponding challenge to the maritime empires of the nineteenth century such as Britain and France as well. Identity was also at stake in these empires. Distinct for these cases, however, is the fact that identity politics were partially articulated through the debate on copyright, the cases of Canada[7] and the USA[8] being perhaps the most prominent. It is therefore no coincidence that in various instances and to varying degrees, copyright in those empires

6 For a useful discussion of the concept of "autonomy" in the professions, see Hannes Siegrist, "Professionelle Autonomie in der modernen Gesellschaft, Wissenschaft und Kultur," in *Professionen, Eigentum und Staat: Europäische Entwicklungen im Vergleich. 19. und 20. Jahrhundert*, eds. Dietmar Müller and Hannes Siegrist (Moderne europäische Geschichte, 8) (Göttingen: Wallstein, 2014), 15–38.

7 On Canada, see Seville, *The Internationalization of Copyright Law*; also Sara Bannerman, "'We Are All Developing Countries': Canada and International Copyright History: Fault Lines in the Map of International Copyright," in *Copyright Future: Copyright Freedom*, eds. Brian Fitzgerald and Benedict Atkinson (Sydney: Sydney University Press, 2011), 79–96.

8 On the US, see Brian Pelanda, "Declarations of Cultural Independence: The Nationalistic Imperative behind the Passage of Early American Copyright Laws 1783–1787," *Journal of the Copyright Society of the USA* 58 (2011): 431–54; Zorina B. Khan, "An Economic History of Copyright in Europe and the United States," https://eh.net/encyclopedia/an-economic-history-of-copyright-in-europe-and-the-united-states/; Zorina B. Khan, *The Democratization of Invention: Patents and Copyrights in American Economic Development 1790–1920* (New York: Cambridge University Press, 2005).

was associated with movements for independence, either cultural or institutional, or both, as Seville has demonstrated in her work on British colonial copyright.[9] This was not, however, the case in the Eastern continental empires. Here copyright did not become the flagship for the articulation of difference, practically and symbolically fought mainly over language, education and cultural (and/or political) autonomy. Moreover, all three Eastern empires applied "soft" and "porous" copyright regimes, particularly regarding the burning issue of translation, which represented precisely the topic that, for real or symbolic reasons, could ignite identity issues. The difference between these two "types" of empire should be sought in the configuration of language and territory. If we were to judge from the cases of Canada and the USA against the backdrop of the British Empire, then it becomes apparent that copyright became a marker of difference in same-language constellations (i.e. among English speakers), triggered on the one hand by the capacity of colonies or ex-colonies of the same language group to produce cheap reprints either for their home market or for export into the empire, or even for the metropole, thus challenging the commercial monopoly of the metropolitan merchants. The situation was aggravated, on the other hand, by the absolute reluctance of British publishers to grant a share of the publishing business to those new, emerging same-language markets. Moreover, those incipient same-language markets were geographically sufficiently remote, sizeable and developed that they could not be easily controlled by the center, and they therefore enjoyed a certain degree of self-rule. In this same-language imperial context, copyright acquired an identity dimension, propelled through an initial process of commercial strife that subsequently acquired a political and cultural dimension. It is no coincidence that in inverse cases—that is, cases where linguistic pluralism prevailed and where translation acquired increasing political, cultural and commercial importance, as was the case with India[10]—it became necessary to diverge from the standards of the imperial copyright regime (the 1911 British Imperial Act conferred 50 years' protection from the author's death also for translations) and allow for local leeway, quite analogous to the experience of the East European empires. In 1914, as a result of significant resistance from the Indian authorities, the Government of India was allowed to enact a modification that limited copyright on translations to 10 years. Contrary to the Indian government's initial wish, it did not apply to all books but only to those published locally, and prescribed that copyright owners retained the power to control translations into any language for 10 years, unless an authorized translation

9 See Seville, *The Internationalization of Copyright Law.*

10 See Lionel Bently, "Copyright, Translations, and Relations between Britain and India in the Nineteenth and Early Twentieth Centuries," *Chicago-Kent Law Review* 82, no. 3 (2007): 1181–1240.

appeared before that deadline. Though the regulation was below the government's initial benchmark, it was a much more reasonable solution both symbolically and practically for a country with the linguistic and cultural wealth of India, which is "itself [...] a concept that *presupposes* the act of translation."[11]

The confluence of a series of factors (cultural, social, economic and technological) in the nineteenth century prompted the intensification of the cross-border traffic in cultural goods, creating the need for a transnational harmonization of copyright law. Legal regulation of the cross-border flows of protected works involved two dimensions: within the empire, and on an international level, between the empire and foreign countries. The combination of these factors induced the British to "tidy up" the imperial copyright regime by harmonizing legislation within the empire, while also synchronizing it with the international regime of the Berne Union. Most studies converge in their assessment that the installation of the British colonial copyright regime targeted in the first place the protection of UK creators and producers and not that of colonial subjects. Moreover, the British government developed an interest in international copyright to the degree that it could promote and protect British interests in the world and its colonies simultaneously.[12] As maintained by Lionel Bently, "international engagement implicated British-colonial relations in interestingly conflicting ways." On the one hand, internationalization appeared to offer a way out of the legal impasse that came about as a result of the occasionally diverging interests of Britain and some of its colonies. Norms would be more readily accepted if they appeared to represent international consensus rather than British norms. On the other hand, negotiating in the name of the whole empire provided Britain with significant international leverage vis-à-vis the Berne Union countries. These considerations also go some way towards explaining Britain's initial reluctance and indecisiveness over whether or not to accede to the BU.[13]

---

11 Rukmini Bhaya Nair as quoted in Bently, "Copyright, Translations," 1239.

12 See Birnhack, *Colonial Copyright* on Palestine and Bently, "Copyright, Translations" on India. On Australia, Catherine Bond, "'Cabined, Cribbed, Confined, Bound In': Copyright in the Australian Colonies," in *Research Handbook on the History of Copyright Law*, eds. Isabella Alexander and H. Tomas Gomez-Arostegui (Cheltenham: Edward Elgar, 2016), 372–90. On Britain, Catherine Seville, "British Colonial and Imperial Copyright," in Alexander and Gomez-Arostegui, *Research Handbook on the History of Copyright Law*, 268–87. As maintained by Birnhack, the "pattern of diffusion of the legal transplant was from the centre to the periphery, utilizing colonial power to achieve the legislative goals all over the many colonies. Local needs were allowed only in the case of the self-governing dominions or on limited local matters. In all other cases, the local pre-colonial law on copyright, if there was any, was simply ignored. Thus the mix of British interests in the homeland, the interest in protecting its authors offshore, and the rising importance of the international copyright treaties, fueled the colonial legislative engine." Birnhack, *Colonial Copyright*, 78.

13 See Lionel Bently, "The 'Extraordinary Multiplicity' of Intellectual Property Laws in the British Colonies in the Nineteenth Century," *Theoretical Inquiries in Law* 12, no. 1 (2011): 192–93.

When it came to copyright regulation, the British Empire was therefore forced to take into consideration, interact with and fine-tune three layers of legislation: (1) British overarching copyright law like the 1911 Imperial Copyright Act; (2) local copyright legislation, where available, like in the self-governing dominions and crown colonies; and (3) internationally valid copyright legislation as promulgated by the BC. Though primarily serving its own interests, coordinating and balancing all three levels was a strenuous task. Colonies had to be consulted regarding amendments to international copyright law and Britain had to secure their endorsement before ratifying such acts in the name of the whole empire.

The BU, in fact, accommodated the structure of empire. Article 19 of the original 1886 Convention provided that "the countries acceding to the Convention had the right to accede also for their colonies and possessions, either by a general declaration covering all colonies or possessions or by specifically enumerating those that were deemed to be included or excluded. With regard to the original members of the Union at the time of the signature of the Convention in 1886, France, Great Britain and Spain declared that their accession included that of all their colonies and possessions."[14] States incorporated associated territories variably: the German Reich brought its protectorates into the BU in 1909, and when Korea was annexed by the Empire of Japan in 1910, its territories were included as well. At the 1928 Rome Revision Conference, however, article 26 of the Berlin Convention relating to its application to colonies and possessions was amended, in accordance with a proposal by the British administration. According to the old text, contracting countries could accede for their colonies and possessions, whether via a general declaration covering all colonies without further specification or by expressly enumerating the specific territorial entities that were included. By contrast, the 1928 text required that the contracting countries identify with precision the colonies, protectorates and other territories in which the Convention applied.[15]

Having initially declared that it acceded to the BC along with its colonies, France did not specify whether this was the case for subsequent revisions of the BC as well. Apparently, and as became evident only in 1930, for reasons requiring further elucidation, France maintained her colonies in a kind of legal grey zone. This appears all the more puzzling and intriguing in view of the fact that France was the driving force behind the institutionalization of international copyright, and went

---

14 Stephen P. Ladas, *The International Protection of Literary and Artistic Property in Two Volumes* (New York: Macmillan Company, 1938), vol. I, 112.

15 Ladas, *The International Protection,* 113.

to great pains to ensure that some of the most remote corners of the world, by force of persuasion and/or coercion, entered the Berne Union's global regime. Therefore, "France ratified the revised Berlin Convention in 1910 without specifying whether this ratification extended to its colonies. The International Bureau thought for some considerable time that this was without significance, being a case of forgotten formality. This was not the position of the French Government, however, for it acceded specifically for all its colonies and protectorates as of May 26, 1930."[16] The existence of this ambiguous regime is confirmed by the fact that French authorities declared the application of international copyright treaties in colonial regions like French West Africa only in the early 1930s.[17] Moreover, it was only with the 1957 copyright law that France incorporated several clauses of the international treaties into its own legislation. Article 81 of the same law envisioned its application in the overseas territories, including the possibility of a reservation to accommodate particularities in the law's local application. The 1957 law was applied in the colonies in a very particular sociopolitical context, characterized by anticolonial struggles and often violent claims for the emancipation of the colonized peoples.[18]

The history of French colonial copyright still awaits its author, and the precise reasons for the belated ratification of the BC in the case of the French colonies can therefore be formulated only tentatively. The non-inclusion of the French colonies into the BC framework appears to have been a purposeful act. Judging from the complications and challenges facing the British Empire, French reluctance probably reflected the desire to avoid "awakening" expectations and "whetting the appetite" of colonial subjects for more cultural, intellectual and political autonomy. This reticence was related on the one hand to fears regarding the interplay between copyright and identity, and on the other to the desire to avoid intricate tasks such as balancing and coordinating the various levels of the legal regime (metropolitan, local, international), and perhaps the concomitant concern that such a recognition would signify greater concessions to the colonies than was actually desired or intended. Such a compound legal arrangement was not only tiresome but also contained ambiguities, which increased the opportunity for external intervention in the French colonial realm. At the same time, in select cases—that is, regarding regions that had emancipated themselves in one way or another from French tutelage—France practiced the exact opposite policy. It incorporated these regions (Haiti, Tunis, Lebanon etc.) into

16 Ladas, *The International Protection,* 113.

17 See Henri Sène, "Le dépôt légal et la législation sur le droit d'auteur au Sénégal: évolution historique et situation actuelle," *Les cahiers de propriété intellectuelle* 23, no. 1 (2011): 342.

18 Sène, "Le dépôt légal," 346.

the BU in a timely manner as singular members with a twofold effect. On the one hand, it strengthened the pool of unionist members favorable to French positions. On the other, it brought previous "slaves" and colonial subjects into "civilization" and by this means anew into the French orbit, symbolically confirming its global enlightenment and revolutionary role, which became its major export success in the modern world.

Moreover, and most importantly, French mercantilism towards its colonies must be understood in the context of the changing circumstances regarding the book trade. It reflected, in the first place, the desire to keep intact a centralized system of publishing, with Paris as its sole and indisputable production and decision-making center. British (London) publishers had targeted similar objectives but ultimately failed to impose such a monopoly upon the colonial peripheries in the long run; French publishers were more successful in this respect. In the second place, it was related to structural changes in the French international book trade. Having experienced a remarkable expansion in the second half of the nineteenth century, this process was reversed around 1900 as the French overseas book trade contracted significantly, witnessing the loss of the American markets (north and south) that were faced with the avalanche of the anglophone world. Russia, a traditional European market, which in the early nineteenth century traditionally topped the list of importing countries for French books, had dropped by the 1900s to rank eleventh.

Asia, Africa and Oceania remained negligible outlets for the French book trade, until the formation of the French colonies and the concomitant establishment of francophone communities (Algeria, Indochina, Senegal, Madagascar), which then successfully furnished new publics. With few exceptions such as South America and the "reserved markets" created by the colonies, the French book was practically absent from the southern hemisphere and the Asian world in general.[19] The markets for French books could be categorized into three groups: (1) European and American francophone countries; (2) developed, non-francophone countries such as the UK, Germany and so on; and (3) the colonies and French zones of influence in Africa and Asia. While French publishing declined in the majority of the most developed foreign markets in the course of the nineteenth century, at the same time it managed to secure an almost exclusive position in the vast francophone markets of the colonial empire. In 1840, Algeria absorbed 1% of French book exports, but owing

[19] Frédéric Barbier, "Le commerce international de la librairie française au XIXe siècle (1815–1913)," *Revue d'histoire moderne et contemporaine* (Livre, Éducation, Savoirs XVIIe–XXe siècles) XXVIII (January–March 1981): 110.

to the introduction of educational laws it reached 9% in the decade from 1880 to 1890. Predicated, moreover, on a one-way exchange, it formed from an economic point of view a particularly favorable market. Tunisia, a protectorate since 1881, the Indochinese Union founded in 1887, Martinique, Guadeloupe, the islands of Mauritius and Reunion and later Madagascar and Senegal constituted at the end of the nineteenth century the main poles of this new market. Whereas in 1821 trade with the colonies made up only 2.4% of exports, it reached 9.8% in the 1900s and grew, due to the favorable balance of exchange, into a vital component for the equilibrium of the French publishing industry.[20]

Rather than being a failure to take account of a technical "formality," the failure to incorporate the colonies into the BU and the BC apparently corresponded to the desire to maintain a strictly centralized regime of book production and distribution (a closed circuit), managed and controlled exclusively and unilaterally by the Paris publishers. On another note, it was linked to the conscious effort to maintain the francophone character of the educated elites in the colonies and ensure the perpetuation of French as a world language. Moreover, francophone literary elites in the colonies should continue to regard Paris as their indisputable publishing center and aim to have their works published and distributed via metropolitan publishers. Contemporary structures in the publishing and creative industries in the francophone world prove just how successful and long-lasting this geocultural-economic model was and still is. The initial intentions of the British in India had been similar. Anglicization had aimed at the creation of an English-educated elite to work for the Indian government. This policy was reversed, however, as soon as the realization prevailed that higher education was helping to create an educated proletariat as the number of qualified Indians far exceeded available positions. Moreover, by educating the various Indian ethnicities in the common English language, the education system, through the eradication of linguistic barriers, was helping them to overcome their segmentation, that is, it was helping them to unite and thereby effectively politicizing them. Remedy was sought in re-ethnicization. Education and publishing in the various Indian vernaculars was therefore encouraged, and so were translations of English works into the various Indian languages, whereby established British publishing houses replicated their structures by founding local Indian branches.[21]

---

20 Barbier, "Le commerce international," 115.

21 Bently, "Copyright, Translations," 1193–1194, 1196–1205.

Strategies of Expansion of Intellectual Property Regimes in Europe and around the World

One of the most fascinating aspects of IP as a legal instrument is its capacity to coordinate multiple, complex, multivalent and at times also contradictory functions in the management and exchange of intangible assets. IP feeds on expansion, scaling up and diversification of technology and commerce. Its capacity to combine and navigate between internal market consolidation and external market expansion is what makes IP distinctive as an instrument of governance: IP can be protectionist, liberal, monopolist, expansionist, statist, corporatist, free trade all at once and interchangeably, depending on one's standpoint, needs and (geographical) location.

The current section shifts focus between (East Central) Europe and other world regions in search of comparisons. Switching between the regional and the global can help to highlight the multiplicity of relevant analytical contexts and scales, as well as the variety of strategies applied. With no pretension to exhaust such compound subject matter, this subsection provides a comparative overview of types, actors, contexts and constellations in the distribution and expansion of specific IP forms, focusing mainly on the relationship between politics, IP regimes and their globalization strategies.

Understanding the workings of international copyright and the BU requires shifting attention to multiple theatres of action, as the global expansion of IP did not rest on a singular and homogeneous strategy to be applied uniformly, but remained flexible and was adjusted to suit political circumstances, the balance of power, short- and long-term objectives, historical legacies, the status of certain regions or countries, opportunities offered by specific situational constellations, and the positionality of other actors, whether allies or contenders; all factors that determined in each case the specific logic and choice of action. Colonial copyright is a prime example of such continuous recalibration strategies. For precisely the same reasons, IP scholars have emphasized that the historical development of international intellectual property is more than the sum of its parts and needs to be conceptualized rather in systemic terms, that is, as a perpetually evolving and mutating regime and/or order.[22]

[22] Peter K. Yu regards the historical development of the international intellectual property regime to be the product of repeated interactions between an evolving set of currents and crosscurrents producing opportunities and crises. He offers a useful discussion of various instruments, strategies, "offensives" and "resistances" incorporating perspectives from both lawmaking and international relations, and moreover from a longue durée perspective spanning the fifteenth to the twenty-first century. Whereas Yu's strength lies indisputably in the period post WWII, in his long-term analysis

In the case of Central and Eastern Europe, which will be discussed in detail in the following chapter, the post-WWI peace treaty offered a unique window of opportunity for "prescribed accessions," and the context was expertly used in order to bring the majority of the newly created and older nation states of the region collectively into the BU regime. By contrast, in the case of China (for which a closer, even if only cursory discussion is attempted in this section), a region which until 1912[23] was in a state of political turmoil, a much cruder form of colonial intervention was applied and a legal structure devised, which arbitrarily pasted together a closely knit, fictional area of intervention. Law in the Chinese case literally concocted and legitimized a terrain of intervention over territories. Quite the opposite strategy was pursued in the case of the (Hispano)Americas. In this region, representing previous European colonies but to a large extent self-liberated in the late eighteenth and early to mid-nineteenth centuries, crude interventionism would have been the perfect recipe for disaster. The Old World had been warned. Through the Monroe Doctrine, American states had delivered a Pan-American programmatic manifesto against European intervention. Moreover, since the late nineteenth century, the American states were self-organizing and closing ranks *in causa* IP. As a result, in the case of the Americas a more refined and subtle strategy was devised. In the spirit of the Enlightenment values that triggered the decolonization of North and South America, a "universal" convention was planned in the interwar period, which would apparently help to "bridge" the copyright systems of the European and American continents but was eventually cancelled due to the outbreak of WWII.[24]

These diverse examples illustrate well the variety and multiformity in the application of means and methods of "persuasion." They demonstrate that IP expansion consisted of a repertoire of changing and adaptable legal regimes, rather than a straightforward frontal takeover, though this last option was not excluded, as exemplified by the case of China. The repertoire consisted of: (1) a web of diverse technologies of coercion and/or persuasion; (2) diffusion and centralization from above with varying degrees of local leeway, as in the case of British colonial copyright;[25]

---

he eschews an evolutionary narrative sequence and discusses IP development as a medley of intentions, strategies, instruments and balances of power. See Peter K. Yu, "Currents and Crosscurrents in the International Intellectual Property Regime," *Loyola of Los Angeles Law Review* 38 (2004): 323–443.

23 In 1912 the Qing Dynasty was overthrown and the Republic of China proclaimed, thus ending 5000 years of dynastic rule in China.

24 The idea of a Universal Copyright Convention was revived in the post-WWII period and materialized in 1952 in quite different circumstances under the auspices of UNESCO.

25 See here Birnhack, *Colonial Copyright*, 22–78.

but also (3) "regime shifting," that is, the "attempt to alter the status quo ante by moving treaty negotiations, lawmaking initiatives, or standard setting activities from one international venue to another," [26] a form of expansion of IP lawmaking via "a rich variety of moves among international lawmaking fora (both within and among discrete regimes and regime complexes) as well as expansions or shifts of issue area boundaries."[27] The preparation of the universal convention with Hispanic America, the inclusion of IP issues in the Versailles peace settlement, as well as the "tuning" between the BU and the League of Nations, all represent good case studies in regime shifting. It appears that the chosen strategy was contingent as much upon available "windows of opportunity" at a given moment, as upon a specific, often colonially inspired classification of peoples and regions within the trajectory of world civilization. Eastern Europe occupied a somewhat middle and liminal status in that hierarchy, being neither truly colonial nor truly sovereign.

A common approach, and one of the most basic expansion strategies, was to put pressure on states to pass their own national copyright legislations, often as a preliminary stage before joining the BU regime. This concerned states that did not as yet dispose of any home copyright legislation or were still contemplating the enactment of a national copyright law. External pressure often precipitated the passing of copyright legislations in several countries. At times, the opposite was true. When the opportunity arose, states were "hastily" brought into the BU *before* they had had the opportunity to pass their own, modern copyright laws. Such was the case, for example, with several novel states of East and Southeast Europe after WWI; the newly reconstituted Polish state is an exemplary case here. Three different copyright laws, reflecting the different political administrations (Russian, Austrian and German), had been in force in the territories of partitioned Poland in the nineteenth century. The postwar state of Poland released its own copyright law in 1926, but had already "become" a BU member in 1920. In fact, when visualizing the geography of the post-WWI accession wave, one is left with the impression that BU membership almost replicated the postwar conception of the "cordon sanitaire."

The enactment of national copyright laws was a vital step towards extorting compatibility and reciprocity. It was a useful, though not indispensable precondition to conclude bilateral treaties, but it represented the sole instrument capable of activating the machinery of the Berne Union, that is, to put the central mechanism of "national treatment" to work. Finally, the existence of national legislation

---

26 Laurence R. Helfer, "Regime Shifting: The TRIPs Agreement and New Dynamics of International Property Lawmaking," *Yale Journal of International Law* 29, no. 1 (2004): 14.

27 Helfer, "Regime Shifting," 17.

served not only home regulation but, quite importantly, it allowed for interventions by which to prosecute infringements locally. Respectively, it must be assumed that some states released national copyright laws as a means to counter or minimize external pressure, influence and intervention, as well as in an effort to set their own terms and standards of regulation. I assume this to have been a major, if not the primary, motivation in the cases of both the Ottoman Empire and China; both passed their first copyright laws in 1910. Characteristically, the Chinese law, which was fashioned largely after the Japanese one, repudiated any kind of international obligations apart from the absolute necessary minimum emanating from bilateral treaties. It did not differentiate between nationals and foreigners; it did not mention translation rights, presuming that works could be translated freely; the law purposely omitted any mention of reciprocity and international protection.[28]

Bilateralism vs. Multilateralism

A common assumption of evolutionary narratives on the historical development of international copyright maintains that the drive for the creation of the multilateral BC is to be contextualized (1) in the foundation hype that propelled the creation of numerous international organizations in the second half of the nineteenth century and was the expression of a pressing need for cross-border harmonization of standards; and (2) concurring with this stance are the perceived "insufficiencies" of the previous condition, especially the insufficiency, and often inefficiency, of bilateral arrangements.

Indisputably, there is a grain of truth in both assertions. Moreover, the legal philosophy of the times endorsed the universalization of law and the overcoming of national particularities, and existing international unions such as the Universal Postal Union (1874) indeed had an inspirational effect and served as role models. Nonetheless, it is too simplistic to take the evolutionary approach at face value. The relationship between bilateralism and multilateralism was not reciprocally exclusive, and bilateral relations and treaties continued to shape copyright relations parallel to the existence of the multilateral arrangement.[29] Moreover, bilateral treaties were not

28 "Études générales, La première loi Chinoise sur le droit d'auteur," *Le Droit d'auteur*, year 25, no. 9, September 15, 1912, 122.

29 The persistence of bilateral agreements, parallel to the workings of the BC, has also been noticed and analysed by Jose Bellido in the case of Spain. See Bellido, "Colonial Copyright Extensions:

only used, as could be expected, in order to regulate the relationships between union and non-union member states, but were similarly applied in reciprocal agreements between union member countries. Consequently, multilateralism should be viewed rather as an additional platform of action, particularly befitting for setting the parameters for overarching coordination, large-scale harmonization and expansion strategies, as well as an instrument of increased legitimating authority.

It is more meaningful therefore to regard bilateralism and multilateralism as complementary arenas of action, that is, as activity platforms that could be used interchangeably, perhaps also as instruments of a specific division of labor in international relations, whereby each tool was applied in order to tackle diverse situations. It appears that bilateral treaties were used as both exploratory forays and spearheads for future developments.[30] Bilateral treaties could set new standards, which though initially valid only in the relationship between two actors, could potentially be elevated to BU standards. Bilateral treaties frequently served as orientation models and prototypes and were often referred to when searching for appropriate solutions to specific problems. The fact that a specific solution had already been utilized in a bilateral treaty automatically elevated it to a plausible and applicable alternative. In that respect, bilateral treaties created precedents that were able to reposition certain propositions from the margins into the center of the copyright debate. Such was the case, for example, with the bilateral treaty concluded between France and Germany at the turn of the century, in which both countries agreed to raise the term of protection for translations to 50 years p.m.a. in their reciprocal relations. Representing at the time a rather marginal option, the 50-year term for translations was eventually raised to the BU standard.

In addition, multilateralism became an attractive option not only because it kept pace with the internationalist tendencies of the late nineteenth century. It was most likely also triggered by the refusal of certain countries in the world peripheries, like Brazil and Russia, to enter into or renew bilateral treaties with European countries such as France and later Germany. In other words, strategies of resistance and obstruction were paralyzing reciprocal relationships, as a consequence of which bilateralism was reaching an impasse and failing to deliver. Regarded from this perspective, the drive for multilateralism in international copyright relations was not the natural culmination of preceding efforts, leading from primitive to complex

Spain at the Berne Convention (1883–1899)," *Journal of the Copyright Society of the U.S.A.* 58, (2011): 520–21.

30 A quantitative as well as qualitative analysis of bilateral treaties for the nineteenth and twentieth centuries would help us to gain a clearer picture of the proportions of this phenomenon.

forms of action, but rather a kind of "leap" forward. It signified the establishment of an additional and different activity platform with greater reach, as well as disciplining and enforcing power; one that could more easily displace, diffuse and overcome individual resistances.

It should not be regarded as a paradox that the correlation worked in the inverse manner as well, that is, that multilateral agreements were regarded as fora that could facilitate a bilateral rapprochement. At the end of the nineteenth and turn of the twentieth century, both France and Spain sought membership of the multilateral Montevideo treaty,[31] which they treated as a means to an end. Diplomatically, the main goal was to attract Argentina and/or Uruguay bilaterally. Their initial intent had been to celebrate particular copyright treaties with each of the Latin American republics. However, the reluctance of Latin America to engage bilaterally, and the Europeans' inability to connect to them multilaterally (i.e. through Berne), forced them to view the Montevideo convention as an instrument that would enable them to engage specific Latin American countries in some sort of copyright relation. In other words, Montevideo provided a lateral route through which to "capture" certain Latin American countries.[32] As thoughtfully summarized by Jose Bellido, such and other instances demonstrate that "standard divisions between 'center and periphery' and between 'multilateral and bilateral' were contingently and constantly negotiated, strategically deployed and imaginatively recreated."[33]

Copyright's capacity to fluently bundle together diverse competences (commercial, cultural, political) and engage prominent stakeholders (intellectual elites, politicians, government officials, state administrations, powerful interest groups) at various levels (intergovernmental, transnational, international, regional) with issues ranging from identity to trade, made it an attractive terrain for diplomatic deployment. Not surprisingly, both the Spanish and the French states initiated discourses, activities and diplomatic exchanges articulated and framed through copyright issues

---

31 The Montevideo treaty was a copyright agreement made in 1889 between seven American states (Argentina, Peru, Bolivia, Brazil, Chile, Paraguay and Uruguay) creating the Union of South American States in the matter of literary and artistic property. Though largely modelled on the Berne Union, it departed from it on several important issues. The Union was not automatically open to all world states and its individual members could decide whether to accept or refuse the accession of European countries. See Ladas, *The International Protection of Literary and Artistic Property*, vol. I (New York: The MacMillan Company, 1938), 635–79; see also Isabella Löhr, *Die Globalisierung geistiger Eigentumsrechte: Neue Strukturen internationaler Zusammenarbeit 1886–1952* (Göttingen: Vanderhoeck & Ruprecht, 2010), 131–39.

32 Jose Bellido, "Montevideo vs Berne: The Rise of an Interpretation in International Copyright (1888–1898)," *Revue internationale du droit d'auteur* 229, (2011): 69.

33 Bellido, "Montevideo vs Berne," 93.

in the late nineteenth and early twentieth centuries, that is, precisely in an era when both countries were retreating from their erstwhile global domination and were on the look-out for different ways to pursue international relations. As persuasively argued by Jose Bellido, it was only after the "disaster of 1898" that Spain started to discern in Latin American countries a fruitful terrain for foreign policy. As a result, it signed a thick network of bilateral copyright treaties with various Latin American countries parallel to the schedule set by Berne, and almost as if disregarding the BC. Obviously Latin America offered Spain a level of international influence that it had not been able to find in Berne, and "providing offices for copyright bilateralism, conveyed different ways for casting political relationships simultaneously to the international efforts in Berne."[34] Spanish activity was undertaken at the fringes of the international convention, and was not an effort to ignore Berne, whose global aspirations, on the contrary, had whetted the Spanish appetite for greater international influence, but rather was an attempt to create and promote alternatives to Berne. The Spanish example was sedulously followed by France, which embarked on the same adventure and signed several bilateral agreements with Latin American countries at the end of the nineteenth century.[35] Spanish, French, British and North American ambitions colluded over influence in the Latin American region. This constellation can perhaps help to elucidate why in the interwar period France zealously pursued the objective of a "universal" copyright convention with the Americas. The initiation of a universal convention under French aegis was without doubt a very prestigious project. Though formally acting through the League of Nations (that is, through the International Institute of Intellectual Cooperation) and the framework of the BU, in reality the French government pursued the goal of a universal convention almost single-handedly, merely incorporating Belgium and Brazil in secondary roles. A different strategy was followed in the case of China. In this case, alliances were mandatory and bilateralism was handier for weaving together the foundations of a quite different type of legal regime.

34 Jose Bellido, "Latin American and Spanish Copyright Relations (1880–1904)," *The Journal of World Intellectual Property* 12, no. 1 (2009): 18.

35 Bellido, "Colonial Copyright Extensions," 520–22.

China

An additional method of expansion—and perhaps the epitome of the colonial philosophy—was to virtually extend the legal regime of the BU by applying bilateral protection agreements over foreign, non-unionist territories. Such a regime was applied to China in the early twentieth century. Law constructed in this case a new form of territoriality, which allowed bilateral contracting states to consider China a prolongation of their own territories and jurisdictions, and provided them with the opportunity to intervene, persecute and punish counterfeits, by their nationals and others, in the same manner as practiced in their own national and/or colonial realms, or bilateral relations. The pioneers of this system were quickly followed and imitated by others.

Using insufficient protection of authors' rights and the established counterfeiting practice of European works in China as a justification, a series of European and regional powers took concerted action to "remedy" the situation. Great Britain took the lead by enacting on February 2, 1899 an ordinance regarding the English jurisdiction in China and Korea, which was replaced in 1904 by article 69 of the China and Korea Order in Council, and consequently amended by the ordinance of February 11, 1907. Its provisions stipulated that any act that would have constituted an infringement by the standards of the copyright law of the British Empire could be brought to the courts of the English jurisdiction in China on the basis of the same legislation, if it had been committed by a British subject against the literary property of an Englishman, and in the cases where reciprocal treatment was guaranteed, action could even be taken against a Chinese or foreign citizen.[36]

On May 19, 1908, Japan and the United States concluded a special (bilateral) treaty, which guaranteed their citizens and subjects the protection of works of literature, art and photography over Chinese territory to the same degree as they were protected in the territories and possessions of each other's country.[37] By "a kind of fiction," the territory of China was considered to be an extension of the territory of the two signatory countries, so that any counterfeit produced by any one of their nationals in China could be prosecuted at the colonial (*tribunaux territoreaux*) or consular courts, as if the act had taken place in the territories or possessions of the other party.[38] The treaty whetted the appetite of France, which concluded a similar

36 "Études générales, La première loi Chinoise sur le droit d'auteur," *Le Droit d'auteur*, year 25, no. 9, September 15, 1912, 123.

37 "Chine, nouvelle loi sur le droit d'auteur," *Le Droit d'auteur*, year 24, no. 4, April 15, 1911, 55.

38 "Études générales, La première loi Chinoise sur le droit d'auteur," *Le Droit d'auteur*, year 25, no. 9, September 15, 1912, 124.

bilateral treaty with Japan on September 14, 1909. Commenting self-importantly in *Le Droit d'auteur* on the extension of the copyright regime, it was noted that "the first elements of a regime of international authors' protection were established in China, *and moreover without any direct action by this country*."[39]

The French-Japanese treaty prompted the Syndicate for the Protection of Intellectual Property to suggest to the French Foreign Ministry the conclusion of an equivalent treaty with the US. Furthermore, the French government was asked to undertake an initiative for an agreement among unionist countries, which would declare the BC applicable in China in the relationships among BU member states' citizens before the respective consular courts of those states. In its response, the ministry deemed it premature to negotiate with foreign governments an extension of the BU in the relationships between foreigners in China, on the grounds that it was not clear whether the laws carrying the approbation of those international acts were binding for French consular courts.[40]

The bilateral treaty between France and Japan (both BU members) provided protection for trademarks, inventions, drawings and copyrights over the territory of China and all French and Japanese dominions. The treaty, which is presented here in more detail in order to offer insight into the workings of such a legal structure, is illustrative of the clout that bilateral treaties could have as legal instruments targeting particular tasks—in this case, the expansion of the signatories' territorial jurisdiction. Moreover, the bilateral arrangement between the two BU members created a new spatial configuration, a territorial area in which France and Japan jointly controlled practically all of East and Southeast Asia. The treaty decreed that:

1. All inventions, designs and trademarks patented or registered by the citizens and subjects of one of the contracting parties enjoyed in China the same protection against all counterfeit by citizens or subjects of the other contracting party as in all territories and possessions of the other contracting party.
2. The citizens and subjects of each of the two contracting parties enjoyed in China authors' rights protection for works of literature and art as well as photographs, to the measure to which they are protected in the territories and possessions of the other party.

---

39 "Études générales, La première loi Chinoise sur le droit d'auteur," *Le Droit d'auteur*, year 25, no. 9, September 15, 1912, 124., Emphasis added.

40 "Chine, nouvelle loi sur le droit d'auteur," *Le Droit d'auteur*, year 24, no. 4, April 15, 1911, 55.

3. If a counterfeit was produced in China by any citizen or subject of the two contracting parties of an invention, design, trademark or copyright enjoying protection by virtue of this treaty, the injured party enjoyed in front of the competent national or consular courts of this contracting party the same rights and remedies as the subjects and citizens of this contracting party.
4. All contracting parties engage in extending to China the treatment that the citizens or subjects of the other contracting party enjoy regarding the protection of tradenames in the territories and possessions of this contracting party in virtue of the convention for the protection of industrial property.
5. The citizens of the possessions belonging to the French Republic and Korean subjects will enjoy in China the same treatment by virtue of this treaty as French citizens and Japanese subjects respectively.
6. It is mutually agreed between the contracting parties that the effects of the present convention will be extended—to the measure that this treaty applies—to every other country where each of them has rights or extraterritorial jurisdiction. All rights resulting from the present convention will be recognized regarding insular and other possessions and the territories under leasehold of the contracting parties, and all legal means foreseen for the protection of the mentioned rights will be considered to apply at competent tribunals.[41]

It deserves to be mentioned that such legal arrangements were officially endorsed by the highest echelons of the BU administration. The territorial expansion of the BU was put into perspective in a celebratory article recounting the Union's foundation on the occasion of the BU's 25th anniversary in 1911. The anonymous author(s) recited the conceptions of the Union's founding fathers such as Numa Droz, who in his 1886 inaugural speech reflected on the Union's impending tasks: to conquer more territories, especially those that remained outside Berne, that is, the USA, the Netherlands, Austria-Hungary, South America and the reluctant Slavs. Summarizing the progress achieved from the standpoint of the year 1911, the article underscored novel forms of territorial expansion: "a kind of territorial prolongation of the effects of the unionist regime deserves to be registered. The extra territorial reach in the case of China." The author(s) praised the already-mentioned French initiative for

[41] "Conventions particulières, convention intéressant un des pays de l'Union. France-Japon. Convention réciproque, en Chine, des marques de fabrique, brevets, dessins et droit d'auteur," *Le Droit d'auteur*, year 24, no. 7, July 15, 1911, 92.

an agreement between unionist states, declaring the BC applicable in the relations between their citizens in China and all other countries "outside of Christianity," where they still held consular jurisdictions. This regime of international protection, which transplanted—at least in the reciprocal relationships between Europeans—the BC in the Far East, though not formally instituted, elicited the interest not only of France but also of Britain, the Netherlands, Germany and Belgium.[42]

Having concluded the bilateral treaty with Japan, France undertook efforts to conclude similar treaties with the US and Portugal. It can be deduced from comments in *Le Droit d'auteur* that the French approach provided something of a role model: "if stipulations similar to the ones negotiated by France are generalized, we will dispose here of a new mode in order to penetrate the Far East with one of the achievements of Western civilization; China will be brought more easily to follow the precious example of Japan, which entered the Union in 1899."[43]

The case of China has been included in this analysis for a number of reasons. Firstly, it illustrates well the global pretensions of the players involved, and their inventiveness in handling legal instruments. Secondly, typologically, the Chinese case elucidates a different and supplementary type of legal regime; one that demonstrates exemplarily the law's capacity not only to erode sovereignty, but also to legitimate and territorialize hegemony. In a manner reminiscent of the capitulations regime imposed on the Ottoman Empire, colonial states found in the case of China the formal and legal formulas to secure their own and their subjects' preferential status, and guarantee their commercial interests in foreign lands. The Ottoman Empire was induced to concede such rights, however, while China was not even consulted. This furthermore reveals the law's practical implication in the expansion of the colonial project, but also its deep intellectual indebtedness to colonialism on the level of mentalities. Thirdly, the Chinese case illustrates well the interplay between bilateralism and multilateralism, and how it was possible to move from one platform of action to the other, and moreover how bilateral agreements could become instructive for other Union members as templates to copy, as well as for the broader development of the Berne Union. Indeed, the net of bilateral treaties over China's territory was to be the preparatory ground for the extension of the BC in the Far East. Fourthly, the Chinese case points at the already-mentioned variance of behaviour adopted, dependent on the respective region in focus. The means and

42 "Études générales, Le vingt-cinquième anniversaire de la convention de Berne du 9 Septembre 1886," *Le Droit d'auteur*, year 24, no. 9, September 15, 1911, 121–122.

43 "Études générales, La première loi Chinoise sur le droit d'auteur," *Le Droit d'auteur*, year 25, no. 9, September 15, 1912, 124.

instruments to be applied per region, or respectively the degree of crudeness sanctioned, corresponded to a hierarchy of civilizations far removed from the theme of the fraternization of cultures and minds that pervaded the BU's official rhetoric and functioned as the Union's window-dressing. Finally, it demonstrates the capacity of IP to structure multivalent and multilevel relations that went beyond mere copyright and trade and included regional diplomacy as well as politico-economic-cultural alliances.

How the specific mode of engaging in copyright relationships could help to design and produce specific knowledge regimes, which in return recast and structured world geographies of empire, dependence, equality, coloniality, liberation, revolution and so on, is one of the fascinating aspects of IP. This was not a prerogative of the Western European colonial states. As already witnessed in chapter three, the East European Empires of the late nineteenth and early twentieth century also opted for particular modes of organizing the circulation of knowledge and print in their realms, and so did Soviet Russia later on.

In conclusion, if we bring together all these strands and dimensions of expansion, it becomes obvious that the BU was not the natural climax of a process of ever-greater protection from primitive to more sophisticated forms of global governance, corresponding more or less to the exigencies of globalization. Neither did it represent a neutral expert forum constantly supplemented and augmented by the entry of new member states and the extension and expansion of subject matter and areas of competence, covering ever-greater areas of creativity. Rather, the BU was a field of power. It consisted of many different theatres of action, running parallel and alongside, through and beneath Berne, and made use of a toolbox of inventive instruments that were chosen to suit the challenge at hand.

Finally, Berne was a big machine that produced and stabilized meaning with respect to the perception and the commercial use of cultural goods, an agenda that it was able to radiate—with greater or lesser success—globally. As witnessed in the case of translation, the BU did not codify authors' rights. Rather, it ensured that a specific business model regarding orderly management in the transnational transmission of texts was naturalized, universalized and legitimized. By codifying the standards and national business models of the advanced and culture-exporting nations, it often elevated them to universal standards, and in turn these different IP regimes helped to structure the global markets for cultural commodities.

Chapter 6

Orchestrated Globalization

The Expansion of Intellectual Property Rights in Southeast and East Central Europe in the Context of World War I

In the late nineteenth and early twentieth century, for reasons already expounded in the previous chapters, the empires of East and Southeast Europe were reluctant to join the newly created international structures for the protection of intellectual property. Aiming in the first place at maintaining equilibrium within their own fragile imperial realms and fostering their own circuits of communication and exchange of information, they eschewed a precipitated accession into the emerging structures of international IP regulation. This condition changed radically with the end of WWI, when, as a result of the post-war Versailles settlement, the newly created nation states of East Central and Southeast Europe were brought practically *en groupe* into the Berne Union. This chapter analyses the development of copyright in conjunction with the consolidation and internationalization of the West and Central European book industries in the second half of the nineteenth and early twentieth centuries. It explores models, modalities and geographies of expansion of the book trade, highlighting the interdependence between commerce, culture and geopolitical sway. Consequently, it concentrates on the arrangements of the post-WWI peace settlement, which effected the purposeful expansion of the BU regime into East Central and Southeast Europe.

The European Book Trade and Its Models

The nineteenth century, and particularly the decades 1850–1860 and 1880–1890, witnessed a wholesale reorganization of the legal parameters in international book trade, a process that went hand in hand with a functional reorganization of commercial practices, means of transport and modes of payment.[1] A combination of factors,

1 Frédéric Barbier, "Le commerce international de la librairie française au XIXe siècle (1815–1913)," *Revue d'histoire moderne et contemporaine* 28 (Livre, Éducation, Savoirs XVIIe-XXe siècles) (January–March 1981): 100.

including the development of new legal structures, an unprecedented improvement in transport and communications and the installation of a more efficient financial system, led, according to Frédéric Barbier, to the unprecedented globalization of the book trade between 1815 and 1914. Significant changes in the world of readers provided the impetus for the structural reorganization that began in 1840. Three phenomena converged to cause an ever-greater production and circulation of print: (1) accelerated population growth, with the European populace growing from 187 million in 1800 to 401 million by the end of the nineteenth century; (2) a concurrent urbanization drive as the proportion of cities with more than 100,000 inhabitants grew from 2% in 1815 to more than 20% in 1901; and finally, (3) an extension of almost universal literacy, which around 1900 reached 80–90% in Western Europe, barring the Mediterranean countries. On top of this, more than 50 million Europeans settled overseas,[2] forming a formidable diaspora and thereby creating new markets that to a large extent determined European book exports. The production and diffusion of printed materials accelerated considerably as a result of this extraordinary expansion of the market: there were 180 million literates in 1800 compared to 544 million in 1900, 64% European and approximately 16% North American. As the population doubled, the number of readers tripled, and the number of books quintupled.[3]

With the substantial expansion of the middle classes, "the backbone of the reading classes," the nineteenth century was the epitome of the "triumph of bourgeois culture." The unprecedented growth of commerce in written texts was due not only to the expansion of education and greater access to cultural goods, but also to the considerable extension of leisure time. During the decades 1830–1880 the book ruled supreme and the written word became progressively cheaper, whereas after 1880 a number of rivals to the written text emerged: the gramophone and the record, radio and cinema, all connected to practices vying for the audiences' attention and a fraction of their leisure time.[4]

Industrialization made paper cheap, and after 1830 a series of technical innovations in printing—improved steam presses, ameliorated lithography, stereotype, monotype and linotype—helped to lower costs and increase quality. Publishing enterprises and production grew, but the "key to wealth in publishing," as pointedly

2 Approximately 36 million in North America, 8 million in South America, 3 million in Oceania, 1 million in South Africa, half a million in the Maghreb. Barbier, "Le commerce international," 104.

3 Barbier, "Le commerce international," 104–105.

4 Donald Sassoon, *The Culture of the Europeans: From 1800 to the Present* (London: Harper Press, 2006), 295.

emphasized by Donald Sassoon, "was not in convincing thousands of readers to buy books, but in getting state backing or establishing a monopoly."[5]

The creation of the BU in 1886 coincided with one of the most dynamic periods in the development of the book industry, that is, the unprecedented expansion of the international book trade, and was profoundly stimulated by it. Through a system of bilateral treaties, several of the continent's leading book-exporting nations had managed by approximately the middle of the nineteenth century to subdue their one-time rival "pirate" nations (particularly those of the same linguistic group) by turning them either into subsystems of their own book trade or into extensions of their own commercial networks. In doing so, they expanded their reach and sphere of influence to a considerable degree. This had been the case for France regarding Belgium[6] and French-speaking Switzerland, but also for Germany with respect to the Habsburg Empire and German-speaking Switzerland.[7] Moreover, having succeeded in disciplining contenders in the peripheries of their own realms (London publishers vis-à-vis Scottish and Irish publishers; Parisian publishers and publishers in the provinces; northern German publishers and the publishers of the south), they then proceeded to consolidate indisputable, dynamic centers of the printing industry in such places as London, Paris and Leipzig, which acted as national coordination centers for their respective book industries. In the second half of the nineteenth century, with the issue of reprinting largely under control (at least in the western part of the continent), book-exporting nations began to regulate their mutual trade relations in the context of the increasing internationalization of their cultural industries.

The creation of the BU was not an undisputed project, and in the late nineteenth century several European powers and states such as Spain,[8] the Scandinavian countries,[9] Holland and initially even Britain remained aloof from the organizational fever of the initiators. As has repeatedly been emphasized by scholars of

5 Sassoon, *The Culture of the Europeans,* 296.

6 Treaties were conducted between France and Belgium in 1852 and 1854. See Pascal Durand, "Éthos reproducteur et habitus techniciste: Naissance du 'modèle' éditorial belge francophone," in *Les mutations du livre et l'édition dans le monde du XVIIIe siècle à l'an 2000*, eds. Jacques Michon and Jean-Yves Mollier (Paris: L'Harmattan, 2001), 251–259; see also Frédéric Barbier, "Les marchés étrangers de la librairie française," in *Histoire de l'édition française*, eds. Roger Chartier and Henri-Jean Martin, vol. 3 (Le temps des éditeurs: Du romantisme à la Belle Époque) (Paris: Fayard, 1990), 310f.

7 See here Norbert Bachleitner, "Tausch, Produktion und Übersetzung im österreichischen Buchhandel im 19. Jahrhundert," in *Est–Ouest: Transferts er réceptions dans le monde du livre en Europe (XVIIe–XXe siècles)*, ed. Frédéric Barbier (Leipzig: Leipziger Universitätsverlag, 2005), 109–123.

8 On Spain see Jose Bellido, "Colonial Copyright Extensions: Spain at the Berne Convention," *Journal of the Copyright Society of the U.S.A.* 58, no. 1 (2011): 501–522.

9 On Scandinavian countries see Eva Hemmungs Wirtén, *Cosmopolitan Copyright.*

intellectual property history, the establishment of an international treaty on intellectual property was neither an obvious nor an inevitable act, and at the time of the treaty's signature, each country's attitude was dictated by its own specific commercial and political priorities and ambitions.[10] Colonial states in decline, such as Spain, and contemporary colonial powers like Britain consented to participate in Berne only after thoroughly weighing the pros and cons of accession, and after having found Berne's international framework sufficiently expedient for structuring their commercial and other relationships with their own (past and present) colonies.[11] In light of the fact that the interests of the participants in the BU project were so diverse, the question could be legitimately raised as to the motives that glued it together. One potential answer is that the key actors/states at a given moment, variable for each, regarded the existence of such a multilateral forum to be more advantageous than not, and moreover, that they regarded the BU to be a convenient, influential and resourceful platform through which to pursue jointly and persistently an international agenda with transnational ambitions, which they would otherwise have been incapable of pursuing individually with any certainty of success.

In broad terms, it could be argued that the BU was constructed around a core of industrial and culture-exporting countries (France, Germany, Britain), which having freed themselves earlier from the corporate bonds of feudal, estates-based society, developed a strong interest in the market-based regulation of intellectual property and played a pioneering role in the solidification and expansion of that institution. From this perspective, the foundation of the BU resembled somewhat the creation of a "cartel," that is, an alliance of states similar to that of a professional alliance whose purpose was to develop binding rules by which to govern and regulate competition among the principal actors. In contrast to a traditional cartel, however, the BU did not represent a closed professional structure. Moreover, its objective lay not in the regulation of prices or the settlement of volumes of production, but rather in the elaboration of spheres of influence and the regulated monopolization of markets.

10 Bellido, "Colonial Copyright Extensions," 521–22.

11 For Britain the priority lay with copyright in English books and the English-speaking colonies. Britain sought means to master its problematic relationship with the US and forestall inter-colonial piracy. See here Catherine Seville, *The Internationalization of Copyright Law: Books, Buccaneers and the Black Flag in the Nineteenth Century* (Cambridge: Cambridge University Press, 2006), particularly pages 22–77; idem, "British Colonial and Imperial Copyright," in *Research Handbook on the History of Copyright Law*, eds. Isabella Alexander and Tomás H. Gómez-Arostegui (Cheltenham: Edward Elgar Publishing, 2016), 268–287; see also Birnhack, *Colonial Copyright*, 22–78. In the case of Spain, the initial negative attitude towards Berne was curbed with the realization that the BC helped to refocus Spanish foreign policy towards copyright and set its international expectations in motion, particularly with respect to the development of copyright in (the lost colonies of) Latin America; see here Bellido, "Colonial Copyright Extensions," 522.

At least, such is the impression given when looking at the deliberations of the International Congress of Publishers.[12] Following a disagreement over the location of the institution's permanent seat at its 1901 Leipzig congress (the French delegation strongly opposed the idea of crowning Leipzig the official printing capital of Europe), the members opted for a compromise. The congress's permanent seat would be internationalized and put under the auspices of the Berne Bureau and its director, Henri Morel, with a seat in Berne. Neither would the publishers create one shared international bulletin for the dissemination of professional information; rather, they decided to undertake a division of labor among themselves by grouping countries and world regions into the following three categories: the German *Börsenblatt für den deutschen Buchhandel* would report on Germany, Austria, Switzerland, Holland and the Scandinavian countries; the French *Bibliographie de la France* would be responsible for France, Belgium, Italy, Spain and South America; and the British *Publishers' Circular* for Great Britain, the British colonies and North America.[13] It becomes apparent, as observed by Thomas Loué, "that there existed in the representations of the publishers three distinct areas, three spheres of influence dominated by the three most developed publishing nations, establishing an international hierarchy of publishing. This also encouraged the eviction of other countries from the executive restricted instruments of the International Congress of Publishers."[14] Though constructed on an elaborate and sophisticated legal edifice, and dependent on mechanisms of negotiation and compromise, the BU reflected more or less the dynamics of the above-mentioned hierarchy.[15] The proliferation of supranational, transnational and international non-governmental structures characteristic of the second half of the nineteenth century reflects, therefore, neither purely altruistic nor purely hegemonic intentions, but rather something of both and in-between. Using internationalism in order to further one's own national interests—that is, "internationalism to the advantage of the nation"—was incorporated into the politics of universalism.[16] Liberal internationalism and nationalism

12 See here Thomas Loué, "Le Congrès international des éditeurs 1896–1938: Autour d'une forme de sociabilité professionnelle internationale," in Michon and Mollier, *Les mutations du livre et l'édition*, 531–43; also Annett Kuhn, "Die Internationalen Verlegerkongresse von 1896 bis 1938: Arbeitsweise, Diskussionsschwerpunkte, Beschlüsse," *Leipziger Jahrbuch zur Buchgeschichte* 12 (2003): 285–99.

13 Loué, "Le Congrès international des éditeurs," 536.

14 Loué, "Le Congrès international des éditeurs," 536.

15 In addition, I would argue that the "technical" dimension that legal discourses took in the process of negotiations (in a certain way also a natural outcome of such processes of codification) often distracts from an examination of the broader cultural, political and economic contexts they were called to regulate.

16 Jürgen Osterhammel, *Die Verwandlung der Welt: Eine Geschichte des 19. Jahrhunderts* (Munich: C.H. Beck, 2009), 733.

were not necessarily antithetical but rather interconnected phenomena in the late nineteenth century and for a good part of the twentieth century, and in that sense, international institutions and sociability were promoted and used as a means for advancing a wide variety of agendas.[17]

IP is a multifunctional instrument, capable of structuring legal, commercial, cultural and diplomatic relations. From the perspective of the leading exporting nations, IP concerned both the expansion of their respective publishing industries and their cultural influence and prestige, and by consequence their ability to project political and geopolitical power. The expansion of the book trade was both a consequence and a symptom of this influence. As pointedly phrased by an Italian publisher at the end of the nineteenth century, "the Italian market will always be limited to Italy, whereas French, English, German books are the world."[18] The geography imposed by the logic of distinct spheres of influence overlapped, intersected and collided with other geographies of the book trade. Such a geography, for example, was imposed by the popularity and reach of world and learned languages, or by the literary field and its most representative literary circles and their locations. Last but not least, different types and genres of publications, particularly those that were both popular and commercial successes, such as novels, serialized novels, newspapers and magazines, encyclopedias, practical books and so on, created an additional and distinct geography of demand and distribution. Publishers were assiduous and fast in copying each other's models (the penny magazine, the pocket book etc.) on a national and international level, thus contributing to the development of a dynamic and competitive sector on a global scale. Power generated a new geography that was both tangible and visible. In the second half of the nineteenth century, most established and successful publishers founded branches abroad in foreign continental capitals and overseas (North and South America, Oceania etc.).

If there was one literary form of the late eighteenth and nineteenth centuries that embodied the notion of European literature and helped to mould European space into a united though uneven literary market, this form was undeniably the *novel*. The absolute and indisputable blockbuster of modern times,[19] the novel was the most centralized of all literary genres. It imposed a geography of publishing where the national center held an almost unchallenged prerogative so that "while

---

17 See here Glenda Sluga, *Internationalism in the Age of Nationalism* (Philadelphia: University of Pennsylvania Press, 2013); also Mark Mazower, *Governing the World: The History of an Idea* (New York: Penguin, 2012).

18 Nicola Tranfaglia and Albertina Vittoria, *Storia degli editori italiani: Dall' Unità alla fine degli anni sessanta* (Rome: Laterna, 2007), 4.

19 Franco Moretti, *Atlas of the European Novel: 1800–1900* (London: Verso, 1998), 158–64.

the consumption of fiction was becoming more and more *widespread*, then, its production was becoming more and more *centralized*, both within each individual nation-state, and within the larger system of European states."[20] This expanding international market, as pointedly argued by Franco Moretti, created a specific and uneven geography of publishing in Europe:

> "a small group of countries (two or three [...])—a very small group that exported intensively in every direction; at the other extreme, a very large group that *imported* a lot, and exported almost nothing. And in between, 'regional' powers [...]. Two, three Europes. With France and Britain always in the core; most other states always in the periphery; and in between a variable group, that changes from case to case."[21] As a result, "Three Europes—probably. And then, in all three, a long and bitter rivalry between the continent's two narrative superpowers. [...] It is the sign of a struggle between the two core literatures, that divides the European system in zones of symbolic influence: a struggle for cultural hegemony, in which France seems to have clearly prevailed [...]. It is as if the Hundred Years' War won by Britain in 1815 had repeated and reversed itself on the cultural front, making of Paris, as it were, the Hollywood of the nineteenth century [...]. Wonderful thing, symbolic hegemony; and no one gives up without a struggle."[22]

Concomitantly to the expansion of publishing, political, cultural, and by extension linguistic influence went hand in hand and reciprocally strengthened each other. From the sixteenth century onwards, the question of universal and learned languages had acquired heightened significance due to the slow decline of Latin and the competition for different vernaculars to be its proper successor. Though both Tuscan Italian and Castilian Spanish had presented potential candidates, it was French that ultimately won the race and established itself by the eighteenth century as the heir to the universality of Latin. French became the language of the European royal courts, the aristocracy and of learned citizens and professionals. It grew to be the language of international treaties and diplomacy, and later of international organizations. With the radiation of the French Enlightenment and literature, French managed to acquire a commanding status (as the lingua franca) in the European public sphere and the literary field[23] through "symbolic hegemony."[24]

20 Moretti, *Atlas of the European Novel*, 165–70. Emphasis added.

21 Moretti, *Atlas of the European Novel*, 174. Emphasis added.

22 Moretti, *Atlas of the European Novel*, 184f.

23 See here Pascale Casanova, *La République mondiale des lettres* (Paris: Seuil, 1999), 69–118.

24 Casanova, *La République mondiale des lettres*, 106; see also Moretti, *Atlas of the European Novel*, 185.

France was able to hold this position until the late eighteenth century, when it began its progressive descent as leader of international culture.[25] Challenges came both from Britain and Germany.[26] Though all book-exporting countries were eager to expand their trade, France was faced with additional problems of a demographic nature. In contrast to developments in England and Germany, France's population barely grew in the course of the nineteenth century.[27] Though French publishers managed inventively to overcome the demographic bottleneck, the French book trade was visibly in a crisis of overproduction by the end of the nineteenth century. The French language was nevertheless able to maintain its leading cultural position. French was a principal language of instruction in the institutions of higher education of the Ottoman Empire (for example at the prestigious Military Medical Academy and the Imperial Law School), held the status of first foreign language in Latin America (not to speak of certain zones of fluid passages between French and Spanish), and was still held in high esteem by the educated elites of East and Southeast Europe.

Next to fashions and cultural influences, the expansion of the book trade was, on a practical level, also predicated upon finding and exploiting loopholes in commercial, economic and/or political arrangements that allowed states and their industries to step into rivals' shoes and challenge their commercial pre-eminence as well as their generic geopolitical position. Moreover, by such means, certain world regions became locations for conducting "proxy wars," that is, spaces where established and contending powers could flex their muscles. Such an opportunity arose, for example, in the early nineteenth century with the end of Spanish domination in

25 Barbier, "Les marchés étrangers," 318. Barbier measures the influence of the book trade through the equilibrium between imported and exported books. In the period from 1850 to 1890, French imports multiplied by 11, whereas exports multiplied only by 4. Following the rise of English to the status of first international language, the bulk of French book exports in the twentieth century will be geared from that moment onwards towards the francophone world. See also Olivier Godechot and Jacques Marseille, "Les exportations de livres français au XIXe siècle," in *La Commerce de la librairie en France au XIXe siècle*, ed. Jean-Yves Mollier (Paris: IMEC/Éditions de la MSH, 1997), 373–79. Their conclusion is quite telling: "Autant d'indicateurs qui soulignent la perte de prééminence de la langue français au cours du XIXe siècle. C'est bien à partir des années 1880-1890, date à laquelle les tonnes de livres à destination des pays francophones dépassent celles à destination des pays non francophones, que la place du français comme langue régionale l'importe sur la place du français comme vecteur d'une culture internationale" (377).

26 Casanova, *La République mondiale*, 105.

27 Whereas during the nineteenth century England grew from 10.5 million inhabitants in 1800 to 21 million in 1851 and 37 million in 1901 (that is, a growth rate of 350%), in the same period France grew by only 33%, from 30 to 40 million inhabitants. Germany counted 29 million in 1838, 42 million in 1875 and 65 million in 1910, demonstrating a growth rate of 120% during those 80 years. See Jean-Yves Mollier, "La construction du système éditorial français et son expansion dans le monde du XVIIIe au XXe siècle," in Michon and Mollier, *Les mutations du livre et l'édition*, 56.

the American continent and the liberalization of trade with the newly established republics. The Spanish empire's disintegration in the first decade of the twentieth century allowed certain countries like France, England and the US to intensify their guardianship and influence towards the new Latin American republics.[28] With Spain in disarray, there was a blooming black market in publications in Castilian, originals as well as translations, produced in France (and other European countries) and illicitly smuggled into Spain, at approximately the same time that France was fighting moral "battles" exporting and defending the concept and the universal sanctity of authors' rights. Being a major producer of books in Castilian—in fact, French-produced Castilian books represented the majority of books imported into Spain from abroad (or illicitly smuggled into Spain via the Pyrenees)— France catered almost exclusively to Hispanic foreign cultural needs, as the importation of scientific and literary culture was materialized predominantly through French editions or translations from French. Either by way of Spanish, or directly via French ports (Bordeaux), pirate editions were further shipped to the Hispanic Americas. The tables were turned for a short period between 1890 and 1900, when, with the crash of French publishing, the Spanish book once again resumed a position of leadership in book exports to Ibero-America.

The obvious loss of French intellectual influence in the course of the nineteenth century, in contrast to the growth of Anglo-Saxon culture, animated French projects of cultural and political colonization in the direction of Hispanic speakers. Aware of new commercial opportunities offered by the need for French books and good translations into Spanish for the rapidly developing Latin American societies, Parisian publishers such as the Garnier Brothers soon oriented their business towards Ibero-America with the intention of "rendering the greatest services to the Latin race." In the 1850s, the number of books published in France and destined for the Hispanic Americas grew significantly. They made up approximately 26.89% of the international trade in French publishing. In fact, the American market represented the second world market for French books.[29] The disintegration of Spain's colonial empire produced substitute candidates. Political turbulence incited foreign interventions, such as the joint British, French and Spanish intervention in Mexico, in whose aftermath French troops imposed Maximilian I as emperor in 1863. Such settings strengthened aspirations for political and cultural hegemony fashioned upon the French model. They furthermore encouraged the expansion of French

[28] Pura Fernández, "El monopolio del mercado internacional de impresos en castellano nel siglo XIX: Francia, España y la 'luta' de Hispanoamérica," *Bulletin Hispanique* 100, no. 1 (1998): 166–67.

[29] Fernández, "El monopolio del mercado internacional," 173–74.

publishers like Rosa y Bouret, who, after settling down in Mexico's capital, monopolized the Mexican book market for centuries.[30] Correspondingly, French publishers like Baptiste-Louis Garnier were instrumental in the development of the book trade and are considered among the founding fathers of book publishing in Brazil. Garnier promoted both local authors and international literature in translation. Interestingly, his attitude towards copyright in the international book trade was neither deferential nor consistent. On the contrary, he employed copyright in a selective and situational manner that was predicated more on his specific business interests and strategies and much less on principle.[31]

Most significantly, it should be remembered that the nineteenth century was the century of nationalities, witnessing not only the creation of different national movements and the codification of new languages, but above all the fragmentation and pluralization of public spheres and the slow development of mass culture. Translations rather than reprints came to dominate publishers' attention and the BU's agenda.[32] French was now required not only to preserve its position as the universal language of cultured elites but also as that of broader social strata. Expanding and maintaining a constant public of French-speaking readers became even more imperative. The creation of organizations like the *Alliance Française* in 1883, the first national organization for the dissemination of a foreign language,[33] targeted precisely that goal.[34] Until the First World War, the Alliance Française functioned as an official diplomatic institution holding the reins of French cultural activity abroad. Its aim was "organizing French linguistic diffusion and creating 'captive' publics in favor of French culture."[35]

Though all culture-exporting countries were equally interested in the juridification of IP, they were able to uphold their respective legal and commercial regimes through a variety of assets. Historical, cultural and commercial legacies and patterns played a role here, for example the traditional connection between the European

---

30 Fernández, "El monopolio del mercado internacional," 175.

31 Indicative is Garnier's correspondence with the Parisian publisher Louis Hachette; see here Lucia Granja and Valéria Bezerra, "Baptiste-Louis Garnier e Louis Hachette: contatos internacionais, direitos autorais e tradução," *Cadernos de Tradução* 43, no. 1 (2023): 1–26.

32 On translations see Hemmungs Wirtèn, *Cosmopolitan Copyright*.

33 In a comparative perspective, the British equivalent organization, the *British Council*, was created in 1930 and the German equivalent, the *Goethe-Institut*, in the 1950s.

34 François Chaubet, "L'alliance française ou la diplomatie de la langue (1883–1914)," *Revue historique* 632, no. 4 (2004): 763–85; see also Janet Horne, "'To Spread the French Language Is to Extend the *Patrie*': The Cultural Mission of the Alliance Française," *French Historical Studies* 40, no. 1 (2017): 95–127.

35 Chaubet, "L'alliance française," 764.

Protestant north (Scandinavia) and Germany or the particular association between France and Romance-language speaking countries. Britain could base the expansion of printing and publishing on the greater capitalization of its industry during the eighteenth and nineteenth centuries as well as the breadth of its empire. In fact, those two aspects seemed to mutually reinforce each other.[36] Germany's expansion was based on a very successful business and book trading model, specifically the wholesale book trade (*Kommissionsbuchhandel/Zwischenbuchhandel*), which it had pioneered.[37] One of its most "organic" zones of activity was East and Southeast Europe.

Though disposing of a centuries-long history, the German publishing industry took off with a particular dynamism in parallel with German industrialization after the 1860s.[38] It aimed at the construction of a zone of economic, cultural and ultimately political influence directed towards the Ottoman Empire and its own colonies. The center of gravity of German printing had shifted by the sixteenth century from the West to the East, that is, from Frankfurt to Saxony and Prussia (Leipzig and Berlin).

The great innovation of the German book trade was its high degree of specialization and division of labor. The wholesale book trade[39] developed almost out of necessity, as a means to overcome the political, economic and administrative fragmentation of the German lands. It guaranteed the swift distribution of books countrywide and acted as the avant-garde in the book trade's growth towards intensified commercialization.[40] As a business model it corresponded ideally to the rising number of published books, the growing number of publishers and booksellers and provided for the commercial integration of huge spaces independent of borders. It represented an amazingly fast and efficient system of book distribution based on

---

36 See James Raven, "British Publishing and Bookselling: Constraints and Developments," in Michon and Mollier, *Les mutations du livre et l'édition*, 19–30.

37 On the development of the "Kommissionsbuchhandel" see Mark Lehmstedt, "Die Herausbildung des Kommissionsbuchhandels in Deutschland im 18. Jahrhundert," in *L'Europe et le livre: Réseaux et pratiques du négoce de librairie XVIe–XIX siècles*, eds. Frédéric Barbier, Sabine Juratic and Dominique Varry (Paris: Klincksieck, 1996), 451–83; Thomas Keiderling, *Die Modernisierung des Leipziger Kommissionsbuchhandels von 1830 bis 1888* (Schriften zur Wirtschafts- und Sozialgeschichte, Bd. 58) (Berlin: Ducker & Humblot, 2000).

38 Numbers are quite indicative here: 9000 titles produced yearly until 1868, more than 15,000 titles in 1882, 20,000 in 1890 and almost 35,000 on the eve of WWI. Frédéric Barbier, "La librairie allemande comme modèle?" in Michon and Mollier, *Les mutations du livre et l'édition*, 37.

39 Simply put, the wholesale book trade was built on the capacity of big wholesalers to procure huge numbers of books from publishers in advance, store them and ship them with extreme speed, using the advantages of an advanced railway system. The wholesale book trade separated publishers from retailers and provided an important and rationalizing intermediary business structure for the book trade as a whole.

40 Georg Jäger, ed., *Geschichte des deutschen Buchhandels im 19. und 20. Jahrhundert: Das Kaiserreich 1871–1918* (Berlin: De Gruyter, 2001), vol. III: 523.

the breadth and capacity offered by extensive trade distribution networks. The city of Leipzig developed into a central node of the wholesale book trade with agencies in Germany and abroad (Zurich, Prague, Vienna, Budapest). Each of these cities had an additional radius of activity, thereby enforcing the geographical extension of the trade networks even further. The model was easily transported into Central and Eastern Europe, where it facilitated the expansion of the German book trade, extending from Zagreb to St Petersburg, but also into the Mediterranean area.[41]

The German model benefited from a series of favorable conditions, which strengthened its position in parts of Slavic Eastern Europe, Romania and Scandinavia. Germany became a natural intermediary between the book-producing zones located in Western Europe and the markets of readers developing on the continent's peripheries.[42] Moreover, the German trade could rely on the presence of a relatively large number of German speakers, who, though dispersed throughout a huge territory in East and Southeast Europe (Baltics, Bohemia, Transylvania, Galicia, Vojvodina, Croatia and Slavonia, Slovenia, Silesia etc.), tended to be concentrated in the urban centers and represented the educated strata of specific socio-economic groups that built the core of a potential readership. Germany, and to a certain degree Austria, naturally benefited from the structural disequilibrium between more advanced countries and developing regions. Furthermore, Germany was a major provider of printing and typographic equipment for the same areas and German functioned as the lingua franca of the book trade and apprenticeship in the printing and publishing professions. Finally, the German book trade was favored by the ascendance of German scholarship and science in the nineteenth century. By the turn of the century, particularly in the fields of the natural sciences, law, technology and philosophy, German was able to establish itself as the almost indisputable leading language of scholarship and research, not forgetting Germany's dominant market position in the production of musical scores. The German model was able to expand all the more easily since it relied mainly on the power, consistency and breadth of national and transnational networks that exceeded the existing political geography and its borders.[43] As succinctly put by Barbier, "at the end of the 17th and above all in the 18th and 19th centuries, Germany, German culture and the German book trade functioned in the first place as the principal natural intermediaries by means of which the 'frontiers' of Westernization were shifted progressively towards Central and Eastern Europe."[44]

41 Barbier, "La librairie allemande comme modèle?," 40f.
42 Barbier, "La librairie allemande comme modèle?," 41.
43 Barbier, "La librairie allemande comme modèle?," 42.
44 Barbier, "La librairie allemande comme modèle?," 45.

The First World War and the Versailles System

In the period between its foundation and the outbreak of the First World War (that is, for almost three decades), the Berne Union had enjoyed certain prestige and status as an international organization for the protection of authors' rights, but it had nevertheless barely expanded enough to corroborate its actual intention, that is, to embody a universal convention. Moreover, it was considered by many—particularly non-European states—to be a predominantly European creation, a treaty dominated by Europe.[45] Next to the ten member states that had signed the initial convention in 1886, another eight had joined in the following years.[46] This expansion was hardly noteworthy in light of the assumption that several smaller member states (e.g. Tunis, a member since 1887, or Haiti) represented satellites of stronger union members[47] or formed integrated subsystems of the established book trade conglomerates, for example Belgium, whose book trade was intricately linked to that of the French. Rising new regional powers in the midst of dynamic modernization and industrialization processes who were conscious of the capacities of new communication technologies and eager to access Western know-how, yet eschew Western domination, such as Meiji Japan, sought membership of the BU. Others, like tiny Montenegro, when faced with expensive membership costs, simply dropped out. This condition changed significantly with the end of the First World War, as its conclusion granted the Union a thrust of new members, including literally the whole region of Southeast and East Central Europe with the sole exception of Russia. The end of the First World War inaugurated a period of deliberate and vigorous expansion that lasted approximately until and including WWII. The Versailles treaties set the stage for a far more comprehensive period of development and intervention in the interwar period. The "prescribed accessions" of the new and old East Central and Southeast European states that took place in the context of the peace treaties reveal the Janus-faced quality of the BU: while on the one hand the Union raised the claim to function as a regulator of globalization, it functioned at the same time as an agent of globalization proper, that is, it purposefully exploited the same structures in order to promote the global expansion of IP.

45 Ulrich Uchtenhagen, "Zur Geschichte der amerikanischen Urheberrechts-Konventionen," in *Die Notwendigkeit des Urheberrechtsschutzes im Lichte seiner Geschichte*, ed. Robert Dittrich (ÖSGRUM, 9) (Vienna: MANZ'sche, 1991), 257.

46 See relevant discussion in Léon Malalpate, *Le Droit d'Auteur: Sa protection dans les rapports Franco-Étrangers* (Paris: Recueil Sirey, 1931), 118–21.

47 "Unter den 10 Gründerstaaten finden sich sieben europäische Länder; die beiden afrikanischen Staaten Liberia und Tunesien sowie das zentralamerikanische Haiti standen unter europäischem Einfluss und dienten vor allem der Stärkung der französischen Stellung." Uchtenhagen, "Zur Geschichte der amerikanischen Urheberrechts-Konventionen," 257.

Judging from the agenda for the post-WWI settlement, it can be broadly argued that the actors' main focus *in causa* IP resided in industrial property (patents and trademarks) rather than in copyright.[48] Authors' rights were clearly of secondary interest and were included at the tail end of more generic arrangements. The First World War created a new set of conditions altogether and raised new issues concerning both the Berne Union's legitimacy and its status postbellum.[49] The opinion was aired that the territorial changes effectuated through the war were bound to affect the Union's structure and make its revision inescapable. Confronted with such perspectives, the Union developed its own argumentative strategies in order to counter the allegations. The BU's official narrative emphasized the status of the BC as an international multilateral treaty. Given this, it was not affected or automatically abrogated by the outbreak of war as bilateral treaties were; different sides to the conflict, both Entente and Central Powers, were members of the Union. Additionally, the Union fashioned itself as a law-abiding gentlemen's agreement passionately sticking to its principles, a circumstance apparently demonstrated by the absence of serious violations and copyright infringements during the course of the war. Though this picture was perhaps a bit too euphemistic,[50] and disregarded confiscations and war provisions that automatically incapacitated copyright owners during the war, it nevertheless had a strong rhetorical effect. The bottom line of this string of arguments was that the Union's regime had remained intact and thus did not need to be enforced anew; the status quo antebellum had neither been injured nor compromised.[51]

The BU was clearly not disinclined to the idea of a territorial extension of its domain in the aftermath of war. The apple of discord concerned not the question of whether or not to expand, but rather the modality of expansion. The mode of thinking developed procedurally and was initially encouraged by arrangements that were peripheral to the war settlement. Such was the case with the commerce and navigation arrangement between Germany and Finland (March 7, 1918), who agreed to

---

48 See here Florian Mächtel, *Das Patentrecht im Krieg* (Geistiges Eigentum und Wettbewerbsrecht, 25) (Tübingen: Mohr Siebeck, 2009). Most recent publication on the treatment of industrial property in the context of the Versailles Treaty, see Nicolas Chachereau and Gabriel Galvez-Behar, "Patents, War and Peace. The resilience of the international patent order through the First World War," *Journal of European Integration History* 29, no.2 (2023): 205–226.

49 See here Isabella Löhr, *Die Globalisierung geistiger Eigentumsrechte: Neue Strukturen internationaler Zusammenarbeit 1886–1952* (Kritische Studien zur Geschichtswissenschaft, 195) (Göttingen: Vandenhoeck & Ruprecht, 2010), 85–113.

50 There had also been violations in the Union's core countries like Britain, France and Germany. For an article sympathetic to the Union's official argumentation, see Isabella Löhr, "Geistiges Eigentum in Kriegszeiten: Der Schutz von Urheberrechten und die Berner Übereinkunft im Ersten und Zweiten Weltkrieg," *Comparativ* 16, no. 5/6 (2006): 234–48.

51 "L'union international après la guerre," *Le Droit d'auteur*, year 31, no. 2, February 15, 1918, 15–17.

guarantee reciprocal protection of industrial and literary property according to the dispositions of the revised Paris Convention of 1911 and the revised Berne Convention of 1908. Similar rules were adopted between Austria-Hungary and Russia concerning industrial property. These regulations signified the implantation of the unionist regime in action, since they provided regulation between unionist and non-unionist countries according to the unionist framework without the parties having entered the Unions.[52]

Two things were clear concerning the post-war arrangements. First, both Unions (Paris and Berne) expected an upgrading of their function through their forthcoming association with the League of Nations. Second, the war settlement offered a rare window of opportunity and it was emphasized that the momentum should not be lost. As underscored by *Le Droit d'auteur*, "this extension of the sphere of influence of our two unions inaugurated properly the role that they will play in the future organization of the League of Nations [...] triggering the closer study of the circumstances around world peace. In fact, it is uniquely on such occasions and not in ordinary times that a measure of such considerable range as the collective recruitment of adherents to our international Unions can start to be calculated with certain chances of success."[53] Territorial expansion was also understood as justifiable compensation for the calamities and difficulties suffered during the war: "the rallying cry of humanity is at the current moment so solemn: law [...] the authors, artists, inventors, industrialists have cruelly suffered from the obstacles imposed upon their work through the world conflict. It is not enough to re-establish the protective regime in whose shade they will be able to materialize their efforts and apply their talents anew. They must have compensation. It is not much to ask to enlarge the terrain where they will exercise their undoubtedly useful activity, naturally on account of peaceful conquests, and thus let reign justice, good faith and loyalty among people in such delicate domains."[54]

The goal was clear: "the glimmers of a new epoch have already appeared on the horizon. The international Unions will become the pillars for the reconstruction of the social edifice, on condition that uniform rules are extended on all issues in such a manner as to augment the force and solidity of those Unions and if, at the same time, their action is enlarged through the participation of a much greater number of states. Our Unions, which are still international, will become universal."[55]

---

52 *Le Droit d'auteur*, year 32, no. 1, January 15, 1919.

53 *Le Droit d'auteur*, year 32, no. 1, January 15, 1919.

54 *Le Droit d'auteur*, year 32, no. 1, January 15, 1919.

55 *Le Droit d'auteur*, year 32, no. 1, January 15, 1919.

It must be mentioned here that articles in *Le Droit d'auteur* were often anonymous. Additionally, Jose Bellido has pointed out how the publication created the normative framework for a standardized and evolutionary understanding of the development of international copyright through classification and comparison between countries and world regions.[56] Due to this anonymity it is often practically impossible to trace either the sources or the agents of the narratives. Though anonymity is a common practice of newspaper editorials, entire sections in *Le Droit d'auteur* were sometimes published without any indication of authorship, somehow evoking the sensation of scientificity, neutrality and unanimity.

Whereas the BU's geographical expansion was clearly on the agenda, the visions of how to go about it differed. Though there were obviously two schools of thought, neither possessed clearly identifiable agency. The perpetrators of these agendas are never named overtly, nor are the positions discussed attributed to specific agents. The first school, most likely identical to the blueprints of the Berne Bureau, preferred a slow, gradual and voluntary accession of new member states. The second was keen on using the framework of the League of Nations, that is, the new framework offered by international law, to the benefit of a speedy extension of the Unions. The first scenario proposed that while waiting for the restart of negotiations on the subject of protection of literary and artistic property by treaty, a clause be inserted into the general peace treaty claiming that the affected countries would come to regulate their reciprocal copyright relations according to the standards of the revised Berne Convention of 1908. Non-union members would be given a kind of special status and the opportunity to familiarize themselves with the workings of the Union in practice. In time, they would be free to decide whether they preferred to return to the system of particular treaties or join the Union's legal regime, which in the past they had rejected as being too advanced for them. More to the point: "convinced of the mutual utility and liberty of the unionist regime, they would spontaneously instigate their accession to the Union under regular conditions. Provisional members would therefore be transformed into regular members to the greatest benefit of the universal republic of letters and the arts."[57]

This school of thought strongly opposed the idea of coercing states into union membership. Indeed, "speaking of the fortunes of the Union after the World War,

---

56 See Jose Bellido, "The Editorial Quest for International Copyright (1886–1896)," *Book History* 17 (2014): 380–405. It is more that ironic than the main publishing organ of the organization for the protection (and emancipation) of authors' rights functioned every so often without identifiable authors.

57 "L'union international après la guerre," *Le Droit d'auteur*, year 31, no. 2, February 15, 1918, 16f.

certain milieus are already obviously occupied with the extension of our 'syndicate,' an extension which they dream to attain not through the slow and painstaking path of ordinary recruitment of new members but through faster and more ambitious means to be furnished by the constitution of the League of Nations [...] [A] coercion of this kind regarding the domain of intellectual rights seems to us to conform little to the historical past and the general tendencies of the BU. Another suggestion, which would reserve for states their liberty of action, would better achieve the envisioned goal."[58]

In order to understand why the gradualist approach failed and the political fast-track solution triumphed, it is necessary to embed it into the logic both of the international law treaty and the new economic and commercial prospects created through the territorial reorganization of the East Central European space.

International peace treaties—and this constitutes a truism ever since the Treaty of Westphalia—do not merely establish peace; they ascertain and sanction new world orders and as such also prescribe the conditions and principles governing the new world order.[59] Connecting intellectual property with the Versailles peace treaties system and the emerging League of Nations meant an enormous upgrading of that institution. These systems endowed IP with a political flavor, which, although always having been present in a rather diffuse manner, had never been as clearly articulated. The new political validation signaled that IP was to become a significant (political) instrument with the capacity to structure and codify international relations. This was in addition to the regulatory function it served vis-à-vis commercial and cultural relations up to that point. The deployment of copyright as an instrument capable of structuring political relationships was no novelty. During the first two decades of the twentieth century, Spain consciously put copyright bilateralism to use, in order to strengthen its (multiple) relations to Latin America, and perhaps also with the ulterior motive of creating a separate Ibero-American multilateral copyright convention as an alternative to Berne (an option, however, that never materialized).[60]

58 "L'union international après la guerre," *Le Droit d'auteur*, year 31, no. 2, February 15, 1918, 16.

59 It is thus not a coincidence that in the case of such major peace treaties, negotiations extend over a protracted period of time. For example, the Versailles system extended from 1919 to 1923, the year that the Treaty of Lausanne, the last peace treaty with Turkey, was signed. Not only do international peace treaties carry the advantage of bringing a substantial number of participants around the same table, both winners and losers (as perhaps no other political forum can do), they moreover have the capacity to dictate and have conditions accepted that under other circumstances would have been unattainable.

60 Jose Bellido, "Latin American and Spanish Copyright Relations (1880–1904)," *The Journal of World Intellectual Property* 12, no. 1 (2009): 1–39.

The First World War changed the geographical map of East and Southeast Europe in a decisive manner. It instigated the demise of the long-lived multicultural empires of the East (Russian, Habsburg and Ottoman), affirmed an ethnicized concept of the nation and saw the triumph of the nation state principle. The end of the conflict witnessed the creation of a series of new states by reorganizing space into new political and socio-economic units. Both winners and losers of the war, including all of the newcomer states of East Central Europe, were obligated via clauses inserted into the Paris peace system to pass national copyright laws and to accede to the Berne Union within twelve months of the coming into force of their respective treaties. The states involved included Austria, Yugoslavia and Czechoslovakia through the *Treaty of Saint-Germaine-en-Laye* (September 10, 1919), Bulgaria though the *Treaty of Neuilly-sur-Seine* (November 27, 1919), Hungary through the *Treaty of Grande-Trianon* (June 4, 1920) and Turkey through the *Treaty of Lausanne* (July 24, 1923). Bulgaria and Turkey would concurrently accede to the 1883 Paris Convention for the Protection of Industrial Property. Austria-Hungary had already been part of that Union. The fact that accessions had been dictated met with the disapproval of several contemporary commentators, who raised doubts as to the ulterior motives behind the accessions.[61]

The success of the design to upgrade and solidify IP by anchoring it to international law was confirmed by a series of additional accessions in the 1920s, which brought an even greater number of East and Southeast European states into the unionist regime. Poland, the free city of Danzig and Greece acceded in 1920, and over the course of that same decade, Romania, Finland and the first South American state, Brazil, joined in. Turkey raised reservations[62] concerning translation rights, a position it would consistently defend in later years, and moreover forewent the one-year deadline from the coming into effect of the Lausanne Treaty. Turkish reservations concerned the freedom of translation of works into the Turkish language, and went beyond a mere reservation about being governed by a previous text of the Convention. On the contrary, accession was to be on the condition that Turkey intended to ignore any provision of the Convention related to translation rights. Turkey's standpoint concerning translation rights appeared insupportable to a number of Union states, and above all to the ALAI.[63] Moreover, its radical

61 See for example Malalpate, *Le Droit d'Auteur*, 147. "Ces accessions forcées aux Unions ont été sévèrement critiquées. Il faut reconnaître que c'est là un procédé assez bizarre, qui ne se concilie guère avec l'esprit qui règne généralement dans une Union."

62 See Stephen P. Ladas, *The International Protection of Literary and Artistic Property* (New York: Macmillan, 1938), vol. I: 119f.

63 Ladas, *The International Protection of Literary and Artistic Property,* 119f.

position on a topic so central to the BU is conducive to the assumption that the Turkish government was consciously practising a policy of obstruction. Turkey remained outside the unionist regime until the early 1950s.

To underscore once more the political implications in the connection between the Versailles system and the BU accession patterns, it is instructive to take a closer look at the case of Greece. Copyright issues had strained bilateral Greek-French relationships since the beginning of the twentieth century and there had been intensified pressure on the Greek government to accede to the BU. Greek "pirating" of French cultural goods resulted in the country falling into disfavor with French authorities, perceptible also in the ensuing distancing of the French embassy in Athens from the Greek government.[64] World War I changed this constellation, yet in unanticipated ways.

Greece was among the winners of the war and the Versailles settlement. On October 27/November 9, 1920[65] the country acceded to the 1908 Rome Revision of the Berne Convention with a series of substantial reservations appended. These reservations concerned the right of translation, the right of performance of theatrical works in translation as well as the right of reproduction of articles from journals and magazines. The most significant reservation, however, concerned the protection of the rights of foreign authors, which in a certain way meant an abrogation of one of the most important pillars of the unionist regime. Foreign authors would enjoy protection only to the degree provided by Greek copyright law. Consequently, the minimum standard of protection provided automatically by the Union's regime was rendered inoperative. In other words, the direct application of the provisions of the Convention, that is, *ex iure conventionis*, was made impossible. The accession was ratified by royal decree (16/March 31, 1921) and not through parliament, which according to Greek jurists was the reason for the institutionalization of such a precarious legal regime. In reality, the ratification created a legal status contrary to the BC to which Greece formally acceded.[66]

With historical retrospection and a dose of historical intuition, the mode and procedure of accession seem to suggest two things: first, that action was taken in

64 See here Manolis Seiragakis, *To elafro mousiko theatro stin mesopolemiki Athina* (Athens: Kastaniotis, 2009), 79–80.

65 Old and new calendar.

66 See Giorgos Koumanos, *Pnevmatiki idioktisia* (Athens: Sakoulas, 1995), 21f. Koumanos's book is a legal textbook and therefore references to the history of copyright in Greece are presented in a rather factual and cursory manner and not via insights gained through archival research. Greek jurists themselves are astounded at the precariousness of the legal regime, which was perpetuated in that form until the mid-1950s. I am inclined to believe that a better and more sophisticated exegesis can be won by placing the 1920 accession of Greece to the BU in the political and diplomatic context of the times, which I will attempt in the following.

haste; second, that accession was not exactly voluntary, but rather (in the best-case scenario) took place as part of a deal. It appears therefore much more instructive to contextualize the act in the framework of developments in and around the year 1920, namely, Greece's participation in the *Treaty of Sèvres* (August 10, 1920). Signed between the Entente and the Ottoman Empire in that same year, the treaty also officially marked the beginning of the partitioning of the latter, a process that had already informally started by 1915. Greece was rewarded with territorial concessions (occupation and administration of the Smyrna enclave, Eastern Thrace and the islands of Imvros and Tenedos) and was therefore certainly grateful and probably indebted to its Entente allies for having helped to materialize its irredentist agenda. It is highly doubtful that Greek diplomats would deny their allies anything that would endanger the country's geopolitical objectives and IP was—from the perspective of this greater political context— simply a trifle. Lastly, the sequence of events (signing of the Treaty of Sèvres in August 1920, accession to the BC in November 1920) seems to corroborate exactly this interpretation (whose pattern fits quite well with the accession pattern of the rest of the Southeast and East Central European countries). It is also interesting to observe the different treatment given to Greece and Turkey regarding their respective reservations.[67] On another note, Greece's accession to the BU had paradoxically unanticipated by-effects. Instead of augmenting the volume of French cultural imports, it led for financial reasons to a reorientation of Greek cultural entrepreneurs towards German cultural production.[68]

67 One can only speculate as to ulterior motives behind this differentiated treatment. Perhaps it was the result of the winner-loser syndrome, or the consequence of an orientalist bias.

68 After Venizelos signed Greece's accession to the BU, French writers demanded as a rule 1000 French francs in advance royalty payments, plus 6% royalties from ticket revenues for the staging of their plays. These conditions made French plays unaffordable for Greek circumstances. The required sums were simply exuberant and signified the economic ruin of any theatrical company if the play was not a guaranteed commercial success. In addition, in the 1920s the currency exchange rate was altogether unfavorable for the procurement of foreign copyrights. Around 1922, the minimum copyright fee for foreign authors was 2500 drachmas. According to Seiragakis, in 1926 the exchange rate between the French franc and the Greek drachma was 1:3 and advance royalties amounted to 1000–1500 francs. He attributes the decline of the staging of foreign (French) operetta performances in Greece in that year to precisely this reason. Moreover, it was observed that plays that had actually been rehearsed and were all set for the stage were sometimes withdrawn out of fear that their revenues were insufficient to pay for the advance royalties. The prohibitive costs meant that stage owners and theatrical entrepreneurs turned to Germany and German plays. Copyright rates for Viennese operettas, for example, were not significantly lower (they amounted to approximately 10% of gross revenues), but no advance royalty payment was required, and this provided entrepreneurs with leeway regarding the exact sum to be paid at the end. Germany's battered economy and lower exchange rates made trade with this country more affordable and attractive, and was the main reason for the reorientation of Greek impresarios and theatre producers towards German cultural production. Seiragakis, *To elafri mousiko theatro*, 79–82.

In summary, the expansion of the BU in the aftermath of the First World War was a conscious, encompassing and calculated internationalization of IPRs and moreover signified a substantial breakthrough for the status of IP as an institution. In one coup it brought about an important territorial expansion of the Union's legal regime, transforming it from a predominantly West European into an overall European affair (excepting Russia). In doing so, it thus augmented not only the legal reach but also the subsequent coding of inter- and cross-cultural relations according to the logic of IP. The conjunction of IP and international law provided both the BU and the institution of IP with surplus value and tied IP even more closely to the principle of nationality. Naturally, the question could be raised here as to whether or not international law itself at the time was conceptualized as a civilizing mission, a position that would fit quite well with the alleged "civilizing" mission of IPRs.[69] The originators of the strategy to politicize IP and use the Versailles system as a floodgate to this end cannot be identified with certainty.[70] In all likelihood the enlargement process is to be credited to the initiatives of France (and its allies) and reflects the intention of France and its cultural industry to ascertain their position and enhance

[69] The narrative topos claiming IP to be an attribute and characteristic of civilized nations is ubiquitous in the late nineteenth and early twentieth centuries. It can be found literally on every second page in the literature of that period, particularly in French works. With respect to international law, see Martti Koskenniemi, *The Gentle Civilizer of Nations: The Rise and Fall of International Law 1870–1960* (Cambridge: Cambridge University Press, 2001).

[70] I found only one laconic reference in *Le Droit d'auteur*, where in a very general manner gratitude was expressed to the ALAI (Association littéraire et artistique internationale) and the "Syndicat pour la protection de la propriété intellectuelle" for all the preparatory and lobbying work they carried out in the context of the peace treaties. "[P]laced at the centre of events, those two institutions worked assiduously and also in a very discrete manner for the extension of the BU. The first started last June a campaign aiming at the representatives of the non-unionist countries, which participated in the conference in order to get them interested in the work of the Union and remains in contact with them in expectation that this awakened interest might be transformed into something more tangible. The second corporation took a political initiative (démarche) with the French ministry of foreign affairs with the goal of obtaining the adherence of the US in the BU." *Le Droit d'auteur*, year 33, no. 1, 15.1.1920, 6. Due to the fact that both organizations constituted non-transparent assemblages of very diverse agents ranging from diplomats and politicians to authors, representatives of professional organizations and lobbies, and were moreover nodal points of networks with far-reaching ramifications, I consider the statement to indicate in fact little about the actual masterminds of the operation. Neither was I very successful in identifying concrete actors in my research in the French Diplomatic Archives in *La Courneuve*. There I concentrated predominantly on the committees dealing with economic aspects of the Versailles settlement. Even there I found no concrete reference to the accession process. It could well be that I overlooked something; the French archival collections on the Versailles treaties are vast and I had to orient myself according to their catalogues. I therefore maintain a certain reservation as to the exhaustiveness of my research. At the same time, I find the opaqueness surrounding the operation of "prescribed" accessions to the BU and the invisibility and anonymity of concrete actors to be quite an interesting indicator.

their influence in the region of *Mitteleuropa*.[71] IP was to be one of the instruments they used to help cement that influence, all the more so since the newly reorganized space also opened up new commercial prospects propelled through the creation of new and multiple national markets.

The enforced accessions therefore served several objectives simultaneously. They presented the BU's unique chance to finally incorporate "the Slavs," who had stubbornly resisted joining the unionist regime, into its legal structure.[72] Though procuring rights to works was not an unknown practice, it was not the rule, and there was a tendency in large parts of East and Southeast Europe (particularly in former Ottoman dominions) to ignore copyrights, borrow and adapt freely, partially due to established practice and mentalities and partially in order to evade costs. At the same time, judging from the geography of expansion, it is indeed hard to overlook the fact that it predominantly concerned territories traditionally belonging to the German book-trading sphere. Attachment to the BU meant a reshuffling of the framework, the parameters, the practices and the priorities governing the regional book trade. It also meant a shift in the logic of governance: a shift from the networked German (quasi monopolistic) commercial regime to a legal regime warranting the ex-territorialization of territorial rights within a system of international obligations and supervision. Next to the political capital to be accrued through the winning over of new allies positively predisposed towards Entente countries, it was also possible to engage them in formal relationships governed by international law. Finally, there were serious revenues to be recuperated, also considered by some—as exemplified by previous quotes—to be a legitimate form of indirect reparations.[73] Political, geostrategic and commercial dimensions and motivations all went hand in hand.

There was indeed a need to hurry, not merely because the post-war settlement offered a unique chance of intervention and the opportunity to enforce legal obligations. New forms of mass spectacle, stage entertainment and musical theatre that had been

---

71 *Nota bene*: even French diplomatic circles occasionally used the German term "Mitteleuropa" to refer to East Central Europe (next of course to "Europe Centrale"). By doing so they referred not simply to a region but also to a *region/power concept* as actually intended by the initial German coinage. This circumstance serves as an additional indicator not only of the preponderance of German mental maps, but also of the awareness within French political elites of the German influence in the area.

72 See here: "Études générales, Le vingt-cinquième anniversaire de la convention de Berne du 9 Septembre 1886," *Le Droit d'auteur*, year 24, no. 9, September 15, 1911, 121.

73 As argued by Daniela Caglioti, the First World War was a "watershed in the conception of property rights" and a proper departure from the liberal conception of the inviolability of property; see Daniela L. Caglioti, "Property Rights in Time of Wars: Sequestration and Liquidation of Enemy Aliens' Assets in Western Europe during the First World War," *Journal of Modern European History* 12, no. 4 (Aliens and Internal Enemies during the First World War) (2014): 523–45.

gestating since the last decades of the nineteenth century—like varieté, revue, operetta, cabaret, comic operas, musical comedies and eventually the musical—mostly French but also Viennese, and from the 1920s progressively also of US provenance, were conquering the stages of the world in their original or adapted versions. The social and cultural elites of East and Southeast Europe had been progressively nationalizing since the nineteenth century, switching from cosmopolitan cultural consumption (often also performed by foreign touring theatrical ensembles) to increased local production, a process that was enhanced after WWI. It was only a matter of time until local cultural creators, who learned quickly by copying tirelessly, could reproduce the same genres on a level professional enough to compete with the foreign prototypes and able to address the needs of national audiences.

At the same time, the period around World War I ushered in a new era of internationalization of media and culture. The last decades of the nineteenth and first decades of the twentieth centuries had witnessed the introduction of a series of innovations (cinema, gramophone recording and radio) that signalled the ascent of a new, technology-led, cultural industry, whose proper application became widespread in the interwar period. In contrast to previous periods, which had, in general, witnessed improvements of already existing technologies, the new broadcasting media heralded a real breakthrough that made possible the recording of images, motion and sound.[74] They buttressed new forms in the private consumption of culture, as well as the spectacular and unprecedented rise of mass entertainment. In contrast to the consumption of the book, the new cultural opportunities required no previously acquired abilities, like reading skills, in order to be appreciated and understood. Rather, relying on the power of image and sound, they could be consumed instantaneously, making it much easier to address, include and attract the lower social strata as well. What is more, the consumption of new genres like silent film or jazz music relied on new international semiotics of image and sound and could thereby be consumed globally, beyond language barriers.

With the expansion of show business, the massification of culture, the proliferation of new media and the German economy in disarray, there were multiple reasons why the timing of the peace settlement was convenient for IP lobbyists. Finally, the whole episode is perhaps also telling with regard to the governance structures of the BU. The fact that the Berne Bureau was unable to maintain and push through its own blueprints for the post-war era (gradual and voluntary enlargement for Southeast and East Central Europe) is a barometer of its actual authority. It appears that not only was

[74] Sassoon, *The Culture of the Europeans*, 595.

it unable to enforce its own concept of a neutral organization standing above politics, but it also succumbed to the political will of stronger actors, whose decisions it embraced in the end. Altogether, the picture points at a feeble and only formally sovereign institution. The system's actual puppeteers remain barely visible in the background.

The motivations of the various actors involved in the international settlement were quite diverse, and what is more, as can be judged by the case of Greece and others, were guided in no small measure by a certain politics of duplicity. What is astounding about this is how little it had to do with copyright as such, confirming the thesis about the politicization of the institution. In their majority, the states that were brought to accede to the BU were net importers of cultural goods with a natural inclination for protectionist policies. As such, they had little interest in the free trade philosophy and the legal symmetry provided by the Union's regime. For small actors (small or newly created states), accession to the BU likely represented the lesser evil. Moreover, it provided them with the opportunity to demonstrate their good will, thus accruing important symbolic and political capital that could be exchanged to promote their own "real political" interests (territorial claims, for example). Most significantly, inclusion into an international law treaty and an international organization such as the BU provided small states and new actors just entering the arena of international politics with the recognition and legitimacy in international relations they so desired. Inclusion in the BU put them definitively on the map of "respectable" nations. Finally, there was one other aspect related to the Union's codification of culture that could possibly appeal to young and only recently consolidated nation states.

As can be ascertained from various expositions in the Union's official organ, *Le Droit d'auteur*, the Union promoted a very specific notion of culture.[75] Its very essence was high and elite culture and it painstakingly perpetrated the cult of the literary genius, whose works both encapsulated the spirit of the nation and also stood as an example of the nation's literary and artistic achievements around the world.[76] This literary classification process was not only hierarchical but also tended to place national literary canons in relation to each other (for example, Bulgaria also has its Goethe). The end result was the sacralization of a pantheon of the leading literary geniuses of the nation, the absolute majority of whom, it goes without saying, were

[75] The journal's articles usually took the form of expositions on copyright developments in relevant countries and customarily also included brief overviews of intellectual and literary developments in these countries.

[76] See Anne-Marie Thiesse, *La fabrique de l'ecrivain national: Entre littérature et politique* (Paris: Gallimard, 2009).

men. Such a codification corresponded quite well with the Herderian principles (one people, one language, one literature) that those young nations would employ in order to retrospectively codify their often enmeshed history and literature.[77] Moreover, this circumstance provides for an interesting observation regarding the mirroring effects of nationalism. Observed from the reverse side of the mirror, that is, not from the side of those who are seeing themselves in it, but from the side of those who are holding the mirror, the nation of high culture was not simply the product of the imagined community of aspiring nations, but also the sole identity offered by the international community for entry into the world of civilization (that is, in order to join the club of "civilized people"). In other words, the proposal offered by the consolidated nation states of Western Europe to the rest of the world was nothing but a mirror image of themselves.[78]

The fact that such considerations weighed into the calculations of national actors is proven by debates on the advantages and disadvantages of accession to the BU that took place in interwar Czechoslovakia. This was a country that could, after all, count itself among the small number of culture-exporting states in the region, even if it was only a modest one in comparison to the core countries. Responding to critical voices pointing at the asymmetrical balance of trade, Czechoslovakia's primary copyright expert, Jan Löwenbach, argued that it was imperative to dodge the derogatory label and potential status of a "pirate state," and stressed the significance of such a step in order for Czechoslovakia to be appreciated internationally as a culturally active, respectable state.[79] The framing of the discourse demonstrates well the degree to which the civilizational rhetoric had both an enticing and a disciplining effect upon its recipients.[80] "Piracy," framed as the complete antithesis of propriety

77 For an interesting discussion on the real and/or retrospectively fabricated influence of Herder, see Marie-Elizabeth Ducreux, "Langue et Histoire. L'Europe centrale entre l'érudition et la tradition, 1760–1810 (ou: quelques réflexions autour de Schlözer, Herder, Dobrovský et Dobner)," in Barbier, *Est–Ouest*, 263–82.

78 It can be argued that world exhibitions since the late nineteenth century had a similar "civilizing" effect. By putting on show the technological and artistic achievements, the splendour and wealth of expanding nation states and the vastness and variety of their colonial empires, they created the stage and the script used in the competition among nations regarding the meaning of progress and national achievement.

79 Jan Löwenbach, "Hospodářské důsledky zvýšené autorské ochrany," *Soutěz a Tvorba* 2 (1929): 43.

80 On how international copyright was aligned with a discourse about "civilization" and "progress," and how this affected the decisions of other world peripheries about whether or not to participate in the Berne Union, see Sara Bannerman, "'We Are All Developing Countries': Canada and International Copyright History. Fault Lines in the Map of International Copyright," in *Copyright Future Copyright Freedom: Marking the 40th Anniversary of the Commencement of Australia's Copyright Act 1968*, eds. Brian Fitzgerald and Benedikt Atkinson (Sydney: Sydney University Press, 2011), online version, no pagination.

and hard labor, has been, and still is, one of the most durable and diachronic motives for the justification of IP discourse. It has moreover helped to cement the aura of political correctness and the morally superior stance that have been associated with IP in international relations.[81]

Though rhetorically the connection between civilization, high(brow), qualitative culture and copyright was underlined, in practice the main areas targeted by international copyright (intervention) were the most commercialized sectors of the cultural economy. The rhetorical framing of copyright (that is, ownership of intellectual labor and the market-based exchange of knowledge) as civilization overrode other forms of productivity in the creation of knowledge and culture. This included concepts such as exchange, reciprocation, gift, association, sharing, emotion, passion or curiosity and largely underplayed the social character of authors' rights. The same rhetoric "blackboxed,"[82] that is, rendered invisible, the commercial and financial interests that were also involved in the regulation of the international IP regime. In fact, though largely regulating the exchange of "commodities," concepts like "market" or "trade" are barely to be found in the international sources. The civilizational rhetoric concealed not only the aspect of power relations in the global production of knowledge but also the deep asymmetries in the distribution of that knowledge.

The post-war period decidedly changed the map of East and Southeast Europe, and along with the creation of new nation states it also inaugurated a new chapter in the history of copyright in the region.

Conclusion

In this chapter, I have proposed viewing the Versailles settlement as a particular breakthrough inaugurating a period with strong *propertization*[83] tendencies. The initiative

81 There are several analyses that offer fascinating perspectives on the historical development of the notion and "practice" of "piracy." Exemplarily, see William St. Clair, "Metaphors of Intellectual Property," in *Privilege and Property: Essays on the History of Copyright*, eds. Ronan Deazley, Martin Kretschmer and Lionel Bently (Cambridge: Open Books Publishers, 2013), 369–95; Mark Rose, "Copyright and Its Metaphors," *UCLA Law Review* 50 (2002): 1–16; several articles in the collective volume edited by Lionel Bently, Jennifer Davis and Jane C. Ginsburg, *Copyright and Piracy: An Interdisciplinary Critique* (Cambridge: Cambridge University Press, 2010); Adrian Johns, *Piracy: The Intellectual Property Wars from Gutenberg to Gates* (Chicago: University of Chicago Press, 2009).

82 For the concept of "blackboxing," see Bruno Latour, *Pandora's Hope: Essays on the Reality of Science Studies* (Cambridge, Mass.: Harvard University Press, 1999).

83 By propertization, I refer to the tendency to increasingly conceive of and regulate relationships

for this offensive came largely from France and reflected the intention to regain the political, economic and cultural ground the state had lost to its main rivals (England and Germany) in the course of the nineteenth century. IP was part and parcel of a much more comprehensive cultural foreign policy and diplomatic practice that had strong geopolitical connotations, at a precise moment in time when the French language (and by extension French publishing) appeared to be losing its universalist hold over the world. Representing a French triumph, it also signaled the beginning of the French decline as the leading force in the regulation of international copyright, a slow changing-of-the-guard and the end of an era in this respect.

Paradoxically, even though the interwar period marked the end of the first period of globalization (1870–1914), at the same time it ushered in an era of increased internationalization of cultural commodities, genres and media, and an intensification of international exchange. On the one hand, this deepened competition between the national content industries, and on the other, it led to intensified efforts for supranational and transnational regulation. Despite the fact that the interwar period witnessed the multiplication of stakeholders in the international trade in cultural goods, with the noticeable entry of the US as a major producer of films and music challenging European supremacy, the French were able to retain the prerogative of action, lead the efforts towards internationalization and set the agenda for IP regulation for most of that period. This constellation changed irrevocably by the beginning of the 1940s with the anticipated creation of UNESCO, which signaled an unambiguous change of leadership and the passing of the initiative regarding international copyright to the Anglo-American block.

Second, I have made a strong argument for the political function of IP (that is, beyond its legal, economic and cultural function). Herewith, I refer to something more than the inclination of diverse political systems to instrumentalize IP to serve their own political/ideological ends. Intellectual Property Rights (IPRs) acquire a distinct political quality when they can assist in the extension and consolidation of new world orders that require a reordering and/or rescaling of territorial space according to the needs of a new or expanding (knowledge) economy. Furthermore, throughout its history, IP has functioned with the capacity to structure political relations both as a coercive and soft power instrument.

---

in culture, science and economics through the property paradigm. Propertization in this context means that exclusive claims to the exploitation, control and use of tangible and intangible assets are regulated and established by means of theories, concepts and norms concerning property. See here Hannes Siegrist, "Die Propertisierung von Gesellschaft und Kultur: Konstruktion und Institutionalisierung des Eigentums in der Moderne," *Comparativ* 16, no. 5/6 (special issue: *Entgrenzung des Eigentums in modernen Gesellschaften und Rechtskulturen*, ed. H. Siegrist) (2006): 9–52.

Finally, I propose viewing the expansion of the institution of IP in East Central and Southeast Europe in the context of the Versailles treaties settlement and the efforts to establish a first Universal Convention in the 1930s as one block or as one interrelated strategy of expansion. The internationalization and universalization of IPRs in the interwar period aimed at "subduing" two of the areas most resistant to the extension of the Berne Union's legal regime: Europe's eastern multinational empires and the Americas, who were at that time organized within an independent and strongly protectionist Pan-American Union. Both initiatives reflect the intention to promote the regulation of international copyright relations according to the Western European liberal model and bring the European and extra-European peripheries into this scheme of cultural exchange. Though complementing each other on a functional level, the two initiatives contrast nicely with respect to the ways in which they were staged and the forums through which they were promoted. This indicates at the same time the possibilities and limits of politics: one based on an international law treaty with the capacity to prescribe rules (Versailles settlement), the other aiming at a Universal Convention necessitating broad international consensus. It was perhaps these different circumstances that determined in each case their real chances of success.[84]

[84] I must clarify at this point that I do not have the capacity to support my argument concerning the Universal Convention with archival material from the Americas. My work focuses predominantly on East and Southeast Europe in the twentieth century. Nevertheless, I would still like to advance the argument concerning the *relative "symmetry" of intentions* between the enlargement process in the context of the Versailles treaties and the Universal Convention. I do this in the hope that this argument might provide the incentive for more detailed research in this direction and that scholars working on North and South America might take up the task.

Chapter 7
Interwar Bulgaria

Before Copyright

The first attempts to regulate intellectual professions in the Bulgarian kingdom (founded in 1878) were linked to the advancement of printing and the press and were directly or indirectly associated with censorship in a manner reminiscent of the Ancient Regime. Conforming with Michel Foucault's typology of the "author function,"[1] which attributes the rise of the legal figure of the author, in the first place, to his ability to carry penal responsibility for transgressive discourses, the appearance of the professional author in Bulgaria was closely connected to penalizing or interdictory objectives. The legal conception of authorship designated less the author's prerogative to control and trade his texts in a market and more the capacity of authorities to attribute texts to the author's person. In the late nineteenth and early twentieth centuries, the figure of the author and consequently the question of authorship and ownership of texts was unstable and inconsistent. Printing acts correlated with politics and were mainly concerned with: (1) the political balance between government and opposition; and (2) the place of the press as an independent force in political life.

Professing to the liberal spirit of the times, the first Bulgarian constitution (the Tărnovo Constitution of 1879) guaranteed the freedom of the press (art. 79) and the absence of censorship. In case of damage or injury, the law established cascading accountability. Liable in the first place was the author, and where absent or anonymous, responsibility plummeted in progression to the remaining stakeholders: the publisher, the printer and eventually the supplier.[2]

---

1 Michel Foucault, "What Is an Author?" in *Aesthetics, Method and Epistemology*, ed. James D. Faubion (New York: The New York Press, 1998), 206–222. See also Vasil Zagorov, "Iz istorijata na avtorskoto pravo v Bălgarija (1878–1948)," *Biblioteka* 1 (2013): 25.

2 Lăčezar Georgiev, *Teorija na knigoizdatelskija process, aspekti, problem, tendencii* (Veliko Tărnovo: Universitetsko izdatelstvo "Sv. sv. Kiril i Metodii," 2001), 44–45.

Applied in Bulgaria in 1881, the 1865 Ottoman press law made private persons liable for periodical publications even if responsibility was carried collectively, for example by a society or an organization. The law was particularly vigilant regarding injuries committed against the king. The same year witnessed the introduction of an obligatory registration of all periodical editions, going hand in hand with the duty of all publishers to deliver—equivalently to the 1865 Ottoman law—an exemplar of every published issue to the Ministry of Internal Affairs, to which responsibility for printed materials was thereafter transferred.[3]

Repressive measures were introduced in 1883 through the law on criminal acts against the prince (decree no. 334/4), while the same year witnessed the publication of the first Bulgarian press law. This law stipulated the liberty to establish printing presses (although it made registration with the district administrator mandatory) and to publish books and brochures, provided that the names of both publisher and printer featured on the publication (otherwise fines between 50 and 300 leva applied). Periodical publications required no special licence but only a written request to the Ministry of Internal Affairs, while the owner of the printing press was required to publish his business's name and signature on every printed copy, otherwise he became liable to imprisonment (between five days and three months) or fines (between 50 and 500 leva) and the confiscation of the entire edition. The law also introduced the practice of the legal deposit. Publishers of periodical publications and books were obliged to donate two exemplars of each new publication to the National Library in Sofia. In legal terms, the law established the shared responsibility of the author, the editor and the publisher. Injuries against the king and the monarchy, state institutions and government officials were severely punished. Though the Bulgarian law was more democratic than its 1865 Ottoman equivalent, it nevertheless clashed on several points with the liberal spirit of the constitution. Control over the author's personality was apparently intensified.[4]

The 1883 law was repealed and replaced in 1885 through the "law-supplement to the penal code concerning offences of the press," which was somewhat more liberal in character. Censorship of the author and his works was abandoned, cascading responsibility established, punishment for defamation of private persons was reduced and penalties for defamation against the government in the press relaxed, if the defendant could prove the legal basis of his action and demonstrate the accuracy of his claims. Obstacles to the establishment of printing presses were removed, barring the

3 Georgiev, *Teorija na knigoizdatelskija process*, 45–46.
4 Georgiev, *Teorija na knigoizdatelskija process*, 46–47.

responsibility to publish the printer's name and location in the publication; non-compliance was punished with imprisonment (up to six months) and fines of between 20 and 2000 leva. Authors were forbidden to publish under pseudonyms, though no sanctions were taken against them. The measure targeted rather the practice of publishing under a "false name," in which case the responsibility for the publication fell onto the publisher. In cases of confiscations, injunctions were filed by legal rather than administrative institutions in order to guarantee a more democratic procedure.[5]

A new press law was issued in 1887, regulating the rights of the author, printer, publisher and purveyor. It placed the figure of the editor ("redaktor") of periodical publications in the foreground, making the divulgence of his name along with those of the publisher and printer of the publication mandatory. According to the 1887 law, it was the editor who carried responsibility for the publication in administrative, legal and penal terms, and his responsibility differed from that of both the author and the publisher. Under certain circumstances, the author could also be held accountable for the injury along with the editor and the publisher, if the latter was a different person than the editor. Interestingly, in the text, the legal person of the editor, designated as "spisatel" (which means author), is made responsible for the publication as the carrier of the author's rights and by consequence of authorial responsibility.[6] These vague and interchangeable roles reflected the incipient process of professionalization in the field of publishing that eventually took a more stable shape in the first decades of the twentieth century.

Changes to the 1887 press law towards the end of the century once again curtailed authors' rights. The most drastic measures concerned the introduction of internal monitoring and censorship, evident in the chief editor's capacity to censor the author, since the former was now made solely responsible for committed injuries instead of the publication's actual author. Incarceration (of one to six months) or a fine (of 100 leva) also threatened the printer, who, motivated by the same concerns, likewise censored publications. Moreover, certification of secondary school education was made a qualification criterion for the publisher's profession.[7] Issued in 1900, the "temporal regulations" evidenced a strong inclination towards censorship, which besides the press encompassed all publications (books, brochures) of a political character. The printer was now placed at the top of the responsibility ladder and asked to certify a series of requirements, such as the publisher's age (at least 30 years old),

[5] Georgiev, *Teorija na knigoizdatelskija process,* 47–48.

[6] Georgiev, *Teorija na knigoizdatelskija process,* 48.

[7] Georgiev, *Teorija na knigoizdatelskija process,* 49.

educational level (higher education) and the editor's residence (which had to be congruent with the location in which the publication was issued). On the grounds of the collaborative principle, both author and publisher were commonly held accountable for the publication. At the same time, fines were raised and it became impossible for one person to be the editor of more than one serial publication.[8]

A major turn for the better came in 1901 when democratic changes in politics affected publishing as well. The old press law and all previous ordinances were repealed and new liberal legislation re-established the freedom of speech. Turning to the Tărnovo Constitution, the law established cascading responsibility of the author (when identified and living in the principality), the publisher (if the author was unknown and not living in the kingdom), the printer (if the publisher was unknown) and the supplier (if the printer was unknown). Missing in this constellation was the figure of the editor. With decision no. 112 (March 23, 1905), the supreme court of cassation specified as "author" the periodical's chief editor, held accountable for all materials of the publication and all articles carrying his signature. The 1901 law affirmed that all Bulgarian citizens of age with a permanent residence in Bulgaria could be "authors" and/or "publishers." All restrictions on the import of foreign literature, books and magazines were removed.[9]

Evidently, the "author" occupied a leading position in the different legislative initiatives of the late nineteenth and early twentieth centuries. Sometimes he was ascribed an independent status, and sometimes he shared responsibility with the other participants of the publishing chain along with the publisher, printer and trader. The figure of the chief editor made its appearance towards the end of the nineteenth century, identified at times as the author, while at other times his competences exceeded the parameters of authorship and he switched position to become the author's censor. The printer was at times also installed as a censor of the author, the publisher and the publication. Though principally targeting the press, regulations were often imposed on authors of books and brochures as well, extending the reach of censorship over the rest of the publishing sector. In the first decades after Bulgaria's liberation, the author and his writings—periodical publications as well as books—were feared. This goes to explain the drastic measures imposed as well as the regular violation of the Tărnovo Constitution and its liberal spirit.[10]

The first provisions regulating the publishing contract appeared in the seventh section of the 1897 Commercial Law. Article 432 stipulated the necessity to conclude

8 Georgiev, *Teorija na knigoizdatelskija process*, 50.
9 Georgiev, *Teorija na knigoizdatelskija process*, 51.
10 Georgiev, *Teorija na knigoizdatelskija process*, 51–52.

a contract between the author and/or his successors in title and the person, who received the exclusive right to reproduce, publish and distribute a literary, technical or artistic work. The law essentially defined the rights and responsibilities of both sides in fulfilling the contract, such as conditions for the delivery of the manuscript and the time schedule for publication, contract duration, the author's right to remuneration, payment schedule and so on, as well as the conditions permitting a lawful abrogation of contract or the terms regulating breach of contract.[11] This first legal codification of the author-publisher relationship, most likely developed under French influence, reflected professional practice according to the tradition of publishing law (*Verlagsrecht*).

The 1921 Copyright Law

The introduction of copyright law in Bulgaria did not come about as the result of local gestation processes but was rather the result of external pressure. By means of art. 166 of the peace treaty signed between the allied and associated powers and Bulgaria in Neuilly-sur-Seine on 27 November 1919, Bulgaria was obligated to adhere to the Washington Act (1911) of the 1883 Paris Convention for the Protection of Industrial Property, and the Berlin Act (1908) of the 1886 Berne Convention for the protection of literary and artistic works, as well as the Berne Additional Protocol of March 20, 1914. In addition, and independently of the above-mentioned obligations, Bulgaria was compelled to recognize and protect all industrial, literary and artistic property of nationals of allied and associated states according to unionist standards no later than July 28, 1914. Faced with the necessity to observe international obligations emanating from the peace agreements, the Bulgarian state prompted the legislation of a copyright law, the motives of which were deliberated in parliament in February 1921 and were finalized with the passing of the first copyright law on July 11, 1921.[12]

Initially, the Ministry of Education had subsumed authorial rights under property rights and the law project was originally conceived under the title "law for literary and artistic property." Though it was unclear whether this initial conception had been intentional or not, it was subsequently identified as inappropriate by the

11 Georgiev, *Teorija na knigoizdatelskija process*, 52–54.

12 *Dăržaven Vestnik*, 20.7.1921, no. 86, 1–5.

examining committee, which laid forth its objections. Whereas the committee shied away from engaging in a fully-fledged theoretical discussion on the nature of authors' rights, at the same time it acknowledged that designations had an impact on and weighted future interpretations of the law, and therefore felt compelled to define its own stance with regard to available copyright definitions.[13]

In its deliberations, the committee observed that the conception of authors' rights as property was quite widespread, and in some cases, such as in French copyright doctrine, it was predominant. Moreover, various references to authors' rights that could be found scattered throughout several Bulgarian laws also treated authors' rights as property. Such was the case with art. 30 of the law on property, ownership and easements (*zakon na imushtestvata, sobstvenostăta i servitutite*), which specified the ownership of scholarly, literary and artistic works; art. 67, which referred to the ownership of [state] treasures; as well as art. 1, which broadly integrated immaterial goods into a notion of property. Finally, art. 373 of the penal code directly confirmed the notion of literary, musical and artistic property. As a result, the commission proposed a change of title to "law on authors' rights" or "copyright law" (*zakon za autorsko pravo*), thereby adopting the modern nomenclature used in most Slavic languages, which reconciled in one expression both the notion of authors' rights and the legal field of copyright law (equivalent to the German *Urheberrecht* or the French *droit d'auteur*).

Objections to the "property" theory were justified on several grounds. (1) Copyright protected the material, as well as the personality and ideational interests of the author. A property right, however, was a pure possession right of a person towards a thing and quite different to personality. As a result, the author's diverse ideational interests were not protected when copyright was categorized as a property right. (2) Moreover, a property right was in conflict with the limited temporal character of copyright, whereas the right of ownership was infinite. (3) Carried to its extreme consequences, the right of ownership could be misleading in various respects, and for this reason, the committee appraised copyright to be the protection of specific material and ideational interests, which the author of a literary or artistic work had in relation to his creation. Eventually, the commission implicitly discarded the property paradigm and explicitly instructed that the designation "literary and artistic property," as well as the codification of authors' rights as property rights, be removed from all official legal texts.[14]

---

13 Stenografski dnevnici, 19. Obiknoveno Narodno Săbranie (ONS), I RS, 39 3, 8/II 1921, 1345.

14 Stenografski dnevnici, 19 (ONS), I RS, 39 3, 8/II 1921, 1345.

The Russian copyright law of March 20, 1911 served as a template for the Bulgarian copyright law and was further adjusted to the specificities of the Bulgarian context. The law protected literary (written and oral), musical, artistic and photographic works without defining their content in detail, thus allowing a flexible and open approach towards future developments. Article 3 excluded from felonies works created on the basis of already existing works, provided that the new work differed significantly from the original. Also excluded were copies produced for personal use, provided that the copy did not carry the initials or the signature of the original author. The concept of "personal use" was deliberately left unspecified and its definition was to be determined in court by case law.

Protected were Bulgarian nationals for their published and unpublished works, issued in Bulgaria and/or abroad. The law protected foreign nationals, whose works had been published in Bulgaria, irrespective of whether the author resided in Bulgaria or not, as well as foreign nationals living in Bulgaria regarding their existing and future works published in Bulgaria.[15]

The initial draft, in line with the Russian law but in violation of the Berne Convention, did not recognize foreign citizens' copyrights. They were protected only partly through art. 32, which prohibited the reprinting (in the original language) of works initially published abroad without the permission of the rights-holders, and afforded them protection according to the laws of the country in which they were first published, with the reservation that the duration of protection was determined by Bulgarian, and not foreign law. Article 44 stipulated the same principle for musical works published abroad. These provisions were ultimately modified to fit BC parameters.

Articles 8 and 9 regulated future works and limited their contractual validity to five years in order to avoid exploitation of the author and his labor. If no time frame was mentioned in the contract, the five-year term was binding; if the contract stipulated a longer term, it was obligatorily reduced to five years. The duration of the term of protection was 30 years p.m.a., which was thought to strike a good balance between the interests of society and the author's pecuniary needs.[16] The 30-year term p.m.a. also represented a deviation from the 50-year p.m.a. standard of the BU.

Article 10 stipulated that copyright could only be transferred with the author's and/or heirs' consent. Creditors were prohibited from redeeming debts through copyrighted works or through copyright itself, unless so authorized by the author and/or his heirs. Personality and moral rights could not be compromised for pecuniary rights. A creditor could, without the author's consent, raise claims to revenues

---

15 Stenografski dnevnici, 19 (ONS), I RS, 39 3, 8/II 1921, 1346.

16 Stenografski dnevnici, 19 (ONS), I RS, 39 3, 8/II 1921,1347.

received by the author from a third person through the transfer of his publishing rights and also regarding the author's published and traded works. These could be sequestered and sold but without the creditor receiving the right to use those works for any other purpose than the one determined by the author, nor was he entitled to republish a work for his own economic benefit.[17]

Copyright could be transferred by contract among the living, by inheritance or through testament. Copyright, if not otherwise indicated by testament, was transferred to the author's heirs. In the absence of heirs, as far as the 10th degree of kinship, copyright was extinguished and works were transferred to the public domain.

The integrity of works was guaranteed and changes in the form and/or contents of works without the consent of the author prohibited, apart from such changes and alterations considered absolutely indispensable and to which the author acting in good faith would have anyway consented to.[18]

Infringements and penalties were handled in a differentiated manner. The legislator avoided addressing concrete retribution measures. Any form of infringement represented a civil penalty requiring retribution, but the scale of retribution varied and was dependent on whether or not the wrongdoing was premeditated. If the infringement was deliberate, then the offender had to carry all costs of the harm inflicted on the rights-holder; if the act was unintentional, however, the responsibility for the injury was limited to the value of the accrued profit. This ruling affected the amount of compensation: if injuries suffered were greater than the acquired profit, the infringer could not be called on to pay more than the profit he had accrued through unintentional copyright contravention. Recompense was decided by the court. A more severe treatment was reserved for reprinting. In this case, the author having incurred damage could claim all unlawful copies and confiscate all machinery and printing plates used for the publication. Similar measures were applied in the case of musical works. Recompense claims could be raised up to five years after the infringement was committed. By contrast, in the case of illegal printing of foreign works, claims could be raised during the entire duration of copyright.[19]

Translations were considered independent works and were copyright protected. Regarding Bulgarian citizens, having published at home or abroad, the initial draft law followed the early BC in securing an exclusive right of translation into other languages only if such a reservation was mentioned in the work's introduction and provided that the translation appeared within five years of the original publication.

17 Stenografski dnevnici, 19 (ONS), I RS, 39 3, 8/II 1921, 1347.

18 Stenografski dnevnici, 19 (ONS), I RS, 39 3, 8/II 1921, 1349.

19 Stenografski dnevnici, 19 (ONS), I RS, 39 3, 8/II 1921, 1349–1350.

The duration of copyright for these translations was only 10 years from the date of publication. Were those conditions not met, the author lost the exclusive translation right. In the initial draft law, foreign authors having published abroad were not protected and could therefore be published in Bulgarian or other language translations without the consent of the author or the rights-holder. The draft was very clear in the intention to deprive foreign authors of copyright protection, an issue that essentially boiled down to the question of translation.

In fact, the parliamentary discussions reveal that there was a strong consensus among Bulgarian statesmen, intellectuals and even jurists that translations were indispensable in order to adequately develop national culture, and that it was the legislator's responsibility to ensure access to foreign works. The commission was conscious of the international trend to reserve the rights of translation and adaptation exclusively for the author for the duration of the copyright period, a trend that the commission found unacceptable. In its exposé, it refuted an understanding of copyright as natural law and instead made a strong case for positive law. Apparently, similar to the case of Russia, the need to refute argumentation supporting a universal, exclusive right of translation helped lawyers to disengage from natural law and cleared the way for the recognition of copyright as statutory law. Discussing the freedom of translation, it was stated:

> This provision is fully justified, when considering [the fact] that in the many years to come, Bulgaria will be in pressing need of translated literature. No general provisions can ascertain that foreign citizens, who published their works abroad, need to be protected by Bulgarian law regarding the translation of their works into Bulgarian, since the content of copyright law, such as the content of any other right, cannot be constructed on the basis of abstract notions, but is the creation of the law maker. He is responsible—when determining the degree of authorial protection—to take under consideration not only the interests of the authors but mainly those of the country's enlightenment and education [needs], the more so, since as it has already been pointed out, translations are considered to be the expression of independent intellectual labor. The recognition of foreign authors' exclusive right to translation would signify the restriction of translated literature, and this would be particularly harmful for the intellectual life of Bulgaria, where there is a great need for translated scholarly literature. The development of [such a literature] is instrumental and imperative for the law-maker, who above all things [and] by virtue of his competence, needs to remove [all] hindrances to such a development, and such will be, without doubt, the recognition of the translating rights of foreign authors.[20]

20 Stenografski dnevnici, 19 (ONS), I RS, 39 3, 8/II 1921, 1351.

In the final parliamentary discussion[21] preceding the publication of the law, objections were raised concerning the fact that the final draft, though making explicit reference to the translating rights of Bulgarian citizens and foreigners published in Bulgaria, deliberately remained silent concerning foreign authors' translation rights. Such a palpable discrepancy—it was underlined—could not stand for long, and was bound to fly in the face of the country's obligation to ratify the peace agreement, which also prescribed Bulgaria's membership of the Berne Union. The danger that *jure conventionis*, that is, unionist law, would automatically apply and override local arrangements was very real. It was wiser to reformulate. As the MP V. Mollov highlighted, the freedom of translation had a long history in Russia, a circumstance for which he had a certain degree of understanding:

> If we support [the freedom of translation] consciously, with the intention to carry on with this policy, I have nothing against such a ruling since our literature, our scholarship currently genuinely need a great quantity of translated works. At the same time, however, I have to underline that according to the peace treaty, we are obliged to adhere to the Berne Convention. And the essence of the Berne Convention is that it provides protection to foreign authors and by consequence if we go ahead with this law, we will need to fulfil an additional requirement, to endorse the Berne Convention, since this has been explicitly agreed upon, and so it is clear that we have two, reciprocally contradicting provisions. [...] article 33 will have to be modified because it will be amended by force of the rule of the Berne Convention.[22]

Countering this position, MP M. Madžarov proposed sticking to the existing phrasing. Accession to the BC was indeed obligatory and had to be ratified, but it concerned only a specific number of states. If Bulgaria endorsed the principle of free translation from other languages, it would "leave a small door open, so as to use the literature of those states, which will not adhere to the convention. For example, Russia will not enter the BC—why not use Russian literature and translate from it?"[23] The final formulation of art. 4 silently endorsed this strategy. It provided foreign authors with protection but conditionally, that is, "only and to the degree that international agreements conceded them such a right."[24] By these means, the issue of foreign authors' translation rights was intentionally left ambiguous. The Bulgarian law only paid lip service to its international obligations and in essence neither truly sanctioned nor

21 Stenografski dnevnici, 19. ONS, II IS, 26 3, 7/VII 1921, 712–718.

22 Stenografski dnevnici, 19. ONS, II IS, 26 3, 7/VII 1921, 715.

23 Stenografski dnevnici, 19. ONS, II IS, 26 3, 7/VII 1921, 715.

24 *Dăržaven Vestnik*, July 20, 1921, no. 86, 1.

suspended foreign authors' rights. Their rights were protected by national and international law, but local legislation and practice remained uncommitted. What needs to be emphasized once more is the broad consensus among Bulgarian statesmen on this issue. Viewed comparatively, what is apparently absent in the case of interwar Bulgaria (in contrast to the Yugoslav and Czechoslovak cases) is the figure of the authoritative copyright lawyer, who by partaking in the international IP networks would have become their local mouthpiece and contradicted local tendencies, perhaps even maneuvered things in a different direction, that is, along a more BU-compliant track. These factors go some way to explain the absence of rigorousness in observing the translation rights of foreign authors in practice,[25] as well as the common habit of translating foreign works second-hand, often from their Russian translation.[26]

The negation of the exclusive property paradigm was most evident in the reasoning on the use of excerpts and quotations in publications. The commission ascertained that there were limits to authorial control and what constituted copyright infringement; not all published literary works could be considered the unbounded property of the author. After all, such an unconditional arrangement worked against the very interests that literary works were predestined to serve, namely the public. Next to art. 3, which regulated permitted uses, art. 39 added a special regulation regarding the legal use of already published foreign texts. Permitted were small excerpts, reprints and summaries of foreign works in their entirety, on condition that such excerpts and reprints were placed within new compositions, which constituted independent works, or within chrestomathies and other composite volumes, compiled for educational, scientific or technical purposes. Criteria for the use of works were the application of moderation and the composition of a new independent and original work. Even greater concessions were made for chrestomathies and other assorted collections and editions of texts on account of their social utility.[27]

---

25 On the absence of regulation in the case of translations, see also Vasil Zagorov, "'Prestăplenie i nakazanie' Reglementirane na otnošenijata avtor – prevodač – izdatel v Bălgarija za perioda 1921–1944 g.," *Izdatel* 12, no. 1-2-3 (2010): 87–89. Zagorov attributes the non-observance of foreign authors' translation rights to the publishers' disregard for the legal framework due to the absence of real enforcement mechanisms (87). Though his observation concerning the non-observance of translation rights for foreign authors is accurate, the imposition of strong sanctions was never the intention of the legislator. As I hope to have demonstrated, the issue was far more complex and rested on a much more fundamental societal consensus on the necessity for cheap access to foreign literature.

26 See here Vasil Zagorov, "Lost in Translation or Lost in Publishing: Introduction of World Literature in Early Modern Bulgarian Publishing via Russian Language Editions," *Publishing Research Quarterly* 33, no. 2 (June 2017): 160–172; and idem, "Knigoizdanie russkogo zarubežija v Bolgarii do 1944 g.: periodizacija – organizacija – problemii," *Izvestija viisših učebnih zavedenii. Problemii poligrafii i izdatelskogo dela*, no. 2 (2014): 65–78.

27 Stenografski dnevnici, 19. ONS, I RS, 39 3, 8/II 1921, 1351.

Article 40 permitted the reprinting of articles and news from newspapers, magazines and other periodical publications. The criterion for use was again moderation and therefore it was prohibited to reprint constantly from the same periodical publication. Also banned was the publication of foreign messages communicated via telegraph and/or telephone if they were subject to such a prohibiting agreement; they could be published in local newspapers only 18 hours after their original disclosure.

Unlike West European copyright, but consistent with its Russian blueprint, the Bulgarian law introduced the notion of folk art and provided compilations of both oral and material popular art with copyright protection for 30 years from the date of publication. Other authors were legally not prevented from conducting their own (original) compilations of the same works (art. 13), and thereby folk art was effectively constructed as belonging to the commons.

Summarizing the basic tenets and tendencies of the Bulgarian law, it is obvious that the law reflected less the intention to raise and solidify rigid property borders in copyright relations, and more the objective to demarcate important areas for the development of national culture, which consequently needed to be encouraged, regulated and/or protected. Though the law secured the notion of authors' rights, it did not as such boost the model of the individual author proprietor, and as discussed earlier in this chapter, in several instances of its reasoning it even questioned the imperative of absolute authorial control. In many ways, this first Bulgarian copyright law was already a departure from the liberal model of regulating cultural relationships, a tendency that would be further strengthened in the course of the interwar period. The law was fairly protectionist: it kept the deterring and penalizing aspects of the law to a minimum; transferred a great deal of the decision making to the court; established a series of exceptions to what constituted law infringement; acknowledged the significance and sovereignty of moral rights in juxtaposition to pecuniary interests; cancelled, in its initial draft, the automatization of the Berne Convention by refusing to acknowledge the reciprocity clause; made broad concessions when it came to education; and constructed folk art as commons. Protection was attributed according to the nationality principle (Bulgarian citizens in Bulgaria and abroad) and according to location (foreigners having published in Bulgaria). It had been one of the legislator's central concerns to secure satisfactory access to foreign texts, mainly with a view to public education. In order to ensure this goal, the law was inadvertently favorable to publishers, as they represented the indispensable link between the production of texts and the public. There is no evidence that the publishers had any significant influence on the drafting of the law. The proclivity to support the publishing sector was rather motivated by *raison d'état*. In the course of the interwar period, the legislator rectified this imbalance, and whereas the state continued to directly or indirectly subsidize the publishing sector, it progressively brought the author under more state protection.

Reflecting, both literally and metaphorically, the novelty of copyright for Bulgarian conditions, the law included provisions regarding practices that were without reference to Bulgarian society's reality and its economy of culture. For example, the law protected the mechanical reproduction of musical works, referring *de facto* to a non-existent cultural industry. The law acknowledged this discrepancy by introducing relevant articles with the words, "in the interest of the *future industry* of mechanical reproduction of musical works."[28] The same goes for films. Being a recipient rather than an initiator of technological innovation, the Bulgarian legislator was also more relaxed concerning the use of new media such as photography. The reproduction of photographs in independent scholarly works, or in order to elucidate texts in compilations and essays serving educational purposes, was free. Importantly, the reproduction of photographs for the purposes of industrial, manufacturing and specialized production was unrestricted.[29] This last point clearly ran against French interests and their efforts to inhibit such practices through apposite international legislation.

Professionalization Processes in Culture

Created literally *ex nihilo*, the Bulgarian state adopted from its formation in 1878 a policy of state patronage towards the arts and sciences. This attitude was reflected in a series of legislative and administrative measures that aimed at establishing and financing cultural institutions and creators. Due to the political constellation, this policy was heightened after WWI and reached its apogee in the dirigiste policies of the 1930s. The exclusive and—in many ways—indispensable role of the state in the modernization process was reflected in diachronic protectionism and substantial and extensive support for culture. While in the immediate post-liberation period this support was relatively free of prescriptive directives, after WWI, governments effectively imposed a strong ideological profile, and progressively from the late 1920s onwards a strong national focus was enforced in which the intelligentsia increasingly took on the role of mediator.[30]

28 Stenografski dnevnici, 19. ONS, I RS, 39 3, 8/II 1921, 1352, emphasis added.

29 Stenografski dnevnici, 19. ONS, I RS, 39 3, 8/II 1921, 1357.

30 Ivan Elenkov, *Kulturnijat Front, Bălgarska kultura prez epohata na komunizma: političesko upravlenie, ideologičeski osnovanija, institutionalni režimi* (Sofia: Ciela, 2008), 76. For a more detailed

Following a worldwide trend, the first decades of the twentieth century, and particularly the interwar period, witnessed the creation and consolidation of professional organizations for most liberal professions and groups involved in cultural production. The Union of Bulgarian Writers was created in early September 1913 with the double aim to actively participate in social life and defend writers' particular professional interests, while the Booksellers' Union was founded in 1923.

Despite the creation of branch-specific unions, professionalization processes were feeble and remained ambivalent mainly due to the limited market for cultural goods. This labile professionalization was reflected in the initial lack of differentiation but also in the ensuing competition and absence of codes of conduct between professional groups, as for example between journalists and authors, or between booksellers and publishers. The absence of a vigorous market sustained porous borders between the different professional groups. As a result, the state often intervened and completed the process of professional regulation, given that self-regulation could not be achieved by relying solely on the dynamics of demand and supply. It is noteworthy, however, that such an approach was not new. Ever since its creation, the Bulgarian state had played a pivotal role in the institutionalization of civil society, culture and the arts. State intervention and administrative engineering compensated for the lack of a dynamic market for cultural goods. The establishment of two major cultural institutions, the state opera and theatre, are textbook examples of this phenomenon. Set up by artists themselves at the end of the nineteenth and beginning of the twentieth century as civil society initiatives, both led an anemic life and were at the point of dissolving when the state intervened and took up their maintenance by transforming them into representative state institutions.[31] This pattern can be observed in the establishment of other institutions as well. Founded in Braila in 1869 as a learned society and likewise representing a civil society initiative, the "Bulgarian literature society" was later institutionalized with state help as the Bulgarian Academy of Sciences.[32]

presentation, see Irina Gigova, "Writers of the Nation: Intellectual Identity in Bulgaria 1939–1953" (Unpublished PhD diss., University of Illinois at Urbana-Champaign, 2005); idem, "In Defense of Native Literature: Writers' Associations, State and the Cult of the Writer in pre-1945 Bulgaria," *Slavic Review* 77, no. 2 (Summer 2018): 417–40.

[31] The Sofia-based group "Sălza i smjah," created in 1892, formed the initial nucleus of the future National Theater, which was officially institutionalized in 1904 by the Ministry of Education under Minister Ivan Shishmanov. The creation of the National Opera took place later and was a more strenuous process. Initiated as an operatic society in 1908, it legally secured a state subvention in 1921 and became a state institution in 1922. See Rumen Daskalov, *Bălgarskoto Obshtestvo 1878–1939* (Sofia: Gutenberg, 2005), vol 2: 410–12.

[32] Daskalov, *Bălgarskoto Obshtestvo 1878–1939,* 410–12.

Though created with the goal to protect and advocate the professional interests of authors, the Union of Bulgarian Writers (UBW) led a weak existence during the greatest part of the interwar period, oscillating between the tasks of a cultural and a professional organization. Next to theoretical and generational differences, internal and personal strife hindered the union's consolidation. After WWI, diverse literary and social agendas split the community of writers into numerous (fluid) circles associated with specific literary magazines (*Misul*, *Zlatorog*, *Hiperion*, *Izkustvo i Kritika* etc.).[33] Though the wars and the early 1920s managed to enlarge the book market to a certain degree, this advantage withered in the succeeding period due to the population's weak consumer spending.

The majority of authors earned their living by exercising different, mostly white-collar professions. Some of the writers and literary critics were pedagogues or philologists having worked for a substantial time as teachers, while another rather small contingent came from the free professions, a circumstance that exercised a certain influence on their culture, style, ideas and aesthetic inclinations. The greatest percentage of writers, however, were active in civil service. Only exceptionally few made ends meet by relying purely on writing and translations, journalistic, publishing and similar activities, that is, from writing as a free profession. In fact, the voices castigating the desolate material conditions of the Bulgarian author and the plight of the literary market multiplied in the late 1920s and 1930s.[34]

The disarray in the UBW triggered the creation of competing associations such as the Club of Bulgarian Women Writers (1930), the Association of Children's Book Writers (1930), the short-lived Union of Proletarian Writers (1931), the Militant Labor Writers (1932) and the Union of Provincial Writers (1934) and even the emergence of a Guild of Historical Writers also in 1934.[35] This boom of associations reflected different things simultaneously: an awareness of the benefits of professional organization, the "neocorporatist" spirit of the depression years as well as the fragmentation among writers. Things took a turn for the better after the mid-1930s as the UBW initiated a strategy of inclusion and rebranding, which ideologically and practically synchronized with state policy and patronage.[36] The fate of the UBW is exemplary of a general trend regarding the life of cultural associations in interwar Bulgaria: "lack of [a] vibrant market, multiple rival societies, entrepreneurial activities,

---

33 Gigova, "Writers of the Nation," 7; Dimităr Ludžev, *Grad na dve epohi, istorija na obštestvenite grupi v bălgarskite gradove v sredata na XX vek* (Sofia: Sv. Kliment Ohridski, 2005), 530.

34 Ludžev, *Grad na dve epohi*, 529.

35 Gigova, "Writers of the Nation," 13.

36 Gigova, "Writers of the Nation," 15–19.

impassioned pleas to society, and finally, the creation of a single professional organization in the early 1930s in increasingly close cooperation with the Ministry of Education."[37] The publishing sector was exposed to a not insignificant number of challenges and equivalent pressures.

Due to the social significance of printing, the state intervened early on, on behalf of printers/booksellers/publishers. It used customs regulation to stimulate literary pursuits but also to strengthen the development of local production and industry. In order, for example, to support the home book binding industry, production abroad of unbounded books in foreign languages was relieved from import duties, whereas taxes were imposed on bounded books. On the other hand, books and materials in Bulgarian language printed abroad, with the exclusion of maps and atlases, were burdened with heavy import duties, thus making foreign competition practically meaningless. Imported printing machines were exempt from customs taxes and the Bulgarian state had already acceded in 1881 to the international postal union which facilitated access to the European network of commercial book exchange.[38]

Seeking to regulate and stabilize a rather disorderly textbook market, the first efforts to create a publishers' union dated back to 1897. This first and rather short-lived union (Bălgarski knižarski suiuz) aimed primarily at bringing the overproduction of textbooks under control, which even after state efforts to standardize textbook production in 1897 did not subside, leading to unfair competition and saturation of the market.[39]

Belated state building also affected the professionalization of book production. Before the creation of the Bulgarian kingdom, the production of Bulgarian books was a cosmopolitan business and books were printed in different locations. It was only with the creation of the Bulgarian state that printers/publishers slowly moved their businesses to the principality. The syncretistic model, in which creating, publishing and selling texts were often united in one person, disintegrated only in the late nineteenth and early twentieth centuries.[40] The assistance of state and communities in helping to build up the educational system and promote literacy, and by doing so also facilitating the modernization of the book, cannot be stressed enough.

At the end of the nineteenth and beginning of the twentieth century, a slow and strenuous differentiation took place between the bookseller, who published books,

---

37 Gigova, "Writers of the Nation," 20–21.

38 Vasil Zagorov, *Bălgarska kniga (1878–1912) ot văzroždenskija ideal do komercializacijata* (Sofia: Za bukvite-O pismeneh, 2014), 31–35.

39 Zagorov, *Bălgarska kniga,* 24–25.

40 Zagorov, *Bălgarska kniga*, 133.

and the publisher, who sought to develop his own distribution network. The ambiguity over whether enterprises related to publishing and book distribution were to be labelled "bookstores" or "publishing houses" is a precise indicator of this weak labor differentiation. The ambivalent meaning of the word "knižar," designating a person involved both in the publishing and selling of books, is similarly an indicator of this rudimentary professional delineation.[41]

The passage from general, patriotic publishing of the awakening period to market publishing took place in the last decades of the nineteenth century. Violating ethical and legal norms, pedagogues proposed their own textbooks or materials to their close acquaintances, or reached percentage deals with local booksellers and then directed students to them. As a result of such strategies, which involved intensive lobbying on all levels, micro-cartels were formed, which were harmful to the educational, publishing and distribution processes. The regulation of the textbook market was therefore the key motivation behind the creation of the "Bălgarski knižarski suiuz" (Booksellers' Union of Bulgaria), which aimed at fixing reduction rates for their own union members and prohibiting price dumping for books sold directly to end customers. As observed by V. Zagotov, the publishers' professional consolidation created the impression that the organization's objective was not the regulation of the market, but rather the domination of the author-publisher-printer-bookseller-reader chain. In their endeavors to secure their own benefits, publishers apparently ignored public interest.[42] In spite of all efforts to control illegal competition, establish a disciplined and principled professional organization and standardize professional qualifications for its members, the union was short-lived. Missing internal discipline and solid professional attitudes, participants were unappreciative of the need for a professional organization. The union disintegrated after only two meetings, as a result of the lack of professional culture and/or the fact that the state standardized procedures in the production, reviewing, printing and dissemination of textbooks largely cancelled the association's initial motivations for the creation of a professional organization.[43]

Though the growth of the book market at the beginning of the twentieth century effected the expansion and differentiation of professional interactions and practices, it equally witnessed a "bewilderment" of commercial relations: publishers favoring specific regional booksellers, fluctuating price reductions in the publisher-trader-reader chain, lack of correctness and systematic bookkeeping regarding books sold

41 Zagorov, *Bălgarska kniga*, 134–35.

42 Zagorov, *Bălgarska kniga*, 153–55.

43 Zagorov, *Bălgarska kniga*, 155–56.

on consignment—all phenomena that rekindled a cycle of illegal competition.[44] The creation of the "Booksellers' Union of Bulgaria" (Knižarski suiuz v Bălgarija) in 1923 represented a second attempt to create a professional organization around the book economy. The union's official newspaper, *Knižarska Duma*, testifies to the fact that the above picture did not change substantially in the 1920s and 1930s. The overproduction of textbooks remained a chronic problem, with publishers and booksellers seeking to offload financial losses onto each other's shoulders, publishers lacking coordination and strategy regarding textbook production, simultaneous circulation of several generations of textbooks, problems with the country-wide placement and distribution networks for books, competition between stationary and ambulant booksellers, the meddling of provincial warehouses in retail book sales,[45] lack of capital, internal strife and the pursuit of diverse agendas within the professional organization, and books traded through generic, non-specialized merchants.[46] Unfair competition such as practiced by the publisher Ignjatov, who sought to circumvent booksellers by selling directly to customers, was particularly damaging to the book trade.[47] Ignjatov, and other publishers, cheated customers by offering reduced books on subscription. It was later revealed that the discounted volumes were simply older editions clothed in new covers that indicated (in fact) a higher price.[48]

Book market conditions in the 1930s were characterized as "chaotic." While the economic crisis took its toll, chronic problems were aggravated due to the disproportionate relationship between strong supply and waning demand, a decrease in the educated strata's purchasing power, the press (newspapers and journals) competing with books for readers, incomplete legal regulation of the publishing profession as a commercial branch, and great fluctuations in book prices. Accumulated problems increased the necessity for regulation and intervention, such as the need to fix book prices and norms for paper, liquidate problematic enterprises and control translated literature, impose union and state control over the production of books, promote mixed participation of booksellers and publishers in the same union, stall the production of brochure literature and the publication of literary works in journals, impede publishers from selling directly to the public, standardize discount rates for booksellers and publishers, institutionalize a qualification (*cenz*) for publishers, eradicate itinerant booksellers, compel booksellers to trade only with

44 Zagorov, *Bălgarska kniga*, 158.

45 *Knižarska Duma*, November 23, 1927, year 1, no. 6, 1–2.

46 *Knižarska Duma*, December 14, 1927, year 1, no. 9, 1–2.

47 *Knižarska Duma*, October 10, 1928, year 1, no. 9, 1.

48 P.K. Činkov, *Sega šte čuete našija komentator* (Sofia: Sineva, 2001), 61.

publications of unionized publishers, and entrust consignment sales only to booksellers with regular accounting records or otherwise deprive them of the right to receive books on consignment.[49] In an attempt to dominate the most profitable sector of the book market, the market for textbooks, and avert the competition between them, three of the leading Sofia publishers (Danov, Hemus and Kazanlăška Dolina) closed ranks in 1933, creating a cartel; they were later joined by the publisher St. Atanasov. The cartel was dissolved in 1937 due to divergences of opinion.[50] Overall, it can be tentatively argued that developments in the publishing sector in the late interwar period show a certain trend towards "deprofessionalization." Nevertheless, this circumstance does not seem to have affected in any way the quality of native literary and scholarly production, which by all accounts reached a high level of maturity in the interwar period.

Copyright as Practice

The introduction of copyright legislation did not really affect the economy of publishing, alter established trade habits or shape the author-publisher relationship in terms more benevolent for the former. The archives of the National Library in Sofia contain the records of several publishing houses from the interwar period,[51] which though often only fragmentary, nevertheless allow an insight into the mundane practices of the publishing sector. Some scholars attribute the inability and ineffectiveness of copyright law to structure more solid professional relationships firstly to the short period in which it was implemented (1920s and 1930s), and secondly to the lack of rigorous penal enforcement.[52] Though both observations are accurate, they overlook the fact that copyright was thoroughly secondary in structuring the relationships between stakeholders, which were configured primarily by the conditions and limits of the existing market.

The structure and contents of publishing contracts contained in the National Library display a great diversity of approaches and treatments. They testify that publishers' behaviour was structured above all by economic considerations, while

49 *Knižarska Duma*, 1935, no. 35, 4.; no. 44, 3–4.

50 Nacionalna Biblioteka, Istoričeski Arhiv, fond 260, a.e. 5, 1–8 and a.e. 6, 1–8.

51 NB IA, fond 260 "Hemus," fond 501 "Čipev," fond 560 "Atanasov," etc.

52 See for example Zagorov, "Lost in Translation," 171. Zagorov has only analysed translated literature, which was probably the most speculative area of publishing activity. For a complete picture, he would need to examine translated and native literature and their correlation.

copyright regulation was incorporated into their rationale only when it promised to bring them an extra benefit or secure for them a particularly profitable monopoly. Though they tried to secure their own advantage and clearly maintained the upper hand in the relationship with authors, Bulgarian publishers on the whole paid honorariums and had done so even before the introduction of copyright law. From the early 1930s there was an increasing and more accurate use of copyright nomenclature in contracts, which evidences a greater familiarity and ease with copyright as an instrument, without signaling a substantial change in publishers' strategies. Some publishing houses, like Hemus, developed and increasingly used standardized contracts in the late 1930s. For the most part, conditions dictated in contracts varied according to the authors' reputation and the estimated or expected success of works. Publishers aimed to obligate and monopolize successful writers and secure the publishing of subsequent editions. Dependent on their estimates, the prospect of publishing future editions was made mandatory, conditional or optional in contracts, with stronger authors being—as far as possible—obliged to produce future editions, with weaker or lesser-known authors/works being left to the discretion and future judgement of the publisher. What constituted an edition and when it was considered exhausted was also quite volatile. Modes and intervals of payment varied. Often, translations were contractually rendered the property of publishers, though they also paid honorariums to translators for new editions every now and then. When existing contracts were convenient, they were usually extended, rather than new ones being drafted.

There were regular payments to heirs of renowned authors like Penčo Slaveikov, Iordan Iovkov, Pejo Javorov, Hristo Smirnenski, Todor Vlaikov and others, and several of them were obviously accustomed to receiving fees. They even negotiated their preferred conditions for payment. For example, Javorov's heir, Ekaterina Neidenova, renounced her right to receive additional free copies (she had already received 20) and asked to be paid (for the remaining 30) in cash instead.[53] From the correspondence, it becomes obvious that heirs developed a habit of asking for fees, and moreover that a certain business developed around heirs' rights, as in cases when several claimants turned up simultaneously, apparently as rightful heirs of deceased authors. Therefore, when negotiating publishing conditions for Hariton Genadiev's translations with his heirs, Hemus emphasized that in the eventuality that additional contenders should come forth as rightful heirs, and should the publishing house suffer losses as a result thereof, all compensations would be carried by the heirs.[54]

[53] NB IA, fond 260, a.e. 16, 183.

[54] NB IA, fond 260. a.e. 19, 1–3.

Publishers did not rely on copyright law so much as a regulatory framework but rather as a deterrent, that is, as a warning in order to avoid dealings in court. Copyright was perceived less as a context for the regulation of the author-publisher relationship, and more as an impersonal warning, the last resort when all means of persuasion were exhausted. Overall, the picture reveals a society that was not particularly fond of copyright litigation. There was obviously still faith in interpersonal agreements and accommodation options and they counted for more. Apparently, it sometimes sufficed to articulate copyright infringement as a threat; there was still more trust invested in the interpersonal relationship. In several instances, Hemus included in its contracts clauses that stipulated that the author or translator and the publishing house would together prosecute any third party involved in the reprinting of the same work. The purpose here was twofold: first, to restrain the author from self-publishing, and second, to prevent him concluding an agreement with another publisher for the same work simultaneously. Authors agreed in the contract that they would pursue infringements of this kind along with, and in support of, the publisher. What was addressed here was in the first place an ethical "contract"; by committing the author, the publisher tried to ensure that he could not play a double game. If ethical pressure did not work, prosecution was the next resort. It could well be that such stipulations reflect earlier practices that had withstood the test of time and had established themselves as standard in the publisher-author relationship.

Remuneration could vary significantly from case to case. In some cases, a fixed fee was proposed based on a calculation of print sheets (1 "kola" equivalent to approximately 16 pages); sometimes a fixed sum was proposed without any allusion to a fixed unit of calculation; and sometimes remuneration was determined on the basis of sales. In a series of contracts, it was mentioned that if for any reason the publishing house was forced to raise the price of the book, authors' honorariums would be raised proportionately. On occasion, the author received a smaller or greater number of exemplars, which he could trade himself. Corrections were either taken on by the publisher or delegated to the author.

Publishers aimed at monopolizing authors in subject areas in which there was a dearth of specialists, as was the case, for example, with dictionary authors. In those sectors there was intense competition not only to engage them first but also to hinder their engagement by another publishing house. Attempts to maintain exclusive, monopolistic rights concerned not only the particular work but also the general disposability of authors. Contracts often contained clauses that prohibited them from engaging in similar activities for other publishers.

Noteworthy in the case of Bulgaria is the absence of rigorous and persistent public debate regarding copyright. Though the plight of the author and his dire living conditions was a continuing topic in the press, copyright was not heralded as the solution. This attitude probably reflects the consciousness among creative elites that their fortunes were predicated less on the clout of copyright and more on the narrow internal market. Even P.K. Činkov, one of the strongest advocates of copyright legislation and a proficient translator, while explaining that before WWI translations were often paid in kind, that is, in the form of a certain number of copies, also had to acknowledge that "that is how we were normally paid, and it was impossible under the conditions prevalent at the time to pay more."[55] Having studied philosophy and law and worked as a correspondent for Bulgarian and German press agencies in Germany, Činkov appreciated German "correctness" when remunerating his services. His foreign experience and background in law were formative experiences that shaped his attitude towards copyright.[56]

Činkov's testimony provides insights into the publishing practices of interwar Bulgaria. Only a few robust and reliable publishers like Hemus paid honorariums regularly for translations and consequent editions, but even those enterprises occasionally faced problems and delayed remuneration of translators. Činkov placed great faith in the capacity of copyright law to streamline publishing practice. If Bulgarian publishers were compelled to pay loyalties to foreign authors, they would be deterred from stealing other people's intellectual labor and would be forced to make better decisions when choosing what to translate. Only by such means would Bulgarian translated literature achieve higher qualitative standards.[57] Though testimonies from the time tend to confirm the problem with the overproduction of translated works, as well as the phenomenon that the same works in translation appeared in different publishing houses, what is interesting in Činkov's thesis is that he proposes authorial permission as a distinctive feature capable of drawing the line between good and bad translations. Read in the inverse, Činkov's stance appears rather as an appeal for a greater professionalization of the translator's occupation.

It is, however, remarkable that even this staunch supporter of copyright law had to lower his sights when dealing with the realities and oddities of publishing in Bulgaria. Interestingly enough, in his own professional practice, he showed himself lenient towards copyright infringements. Having completed a translation of Erich Maria Remarque's *Die drei Kamaraden* on demand of the publisher Mirčo

55 Činkov, *Sega šte čuete našija komentator*, 48.
56 Činkov, *Sega šte čuete našija komentator*, 52.
57 Činkov, *Sega šte čuete našija komentator*, 52 and 59.

Smrikarov, the latter, due to lack of means, decided to shorten the translation. The book's size had grown way beyond his initial calculations and the publisher lacked the means to finance the printing of the entire manuscript. He assured the translator, however, that in the consequent edition he would include the entire translation. Činkov, in his memoirs, praises him for keeping his word. In the next edition, the publisher indeed included the whole translation and paid for the translated passages he had omitted in the first one. Činkov reports the incident with a sympathetic ear, though—strictly speaking—Smrikarov had *de facto* committed a double infringement: both against the original author and the translator.[58] Moreover, the same Činkov, as editor of the periodical *Čas*, prioritized the exigencies of publishing and literature over formalistic copyright rules. Seeking to embellish a contribution honouring the poet Hristo Smirnenski with the poet's picture, Činkov, after going to great pains, managed to find through their common friend Aleksander Dobrinov a group photograph from which they were able to isolate Smirnenski's portrait. Because the photograph had faded, Dobrinov, a caricaturist by profession, intensified the contours and colours and, in order to increase contrasts, scratched with a paper knife something that looked like a scarf around the poet's neck. By such means "Hristo Smirnenski [got to wear] a scarf, which he had never worn in his life, but which made the picture very effective. Precisely, this artistically falsified picture [...] we reproduced in the *Čas* newspaper and as a postcard."[59] To top it all, the brother of the deceased Smirnenski claimed in the name of Smirnenski's family and his competence as the poet's legal heir a fee for the publication of the picture. An infuriated Činkov declined, explaining that the published portrait had not been in the family's possession and moreover the end result had been significantly retouched. Whereas the artist who had supplied and embellished the photograph to honor his friend and poet did not even think of asking for a fee, the brother, who had contributed nothing to obtaining the portrait, was raising copyright claims to the picture.[60] In both instances described above, Činkov was having problems reconciling in himself different codes of behavior: the ethical, the intellectual and the commercial.

Heirs recognized the relevance and developed an appreciation for the "value" of copyright more quickly than authors. The following incident demonstrates well both the rising authority of heirs and how unprincipled the publishing game could be in Bulgaria, even when dealing with Bulgaria's most successful and professional

[58] Činkov, *Sega šte čuete našija komentator*, 65.

[59] Činkov, *Sega šte čuete našija komentator*, 176.

[60] Činkov, *Sega šte čuete našija komentator*, 177–78.

publisher. Having had the original idea to produce a book entitled *Vazov for Children*, that is, a compilation of texts by Bulgaria's most prominent belletristic author that would be accessible to children, Činkov contacted to this end the renowned publishing house Hemus. Though the initial manuscript attracted the attention of the publisher, he later turned it down, only for Činkov to find out that the publisher had in the meantime contacted Vazov's legal successor, his son Boris Vazov, in order to get authorization for the same kind of publication but of his own making. In the end, the project was dropped, not because Hemus had stolen Činkov's initial idea, but because Vazov's son demanded an exuberant sum for copyrights. One last remark on this account: Činkov, though himself such a conscious advocate of copyright issues, prioritized here the intellectual value of labor and compiled a manuscript consisting of Vazov's texts in adaptation without having previously sought the legal heir's permission. So much for the record of one of Bulgaria's warmest and most vocal copyright proponents in the interwar period.

How copyright, in practice, came to represent a publisher's rather than an author's right is one of the most interesting aspects of this story, but one that has international equivalents. Having received permission for an authorized translation of Bernard Kellerman's *The Schellenberg Brothers*, Činkov proposed the translated work to the publisher Yurukov, who turned it down. Consequently, he proposed the same translation to the publisher Ivan Ignjatov, who accepted and drafted a contract with him, explicitly mentioning that the translation was authorized. It was later found out that Yurukov had included the title in his series "Mosaic of Important Contemporary Novels." Ignjatov rushed to inform him that his translation was illegal, since he had received official authorization for it, and could moreover stop Yurukov from publishing his version on the grounds of the Berne Convention. Though no national copyright law had yet been released, the Berne Convention was already in force due to the Neuilly agreement. The turn of events pleased Ignjatov, who managed to thwart the plans of his competitor. Upon Činkov's inquiry as to why he did not mention on the cover that the translation was authorized, Ignjatov replied: "I am not mad to mention that your translation is authorized. For me, it suffices that by such means I can eliminate competition. If I stress that your translation is authorized, this means to underscore that all other translations I publish are not authorized."[61]

It is not for their anecdotal nature that the above incidents are included in this analysis, but rather because they clearly demonstrate the various codes and currencies of culture in Bulgarian society when applying the language and instrument of

[61] Činkov, *Sega šte čuete našija komentator*, 56–58.

copyright. Furthermore, they demonstrate well the tension between legal prescription and actual practice, as well as the tension between social and formal norms and how they were negotiated on a local level. Finally, they throw light on the social actors that first grasped the significance of copyright. Against all expectations, these were not the authors. A limited analysis of contracts from the interwar period tends to confirm the picture gained above. The social actors that learned most quickly to speak the language of copyright and understood how to raise and enforce claims based on copyright were primarily publishers and heirs, and as we will witness later in this chapter, also native and foreign private collecting societies.

Copyright and Culture in the 1930s

The protectionist attitude towards local authors was enhanced in the 1930s and early 1940s in the context and spirit of nationalism and corporatism of that period. World War II, and the kingdom's agenda to promote the union of all Bulgarians in one state, mobilized society "and created a potent, if short-lasting, unity in purpose among citizenry, state and cultural producers. As a result, the ignominious war years became the best period of the decades-long existence of mainstream literati in terms of financial security, social visibility, cultural and moral authority."[62] Framed under the banner of Bulgarian "cultural unity" and constructed on the basis of mutual advantages, the relationship between government/state and cultural elites was reciprocal. The state sought to win over authors for its propaganda purposes, while authors used state patronage to bolster their reputation, augment their moral authority and visibility and secure better material conditions.[63] The state committed itself to supporting cultural production, and along with other measures actively subsidized the Bulgarian Writers' Union starting from 1938. Authors participated in the regime's various cultural campaigns, from official ceremonies to public readings, official trips to newly acquired territories, enlightenment campaigns among the population, literary publications on the "newly-liberated lands," literary readings in schools and reading clubs, and public commemoration practices. In order to raise cultural awareness and secure ideological conformity, a "Cultural Week" was introduced and celebrated in the Bulgarian countryside, while the sponsored "Week of the Bulgarian

62 Gigova, *Writers of the Nation*, 22.
63 Gigova, *Writers of the Nation*, 22.

Book" underlined the contribution of the Bulgarian book in raising the cultural and material status of the population. From 1940 a policy of centralizing cultural life along the lines of the German model was implemented, with increased state supervision, censorship and spending over society and culture. The culmination of this policy was the creation of the National Chamber of Culture, inspired by the Reichskulturkammer, aiming to unite all cultural producers and their organizations under an umbrella agency that would harmonize their professional interests with those of both the nation and the state.

The 1921 copyright law was amended and supplemented in 1936 by decree no. 446.[64] It revised art. 39 on compiled editions, which had enabled the free use of excerpts and short essays by foreign authors in edited volumes of educational, scholarly and/or technical purposes such as chrestomathies. The article was amended to specify that for the same kinds of publications, Bulgarian publishers were now obliged to remunerate Bulgarian authors for the use of excerpts from their works, according to the stipulations of a specific rule-book (*pravilnik*).[65] The rule-book stipulated detailed remuneration tariffs, in some ways anticipating later communist practice. For example, a published excerpt of prose literature (stories, accounts, biographies, dialogues etc.) up to one page in length was remunerated at 200 leva, with lengthier excerpts at 250 leva. Fees for the placement of poems amounted to 200 leva. Remuneration was due at the latest by mid-March of the school year for which the teaching materials had been developed. Authors or their heirs received their payments directly from the publisher. The term of protection was the same as stipulated by the 1921 law.[66]

Being directly prescriptive, the 1936 amendment reflected more than just a heightening of the legislator's protectionist disposition. The legislator blatantly blackmailed publishers into obedience as the Ministry of Education declined to print and circulate the new edition of any textbook whose publisher had neglected to remunerate Bulgarian authors within the time frame and according to the

64 *Dăržaven Vestnik*, October 30, 1936, no. 246, 4257.

65 *Dăržaven Vestnik*, 2.12.1936, no. 274, 4638.

66 How ideological preconceptions can taint the writing of history is well demonstrated by post-communist accounts on the historical development of copyright in Bulgaria. For example, Bulgaria's foremost expert in copyright issues and eminent copyright lawyer Georgi Sarakinov, in his short account on copyright history included in the introductory pages of his commentary on recent copyright legislation, attributes the tradition of remunerating creators on the basis of fixed tariffs to communist practice: "It should be underscored that very soon after 9 September 1944, the state began to standardize authors' remuneration. The first obligatory tariffs, concerning in the first place authorial labor, date from 1946 and 1947." Georgi Sarakinov, *Avtorsko pravo i srodnite mu prava v Republika Bălgarija* (Sofia: Sibi, 2005), 24 ff.

instructions specified. These punitive measures were directly written into law. The ministry withheld sanctions only when there was disagreement concerning the work's authorship, when the author and/or his heirs were unidentified, or when their postal addresses were unknown. In such cases, the publisher was obligated to deliver the fees to the Ministry of Education, where they were deposited for three years in the name of the rights-holder. After extinction of this term, and if unclaimed, the sum was transferred to the "fund for the social and cultural support of teachers."[67]

This top-down management, as well as the fear of sanctions, obviously produced results. From the late 1930s the association of publishers, booksellers and warehouses was entrusted with the task to monitor and register the frequency by which authors' texts were included in educational materials and to devise remuneration tables accordingly. Starting in 1937, ninety-three Bulgarian authors were remunerated, receiving a total amount of 219,700 leva.[68]

I was unable to find sources indicating the initiator of the proposal, but it can be assumed with almost absolute certainty that the authors' association had a hand in its formulation. How the legislator handled the remuneration of Bulgarian authors in the 1936 law revision provides an interesting starting point for reflection on the legislator's modus operandi. Indisputably, this last amendment reflected the protectionist and corporatist spirit of the times and was the apogee of state intervention. Yet, the specific way of handling the issue also demonstrates pragmatism regarding social practices in the field of cultural production. This becomes evident if one considers the alternatives. A conventional mode of regulation would have been to legislate copyright protection for the use of domestic authors' works and subsequently penalize violations thereof. Infringement cases would have to be brought to court, costing money and time. It is uncertain and highly doubtful whether authors would resort to or could afford to take legal measures against publishers. The legislator chose not to follow this costly, formal juridification track with uncertain outcomes. Rather, he picked the shortest path and opted instead to intervene directly into the field of practice in a way that had an unequivocally disciplinary effect upon the publishers.[69] The measures were prescriptive, even paternalistic in comparison to liberal

67 *Dăržaven Vestnik*, December 2, 1936, no. 274, 4638.

68 Zagorov, *Bălgarska kniga*, 33–34. Zagorov misguidedly considers the payment of royalties to Bulgarian authors to be the result of legislative changes in the commercial sector, which led to the professional consolidation of Bulgarian booksellers. In fact, as demonstrated above, the publishers changed their attitude only after they were blackmailed into obedience. The act had little to do with professionalization but was rather the result of top-down measures and direct state intervention.

69 It is worth mentioning that such kinds of behaviour, i.e. practical forms of penalization and disciplining rather than the "orthodox" path of legal litigation, have a long history in the field of publishing. In the eighteenth century, publishers often "punished" pirate publishers through public

contract law, but in the given context, apparently more effective. Forecasting the policy of the communist regime, it is possible to witness already in the late 1930s a de-specialization of copyright law, with emphasis being shifted from abstract legal normification towards regulation of the field of practice.

The final revision of the copyright law before the communist takeover took place in 1939, and reflecting the spirit of its times, brought the state and its institutions to the fore.[70] The law regulated works made for hire by employees in state service, in designated and/or autonomous institutions, and declared their copyrights to be employer (state) property and perpetual (i.e. they could not cease to subsist). If the institution carrying the copyrights ceased to exist or was reformed, relevant rights were taken over by the organization or institution closest to its original duties (art. 4). Whoever infringed upon these rights had to recoup not only inflicted losses and damages but also pay a fine ranging from 10,000 to 100,000 leva, while for all other violations fines varied between 200 and 30,000 leva (art. 26a). Artistic creations produced for hire by artists in state or communal service, as well as those created by conscripted artists, were also considered state, respectively communal property, if the task was preordained and assigned to them on duty (art. 52).

The 1939 amendment, according to Ljuben Vasilev, pioneered the option for public-legal personalities (*publično-pravni yuridičeski ličnosti*), that is, state institutions, to become carriers of copyrights.[71] Though similar tendencies could be observed in Italian, German and French law at the time, the Bulgarian law went a step further by removing all conditionality present in the laws of the other states. In the Italian law, for example, state ownership of copyrights depended on whether the work had been published with public money or on account of the state, while in the German case it applied only to cases where no author was clearly mentioned as the work's creator. In the Bulgarian case, the legislator considered the publication of a work to be, in legal terms, unconditionally a creative act. It was for this reason that unpublished works were also protected and their original copyrights rested with the state.[72]

---

shaming and truthful negative gossip. Sometimes they threatened pirates directly by paying them private visits, placed newspaper advertisements attacking unscrupulous publishers and warned the public against purchasing pirated texts. See Matthew Birkhold, *Characters Before Copyright*, 75. Michael Birnhack also reports on similar practices and the power of social norms in the regulation of the relationships between publishers, between authors, but also between publishers and authors in Mandate Palestine; see *Colonial Copyright*, 148–57.

70 *Državen Vestnik*, April 1, 1939, no. 73, 1–2.

71 Ljuben Vasilev, "Kritični beležki vărhu reformata na bălgarskoto avtorsko pravo," *Yuridičeski arhiv* 11, (1940): 249.

72 Vasilev, "Kritični beležki vărhu reformata," 252–54.

The law sought further to protect authors from exploitative contracts. Article 8 of the copyright law on the transfer of copyrights and the written contract was amended to specify that copyrights could only be transferred for a precisely defined (limited) term and declared void all contracts in which copyrights were transferred in perpetuity. In order to strengthen the revenues of authors and creative unions, and in anticipation of a *domaine public payant* regime, the law transferred after the end of the term of protection the copyrights of deceased authors to their professional organizations. Article 5 prescribed that after the expiration of the 30-year term p.m.a., copyrights were consequently transferred for another 20 years to the Unions of Writers, the Society of Bulgarian Composers "Săvremena Musika" and the Union of Bulgarian Artists respectively. If in the meantime those unions had ceased to exist, copyrights were transferred to the Academy of Sciences.

Reacting to an incident regarding film copyrights that will be analysed later in this chapter, the 1939 amendment further supplemented art. 14 on films. The new formulation declared film copyright to rest with the film producer, who retained copyright for 25 years from the film's release date. Most importantly, and as a direct reaction to foreign intervention, the article stipulated that film copyright included the right to project the film and incorporated all speech acts and music, which invariably constituted part of the film.

The amendment also applied to photographs. While retaining the initial stipulation of the 1921 copyright law, which protected photographs for a five-year term from the date of publication, the 1939 amendment made a specification for professional photographer-journalists, who were granted a 25-year term of protection for their works, with the exception of photographs created by state institutions and agencies, whose replication, exhibition and reproduction could only be authorized by state institutions and authorities (articles 60 and 61).

Through both convenience and necessity, the reality of war strengthened the relationship between the state and creative elites. The state was not only the most resourceful institution in dire times, but also the one most capable of directing the flow of financial means in the field of culture. The 1939 amendment of the copyright law, which bequeathed the management of deceased authors' copyrights after 30 years p.m.a. to the creative unions for another 20 years, was the result of strong negotiations and lobbying on the part of the writers' union. Publishers were brought to accept these conditions.[73] A series of additional measures sought to strengthen the position of the Bulgarian author: the collaboration between the Supreme

73 Gigova, *Writers of the Nation*, 56.

Congress of Reading Clubs and the Ministry of Education secured the creation of a regularly updated list of indispensable titles that had to be available in all libraries countrywide; the ministry commanded the increase of staged plays by Bulgarian authors and gave 5% of the gross earnings to the author; and finally, it directly helped individuals by either purchasing their books or by granting donations to the needy.[74]

It is noteworthy that the legislator did not yield automatically to the wishes of creative elites. Judging from a document likely dating from 1935 and addressed to the Ministry of Education, fine and graphic arts' creators complained about the inadequate and lenient treatment of copyright infringements and requested far more rigorous measures. Among them was the right to confiscate illegal reproductions of their works (often used in textbooks), justified on the grounds of illegal reproductions and the demand that infringers carry criminal responsibility.[75] None of these demands was integrated in the 1936 or 1939 law amendments, which could be understood as an indication of the legislator's unwillingness to incorporate them. One possible interpretation is that the artists' demands went too far in criminalizing transgressions, an intention that had been lacking in the Bulgarian legislator's philosophy from the beginning. That would be the conclusion if one were to draw a comparison with the treatment of publishers in the case of belletristic authors. The legislator compelled publishers to remunerate authors but did not criminalize them, which would have been an alternative way to handle it.

The official stance of the Bulgarian state regarding the BU, as reflected through the opinion of its civil servants, remained largely unchanged. Recommending Bulgaria's participation in the upcoming 1939 diplomatic conference in Brussels, charged with the development of a universal convention, the chief of the ministry's cultural section in his report recapitulated Bulgaria's relation to the Berne Convention, as well as the position of the Bulgarian state in the international division of labor in the field of culture. Commenting on the fate of small states, the author stressed their inclination to make reservations, "with the goal to guarantee a safe and benign development for their national culture. Small states predominantly resort to reservations regarding translations and the use of other intellectual goods in order to secure minimum payment, or even to evade the payment of loyalties. These reservations are very substantial because small states do not export, but usually import cultural products, and by consequence, especially if they are poor, they are incapable of paying expensive European honorariums, which impede the development of national

74 Gigova, *Writers of the Nation*, 54–55.

75 Centralen Dăržaven Arhiv (CDA) Sofia, f. 177, op. 2, a.e. 1056, 57f.

arts. Exactly this is the condition of Bulgaria, which did not sign the 1908 revision of the BC. After the Neuilly peace treaty, Bulgaria was forced to sign the Berne Convention and release a copyright law."[76] Bulgaria's participation in the upcoming conference was meaningful. By means of such an extensive introduction, the chief of the ministry's cultural section had wanted "to draw attention to the seriousness of the issue, especially for us, Bulgarians. We have to be extremely cautious. Our creators barely manage to make a living and do not export their products. And this again, which can be exported, is not profitable to such a degree as to commit us to pay loyalties to foreign authors."[77]

Copyright law in interwar Bulgaria evolved in successive waves of protectionist policy that in the late 1930s and early 1940s properly ebbed into a dirigiste programme. From its introduction in 1921, copyright was applied less as an instrument regulating free competition, but rather the contrary, in the first place as an instrument supporting national culture, and in the second, as guidelines organizing in a prescriptive manner the place and conduct of actors in the cultural field and industry. This tendency, which was enhanced in the late interwar period, coincided with a rapprochement between creative elites and the state that was mediated through the national agenda and translated into increased state patronage. Since the creation of the Bulgarian state, and throughout the interwar period, the state took up the role of legal demiurge of social relations in the field of culture, as well as the role of broker of the cultural economy, ensuring, under the conditions of a restricted market, the circulation and placement of cultural goods and the material survival of their creators. Though at first glance the system of culture seems to operate in an autonomous and self-sustained way in the interwar period, it was in fact the invisible and benevolent hand of the state that constantly oiled the junctions of the system of culture and education, underwriting its continuation in multiple ways.

Law and Territory: The Space of the Union

Through their accession to the Berne Union, states entered into a legal regime as well as into a series of formal relations with the union's structures. These are usually well documented in diplomatic exchanges and conference meetings and represent

[76] CDA Sofia, f. 177, op. 2, a.e. 1056, 134.

[77] CDA Sofia, f. 177, op. 2, a.e. 1056, 134–135.

the web of relations that form the BU's formal sphere of activity. These kinds of activities can be traced and reconstructed most easily via the official archival repositories of international organizations.

Additionally, as the sum of its members, the BU also embodied space, that is, the territorial reach of its realm and legal regime. Most importantly, as an intergovernmental and supranational organization, the BU did not only represent transnational space; through a thick network of social relations, it also produced space. One such manifestation of a spatial configuration we already encountered in the chapter on international comparisons and expansion (chapter five). Through a web of bilateral treaties, a group of select states encircled the territory of China with the explicit purpose of creating a fictive, yet legally sanctioned space of intervention.

A different and additional formula for constructing space was meddling with what could be called the informal sphere. This concerned an amorphous and malleable grey zone of activity, which though assembled and legitimized through the union's authority and regime, and while clearly exploiting the union's territorial reach, was not necessarily identical to the union's official structures (the degree of coalescence of interests is anyway very hard to determine). It was a busy universe populated by multiple and entrepreneurial actors, such as internationally operating collecting societies, private and entrepreneurial agents, international authors' associations, various organizations of corporate interests, pressure and lobby groups, to name just a few of the actors involved. Their goal was persuasion and intervention. Squeezing themselves into that constructed, uncontrolled space between nation states and the BU, using and misusing BU authority, they managed to continuously enlarge and steer the grey zone, promoting on the one hand their own specific professional interests and models and attempting, on the other, to influence the agendas for future developments. Interest groups, also in competition with one another, worked even more aggressively towards securing their lead on a global scale. By recruiting national agents, that is, representatives on the nation state level (this had been a common practice of the ALAI as well, for example), or even by setting up proper branch offices and agencies, they constructed far-reaching and influential transnational networks. By these means they not only transported their agendas, worldviews and competition to other contexts but also tried to influence national developments in their favor.

The reasons why this space of intervention is interesting in the context of this story, but also as a more general reflection on the constitution of international relations, are twofold. Firstly, because these kinds of informal relations are often invisible and therefore harder to document. Their influence, however, is as important and far-reaching as the official story of the BU and should not be underestimated. Secondly, because action provokes reaction, and intervention activates countermoves. Interest groups, ensconced in BU attire and often backed formally or informally by their respective governments, intervened uninhibited on the level of nation states, often trying to enforce specific interpretations of legal doctrine, frequently concerning open-ended topics, whose legal codification was still pending or ambivalent. Starting their persuasion campaigns from the peripheries (perhaps also using them as testing grounds), they tried to work themselves into the center of decision making by creating precedents. They moreover put pressure on national authorities and tried to hamper legislation change on a national level when it did not serve their particularistic interests. In some cases, as I will demonstrate shortly, they met with little success. These actions did not remain unanswered. They provoked a transnational wave of reaction by states facing the same dilemmas and pressures, states looking to other states' legislations and legal decisions as orientation and legitimization for resistance.

Such a constellation informed the background of the following incident that took place in the late 1930s, and revolved around the status of "talkies" (talking pictures) and the innovation of sound film, which, representing only a recent invention (since the late 1920s) with incomplete legal regulation, was still open to speculation. The passage from mute to sound film had destabilized the previous status of cinematographic works, as it had added new components to films that were open to various interpretations and remuneration claims. Up to that moment, the screening of silent films had almost always featured live music, with cinemas usually paying a fee to the performing musicians for the music. What happened when music became integrated in the film through synchronization?

The issue involved the question of whether music reproduced in films entitled composers to additional remuneration on the part of cinema owners when they screened films containing their compositions. This was the interpretation that SACEM (La Société des Auteurs, Compositeurs et Éditeurs de Music) had managed to enforce in France,[78] Italy, Britain, Germany and the Austrian Empire (that is, the core of music-producing countries), and was now trying to establish internationally, relying on the provisions of the BC and the absolute right of authors to control the fate of their works. According to this interpretation, music in films consisted of diverse rights, and whereas the reproduction right could be ceded to the producer, the composer still held the right of public performance.

---

[78] Jean-Jacques Lemoine, *La Société des Auteurs, Compositeurs et Editeurs de Musique 1850–1950* (Bar-sur-Aube: Lebois, 1950), 43–49.

Having represented only a perfunctory claim until the early twentieth century, the right of public performance rose to great prominence after the 1920s due to the broadcasting revolution, the extensive diffusion of the gramophone and the radio, and through the realization of the enormous revenues that could be recuperated through it for the music industry.[79] In fact, the "right of public performance" became for the audiovisual era the equivalent of that which the "right of reproduction" had been for the printing era, a panacea opening doors to various interpretations and the purposive installation of "toll stations."

SACEM was seeking to enforce an interpretation whereby music performed in films was subsumed under the category of public performance and had therefore to be compensated accordingly.[80] In addition, SACEM constructed its claims by relying on the difference/changes that emerged in the process of transmission from one context/language to another, for example as a result of dubbing (*doublage*). On these grounds, SACEM started to prosecute, impound and impose penalties on Bulgarian cinema owners, who collectively protested to the Ministry of Education requesting revision of the existing copyright law. They argued that music in sound films was one constituent part of the whole oeuvre, whose rights resided with the film's producer. Moreover, composers were usually paid for their compositions in advance. Demanding additional compensation meant "transforming cinema owners into concert impresarios."[81] Needless to say of course that Bulgaria had nothing like a home cinematographic industry (which was first properly built up during communist times) and was a net importer of films. Apparently, as the Union of Bulgarian Cinema Owners could demonstrate, Bulgaria was not a solitary case. During the 1930s, SACEM had undertaken similar offensives in a number of countries (Holland, Finland, Egypt, Greece), where local courts had dismissed the charges.[82] Based on these precedents, the copyright law amendment proposed that film rights rested with the producer for 25 years from the date of the film's release. This right included the right to screen the film and to reproduce during the screening speech and music, which constituted an integral part of the film. The Bulgarian initiative provoked an energetic reaction from SACEM, which through its Italian branch and the president of the Italian Society of Authors and Composers requested the repeal of the amendment. SACEM's rebuke amply used the BU as a legitimation framework,

[79] See Benedict Atkinson, *The True Story of Copyright: The Australian Experience 1905–2005* (Sydney: Sydney University Press, 2007), 112–16.

[80] CDA Sofia, f. 177, op. 2, a.e. 1056, 22–26.

[81] CDA Sofia, f. 177, op. 2, a.e. 1056, 41.

[82] CDA Sofia, f. 177, op. 2, a.e. 1056, 39–40.

while performing a wide register of meanings of the concept of "international." On the one hand it was claimed that Bulgaria was part of the BU and could therefore not repudiate its international obligations, and on the other, the country was admonished to consider its international prestige. Warning that "the system to which we have been referring, and which would be completely upset by the Bulgarian project law [i.e. the planned amendment] is based on international legal rules, which govern almost all European countries, among them also Bulgaria, that is to say, the regime of the international convention of Berne. [...] I am convinced that the noble goals, that is, the fruitful cultural exchanges between nations and the *defence of the most sacred of all properties*, which motivated Bulgaria to adhere to the international BC in the first place, will by no means be ignored in the interests pursued so actively by your ministry."[83] Informed in a timely manner by the Confédération International des Sociétés d' Auteurs et Compositeurs (CISAC),[84] Bulgaria's handling of the issue immediately provoked the interest of the Czechoslovak authorities, who requested additional information on the amendment of the copyright law.[85] It is to be assumed that Czechoslovak interest in the Bulgarian copyright amendment was motivated by similar preoccupations and/or nuisances. It goes without saying, of course, that the regulation of music in talkies represented a conundrum that vexed stakeholders on an international scale; the Bulgarian incident was neither singular nor exceptional. However, it also worth bearing in mind that these issues did not emanate from the Bulgarian reality. The incident did not reflect a conflict between Bulgarian creators and Bulgarian cinema owners. Rather, it was a conflict over how international industries split the spoils on a world scale and which rights register to activate in order to secure the flow of payments. Peripheries were drawn into the conflict only as consumers, not as active members.

While the above-mentioned incident fittingly demonstrates the dynamics in the attempt to extend propertization regimes on an international scale, the next one, which also involves the medium of film, is rather indicative of the complex intertwining between commercial interests, film rights and politics. In November 1933, the French Cinema Society protested to the Bulgarian Foreign Ministry against the ban it imposed on the screening of the French film "The Angels of Hell." The French Cinema Society had heavily invested both in the film's production and in procuring monopoly rights for the film's screening in Bulgarian cinemas. The film's

83 CDA Sofia, f. 177, op. 2, a.e. 1056, 22–26, emphasis added.

84 The "International Confederation of Societies of Authors and Composers" (CISAC) was created in 1926 in Paris and is an umbrella association of authors' collective management organizations.

85 CDA Sofia, f. 177, op. 2, a.e. 1056, 29.

interdiction had been the result of the German legation's protest to the Bulgarian Ministry of Public Education, claiming the film to be intrusive to the honour of the German army. As the French Cinema Society responded, this reasoning was only a pretext because "in reality, the German legation's intervention had to all appearances a commercial character in favor of the German Film Society, UFA, which in the current crisis was seeking to eliminate the competition by another society."[86] Having exposed the German arguments as a ruse, the French Cinema Society underlined the financial damage it was about to incur and ended its exposé with a warning: "it is therefore true that on the simple demand of the German legation, whose purpose was to avoid competition by a rival cinematographic society, the Bulgarian government brings upon a French society considerable damage. This is a signal that will not fail to attract the interest of my government."[87]

Who Gets to Profit?

One crucial issue when dealing with international copyright is the question of whom copyright serves in the first place and who gets to profit the most from its application. If a certain form and degree of commodification of cultural goods is considered permissible, necessary and/or acceptable, several episodes analysed in this book also demonstrate that copyright all too often stimulated speculative economic practices, revolving around the business of rights, and moreover, that it is often indeterminate where royalty payments went, and if, and to what degree, creators truly profited from them. While this phenomenon will be dealt with more extensively in the next section on Yugoslavia, an analogous story of smaller magnitude can also be encountered in the case of Bulgaria. The protagonists in both stories were local private agents acting as proxies for copyright-holders either in the form of international collecting societies (in the case of Yugoslavia) or international publishing houses/theatrical agencies (in the case of Bulgaria).

In 1937, the Austrian embassy in Sofia sent a notice to the Bulgarian Ministry of Education bemoaning the fact that for some time the National Theater in Sofia had been staging plays by Austrian authors without paying royalties.[88] The copyrights for the 11 plays in question belonged to the Viennese publishing house Eirich,

86 CDA Sofia, f. 177K, op. 2, a.e. 509, 73f.
87 CDA Sofia, f. 177K, op. 2, a.e. 509, 74.
88 CDA Sofia, f. 177K, op. 2, a.e. 1116, 6–7.

and the debt accrued for the years 1933–1937 amounted to 300,000 leva. Eirich's local representative in Sofia was the private copyright agency Apra, which mustered the Austrian embassy's help in order to get Bulgarian authorities to pay the debt. During negotiations with Apra, the National Theater had agreed to pay royalties for the staging of all future plays, but was currently unable to pay off liabilities. Dissatisfied with the outcome of the negotiations, Apra goaded the Austrian embassy to urge payment of the debt, otherwise it would press charges against the National Theater; after all, Bulgaria had been a member of the BU since 1921.

The message was received by the ministerial authorities, who issued a directive to refrain from the staging and performance of plays when copyright questions had not been clarified in advance. As Nikola Balabanov, head of the section for national culture and arts, explained,[89] after WWI there had been a lively interest in the procurement of theatrical plays. Special agencies and publishers had been created for this purpose, disseminating plays in manuscript form against payment. Most of these enterprises eventually closed down, but a couple survived in Vienna, Berlin and Paris and they continued to supply the world with plays. Dramatic publisher Eirich belonged to the last category and was one of the main suppliers of plays in Bulgaria. The publisher procured rights to theatrical plays and then offered them against payment to theatres worldwide. Various representatives of publishers had popped up in different countries, Bulgaria included, where several of those proxies practicing speculative business had periodically demanded royalty payments from the National Theater and several provincial theatres. The sum total claimed from Bulgaria was over 1 million leva, of which only a very small amount had been paid by the National Theater and some provincial theaters; it was to be expected that the rest would soon be requisitioned. For example, even with the support and intermediation of the Czechoslovak embassy, just for the presentation of the play "Vărhu leda," the National Theater was asked to pay 36,000 leva, which it promised to do.

Apra, headed by former opera singer A. Sladkarev, had become Eirich's new representative in Sofia, and Sladkarev claimed 300,000 leva from the National Theater for the staging of 10 plays on the publisher's behalf. Before Sladkarev, Eirich had contracted another agent in Bulgaria and the ministry was seeking to reach an arrangement with him, hoping to settle for a more reasonable sum. Moreover, the ministry sent a special envoy to Vienna in order to contact Eirich directly, and managed to reach a settlement with him for 5000 schillings (80,000 leva) on condition that all staging of Eirich plays be stalled immediately. As the ministry official

[89] CDA Sofia, f. 177K, op. 2, a.e. 1116, 25.

commented, it thereby managed to save almost 1 million leva and could expect to achieve more convenient prices for the future procurement of plays. Soon after, the theatre publisher Georgi Marton revoked Apra's representation mandate. In a letter sent to the National Theater in 1938, he informed the theatre's management that he had repealed Apra's right to collect royalties and draw up contracts, and had meanwhile handed the exclusive right of representation to the publishing house Kazanlăška Dolina.[90] Because available evidence is fragmentary, it is hard to determine the exact causal circumstances of the story: was Sladkarev acting on his own initiative when he demanded exuberant sums? He had obviously taken over from a previous agent. What kind of arrangement was there between local agents and international dramatic publishers? What can be ascertained with confidence is that there was a serious discrepancy in the various sums that were handled in this story, and this discrepancy is indicative of the elastic profit margins that could be achieved through speculative trading in performing rights. Conspicuously missing from this story once more is the author. Finally, the story is a reminder of the fact that partaking in international culture can be an expensive sport for countries with limited resources.

---

[90] CDA Sofia, f. 177K, op. 2, a.e. 1116, 28.

Chapter 8

Interwar Yugoslavia

Voices calling for the amelioration of the livelihood of creators and copyright protection had been sporadically raised before the creation of the *Kingdom of Serbs, Croats and Slovenes* (i.e. the first Yugoslavia) in 1918.[1] Since the late nineteenth century, intellectuals had been critical of the poor material conditions and adverse professional relations facing the creative strata. Though demands for a copyright law were already being made in the first decade of the twentieth century and were regularly reiterated in public manifestos promulgated by writers and their professional organizations, the first copyright law was passed only in 1929. Paradoxically, the enactment of copyright legislation did not significantly transform Yugoslavia's economy of culture. Though the demand for copyright protection had been raised from within the ranks of the fledgling cultural and intellectual professions, the materialization of the law was ultimately the outcome of international developments within the context of the post-WWI diplomatic settlement. In other words, the law was activated and harnessed more by forces from outside the country than by local actors and/or domestic professionalization processes.

The Yugoslav case is interesting for a number of reasons. Due to the particular ethnic make-up and the diverse historical legacies incorporated into the Yugoslav state, the entanglement of identity with professionalization processes is underscored. In other words, it exemplifies how complex ethnic settings can encourage but also complicate, decelerate and even obstruct professionalization processes. By the same token, in a roundabout way, it underlines just how important the components of consolidated identity and nationality are for the stabilization of the notion of IP. As in the case of Bulgaria, this chapter shows that factors other than copyright were more conducive and incentivizing for the development of domestic culture, while copyright only modestly promoted the professionalization of literature and the arts. The copyright law that was introduced in 1929 in Yugoslavia was on paper a

[1] In this chapter, for the sake of simplicity, I often refer to the Kingdom of Serbs, Croats and Slovenes (1918–1929) and the Kingdom of Yugoslavia (1929–1941) as the first Yugoslavia or simply Yugoslavia in order to designate the state structure that existed from 1918 to 1941.

modern piece of legislation that aimed to establish robust, exclusive authors' rights. As will be witnessed in this chapter, in practice, it contributed moderately towards improving the livelihood of local creators, but primarily favored intervention on behalf of foreign authors, and for this reason it had to be reconsidered and modified. Finally, this chapter emphasizes that the timing for an institution to be introduced into a local culture/setting, and respectively, the timing for a local regime to connect to international structures, can be decisive. This concerns, for example, cultures and states with little or no experience of operating such a complex legal instrument as copyright, or societies whose cultural creators have not yet consolidated their own professional position or had time to develop strong domestic syndicalist structures and representative institutions, or again societies whose economies of culture are not predicated or organized on the basis of strong and dynamic capitalistic exchange.

Created in 1918, the Kingdom of Serbs, Croats and Slovenes (Kingdom of SCS, renamed the Kingdom of Yugoslavia in 1929) unified a broad array of territories, traditions and cultures. Populations and regions that had existed for centuries under the reign of various empires brought to the new state different life experiences, political cultures and political systems, agricultural regimes, methods of communication, monetary and taxing systems, languages, scripts and religions, legal traditions, modes of production and forms of ownership, zones of economic development and finally professional and social structures, profoundly complicating the integration and consolidation of the new state formation.[2] The following section offers a cursory reading of professionalization efforts among a select group of creative elites such as writers, musicians and actors, but also of the newly institutionalized domain of film production, with the aim to evaluate the dynamic of cultural occupations, their status in Yugoslav society and the cultural market, and their relationship to political power and the state in an effort to analyse the factors that contributed to or impeded their professional development. In a roundabout way, by embedding professionalization processes within the social and cultural context of interwar Yugoslavia, this section seeks to answer the question of why copyright remained of secondary significance.

[2] Ljubodrag Dimić, *Kulturna politika Kraljevine Jugoslavije 1918–1941* (Belgrade: Stubovi Kulture, 1996), vol. I: 24–25.

Labile Professionalization

Several factors affected the professionalization efforts of authors and artists in the lands that came to constitute the first Yugoslav state. The most significant were: (1) the absence (or belated establishment) of institutions of higher learning and academic training in specific arts and the lack of relevant infrastructure; (2) regional discrepancies and diversity of experience regarding both elite and popular culture, cultural traditions and patterns of consumption due to prior and distinct imperial legacies; (3) the frailty of local cultural markets and the almost simultaneous institutionalization of highbrow and entertainment culture in the interwar period, resulting in fluid professional boundaries on the one hand, and intense competition for resources on the other; (4) the dynamic presence and surplus of actors involved in cultural production in relation to the capacity of the cultural market to absorb and remunerate their labor; (5) limited state resources for culture; (6) the destabilizing effects and prevalence of the national question; and, finally, (7) both the economic crisis of the late 1920s and the acute state crisis of the 1930s.

Before the creation of the Kingdom of SCS, several authors' organizations sprouted up locally in the late nineteenth and early twentieth centuries. They were, however, often short-lived and had to be resuscitated several times. Most unsuccessful were efforts towards the creation of a countrywide authors' association after the creation of the Kingdom of SCS in 1918. Revolving around the dilemma of the appropriate form of political organization of the South Slavs, the national question remained central and moreover metamorphosed several times in the period under examination: before the creation of the Kingdom of SCS, it concerned efforts to unify all South Slav authors for the higher purpose of creating a common state; after the creation of the state, it concerned the concrete organizational structures that such an association should develop, as well as the ideological foundations of the new state. Those conceptions varied significantly and ranged from diverse, voluntary or imposed conceptions of Yugoslavism to various centripetal forms and shades of nationalism by the end of the 1930s.

Copyright protection as an intellectual claim was formulated early in the case of the Serbian Kingdom (1882–1918). Dissatisfaction stemmed from disrespect for the rights of authors, whose works were reprinted without their knowledge and permission and often without remuneration. Authors were exposed to great material insecurity, and though literature was beginning to have a growing influence upon the reading public, it was almost impossible for authors, even the most prominent among them, to make a living as professional writers. Employment as a reviewer for the state printing house was among the most stable intellectual occupations.[3] The first efforts towards self-organization took place in 1892 with the creation of the Society for the Support of Needy Serbian Artists and Their Families (Društvo za potporu iznemoglih srpskih umetnika i njihovih porodica), which aimed to prod the state into developing some sort of social security for incapacitated and aged artists.[4]

Due to the relatively low degree of specialization and professionalization, the first societies and associations formed were all-inclusive organizations that were not split into artistic branches. Until 1912, approximately 10 societies for the organization of authors, artists, journalists and academics were created, lasting for varying amounts of time: the Art Society (Društvo za umetnost) was founded in 1883, the Literary and Artistic Union (Kiževničko-umetnička zajednica) was founded in 1892 and dissolved in 1897, while the Society of Serbian Writers and Artists (Društvo srpskih književnika i umetnika) was founded in 1902; all were forerunners of the Serbian Literary Society (Srpsko književno društvo) created in 1905. The Art Society and the Literary and Artistic Union encompassed generically writers, literary men, musicians, painters, sculptors and theatrical artists. All associations raised the issue of protection of literary and artistic property against encroachments from commercially minded intermediaries. However, most of these organizations were generally inactive and short-lived.[5] The foundation of a Croatian writers' association advanced in a similar manner. The Society of Croatian Writers (Društvo hrvatskih književnika) was founded in 1900 and emerged from a series of consequent splits from the initial, generic Artists' Society (Društvo umjetnika) which was founded in 1871, then transformed into the Society of Croatian Artists (Društvo hrvatskih umjetnika) in 1897 and subsequently became the Club of Croatian Artists (Klub hrvatskih umjetnika), until it finally consolidated at the turn of the century into the Society of Croatian Writers. Even this last formation had to acknowledge the pivotal role of Matica Hrvatska, the "national" all-encompassing organization with a claim to represent the Croatian creative intelligentsia.[6]

The first decades of the twentieth century stood under the banner of South Slavic unity and witnessed close collaboration between creative elites, evidenced through a series of regular conferences (e.g. 1904 in Belgrade and 1905 in Zagreb) held by Serbian, Croatian, Bulgarian and Slovenian writers, artists and journalists whose goal was to promote literary and artistic collaboration among the South

3 Milovan J. Bogavac, *Udruženje srpskih književnika, 1905–1945* (Belgrade: Mrlješ, 2007), 18.

4 Bogavac, *Udruženje srpskih književnika*, 21–22.

5 Bogavac, *Udruženje srpskih književnika*, 48.

6 For a concise history of the Društvo hrvatskih književnika, see its website: http://dhk.hr/povijest-dhk.

Slavs.[7] Their cooperation frequently stumbled upon practical issues such as the dilemma of whether an all-South Slavic organization should be organized according to centralist or federative principles.[8]

The Serbian Literary Society, uniting authors in the broad sense, developed the first coherent professional programme, focusing on pragmatic issues related to the material security of its members: to unite all Serbian authors, defend their professional interests, regulate their reciprocal relationships with publishers and the public, improve conditions for intellectual labor, and support and provide care for its members and their families.[9] Maintaining clear professional demarcation lines, however, proved to be difficult, and strong antagonism developed between writers' and journalists' organizations, though authors often belonged to both. The Serbian Journalists' Association (Srpsko novinarsko udruženje) split in 1905 and in the following year (1906) witnessed the creation of a parallel organization, the Society of Serbian Journalists and Publicists (Društvo srpskih novinara i publicista), created in part by members of the Serbian Literary Society.[10] In 1911, younger authors revived the Society of Serbian Writers (Društvo srpskih književnika); they also sought to end abuse and exploitation and recommended to this end state protection and recognition of IPRs.[11]

After WWI and the formation of the Kingdom of SCS, a new context arose and efforts were rekindled with a view to the creation of an all-Yugoslav writers' organization. Faced with the need to amalgamate all existing organizations and extend activity over the entire country, the question arose anew of how to go about such a feat: should one comprehensive organization be created for the whole country, or should regional sections unite? In other words, the question of centralism vs. federalism, which eventually came to dominate the political discourse and practice of the first Yugoslav state, was reflected in the case of the writers' organization as well.[12]

After the war, Serbian writers organized in the wake of painters, sculptors, actors and musicians. The Writers' Association (Udruženje književnika) was re-established in 1920 and pursued both practical and ideational objectives: to protect the material interests of authors, to safeguard authors' interests after Yugoslavia's entry into the Berne Union, and to help materialize the Yugoslav idea via the creation of an

7 Bogavac, *Udruženje srpskih književnika*, 54.
8 Bogavac, *Udruženje srpskih književnika*, 96.
9 Bogavac, *Udruženje srpskih književnika*, 86.
10 Bogavac, *Udruženje srpskih književnika*, 136.
11 Bogavac, *Udruženje srpskih književnika*, 149–50.
12 Bogavac, *Udruženje srpskih književnika*, 177.

appropriate, countrywide literature.[13] The introduction of legal measures was envisaged to help regulate the relationship between publishers and authors, to offer legal protection in cases of legal disputes and to create optimal conditions for the publication and circulation of books. The association's quest for state protectionism—that is, state aid for the sick and needy, the creation of a fund on behalf of deceased authors' families and, finally, the introduction of customs dues for imported books published abroad—was unambiguous.[14]

This final measure, the imposition of an import tax on books published abroad, targeted a well-established practice whereby publishers preferred to publish works abroad, in Vienna, Prague and other places, to benefit from the favorable currency exchange rates that made publishing abroad cheaper. On account of such benign conditions, they pocketed all profits while paying authors the meagre honorariums their books would have provided if they were actually published in Belgrade; the same strategy was followed regarding the pricing of books. Thereby they deprived the state of customs duties and harmed both authors and the public. While seeking the imposition of duties on imported works, authors' societies in Belgrade, Zagreb and Ljubljana sought to secure their own advantages and determine which imported works were useful for local literature and should therefore be exempted from customs duties. The aim of Yugoslav authors was to exempt their own works when they were published more cheaply abroad and subsequently imported into the country, while ensuring that foreign works and imported literature in translation were properly taxed. Subsequently, local literary works were successfully relieved from customs duties when published abroad, and were only charged a sum corresponding to the quantity of imported paper.[15]

Though writers' organizations resumed syndicalist pursuits, their activity was too erratic to produce substantial results and tackle real problems such as the professional relationship between author and publisher. Moreover, fragmentation prevailed, not only between different regions, but also within the same regions. The Serbian Literary Society was renewed in 1925, while the Association of Serbian Writers was re-established for the fourth time in 1927. The latter's programme included important practical measures: to promote legislation that improved conditions for literary labor, to create an authors' fund, to defend and provide its members with legal support and counselling on IP rights and interests, to negotiate satisfactory remuneration standards and defend dramatic authors' performance rights, and to

13 Bogavac, *Udruženje srpskih književnika*, 178.

14 Bogavac, *Udruženje srpskih književnika*, 180.

15 Bogavac, *Udruženje srpskih književnika*, 181.

optimize the relationship between authors and the public.[16] Despite the fact that the association hosted some of the most prominent Serbian authors, it soon disintegrated and fell into passivity from 1931 onwards. Attempts to establish a countrywide professional association were initiated with the creation of the Kingdom of SCS and were repeated regularly, for example through the 1919 venture of the Croatian Writers' Association, which, however, brought few tangible results. Though all regional associations apparently endorsed collaboration and rapprochement, opinions differed as to the degree of desired centralization or autonomy. All regional associations therefore proceeded with the formation of their own Poets, Essayists, Novelists (PEN) sections.[17] The inability to unite professionally in the case of the Yugoslav writers is particularly intriguing, given the fact that their association was greatly coveted and supported by the educational authorities, who regarded it as an important aspect of the state's cultural policy and a significant ingredient for the integration of Yugoslav society.[18] Writers were not a singular case, and similar dissonance could be observed in other creative fields as well.

Though certain arts groups temporarily achieved better coordination—such was the case in the graphic and decorative arts as well as in architecture, where in the 1920s artists held several mixed countrywide exhibitions[19]—they nevertheless failed to sustain a countrywide visual artists' association. Rather, they maintained small regional societies, often representing nothing more than artistic cliques. Responsible for this organizational failure was the classification of artists on the basis of party politics, and the periodically strained relationships between the different national centers, mainly due to the exchange of unflattering art criticism between them.[20] The only writers' organization that was evidently more successful and managed to act as a united front was the Association of Yugoslav Theatrical Authors (Udruženje jugoslovenskih dramskih autora, UJDA). Having a stake in defending the regular collection of royalties from theatres, dramatic authors managed to act in concert on the basis of their common interests and professional concerns. We will encounter them again later in this chapter in connection with copyright law. Disputes between authors intensified in the 1930s as their associations were additionally burdened by

16 Bogavac, *Udruženje srpskih književnika*, 201.

17 Bogavac, *Udruženje srpskih književnika*, 191, 195, 208, 215.

18 Dimić, *Kulturna politika*, vol. III: 295.

19 Dimić, *Kulturna politika*, vol. III: 268–69; see also Andrew Baruch Wachtel, *Making a Nation, Breaking a Nation: Literature and Cultural Politics in Yugoslavia* (Stanford, Calif.: Stanford University Press, 1998).

20 Milosav Janićijević, *Stvaralačka inteligencija međuratne Jugoslavije* (Belgrade: Institut društvenih nauka – Centar za sociološka istraživanja, 1984), 40.

political sectarianism, divisions among elder and younger generations, between left and right, as well as among leftist groupings.[21]

As already witnessed, the claim for copyright protection had formed part of the agenda of various authors' societies from early on, and in 1928 a germane association was even created, the Association for the Protection of Literary and Artistic Property (Udruženje za zaštitu književne i umetnicke svojine). Probably representing a branch of the ALAI (its title would seem to indicate such a connection), it had little real impact and was soon abandoned. Though the institutionalization of a copyright law was obviously a staple in the Yugoslav writers' catalogue of demands and had been on the agenda of the Ministry of Education, when the law was finally introduced in 1929, for reasons that will be explained later, it had a negligible effect and did not even lead to a solidification or stabilization of authors' organizations.

It can be claimed that the public discourse on copyright was mostly phrased in broad and generic terms and rarely boiled down to concrete practical issues or palpable cases. While addressing, on the one hand, the real need to stop abuses and exploitation, it intermingled, on the other, with a discourse demanding state protectionism and anticipated the active role of the state in securing not only legal regulation but also the material welfare of writers through a series of social measures such as funds, pensions and so on. A general, equivocal appeal to IP was common, more as an institution that confers "respect" and stabilizes the "status" of intellectual professions than as an instrument for concrete problem solving in the context of market relations. In other words, there was a strong symbolic connotation to the claim for copyright recognition that appeared to confirm and attribute respectability to the profession of the author. The association of property with propriety was an internationally, widely disseminated conviction and discursive topic in the late eighteenth and nineteenth centuries. In the local setting, it reflected a society that was just learning to operate with the various valences and facets of value contained in property. Authors' rights in the nineteenth and twentieth centuries were internationally coded as the epitome of progress and were regarded as a milestone in the establishment of creative and artistic autonomy. Rarely was the question raised of actual measurable gains for authors, or which stakeholders actually profited from the implementation of IP, and how. Rather, the civilizational discourse radiated a strong symbolic message to the world, wherein the liberal figure of the "proprietor" automatically connoted the respectable, sovereign and accomplished individual/

[21] Bogavac, *Udruženje srpskih književnika*, 231–37. On internal disputes among the literary left, see Stanko Lasic, *Les intellectuels et la contrainte idéologique: Conflits internes de la gauche littéraire en Yougoslavie 1928–1952* (Paris: Editions Denoël, 1974).

creator. At times this symbolic coding and concomitant undertones were all the more readily absorbed in societies in the (world and European) peripheries, eager to join the path of "civilization." Moreover, in regions and societies where dissociation from physical labor, the process of labor differentiation and urbanization were advancing only slowly, accentuating the symbolic worth of intellectual labor and commanding respect for it was *a fortiori* essential.

In 1937–1938, for reasons related to the amendment of the copyright law to be discussed later, efforts to create an association of Yugoslav writers were rekindled. Essentially representing, however, an initiative of the Serbian Writers' Association, it failed to appear representative of the whole country. The following year (1939), this time on the basis of a Zagreb initiative, the Association of Authors of the Kingdom of Yugoslavia (Udruženje autora kraljevine Jugoslavije) was founded. It issued a Literary Memorandum (*književni memorandum*) that confirmed the unfavorable status of authors and deplored the following: the general lack of respect for intellectual labor, absenteeism of the state and the public, the dearth of sophisticated periodicals of literary criticism and publishers' ineffective business models. The catalogue of remedies proposed included full independence from publishers by establishing a self-managed, author-owned publishing enterprise, which would tentatively be willing to cooperate with existing publishers upon condition of a strict regulation of authors' fees. Contrary to established practice, the enterprise would not cash in on percentages or royalties but would institutionalize a system in which every literary work (with the exception of magazines and dailies) would be remunerated according to fixed units such as print sheets, percentages or a surtax, envisaged as the "literary dinar." The literary dinar would be assembled from customs dues on imported cultural products and would flow into the association's fund. Finally, the association would establish its own translation agency in order to facilitate a worthy exchange of domestic and foreign literature.[22]

Unsurprisingly, the Association of Serbian Writers advanced analogous claims. Enumerating authorial demands in the late 1930s, the association's president, Milan Bogdanović, compiled a long and detailed list: to liberate writers from the mercy of publishers; authors' fee rates to be determined by the writers' association rather than through the arbitrariness of publishers; the association to control book sales and curb publishers' abuses; authors to create and manage their own cooperative publishing enterprise and liberate themselves from the grasp of both booksellers and publishers; the implementation of authors' rights; to promote the translation

22 Bogavac, *Udruženje srpskih književnika*, 318–22.

of domestic literature into European languages; to mediate in every respect between authors and the public; to organize a fund for disabled authors; to care for the impoverished families of deceased authors; to secure pensions for intellectual workers; to establish an authors' residence to support writers' labor; and to create propitious conditions for intellectual professions such as improved working conditions and support for travel that should instigate a comprehensive dynamic around creative processes.[23]

Apart from those already mentioned, numerous other societies and associations populated the uncoordinated Yugoslav cultural landscape before WWII. Among them were the Society of Humoristic Authors (Društvo humorističkih pisaca, 1933, Belgrade), the Club of Free Writers and Artists of the Kingdom of Yugoslavia (Klub slobodnih literata i umetnika Kraljevine Jugoslavije, 1939, Belgrade), the Union of Russian Writers and Journalists (Savez ruskih književnika i novinara, 1932, Belgrade), the Serbian PEN section (Belgrade), the Writers of the Hermagoras Society (Društvo književnika sv. Mohorja, Celje), the Slovene PEN section (Ljubljana), the Club of Croatian Writers (Klub hrvatskih književnika, Osijek), the Croatian Literary Society of St. Jerome (Hrvatsko književno društvo sv. Jeronima, Zagreb), the Association for the Advancement of Children's Literature (Udruženje za unapređenje dečije književnosti, Zagreb), the Croatian PEN section (Zagreb) and the Croatian Pedagogical Literary Assembly (Hrvatski pedagoški književni zbor, Zagreb).

The Second World War brought these activities to a standstill and radically altered the scenery. With the establishment of communist power, republican authors' associations were compelled, as soon as possible, to harmonize their regulations with the new statutes of the Union of Writers of Yugoslavia (Savez književnika Jugoslavije), which were endorsed during the union's congress in November 1946.

Cultural Professions, Professionalization and Higher Education

The present section outlines the historical development of select cultural occupations and their professionalization efforts, concentrating largely on the case of Belgrade, though it also highlights broader trends concerning the professionalization

[23] Bogavac, *Udruženje srpskih književnika*, 217–18.

of cultural occupations in the first Yugoslav state. The focus is not on the reconstruction of the cultural and intellectual history of the arts but rather a sociological perspective on the artistic professions, including efforts to establish professional associations and their agendas. Diverse patterns of historical development and cultural influences meant that other regions and metropolitan centers like Zagreb and Ljubljana had more long-standing and evolved traditions in certain artistic genres such as theatre or operetta than Belgrade, but the Serbian capital functioned as Yugoslavia's administrative center. Finally, when considering the complexity of the Yugoslav mosaic, it is useful to keep in mind that there were noteworthy regional discrepancies regarding influences and traditions even within the same ethnic groups.

For the young Yugoslav state, the interwar period became a time of high cultural creativity, openness and collaboration, exemplified in the striving for unified artistic expression in all artistic fields, as well as pluralism of expression concerning the choice of artistic languages and applied media.[24] This explosion of creativity, however, can easily obscure the fact that most cultural institutions were relatively recent creations, established gradually and with great perseverance mostly in the late nineteenth century, while most institutions of higher learning like music and arts academies were officially launched in the 1930s. Moreover, the interwar period was characterized by a clash of antithetical processes such as striving for freedom of artistic experimentation, coupled with the need to operate largely in an environment of social and creative conservativism.[25] Struggling to stabilize their professional grounds and make ends meet in this context of limited educated audiences and belated institutionalization of cultural fields as academic disciplines, creative elites in interwar Yugoslavia were faced simultaneously with competition from market-oriented entertainment culture with a strong mass appeal. Though entertainment expanded options of economic independence and professional pursuits for creative elites, it was simultaneously carried by strong transnational fashions and internationally active artists that posed significant competition to local groups. Even if on the rise, the urban middle classes were neither numerically strong enough to nourish and finance the arts long term, nor was there a self-sustained market for cultural

24 Jelena Milojković-Djurić, *Tradition and Avant-Garde: The Arts in Serbian Culture between the Two World Wars* (Boulder, Colo.: East European Monographs, 1984) (East European Monographs, no. CLX), 9–10.

25 On interwar modernism in Serbia, see "Introduction," in *On the Very Edge: Essays on Modernism in the Arts and Architecture of Interwar Serbia (1918–1941)*, eds. Jelena Bogdanović, Lilien Robinson and Igor Marjanović (Leuven: Leuven University Press, 2014), 1–29. On the effects of cultural conservativism on the arts, see Ivana Vesić's analysis of the fortunes of operetta theatre in Belgrade in the interwar period: Ivana Vesić, "Under Political and Market Pressures: The Staging of Operetta in Interwar Belgrade," *Musicology* 33 (2022): 121–52.

products. It is against this background that the professionalization of cultural occupations took place, and it goes to explain, on the one hand, the lability of professionalization processes, and on the other, the expectations for state intervention in securing the existence of cultural professions.

Notwithstanding the fact that centers of generic higher learning were established by the nineteenth century (the Jesuit Academy in Zagreb transformed in 1874 into the University of Zagreb, for example, and the Higher School/Velika škola in Belgrade transformed in 1905 into the University of Belgrade), most arts fields were short of local higher training institutions. Before WWI, only two music schools were established in Belgrade, either as a private or civic society initiative (the Serbian Music School in 1899 and the music school of the Stankovic Singers' Society in 1911). Due to the absence of music academies and conservatories, it was impossible to provide professional education for symphonic and operatic orchestras, opera singers and middle school music teachers. As a result, composers often simplified or rewrote their compositions, while orchestras (for the National Theater, for example) remained incomplete and often employed foreign musicians.[26] The first Serbian school for design and painting was established in Belgrade in 1895 by the Czech artist Kiril Kutlik, a former student of the Prague and Vienna academies, and was modestly financed by the educational authorities.[27]

In the years after WWI, intellectuals educated abroad brought home the spirit of big intellectual rebellions and the search for new values through a whole series of avant-garde movements. At the beginning of the twentieth century, and even after WWI, employment in high schools and middle schools as fine arts or music teachers was the only secure form of employment for many artists who had completed their higher education abroad. New impetus came in the 1920s, with the creation of an Arts Department at the Ministry of Education, spearheaded by Branislav Nušić, and the foundation of institutions encouraging the expansion of new organizational structures. Created in 1922 through the concerted efforts of intellectuals, the Association of Friends of Fine Arts "Cvijeta Zuzorić" staged local works, organized exhibitions, sponsored open music competitions and raised funds in support of needy artists. A landmark was set in 1925 when faculty members of the University of Belgrade founded Collegium Musicum, the University Chamber Music Society, aiming to educate the musical taste of the student body and cultivate chamber music.

26 Milojković-Djurić, *Tradition and Avant-Garde: The Arts in Serbian Culture*, 13–14.

27 Jelena Milojković-Djurić, *Tradition and Avant-Garde: Literature and Art in Serbian Culture, 1900–1918* (Boulder, Colo.: East European Monographs, 1988) (East European Monographs, no. CCXXXIV), 36–38.

Nevertheless, several factors prevented the growth of musical life in Belgrade, not least the shortage of understanding and support for the development of musical education and fine arts in general. Due to the unreceptive environment, music conformed to dominant local tastes and was mostly vocal.[28] Young authors and artists remained in general without an audience and had difficulties challenging the canon. Contextual conditions were so discouraging that many artists became decorators and portrait painters for the middle classes. By the 1930s the quality of arts had improved significantly compared to the situation before the war, but this artistic upsurge did not find adequate reflection in society. Moreover, the appropriate infrastructure was missing; there was no permanent concert hall in Belgrade and visual arts exhibitions often took place in school assembly rooms and corridors. The lack of moral and material gratification induced many to emigrate abroad, particularly painters.[29]

From the beginning of the century, the growing demand for musical performances had barely been met by the only symphonic body available in Belgrade, the Orchestra of the Royal Guard. Employed indiscriminately, it played at festive parades and balls, at the Royal Palace, in movie theatres, at the National Theater and in concerts. The formation of the Belgrade Philharmonic in 1923 was therefore acknowledged as a great feat, particularly in light of the absence of a tradition of instrumental musicianship in Serbia. The instrumentalists of the Philharmonic, however, were not permanent employees and were poorly remunerated, while their profession lacked social prestige. A third orchestra, the Radio Orchestra, was established in Belgrade in the 1930s.

The first opera seasons arrived in the National Theater only prior to WWI, while the Belgrade Opera was founded in 1920. Similar to other art ensembles, it had no premises of its own and performances took place irregularly in the halls of the Kasina and the Menaž theatres. For its orchestral needs, members were drawn from the Royal Guard, while the operatic choir was made up of actors participating in popular theatrical plays that involved singing. Actors with natural singing voices became operatic soloists in supporting roles. The lead singers were usually foreigners, most of Russian origin. In spite of the need to secure young talent for the growth of the opera company, the education of fledgling artists was not supported. Overall,

---

28 On the development and codification of vocal music as the most representative national musical genre in Serbia until WWI, see Bilhana Milanović's article on the work and impact of Stevan Stojanović Mokranjac: Bilhana Milanović, "Disciplining the Nation: Music in Serbia until 1914," in *Serbian Music: Yugoslav Contexts*, eds. Melita Milin and Jim Samson (Belgrade: Institute of Musicology, Serbian Academy of Sciences, 2014), 47–72.

29 Milojković-Djurić, *Tradition and Avant-Garde: The Arts in Serbian Culture*, 17–25.

there was an insufficient number of native artists compared to the disproportionate number of Russian singers, ballet dancers, orchestra and choir members, as well as conductors.[30] Development of the arts was boosted by migration, including the influx of 10,000 Russian émigrés between 1918 and 1921 and the internal migrations of Yugoslav-oriented artists to the new capital.[31] The establishment of the Opera and the Belgrade Philharmonic once again posed the question of the professional training of young musicians. An official plan for a music academy was announced in 1921 but failed to materialize, as did renewed efforts in 1929. It was only in 1937 that the Academy of Music and the Academy of Fine Arts were finally founded in Belgrade.

Their institutionalization was not easy, and due to financial troubles, the placement of new teachers and the purchase of necessary musical instruments for the music academy soon stalled. In a well-known pattern, civil society intervened to salvage the situation; composer/teacher/rector Kosta Manoljović took a loan from bookstore owner Sveta Rajković in order to resume construction of the academy.[32] As can be deduced from this inevitably cursory analysis, the establishment of cultural institutions and the professionalization of artistic and creative occupations was neither trouble-free nor linear in interwar Yugoslavia.

The Social Status of the Creative Intelligentsia

Yugoslavia's creative intelligentsia[33] were among the 287,870 civil servants and employees registered in the 1932 census. Already in the interwar period, the state represented the largest and most prominent employer for creative individuals. Research on the interwar period conducted by Milosav Janićijević in the 1960s reveals that 64.5% of writers and publicists belonged to the strata of civil servants,[34] 76.2% of visual artists

30 Milojković-Djurić, *Tradition and Avant-Garde: The Arts in Serbian Culture*, 42–43.

31 Ivana Vesić, "Popular Culture and Cultural Policies and Narratives in Interwar Yugoslavia," in *Urban Popular Culture and Entertainment: Experiences from Northern, East-Central, and Southern Europe, 1870s–1930s*, eds. Antje Dietze and Alexander Vari (New York: Routledge, 2023), 201.

32 Milojković-Djurić, *Tradition and Avant-Garde: The Arts in Serbian Culture*, 47.

33 The following section draws largely on Janićijević, *Stvaralačka inteligencija*, 37–45 and Dimić, *Kulturna politika*, vol. III: 289–338.

34 The composition of the writers' and publicists' group according to their main profession for the years 1918–1941 in detail: (1) Civil servants with low or intermediary education and teachers = 17.7%; (2) Civil servants with higher education = 31.5%; (3) Civil servants in leading positions = 13.8%; (4) Diplomatic service, ambassadors, senators, ministers = 4.5%; (5) Journalists, publicists, editors = 23.3%; (5) Liberal professions (attorneys, pharmacists etc.) = 5.2%; (6) Professional writers (outside of the state service and the liberal professions) = 7.1%. See Janićijević, *Stvaralačka inteligencija*, 37.

were state employees, that is, about three-quarters were employed as arts teachers in middle, high and higher schools and less than a quarter in specialized posts in state government and cultural institutions, while 90% of musicians were employed by the state. The socioeconomic structure and the degree of cultural development of Yugoslav society meant it was impossible for the creative intelligentsia to make a living exclusively from creative labor, prompting many to seek employment in state service. The intellectual elite's social status was quite diversified to allow for generalizations. Employees in education did not live comfortably (around 40–50% of writers, 72.3% of painters and sculptors, a significant number of musicians and lower-level academics). Particularly uncertain and unenviable was the situation of theatrical artists (actors, opera and ballet artists, directors). At the same time, diplomatic ambassadors, senators and ministers (4.5% of writers) had a significant income, which allowed them a privileged position in society. It is therefore unsurprising that diplomatic service was in great demand among intellectuals in the Kingdom of Yugoslavia.[35]

How strenuous it was for artists to make ends meet from arts alone, and how restricted the arts market was, is evidenced by several facts. Not a single painting was sold in the context of the 6th Yugoslav artistic exhibition in Novi Sad (1927), though the artist to population ratio at the time in the Kingdom of SCS was approximately 250 painters and sculptors to 13 million citizens. The situation in other branches of culture was comparable. Poetry collections were printed in such limited editions that they barely covered publishing costs. Intellectuals usually considered civil service employment a blessing though it could be contrary to the artistic nature. At the same time, the state was unable to make full use of the intellectual potential available.

Enter Entertainment

Belgrade's connection to the transnational networks of foreign entertainment in the interwar period has been analysed in detail by Jovana Babović.[36] In the 1920s

[35] Besides motivations related to the arts, like proximity to foreign artistic movements, it was material considerations (i.e. an income nearly 10 times higher than the average civil servant's salary) that motivated intellectuals to join the diplomatic service. Among the most prominent were Jovan Dučić, Milan Rakić, Ivo Andrić, Rastko Petrović, Branko Lazarević, Božidar Purić, Anre Tresić Pavičić and Isidor Cankar. Equally popular was the position of cultural attaché in Yugoslav embassies abroad (Miloš Crnjanski, Stanislav Vinaver, Božidar Nikolojević, Josip Sibe Milačić, Risto Ratković a.o.).

[36] Jovana Babović, "Entertaining the Yugoslav Capital: Culture, Urban Space, and Politics in Belgrade between the Two Wars" (PhD diss., University of Illinois at Urbana-Champaign, 2014). In this chapter, I quote from Babović's dissertation manuscript, which has since been published in book

and 1930s, Belgrade was more synchronized with the world than ever before. Babović demonstrates how the presence of foreign entertainment in interwar Belgrade bridged the gap between the Yugoslav capital and its urban European contemporaries by producing a sense of temporal synchronicity, even though this exchange was in several respects asymmetrical.[37]

Relative to prewar repertoires, interwar entertainment was overwhelmingly imported, while technology made it quicker, cheaper and more easily distributed. Entertainment challenged the definition of culture in interwar Belgrade because, unlike the arts and state culture, it did not aim to enlighten or educate, but appealed rather to the tastes of the public with the allure of big city spectacle.[38] The result was an ensuing power struggle between cultural elites and their professional organizations, on the one hand, and entertainment artists, networks and entrepreneurs, on the other, over the content, the significance and place of culture, the right to (state) patronage, and finally over social and cultural legitimacy. Entertainment presented a challenge to the established aesthetical, institutional, artistic and class hierarchies. According to Babović, it defied the cultural hegemony of the educated bourgeoisie and petite bourgeoisie, and threatened their moral and intellectual leadership. Professional associations took up the struggle against entertainment by framing it as subordinate to "learned" arts. They responded with alarm not only because its availability and accessibility challenged the salience of the arts and its patronage, but also because it threatened to unravel the class relations that were implied in the maintenance of cultural, national and moral hierarchies. Professional associations levied their power to maintain these hierarchies, by enforcing strict membership rules and excluding entertainers from the financial and practical privileges they carried.[39]

Babović has appropriately identified the struggles for the prerogative to define the field of culture, and the battles for the entitlement to occupy strategic positions within this field, which she attributes to the challenge that entertainment posed to established social and cultural hierarchies in interwar Belgrade. However, when taking into consideration the previous expositions on the inability of authors to sustain their organizational structures and maintain countrywide unions, the belated establishment of institutions of higher learning and the lack of professional options for

form as *Metropolitan Belgrade: Culture and Class in Interwar Yugoslavia* (Pittsburgh: University of Pittsburgh Press, 2018). There are differences in content and structure between the thesis and the book, but since my research was completed before the publication of the book, I decided to remain consistent and quote only from the initial text at hand, that being the PhD manuscript.

37 Babović, "Entertaining the Yugoslav Capital," 47–54.

38 Babović, "Entertaining the Yugoslav Capital," 64.

39 Babović, "Entertaining the Yugoslav Capital," 115–16.

highly qualified personnel in the arts, it should be clear that the typical professionalization struggles described by Babović came about less as a result of entertainment culture displacing "the unquestionable salience of the arts in the city,"[40] and more because, on the contrary, entertainment challenged only recent, unstable, fluid and unconsolidated structures in the literary and artistic professions. The associations' claim to the exclusive right to control the professions arose from competition for scarce resources and the absence of noteworthy upper-class clients and patrons, both conditions that elevated the state to a more than significant resource. Though entertainers vied likewise for state patronage, they could partially rely on the market and its consumers to remunerate their services.

Associations and the State: Professionalization, Protectionism, Ideology

The conflicts over pre-eminence and resource allocation that erupted in interwar Yugoslavia between cultural associations and representatives of the entertainment industry were typical examples of professionalization struggles over jurisdictions and functions, symbolic and material assets.[41] According to McClelland, Merl and Siegrist, a professionalization agenda is likely to develop from the following concerns: (1) awareness of a need to "raise," define or make a professional group more exclusive; (2) demands by professionals and their groups for increased educational or examination requirements needed to enter the profession (who sets standards for study, examinations, licensing?); (3) professional interaction with outside (e.g. state) influences on certification, educational requirements and the regulation of professional behaviour ("professional ethics"); (4) evolution of a career pattern ("ladder") and its complexity; (5) dealing with competition from practitioners

40 Babović, "Entertaining the Yugoslav Capital," 220.

41 The history of professions and professionalization developed quite dynamically in the 1980s and 1990s, whereas ever since the early 2000s there has been a significant renewal of the history of professionalization focusing on the creative/artistic professions and industries. Here only exemplarily: Martin Rempe, *Art, Play, Labor: The Music Profession in Germany (1850–1960)* (Studies in Central European History, vol. 73) (Leiden: Brill, 2023); Dorothea Trebesius, *Komponieren als Beruf: Frankreich und die DDR im Vergleich 1950–1980* (Modern Europäische Geschichte, vol. 4) (Göttingen: Wallstein, 2012); Juliane Scholz, *Der Drehbuchautor: USA-Deutschland* (Bielefeld: Transcript, 2016); Dietmar Müller and Hannes Siegrist, *Professionen, Eigentum und Staat: Europäische Entwicklungen im Vergleich 19. und 20. Jahrhundert* (Modern Europäische Geschichte, vol. 8) (Göttingen: Wallstein, 2014).

outside the profession in the market for services (degree of monopolization of the market by professionals as opposed to "quacks" or "unqualified practitioners"); (6) the degree of autonomy of a profession (e.g. did it, or other agents such as the state, determine the conditions of the profession?), including autonomy vis-à-vis clients and the degree to which professionals were self-employed or salaried; (7) social prestige of the profession; and (8) the degree of modernity of the profession (when did the profession become a life-long and exclusive occupation?).[42] Several of the above-mentioned criteria, at times in combination, were relevant in the Yugoslav story. As argued persuasively by Andrew Abbott, because jurisdiction is exclusive, "professions do not come about independently, but rather *interdependently*," meaning that a "move by one inevitably affects others."[43] Though domestic entertainment likewise challenged professional hierarchies, imported entertainment inadvertently created an additional cleavage.

In the context of a widening and expanding urban audience and the proliferation of new consumption opportunities offered by novel technologies in sound and image, domestic creative associations sought to gain and maintain a monopoly in the organization, privileges and definition of the arts. Their efforts took place in tandem with the state and there was a reciprocal instrumentalization between them in their quest for legitimacy: the state used the associations' efforts for its own ideological project of state building, particularly after the establishment of the dictatorship by King Alexander in 1929, while the associations sought to advance and solidify their monopoly claims with the help and institutional protection of the state. Aligning their professionalization agenda with state ideology, many creative associations were eventually sidetracked, as soon as state ideology was changed, dropped or became irrelevant. Though it developed a utilitarian attitude towards culture, the Yugoslav state's interwar cultural policy was undersized and lacked cohesion as state institutions and agencies were overwhelmed with myriad challenges such as new borders, fragmented political parties, a volatile political climate, nationalism, and an unstable economy burdened additionally by the 1929 world financial crisis.[44]

Though the dividing lines between highbrow and lowbrow culture were in practice far less rigid than suggested in the professionalization debates, discursively, they were constructed noticeably as antipodes. Objections to entertainment

42 "Introduction," in *Professionen im modernen Osteuropa / Professions in Modern Eastern Europe*, eds. Charles McClelland, Stephan Merl and Hannes Siegrist (Berlin: Duncker und Humblot, 1995), 17ff.

43 Andrew Abbott, *The System of Professions: An Essay on the Division of Expert Labor* (Chicago: University of Chicago Press, 1988), 86.

44 Babović, "Entertaining the Yugoslav Capital," 87.

were rhetorically fashioned as a devaluation of legitimate arts, and cultural elites professed to a specific order of knowledge which entitled them to special rights: privileges with regard to education, control of access to the professions and the practice of the professions, ethical monitoring and a livelihood superior to commercial occupations and handicrafts.[45] One of the most commonly applied qualification criteria drew a clear line of distinction between "learned" and "untrained" professions and the concomitant claim to exclude artists lacking qualifying training from the advantages of state protection. By way of illustration, but by no means representing a singular phenomenon, the Belgrade branch of the Association of Yugoslav Musicians lobbied in 1920 for an amendment to the state's blanket taxation on culture, on the grounds that it was inequitable to treat artists with high and lengthy education in a similar way to cinemas and circuses. Association members, therefore, had to be exempted from the 10% standard cultural tax, which then had to be increased for entertainment in precisely the same proportion as it was reduced for "learned" culture.[46]

Most professional associations were active and vocal in their quest to demarcate these differences. In so doing, they reproduced "the qualifications required for group membership as the qualitative measures for the arts."[47] In the late 1920s, most cultural associations demanded proper training as a prerequisite for membership of their ranks. In 1929, the League of Musicians announced that orchestra directors were required to complete mandatory training and exams before being certified by the organization; the Association of Dance Teachers accepted only certified teachers; and the Association of Authors dismissed private theatres as dilettante and non-national.[48] Cultural associations tried to control not only access, but also the nomenclature of cultural professions. Professional associations zealously guarded the attribute "umetnik" (artist) for serious culture, while employing the more generic term "artist" to designate a performer, that is, somebody with talent and skills but lacking formal training or artistic merit. In this vein, the Association of Actors complained that performers were undermining the sphere of state-endorsed art theatre (*umetničko pozorište*) and requested the issuing of separate work permits for arts and entertainment.[49]

---

45 Hannes Siegrist, "Professionalization/Professions in History," in *International Encyclopedia of the Social and Behavioral Sciences*, eds. Neil J. Smelser and Paul B. Baltes (Oxford: Pergamon, 2001), vol. 18: 12155.

46 Babović, "Entertaining the Yugoslav Capital," 85.

47 Babović, "Entertaining the Yugoslav Capital," 116.

48 Babović, "Entertaining the Yugoslav Capital," 116–17.

49 Babović, "Entertaining the Yugoslav Capital," 81–83.

To the degree possible, the state provided employment and financial support to the creative professions. Theatres, orchestras, studios, schools and so on were usually endowed with a coveted state-endorsed privilege (*povlašćenje*) that entitled them to reduced taxation, a guarantee of employment and state funding. The state was also able to influence the entry and sojourn of foreign artists through its legislation on labor and citizenship, which slightly favored Yugoslav cultural workers, but provided only for limited accountability of the state in shaping the market.[50]

At first glance, the sphere of culture in the Kingdom of Yugoslavia enjoyed autonomy and resisted the efforts of state authorities to direct, and ultimately subordinate it to the interests of state politics and official state ideology. Nonetheless, the country's political and economic conditions provided state cultural policy with a great variety of possibilities to influence and control creators and their artistic and political engagement. Awareness of creators' existential dependency on civil service, expectations regarding endowments, procurement of works, takeover of printing costs, awards, as well as the prevailing organizational structures of artists, the formation of tastes, political repression and more, all provided a good mix of distress and stimulation, which consciously or unconsciously influenced artists.[51]

The following section analyses the multifarious ways and means that helped to structure the relationship between creative intellectuals and the state, by taking a closer look at the agendas of associations such as the unions of dramatic authors, actors and choir singers as well as the state's approach to the film industry. Analysis confirms that most cultural associations advocated "closed" professions.[52] Furthermore, it highlights the close intertwinement and reciprocity between professionalization claims, the prerogative for protectionism and state ideology—in a nutshell, how the process of professionalization advanced under the protective guise of the state and in close alignment with state ideology.

Endowments and procurement of works were commonly used to subsidize and concurrently influence creators. In the 1930s, the majority of renowned intellectuals received some kind of state support, even if only symbolically. The Ministry of Education endorsed, for example, a special royalty rate for Miroslav Krleža, a well-known leftist and opponent of King Alexander's regime, which amounted to 20%

50 Babović, "Entertaining the Yugoslav Capital," 87, 90, 100–103, 122.

51 Dimić, *Kulturna politika*, vol. III: 289.

52 The demand for occupational closure was frequent at the time. See, for example, the history of the Greek Actors' Union (Somateio Ellinon Ithopoion): Manolis Seiragakis, "Theatrikoi asteres, peitharhia kai kratos: To epaggelma tou ithopoiou ston Mesopolemo," in *Doulevondas ston horo tou theamatos: Elliniko theatro kai kinematografos, 19os–20os aionas*, eds. Elisa Anna Delveroudi and Nikos Potamianos (Rethymno: Panepistimio Kritis, 2020), 53–77.

of all proceeds for his scenic works staged in Belgrade and Zagreb. Such opulent remuneration was a rarity and a privilege; other dramatic authors contented themselves with a one-time payment of special royalty rates for the premieres of their plays. The state stimulated and buttressed connections with foreign countries and to this end supported booksellers, translators and writers. Occasionally, as a sign of appreciation, the ministry procured authors' books. Financial support served more as a temporary stimulus and form of aid rather than a long-term, permanent source of income. Prizes and decorations performed similar functions.[53]

Artists received modest subsidies for the organization of exhibitions (leasing of space, utility expenses etc.), maintaining contacts with foreign artists or for the purchase of necessary materials (for paintings and sculptures). The ministry procured art works in order to support destitute artists and increase its own art collection, though ideological considerations partially influenced the selection of works. The extensive number of exhibitions and procurements between 1929 and 1931 points towards the regime's eagerness to entice artists and present the royal dictatorship as a system able to serve artistic life in a more systematic and active manner. Of all visual artists, the sculptor Ivan Meštrović received the greatest state commissions and income. Policy planners attracted and instrumentalized artists by commissioning works related to the Karadjordje dynasty, and/or expanding on historical themes, which, though not particularly imaginative, were well remunerated. National and cultural societies initiated the construction of new public monuments, which received a new impetus after the establishment of the royal dictatorship. Collective organization of the creative professions formed a constituent part of state policy. Through their works, artists' organizations were expected to confirm and buttress the ideology of Yugoslavism in all spheres of life. Participation in the Yugoslav state-building project signified for creators greater authority and respect for their works, social security and favorable conditions for the collective protection of their interests. The heterogeneity of professional associations and their lack of professional unity, however, weakened and partially frustrated the state's objective to control them.[54]

---

53 Dimić, *Kulturna politika*, vol. III: 293–294.

54 Dimić, *Kulturna politika*, vol. III: 295–99.

Theatre

In 1929, a few months before the Yugoslav copyright law entered into force, a group of Belgrade-based dramatic authors led by Ivan Vojnović composed a short rulebook containing the statutes of the association of dramatic authors and composers for the purpose of mutually protecting their moral and material interests (August 15, 1929). The rulebook was endorsed by state authorities in June 1930. Various sources provided inspiration for its statutes: the new copyright law, related associations abroad as well as the structure of comprehensive international unions like CISAC served as models. The Association of Yugoslav Dramatic Authors (Udruženje jugoslovenskih dramskih autora, UJDA) included in its ranks two generations of authors from several literary and theatrical centers (Sarajevo, Zagreb, Ljubljana, Belgrade). By September 1930, it counted 39 regular and 15 irregular members, among them 46 authors and translators and 8 composers. In an admixture of idealism and expediency, UJDA pledged its allegiance to Yugoslav ideology and literature and firmly espoused the principle of Yugoslav territorial and national unity. Conscious that Yugoslav drama lacked popularity abroad, UJDA sought to promote and strengthen relations with foreign countries. Its priority, however, was to consolidate domestic artistic production and its predominance in domestic repertoires, ensure the development of domestic theatre and music and guarantee the livelihood of native literary, artistic and other intellectual professions.

Importantly, the association proposed the institutionalization of literary-artistic councils (*književno-umetnički odbori*) alongside the country's national theatres. Manned and operated by professionals, the councils would function as mediators between theatre management and authors and as agencies overseeing the quality of theatrical repertoires. Given that the state's principal motivation behind the subsidy of national theatres was to strengthen national culture, the association impelled domestic stages to tend, in the first place, to domestic drama and music. Inventories of theatrical productions demonstrated a disproportionate relationship between domestic and foreign repertoires: 40% domestic to 60% foreign in the case of drama, 10% domestic to 90% foreign in the case of operas; among the councils' primary demands was a reversal of this policy.

The association paid special attention to the translation of theatrical works. In its desire to control both the availability and quality of foreign works in translation, it insisted on a policy of a singular quality translation for each foreign theatrical play. UJDA's Yugoslav orientation prompted the state to take the protection of domestic and foreign creators seriously, and the ministry issued instructions to all cultural institutions to respect copyrights and acquire permissions for the use of works in advance. Particularly fruitful was the association's cooperation with the state in the field of cultural propaganda abroad, an issue of special importance to the dictatorship, by means of which it hoped to link cultural with political objectives. UJDA would promote Yugoslav theatrical plays abroad, while the state was expected to carry the expenses, such as authors' remunerations and membership fees for international unions. UJDA was particularly active in the so-called "cultural small Entente," an association of states which, seeing its expectations from the West unmet, organized on the basis of self-help, hoping to fill gaps in regional diplomatic and economic cooperation through planning and teamwork in the field of culture. In accordance with these goals, the association invited domestic educational authorities to significantly strengthen the repertoires from Poland, Bulgaria, Romania and especially Czechoslovakia in domestic theatres. Reciprocally, translations of Yugoslav texts into their languages had to be bolstered and foreign translators guaranteed minimum remuneration. In the context of cultural policy and international cooperation, cultural exchanges among these countries would include alternating visits by theatrical ensembles.

UJDA raised a whole array of issues, such as the enactment of special legislation on theatre, promotion of a domestic repertoire, systematic alternation of Serbian, Croatian and Slovenian repertoires between the country's theatres, stimulation and staging of young authors' works, institutionalization of literary-artistic councils alongside all national theatres, prohibition of foreign operettas, augmented opportunities for young talents to create new theatres and stages, and finally the demand to channel revenues from copyrights into the hands of neglected and destitute intellectuals and their families, and thereby prevent the flow of royalties into the hands of private agencies on the look-out for profit.[55] This last issue will be examined in greater detail in the following section dealing with the copyright law.

Actors

The Actors' Association was among the most effective and influential Yugoslav cultural unions. Their pattern of professional demands, promoting monopolization, centralization and control of culture with the help of state authorities, strongly

[55] Dimić, *Kulturna politika*, vol. III: 300–305.

parallels UJDA's agenda. In the 1930s, the association exercised almost absolute control over the activity of entertainers, foreign and domestic, in Yugoslavia.[56] Especially during the royal dictatorship, it advanced to become a significant partner of the Ministry of Education, with whom it developed a strong symbiotic, mutually beneficial relationship: actors expected the ministry to use its clout to defend theatrical art and its representatives, while educational authorities anticipated that the association would promote and diffuse some of the regime's basic postulates, above all the idea of integral Yugoslavism through theatre.

Actors' efforts went in two directions: on the one hand, they aimed to obtain and secure professional advantages from the regime, and on the other, to promote the association's conceptions and expand subject matter to include topics attractive to the state. Next to a new law on theatre, their agenda included legislation on social security and a pension fund for artists. The policy of closing down regional theatres due to budgetary cuts was to be reversed and replaced with a stable theatre strategy based on permanent employment. In tune with the regime's ideology, the association advocated the standardization of theatrical texts and the purification of literary language in order to facilitate the exchange of cultural values within the country. To have a long-lasting impact on the population, the Actors' Association fostered the creation of regional (*banovski*) theatres, and monitored the quality of actors' ensembles and their theatrical repertoire.

Among the association's most important initiatives was the creation of an authorized Yugoslav artistic exchange agency (*povlašćena jugoslovenska umetnička berza*), tasked with the supervision of all visits by domestic and foreign theatrical artists in the territory of Yugoslavia. This arrangement furnished advantages for both sides: it provided artists with an ideal instrument to protect their interests, and the regime with the means to complete its centralization plans and control theatrical life along the lines of its cultural and artistic policy. The exchange agency pursued some explicitly monopolistic and protectionist goals, such as: to impede abuses during foreign artists' visits to Yugoslavia; to cooperate with analogous organizations in foreign countries to prevent the entry into Yugoslavia of nonqualified or suspect individuals under the guise of artistry; to establish high selection criteria and secure visits from first-class artists; to thwart swindles by employers or unscrupulous intermediaries that may harm Yugoslavia; to facilitate a fast professional reintegration of unemployed theatre employees; to strengthen the association's financial resources through the collection of taxes; to support poor and aged artists; and to raise the general level of performing arts.

56 Babović, "Entertaining the Yugoslav Capital," 120–21.

Moreover, the governance of culture by virtue of centralization and control was sanctioned through ministerial decrees (June 30, and October 12, 1931), postulating that all arrangements and performances by domestic and foreign artists in the kingdom could be carried out "only" and "exclusively" via authorized artistic agencies. The authorized agency fulfilled its role quite successfully. Vienna was soon established as a center serving the kingdom's cultural needs and connected with equivalent agencies in other European metropolises. The agency extended its radius of activity into a good part of Southeast and Central Europe and maintained special relations with Bucharest, Sofia, Athens and Istanbul, which pledged to book all engagements exclusively through it. By such means, the agency was able to influence inter-Balkan relationships, a circumstance congruent with the regime's political agenda. The amelioration of its members' social conditions through the creation of a central pension fund and the education of the masses by way of exposure to quality theatre represented additional spheres of the agency's activities.

The agency's influence weakened proportionately to the regime's decline, and even before the end of the dictatorship numerous theatres reclaimed their independence to determine and organize their own visits by foreign artists. In order to avoid anarchy, the ministry insisted that permission by the educational authorities had to be sought before concluding any agreements with foreign artists, particularly when state-funded theatres, whose purpose was to consciously promote national arts, were concerned. Visits had to be harmonized with the ministry's general policy, particularly regarding states with which Yugoslavia entertained reciprocal cultural relationships, such as Czechoslovakia and Poland. As political life resumed after relinquishing the ideology of integral Yugoslavism, state care for theatres and the performing arts diminished.[57]

The fate of the South Slavic Choral Union (Južnoslovenski pevački savez) resembles in many ways the development of the associations analyzed so far, and the short elucidation of its history here serves no other purpose than to confirm that the attitudes towards professionalization in the arts described hitherto were not singular cases, but rather represented a common pattern among the mainstream cultural institutions in interwar Yugoslavia.

The union was created in 1924 and subsequently formed part of the All Slavic Choral Union (Sveslovenski pevački savez) founded in 1928. Initially, and for a limited period, it received financial support from educational authorities. Having a clear ideological orientation, the Savez professed to national unity and the formation

[57] Dimić, *Kulturna politika*, vol. III: 306–312.

of a single national consciousness, while it rejected any particularistic or localist conceptions and emphasized the need to develop a unified South Slavic musical ideology. It fought in the first place for preferential treatment within the state, aiming to become the arbiter of chorus singing in the kingdom and a privileged ambassador of Yugoslav choral culture abroad. In 1929, it suggested a series of measures to promote musical culture and advance state and national interests. It advocated to exempt choral concerts from state taxation, ease the planning of concerts, and to allow only state accoladed choirs to travel abroad and participate in foreign singing contests.

In its desire to influence state cultural policy, the Savez sought to enforce monopolies. It wanted strict regulation of state funding for singing societies, participation in international events to be reserved only for certified societies belonging to the union, for the union to approve and control the repertoire of concerts abroad, and for a Yugoslav or alternatively Slavic orientation of the choirs' repertoires to be mandatory. It supported the enforcement of the unison of all choirs through legislation, as well as the representation of Yugoslavia in the All Slavic Choir Union through a single choir. It wanted a permanent state subvention in favor of the union, and exclusion of all non-union member choirs from financial aid, with the union managing and allocating all financial subsidies single-handedly. Exchange with foreign arts and cultures was to be both promoted and controlled, but domestic creators were to be given indisputable precedence.

As state support foundered after 1931, the union regularly reached its limits and survived only through the material sacrifices of its members. Not realizing that the tide had turned, it continued to serve the ideology of integral Yugoslavism, which in the 1930s progressively lost its *raison d'être*. The union shared the fate of other equivalent Yugoslav and Slavic organizations (like Sokol), which the state stifled and oppressed in the second half of the 1930s.[58]

How the state sought to control new media, and inversely how foreign media industries competed for control of foreign national markets, is best demonstrated in the case of the film industry. Domestic film production throughout the interwar period remained limited and underdeveloped. Enjoying great popularity, the screening of films basically relied on imported films. Overall, neither the state nor domestic investors had much interest in the development of the home industry. The kingdom regarded film more as a branch of commerce than as a cultural asset, and collected a 40% tax on cinema revenues. Domestic distribution companies were financially

[58] Dimić, *Kulturna politika*, vol. III: 312–23.

linked to foreign distributors, whose films they screened on a monopoly basis across the whole country. Local distributors were mainly interested in the placement of foreign films, which guaranteed the greatest profits, and avoided the uncertainties of investments in domestic production. They were also deterred by the low level of technical and technological expertise. Moreover, the poor quality of domestic films, their technical simplicity and other factors did not meet the public's taste. Finally, the state taxed domestic films at the same rate as imported films, thereby stimulating film imports.

The irrelevance of motion picture copyright in the context of interwar Yugoslavia is demonstrated by the fact that for the longest time, the state's main concern with respect to film remained censorship and control, a policy that was likewise continued under the dictatorship. A closer look at the censorship stipulations provides an insight into the regime's priorities, which can appear surprising. Next to anticipated anxieties, such as the corruption of morals, the offence of ethnic and/or religious feeling, the disturbance of public order and security, and the pernicious effect on people and the state, as well as the prohibition on altering monologues, dialogues, titles and subtitles in films, the censor was particularly vigilant about translations, and more specifically the language and script in which they appeared in films. To this end, all subtitles and texts in films "had to be communicated in state language [*na državnom jeziku*] and be thoroughly edited with respect to grammar and style." With regard to scripts, subtitles and texts, film acts had to appear alternatively in Cyrillic and Latin script and alternate between them with each change of act, or otherwise appear in both scripts simultaneously. Considering both scripts equal, it had to be ensured that if priority was given to Cyrillic in one act, then Latin was given precedence in the next one, and vice versa.[59] These stipulations clearly demonstrate how mass media and censorship were employed with a single purpose in mind: to influence Yugoslav state building, and demonstratively perform ethnic equality in public. Finally, the absence of a local cinematographic industry rendered the employment of copyright as a regulating instrument of creative labor or the practices attached to it rather superfluous.

State legislative initiatives in the late 1920s and early 1930s mainly targeted control. Such was the motivation behind the envisioned Institute for National and Cultural Action, which was expected to regulate everything to do with film—production, distribution, screening, control of the local cinema network—as well as

[59] Archiv Jugoslavije, Ministarstvo prosvete Kraljevine Jugoslavije, fond 66, fas. 383, a.j. 622, Pravilnik o cenzuri filmova, Ministarstvo prosvete, February 22, 1932.

conduct propaganda for Yugoslav film abroad. Parallel efforts were made to boost local film production, as with the law on film turnover, which ordered cinema owners to maintain a certain symmetry between the screenings of foreign and domestic films; along with the screening of every imported film, it was obligatory to screen a certain percentage of a local film as well.

An additional effort towards control and regulation was the creation in 1931 of the State Film Centre (Državna filmska zentrala). The center gave expert assessments regarding permits for distribution companies (import and placement of films), and for film production and processing companies. It advised ministries on film-related issues and helped young talented film workers to perfect their skills. All films intended for the screen had to be registered with the center. In accordance with state ideology, the regime instrumentalized Yugoslav film for the purposes of furthering society's integration. Disgruntled by the limitations imposed on foreign films by the law on film turnover, the powerful American distribution enterprises reacted with a boycott of the Yugoslav film market. They subsequently withdrew American films, which normally amounted to approximately 200 films per year, from the Yugoslav film distribution network. This vacuum was quickly filled by German films, which dominated Yugoslav cinemas and along with Austrian and Hungarian films radiated a strong propaganda content in the 1930s. Under the effect of the economic crisis, the state abandoned its extortion policy towards distributors and removed protectionist regulations that favored domestic films, which effectively led to their further decline. Overall, the state lacked the means to effectuate greater influence on domestic film production and enable the synchronization of foreign talkies with "state" language.[60]

The 1929 Copyright Law

Two different copyright laws were valid in the lands that eventually formed the Kingdom of SCS. Austrian copyright law applied in the territories that had once been under the jurisdiction of the Austrian Empire, and Hungarian copyright law in the lands that had belonged to the Hungarian Kingdom. Copyright protection in the Habsburg Empire was introduced with the royal patent of October 19, 1846 for the protection of literary and artistic property against illegal publication and reproduction. In tune with the spirit and stipulations of the civil code, the patent recognized creators' absolute right to their work, but simultaneously through

[60] Dimić, *Kulturna politika*, vol. III: 326–37.

a series of particular regulations on translations and adaptations, public displays and reproductions, relativized an exclusive authorial regime. The term of protection p.m.a. lasted 30 years, and 10 years for public performances. The patent was amended through the law of December 26, 1895, which remained in force in the Austrian territories that formed the new Yugoslav state until the introduction of the 1929 law. The 1895 amendment introduced some novelties such as the extension of protection to photographs, while it did away with the author's express reservation concerning the performance of theatrical works and the graphic artist's duty to explicitly reserve the right of multiplication and reproduction in order for both categories of works to be apt for copyright protection. The exclusive right of translation had to be unequivocally reserved in the work, and the translation completed within three years of publication of the original. The translated work enjoyed protection for five years. The Hungarian law of April 26, 1884 differed in a series of issues. Copyright protection lasted 50 years p.m.a. The author had to explicitly reserve the right of translation, initiate by himself the work's translation into a foreign language within the first year of publication of the original and complete it within three years. It is understood that authors and works that did not comply with the above regulations could be freely translated. Finally, there was no end to the term of protection for translators. Both regimes demonstrate the centrality of translation and its preferential treatment with a twofold objective: to facilitate access to (the latest) knowledge and to enhance the advantage of local intellectuals/authors/translators.[61]

With the end of WWI, the Kingdom of SCS was obligated via clauses included in the peace treaties (art. 274 of the treaty of Saint-Germain-en-Laye and art. 257 of the treaty of Trianon) to grant its citizens copyrights to the same extent they had enjoyed under the laws of Austria-Hungary and to which they were partially bound through reciprocal treaties with France, and ultimately to pass (new) legislation on IP protection. It is noteworthy, if not completely paradoxical, that the arrangement sanctioned the perpetuation of the empire's copyright regime, which these same treaties had just helped to dissolve. On the one hand, they were abolishing the *old world*, but oddly enough, ensuring on the other that existing bilateral obligations remained intact. Moreover, the intention was apparent to avoid the uncertainty of a legal void and secure the seamless passage from one copyright regime to the next, whereby the parties affected were given little choice concerning the modality of transition. Political formations like imperial states could disappear, but their international obligations had to be perpetuated.

61 Janko Šuman, *Komentar zakona o zaštiti autorskog prava i međunarodnih propisa* (Belgrade: Geca Kon, 1935), 8–9.

Legislation on industrial property was given prime consideration with the release of a related law on February 17, 1922.[62] Consequently, the Ministry of Education commissioned two expert lawyers, Dr Milorad Stražnicki of Zagreb University and Dr Janko Šuman, president of the Bureau for the Protection of Industrial Property in Belgrade, to draft a copyright law, which was submitted in the spring of 1926 and subsequently distributed to relevant cultural associations, interest groups and law faculties for deliberation. The draft law was completed by the end of 1927, but in anticipation of the 1928 revision congress of the BC in Rome, the ministry decided to wait for deliberations in parliament in order to supplement the draft and update the law according to the latest international standards. In the congress's aftermath, the Yugoslav delegates suggested a number of amendments to the draft law, particularly with regard to moral rights. That same year, the ALAI's annual congress was held in Belgrade, where the draft was discussed in detail by international experts, who, in spite of certain suggestions for modifications, praised it highly, with the French delegates even classifying it as a "loi type," a model law.[63] During the same congress, the Minister of Education was urged to accelerate the passing of the copyright law, but the change of political regime, that is, the establishment of the royal dictatorship, put the brakes on the process. Two modifications were inserted before the law was finally handed in and signed by the king. The first concerned the regulation of translations, and the second the creation of an expert council to consult state authorities on copyright issues in cases of civil or criminal disputes. King Alexander signed the law on December 26, 1929 and Yugoslavia's accession to the BC was ratified by law on March 22, 1930.[64]

The law's creators refrained from reflecting on theoretical questions such as the precise nature of authors' rights or definitions of what constitutes a work of literature, art or photography. The legislator did not specify his standpoint on doctrinal legal inquiry, though it was acknowledged that Joseph Kohler's doctrine of *Immaterialgüterrecht* formed the broad basis of the involved jurists' worldview, thereby confirming the dual influence of both German legal doctrine and legislation. Rather, it was expected that legal practice and scholarship would eventually help to bring greater clarity of interpretation, and thereby guide and help to develop the judiciary. The legislator emphasized the incessant innovation generated through intellectual

62 Regulation of November 15, 1920, *Službene novine*, no. 265, respectively see law of February 17, 1922 on the protection of industrial property, *Službene novine*, no. 69; accession to the international Paris treaty of March 20, 1883 on the protection of industrial property, *Službene novine*, February 19, 1921, no. 38.

63 Šuman, *Komentar zakona*, 10–11.

64 *Službene novine*, July 9, 1930, no. 153–LVII.

works, which, in combination with the continuous development of new technologies, prevented a rigid and ultimate definition of the nature of copyrights. The provisions of the BC, especially those of the Rome revision, as well as the copyright legislation of states that acceded to the BU after its 1908 Berlin revision, and finally some regulations of the Russian copyright law of March 20, 1911, served as templates for the new Yugoslav law.[65]

The 1929 law[66] was based on a combination of the citizenship, territoriality and language principles. It provided protection for works first published in the Kingdom of Yugoslavia, published and unpublished works by Yugoslav citizens irrespective of the location in which they were first published, whether in Yugoslavia or abroad, and finally for all works in Serbo-Croatian-Slovene language published by foreign citizens abroad. This last point followed the prototype legislation of the Polish copyright law, and was meant to address the works of Yugoslav immigrants who had taken on a different nationality (art. 1). Foreign citizens' published and unpublished works abroad were protected by the relevant regulations of international agreements, and in the absence of such, only when reciprocity between Yugoslavia and another state was guaranteed (art. 2). With Yugoslavia's entry into the BU, all existing international treaties, such as those signed with Germany, Austria, France, Czechoslovakia and Hungary, lost their *raison d'être*.

The law protected literary and intellectual works and enumerated to this end an open-ended list of relevant categories of works, allowing therefore for additions (articles 3 and 4). It acknowledged an original right for adaptations and translations, whereby the acquiescence of the original author was presumed. Importantly, Yugoslavia made a reservation regarding translations and adaptations, which departed from the concept of exclusive authorial rights. If the original author declined to translate a work into the local languages for a period of 10 years, or prohibited a work's translation and circulation, it was permitted to translate his work into the local languages without the consent of the original author (art. 6).

65 Several European copyright laws were consulted and taken into consideration in the drafting of the Yugoslav copyright law. These included the Swiss copyright law of December 7, 1922, the Austrian copyright law of August 31, 1920, the Hungarian copyright law of December 31, 1921, the Romanian copyright law of June 28, 1923, the Greek copyright law of July 17, 1920, the German copyright laws of June 19, 1901 and May 25, 1910 and those on artistic copyright of January 9, 1907 and May 22, 1910, the Swedish copyright law of May 30, 1919, the latest Czechoslovak copyright law of November 24, 1926, the Polish copyright law of March 29, 1926, the British copyright law of December 16, 1911 and the New Zealand copyright law of November 22, 1913.

66 *Zakon o zaštiti autorskog prava (sa pravilnicima)*, Ministarstvo prosvete Kraljevine Jugoslavije (Belgrade: Državna štamparija Kraljevine Jugoslavije, 1930). The law appeared officially in *Službene novine*, December 27, 1929, no. 304–CXXIX.

The historical development of translation rights in the lands that came to constitute the Kingdom of SCS had been diverse, but terms of protection had generally been fairly short. While in the territories under Austrian and Hungarian rule the author had to reserve the right of translation, which was consequently valid for three years, in the Kingdom of Serbia and the Principality of Montenegro there had been no restrictions at all concerning translations.[67] The legislator credited the particular conditions in Yugoslavia for the specific treatment of translation rights. Owing to the old legal regime, domestic literature had been accustomed to rely on translations, which not only greatly enriched home literature but also provided a significant source of income for domestic intellectuals/translators. Other countries such as Estonia, Ireland, Italy, Japan, Holland and Greece had made similar reservations concerning translation rights.[68] With the enactment of the new copyright law a gap opened up between the old and new translation regimes, which left space for contradictory interpretations. The countries with which commercial treaties had been signed before the entry into force of the 1929 law—that is, Czechoslovakia, France, Germany and Austria—insisted that the new regulation on translation did not affect previous agreements, and strove to discard the 10-year restriction on translation copyright. Yugoslav jurists, however, held onto their own interpretation.[69]

The author and/or his heirs could transfer copyright of an existing or future work, in its entirety or in part, to a third party. Following the example of the Austrian and other laws, it was impossible, as a rule, to contractually transfer copyrights for all future works or specific types of works. In such cases, the contracting parties had the right to withdraw from the contract after the lapse of one year, if no other limit was contractually set. The parties could not waive the right to discharge the arrangement (art. 15).

Moral rights were protected in articles 16, 17, 18 and 20. Ownership did not automatically entitle an owner to all rights, or in other words, even in instances where a literary and/or artistic work was sold or changed ownership, moral rights remained with the original creator (art. 16). Article 17 safeguarded the right of attribution (the name of the author) and the preservation of a work's integrity, forbidding alterations, mutilations or changes of title. The right to put a name, signature and/or mark on art works and/or their copies could be exercised only by the artist personally (art. 18). Copyright could not in itself be subject to enforcement against the author and/or his heirs. Only profit stemming from the use of a work could be subject to enforcement measures (art. 20).

---

67 Šuman, *Komentar zakona*, 80.

68 Šuman, *Komentar zakona*, 82.

69 Šuman, *Komentar zakona*, 83.

The author benefited from a robust and extensive bundle of exclusive rights, which, next to the classical prerogatives, included the republication of works in their original or altered form, translation into foreign languages, reversed translation into the original language, processing of a work from one genre of literature into another, processing of musical works into vocal and other instruments, transfer into mechanical recitation instruments and the prerogative to authorize the public performance of works through those instruments, the public performance/presentation of literary works in cinematography and radio, the reproduction and exposition of artistic works, the documentation of works of architecture or civil engineering in plans, sketches and buildings, and finally the reproduction of cinematographic works in a different literary or artistic work (art. 22). Personal use of copyrighted works without legal liability was allowed under specific circumstances, for instance when refraining from publicity or commercial purposes (art. 23).

Fair use provisions were enumerated in articles 24–35. Exceptions to authors' exclusive rights included the conditional use of certain categories of articles and news in the press, uses of literary, artistic, photographic and musical works for educational purposes (included was the threshold for quotations), licit reproductions of publicly exhibited art and the public use of portraits and photographs for specific purposes. Naming of the original source was mandatory at all times. The term of protection spanned the author's lifetime plus 50 years p.m.a. for most categories of works. Exceptions concerned photographic works, which were protected for 20 years, and films, whose term of protection varied according to their classification, that is, as potential literary, fine arts or photographic works.

Copyright infringements were dealt with in 22 articles in section 4 and foresaw monetary fines, imprisonment or a combination of the two. It was not only transgressions that were penalized, but also attempts thereof. Specific infringement cases could be settled by agreement. Moral rights were defended by the author and his heirs, and in the absence of both, by cultural and academic institutions such as academies, universities or relevant associations. Earnings from monetary fines were to be used to finance the Fund in Support of Impoverished Authors and Their Families. The law also applied retroactively, with particular conditions governing specific time frames. Finally, the Ministry of Education instituted an expert commission consisting of prominent authors, artists and jurists to assist state authorities and courts with the implementation of the copyright regime. With the entry into force of the 1929 copyright law, all previous particularistic and regionally active copyright laws (laws of December 26, 1895, February 26, 1907 and the 1884 law) were repealed.

The Dawn of a New Era: From Print to Audiovisual Media

By the end of the first decade of the twentieth century, acceptance by the BU member states that copyright protection could be applied to formats other than physical books opened the door for rising industries that fixed works in records and film to control the multiplication of copies. Two BC revision conferences were instrumental in determining developments in the new field of audiovisual technologies: the 1908 Berlin Act and 1928 Rome Act. The rights to mechanical reproduction, public performance and broadcasting represented in the first decades of the twentieth century the three key areas of contention in copyright regulation.

The revision conference in Berlin was a seminal step towards the expansion of copyright prerogatives. It enlarged the scope of authors' rights to include a series of transformative processes (translations, adaptations etc.), did away with formalities and expanded the term of protection to 50 years p.m.a. Most significantly, authors (composers) were granted the exclusive right to authorize mechanical recordings of musical works and the public performance of those works. Yet, this concession sparked the reaction of the phonographic industry, determined to fight the battle for the interests and investments of producers. Until that moment, the concept of copyright had theoretically rested on the primacy of authorial entitlement, but as eventually became clear in the case of mechanical reproduction, authors "would have to deal with a ruthless industry not inclined to give much weight to considerations of moral rights or natural justice."[70] Though the ensuing conference text was a compromise, it somehow undercut absolute authorial sovereignty. It gave member states the prerogative to decide how the mechanical right would be granted, meaning that a country had the option of introducing a compulsory licensing scheme that would allow reproduction even without authorial consent. It could even grant a parallel copyright in mechanical reproduction to more than one manufacturer.

Had the BU not recognized the author's mechanical copyright, it is uncertain whether the industry would have bothered with copyright regulation. "In any event, in securing provisions in the Berlin text for countries to impose reservations and conditions on the right, the industry's representatives established a pattern of active persuasion imitated by different industries in the future. They also ensured that their industry and the fledgling film industry could expect, over time, to receive the

[70] Atkinson, *The True History of Copyright: The Australian Experience 1905–2005* (Sydney: Sydney University Press, 2007), 33.

benefits of property rights. And what could in principle extend to these industries could extend also to the broadcasting industry and any other industry reproducing or disseminating works."[71] The BU's legal regime and territorial reach substantially aided the expansion of the phonographic industry.

Next to the mechanical reproduction right, the right to public performance was among those that the technological revolution catapulted to unexpected prominence. Performing rights had generated income for rightsholders in dramatic and musical works even in the nineteenth century. Sales of sheet music for domestic performances had been the primary source of income for music publishers, but rights to popular works (plays, opera, music) also brought returns. Income was generated through contractual agreements between copyright holders and contracting entities for the use of works.[72] However, the nineteenth century had been driven by the belief that copyright law existed in order to allow the owner to control the production and supply of books. Though attracting the same rights, dramatic and musical property were considered to be subsidiary products to books. The advent of the gramophone and the radio radically transformed this worldview.

At the beginning of the twentieth century, stakeholders such as musical authors and publishers had little interest in the merits of performing rights, concentrating rather on their dispute with record manufacturers over the proposed compulsory recording licence. The advent of the gramophone and the radio decisively transformed their attitude. "Public performances of music to mass audiences, whether disparate listeners to records played publicly, or the aggregated mass of radio listeners, created growing demand. Control of the public performance right thus delivered an extraordinary windfall. The entertainment venues and radio stations that wished to supply the demand were forced to negotiate like supplicants with holders of the performing right."[73]

Finally, control over the broadcasting of copyrighted works was a central concern of the BC revision conference in Rome in 1928. Whereas regulation of the other two rights (mechanical reproduction and public performance) had been decided essentially to accommodate the interests of authors and the phonographic industry, control over broadcasting brought the issue of public access to the fore. Opposing absolute authors' rights in broadcasting, the sturdiest proponents of public access came paradoxically from world peripheries, the newly acceded BU members Australia

71 Atkinson, *The True History of Copyright*, 33.

72 Atkinson, *The True History of Copyright*, 89.

73 Atkinson, *The True History of Copyright*, 91.

and New Zealand. Their motives were diverse. Representing young, spacious countries, they were naturally predisposed towards open communications, but it was predominantly their negative experience with a rapacious native performing rights society (Apra, a sister society of the British Performing Rights Society),[74] a similar experience to the one we will encounter in the case of Yugoslavia in this chapter, that spurred their resistance to exclusive authors' rights to broadcasting. It was feared that recognition of an unqualified broadcasting right would strengthen collective management organizations (CMOs) that would then arbitrarily raise fees for the broadcasting of music. The Rome BC conference brought two amendments: (1) codification of authors' moral rights, and (2) recognition of the author's right to authorize the diffusion of his works via radio (art. 11bis, par. 1), but also the power of national legislatures to control the exercise of this right (art. 11bis, par. 2). Though representing a compromise, paragraph 2 was a "victory" for the countries that insisted on the need to keep the innovations of the radiophonic field under public control and free from domination by commercial and financial corporations.[75]

The expansion of public performance of music via mechanical instruments was the reason for the particular expansion of the model of collective rights administration in the interwar period. The collection of societies' surging revenues from licence fees kept pace with the ongoing growth of the copyright industries and the explosion of mass entertainment.

Applying the Law, Interpreting the Law

Through the passing of the 1929 copyright law, a modern and well-conceived piece of legislation was enacted in the Kingdom of SCS, which had to consequently be applied and therefore interpreted in practice. Since the turn of the century, and especially in the interwar period, the rise and diffusion of new audiovisual technologies and the concurrent development of mass consumption of culture effectuated a shift in the preoccupations of copyright. During the previous era, in the heyday of print technologies, the heart of the matter had been to control the (illicit) reproduction of prints, to thwart pirate publishers and the (illegal) reprinting of works. The copyright regime of the print era had been stabilized by teasing out and capitalizing

[74] Atkinson, *The True History of Copyright*, 97–122.
[75] Atkinson, *The True History of Copyright*, 127.

on the tension between "content" and "form" (the idea vs. the concrete form of expression) and the separation of the intangible content from the tangible object (the printed book). The author's exclusive right of ownership was founded on, besides the notion of "labor," the proposition of "originality," denoting the particular "form" that the author had given to his/her creation. Hence, the epistemological criteria applied in order to substantiate exclusivity were *inherent in the work*. In parallel, an abstract notion of the "public" as the "welfare of the people" existed in the foundation of copyright as in the Statute of Anne. The agents and activities that copyright sought most eagerly to control were pirate publishers, unauthorized theatrical performances and translations.

With the rise of new technologies of mass consumption related to sound and music, the above configuration was substantially altered. Multiplication, commercialization and simultaneous "privatization" of the means of broadcasting, in connection with the use of appliances such as the radio and the gramophone, which could be consumed in a variety of milieus, from the privacy of the living room to social gatherings in coffee shops and as far as mass events like trade fairs, affected a mutation with respect to the notion of the "public." A novel *private-public dichotomy* moved to the foreground, with "public" now signifying not so much general welfare as had traditionally been the case, but increasingly and predominantly a *consuming and measurable entity*. In addition to the notion of "public interest" that already existed, the "public" could now also be applied as a yard stick to determine barriers to access. Many of the elaborations of copyright laws in the interwar period, Yugoslavia's included, revolved around the issue of what constitutes a "public" (performance, act, concert, execution, broadcast etc.), always in reference to the new diffusion media.[76] The exclusive right of the author was no longer grounded solely upon criteria inherent in the creation itself (labor, form etc.), but now also and increasingly upon *criteria external to the creation* (purpose, venue, space, size of the public). This was a new shift in the configuration of copyright; after all, during the era of the predominance of print technologies, nobody had ever thought of the practice of public reading, which had been such a common habit in the early modern period until well into the nineteenth century, as constituting a copyright infringement, in spite of its indisputably publicly consumed and sociable character. For obvious reasons, the fate

76 This observation is all the more interesting when considering the fact that the public performance of music was not conceptualized in copyright terms until the end of the nineteenth century, and that as Michael W. Carroll convincingly argues, the battle to reallocate rights in music developed more or less independently, and cannot be traced back, or be equitably compared to, the elaboration of copyrights in the case of printed books/works. See here Michael W. Carroll, "The Struggle for Music Copyright," *Florida Law Review* 57 (2005): 907–961, here 947–48.

of new media such as sound reproduction technologies and/or cinema at the dawn of the twentieth century was quite different. It is also no coincidence that provisions regulating the private use of cultural commodities arose and became widespread in precisely this period. The idea of private use as being outside the copyright owner's monopoly right was in previous periods so evident and obvious that it did not need to be mentioned in copyright acts. It was only with the tension between private and public coming to the fore that private use had to be explicitly codified.[77] Moreover, new reproduction technologies jeopardized established professional structures, and the stakeholders affected tried to use the public-private dichotomy in order to regulate anew professional relationships, as was the case with the rising numbers of unemployed musicians. In this vein, the Nordic Musicians' Union suggested in the 1930s a labor division predicated on the distinction between private and public; gramophone records would be produced for use in private homes, whereas musicians would dominate performances in public.[78]

Disciplining and controlling the ambiguous space originating from the private-public dichotomy, and the fortification of moral rights through international codification as the absolute extension of the author's personality, were the two components that helped the copyright regime expand and prevail in the ascending audiovisual era and in the context of mass society in the twentieth century. As perspicaciously observed by M. Birnhack, an additional requirement of the new media era was the necessity to assure the existence of a "bridge" linking copyright owners to institutional users. In the print age, the players had directly depended on each other to conduct their business; the author could not publish without the publisher, the publisher could not publish without the author. This was no longer the case in the new audiovisual era, where the relationships between players had become both detached and independent. Collecting societies, cinemas and café owners were no longer dependent on each other. "The initial state of the relationship between the copyright owners and the institutional users was of two separate parties: the cinema could do without the copyright owners. The mission of the copyright owners was to shift this preliminary state into one in which the institutional users had to rely on them. The law created the dependency."[79] The conceptual private-public dichotomy assisted the law in this mission.

---

77 See here Katarzyna Gracz, "Opposing the Expansion of Copyright Law," 274.

78 Rasmus Fleischer, "Protecting the Musicians and/or the Record Industry? On the History of 'Neighbouring Rights' and the Role of Fascist Italy," *Queen Mary Journal of Intellectual Property* 5, no. 3 (2015): 332.

79 Birnhack, *Colonial Copyright*, 186.

This is not to say that delineating the "public" proved to be an easy task in interwar Yugoslavia, or elsewhere for that matter; quite the contrary.[80] The expert commission had to pass judgement on a series of ambiguous cases involving mainly the playing of music, and though it gave its expert opinion on how to handle them practically, the one thing it most consistently and expressly avoided doing was to define what "public" (*javnost*) meant, not least because there was no unanimity either among legislations or in juridical practice. Legal codifications of the "public" differed widely among countries. Italian legislation, for example, was particularly vigorous; art. 10 of the February 7, 1925 law defined as public performance any event concerning a group beyond the ambit of a family. German and Austrian definitions were more relaxed; "public" was considered to be the execution of musical works that was accessible to an unlimited number of listeners.

Replying to an inquiry by the Army and Navy Ministry regarding IP remuneration in the case of performances of military bands serving official occasions and state events such as military parades or troop marches, the commission defined them as public events and saw the bands liable to payment. To this end, it suggested different approaches, from reaching an agreement with the domestic collecting societies regarding a fixed lump sum to negotiating with army-friendly authors a reasonable remuneration fee. Simultaneously, the playing of music within the space of military barracks or in secluded military circles like reading rooms or officers' quarters, intended exclusively for military personnel and their families, when they were not attended by third parties in indefinite numbers, should not be considered "public" performances and was therefore exempt from IP payments. Interestingly, "public" here is not understood in terms of utility (like the service of the band to the nation or the city inhabitants, for example), but solely in terms of enclosed or unenclosed spaces, and large or small numbers of consumers.[81]

A different rationale was followed with respect to the inquiry of the Central Secretariat of the Chambers of Labor (Centralni sekretarijat radničkih komora) that goes to demonstrate how volatile such decision-making and interpretation could be. The secretariat addressed the Ministry of Education, inquiring whether radio and gramophone playing in public spaces was indeed burdened with a compulsory tax,

80 The issue of boundaries between private and public spaces in connection with the definition of public performance, the various shifts of perspectives, enforcement challenges and enacted strategies in the realm of music are also the focus of Jose Bellido and Fiona Macmillan, "Music Copyright after Collectivization," *Intellectual Property Quarterly*, no. 3 (2016): 231–46.

81 AJ, fond 66, fas. 408, a.j. 654, Exchange of correspondence: Letter from the Army and Navy Ministry to the Ministry of Education, 1.12.1931, and Letter from the Ministry of Education to the Army and Navy Ministry, 10.4.1932.

and moreover, whether it was mandatory to pay a daily fee per association member (50 para was the fee demanded by collecting societies) when listening to radio or music reproduced by gramophone records. The secretariat pointed at the compulsory radio tax, which was paid on a regular monthly basis to the post authorities, and demanded that authors' fees be paid by the agents that reproduced the author's music in the first place, that is, the broadcasting stations and gramophone record factories. Being asked to pay repetitively for a record procured on a single occasion but played frequently was found to be excessive. The secretariat raised the question of ceilings for compulsory payments and whether "there was a value limit to the price of works protected by IP."

The answer of the expert commission was in part predictable. Officially, the author benefited from both exclusive rights: (1) to authorize the execution of his works via mechanical reproduction and radio, and (2) to sanction their public performance. Such were the provisions of the BC; it was, however, a different question whether the remuneration demanded by the collecting societies was just and appropriate. Yet another question was whether the execution of music via mechanical instruments or radio in workers' reading rooms, unions and cultural institutions constituted a public performance. Here the criteria applied by the expert commission were: a limited number of listeners, belonging to a closed circle entertaining a specific connection, such as members of an association, but also when, in the context of a specific social group, a particular connection existed between the listeners and the performers. Such instances, it was explained, did not constitute public performances. According to the expert committee, it was this last interpretation of the notion of "public" that had to be applied in the context of Yugoslavia, where "the cultural level of the population, eager for science and art, requires that musical works all the more, and to the extent possible free of charge, are made accessible to broad layers of the population, so that the arrangement of musical performances in the narrow circle of workers' reading rooms and other associations, when limited to their own members, should not be considered a public performance."[82] Here again, though the criterion of a limited number of participants was applied consistently, the argumentation was substantiated by a parallel utilitarian understanding of "public" as the welfare of the people.

Exploring the limits and the ambiguity of "public" was not a prerogative of the jurists. Social subjects and commercial agents also had an interest in testing and

[82] AJ, fond 66, fas. 408, a.j. 654, Letter from the Central Secretariat of the Chambers of Labor to the Ministry of Education, 29.2.1931, and Letter from the Expert Council for Authors' Rights to the Ministry of Education, 5.3.1932.

defining the borders between private and public, namely in their own interest. Zagreb's commercial chamber intervened on behalf of vendors of mechanical sound devices like gramophones and radios, requiring a waiver of copyright fees when retailers played music demos in their shops and at commercial fairs. Playing music samples in order to persuade customers to buy was the very essence of business and could by no means be categorized as public performance. The chamber insisted that their trade find special mention and regulation in the rulebook attached to the copyright law, and consequently, that vendors of mechanical music instruments and records be exempt from copyright fees when broadcasting music in stores and at fairs. In this case, the commission opted for a Solomonic solution, which nevertheless demonstrates how precarious such categorizations of space could be. Thereby, the performance of music within the confines of a store selling audio devices should not be considered a public performance; however, the moment the vendor placed the mechanical instrument or the loudspeakers outside his store, where music was accessible not only to the customers but to an indefinite number of listeners, he was liable to copyright fees. Moreover, music broadcasts during fairs, presented not in confined spaces but in the open, even if solely serving advertisement purposes for those mechanical instruments, were to be considered public performances and required the author's permission.[83]

Naturally, the area in which the greatest confusion and discontent prevailed concerned the sphere of gastronomy, and the catering of food and drink. At the heart of this debate was the attribution of responsibility for paying IP fees for live or broadcast music in such locations, as the actors involved—tavern owners, band leaders, events organizers and musicians—each denied responsibility for copyright fees and tried to offload it onto the other groups. Even greater confusion concerned locations using radio broadcasting, since radio subscribers were required to pay a monthly subscription fee to the local radio company, which was in private hands until the 1930s.

This short exposition into concrete instances involving the application of the copyright law offers an interesting insight into the messy reality of everyday life and the exigencies regarding the law's interpretation. They testify, on the one hand, to the conventional difficulties when operating with new legislation in practice and the challenges this can bring. On the other hand, they attest to the practical difficulty of ordering space according to clear-cut, unequivocal and unwavering criteria and

83 AJ, fond 66, fas. 408, a.j. 654, Letter from the Chamber of Commerce, Zagreb to the Ministry of Education, 23.1.1932, and Letter from the expert commission on copyright to the Ministry of Education, 10.3.1932.

categories. Moreover, they reveal copyright's capacity to structure and frame "space" according to measurable and comparable units, an aptitude of copyright already witnessed in the way it frames and legitimizes (the) nation(al territory). Finally, they demonstrate the multifarious dimensions of space, as well as the tensions between physical and social, official and unofficial, private and public space—just some of the opposing poles capable of producing spatial grey zones.

Moral Rights

On a final note, the pre-eminence of moral rights as a particular objective of international copyright regulation in the interwar period deserves special attention here. Interest in so-called "moral rights"[84] was not a concern of the twentieth century. On the contrary, complaints about works being arbitrarily and clumsily edited, abridged, modified, renamed, rewritten and so on were recurrent in earlier periods, and it should not be forgotten that up until and including the nineteenth century, publishers often took the liberty of modifying works at will before printing. By the late nineteenth and turn of the twentieth century, several shifts in the conceptualization of copyright were taking place, such as a limit to the acceptance of textual violations, as well as the realization that a conception of authors' rights as purely pecuniary rights was inadequate. The increased importance attributed to moral rights in the interwar period, however, is closely linked to technological innovation, the expansion of consumption options via mechanical transmission devices, and the multiplication of involved stakeholders either claiming financial compensation for their services (e.g. the record industry, collecting societies etc.) or defending other values than property (e.g. public broadcasting), and demanding a say in the division of the spoils and/or the modality of copyright regulation. Moral rights meant a strengthening of the figure of the author (diachronically, it represented the position most strongly advocated by France) as the authoritative and ultimate decision-maker, able to determine questions of access, transfer and remuneration of copyrights, precisely at a time when the pre-eminence of the author figure was being called into question.

84 Moral rights refer to the rights of *attribution* (i.e. to be identified as the creator of a work), *disclosure* (i.e. the right to decide when and whether to publish a work), *withdrawal* (i.e. the right to withdraw a work from circulation) and *integrity* (i.e. the right to preserve the integrity of a work).

New technological opportunities increased and expanded the range of transmission, transmittal, broadcasting and reproduction options, of and between works, in a manner unprecedented in comparison to the period of supremacy of print technologies. New categories of stakeholders emerged with a claim to copyright protection, such as the group of performing artists, thereby providing competition to a "pure" definition of the author. Through phonogram and public broadcasting, performances could now be fixed and disseminated beyond the confines of concert halls and public venues. The question arose of whether performers could be regarded as authors of their performances and claim compensation. The issue was first discussed during the Rome revision conference, where no consensus was reached. The French delegation in particular insisted that performers were not authors and performances should not be considered works within the framework of the BC.[85]

Moreover, the internationalization of moral rights—more precisely, the upgrading of moral rights as a legal issue of international relevance in the postwar period—took place in the context of a concrete socioeconomic constellation that involved precarious balancing. There was a need to counter the mercantilist reflexes of national governments after the Great War and ensure the advantages and practice of free trade in the traffic of intangible commodities, while at the same time restraining the trend towards nationalization (i.e. public ownership) of the new communication media. In the interwar period, both the notion of property and processes of propertization were challenged though the rise of new social visions and social subjects. If in the print (liberal) era it was widely considered that protecting (i.e. propertizing) the author was equivalent to contributing to the public good (the author is incentivized to create useful works for the community), such a correlation could no longer stand its ground in the era of mass politics and mass society.

Characteristically, in the literature of the times, moral rights were often discussed in relation to the introduction of obligatory licences for radio, which were welcomed by some governments, such as those of Norway and Czechoslovakia,[86]

---

85 In later years both the ALAI and CISAC reiterated arguments against the extension of authors' rights to performers, in contrast to the ILO, which developed a sympathetic ear for the claims of the musicians' and actors' unions. Indeed, performers were not integrated into the BC framework. International protection of performers' rights was subject to separate treaties like the Rome Convention of 1961 and the WIPO Performances and Phonograms Treaty of 1996. See here Sam Ricketson, "Rights on the Border: The Berne Convention and Neighboring Rights," in *Copyright Law in an Age of Limitations and Exceptions*, ed. Ruth L. Okediji (Cambridge: Cambridge University Press, 2017), 352–353.

86 Both countries favored a provision that after the passing of one year, legislation should allow the radio diffusion of works, without the author's consent but against an equitable remuneration for the work's use. Authors had the right to withhold permission only on the grounds of very important and exceptional reasons.

but vehemently opposed by a number of stakeholders as well as international societies such as the ALAI. The resolutions from its Budapest congress in June 1930[87] declared compulsory licenses to be "in essence, a serious violation of the author's moral rights," and invited its various national sections to act upon their governments in order to refuse the application of obligatory licenses in radio diffusion, as well as amendments of relevant BC articles. In art. 11, in connection to public broadcasting, reference was made to a "competent authority" which, in the absence of an agreement, should decide a fair reward for the author. This authority, the ALAI insisted, should be a regular or elected court rather than an administrative body. On the contrary, in order to decide such questions, the League of Nations should initiate international conventions, arranging for the creation of mixed international courts with a seat in Berne, in order to litigate cases between member states. Their decisions should be binding for all union countries.

In the same context, the ALAI postulated the need for unrestricted and broad circulation of literary and artistic works and considered duties or other kinds of import taxes to be unjustified. It was necessary therefore to create and ensure an unconditional, customs-free regime for intellectual works disseminated via mechanical process. Naturally, as the association repeatedly stressed, unrestricted tax-free access to foreign markets by no means signified circumventing existing national bans or local censorship, or encroaching on public order or a country's good morals.

It is worth pointing out a few issues of interest here. The central point in the case of compulsory licences for radio also revolved around the "private-public" dichotomy, and more specifically around the question of who has the prerogative to determine access: the private person or the public authority. Practically, obligatory licences meant the capacity to override the author's absolute ownership right, which signified a fracture in the otherwise absolute construction of authors' rights as an impenetrable bastion. The preference of organizations like the ALAI for a juridification of the regulation of relationships, instead of a practical and/or administrative approach, is also clear. Furthermore, the predilection that litigations concerning the generic area of radio broadcasting be regulated essentially by private and/or international law, or in other words by law that circumvents national jurisdiction and/or public law, is obvious.

This example also clearly demonstrates a further paradox of copyright: that it is possible to uphold and defend moral rights as the supreme expression of the personality of the author, as rights that need to be universally defended and respected,

[87] AJ, fond 66, fas. 408, a.j. 655, Report ALAI congress in Budapest, June 1930, objectives and resolutions.

while at the same time arguing that obeying national censorship standards is perfectly legitimate. Finally, I would like to raise the tentative hypothesis that the international codification of moral rights in the interwar period was ultimately an attempt to "prolong" a theoretical conception of IP rights as "natural rights," precisely at a moment in time when the conceptualization of IP rights as statutory rights was gaining ground internationally, thereby altering the argumentative grounds and the foundations of legitimacy for IPRs. Whether it was a "pure" coincidence that the above-described developments in international legal codification were taking place in parallel to a process whereby both the state and private industry were competing over the encouragement of innovation and the prerogative to determine regulation in the field of communications needs to be substantiated by further research.

Applying the Law: Organizational Structures, Social Agents and Practice

This section[88] deals with the phenomenon of private collecting societies in interwar Yugoslavia, and though it has an amusing plot, the story was not included in order to indulge the reader in anecdotal entertainment. Rather, its reconstruction is meant to be instructive in several ways.

In the first place, it demonstrates quite lucidly that the sole existence of IP rights effectuates *per se* very little within a given context. Rather, it is the ways in which IP rights are practically organized and applied that determines who effectively profits from their existence. Second, it demonstrates that the organization of IP rights necessitates regular revisions, adjustments and control in order to remain balanced, and moreover, that an IP system can very well fail in its noble purpose, that is, to protect authors and secure their remuneration, as well as guarantee fair access to end users. Furthermore, a thoroughly liberal IP system without regulation, auditing and appropriate redistribution and balancing mechanisms can easily degenerate into the rule of the strongest. This section also testifies to the intrinsic danger that copyright can turn from an instrument of support and remuneration for cultural creators into a banal capitalistic business motivated solely by profit. Third, it tells a story about the

88 An earlier version of this section appeared in German as "Das Recht am geistigen Eigentum im Jugoslawien der Zwischenkriegszeit. Internationaler Institutionentransfer zwischen rechtlicher Normierung und sozialer Praxis," *Zeitschrift für Ostmitteleuropaforschung* 61, no. 3 (2012) (Institutionenwandel und Rechtstransfer im 20. Jahrhundert, eds. Hannes Siegrist and Stefan Troebst): 356–78.

application of IP rights in a European periphery, and thereby draws attention to the different contextual conditions into which this institution was embedded and why they matter. Yugoslavia was one of the many countries that through its incorporation into the international IP regime became part of the international division of labor in the cultural industries, an arrangement that clearly favored strong players and their quasi-colonial approach towards weaker players. The international IP system (through a variety of formal and informal instruments) had the capacity to structure repertoires and install a royalty-extracting machine, which sooner or later provoked local resistance, a pattern already witnessed in the case of the Australian collecting society ARPA, but also in the previous chapter concerning music and the screening of talkies in Bulgaria, and as will be analysed in detail in the present chapter on Yugoslavia. Fourth, and in connection to the above, it demonstrates how asymmetries of culture condition the application of legal instruments, and moreover, points to the paradox that the internationalization of IPRs in the aftermath of WWI could cause a counter-reaction similar to a renationalization, and how intertwined those processes were, as will be witnessed in this chapter.

The first collecting societies founded in the Kingdom of SCS in the early 1920s were private agencies such as the Association for the Protection of Literary and Artistic Property (Udruženje za zaštitu književne i umjetničke svojine) of Josip Nagy and Srećko Albini with seats in Zagreb, and later also in Belgrade and Ljubljana. In the early phase, Zagreb was apparently a mainspring of such activities, a circumstance likely related to the greater exposure of the previous Habsburg territories to the notion and practice of IP rights in comparison to the Ottoman dominions. These first societies were usually founded by a particular type of artistically inclined and engaged professional (for example, Srećko Albini was a composer, conductor and music publisher), who entertained multiple (not always transparent) connections to art and spectacle, and who in addition had a sense for the practical, enterprising and commercial side of cultural business. They were moreover associated with foreign artists, impresarios, collecting agents and societies and well acquainted with the international market in cultural goods. The early societies had little authority, which probably explains why they were not consulted regarding the drafting of the 1929 copyright law. They nevertheless insisted on having their voice heard, arguing for the necessity to accelerate the law's enactment and provide authors with strong and exclusive copyrights. Unfettered authorial protection was the current trend in most modern legislations such as the Czech and Polish copyright laws, and the association argued against "useless and unnecessary restrictions," such as the government's reservation in the case of translations. On the contrary, only strong authorial rights benefited all sides: they protected authors against publishers, they regulated competition among publishers and brought an advantage to the reading public. Framing the protection of authors as a noble mission, the fulfilment of which automatically legitimized any action, the association prodded the government to fulfil its international obligations without delay.[89] Also founded in Zagreb in the 1920s was the Yugoslav Joint-Stock Company for the Use of Authors' Rights (Jugoslovensko dioničko društvo za izkoriščivanje autorskih prava) by Silvestar Bakarčić.

Owing to the absence of any previous or substantial experience in the handling of copyright issues, copyright protection in the Kingdom of SCS had to be set up practically from scratch. These efforts coincided with the labors of foreign authors' associations and CMOs, who at the first opportunity sought to extend IP protection for their authors in the newly created state. Due to a synergy of reasons, therefore, several agencies were quickly set up as proxies. Albini founded the Author-Central for Copyrights (Autor-Centrala za autorska prava) in Zagreb, where the Association of Yugoslav Music Authors (Udruženje jugoslovenskih musičkih autora, UJMA) was also established, representing a substantial number of Yugoslav composers and functioning practically as their national association. At the same time, agencies came into the picture in Belgrade as well. The lawyer Vesa Marković claimed the representation of the "French authors' society," most likely indicating SACEM, while the journalist Todor Paravos founded the collecting society Agency-Author for the Protection of Authors' Rights in the Kingdom of Yugoslavia (Agencija-Autor za zaštitu autorskog prava u kraljevini Jugoslaviji).[90] UJMA soon transferred its copyrights to Autor-Centrala. Three collecting societies therefore existed by the time of CISAC's (Confédération Internationale des Sociétés des Auteurs et Compositeurs)[91] interwar conference in Budapest: Albini's Autor-Centrala, the agency of Vesa Marković, and Paravos's Agencija-Autor. During the conference and in the presence of other foreign authors' societies, negotiations took place aiming at a fusion of the three Yugoslav societies, but with little success. Soon after, Marković partnered up with Paravos under the label of Agencija-Autor, so that effectively two collecting societies remained active: Autor-Centrala and Agencija-Autor. At the end of 1930, Silvestar

89 AJ, fond 66, fas. 409, a.j. 657, Letter from Udruženje za zaštitu književne i umjetničke svojine u Zagrebu to the Minister of Education, B. Maksimović, November 27, 1929.

90 *Jugoslavenski autor, glasilo Autor-Centrale za autorska prava i Udruženja Jugoslavenskih muzičkih autora* 1/2 (1932), 1.

91 The International Confederation of Societies of Authors and Composers (CISAC) was founded in France in 1926 by 18 European authors' societies, at the time representing mainly the dramatic arts, but its areas of competence were progressively expanded to include all kinds of performing rights. It is currently the largest international network of authors' societies functioning as a CMO.

Bakarčić took over the management of Autor-Centrala and proposed during the CISAC conference in Paris in February 1931 a division of Yugoslav territory so as to avoid conflicts with Agencija-Autor. CISAC accepted his proposal, and handed over to him personally the prerogative of representation. Subsequently, Bakarčić founded a new collecting society, the "Autor-Centrala for Authors' Rights S. Bakarčić" (Autor-Centrala za autorska prava S. Bakarčić) and liquidated the old agency. CISAC's subsequent conference in Rome, in November 1931, confirmed Bakarčić and his Autor-Centrala as sole representatives for the entire Yugoslav territory.

In parallel to the above-mentioned developments, additional aspirants continued to pop up, fashioning themselves as proxies of foreign societies. In November 1931, a certain Belgrade lawyer by the name of Milan Fotić addressed the Ministry of Education and requested a certification testifying that he was the official representative of the French authors' association "Société des gens de lettres," to which end he handed in a relevant warrant.[92] Whether such single incidents were the result of opportunists functioning as self-appointed proxies, or whether they were actually instigated on the initiative of foreign societies, is not always evident. What is clear is that among the prominent protagonists of this story, lawyers can be encountered with a certain regularity.

Collecting societies pursued similar strategies in their objective to inculcate in users the as-yet-unfamiliar notion of exclusive copyright; their objective was to discipline social subjects by enforcing the internalization of pertinent values. Whereas familiarizing the public with a novel notion such as IP rights was undoubtedly a demanding task, the agencies were overzealous in imposing a notion of copyrights in which access to and use of culture were rigorously conditional upon payment of tolls with collecting societies representing the official doorkeepers. Discipline was also rehearsed by making the law conspicuously visible. Letter templates used by Autor-Centrala for regular correspondence contained a printed column inserted on the letter's left margin, next to the state's coat of arms, which recapitulated excerpts of the copyright law, particularly paragraphs enumerating sanctions against infringements. Such practices illustrate well the multiple and intersecting layers of legitimization strategies: repetition, constant visualization and ubiquity of sanctions, and self-legitimization of the agencies through appeals to law, order and the state.

In their efforts to monopolize copyright management in Yugoslavia, both agencies begged favors of the state and tried to instrumentalize state authority, in a pattern already encountered in the introductory section on Yugoslav cultural

92 AJ, fond 66, fas. 409, a.j. 659, Letter from Milan Fotić to the Ministry of Education, November 25, 1931.

associations. Agencija-Autor's letterhead carried the epigraph "Under the supervision of the Ministry of Education," while the agency had its rulebook officially endorsed by the ministry,[93] arousing thereby the envy of its competitor Bakarčić, who protested against Agencija-Autor's preferential treatment and demanded similar recognition for his agency.[94] In his petition to the Ministry of Commerce and Industry asking for permission to likewise carry the state emblem, Bakarčić explained that the goal of Autor-Centrala was, "through cultural alertness, to foster our literature and culture in the spirit of national and state unity, domestically and abroad." Bakarčić concluded ardently that being able to pursue this feat under the aegis of the state would be of great moral value.[95]

Reactions to the agencies' unprincipled manner of conducting business were not long in coming, and included a wide range of social actors from the world of commerce and the professions as well as civil society. They criticized the fact that regulations were set up by a private agent, as well as the state's failure to take the initiative in setting up operational guidelines. Paragraph 5 of Agencija-Autor's rulebook in particular aroused strong objections; it sanctioned the intervention of state authorities in the interim period before litigation could take place in court, and thereby, so social actors feared, opened the door to police interventions.[96] Collecting societies, depending on their respective interlocutor, availed themselves of a double discourse as a legitimization strategy: in regard to society, they presented themselves as official representatives of state authorities (though in reality they were private enterprises), while in regard to the state, they referred to the international obligations that Yugoslavia had incurred as a member of the Berne Union.

Arranged in such a manner as to be comprehensible at first glance, Agencija-Autor's information sheet presented a combination of these legitimization strategies on a visual level: while the top half of the sheet addressed the domestic components of authority, that is, excerpts from the agency's certification and its rulebook, printed along with the state emblem and the ministry's header, the lower half comprised the international components of authority. The main authority and point of

---

93 AJ, fond 66, fas. 408, a.j. 659, Uverenje, Certification of the Ministry of Education issued after the request of T. Paranos, officially endorsing the foundation of his agency, April 9, 1930; see also *Pravilnik* May 9, 1930.

94 AJ, fond 66, fas. 409, a.j. 657, Letters from Autor-Centrala to the Ministry of Education, November 17, 1931 and July 2, 1932.

95 AJ, fond 66, fas. 408, a.j. 653, Letter from the Ministry of Commerce and Industry to the Ministry of Education, October 8, 1929.

96 AJ, fond 66, fas. 408, a.j. 656, Joint letter from Radio A.A., the Yugoslav Choir Union, Cinemas *Korzo*, *Urania* et al. to the Ministry of Education, April 17, 1931.

reference here was SACEM, while the sheet also included a list of the societies that made up the "kartel," on whose account authors' fees were collected in Yugoslavia, those being: Genossenschaft zur Verwertung Musikalischer Aufführungsrechte (Berlin), Sociedade Brasileira de Autores Teatrais (Rio de Janeiro), American Society of Composers, Authors and Publishers (New York), Société des Auteurs, Compositeurs et Editeurs de Musique (Paris), The Performing Right Society Ltd. (London), Magyar Szövegírók, Zeneszerzők és Zeneműkiadók Szövetkezete (Budapest), Società Italiana degli Autori ed Editori (Rome) and Sociedade de Escritores e Compositores Teatrais Portugueses (Lisbon). Below them were listed the categories of events and tariffs applied, calculated in percentages that were deducted from gross realized income as follows: (1) Concerts (secular or spiritual), spectacles-concerts, balls, balls-concerts, dancing places, casinos, music-halls, dance schools, game performances etc. = 6%; (2) Variety shows, bars, arias inserted in revue theatres etc. = 5%; (3) Symphonic concerts = 4%; (4) Cinemas = silent films 2% and talkies 3%; (5) Coffee shops, restaurants, pubs, hotels = 3%; (6) Circuses, ringspiel, carousel = 2%; (7) Places of worship = spiritual concerts 6.6%, weddings and funerals, a fixed sum according to the church's significance.

In addition to the above tariffs, a 10% fee was levied "in favor of the societies' pension funds." The formulation was very general, and it was not specified which societies were referred to, whether domestic or foreign ones, or the exact modality of distribution. The 10% fee included literally *any* kind of event, performance and/or venue, from theatres and pubs to schools and universities, parks and public promenades, ports and racing grounds, all kinds of musical performances, whether vocal or instrumental, civic or military, mechanical or organized, and all kinds of societies, whether charity, patriotic, artistic and so on. It literally left no aspect of social life untaxed.[97]

The agencies readily posed as representatives of the entire world music and theatre repertoire and eventually provoked the distrust of business, trade and arts professionals, who increasingly turned to the Ministry of Education to specify and qualify the agencies' claims. Via their reports, protests and requests, the ministry gained insight into the agencies' practice. One such example was the case of the owner of the Belgrade hotel Srpska Kruna, Đorđe Popara. When he asked Agencija-Autor which composers the agency represented, and which criteria were applied for the calculation of tariffs,[98] he was informed that "the agency represented more or less the composers of the entire world, also the national ones," and that for a fixed

[97] AJ, fond 66, fas. 409, a.j. 659, Information sheet of Agencija-"Autor," 1930.

[98] Archiv Jugoslavije, fond 66, fas. 408, a.j. 656, Letter from the hotel owner Đorđe Popara to Agencija-Autor, May 13, 1931.

monthly fee of 1155 dinars he was eligible to perform any piece of music in his hotel.[99] Subsequently, Popara turned to the Ministry of Education to authenticate the claim, and demanded a written confirmation that Agencija-Autor was indeed authorized to represent the entire world repertoire and that upon payment of the requested sum he was entitled to play any music on the premises of his hotel.[100]

Theatre was not spared from shady dealings with copyrights either, as the official association of Yugoslav theatrical authors (UJDA) was about to find out. In the spring of 1931, they were contacted by the Theater Agency of the Association of Polish Dramatic Authors (Agencja teatralna zwiazku autorow dramatycznych polskich), and invited to deliver the fees for the performance of the play "The Morality of Mrs. Dulska" by Gabriela Zapolska.[101] There is no doubt that the theatre had paid the fees for the rights to the play, but not to UJDA, which had been officially authorized by Zapolska's heir, Ms. Lewicka, to represent her in Yugoslavia. Instead, royalties had been cashed by Srečko Albini, who claimed that through his contract with the Viennese theatre publisher Otto Eirich, he was officially authorized to collect royalties for Eirich's entire portfolio of works in all Yugoslav languages, Zapolska's play among them.[102] Upon intervention by the authorities, Albini was asked to contact Eirich anew in order to confirm the authorization, which he ostensibly did. Albini claimed that Eirich had allegedly concluded a contract with Zapolska in 1908, which also authorized him to collect author's fees in Yugoslavia, while the author's heir claimed on the contrary that Zapolska's rights had been transferred to the agency of the Polish dramatic authors. Albini lamented being unable to furnish a legalization of the document, but royalties had been so insignificant and legalizations so expensive that it was simply impossible to supply them for every single document. However, he was, as he assured the local educational authorities in Zagreb, certainly in possession of the original documents, which he had quoted in his initial defense.[103] After a thorough examination of all documentation, the authorities concluded that UJDA was Zapolska's lawful representative in Yugoslavia and called on Albini to address the issue of royalties.[104] In the

99 Archiv Jugoslavije, fond 66, fas. 408, a.j. 656, Answer from Agencija-Autor to Đorđe Popara, May 14, 1931.

100 Archiv Jugoslavije, fond 66, fas. 408, a.j. 656, Letter from Đorđe Popara to the Ministry of Education, May 15, 1931.

101 AJ, fond 66, fas. 409, a.j. 659, Letter from the Theater Agency of the Association of Polish Dramatic Authors to UJDA, Belgrade, April 13, 1931; also Letters of June 23, 1931 and November 21, 1931.

102 AJ, fond 66, fas. 409, a.j. 659, Letter from the Theater Agency of the Association of Polish Dramatic Authors to UJDA, Srečko Albini, Zapisnik, November 27, 1931.

103 AJ, fond 66, fas. 409, a.j. 659, Letter from the Theater Agency of the Association of Polish Dramatic Authors to UJDA, Zapisnik, December 19, 1931.

104 AJ, fond 66, fas. 409, a.j. 659, Letter from the Theater Agency of the Association of Polish Dramatic Authors to UJDA, Letter from the Ministry of Education, Belgrade to kraljevska banska uprava savske banovine, prosvetno odelenje, Zagreb, December 31, 1931.

wake of repeated instances such as these, numerous complaints and appeals reached the Ministry of Education between 1930 and 1931.

In the meantime, both agencies nominated representatives and authorized them to collect royalties in regions and *banovinas*[105] where they had so far been absent. They in turn often calculated fees arbitrarily and double-billed clients, as they both repeatedly charged the same institution, organization or company for the same event/performance. As incidents accumulated and the agencies' proxies became bolder, the Chamber of Commerce and Industry was compelled to intervene. Such was the case, for example, with an inquiry by the association of restaurant and hotel proprietors, which demanded clarification as to which of the three agents, all officially presenting themselves as proxies of Autor-Centrala, was the rightful and authorized representative for the Vardar banovina.[106] Catering and tourism also switched to defence mode and consulted the Ministry of Education directly; Petar Skipić, an innkeeper from Subotica, asked the ministry for a catalogue of all protected authors and their works, claiming that "the representatives of Autor-Centrala inquired fees for all musical works, irrespective of whether their authors were protected by copyright or not."[107]

Cultural institutions were also not spared from the arbitrariness of collecting agencies. In 1931, the national theatre of Zeta banovina in Dubrovnik urgently appealed to the Ministry of Education for help, as it was being charged by both branches of Autor-Centrala in Zagreb and Belgrade to pay fees for one theatrical play. While the theatre had recompensed the Zagreb agency with 5% from box office earnings, the Belgrade branch demanded 7.5%. As they emphasized, this was not the first time the theatre had been double-billed.[108] The national theatre in Belgrade reacted alike, and proposed that the Ministry of Education introduce an official index, obligating collecting societies to register the authors and works they legitimately represented. Such an official directory, accessible to all theatrical directors, would deter the agencies from raising arbitrary claims. Among the agencies' common practice was to pose as official rights owners in advance, before they had actually acquired authorization for a theatrical play, and then acquire the rights retrospectively.

---

105 "Banovina" was the designation for a province in interwar Yugoslavia. After King Alexander I established the royal dictatorship of January 6, 1929, he proceeded with a programme of state centralism, including the redrawing of the internal, administrative divisions of the state. The 33 existing oblasts were replaced by nine provinces called banovinas, and their borders were intentionally drawn in such a manner as to correspond neither to ethnic nor to previous imperial borders.

106 Letter from the Chamber of Commerce and Industry to the Ministry of Education, no. 1120, February 20, 1931.

107 Letter from Petar Skipić to the Ministry of Education, January 2, 1932.

108 Telegram from the theatre of Zeta banovina to the Ministry of Education, no. 1-1576-101-15-16-15, 1931.

In such cases, theatre managers risked paying high sums for authorizations, since the agencies ultimately offered the plays to those willing to pay the highest price, and by such means created precedents.[109] The agencies' representatives behaved increasingly brazenly: they disrupted running performances, prohibited planned performances, confiscated musical instruments, and even used their authority to settle personal scores. They went so far as to interrupt a spectacle of the national youth organization Sokol, provoking the wrath of the Minister of Education.[110]

Faced with a mounting number of abuses, the Ministry of Education was forced to intervene. Via circular letter (October 30, 1931), it invited all collecting societies and agencies to deliver credible evidence regarding all foreign and domestic authors they represented, and furthermore to document this authorization. As of January 1, 1932, agencies could only collect royalties for authors who were officially registered with the Ministry of Education.[111] Simultaneously, the ministry sought the advice of the expert commission in order to find long-lasting solutions and develop uniform standards concerning copyright application.[112]

Agencies were now obligated to supply documentation regarding their licensing agreements, and not surprisingly, this requirement easily exposed the iniquitous practice behind the facade. Srečko Albini handed in no original certificates but only indirect attestations. He delivered to the ministry long lists of his partners and affiliates, allegedly compiled on the grounds of original documents that had been formally authenticated by a notary. Interestingly, the partners listed were in their absolute majority publishers, copyright agents and sometimes heirs; authors' associations or individual authors were almost completely absent. As he explained in his correspondence with the ministry, he "represented for more than 10 years the majority of the local, and soon, all foreign authors, their societies and publishers," while during this period, according to his self-evaluation, he had rendered an "immense service" to local authors and theatres by promoting and propagandizing domestic works abroad, and also furnished domestic theatres of modest means with the appropriate foreign repertoire. Moreover, he supplied theatres with loans necessary for their everyday business. Discretion and loyalty towards his partners and clients inhibited him from handing in original documents, but in any case, the ministry had "only required"

109 AJ, fond 66, fas. 409, a.j. 653, Letter from the national theatre in Belgrade to the Ministry of Education, no. 2976, July 16, 1931.

110 AJ, fond 66, fas. 409, a.j. 656, Letter from the Ministry of Education to the municipal administration of the city of Belgrade, no. 56941, December 10, 1931.

111 AJ, fond 66, fas. 409, a.j. 657, Circular of the Ministry of Education, no. 3-1348, September 30, 931.

112 AJ, fond 66, fas. 409, a.j. 657, Letter from the Ministry of Education to the expert commission, no. 54991/31.

credible proof of the right to represent individual clients. Consequently, the ministry ought to put these concerns to rest, and hasten to provide him with the necessary certificates before his business began to suffer loses. Finally, the ministry ought to issue him a "general authorization for the representation of authors' rights, so that he, in this capacity, can tend to his business undisturbed, in the sense of our law for the protection of authors' rights, and the Berne Convention, and represent all copyrights that have been entrusted to him by their owners or will be entrusted to him in the future."[113] However, by the end of 1931 the ministry had already decided to deprive Albini of any certification on the grounds that the documents he had submitted were insufficient: they conveyed neither the kind of rights he was entitled to nor the persons to whom those rights were attached.[114] Indeed, in this story of profuse plenipotentiaries and alleged authorizations, it required some effort to locate the author, hopefully somewhere at the end of this long line.

In the 1920s, two nationwide authors' organizations were created that marked the beginning of genuine local authors' associations: the Union of Yugoslav Dramatic Authors (UJDA, Udruženje jugoslovenskih dramskih autora) and the already-mentioned Union of Yugoslav Music Authors (UJMA, Udruženje jugoslovenskih musičkih autora). UJMA had delegated the rights management of its members to Autor-Centrala, as did UJDA in 1931, after an infelicitous collaboration with Agencija-Autor. Both associations lacked the resources to organize and self-manage the collection of royalties. Due to the fact that Autor-Centrala had specialized in the sphere of so-called "small rights," that is, licensing the performance of musical works, and therefore had little experience of "grand rights," that is, authorization of dramatico-musical works for the stage such as plays, operas, musicals and so on, it decided to employ Vladimir Velmar-Janković, the secretary general of UJDA and simultaneously a member of the expert commission on copyright, as its general manager.

Overall, Agencija-Autor and Autor-Centrala followed similar strategies and aimed at monopolizing the domestic market, winning over local creators, while obtaining and maintaining the favor of foreign collecting societies, whose agents in essence they were. Most importantly, the interests of domestic agents and foreign actors coincided, given that the latter strove as far as possible to monopolize national markets. In order to secure the monopoly of representation within the national market, the existing private CMOs in Yugoslavia pursued a policy of obstruction

113 AJ, fond 66, fas. 409, a.j. 659, Letter from Srečko Albini to the Ministry of Education, January 14, 1932.

114 AJ, fond 66, fas. 409, a.j. 659, Internal Ministry correspondence, no. 1495, January 18, 1932.

and started founding shadow pseudo-associations. Agencija-Autor created to this end the Association of Yugoslav Composers (Udruženje jugoslovenskih kompositora, UJK) in 1930 as a counterweight to UJMA. Later renamed the Union of Yugoslav Composers and Music Publishers (Udruženje jugoslovenskih kompositora i izdavača musike, UJKIM), it remained largely insignificant.[115] Autor-Centrala equally tried its hand at generating authors' societies. Bakarčić founded the Central Union of Yugoslav Authors (Centralno udruženje jugoslovenskih autora), which was, however, eyed suspiciously by the Ministry of Education from the start. Against the background of a lawsuit filed against him, Bakarčić founded the Central Cooperative of Yugoslav Authors (Centralna zadruga jugoslovenskih autora), and claimed that it already enjoyed CISAC membership, and would, after having completed the necessary formalities, take over licensing on behalf of several foreign authors' societies. Subsequently, Autor-Centrala empowered the new organization based on the ministerial accreditation of 1932. Lacking direct ministerial authorization and therefore expecting complications with the collection of royalties, Autor-Centrala supplied the Central Cooperative with a general power of attorney.[116]

At the beginning of the 1930s, the juggling act between rights and plenipotentiaries took on unrestricted and somewhat grotesque features. Rights became a commodity that was transferred, repackaged, traded and bequeathed at will.[117] Authors' rights represented a new terrain of activity, and the agents involved were keen to explore the financial opportunities it offered, as well as testing the limits of how far they could go without any consequences. As is evident from the above exposition, copyright law did not serve the purpose of defending authors' rights, but rather the opposite; it accelerated the commodification of cultural rights in the "wrong" direction and for the benefit of the "wrong" actors. The law, moreover, abetted the process of handling rights as property, thereby transforming them into a tradable good. The propertization strategy proceeded in a crude fashion similar to the conquest of the "Wild West"; all territory that had not been previously occupied by others was colonized, and whoever arrived first claimed titles of ownership, irrespective of whether propertization was necessary, equitable or meaningful. Things became even more muddled at the end

115 AJ, fond 66, fas. 409, a.j. 656, Letter from Agencija-Autor to the Ministry of Education, January 12, 1931.

116 AJ, fond 66, fas. 409, a.j. 657, Letter from Autor-Centrala to the Ministry of Education, September 28, 1933.

117 In 1933, for example, Albini's niece, Julija, suddenly emerged, claiming she was the legitimate heir of all her uncle's licences, which he had transferred to her, and requested that the ministry furnish her with a relevant certification, testifying that she had formally taken over her uncle's business. AJ, fond 66, fas. 409, a.j. 659, Letter from Julija Albini to the Ministry of Education, and Confirmation (uverenje) from the Ministry of Education to Julija Albini.

of 1931/beginning of 1932, when numerous authors overwhelmed the Ministry of Education with letters of authority, demanding the transfer of their copyrights from Agencija-Autor to Autor-Centrala and asking the ministry for an official confirmation of the transfer. Caught by surprise, the astounded ministry invited authors to clarify their legal relationship with their representatives, which was a precondition in order to transfer their rights from one agency to another.[118]

The situation came to a head in 1933, when Velmar-Janković became the target of a defamation campaign by Bakarčić, and in response informed the Ministry of Education about the business affairs of Autor-Centrala and UJMA's ongoing legal action against Bakarčić. Velmar-Janković's report was a real eye-opener for the ministerial authorities.[119] UJMA's lawsuit against Bakarčić declared the latter guilty of acting against the interest of national associations, which he tried to sabotage and divide. By deliberately spreading the rumour that UJMA was about to dissolve, he filed for the association's insolvency, only to subsequently snatch UJMA's business away. The audit of his accounting records discovered multiple cases of embezzlement: he calculated and distributed fees arbitrarily, often on the basis of fictitious concert programmes; he undeservedly retained a share of the revenues for his agency (Autor-Centrala); and alongside the agreed rate of 50%, he withheld an additional 15–20% from authors' fees, for unspecified and unidentifiable expenses. The verdict declared him guilty of intentionally damaging UJMA, whereby "the dealings of Autor-Centrala had a devastating effect upon the association."

In his report to the ministry, Velmar-Janković emphasized the unsuitability of private agencies as administrators of copyrights on the national level. Functioning as proxies of foreign cultural and business interests, the agencies neglected and displaced domestic cultural production. He pressed for the immediate amendment of the copyright law, as the agencies were corroding the already weak native associations and blocking domestic development. In 1932, UJMA was denied membership of the "international authors' organization" [probably implied here was CISAC], on the grounds that multiple authors' societies evidently existed in Yugoslavia. Obviously, Bakarčić's propaganda had been successful in convincing foreign cartels that authors' societies active in Yugoslavia were particularistic groups, and not national associations. The mode of operation and the arrangements between international CMOs and national branches and/or collecting societies have not been researched in a systematic way. It is plausible that it was more convenient for foreign cartels,

---

118 AJ, fond 66, fas. 409, a.j. 654, Letters from Autor-Centrala to the Ministry of Education, September 26, 1931 and February 10, 1932.

119 AJ, fond 66, fas. 409, a.j. 657, Letter from Velmar-Janković to the Ministry of Education, April 18, 1933.

depending on the case at hand, to sidestep national authors' representations, preferring instead to deal with the more compliant and entrepreneurially minded private collecting agencies.

Nationalization as a Defense Strategy

In the meantime, the voices of authors, social actors, institutions and representatives of cultural establishments denouncing abuses and demanding state regulation swelled.[120] The expert commission informed the Ministry of Education that both UJMA and UJDA had deprived Bakarčić of their mandate of representation and emphasized the urgency to protect domestic creators by passing a law regulating the activity of collecting societies, that "without such a law, it is impossible to withstand the pressure of foreign cartels and their capital."[121] In addition to the law on the supervision of copyright implementation, the expert committee suggested a number of supplementary measures, such as enhancing support for the public good through the introduction of a mandatory subscription system, and a more systematic regulation of the relationship between authors and publishers and concerning the modalities of transfer of authors' rights.[122]

In its justification of the "law on the more vigorous supervision of copyright implementation," the expert commission corroborated the shortcomings of the existing copyright law and the abuses that occurred in practice. Intermediary agents had turned the tables on authors, for whose benefit copyright law had been introduced in the first place. International experience had shown that in all places in which intermediary organizations were founded on primarily commercial principles, sooner or later they came into conflict with the vital interests of authors. When financially powerful, those enterprises (and agencies) functioned as private businesses; they exploited authors or committed them for longer periods via inequitable contractual terms.

From the beginning, both Yugoslav associations (UJMA and UJDA) had to stand their ground against the representatives of foreign authors' cartels, whose foremost concern had been to cause disarray in the fledgling national associations

120 AJ, fond 66, fas. 409, a.j. 653, Letter from the chairman of the Choirs' Union to the Ministry of Education; Letter from Kresimir Baranović, director of the Zagreb Theater and Opera to the Ministry of Education (both undated).

121 AJ, fond 66, fas. 409, a.j. 657, Telegram from the expert commission to the Ministry of Education, Zagreb, no. 6-673-70-8-12.

122 AJ, fond 66, fas. 409, a.j. 653, Letter from the expert commission to the Ministry of Education, July 4, 1932.

and compromise the trust of domestic authors in their native unions. The agencies aimed further at limiting the national repertoire, particularly in the realm of music, and weakening domestic cultural production. Finally, they artificially inflated authors' fees, thereby cashing in higher royalties in the name of foreign collecting societies, which caused a flight of domestic capital abroad.[123]

Building on the latest European experience, the amended law transferred the organization and management of copyrights to the hands of the native authors' unions, thereby creating a national monopoly of representation. The Yugoslav solution was in fact copying a Dutch recipe;[124] vexed by similar problems, the Netherlands amended their copyright law in 1932. Prior to that date, two nonprofit societies had operated in the Netherlands, the native BUMA (Het Bureau Voor Muziek-Auteursrecht) and the French society SACEM.

BUMA had been formed by the trade union of Dutch composers of "serious" music (Genootschap van Nederlandsche Componisten) and the association of Dutch music dealers and publishers (Vereiniging van Muziekhandelaren en -Uitgevers in Nederland), and represented highbrow Dutch music and some foreign repertoires. SACEM also maintained a branch office in the Netherlands and controlled most Dutch "light" music, in addition to its own large national repertory and most foreign music. The presence of the two competing societies wreaked havoc, particularly among users, and as the situation escalated alarmingly, the Dutch government saw itself forced to intervene. In 1932, it amended the copyright law by adding article 30(a), which provided that the Ministry of Justice's permission was essential in order to engage in the business of collecting performing rights in music, and moreover that licences issued by unauthorized intermediaries were void.[125] The amendment could be further supplemented by royal decree, while control over intermediaries was enhanced and a consultation mechanism with all interested parties introduced. In 1933, the Dutch Ministry of Justice issued a decree giving BUMA the necessary authorization, which effectively meant that SACEM, which had failed to obtain permission for its operation, was forced to cease acting as a performing rights organization in the Netherlands. As a consequence, the French society transferred its

123 According to the testimony of one such agent, who collected royalties for foreign performing rights societies, approximately 800,000 dinars had flowed abroad in a period of eight months. The agent explained that he retained 50% for himself, which signified that the actual revenues from royalties were 1,600,000 dinars for eight months, quite a respectable sum, none of which flowed to the local creators. AJ, fond 66, fas. 408, a.j. 653, Explanation (obrazloženje), footnote 1, 2ff.

124 AJ, fond 66, fas. 408, a.j. 654, Explanation (obrazloženje) of the law on copyright mediation, 3.

125 Stanley Rothenberg, *Copyright and Public Performance of Music* (The Hague: Martinus Nijhoff, 1954), 115.

repertory for the Netherlands to BUMA, which in the absence of other authorizations acquired a monopoly in representation.[126]

Because we lack comprehensive, scholarly histories for most of the organizations included in this story, such as SACEM, CISAC, BIEM, SACD and so on, as well as histories of their entanglements and interconnections, it is only possible to reach tentative conclusions and raise some hypotheses concerning their activity for the period under discussion. Undoubtedly, the creation of supranational structures such as the BC and the BU and the juridification of international copyright helped societies like SACEM to expand. They aimed, on the one hand, at structuring and enforcing the general rules for the international expansion of the music industry, and on the other, at securing the flow of revenues, among other things, also according to their particular cartel interests. We know (though we lack relevant research on the topic) that in the late 1920s, several European performing rights societies, among them the British, French, German, Italian and Austrian ones, joined forces to form a cartel, whereby each society was responsible for copyright in "its" territories, while also practising cross-representation and cooperation.[127] These collecting societies as the forerunners obviously benefited from existing organizational "lacunas" in the different national contexts. They established themselves almost as "parasitic" organisms complementing, replacing, and potentially displacing, domestic performance rights societies, a circumstance that allowed them to promote a repertory tailored to their own interests. This was the common feature that triggered state intervention in the cases of both the Netherlands and Yugoslavia.

The "Law on Copyright-Legal Mediation and Supervision over the Application of Copyright Protection" (Zakon o autorsko-pravnom posredništvu i nadzoru nad primenom zaštite autoskog prava) forsook the liberal system of copyright intermediation and introduced a system of state concessions, placing the supervision of copyright implementation under the control of the Ministry of Education. To this end, the ministry would furnish concessions only to local authors' societies on condition that they had existed for at least three years. The new provisions barred legal and natural persons from acting as intermediaries, essentially creating a monopoly of representation. Four months after the new law was enforced, all existing contracts between creators and mediators, unless terminated earlier by expiration date, would be declared void (art. 3). All existing collecting societies and agents lost their working permits, irrespective of the legal basis of their business (art. 4). After

126 Rothenberg, *Copyright and Public Performance of Music*, 116.

127 See here Birnhack, *Colonial Copyright*, 167.

consulting with the expert committee on copyright, the ministry would issue a statute regarding all provisions governing copyright mediation, particularly the mode and conditions of operation, supervision, as well as the endorsement of tariffs for copyright remuneration (art. 5). Violations would be subject to fines of between 500 and 40,000 dinars, while payments would be directed to the state aid fund for destitute authors and their families (art. 6). All contracts concluded with mediating agents lacking ministerial permission were invalidated (art. 7). Any other legislative provisions that possibly touched upon copyright mediation but contradicted the new law lost validity (art. 8).[128]

The commission took a holistic approach that also included end users and their protection, while its focus was directed less on the singular and individual creator and more on the system of culture as a whole. In its explanation, the commission clarified that the law had "a distinct social tendency," the objective of which was to protect "the entire class of authors" and the "general public as end users of works," against a small number of capital-rich intermediaries.[129] The goal was to assist authors in developing self-help organizations that would make them professionally and financially independent, that is, able to warrant and extend social services to their members, and thereby replace state subventions.

Without delay, existing collecting societies had to subordinate themselves to the national authors' associations and conduct business through them. Up to that moment, agencies had functioned mostly opportunistically, picking and adopting various statutes and regulations from different laws. Collecting societies therefore invoked different legal authorities and regimes: some functioned in their own right, simply on the basis of warrants; others had received special authorization through the Ministry of Education; while yet others were pure joint-stock companies or commercial firms. This lack of a binding arrangement created confusion, and collecting societies referred, depending on their needs, to both the Ministry of Education and the Ministry of Commerce. In order to curb the agencies' random behaviour, the new law established the exclusive right of the Ministry of Education to issue licences and supervise the practice of copyright mediation. Authors' associations were given precedence in the distribution of licences. In order to facilitate negotiations, authors' organizations were divided into sectors. Licences were handed to one union per sector, usually the most representative in terms of membership. Only when such an association was lacking were other forms of copyright mediation to be considered, and in all cases the ministry's authorization was indispensable.

---

128 AJ, fond 66, fas. 408, a.j. 654, Draft law on copyright-legal mediation.

129 AJ, fond 66, fas. 408, a.j. 654, Explanation (obrazloženje) of the law on copyright mediation, 3.

The law on copyright-legal mediation carried the imprint of cultural and economic protectionism, and was propelled by the need to protect authors, end users and the domestic cultural sphere in Yugoslavia. As evidenced by the above analysis, the introduction of IP hardly contributed to the betterment of the position of the domestic author in Yugoslavia, but rather confirmed the supremacy of the advanced, exporting nations, who converted local collecting societies into their import agents. International juridification thereby established an asymmetrical power relationship that was predicated on the geographical expansion of IPRs, and aimed at helping established cultural cartels to expand and monopolize the world market for creative industries.

The 1936 Yugoslav law signified a departure from the liberal model of a self-regulating market, and saw the integration of the state as an equal partner and indispensable supervising authority required to guarantee efficient and impartial protection of authors' rights. Authors' self-government and centralization in the administration of IPRs were the two components that accompanied the shift from a regime of private collecting agents towards a monopoly of national copyright regulation. If the enactment of the initial 1929 copyright law denoted a "first" nationalization of international copyright in Yugoslavia, which at the time converged with a purposeful internationalization strategy, the supplementary 1936 law and its enhanced protectionist character designated a "second," deeper nationalization that in many ways extended and corrected the shortcomings of the first one, and represented an adaptation of the law to the exigencies of the local context.

As was to be expected, the new law provoked reactions and witnessed efforts by existing collecting societies to obstruct the legislative process. Representing a joint creation of Autor-Centrala and the French society for mechanical reproduction rights EDIFO, the Yugoslav Joint-Stock Company for the Use of Authors' Rights (Jugoslavensko dioničko društvo za iskorišćivanje autorskih prava, IDAP) managed mechanical rights for foreign and domestic authors. It charged domestic record factories licence fees for manufactured and marketed records for all authors worldwide. IDAP had also briefly represented the mechanical rights of UJMA members, because during the period when Autor-Centrala had functioned as the legal representative of UJMA, it had transferred the mechanical rights of UJMA to IDAP for a 10-year period. In its letter, IDAP addressed the Minister of Education in the name of eminent foreign performing rights societies, such as EDIFO (Édition phonographique et cinématographique) and BIEM (Bureau international de l'édition musicomécanique), and demanded that he scrap the expert commission's proposal for an amendment of the existing copyright law, that the proposition "would harm all foreign authors, and particularly those Yugoslav authors who were not, and did not wish to become, members either of UJMA or UJDA." Besides, the endorsement of the proposal "would signify a critical violation of the provisions of the existing national law on copyright protection and the Berne Convention legislation, in connection to which our state, among other states, has taken on obligations which cannot be cancelled in the name of one domestic society, one moreover which does not represent even half of Yugoslav authors."[130]

In the interwar period, several processes came to a head: at long last, Yugoslav authors had fairly propitious conditions (creation of relevant institutions of higher learning, burgeoning cultural establishments, expansion of the entertainment sector, proportionate growth of the urban middle strata, programmatic state building with the ensuing need for representative arts and so on) to advance their professionalization agenda. The struggle for professionalization of Yugoslav culture and arts, however, took place in a period of intense transnationalization of cultural "idioms," new technical means of diffusion and dissemination, and international expansion of new content industries. As a consequence, the struggle for professionalization was fought on two parallel fronts: with various domestic stakeholders, but also with stronger foreign parties, who pursued their own agendas and interests, and occupied a prominent position in the international division of labor in the cultural industries. The purposeful internationalization of copyright in the early twentieth century was their doing, and copyright became more an instrument serving their ends than a vehicle for domestic consolidation and emancipation of Yugoslav creators. Noteworthy in the realm of IP and global history, furthermore, is the interdependence of internationalization and nationalization processes, not as opposing and contradictory, but rather as mutually enforcing and entangled processes. As this story makes clear, the impetus towards nationalization in the realm of copyright management is not to be credited to the prevailing economic philosophy of the interwar period, that is, to economic nationalism; rather, it represented a reaction induced through real-world experience and impulses coming from below, from the field of practice. Similar to the case of the Bulgarian cinema owners in the previous chapter, efforts to extract excessive surpluses or impose disadvantageous models set local reflexes in motion. Local actors sought and found examples of resistance, which they emulated. Interestingly, resistance was headed less by local creators/authors and more by users and end users.

130 AJ, fond 66, fas. 409, a.j. 657, Letter from the Yugoslav Joint-Stock Company for the Use of Authors' Rights to the Minister of Education, February 2, 1933.

As observed in other cases too,[131] it was primarily foreign players, that is, foreign collecting societies (and their local agents), that triggered the application of the law and profited most from its early enactment. In my research, I did not come across important litigation cases that had been initiated by local authors or creators; this I deem to be indicative of the limited use and application of the law by local actors.[132] As also became clear from the course of events that led to the amendment of the Yugoslav copyright law, the major protagonists of this story were not the local authors/creators.

The enactment of the copyright law did not help to structure more productive and/or reliable relations between local creators, publishers and end users. In the realm of print culture and production, there are no indications that the copyright law effectuated any substantial change in the equipoise between publishers and authors. The examination of a limited sample of contracts reveals that after 1929, business continued as usual and publishers generally retained the upper hand in the formulation of contractual conditions. Contracts issued by the powerful Serbian publisher Geca Kon in 1931 do not even use copyright nomenclature, but rather reiterate customary commercial practices: in the case of Dragoljub Filipović's poem collection *Peonies from Kosovo*, Kon declared the work the "property of the publisher,"[133] paying him a one-off fee for the manuscript. Even in the case of such a prominent author and protagonist of the copyright cause as Branislav Nusić, Kon issued a contract for his collected works, through which he "bought" the rights to all Nusić's works once and for all and subsequently paid him a regular amount each year from sales returns.[134] Undoubtedly, the overlap with the world economic crisis created unpropitious timing for the introduction of copyright. However, as symptomatic as such a coincidence can be, it is also instructive of a more structural conclusion that it is ultimately the economy that structures copyright and not the other way around.

A slightly different picture can be observed in the case of music, on account of the fact that as a creative field it can be practiced and consumed with greater frequency and, moreover, publicly. Research on composers' and arrangers' income

131 See here Michael Birnhack's analysis of the introduction of copyright in Mandate Palestine (*Colonial Copyright*, esp. 186).

132 This is my temporary conclusion, but I will gladly revise my opinion upon substantial evidence proving otherwise.

133 "Kniga koje je predmet ovoga ugovora *ostaje izdavačka (knjižarska) svojina g. Geće Kona*, odnosno firme Geće Kona," in Velimir Starčević, *Knjiga o Geći Konu* (Belgrade: Prosveta/Admiral Books, 2009), 22. Emphasis added.

134 "Branislav Nusić *predaje g. Geći Konu po spisku celokupno svoje stovarište do sada izdatih knjiga* po sledečim islovima...," in Starčević, *Knjiga o Geći Konu*, 66. Emphasis added.

for the years 1937–1939 concludes that the average amount of royalties earned annually was approximately 2000 dinars, whereby the majority received significantly lower sums, and only a very small percentage (approx. 5%) had higher earnings in the range between 10,000–15,000 dinars. Compared to the average worker's salary for the period, it meant that composers could earn annually approximately 1 to 1½ times the income of the highest paid workers. The majority, however, earned their income in the field of education and culture, with royalties forming a modest, and in few select cases, a non-negligible supplement to their basic income.[135]

On the domestic front, the last law amendment made little difference. Rather, it was symptomatic of the deep cleavages caused by the national question in the late 1930s that even the legislator's benignant intervention on behalf of cultural creators was unable to bridge the ideological fissures among the country's intellectual elites. It forms both an irony and a paradox of the Yugoslav story that though the legislator at long last deposited copyright management into their hands, on the sole condition that it be administered by united, countrywide professional unions, the individual associations were unable to put their divergencies aside and unify in order to ultimately profit from the materialization of their long-standing demand. The purpose of the Law on Legal Mediation and Supervision had been to curb abuse and arbitrariness in the regulation of IP. For this reason, the legislator handed the right of IP representation over to the oldest professional writers' organization, covering the kingdom's entire territory. Not even this important pragmatic and practical issue, directly affecting their material well-being, was able to unite writers' associations, which once again brought up the question of a common union.[136] In the end, this observation raises the question of how fundamental a claim the call for the attainment of copyright actually was. It also underscores how unrealistic, impractical and solipsistic intellectuals can ultimately be. Finally, it confirms beyond doubt the centrality of the national question as an important identity issue and a major cleavage that obstructed the emergence of concerted common action and the realization of professional solidarity.

135 Ivana Vesić and Vesna Peno, *Između umetnosti i života, O delatnosti udruženja muzičara u Kraljevini SHS/Jugoslaviji* (Belgrade: Musikološki institut SANU, 2017), 64–65.

136 Bogavac, *Udruženje srpskih književnika*, 244–47.

Chapter 9

Interwar Czechoslovakia

Introduction

On account of its territorial extension, the newborn state of Czechoslovakia that came into being in 1918 incorporated in its realm two different legal systems: on the one hand, Austrian law valid in Bohemia, Moravia and Silesia, and on the other, Hungarian law valid in Slovakia and Carpathian Ukraine. This dualism was reflected in the sphere of copyright law as well, where two different legislations encountered each other: the Austrian copyright law of 1895 (amended in 1907) and the Hungarian Law Nr. XVI of February 26, 1884. Being at variance with one another, as much with respect to their scope of application as with their terms of protection, the homogenization of the two laws was duly perceived as a priority. Most significantly, article 20 of the postwar peace treaty, signed on September 10, 1919 in Saint-Germaine-en-Laye, obligated Czechoslovakia to enter the 1886 Berne Union for the Protection of Literary and Artistic Works (revised in 1908 in Berlin and amended in 1914 in Berne), 12 months after the signing of the peace agreement. Consequently, the BC became effective in Czechoslovakia on February 22, 1921, and the act was confirmed by law on November 10, 1921 (Nr. 401 Slg.).

Czechoslovakia's entry into the BU in the revised Berlin version bore direct and unfavorable consequences for Czechoslovak authors, since the unionist protection standards which now applied to foreign authors surpassed those offered by the existing legislation to local authors. There was divergence on a number of issues: the BU had dropped, for example, all internal formalities as a precondition for the application of copyright protection in its member states, and there were also differences concerning the extent of protection for translations. Interrelated motivations were therefore at work in the drafting of the 1926 Czechoslovak copyright law: it was supposed to rectify the above-described disequilibrium between local and foreign authors, harmonize the two domestic (Austrian and Hungarian) legislations, and accommodate modern developments by introducing changes, particularly regarding new reproduction technologies.[1] Though a first draft was handed in already in October 1920, debates and adjustments of the copyright law dragged on for approximately six years, so that the finalized version was passed only on November 24, 1926 and entered into force on May 1, 1927.

Next to local exigencies and the international obligations emanating from the application of the Saint-Germain treaty, international pressure, coming mainly from France and voiced through French diplomatic channels, had the desired admonitory effect upon Czechoslovak politicians and legislators. French discontent arose principally from the delay in finalizing and adopting a national copyright law, which was an indispensable precondition for activating legal protection for foreign authors. In 1925, the French Authors' Society inquired into the current state of copyright law in a polite yet unambiguous tone: it was certainly laudable that Czechoslovakia had been among the first countries to fulfil all diplomatic formalities and join the nations adhering to the Berne Convention, but it was far from sufficient: "this membership of principle did not meet requirements. There can be no real literary protection unless a country's interior [national] legislation guarantees such protection."[2] It was truly regrettable that a full five years after the signing of the Saint-Germain treaty, it was still possible to reproduce or translate French works without French authors profiting from any greater protection than that offered by the old Austrian law, which permitted unconditional reproduction or translation of undeposited works, while deposited works could be reproduced or translated after just five years. Though certain conscientious Czechoslovak editors did pay royalties for reproductions and/or translations, this happened only on the basis of individual courtesy and was not legally binding.

Furthermore, French law protected "literary property" not only among the living but also post mortem auctoris (p.m.a.); though not all BU member states endorsed the 50-year term of protection, the latest BU Congress in Berlin had recommended extending this term to all national legislations. "We have no doubts that the Prague government is inspired by this vow." Unfortunately, Czechoslovak as well as other East Central European publishers accepted only the 30-year term of protection, refusing to recognize an extension of the rights of heirs. The case of Guy de Maupassant, whose works fell into the public domain in that current year (1925),

1 Inka Schwanke, "Die Entwicklung des Urheberrechts auf dem Gebiet der heutigen Tschechischen Republik und seine Annäherung an den Schutzstandard der Europäischen Union" (Master's diss., Charles University Prague, Faculty of Law, July 2002), 27.

2 Národní archiv, Ministerstvo spravedlnosti, karton 1813, Letter from the Société des Gens de Lettres, July 17, 1925.

was exemplary of this problem, and emphasized the need to remedy the situation. The cordial relationship between Czechoslovakia and France, exemplified in the person of President Masaryk, required that the Prague parliament and government, encouraged by the president personally, prioritize the enactment of the copyright law because without it, "membership in the Berne Convention was nothing but a vain manifestation." From the incident of French intervention in the name of Guy de Maupassant's heirs, and in conjunction with the build-up of pressure to extend the term of protection p.m.a., we can get a glimpse into the repertoire of bilateral exchanges. Furthermore, we are left with the impression that the expansion of the copyright regime did not so much serve the purpose of protecting creators, but was rather transformed—at least in this case—into a convenient form of rent-seeking, particularly congenial to the interests of authors' heirs. Unsurprisingly, there was nothing original about the French claim. Historically, the extension of copyright's term of protection has repeatedly been the result of heirs' petitions and their often less visible lobbying efforts.[3]

The 1895 Austrian copyright law being the more modern of the two legislations furnished the basis for the new Czechoslovak copyright law,[4] which also took foreign legislations, notably the German laws of 1901, 1907 and 1910, into consideration. The draft law was modified several times, while being debated between the Senate and House of Representatives. Whereas with regards to content and structure it reflected its blueprint, the 1895 law, it nevertheless contained contemporary innovations that manifested the law's Zeitgeist.[5]

The 1926 law represented, as is often the case with such codification processes, a compromise. Before being finalized, it engendered broad debates, which are symptomatic of the breadth of opinions and testify to the willingness to also consider more radical solutions than those which prevailed in the end. In contrast to the Bulgarian and Yugoslav cases, the copyright debate in Czechoslovakia was fought along

3 Such had been the case, for example, in 1857, when upon the request of Pushkin's widow, the council of state extended the copyright term from 25 to 50 years p.m.a. in Russia. Some heirs' lobbying efforts were less successful, for example the attempts by Wagner's heirs to extend protection for Richard Wagner's operas, the famous "Lex Cosima." See https://www.faz.net/aktuell/feuilleton/buehne-und-konzert/geschichte-des-parsifal-der-gralsraub-von-bayreuth-12762788.html. The extension of the term of protection to fit the interests of specific stakeholders or entrepreneurs is best exemplified by the Sonny Bono Copyright Term Extension Act of 1998 in the US, which is perhaps the most blatant example of the extension of the term of protection to the benefit of a corporation. See here https://alj.artrepreneur.com/mickey-mouse-keeps-changing-copyright-law/.

4 On Habsburg copyright legislation as a formative framework for the subsequent development of Czechoslovak copyright law, see Valentin Urfus, "Počátky novodobého autorského práva," *Documenta Pragensia* 10, no. 2 (1990): 335–43.

5 Schwanke, "Die Entwicklung des Urheberrechts," 28.

political lines as well, that is, the positions expounded also correlated to political worldviews. As the law was debated in the early 1920s, the model of Soviet Russia had a bearing on the discussion, both as an inspiration and/or a deterrent. During the interwar period, theoretical and doctrinal debates on the nature of copyrights (natural law vs. statutory law, pecuniary vs. moral rights etc.), which had dominated so much of the late nineteenth and early twentieth century, receded substantially. Such deliberations barely informed the legislation of copyright in Eastern Europe in the interwar period, which by and large showed an inclination to adopt and adapt German solutions either in the form of laws or doctrines (for example, the widespread doctrinal position of Josef Kohler's *Immaterialgüterrecht* or Gareis and von Gierke's moral rights theories).[6]

In light of developments in the Soviet Union, however, older and newer, utilitarian, nationalistic and public law-related discourses regarding public benefits and uses of intellectual works now resurfaced in Western and Central Europe, but from a new angle. While the pragmatic approach to copyright, that is, the tendency to abandon excessive theoretical discussions and concentrate more on the practical handling of authors' rights regulation, was an international trend, the Soviet model rekindled earlier, utilitarian discussions (which had taken place in the age of revolutions, i.e. the late eighteenth and early nineteenth centuries) on the scope of copyright: what kind of right was copyright? A public or a private right? And whom should it serve? The Soviet model in its initial radicalism of the 1920s (nationalization of works, abolition of private publishers and centralization of publishing, curtailment of the rights of heirs, shortening of the term of protection p.m.a., compulsory licenses for broadcasting etc.), though acknowledging copyright as a private right, subordinated it to the primacy of the collective, underscoring its social and public character.[7] This framing best served the purposes of revolution and economic restructuring. From that perspective, the Soviet model stood in contradistinction to the propertization tendencies of the BU, and in a certain way served as its (global) antipode. The Soviet model served, also in the Czechoslovak case, both as a point of reference and friction, enabling local actors to delineate their own concept of the organization of culture as they debated various modalities of regulation. While the Soviet model did not lack sympathies, even among its critics, the majority of protagonists in the Czechoslovak copyright debate judged that it somehow went too

6 For useful introductions to the doctrines, works and biographies of leading German copyright jurists like Josef Kohler (1849–1919) and Karl von Gareis (1844–1923), including bibliographies of their main works and references to secondary literature, see Simon Apel, Louis Pahlow and Matthias Wiessner, eds., *Biographisches Handbuch des Geistigen Eigentums* (Tübingen: Mohr Siebeck, 2017).

7 See Serge L. Levitsky, *Introduction to Soviet Copyright Law* (Leyden: A.W. Sythoff, 1964), 11–27.

far. Their concerns revolved essentially around two issues, namely (1) the enhanced and monopolistic role of the state, and by consequence, (2) the politicization and ideological constraints imposed upon the arts. The Czechoslovak approach to copyright was shaped therefore by a multiplicity of obvious and less obvious factors. If the Austrian and German prototypes as well as the Soviet benchmark played a conspicuous role therein, other aspects, such as the structure of the political system, the ideological orientation of the state and the significant role attributed to culture, and the imperative to secure and consolidate Czechoslovakia's international recognition as a state, are less obvious but equally decisive components that helped to shape the consensualism that characterized the more general attitude of interest groups, including the stakeholders of the copyright regime, in interwar Czechoslovakia.

Authors Get Organized: Syndicalism and Lobbyism in Tandem

Creative unions developed into strong players in interwar Czechoslovakia. With time they grew into keen pressure groups that were able to push their agenda and enforce their conditions, ultimately promoting a very pro-author, protectionist regime. In cooperation and collaboration with copyright lawyers, they constructed extensive networks that carried and communicated their objectives both to the broader public and to the higher echelons of politics, that is, the relevant governmental bodies and parliamentary committees.

Some scholars attribute the timely efforts towards unionist organization among the creative strata in the case of Czechoslovakia to the absence of a strong patronage system. Due to the fact that the Czech business elite did not prioritize a more purposeful support of Czech culture, intellectuals gravitated towards kindred occupations like journalism and pursued careers capable of providing them with some sort of financial security. Being increasingly dependent for a living upon a literary market, intellectuals compensated for the available risks by uniting into associations and working together to better defend and advance the interests of their guild. By this means, authors' and artists' traditional individualism intersected with traditional ideas of collective solidarity.[8] Despite the credibility of the aforementioned thesis, it was without doubt the

---

8 Marek Krejčí, "Stát coby patron umění? K státní kulturní politice v první polovině 20. století," in *"O slušnou odměnu bude počováno...". Ekonomické souvislosti spisovatelské profese v české kultuře 19. a 20. století*, eds. Tomáš Breň and Pavel Janáček (Prague: Ústav pro českou literature AN ČR, v.v.i., 2009), 130.

social policy of the Czechoslovak state that provided the impetus for strong syndicalist organization in the interwar period. The experience of WWI transformed traditional world views. In the 1920s and 30s there was greater acceptance for leftist ideas and a strong belief in the capacity of the state to engineer social justice. As exemplified in the thought of its most articulate proponents such as the economist Karel Engliš, social policy was understood as a practical endeavour that purposely employed the capacities of the state and the law in order to mould an ideal social structure. In practice, this resulted in a synergy between state welfare and the voluntary sector. The state reckoned with this interconnection and delegated certain tasks of public administration to voluntary associations, thereby creating extensive organizational networks and structures, such as those that will also be encountered in the case of the local copyright regime described in this chapter. They were financed through diverse means assembled from different sources, including state subsidies, donations, cultural activities and fundraising. An additional, important pillar of social policy in the interwar period was the introduction of the "Ghent system," which granted social benefits such as unemployment subsidies only to unionized workers, effectively promoting the broadest possible syndicalization of the workforce.[9]

The efforts of creative elites towards unionist organization predated the establishment of the Czechoslovak state. In its constitutive meeting at the end of 1917, on the initiative of the Association of Czech Belletristic Authors "Máj," the later Syndicate of Czech Writers decided on the creation of a comprehensive union in order to promote professional matters, and assembled to this end a broad array of actors involved in cultural production and affairs. Apart from members of "Máj," it included members of the Czech Academy, the Club of Dramatic Authors, the Circle of Czech Authors, the Association of Czech Belletristic Authors, the journals *Svatobor* and *Zvon*, as well as the cultural organization "Umělecka Beseda." With the creation of the Czechoslovak state, the syndicate took up systematic activity as an association and initially pursued three goals: (1) the revision of old contracts on the basis of new arrangements, (2) the establishment of a minimum fee, amounting to at least 10% of the retail price of books, and (3) the sanctioning of measures to control the size of an edition. From 1918, the syndicate initiated regular discussions with the Union of Booksellers and Publishers in Prague, where in joint meetings major questions concerning the publisher-author relationship were discussed. In 1918, the

9 František Čapka, "The Essence of State Social Policy in Czechoslovakia in the Years of the First Republic (1918–1938)," *Czech-Polish Historic and Pedagogical Journal* 9, no. 1 (2017): 22–25; see also Jakub Rákosník, "Gentský system v období 1. Československé republiky," *Časopis Národního muzea, rada historická řada* 170, no. 3–4 (2001): 84–105.

association's statute (and name) was changed to include not only belletristic writers, but authors in the broadest sense of the term, including musical composers, and was renamed the Syndicate of Czech Writers and Composers (Syndikát českých spisovatelů a hudebních skladatelů).[10] The syndicate quickly established expert groups on professional matters and institutionalized a division of labor that allowed for the emergence of specialists and spokespersons on focused topics with advanced knowledge and competence, such as dealings with publishers, legal protection, periodical publications, translations, music, contacts with foreign countries, theatre, scholarly and expert literature and so on. It further concentrated on two issues: a speedy revision of the copyright law and a uniform collective publishing agreement.

Regarding old contracts, the syndicate initiated activities that came to a positive conclusion with the passing of the law on the publishing contract. On the basis of its negotiations with publishers, the syndicate provided its members with a model publishing contract. The publishers, however, discontinued negotiations, mainly objecting to the syndicate's demand that remuneration be calculated in percentage rates based on the book's retail price. Moreover, they eschewed the claim to determine fee rates independently for each edition, which would have meant reversing the established practice, where fees established once also extended to all future editions. Although the model contract did not come to pass, it nevertheless summarized most key points of interest and furnished authors with a prototype for negotiations. When a number of publishers eventually came to accept the 10% reward based on retail price, the syndicate could pride itself on its sensible strategy.

From 1921, the syndicate started to receive subventions and material support from various donors (the state and bank institutions) and was able to tap into state funds, securing, for example, a decent share of the Masaryk fund. Support targeted both authors and their families, as was the case with the 1918 food donations offered by the American Charitable Society in New York to the benefit of destitute intellectuals in the Czechoslovak Republic.[11]

In 1919, upon the passing of the law on municipal public libraries, the syndicate intervened actively both with the Ministry of Education and with the Educational Union (Osvětový svaz) to help select the classical works that would build the foundation of the libraries' collections. It interceded successfully with all permanent theatres on behalf of translators of theatrical plays, arguing for a uniform fee regulation on the basis of royalties, a settlement with considerable advantages for translators in

10 "Výtah z jednatelské zpravý za období 1918 až 1928," *Věstník Syndikátu českých spisovatelů*, December 30, 1929, no. 10–11, 1.

11 "Výtah z jednatelské zpravý za období 1918 až 1928," 2–3.

contrast to the established system of fixed honorariums. From the mid-1920s, the syndicate, along with the Czechoslovak Dramatic Union, coordinated action and intervened with the artistic directors of the National and Stavovské Theaters urging them to include greater ratios of Czechoslovak authors in their repertoires.

A breakthrough in the syndicate's negotiations with publishers was achieved in 1921, when they reached a collective agreement on minimum remuneration. The fee tariffs agreed[12] not only established a minimum pay rate, but also detailed the precise mode of calculation for different types of works, such as prose and poetry, works having previously been published in magazines or unpublished works, translations of prose or verse, commissioned or non-commissioned translations and so on, and delivered standardized calculation formulas based either on the work's retail price or on the number of print sheets, lines or characters. For example, poems printed in book layout were remunerated in the same manner as prose; the fee for a poetry book had to be calculated on the basis of an edition of at least 2000 copies, even if the actual edition was smaller.[13] In 1922, the syndicate succeeded in extending the collective agreement to translations, with publishers basically agreeing to pay fees for the second and subsequent editions as well: half the amount of the original fee for independent, non-commissioned translations, and a third of the original remuneration in the case of translations contracted by the publisher. Corresponding efforts were put into raising the fees for magazines and periodicals, an action that achieved partial success when certain magazines such as *Svon*, *Cesta* and *Pramen* accepted higher tariffs.

The syndicate led concerted information and propaganda campaigns regarding issues vital to its interests, such as the regulation of old contracts, the law on the publishing contract, the duration of the term of protection and others, and intervened several times in parliamentary circles, relevant legislative committees and political parties, either defending its own professional interests or as a counter-reaction to corresponding publishers' campaigns.[14] Authors and publishers fought intensive, circuitous, competitive battles, overbidding themselves in their efforts to influence both the political establishment and legislative bodies and tip the scales in their favor.

Various aspects of social security, such as pensions, invalidity and old age insurance, became further areas of intense syndicalist activity and were tackled systematically from the early 1920s onwards. Bidding for state support on behalf of its members (authors and composers), the syndicate entered into intensive

12 "Sazby honorářové," *Věstník Syndikátu českých spisovatelů*, April 15, 1926, no. 8, 13.

13 "Sazby honorářové," 13.

14 "Výtah z jednatelské zpravý za období 1918 až 1928," 3–4.

competition with neighbouring professional unions such as the union of creative/graphic artists, who laid claims to the same state funds.[15] Solomonic decision-making in order to accommodate all bidders was often the only way out of the conundrum for state authorities, which were forced to develop selection criteria in order to reduce the pool of potential beneficiaries.[16] Age and sickness pensions finally materialized in 1925, and the following year there was even a raise in the original annual pension from 2400 to 3400 Kč. In order to support and aid the recovery of authors and composers from illness and physical injury, a recovery fund (*ozdravovaci fond*) was founded in 1922. Its original assets were formed from accumulated deposit interest and value vouchers on the initial capital, but with time its income sources diversified to include yields from the state charitable lottery and donations from private persons. While in 1921 the fund's assets amounted to 74,440 Kč, by the end of 1927 they had grown to 142,456 Kč.[17]

The syndicate negotiated with administrative authorities such as the Land Authority Registry in order to secure a share of expropriated real estate for the benefit of its members, aiming at the creation of a retreat center for writers, composers, graphic artists and journalists. Though it turned down several options in the interwar period (initially Mysliboř castle and later the hunting castle of Jemčina) as inappropriate, this initial idea lived on and did actually materialize in the communist period.

Alongside the law on the publishing contract, the syndicate actively supported authors' rights and pressed for the acceleration of parliamentary procedures leading to the promulgation of the new copyright law. To this purpose, it put forward a relevant request to the presidium of the National Assembly, the Ministry of Education and the Ministry of the Interior. In concerted action, several relevant societies and associations, including the Association of Czech Belletristic Authors "Máj," the Circle of Czechoslovak Writers, the Syndicate of Graphic Artists, IV Academy Class and Umělecka Beseda, closed ranks in support of the proposal. It is worth underscoring that several of these organizations were occasionally in competition with each other over the distribution of state means, but under expedient circumstances they evidently also cooperated closely, functioning as pressure groups towards the state, political elites and parties. Enjoying the broad support of leading figures in state and public institutions, of lawyers and politicians, such as the Minister of Foreign Affairs Edvard Beneš, they actually managed to speed up the process, so that the enacted copyright law of November 24, 1926 entered into force on May 1, 1927.

15 "Výtah z jednatelské zpravý za období 1918 až 1928," 5.

16 "Výtah z jednatelské zpravý za období 1918 až 1928," 5–6.

17 "Výtah z jednatelské zpravý za období 1918 až 1928," 15.

The syndicate also joined ranks with the state collecting society, OSA, and together they promoted a legal regime characterized by stronger propertization tendencies to the benefit of the author. Consequently, they sought to enact the 50-year term of protection, eliminate compulsory licence regulation as well as frustrate the exemption of charitable concerts from royalty payments. The fact that they were successful in enforcing all three objectives testifies to their power and perseverance.[18]

The Law on the Publishing Contract

Though work on the Czechoslovak copyright law started in a timely manner, as early as 1921, it was in fact the law on the publishing contract (*zákon o nakladatelské smlouvě*) that was passed first, in 1923, in a certain way also reflecting the philosophy and priorities of the legislator. Following in the steps of its precursors and modelled along the lines of the German and Austrian *Verlagsrecht* tradition, the Czechoslovak law on the publishing contract went even further and regulated with precision and in great detail the contractual obligations between publisher and author, leaving little room for ambiguity. It set the tone for the pro-author policy that was characteristic of Czechoslovak interwar development. Though it did not officially suspend contractual freedom as was later the case with communist copyright, the law was highly regulative (standardizing) and its mandatory spirit was akin to developments in the communist period that succeeded it.

Until 1923, the provisions of the Austrian civil code of 1811 (Kaiserliches Patent), in its 3rd revision of 1.1.1917, had been valid in Cisleithania (the northern and western part of the Habsburg Monarchy), while the provisions of the Hungarian commercial law of 1875 had been in force in Slovakia. The civil code initially dealt with the publisher's contract in eight short paragraphs (no. 1164–1171), which were included among the provisions on wage contracts.[19] Next to the legal definition, it contained essentially a list of reciprocal rights and obligations, which stipulated that the author was obligated to deliver the manuscript according to the concluded agreement and the publisher was obligated, after having received the manuscript, to pay the agreed remuneration; if no precise remuneration had been agreed upon, the publisher paid an appropriate remuneration according to general

18 "Výtah z jednatelské zpravý za období 1918 až 1928," 8.

19 Jan Löwenbach, *Autor a nakladatel, K chystanému zákonu a smlouvě nakladatelské* (Prague: Tiskem a nákladatelem pražké akciové tiskárny, 1921), 5.

principles. If the author failed to deliver a work on time, the publisher could deviate from the contract, and if the delay was on account of the author, the publisher could claim damages. Had there been agreement on the number of printed copies, the publisher was obliged to conclude a new agreement before publishing a new edition; had the size of the edition not been subject to an agreement, the publisher could print infinitely during the period of the contract's validity. If the foregoing edition had not sold out, the author could reissue the work only if he compensated the publisher for the remaining copies. Any changes inserted into a new edition had to be subject to agreement. If the book was commissioned by the publisher (work for hire), the author was only entitled to the agreed remuneration but not to the publication itself. Regulations were valid for literary and musical works, maps and topographical drawings.

These provisions were partially amended and supplemented by the copyright law of 26 December 1895, which in articles 8 and 9 handed over to the author the right of disposition concerning contributions in collective and periodical works, while articles 16 and 20 allowed the termination of the publishing contract for certain categories of works, and determined a three-year intermediary period, after the expiration of which original rights reverted to the author; the provisions of section IV on reprints were turned to the favor of the author.

The third and last amendment brought only minor changes (art. 1172 and 1173 of the civil code): it extended the concept of the publishing contract to all artistic and photographic works and clarified that the publisher was only entitled to one edition. If the size of the edition had not been fixed, the author could—upon indemnification of the publisher—dispose of the work prior to the edition selling out.

The provisions of the Hungarian law on the publishing contract were far more detailed and could be regarded as a yardstick for the degree of formalization of relations in the publishing sector. They mentioned "features" that had to be commensurate with the purpose and meaning of the work and foreshadowed the idea of the "apposite" price, meaning that the rate charged for a book ought not to discourage sales of the work. The contract allowed only one edition; if the contract was valid for more editions, the publisher was obligated upon sellout to issue a new one immediately. Should the publisher delay in fulfilling his task, the author had the same rights as in the Austrian law (art. 520, 522 and 523, i.e. could terminate the contract). In the case of a new edition, notwithstanding anything to the contrary, the terms of the first edition applied (art. 521). The right to collected works was reserved to the author (art. 524). The payment of a fee was always presumed, even if not expressly formulated; its amount was determined by court, upon hearing from an expert;

it was due when the work was submitted; if determined by print sheets, it was payable when the work or section was printed (art. 525 and 527). The publisher was obliged to pay fees, even if the work (in his possession) was accidentally destroyed, or if a personal accident prevented the work from being published and the author was unable to place it elsewhere (art. 528, 529). The contract was terminated if the work was destroyed before the contract was submitted to the author, the author died or if he was prevented from completing the work, or if the purpose for which the work was intended was foiled (art. 531). The majority of these provisions were included verbatim in the new Czechoslovak law on the publishing contract.

Efforts to reform the law on the publishing contract during the Habsburg Monarchy had failed due to lack of coordination. It was only after the creation of the Czechoslovak Republic that the Syndicate of Czechoslovak Authors took more consistent action. Through long and strenuous negotiations with the Czech Association of Booksellers and Publishers, it laid the foundation for collective bargaining. With this process ongoing, the Ministry of Justice proposed a draft for a new copyright law with a view to Czechoslovakia's obligation to enter into the Berne Union. This action provided the external impetus for an amendment of the law on the publishing contract, "whose inadequacy was felt even more directly among literary and artistic circles than the necessity to reform copyright."[20]

The first draft of May 1920 was sent out for inspection to relevant authorities and interest groups by June of the same year. Its overall structure and individual provisions were taken—with minor changes—from the German Publishing Act (*Verlagsrecht*) of 19.6.1901. The German prototype was supplemented with small adjustments pertaining to local needs, and included some variations in relevant regulations of the Swiss law (art. 380–393, civil law of 30.3.1911), as well as some suggestions made by the Syndicate of Czechoslovak Authors.[21]

The syndicate's main concern was the fate of older contracts and it effectively suggested measures to invalidate them. The proposal demanded that all contracts in which the author had assigned the original rights for a second or all future editions free of charge or for a one-off fee be declared void. Authors should, at any time, be able to terminate by registered letter all contracts concluded before the new law's entry into force, and prompt the cancellation of the contract with the sellout of all remaining copies. Anyone who, after having received notice, continued printing was thus producing non-authorized reprints. The ministry was sceptical about accepting such a radical solution, but stipulated that in the case of old agreements free of charge or with

20 Löwenbach, *Autor a nakladatel*, 8.

21 Löwenbach, *Autor a nakladatel*, 14–15.

one-off remuneration, the new law would apply for all subsequent editions, that is, new editions would be governed by the new remuneration rates agreed between the authors' and publishers' organizations or royalty payments decided by expert groups in court. Finally, the syndicate suggested that contracts for the operation of musical or theatrical works, whose remuneration was agreed as a one-off fee, be terminated with the lapse of 15 years after the work's inaugural performance.[22]

The main features of the 44-article law on the publishing contract[23] were, on the one hand, the conspicuous effort to regulate with the highest possible precision potential areas of friction or grey zones, and on the other, the inclination to regulate in a manner particularly favorable to authors. The law is presented in this section in greater detail with the intention to demonstrate the far-reaching prerogatives that authors were able to broker in interwar Czechoslovakia. Reiterating standard obligations (rights of reproduction, distribution etc.) according to the traditional division of labor between the author and the publisher, the law on the publishing contract nevertheless reserved to the author and his heirs a whole series of reproduction rights, significantly relativizing the publisher's property regime. As a consequence, authors and their heirs were at all times entitled to: (1) issue a work in a comprehensive edition, after 15 years from the end of the calendar year in which the work was published, or even earlier if the editions to which the publisher was entitled were already sold out, or if the author or the publisher of the collected works had purchased the remaining stock; after 10 years, the publisher was obliged to deliver leftover copies at shop price and with a bookshop discount; (2) translations of their works into other languages and/or processing into other dialects; (3) processing into other genres, for example from a narrative form into a dramatic form and/or vice versa; (4) processing of musical works unless they concerned a mere transfer to another key or register; (5) cinematographic or similar works based on a literary, artistic, musical, graphic or photographic work; and (6) works created through the transfer of a literary or musical work to mechanical recitation.

Section 9 guaranteed additional powers to the author: article 1, though restraining the author's right of disposition for the duration of the contracted editions, allowed the creator after 10 years to purchase the remaining copies at a reasonable and reduced price and to freely dispose of them. Article 2 allowed the author or successor in title to freely dispose of contributions published in "generic works" (*v občanských dílech*, i.e. journals, yearbooks, calendars), a year after the end of the

---

22 Löwenbach, *Autor a nakladatel*, 15.

23 Zákon o nakladatelské smlouvě ze dne 11.5.1923, Sbírka: 106/1923 Sb., Částka: 46/1923. https://www.epravo.cz/vyhledavani-aspi/?Id=3315&Section=1&IdPara=1&ParaC=2.

calendar year in which they were originally published, as well as use those contributions for other purposes for which the author had received no remuneration, even though the exclusive publishing right had been granted. Article 4 stipulated that though a publisher may have been granted an exclusive reproduction right, the author was eligible to print reproductions of his work in articles dealing with his artistic activity or providing examples thereof. If the original work was in the publisher's possession, he was obliged to allow the creator to reproduce the work to that end without compensation.

Section 10 limited the right of the publisher to only one edition. If, however, he had received rights to several or all editions, the same contractual conditions applied to them as for previous editions, unless the author explicitly reserved something different (art. 1). If the number of copies for literary or musical works had not been agreed upon, the publisher was entitled to make an edition of 1000 copies (art. 2). On the other hand, according to article 3, he was also obliged to make the agreed or legally specified number of copies. Once the production of the edition had been completed, the publisher was prohibited from making any further prints except in very specific cases determined by sections 15 (art. 2) and 34.

Additional obligations of the publisher were elucidated in section 13. Had he been granted a publishing right for several or all editions, the publisher was obliged to organize a new edition, as soon as possible, once the previous edition had been sold out, and moreover, one commensurate with the latest technical standards of production (art. 1). The publisher was discharged of this obligation only by force majeure or when conditions affecting the whole publishing industry hindered the reproduction or sale of the work. Yet, even in those cases, the publisher was obliged upon request to pay the client the entire agreed remuneration, regardless of when the work could be delivered (art. 2). A work was considered sold out if the publisher, on his own initiative, notified the author via a proper commercial letter, or if the author requested relevant information in the form of a registered letter and the publisher failed to answer the author's query within four Sundays (art. 3). If the publisher failed to reissue the sold-out work—without the author carrying any responsibility for this failure—within two years of the submission of the complete manuscript or original work, the author had the right to claim damages and either withdraw from the contract or insist upon its fulfilment. If he withdrew from the contract, he could freely dispose of the work and also request that the work be returned to him; this also applied if the sold-out work, for which the publishing right had been granted for several or all editions, had not been reissued after two years without the will or guilt of the author within a period of time subsequently agreed.

Options and limits of the publisher were also dealt with in section 14. If several works by the same author were individually put into circulation, the publisher was not entitled to publish them, either as collected works or in a collective work (art. 1). Similarly, a publisher who had been granted the publishing right for the publication of the collected works or a certain group of works by the same author was not entitled to publish any of them individually (art. 2). If a work, however, was free for the duration of the original right, the publisher was also allowed to publish the works in aggregate or individual form.

The law on the publishing contract also contained provisions on damaged and/or lost copies (section 15), on moral rights (section 17), on the technical implementation of reproduction and the author's veto rights to it (proofreading, corrections etc., section 19). The price of the work was also an issue. Section 20 stipulated that it was at the publisher's discretion to determine a commensurate price, but it had to be such that it did not discourage sales of the work (art. 1). The publisher could increase the agreed sale price only with the client's consent. Inversely, in case of price reductions, the publisher did not need the author's consent, unless the reduction affected the author's legitimate interests (art. 2).

Sections 21 to 23 dealt directly with the question of remuneration. The publisher's obligation to pay the arranged fee was not as markedly pronounced (as in the German prototype), but it was referred to indirectly in the first sentence of section 21, which stipulated that "if no remuneration had been expressly agreed, it was always assumed that the work had been delivered in return for payment, unless the circumstances suggested otherwise." According to Jan Löwenbach, lawyer, music critic, poet, librettist, translator of German and a central figure in setting up the copyright structure in post-WWI Czechoslovakia, this provision was clearer and more favorable to authors than the Swiss and German legislations. Whereas the German law only spoke of an "appropriate/proportionate remuneration in money," the Czechoslovak law contained more tangible provisions and ordained that the amount had to be paid which had been fixed between the syndicate and the booksellers' union as a result of their collective agreement, unless other agreements interfered. Moreover, the same tariffs also applied to those who were not members of these organizations, unless the contracting authority (author) would have benefited more from the remuneration agreed between the other unions of which both parties were members. In the absence of such an agreement, the court decided on the proportionality of remuneration via expert review.[24]

24 Löwenbach, *Autor a nakladatel*, 27–28.

The law further determined when remuneration was due (sections 22 and 23), covering all eventualities, that is, cases of fixed or non-fixed remuneration, all possible forms and formats of delivery (whole manuscript, sections, booklets, printed sheets etc.), as well as cases where fees were entirely or partly regulated by sales, in which case it sanctioned the author's access to the publisher's accounting records. It reserved a right of remuneration to the author (section 26), who had concluded a contract and delivered a work in its entirety or in part, even if the purpose for which the work was initially intended was terminated. The same applied if, for any reason, the contracted work was not produced. Furthermore, it regulated rights and obligations for both parties in cases where the publisher's business was transferred to third persons, heirs or went bankrupt (sections 29 and 38). It was a fundamental achievement of the syndicate that the new law on the publishing contract entailed certain legal regulations that the contracting sides could not sidestep, and which therefore applied as law enforcement. Such enforcement provisions also applied to old contracts.

The law on the publishing contract was publicly debated, and though a variety of opinions were aired, views nonetheless converged towards a common denominator: a dislike of economic liberalism, with attitudes fluctuating between a more moderate center-left and a more radical left. Views converged that the contemporary relationship between author and publisher was fundamentally problematic and exploitative. Equally shared was a largely protectionist attitude towards creators, while differences concerned rather the degree and areas of state intervention in the proposed solutions. Interestingly, several of the proposals were discussed against the backdrop of the Soviet paradigm.

Among the most vocal protagonists in the debate, Vàclav Tille, academic, literary historian and member of the advisory committee for literature, energetically defended the need for fair contractual relationships. Contracts had to free authors from undignified servitude by structuring equitable relationships in the publishing business (and other creative fields), with partners having their common share in both profit and loss. For Tille, one of the major problems in the publishing industry was the market value of works and the reluctance of publishers to publish certain works.[25] As Löwenbach pointed out, however, this was in essence a defect of all legal relationships based on the freedom of contract and governed primarily by the law of demand and supply. The requirement that a publisher be forced to publish a certain work was difficult to implement. Moreover, it raised the question of

---

25 Löwenbach, *Autor a nakladatel*, 9.

whether such an approach ultimately served the interests of art.[26] Tille demanded that the law declare the written contract between author and publisher mandatory, and moreover, make the contract's validity conditional upon the insertion of contractual provisions which established to the benefit of the author a profit percentage from gross sales for each copy sold. Finally, the 30-year term of protection p.m.a., which transformed works into general property, had to be changed effectively.

Making the written form mandatory for contracts was desirable but also debatable. Apparently, as reported by Löwenbach, only Britain had enforced the written form for publishing contracts. Neither the German nor the Swiss copyright law contained such provisions, and the Czechoslovak government was reluctant to make the written form the basis for the validity of the publishing contract, pointing out that far more serious contracts were negotiated orally, which did not prevent the parties from making a written contract or confirming the arrangement in writing. The new law on the publishing contract contained amply detailed rules of a mandatory nature that would sufficiently secure the author's protection without going into the details of the contract. Nonetheless, in Löwenbach's view, the future belonged to the standardized contract: "After all, we are convinced that once the law comes into force, it will evolve through the action of the organizations of both parties [meaning, writers and publishers] in our country as elsewhere, in the *form of common type contracts*, so that the written contract will surely become the rule."[27]

Establishing a fixed percentage of profit from sales was bound to be difficult, considering how differently it would have to be graded in order to match the interests of all authors, as well as the various fields and types of works. The current law's general formulation was quite successful: in the absence of other arrangements, it declared the fee tariffs agreed between the organizations of authors and publishers obligatory. In that respect, it went much further than the German law. Some industries and countries had adopted the percentage of profits (from the retail price of sold products, not from gross sales) as a benchmark and it had proven to work well. However, the law came close to such an understanding when it stipulated that the terms agreed, including the fee, always applied to only one edition (1000 copies). And sometimes, noted Löwenbach, a pre-determined and fixed fee was, on the contrary, more advantageous for the author.[28]

Finally, the issue of the term of protection after the author's death was de facto a challenge and did not lend itself to easy solutions. The question was "so closely

---

26 Löwenbach, *Autor a nakladatel*, 9.

27 Löwenbach, *Autor a nakladatel*, 10–11. Emphasis added.

28 Löwenbach, *Autor a nakladatel*, 11.

related to basic concepts of the current private law order, namely the new regulation of the right of inheritance, and for the moment being, no state, except Soviet Russia, has been able to bring the interest of universality into proper compliance with the interests of the author and his heirs."[29] Some authors' unions in Germany and Norway had recently suggested that after a certain period p.m.a., the rights of authors should pass to the state. Naturally, the state could not substitute the publishers (such a solution would be poor and bureaucratic), but authors' rights could be publicly auctioned from time to time. Dealing here with one of the most controversial questions in the realm of authors' and private rights, Löwenbach warned of exposing the Czechoslovak state and arts to the role of a "guinea pig," before sufficient experience had been gathered by the application of different models. Tille further suggested that the parliament ought to follow the French model and raise select individuals to the status of "publicly valuable/beneficial" writers on the basis of proposals made by the Ministry of Education or groups of deputies. All existing contracts governing their works would have to be cancelled; the ministry would set up new contracts and establish standardized editions, which would also safeguard heirs' interests. If no heirs existed, the state would take over. In conclusion, Tille proposed some additional secondary requirements such as: termination of the contract after the death of either party, establishment of minimum fees, as well as the expert assessment of fees. Löwenbach countered both sceptically and affirmatively: on the one hand, he pointed at latent perils arising from a too-tight embrace between the arts and government, and pondered the potential consequences if "art were classified according to a temporary constellation of power." And on the other, he carried Tille's thoughts further, suggesting an intermediary form of *domaine public payant*: after the end of the term of protection, publishers should be given the option to preserve their rights through the payment of a state licence fee, the earnings from which would then flow into the copyright fund administered by the Ministry of Education.[30]

More radical, leftist designs were not absent from the debate, and outlined the other end of the spectrum of opinion. Linking book production to the general mode of capitalistic production, the anonymous writer envisioned a holistic systemic transformation that would inevitably overturn the publishing world as well. The abolition of capitalist social order would equally put an end to anarchical writing and publishing, as it decoupled book production from publishers' profit considerations. The new system would radically help to eradicate authorial misery by separating quality from non-quality works, while the People's Commissariat would

29 Löwenbach, *Autor a nakladatel*, 11–12.

30 Löwenbach, *Autor a nakladatel*, 12.

confiscate and expropriate all valuable books, old and new, and reissue them in optimal design. Ephemeral books (easy reads) would remain free. Though not indemnified, publishers would be allowed to make a living by pursuing another profession. Expropriated authors and their families would receive compensation. The misery of underpriced, quality arts would thus come to an end. Interesting in this exposition, as well as in the one preceding it, is the demand for a clear demarcation between good/valuable and ephemeral/inferior works.

While pondering these stances, Löwenbach raised questions of agency: "who will then decide the price of books for the People's Commissariat, and on what grounds: their ethical, social, artistic or other positive worth? Will a state index of useful books be set up? In Russia, a vast and avid country with a huge literature, whose values are beyond dispute, the solution was not as difficult as in our country, where every book can be potentially disputed. And what about foreign literature and art, will they also be expropriated? Or can we do without them? You and such questions invoke this optimistic, straightforward solution. However, it assumes a fundamental change in the daily legal order but neglects that the main feature of art is freedom, that artistic values cannot remain equivocal, and that our circumstances culturally, artistically and psychologically do not contain the possibilities of such a solution." Moreover, the question of how to practically bring a fundamental change to the relationship between author and publisher could not sidestep other dilemmas. For example, "consider that the writer became in fact an official of another publisher—the state—and that the psychological stimulus of his artistic activity would be largely paralyzed."[31]

Debating Copyright

Arguments corroborating the amelioration of copyright protection in the Czechoslovak Republic usually arose from the wish to improve the social condition of authors and creators. There was a broad consensus on this issue, running more or less through the entire political spectrum. WWI had increased faith in the interventionist and regulatory role of the state, and the Czechoslovak elite was, broadly speaking, leftist inclined and social-minded, a characterization that could even be extended to include parties, which according to formal political classification could be categorized

31 Löwenbach, *Autor a nakladatel*, 13.

rather as right-wing, such as the Czechoslovak National Democratic Party. Though less liberal models (such as the Soviet one) also played a role, efforts were channelled primarily towards developing a state policy on copyright that would furnish practicable solutions. Copyright amendment was framed as an issue of public interest and moreover as a national and unquestionable necessity. A purely statist solution and the consequent nationalization of cultural production, though not absent from ongoing debates, were perceived to be excessive. The involvement of the state, however, was self-evident and was considered indispensable, the main apprehension being that state intervention be practiced with caution and temperance.[32]

The need for improvement of authors' social position in the newly established republic was argued on multiple grounds: historical, social and ethical. The line of argumentation correlated largely with historical facts: ever since the times of "Bílá Hora,"[33] the country's foremost intellectual elite had been deprived of the recognition it duly deserved. In contrast to the experience of writers in other countries, Czech and Slovak authors never attained a prestigious social position. Formed as a group at the beginning of the nineteenth century, the intellectual elite selflessly offered its services to help assemble the nation, "and the sacrifice that [the author], as a rule, brought to his paid profession was the sacrifice of enthusiastic idealism for the homeland."[34] In that early phase of national awakening, publishers and authors were united in their patriotic mission, a circumstance that pushed the economic and legal dimensions of their relationship into the background. It was only at the turn of the twentieth century that society slowly came to realize that an economic value could be attached to cultural and intellectual goods. Publishers accommodated themselves faster to the new economic realities and broadened their activities, whereas authors remained socially "stuck" in the same conditions as in the Enlightenment period.[35] The aim of copyright reform was therefore to strengthen the authors' position, and guarantee decent remuneration and fair contracts between authors and publishers.

The need to publicly substantiate the social value of intellectual labor was argued at different times in the debates that took place in the Senate, echoing voices

32 Hana Beránková, "Kolektivní správa autorských práv – slepá ulička v institucionálním vývoji?" (PhD diss., Prague University of Economics and Business, Faculty of Economics, 2010–2011), 27–28.

33 The Battle of the White Mountain took place on November 8, 1620 and represented an important battle in the early stages of the Thirty Years' War, as it marked the victory of the Roman Catholic Habsburgs over the Protestant Union. The battle, which ended with the crashing defeat of the troops of the Bohemian estates by Emperor Ferdinand II and his allies, enabled the House of Habsburg to end constitutional rule in Bohemia and enforce the Counter Reformation, which effectively meant the re-Catholicization of the Czech lands.

34 Löwenbach, *Autor a nakladatel*, 7.

35 Löwenbach, *Autor a nakladatel*, 7 ff.

from across the political world. Senator Josef Böhr of the German Christian Social People's Party emphasized the need to acknowledge the merit and effort invested in intellectual work, "which was even less appreciated than many simple handicrafts routinely performed for years in a row."[36] Senator Victor Dyk of the National Democratic Party underscored the social aspects of authors' rights. Advocating the extension of the term of protection from 30 to 50 years, he justified it on the grounds of "social justice," intended to bolster the economic position of the author's offspring. Socialist deputies (e.g. Senator Jiří Pichl) emphasized the commitment of their political party even more candidly: "We therefore welcome this law as democrats and socialists, who have always advocated public intervention [concerning issues] where the upsurge of the nation's cultural forces and the improvement of the conditions of all agents of progress is at stake."[37]

Though some of the (more radical) proposals missed the mark, it is worth revisiting them as indicators of the breadth of conceptions and designs available. Behind them, serving as a template, it is at times possible to discern Soviet influence. The nationalization of expired copyrights was proposed by article 47 of the initial copyright draft law of 1920 (Tisk 227), which recommended that copyrights pass over to the state after the end of the official term of protection. Revenue assembled from royalty payments and infringement fines would then flow into a cultural fund for the support of authors and artists.[38] The proposal was put on the table by the Ministry of Finance and supported by the Ministry of Education and National Enlightenment. Wishing to replace existing practice, whereby expired works could be reproduced by anybody, "often benefiting individuals that far from deserved it," the proposed measure envisaged the nationalization of specific works of particular merit to the national community. The fund's proceeds would serve the promotion of literature and the sciences in general, or they would be allocated to support individual destitute authors and artists. Heavily criticized, particularly by the Syndicate of Czech Authors and the Association of Czechoslovak Publishers and Booksellers, the article was eventually dropped. In fact, it was already missing in the follow-up discussions of the law's draft (Tisk 760 and Tisk 1099). Prolonging copyright indefinitely to the benefit of the state, so went the argument, contradicted the BC, whose

36 All sources pertaining to footnotes 36–52 emanate from the records (parliamentary discussions, law drafts and explanatory notes) of the National Assembly of the Czechoslovak Republic (Národní shromáždění republiky Československé) and can be found online in the Joint Czech-Slovak Digital Parliamentary Library (https://www.psp.cz/eknih/index.htm). NS RČS 1925–1929, Senát, Stenoprotokoly, 49. schůze, část 2/2, November 18, 1926.

37 NS RČS 1925–1929, Senát, Stenoprotokoly, 50. schůze, část 1/3, November 24, 1926.

38 NS RČS 1920–1925, Senát, Tisk 227, October 8, 1920, Vládní návrh.

term of protection lasted for the author's lifetime plus 50 years p.m.a. Moreover, after the expiration of the term of protection, copyright wandered into the public domain, which was already a form of "nationalization." Ensuing competition among publishers guaranteed low prices, and by consequence, broad and easy access to the public. A takeover by the state would violate this principle and probably boil down to expensive overheads, lack of business management and subsequent minor returns for the cultural fund. Fiscalism, protectionism and the likely (political) suppression of (uncomfortable) works were all conceivable outcomes of such a policy.[39]

A further proposal advanced in the early stages of the law's crafting concerned compulsory licences for musical works. Drawing inspiration from paragraphs 20 and 22 of the German copyright law of May 22, 1910, the 1920 Czechoslovak draft law proposed with article 36 an equivalent measure. It obligated any author who had already authorized the transfer of his/her work into mechanical instruments to grant anyone else a license for the same work in exchange for a reasonable fee. Unless there were objections concerning the artistic or technical performance, and provided that the third party was a proper resident and/or maintained their business headquarters in Czechoslovakia, they qualified for permission to commercially diffuse a work against an appropriate compensation.[40] The measure was justified on the grounds of anti-monopoly policy. As a result of a poll among interested groups, who subsequently opposed it, the provision was omitted in the printed governmental draft (Tisk 227 of 1920). However, the Senate restored the bill in the resolution of November 3, 1921 (Tisk 1099). It was nevertheless strongly opposed by composers' and professional circles, who condemned it in accordance with the views perpetrated during the Berlin (1922) and Amsterdam (1924) congresses of music authors' societies. In the prevailing view, compulsory licenses in practical terms meant an amputation of authors' rights on behalf of the phonographic industry; they accommodated in particular the interests of foreign industries. For precisely these reasons, the provision had failed to make headway in France, whereas in the states in which the compulsory licence had been introduced (Germany, England, Switzerland, Austria) this had happened against the will of their copyright organizations. This last view ultimately prevailed and was adopted by the expert committees involved in the law's drafting; the issue of compulsory licenses was consequently completely dropped.[41]

39 NS RČS 1920–1925, Senát, Stenoprotokoly, 58. schůze, část 2/2, June 14, 1921.

40 NS RČS 1920–1925, Tisk 760, 19.5.1921. Zpráva ùstavně-právního výboru o vládním návrhu zákona o původcovu právu k literárním, hudebním, uměleckým a fotografickým dílům,; see also NS RČS 1920–1925, Senát, stenoprotokoly, 58. schůze, část 2/2, June 14, 1921, Zpráva ùstavně-právního výboru o vládním návrhu zákona o původcovu právu k literárním, hudebním, uměleckým a fotografickým dílům.

41 Jan Löwenbach, *Právo autorské, komentované zákony československé republiky* (Prague: Československý kompas, 1927), 138–39.

The subject that was debated for the longest and most controversially was the appropriate term of protection post mortem auctoris. The two preceding domestic laws prescribed two different solutions: whereas Austrian law stipulated the 30-year term, Hungarian law applied the longer 50-year term. Proposed during the early negotiations of the governmental draft law (October 8, 1920, Tisk 227) was the 50-year term.[42] However, in the bill's first round of correction (Tisk 760), and as a result of the interventions of the Union of Czechoslovak Judges and the Association of Czechoslovak Publishers and Booksellers, the shorter 30-year term was advanced. Advocates of this solution indicated that the 30-year term represented the Austrian standard, and moreover, that a shorter term would make the works of important authors cheaper and more easily accessible to the public. Furthermore, it was indicated that adjacent countries such as Germany and Austria had opted for the 30-year term; the discrepancy in the term of protection could potentially become a disadvantage for Czechoslovak works, which under a longer protection regime at home could be easily and cheaply reprinted in the neighbouring countries, especially with regard to music.[43] Finally, the Association of Czechoslovak Publishers and Booksellers claimed that the longer term would diminish Czechoslovakia's competitive advantage.[44] This resolution of the Senate was confirmed in June 1921,[45] while the corrected version of November 1921 (Tisk 1099) also stipulated the 30-year term.

Making the argument on behalf of Czech authors, Senator Dr František Mareš, affiliated to the Association of Czech Authors "Svatobor," vindicated the 50-year term by drawing a parallel to material property. The fact that the 30-year term was promoted by stakeholders such as publishers and judges was reason enough to be suspicious, whereas the lofty arguments about cheaper and easily disseminated books were not confirmed by practical experience. How was it that owners of companies or factories could claim absolute ownership and bequeath their property to their heirs forever, and "nobody compels them, when their business runs well, to transfer it to the public after 30 or 50 years. Only authors have to serve society and the whole nation."[46] Though serving the nation was undoubtedly a vocation and an honor, authors and their progeny needed no less support on the practical level.

While one side highlighted the social status of the creator and his descendants,

42 NS RČS 1920–1925, Tisk 227, October 8, 1920, Vládní návrh a důvodová zpráva, Zákon o původcovu právu k literárním, hudebním, uměleckým a fotografickým dílům.

43 NS RČS 1920–1925, Senát, Tisk 760, 19.5.1921, Zpráva ùstavně-právního výboru o vládním návrhu zákona o původcovu právu k literárním, hudebním, uměleckým a fotografickým dílům.

44 NS RČS 1920–1925, Senát, Stenoprotokoly, 77. schůze, část 1/2, November 29, 1921.

45 NS RČS 1920–1925, Senát, stenoprotokoly 58. schůze, část 2/2, June 14, 1921.

46 NS RČS 1920–1925, Senát, stenoprotokoly 77. schůze, část 1/2, November 29, 1921.

the other argued against the danger of monopolies. Senator and law professor Robert Mayr-Harting of the German Christian Social People's Party claimed that the 30-year term represented the good Central European average of protection and saw no need to give it up. Maintaining strong exclusive copyright protection could lead to monopolies in the arts, a circumstance that had to be avoided through the use of compulsory licenses: if a similar right was assigned to one entrepreneur, any other trader should have the right to request that his business also be granted the same right, at least for the same fee.[47]

Other arguments again corroborated the 50-year term; it was the standard applied in Hungarian law and, most importantly, it was advocated by international treaties such as the BC. Other West European states such as Britain, France, Belgium and Sweden, as well as the majority of "civilized countries," also applied the 50-year term. Moreover, a longer period of protection would prompt publishers to grant outstanding talents more favorable terms and remunerate them more generously for they could then assert their rights for longer. A prolongation of the term of protection was to the benefit of both authors and artists.[48]

Conclusively, after five years, with deliberations resumed in 1925 under a new expert subcommittee and concluded in June 1926, the term of protection was extended from 30 to 50 years. The decisive argument, after a comprehensive comparative study of the most recent copyright laws, was conformity with international standards, since new legislations were increasingly adopting the 50-year term.[49] The end result was not welcomed by everybody. Commenting on the six years of back-and-forth between the Senate and House of Commons, Senator Dr Karl Heller of the German Social Democratic Workers' Party criticized the prolonged term, claiming that it inhibited important works from reaching the public at accessible prices and at the earliest date possible. If an author composed a work at the age of 20, and died at the age of 70, the work—calculated on the basis of the 50-year term—would remain locked in for 100 years. This represented an excessively long period.[50]

Judging from the overall development of the debate and the law's final draft, it can be concluded that authors' organizations (Syndicate of Czech and Slovak Authors) and their representatives (e.g. Senator Viktor Dyk) were able to decisively influence the law's orientation. The fact that they managed to frustrate three pivotal regula-

47 NS RČS 1920–1925, Senát, stenoprotokoly 77. schůze, část 1/2, November 29, 1921.

48 NS RČS 1920–1925, Senát, stenoprotokoly, 77. schůze, část 1/2, November 29, 1921.

49 Poslanecká sněmovna N.S.R.Č. 1926, Tisk 447, 15.6.1926, Zpráva výboru ústavně-právniho k usnesení senátu (tisk 1) o vládním návrhu zákona o původcovu právu k literárním, uměleckým hudebním a výtvarným a fotografickým dílům.

50 NS RČS 1925–1929, Senát, stenoprotokoly, 49. schůze, část 1/2, November 18, 1926.

tions that would have curbed authors' rights should be understood as an indicator of their influence and the pro-author inclination of Czechoslovak statesmen and copyright lawyers. Dropping the provisions regarding compulsory licences and the nationalization of works p.m.a., as well as the extension of the term of protection p.m.a. to 50 years, were properly their victory. In fact, in their view, certain issues were far from sufficiently regulated and protection did not go far enough: though the law protected musical works and their mechanical recitation (art. 7), it did not, for example, provide protection for literary works broadcast via radio; serious objections were also voiced regarding the recognition of an original right to creators, who processed existing originals into new original works (this concerned art. 23, 24 and 33).[51] Obviously, the legislator did not yield to all demands, and the far-reaching propertization sought by authors, and later in the 1936 amendment of the copyright law, moved rather in the opposite direction, by confirming and formally strengthening the already substantial role of the state.

The 1926 Copyright Law

The law was the result of close collaboration between Czech and German deputies and experts, and this "unanimity" provided an additional reason for enthusiasm, proving just how "fruitful and reasonable German collaboration is for the state." It was this cooperation that was credited for the carefully negotiated and subsequent fine-tuning in the legislating process. It points also to the various transfer channels that impacted the law's drafting.

Combining territorial and ethnic criteria, the first copyright law[52] protected literary, artistic (musical and graphic) and photographic works published in the territory of the Czechoslovak Republic, as well as works of Czechoslovak citizens abroad both published and unpublished (art. 1). Foreign citizens enjoyed protection in Czechoslovakia for their published and/or unpublished works according to the content of state treaties or on the basis of reciprocity guaranteed by foreign states (art. 2). Copyright was defined, on the one hand, positively through the attribution of exclusive rights to creators, and on the other, negatively by delineating

51 NS RČS 1925–1929, Senát, stenoprotokoly, 50. schůze, část 1/3, November 24, 1926.

52 Zákon ze dne 24. Listopadu 1926 o puvodksém právu k dílům literárním, uměleckým a fotografickým (o právu autorském), no. 218, Sbírka zákonů a nařízení státu československého, částka 105, ročník 1926, December 18, 1926, 1003–1015.

legal licences through the enumeration of free uses. Such provisions were included in article 44 on copyright encroachment, article 16 touching upon different aspects of moral rights and article 57 on the right of compensation in infringement cases.

The law particularly highlighted moral rights and protected them in different arrangements and contexts. Though par. 1 of article 16 sanctioned the limited or unlimited transfer of copyrights to other parties, it reserved the protection of non-proprietary interests to the transferor. If the transferred rights expired in the person of the transferee or his legal successors before the end of the term of protection, they reverted to the transferor in their original form for the remaining period. Paragraph 2 inhibited the acquirer of copyright from making additions, abbreviations or any changes to a work, its title or authors' name unless envisioned so by agreement. Only changes that the author him/herself in good faith would have been unable to refuse were permissible. This provision was valid for publicly performed theatrical, musical and cinematographic works. Most importantly, par. 3 raised the issue of national cultural patrimony in both symbolic and practical terms. With a view to works of overall significance for educational progress and the arts, the law prohibited any intervention in the works of deceased authors that would have diminished either their importance or value. Upon the author's death and in the absence of a legal heir, or upon the latter's failure to intervene commensurately, public or private associations were entrusted with the unlimited protection of the deceased author's rights with the purpose of preventing, prohibiting or prosecuting any misuse or misrepresentation of the author's works.

Moral rights considerations were also included in the provisions on co-authorship (art. 10) and legal enforcement (art. 14). The latter in particular prescribed that copyrights belonging to the author, his heirs or legatees could not be used to satisfy claims for damages or as collateral for cash claims against other persons (par. 1). The same applied to original works protected by copyright law, except for works purposely made for sale, such as buildings and graphic arts. However, even when law enforcement was possible, as in the cases of copies and replicas of already published works or fine arts works destined for sale, the moral rights of the creator had to be taken into consideration and protected (par. 4). In addition, article 19, regulating the relationship between authors and owners, though it recognized the owner's legitimate proprietary interests, simultaneously emphasized his obligation to respect the author's assertion of his original, non-proprietary interests if they were found to be more important than the competing interests of the owner. Moral rights were also included in provisions regarding user licences: article 29 made certain free uses conditional upon their appropriate use, that is, it forsook uses that degraded the artistic value of a work. Moreover, article 33, par. 7 imposed a limitation on the owner's right to exhibit works if public display was considered damaging to the creator's artistic reputation.

Additional provisions regarding the integrity of works were included in the Czechoslovak civil code. The owner could be made liable for incurring intentional damages to works and expropriation was maintained as an option that could be activated in cases where a work's destruction touched upon the interests of the general public.[53]

Similar to the law on the publishing contract, the copyright law included provisions regulating remuneration. Regarding musical works, article 30 brought collecting societies into effect. Instead of filing indemnity claims, local authors who were members of a collecting society could demand a commensurate fee for the unauthorized performance of their works (par. 1). If both parties were members of associations that had already negotiated a collective agreement between them, remuneration was determined by the stipulations of this arrangement. If no such agreement existed, fees were determined on the basis of tariffs established by the local collecting society; tariffs were first endorsed by the Ministry of Education and National Enlightenment and subsequently published in the first quarter of each year in the official gazette of the Czechoslovak Republic (par. 2). Additional specifications replaced these provisions concerning fixed fees with remedies as in article 57 on the right to compensation or article 58 concerning lawsuits in civil courts.

Members of foreign collecting societies could exercise their rights in the territory of Czechoslovakia only through domestic collecting societies. Foreign creators, just like domestic creators, had a choice in how to go about the protection of their copyrights, though non-membership of a domestic collecting society meant de facto less favorable conditions, since the remuneration was linked to the tariffs of the domestic collecting society.[54] Such an arrangement had two sides: it signified on the one hand that payment claims could not exceed local tariff standards, but it also put a ceiling on royalty payments, which in the case of payments to foreign collecting societies was indubitably a domestic advantage.

The law moreover institutionalized through article 62 the function of expert councils. Established by the government, they provided expert opinions on copyright matters at the request of the courts. Their statute and rules of procedure were regulated by ordinance.

53 Schwanke, "Die Entwicklung des Urheberrechts," 33.

54 Schwanke, "Die Entwicklung des Urheberrechts," 30.

Conformity to the framework of the Berne Convention usually translated into an enhancement and expansion of protection, having a bearing on both the term of protection and the extension of subject matter. The term of protection was therefore raised from 30 (as in the Austrian laws of 1846 and 1895) to 50 years p.m.a., whereas in the case of posthumously issued works, which were published during the last 10 years of the term of protection, copyright protection was extended from 5 to 10 years (art. 38, paragraphs 1 and 2). All formalities and legal requirements in order to obtain copyright were dropped. Concerning articles and news in newspapers, article 24 allowed the use (republication) of individual articles unless expressly prohibited in the initial medium; the indication of the initial source was mandatory. Reservations, however, concerning the publication of feuilleton novels, stories and poems as well as treatises of scientific, technical or artistic content published in newspapers and magazines were dropped, and their protection rendered unconditional save with the author's authorization. Copyright in musical works was also extended to cover radio broadcasts; the licence provisions of the 1895 Austrian law, which stipulated that the production and public use of instruments for mechanical reproduction of musical works constituted no copyright violation, were revoked. In the case of visual arts, the new law brought the express recognition of an exclusive exhibition right and though it narrowed down previous provisions on free uses, it allowed mechanical or optical representation for educational and scientific purposes, as well as public lectures with non-profit or charitable objectives (art. 33, paragraphs 5 and 6). Leaning on the French copyright law of May 20, 1920, article 35 introduced the notion of a *droit de suite* (a right to follow), permitting artists or their heirs to receive a fee on the (disproportionately high) profit resulting from the resale of their works. The claim was decided in court, which considered the assets of both sides and could ascribe a maximum 20% net profit; the right expired three years after the claimant had gained knowledge of the sale and 10 years after the actual sale.

Debating the Effect of the Berne Convention

Czechoslovakia's accession to the Berne Union was not greeted with unanimous enthusiasm. In an article printed initially in the periodical *Hospodářská Politika* [Economic policy] and reprinted in *Soutěž a tvorba* [Competition and creation], the anonymous author measured pros and cons against the economic effects emanating from the country's inclusion into the international copyright system.

In particular, the enhanced protection of foreign works and translations created asymmetric relations whereby imports evidently outstripped exports: "from our authors, it is Karel Čapek, Josef Čapek, Stanislav Langer, K.M. Čapek-Chod and at times perhaps a couple of others who get translated, but all this is far from balancing our payments abroad for authorizations." The bottom line of this calculation was that the previous (Austrian) law was economically and culturally more benign to Czechoslovak interests.[55]

Taking up the discussion, Jan Löwenbach emphasized that the enhanced protection resulting from the country's accession to the Berne Convention should not be measured solely in economic terms. He underlined the symbolic significance of Czechoslovakia's membership of the Berne Union, embedding the country into the international state system and the intertwinement of geopolitical status and culture. It was true that the flow of royalties was asymmetrical, but "that is the fate shared by all small states, whose literature, music, arts, whether in terms of quality, [or] in terms of export organization cannot compete with the big, traditional cultural states. Were Czech literature, music and arts to enjoy abroad the same reputation as Czech glass, porcelain, textiles, sugar, beer and so on, the economic question would be solved. How can [we] then possibly compensate in the fields of literature and the arts?"[56]

It was not only that Czechoslovakia was obligated to enter the Berne Union as a result of the peace treaty. If Liberia, Haiti or New Zealand—that is, countries barely disposing of an export capacity in cultural assets—became members, then it was evident that Czechoslovakia could not abstain from membership without risking being permanently and inexpediently categorized as a "pirate state." Abstaining from the union only deprived foreign authors of protection in Czechoslovakia, and the alternative option was to regulate cultural relationships through bilateral treaties as practiced with non-union members like the USA or Yugoslavia. Czech lawyers were right all along in their insistence that Austria enter the BU, a demand that was turned down only in order to accommodate the Slavic nations' need for free access to foreign knowledge via translations. This attitude had only contributed to Austria's classification as a "second class state." Had Czechoslovakia maintained the previous legal regime, it would have "meant voluntary self-declassification." It was therefore all the more evident that foreign authors had to grant their permission for translations and naturally be remunerated for them; any economic consequences arising from this constellation were currently irrelevant. According to Löwenbach, fees for translations were reasonable, and moreover, they were neither prohibitive

55 "Hospodářské důsledky zvýšené autorské ochrany," *Soutěž a tvorba*, 1929, year 2, no. 3–4, 42.

56 "Hospodářské důsledky zvýšené autorské ochrany," 42.

nor prevented the overproduction of poor-quality translations circulating in the Czechoslovak book market. Finally, the mutual protection offered to authors through the BC was also an economic and cultural asset that would hopefully bear fruit in the future.[57]

Such an optimistic assessment was not shared by Adolf Červinka, poet, prose writer, dramatist, translator and legal expert, who acted as the longstanding secretary of the Syndicate of Czech Writers and Composers. In his view, though discursively constructed as a legal issue, international authors' protection represented an economic issue par excellence; moreover, it clearly favored foreign authors as it enhanced the protection for unionist authors in the states belonging to the Berne Convention.[58] At play here was international business in literary and artistic creations, in spite of the alleged idealism of the ALAI, "which also has a branch here, nothing but business, and very much branched so. In this business, those states have priority whose works are translated the most, whose dramatic works dominate theatres, and whose films are most screened, that is, England and France. Those two states are the greatest exporters in the fields of literature, film and the arts, and they naturally have a vested interest to see the works of their citizens fully respected abroad, that is, that authorization fees are paid for translation permissions, for performances of theatrical and musical works and for film screenings."[59]

The international convention, according to Červinka, had to be considered through the prism of economic principles with statistics in hand, and not only through scholarly fondness for copyright issues. When negotiating international copyright regulation, negotiators had to take their own country's decisive economic and cultural issues under consideration. Not all French or English literary imports were valuable or advantageous for (home) culture. Often imported goods represented poor fashions and tastes, which always found a grateful audience, on account only of the fact that they were imported from abroad.

Statistics were useful tools. Authorizations for fashionable French novels cost between 1000 and 1500 French francs. Significant sums left the country for the authorization of theatrical plays, yet by far the greatest share of royalties was paid for film authorizations. A total of 5695 works were published in 1927 in Czechoslovakia; 4436 were published in the Czech language, while 676 were translations. It must be remembered, however, that translations of belletristic works were printed in much larger editions than local works, that is, in numbers two or three times greater.[60]

57 "Hospodářské důsledky zvýšené autorské ochrany," 43.

58 Adolf Červinka, "Ještě několik slov o Bernské úmluvě," *Soutěž a tvorba*, 1929, year 2, no. 3–4, 43.

59 Červinka, "Ještě několik slov o Bernské úmluvě," 43.

60 Červinka, "Ještě několik slov o Bernské úmluvě," 44.

"Our political friends can become at times our economic foes"; it was therefore potentially misleading to be guided only by feelings of solidarity towards allied countries. Reparation payments were a comparable example. In the peace negotiations, Czechoslovakia submitted to the Berne treaty without proper clarification of the scope of these regulations. "For our circumstances," as much for translators as for publishers, the convention was a heavy toll imposed by the victorious treaty on a friendly state. The existence of an additional treaty (January 18, 1921) with France was no special advantage for Czechoslovakia either. Concerning contracts for the use of literary property between French and Czechoslovak nationals, it was agreed that licences had to be renewed no later than six months after the contract came into effect. In Czechoslovakia, most publishers missed this deadline, which was too short and insufficiently publicized, and as a result there was a collision between older publishers, pre-war French translations, and publishers who obtained authorization after Czechoslovakia's accession to the Berne Convention.

Disregard for the inviolability of acquired rights was, according to Červinka, quite natural in view of local conditions, that is, being a country with a passive balance in international trade in literary and artistic works. Czechoslovak authors who were translated into other languages "could be counted on the fingers of one hand." The capacity of local culture in relation to international competition was often overestimated, as in the case of theatrical plays: they were promoted in such a fashion that potential customers had to purchase all locations of the performance (instead of one purchase valid for several theatres), as was the practice in Czechoslovakia, and this in turn induced them into thinking "that our art is triumphant abroad."

Selling quite nicely, piles of translated works were killing domestic literary production, though they required double payment of fees, to the foreign author for authorization and to the domestic author for translation. The same was true of films; local production was unable to assert itself in any way, so foreign films, especially German and American, predominated.

Such an overwhelming willingness to cooperate had prevailed at the peace conference that Czechoslovakia made no reservations concerning domestic circumstances, either regarding translations or transitional provisions, in particular with a view to the legitimately acquired rights to prewar translations. The failure to protect domestic interests had evidently led to enhanced entitlements by foreign publishers, who used the new framework of the BC to raise claims.[61]

61 Červinka, "Ještě několik slov o Bernské úmluvě," 44.

In a pessimistic tone, and not without a tinge of irony, Červinka commented on contemporary developments: "Now they have to ratify the decisions of the Rome Act. I have no doubts that pressured by our political friends, everything will go smoothly again, and our legislators will calmly vote once more to accept this Rome conference resolution, which will again have far-reaching economic consequences, as if it were merely an act of international politeness."[62] He proposed creating a cultural fund to support domestic literature that would be composed of collected fees on free works—in the same vein as designed by the Lex Herriot in France—and a 10% deduction from authorization fees paid abroad. By such means, domestic authors would receive some kind of compensation for the damages they incurred from the "translation fever." The proposal was eventually turned down by the Syndicate of Czechoslovak Writers due to reactions by foreign authors' representatives. The asymmetrical relationship vexed Červinka, who emphasized that authorization fees flowed abroad untaxed, whereas domestic authors had to pay an income, a turnover and, under certain conditions, also an earnings tax. In Czechoslovakia, as in other countries, it was seriously contemplated to introduce fees on foreign films in favor of the still weak domestic film production. But as Červinka emphasized, "even this impetus atrophied, due to the inability or the unwillingness to perceive these issues as economic matters, and [to acknowledge] that the cultural value of literary and film imports is sometimes a mockery of true culture and public morality."[63]

Červinka's assessment was countered by legal scholar, Otto Gellner, who questioned the logic of his economic analysis. The importance of royalties in the balance of trade was overrated, and though payments for patents were much higher, nobody ever argued seriously quitting the system of patent protection. In the same vein as Löwenbach before him, so also Gellner maintained that it was only natural for Czechoslovakia to follow modern legal and cultural developments.[64]

A Closely Knit Network of Actors

A thick network of cooperating actors played a decisive role in linking professional interests and decision-making echelons in the organization of culture; they also mediated between the different structures and institutions of society and the state

62 Červinka, "Ještě několik slov o Bernské úmluvě," 44.

63 Červinka, "Ještě několik slov o Bernské úmluvě," 45.

64 Otto Gellner, "Hospodářské důsledky zvyšene autorské ochrany," *Soutěž a tvorba*, 1929, year 2, no. 3–4, 45.

in interwar Czechoslovakia. This closely knit group, consisting of politicians, men of letters, creators and pedagogues, lawyers, diverse professionals from the field of culture, civil servants and syndicalist leaders, at times uniting several functions in one person, circulated both vertically and horizontally between interest groups, civil society, institutions and the state as they coordinated and balanced interests within the Czechoslovak Republic, but also represented the country in relevant international organizations abroad.

As a result of these overlapping activities and the specific configuration of political culture and practice in interwar Czechoslovakia, the circle that handled the copyright issue, though coming from different political and ideological corners, shared a common horizon of expectations and represented the country abroad with a consistent commitment to state building. Despite the fact that they acted as a transmission belt, transporting international copyright discourses home, at the same time, and as pointedly formulated by Jan Löwenbach in the previous section, they were conscious of the need for the Czechoslovak Republic to persevere internationally as a cultural state. This intertwined, and at times also overlapping system of interests—also because of concerns regarding the corrosive effects of political radicalization in the interwar period—was keen on cooperation, and regarded the mechanisms of culture as a state-building instrument, relevant for the state's internal and external orientation. Copyright regulation was one of the vehicles serving the above logic, and the pro-author proclivity of the copyright regime was meant to strengthen society's creative strata at the service of the aforementioned priority.

The central role of President Tomáš Garrigue Masaryk in shaping state philosophy and practice, as well as the meticulously concocted and widely disseminated image of him as a charismatic personality and chief exponent of a liberal democratic, ethnically inclusive interwar Czechoslovakia, have in the meanwhile become part of the historiographic mainstream.[65] Masaryk's specific application of the "realism" concept to politics, and the prerogative he gave to "culture" as a morality-inducing, educational instrument for politics—in fact, the amalgamation of politics with culture in his worldview—generated the particular validation that intellectuals and men of letters received in the Masarykian political universe.[66] For the generation of intellectuals that was inspired by his worldview and came to bear the name of

65 Andrea Orzoff, *Battle for the Castle: The Myth of Czechoslovakia in Europe, 1914–1948* (Oxford: Oxford University Press, 2009); also Peter Bugge, "Czech Democracy: Paragon or Parody?" *Bohemia* 47, no. 1 (2006–2007): 3–28.

66 See here Michal Kopeček, "Czechoslovak Interwar Democracy and Its Critical Introspections" (Forum: Demokratieverachtung / Contempt of Democracy in Europe), *Journal of Modern European History* 17, no. 1 (2019): 7–15.

"the pragmatic generation," or more colloquially "the Čapek generation," the liberal democratic, humanitarian project of the president-philosopher would be put into practice through a politics of consensus and compromise.[67] Rather than the result of open, but uncertain, democratic debate, consensus and compromise were pragmatically reached through the establishment of two informal political structures that gave Czechoslovak interwar politics the consensualist outlook that could also be observed in the copyright discussion. These extra-constitutional power centers were: (1) the institution of the "Pětka," an unofficial group of top politicians from the five major political parties (i.e. the Agrarians, National Democrats, the People's Party, the Social Democrats and the National Socialists) that decided among them, in advance and in secret, the political agenda before it reached parliament. Its goal was "to make governance efficient by reaching binding political compromises and securing a majority for them in Parliament."[68] (2) "Castle (*Hrad*) politics," designating "a politics based on the informal authority and charismatic personality of the president and his adherents and enacted through his personal influence on political parties, institutions, and the press."[69] The "Castle" stood for a variety of ideological positions and political approaches, the common denominator of which was the defence of the country's westward and European orientation. As a result, the diplomatic policy applied by Foreign Minister Beneš sought to strengthen bilateral agreements with other European states and anchor Czechoslovakia firmly in European and international organizations like the League of Nations and the Little Entente.[70] This general context goes some way to explain, among other things, the interest of the Czechoslovak elite in the regulation of international copyright and also their zealous participation in the structures of international organizations.

The network active in the establishment of the copyright regime, which de facto reached directly all the way up to the Minister of Foreign Affairs Edvard Beneš, consisted of overlapping concentric circles of organizations and their representatives, associations, expert groups and individuals, who acted and interacted as interest and pressure groups. A broad array of cultural clubs, associations and organizations populated interwar Czechoslovakia, and the most important among them closed ranks concerning professional issues, such as the copyright law and the law on the publishing contract. Some of the most prolific were: *Společnost spisovatelů,*

---

67 Kopeček, "Czechoslovak Interwar Democracy," 10–12; also Ort, *Art and Life in Modernist Prague*.

68 Bugge, "Czech Democracy," 14.

69 Kopeček, "Czechoslovak Interwar Democracy," 10.

70 Andrea Orzoff, "Das Personal und das Vokabular der Demokratie: Die Erste Tschechoslowakische Republik," in *Normalität und Fragilität: Demokratie nach dem Ersten Weltkrieg*, eds. Tim B. Müller and Adam Tooze (Hamburg: Hamburger Edition, 2015), 445.

skladatelů a nakladatelů (The Society of Writers, Composers and Publishers), *Společnost hudebních skladatelů v Praze* (The Society of Prague Music Composers), *Unie československých hudebníků* (The Union of Czechoslovak Musicians), *Jednota hudebních stavů* (The Association of Musical Professions), *Deutscher Musikerverband* (German Musicians' Union), *Literární odbor Umělecké Besedy* (The Literary Section of the Art Forum) and *Syndikát československých spisovatelů a hudebních skladatelů* (The Syndicate of Czechoslovak Writers and Composers), with this last organization becoming an assembly point and general coordinator of the creative strata's syndicalist and lobbying activity. These groups were supplemented by official and semi-official organizations such as the *Ochranné sdružení skladatelů, spisovatelů a nakladatelů hudebních děl* (The Association for the Protection of Composers, Writers and Publishers of Musical Works), the Czechoslovak collecting society best known by its acronym OSA, with a virtual monopoly in the collection of royalties, and the Czechoslovak branch of the ALAI established in 1927.

Cooperation between the state and interest groups was perceived as desirable and necessary, with lawyers playing a prominent role in maintaining the coherence of the copyright discourse and making sure that it was periodically updated, while they also oversaw the implementation of the copyright regime.[71] Lawyers, for example Jan Löwenbach and Karel Hermann-Otavský, functioned as specialists in various expert committees, a circle that also included university professors such as Otto Frankl and August Miřička, who consulted the Chamber of Deputies. This circle regularly contributed to the journal *Soutěž a tvorba*, the major public platform for copyright discussions and the main bulletin board communicating copyright infringement litigation to the public. In 1927 and 1928, Literární odbor Umělecké Besedy frequently organized public debates on copyright attended by an established circle including Viktor Dyk (senator and chairman of the syndicate), Adolf Červinka (writer and secretary of the syndicate), Jan Löwenbach, Karel Hermann-Otavský, Rudolf Marek (writer), Burda (representative of the Ministry of Posts, Daneš (representative of the Ministry of Education) and others. The state-promoted special advisory committees were another intersecting point for interest groups. Though not involved in the legislative process, the advisory committees were institutionalized by law and provided on demand expert opinions of a technical nature to judges in copyright infringement cases. Such bodies united, for example, the directors of OSA, members of the Czechoslovak branch of the ALAI, ministry officials, university professors,

[71] Hana Beránková, "Interest Groups and Their Influence on the Czechoslovakian Author's Rights Act," in *Good Governance and Civil Society: Selected Issues on the Relations between State, Economy and Society*, ed. Adam Jarosz (Newcastle upon Tyne: Cambridge Scholars Publishing, 2015), 260–262.

directors of music schools and academies, composers and critics. Indicative also is membership of the local section of the ALAI, an additional junction of the networked public sphere. It comprised of an illustrious list of expert intellectuals such as Chairman Karel Hermann-Otavský and members Dr Hanuš Jelínek, Prof. Dr Václav Tille (member of the advisory committee for literature), Jan Löwenbach, Karel Balling (director of OSA), Eduard Weinfurter (member of the advisory committee for literature), K.M. Čapek-Chod (famous writer), legal experts Dr Otto Gellner and Prof. Dr Karel Kadlec (specialist in Slavic Legal History), František Khol (of the Dramatic Union), Karel Scheinpflug (member of the advisory committee for literature), Prof. Dr O. Sommer (lawyer), J. Štokolovský (chairman of the Syndicate of Fine Arts, and member of the advisory committee for fine arts), architect Otakar Novotný (member of the advisory committee for fine arts), legal scholar and rector of Brno University Prof. Dr Franz Weyr, Miroslav Rutte (of the Dramatic Union) and J. Riedl. Recruits from the same circle represented the Czechoslovak authors' societies at the international meeting of the International Confederation of Societies of Authors and Composers (CISAC) in 1927 and 1928 (Jan Löwenbach, Karel Balling and representatives of the Dramatic Union).[72]

Though this kind of "thick network" activity is not unique to Czechoslovakia—in fact, other cases such as France and Germany demonstrate analogous forms of multilevel entanglements in the constitution of their respective copyright regimes—the case of Czechoslovakia contrasts with the two other cases under scrutiny in this research. Though more systematic comparative conclusions will be drawn in the summary, it suffices to underscore here the alignment of the copyright project with the broader political statehood design, that is, the connection between consensual politics and culture as constituent parts of the "realistic" state-building philosophy of interwar Czechoslovakia; all factors which directly or indirectly related to the country's geopolitical position and mission. Despite the existence of different schools of thought concerning the role of the state (e.g. complete eradication of the market for cultural goods advocated by the radical left, or the restrained state protectionism advocated by the center, left and right), the de facto imbroglio between interest groups and the state optimized their cooperation and mutual interpenetration in the interwar period. All this goes some way towards explaining the prevailing pro-author attitude of the official copyright regime, which in the view of some researchers even went too far in accommodating the needs of the creative strata, possibly even to the disadvantage of the public and end users.[73]

---

72 Beránková, "Interest Groups," 265–66.

73 Beránková, "Interest Groups," 266; idem, "Kolektivní správa autorských práv," 69–73.

It is hard to evaluate the contribution of the institution of copyright to the improvement of creators' fortunes and the dynamic of culture in interwar Czechoslovakia. Though it is tempting to view copyright as the self-evident milestone in the development of the cultural field and the perseverance of authors' rights, the professionalization of authors in the interwar period was rather the result of a combination of socioeconomic, cultural, intellectual and—as already mentioned—also political aspects.[74] Among these factors, the following need to be underlined: (1) in the first place, the relative wealth of Czech society. Progressing industrialization in certain regions (Bohemia, Moravia) was matched by a satisfactory development of the agricultural sector, as well as the newborn state's capacity to recover quickly from the separation of its territories from the Habsburg Empire. The First World War and the Great Depression weakened but did not ruin its economy. (2) The high value ascribed to literature by cultural elites and the educational system, partly due to its role in the politics of the national revival. The result thereof was a long-lasting cult of the book and its treasuring as cultural practice, values that were reflected, for example, in the build-up of family libraries even in working-class households. (3) The top position of print among mass media and the close relationship between journalism and literature, the opulent structure of national and regional press and its countrywide dispersal, whereby the regional press constituted different circuits, which in their turn encouraged the demand for literary texts. (4) Sustained sponsorship by civil society through relief and subsidy measures provided by literary and educational foundations and associations established during the liberal era (i.e. from the 1860s onwards), including Matice česká, Svatobor, Česká akademie pro vědy a umění,[75] Máj and others. (5) State sponsorship as a result of the First Czechoslovak Republic's (ČSR) cultural policies, such as the set-up of the public libraries network in 1919, requiring that all municipalities, regardless of their size, establish their own public library, or the governmental promotion of national literature through the award of State Literary Prizes by the Ministry of Schooling and National Education. Support for culture was also meant to embolden the image of direct communication between the political establishment and the cultural communit(y/ies). In practice, this translated to the subsidization of artistic life via the support for cultural associations.[76] (6) Attainment of a certain degree of cultural differentiation and maturity

[74] Email correspondence with Pavel Janáček September 25, 2016. In the section that follows, I summarize and recapitulate several of his arguments and draw my ensuing conclusions from his insightful comments on the professionalization of authors in the interwar period.

[75] On the sponsorship of the Czech Academy for Sciences and Arts (ČAVU), see Blanka Hemelíková, "Parnas sobě? Ceny, podpory a stipendia literárního odboru ČAVU v letech 1890–1921," in Breň and Janáček, *O slušnou odměnu bude počováno*, 101–129.

[76] Krejčí, "Stát coby patron umění?" 136.

that helped authorship to gratify the differentiated needs and tastes of various readers, the openness of literary culture to foreign texts, the development of the market for popular reading matter and its tight connections to cultural transfers from Germany, Western Europe as well as the US. (7) Accomplishment of high literacy rates but also of "literary literacy," denoting the ability to read, recognize and understand certain conventions of language and therefore produce literary meaning. (8) The writers' long-term experience of the liberal literary market, which stimulated their turn to syndicalist forms of organization like the Syndicate. More than the effect of copyright, the amelioration of authors' fortunes was rather the result of legislative action and practical measures taken in the sphere of labor relations, such as the law on the publishing contract as well as the negotiations of syndicalist organizations with the state and the publishers' guild, which resulted in collective agreements on minimum remuneration and/or percentage payments from sales. Research corroborates these observations, indicating that authors' fees started to rise from 1922 onwards, that is, after the signing (at the end of 1921) of a collective agreement on percentage payments calculated on the basis of the book's price and multiplied by the size of the edition. In the 1920s, the average fee was 10% of the paperback price, paid upon the printing of the book for the whole edition. Fees varied between 8% and 15% with latter percentages being paid to the most prominent authors, like the Čapek brothers.[77]

Finally, if copyright affected the professionalization of authors, it influenced perhaps to an even greater degree the professionalization of jurists. They are conspicuously present in the Czechoslovak story, and in greater numbers than in the other two cases under scrutiny, which is one of the reasons for the much greater specialization in this legal field in interwar Czechoslovakia. Moreover, it involved a circuit of jurists ranging from academic circles to practitioners. The establishment of the copyright regime generated a need for expert knowledge to be applied both internally and externally. The implementation of new rights generated a greater need for legal communication and consultation concerning their lawful application, as in the case of copyright litigations, but also concerning the country's adequate legal representation with a view to international law.[78] There was therefore a circular legitimizing logic in place, which can also be interpreted as the conscious creation of a professional opportunity through specialization: copyright was important, therefore the presence of experts was indispensable; and inversely, the professional

[77] Michal Jareš, "Autorské honoráře ve světle vzpomínek nakladatelů," in Breň and Janáček, *O slušnou odměnu bude počováno*, 147.

[78] Beránková, "Kolektivní správa autorských práv," 51.

authority and activity of copyright jurists confirmed the significance of copyright. Actions like attuning the local with the international copyright regime, or legislating copyright in the national context, were usually preceded by workshops or conferences of the Czechoslovak branch of the ALAI and/or professional meetings of the Czechoslovak lawyers' organization. This goes to confirm that copyright was treated as a national issue, and moreover, an issue involving the entire lawyers' guild and not only a few select individual specialists acting in isolation. The fact that Czechoslovakia's foremost copyright lawyer (Jan Löwenbach) was himself actively involved in cultural production was a felicitous circumstance; it explains his vested and genuine interest in the fortunes of artists, his in-depth understanding of the workings of the cultural industry, his multifarious network connections to men of letters and cultural producers and his comprehension of the correlation of geopolitics and culture.

Amendment of the Copyright Law in 1936

Before the establishment of the communist regime, the 1926 copyright law was amended one last time in 1936. The revision was motivated, on the one hand, by the need to endorse and integrate changes brought about by the 1928 Rome revision of the BC, which were a precondition for participation in the upcoming 1936 ALAI conference in Brussels. On the other, there was a need to update regulation arising from the development of new technologies in the dissemination of works.[79]

Among these priorities was radio broadcasting, which had been the subject of comprehensive discussions during the Rome conference. As discussed in an earlier chapter, the author's right to authorize the use of his work was acknowledged in principle (art. 11a), but there was lack of unanimity among union members concerning the regulation of radio. Representing something of an exception to copyright's principle of exclusivity, and in a certain way also contradicting the convention's preceding paragraph, section 11b of the revised text gave individual unionist states the prerogative to decide the conditions under which radio broadcasts would be regulated at home. During the Rome negotiations, the Czechoslovak representatives spoke in favor of a statutory license to the benefit of radio companies, but with some exceptions.

79 Poslanecká sněmovna N.S.R.Č. 1936, IV. volební období, 3. zasedání, 383. Zpráva výboru ústavněprávního o usnesení senátu Národnhího shromáždění republiky Československé (tisk 351) o vládním návrhu zákona (tisk sen. 64 a 118), kterým se mění a doplňuje zákon ze dne 24. listopadu 1926, č. 218 Sb. z.a.n., o původském právu k dílům literárním, uměleckým a fotografickým (o právu autorském), 1.

The 1926 Czechoslovak copyright law was amended through the law of April 24, 1936, Nr. 120 Slg. In order to accommodate changes resulting from the Rome revision of the BC, articles 21, 27, 31 and 36 were supplemented regarding the exclusive right of authors to disseminate their works via radio and other technical instruments. At the same time, the law limited the author's exclusive right through the introduction of a compulsory licence. Article 16 was supplemented with an additional paragraph (16a), which stated that authors of literary, artistic and photographic works could decline the distribution of their works via radio *only* if the refusal was justified by the work's nature or the creator's non-proprietary interests. In any case, the author was entitled to appropriate remuneration, possibly determined by court, and the licence was valid only for domestic state-owned radio companies or equivalent ones operating under the supervision and/or with the participation of the state. The measure was justified on the grounds of public welfare and the need to meaningfully resolve the conflict between public and copyright-owner interests. As far as literary works were concerned, works not fully published were excluded from the licence.[80]

The catalogue of protected works was extended to include plans and drawings, complete or partial (architectural) designs of municipalities and/or larger spaces, unless they were of a purely technical nature (art. 4, par. 2), and article 18 was supplemented to ensure reasonable remuneration for the transfer of those rights. In order to accommodate changes in article 9 of the revised BC concerning news and articles in newspapers and magazines, article 24 of the Czechoslovak law was modified. The amendment extended copyright to all articles, novels, short stories, stories and poems, as well as all treatises of entertaining, scientific, technical or artistic content published in newspapers and magazines, which from that moment on explicitly required authorial consent in order to be republished.

With article 30, "on the implementation of rights by professional associations," the monopoly position of the home collecting society, OSA, was officially consolidated. As announced in the official state bulletin, the Ministry of Education and National Enlightenment bestowed on it the exclusive right to grant permissions for the use of works, collect operating fees and represent interests regarding: (1) public non-theatrical operation of protected musical works with lyrics or without lyrics, the public recitation of such works by instruments or their devices intended for mechanical recitation; (2) use of such works for transfer into instruments or their equipment for mechanical recitation; (3) broadcasting of such works through radio or other technical instruments. Theoretically, authors and/or their heirs could

80 Ibid., 2.

authorize the permission themselves, that is, if they wished to do so, they could circumvent OSA, but the collective management organization remained clearly the more expedient option. OSA was awarded this exclusive right by official decision on September 10, 1936.[81]

OSA: The Association for the Protection of Composers, Writers and Publishers of Musical Works

A major reason contributing to the timely and expedient expansion of the copyright regime in the case of Czechoslovakia, in contrast to Bulgaria and Yugoslavia, was unquestionably the earlier development, greater professionalization and expansion of the field of music (and related industry) in this country. Music, especially performed music, was the prime mover of copyright and this also goes to explain why copyright-related organizations, like OSA, were institutionalized earlier in Czechoslovakia than in the other two cases in comparison. The creation of the republic in the interwar period coincided with the spread of new technologies like radio and sound film that helped to further consolidate the role of the Czechoslovak collecting society.

The first calls for the creation of a Czech collecting society were voiced already in the Habsburg Empire. At that time, certain music authors were represented by the Viennese AKM and/or the Berlin-based GEMA, but many composers—among them Bedřich Smetana—were not represented at all; most popular music composers belonged to that category. Composers and publishers were initially hesitant regarding the foundation of a copyright association, fearing that overhead costs would endanger the payment of royalties. The idea was, however, openly supported by popular music authors, who having little to lose became the driving force behind OSA's establishment.[82]

The Association for the Protection of Czechoslovak Composers, Writers and Publishers of Musical Works (*Ochranné sdružení autorské československých*

81 Schwanke, "Die Entwicklung des Urheberrechts," 39.

82 Some of the information provided in this section is drawn from the official website of OSA, which on occasion of the organization's centennial celebration designed an elaborate website with an outline of the major highlights of the organization's history (1919–2019). See here https://www.100letosa.cz/#1800. Its historical narrative is doubtless very informative and professionally crafted, but it should nevertheless be kept in mind that the website presents an official self-representation of the institution and not a critical engagement with its history. OSA's development since the 1980s has been an issue of debate.

skladatelů, spisovatelů a nakladatelů hudebních děl) was created in 1919 as a mutual project of the Club of Czechoslovak Composers, Publishers and Librettists (*Klub československých skladatelů, nakladatelů a textařů*). After initial difficulties, the organization developed rapidly in the 1930s. The rise of OSA was significantly aided by the passing of the 1926 copyright law, which brought collecting societies into effect and gave priority to collective agreements and official tariffs. With the new copyright law, OSA became a significant social factor in the life of Czechoslovak composers, receiving recognition at home and abroad. In fact, before 1926, OSA had had no legal grounds for collecting royalties, and end users were reluctant to pay fees and often issued complaints.

OSA's monopoly position[83] was enforced by the 1936 copyright law amendment, which endowed OSA with the exclusive right to grant permissions for the use of works in Czechoslovakia. The organization assessed authors' rights, acted against copyright infringements and collected royalties, dealing essentially with small rights. Consisting of a 12-member board of directors (6 composers, 3 authors, 3 publishers and 4 replacements), it maintained branches in Prague and Bratislava and had its own network of confidants. OSA disposed of a welfare fund and represented approximately 1200 Czechoslovak authors. Records from 1937, for example, show that that same year OSA concluded 6000 one-year general contracts and approximately 48,500 contracts for the use of individual works. By 1940 it had developed a sizeable bureaucratic apparatus of approximately 70 employees. The organization reinvested profits and boasted that its unprecedented, self-generated growth was independent of state subventions.[84]

OSA played a seminal role in disciplining and accustoming societal actors to the payment of royalties. It sent out letters of admonishment and control teams that verified the accuracy of announced repertoires, and made sure that relevant and exemplary court decisions on infringement cases found their way into the press and acted as deterrents (for example in the pages of *Soutěž a tvorba*). A substantial, recurrent practical problem was determining who was responsible for performed music, since individual groups of stakeholders (innkeepers, organizers, bandleaders etc.) denied responsibility and tried to offload it onto the shoulders of the others. It also concerned the capacity

83 There are differences of opinion regarding the business structure and nature of OSA. The official OSA website, for example, claims that the collecting society was always organized as a cooperative and non-profit civic organization. On the contrary, Hana Beránková argues that OSA's operation could not be compared to cooperative activity and that the organization functioned as a joint venture and limited liability company. Beránková, "Kolektivní správa autorských práv," 42–43 and idem, "Interest Groups," 261.

84 Beránková, "Kolektivní správa autorských práv," 44–45.

of OSA to exercise authority and structurally control the field of entertainment. Initially, the lack of clarity provoked confusion, bad blood and litigations. With time, the conception crystallized that operators and organizers carried responsibility for events and performed music, but innkeepers and pub owners were also kept in line. The liability of operators was asserted via governmental order (January 25, 1939), which confirmed the organizers' responsibility to duly inform OSA by attaching all relevant information when applying for admission regarding the organization of an event.[85]

Fee rates were derived either from collective contracts between OSA and certain professional groups or by fixed rates developed in collaboration with the Ministry of Schooling and National Education. OSA collected royalties for four operations: live performances, transfer to mechanical recitation tools, use in films and radio broadcasting. Collective rates were lower than usual; they were established through mixed commissions, composed equally of OSA representatives and representatives of the various corporations. In order to negotiate with OSA, each creative sector had to set up its own negotiating team. Fee rates, tariff categories and collective agreements were meticulously regulated, and in the early 1940s (i.e. during the protectorate), even more stringently as they also had to be endorsed by the Supreme Pricing Authority (Nejvyšší úřad cenový). During the protectorate and WWII, the association's activities were taken over by the German STAGMA,[86] but the management protected the archive and economic resources from liquidation. After WWII, the association's activities were restored and expanded.

85 Beránková, "Kolektivní správa autorských práv," 60.

86 During the protectorate, fees for the use of musical works in films varied between 18 and 50 K for works represented by STAGMA. Filmmakers were also obliged to pay music composers a percentage (for example 20%) of the original royalties for each new version of the film within three months of the film's release abroad. According to the 1944 contract between STAGMA and the Czech/Moravian Film Center, cinematographers seeking permission to use musical works had to pay 4% of gross income after having deducted the entertainment tax. Even if cinematographers forsook this option, they still had to pay a flat fee amounting to 300 K. The contract stipulated further that the Film Center had to disclose all information on the cinematographers to the protectorate. All measures came into effect only after having been approved by the Supreme Pricing Authority. As already mentioned, professional groups built their own teams to negotiate with OSA. The priority of negotiating collective agreements provided for an additional incentive to act collectively. Associating and negotiating with OSA was therefore the most advantageous strategy for members of certain professions. Beránková, "Kolektivní správa autorských práv," 46.

The Protectorate

The Protectorate of Bohemia and Moravia was established in March 1939 following the German occupation of the Czech lands. Paradoxically, the period of occupation (the first half of the 1940s) brought about increased state support for culture. As a result of the ensuing conflict with resistance forces, efforts to indoctrinate Czech society were strengthened, especially after the establishment of the Ministry of Schooling and National Education led by Emanuel Moravec.[87] During the protectorate's early period, authors revived the idea of a cultural fund to be built through subsidies from libraries and publishers. The fund would function as a sovereign legal entity, directly subordinate to the Minister of Education but otherwise autonomous in relation to the administrative apparatus of the Ministry of Schooling and National Education. Its expenditure would be decided by an independent committee, represented evenly by delegates of all artistic associations.

The fund's potential beneficiaries were intentionally defined quite broadly to cover creators and their extended families, and the benefits covered work and age incapacity, unemployment and disease, various forms of rehabilitation, and with a view especially to women, financial assistance for childbirth or abortion. Writers could claim support for diverse needs, ranging from convalescence visits to social institutions and health facilities to malnutrition, parenting, caring for poor relatives, indebtedness, funeral expenses, natural disasters and other particular events. Due to the fact that its formation was independent of government subsidies, state authorities were not inimical to the fund's creation and moreover regarded it as an opportune measure to curb publishers' resistance to new levies on literature. This approach effectively meant partially shifting the financial burden onto the shoulders of cultural consumers. On the basis of a levy, whereby public libraries would forward 20 Hellers to the Syndicate for every book taken out on loan, the proposal questioned the whole system of public librarianship laboriously built up from the creation of the first Czechoslovak state; librarians pointed out several problems, ranging from financial burdens to the discouragement of reading.[88]

Within the framework of new legal regulations, authors pressed to normalize the enforcement of authors' fees, which corresponded to general trends in the protectorate's managed economy. Upon delivery of the manuscript, authors could automatically claim payment of half the fee, irrespective of any other circumstances

87 Krejčí, "Stát coby patron umění?" 140.

88 Krejčí, "Stát coby patron umění?" 140.

concerning the book's publication. The ministry endorsed these claims, pointing at the specificity of the literary market and the heterogeneous level of production. In the 1940s, the idea of an exclusive authors' union was promoted, aiming to monopolize the representation of authors and thereby disadvantage and isolate those intellectuals standing outside the association. In the context of discussions concerning the publishing contract, the Syndicate demanded a fee amounting to 10% of the work's retail price.[89]

With the end of the war, the Ministry of People's Enlightenment was replaced by the Ministry of Information, which played a central role in the organization of culture in the postwar period. The ministry's approach was predicated on the conceptions of resistance groups, whose intellectuals reckoned with the withdrawal of the state and intended to entrust the administration of culture to artists' self-governing institutions. They were headed by prominent artists who were able to recoup for culture a greater share of the state budget, and also attracted sympathy for the Communist Party, which de facto controlled the ministry. Additional factors, such as low social esteem for literary works and the effects of the economic crisis on unemployed intellectuals, nurtured distrust of market mechanisms and the capitalist economy of the interwar period. The planning of culture, to be devised and materialized by a special department of the State Planning Authority under the leadership of the author K.J. Beneš, would therefore replace market spontaneity in the liberated republic. The pluralist system of writers' associations was gradually reduced to the benefit of creative associations that had a profound influence on the everyday life of writers: union membership meant recognition of the status of writer, which in turn, in the context of postwar conditions, could be associated with diverse exigencies: from aid in order to release the funds of fixed deposits, find solutions to housing problems, award or adjust pensions to simple everyday issues like being able to profit from the extraordinary rationing of cigarettes and coffee.[90]

With the progressive liquidation of private publishing houses and the monopolization of the publishing market, receiving the association's recommendation became ever-more important for the publication of manuscripts or the renewal of editions of older works. Moreover, deserving artists received special recognition and were bestowed with the honorary title of "national artist," which was legally coupled with the right to a lifelong honorary pension and state support for publications.

---

89 Krejčí, "Stát coby patron umění?" 141.

90 Krejčí, "Stát coby patron umění?", 141.

Broad Contours of the Czechoslovak Copyright Regime before Communism

The system of culture and the copyright regime that were put in place during the interwar period can be broadly qualified as *pro-author* and *state-protectionist*, with the second tendency essentially enforcing the first. In spite of strong competition among different interest groups and divergent political ideologies (and visions), the priority of political and cultural state building provided the broad context for the consensualist politics that prevailed in interwar Czechoslovakia. The earlier syndicalization (practically all groups involved in cultural production had initiated professional organizations before the creation of the first Czechoslovak state), greater experience and longer exposure to liberal politics led creative groups to quickly seek regulation and accommodation. This attitude was moreover backed and encouraged by the state, both ideationally and practically: ideologically, it was justified on the grounds of the beneficial historical role that creative elites had diachronically played in supporting nation and nation state building, as well as the central demand to finally do social justice to cultural creators; practically, through the interlocked character of interest groups, corporations, political parties and the state, which made such policies feasible. Ultimately, it was the positive valorization of culture as a constructive asset to both national and geopolitical development that provided the proper breeding ground for such policies.

Quite characteristic of this attitude is the preoccupation with music education, the extensive attention it received in parliamentary debates, as well as the multiple, even if unmaterialized legislative projects concerning the development of music professions. These efforts testify to the importance attributed to music, not as a narrow professional field but as a project of national significance. Recurrent among the topics of discussion were the inadequate quality of private music teachers and singers, the need for quality control of both groups, their structure of education, the funding of music schools, professional competition between military and civil orchestras, professional integration of new music graduates and other topics—in other words, a breadth of topics bearing upon not only the expert education of musical professionals but also the musical edification of the popular masses. Though a proposal for a state-controlled system of musical education did not pass, parliament nevertheless adopted a resolution concerning the musical re-education of the nation. As maintained by Beránková, there were at least three important legislative proposals in the interwar period touching upon the amelioration of the field of music and its professional organization. The most important were the proposal by Mayr-Harting concerning the creation of a "musical chamber" (*hudební komora*), the proposal by R. Beran for "the protection of the musical guild" (*ochrana stavu hudebnického*), envisioning the enactment of legislation regulating the teaching of music and singing, and the proposal by V. Sladky propagandizing free musical education for poor but talented children at public expense. These proposals had in common the desire to set up concrete administrative measures to enforce a state-supervised professionalization of music and ultimately restrict branch-internal competition. Had the proposals become law, they would have paved the way for a compulsory, hierarchically organized, professional, state-qualified musicians' guild, functioning according to prescribed and strict rules under the supervision of the authorities. Similar to belletristic authors, there was apparently sufficient support from musicians, who were willing to change the institutional framework and made concerted efforts towards a state-regulated pension. According to Beránková, even without these initiatives, the bureaucratic organization of the music profession was inaugurated with the beginning of the history of the Czechoslovak state, long before the wave of forced étatization in 1948.[91]

The organization of culture in interwar Czechoslovakia was based on a model that favored a strong regulation of labor relations and upheld the autonomy and self-management of creators, but under the auspices and with the help of a state-bestowed and state-supervised monopoly. A broadly shared philosophy of state protectionism corroborated this attitude towards the arts. Creative unions were quite successful in promoting their agendas and pursued a strategy of greater propertization, by seeking an ever-greater extension of their prerogatives. To this end, they aligned themselves with lawyers and international organizations, an alliance that provided each of these stakeholders with reciprocal legitimacy. In order to face post-WWI multilateral challenges, Czechoslovakia was dependent upon international recognition, and as a consequence sought to strengthen its geopolitical standing by anchoring its policies more firmly in international organizations, as well as by aligning itself with broad universalist projects. Last but not least, the country's strong political and cultural orientation towards France could be considered an additional reason that goes some way to explaining Czechoslovakia's affinity for international copyright, a longtime favorite of French diplomacy. All these factors indeed played into each other in the construction of the copyright regime of the First Czechoslovak Republic.

---

91 Beránková, "Kolektivní správa autorských práv," 31–34.

Though operating under market conditions, the interwar Czechoslovak copyright regime was Janus-faced. While being "extrovert," that is, it lined up and coordinated with international authorities and structures, it was simultaneously "introvert," that is, international collaboration was practiced in a manner that nevertheless warranted the beneficial and preferential treatment of local authors/creators, not least by prescribing the conditions and channels through which foreigners could assert their rights in Czechoslovakia, for example by obligating foreign authors to accommodate local fee tariffs or by obliging them to negotiate only with local official copyright structures. In its internal orientation, it was no less protectionist, keeping a close watch over the influence of free trade agents like intermediaries and publishers. From the beginning, and in contradistinction to other collecting societies like GEMA, in which publishers maintained a strong influence over the society's management in the interwar period,[92] publishers in the Czechoslovak case constituted only one quarter of OSA's management.[93]

The basic features of this regime, such as the close cooperation between interest groups and the state (as in the setting up of remuneration fees and tariffs), a certain degree of institutional centralism as well as features of a centrally planned economy, the tendency towards mandatory law, as well as the protectionist, pro-author attitude, were enhanced during the protectorate. Though the communist takeover diminished institutional pluralism, eradicated private entrepreneurship and enforced ideological conformity, it did not substantially change the basic design of the economy of culture, that is, creators' autonomy based on state-bestowed monopoly and protection. On the contrary, it could be argued that the ground had already been laid for the subsequent, more étatist version of creators' professional organization.

---

92 See here Louis S. Pahlow, "Industrialized Music Brokers as Competing Market Players: The Administration of Music Rights in Germany (ca. 1870–1930)," *Popular Entertainment Studies* 6, no. 2 (2015): 62.

93 OSA official webpage, https://www.100letosa.cz/#1800.

Chapter 10

Comparative Perspectives on National, Regional, International and Transnational Trajectories up to and Including the Interwar Period

This chapter brings together several threads of analysis and places copyright development in East Central and Southeast Europe in regional, European and international context. Through comparative juxtaposition, it illuminates select topics such as the role of continuities, traditions, strategies, actors and stakeholders, master narratives and institutional paths, and presents theses and conclusions regarding the trajectory of copyright development in the late nineteenth century, up to and including the interwar period. Among the themes discussed are strategies of governance in the Berne Union, the influence of imperial legacies in the conception of national copyright legislation, the rise of new media in the twentieth century and their effect on copyright regulation, the nature of copyright regimes in interwar Bulgaria, Yugoslavia and Czechoslovakia, trends regarding social rights and the regulation of intellectual labor in the interwar period, the rise of collecting societies and intermediary agents from the late nineteenth century, as well as the outlook and artistic philosophy of intellectual avant-gardes in the interwar period.

Governance Strategies of the Berne Union

The BU's eastward expansion in the context of the Paris Peace Conference took the form of "prescribed accessions," and was a conscious and intended internationalization of IPRs, promoted by energetic lobbying actors such as the Syndicate for the Protection of Intellectual Property and the ALAI. Having stood initially on opposite sides, these two organizations (the Syndicate and the ALAI) reached a compromise around 1900 that also involved cooperation regarding IP internationalization.[1] Their mutual cooperation as pressure groups in the Versailles settlement confirms this

1 Jose Bellido, "Montevideo vs. Berne," 45–47.

change of policy. An additional motivation for the BU's "hasty" eastern expansion, concurrent to the many reasons already elucidated in previous chapters, could well have been Berne's justified concern regarding its stagnant membership, and the pressure to demonstrate "success" and "growth," particularly with a view to independent organizational initiatives in the Americas, which Europeans were increasingly interpreting as "competition" or even as an "obstacle" to Berne.[2] The peace treaties offered a unique window of opportunity to promote and expand the BU regime, and actors took advantage of the synergies offered by the combination of diplomatic context, state backing and international law enforcement mechanisms. The case of the East Central and Southeast European "accessions" points at the policy of internationalization as an expansion strategy. Reactions from the states concerned were mixed and varied. At the time, the majority of East Central and Southeast European societies had limited experience, if any, of the application and operationalization of copyright; they therefore had different and varying degrees of acquaintance with and inclination towards applying copyright in the regulation of their inner and interstate relations.

When legislating in Berne, the hegemonic nations were codifying according to their own needs and the more advanced, up-to-date standards of their own cultural industries. At the same time, they consciously denied other peoples and world regions the option of going through the intellectual and cultural gestation processes that they had experienced while building up their cultures, literatures and industries. Having profited from protracted periods of mercantilist state policies and fulsome copying of foreign models and manufactures in the eighteenth and nineteenth centuries, they emerged during the first phase of globalization with the complementary needs to expand and to provide rules for this expansion on a global scale. Far from being simply anarchic, the appropriation of texts in the early modern period often underlay implied literary conventions and rules of conduct.[3] Inventive translations altering and complementing the initial text, modifications, omissions or supplements, imitations, abridgements and copying, translations from one language to another and from one genre to another, what Roger Chartier has termed "textual migrations"[4] and so on, all represented practices and approaches that at a different time had helped these cultures, literatures and industries to grow. Having

2 Bellido, "Montevideo vs. Berne," 49–51, 71–77.

3 See here Matthew H. Birkhold, *Characters before Copyright: The Rise and Regulation of Fan Fiction in Eighteenth-Century Germany* (Oxford: Oxford University Press, 2019).

4 Roger Chartier, *Won in Translation: Textual Mobility in Early Modern Europe* (translated from French by John H. Pollock) (Philadelphia, PA: University of Pennsylvania Press, 2022), vii.

entered a different phase of capitalistic development, one where international trade in cultural commodities became coterminous with the mass consumption of stabile and recognizable products as components of national culture and economy, the core countries recodified hybridization processes as transgressions. The BU's codification designs mirrored these metamorphoses and power relations. This circumstance is reflected not only in the fact that a one-size-fits-all regime gradually prevailed and all obstacles to the automated application of rules (like formalities and reservations) were effectively removed, but also in the observation that the core countries consciously endorsed and codified concessions and/or exceptions beneficial to their own interests. In a process that could be described as "cherry-picking," they ensured in different instances that their own vital interests were safeguarded, even if they contradicted the general rules.

An illustrious example of such preferential treatment is the British enforcement in 1914 of an "Additional Protocol" by way of exception to the BC.[5] It contradicted the stipulation of the 1908 Berlin Revision of the BC which granted authors of non-union countries the benefits of national treatment if their work was first published in a union country, and unionist treatment in all other member countries. This provision was disadvantageous to Great Britain and the British dominions as it obliged them to protect the works of American authors who published within the realms of the British Empire and also granted them unionist protection if they were published in any other union country. The British reaction must be interpreted against a dual background: on the one hand, North America had declined all along to enter international obligations that would have granted protection to British authors in the US; on the other, the first act that granted protection to foreign authors in the US, the 1891 Chase Act, imposed, on the insistence of the local printing industry, the obligation that in order to enjoy copyright, foreign works had to be printed from type set within the limits of the United States, which effectively meant that works printed outside of the US were deprived of protection. This conditionality was removed for foreign authors in 1909 but was preserved for works in the English language, which amounted to discrimination against Britain, its dominions and colonies. Threatening to withdraw from the union, Britain was able to sway the BU into adopting an "Additional Protocol," which granted to each member state "the right to restrict, within its territory, the benefits of the Convention with regard to authors of a non-member country."[6] Representing an arrangement completely tai-

---

5 See here Stephen P. Ladas, *The International Protection of Literary and Artistic Property*, vol. I: 94–97. For the original text, see "Additional Protocol," https://wipolex.wipo.int/en/text/278726.

6 Ladas, *The International Protection*, 96.

lored to the needs of Britain and its empire, the protocol constituted "a restriction of the regime of the Union by granting power to a member state to limit the protection of the works of authors, nationals of a non-member country, who at the time of publication were not domiciled in a country of the Union. This power could be exercised when the non-member country did not sufficiently protect works of authors belonging to the member country."[7]

The French and German publishing industries likely profited from the same stipulation that irritated the British in the first place, that is, the possibility offered to foreign authors of non-union member states to have their works protected when published first or simultaneously in a union country. Representing a center of publishing for authors of diverse nationalities and languages, like the Spanish-speaking world of South America for example, French publishers had an interest in securing a primacy not only in the trade but also in the rights to those works. The same was true for German publishers regarding the vast world of German, Slavic and other speakers in the Eastern European empires that had their works published in the German lands. What initially constituted article 3 of the original 1886 BC and its 1896 Paris revision, and eventually came to stand as article 4 of the Berlin revision (1908) and then more explicitly elaborated as paragraph 3 of article 4 of the 1928 Rome revision, accomplished precisely this. It declared as the country of origin of unpublished works the author's country of origin; for published works, the country of first publication; and for works published simultaneously in several union countries that country whose legislation provided for the shortest term of protection. Most importantly, for works published simultaneously in a non-union and a union country, it was the latter (i.e. the union country) that was considered exclusively the work's country of origin.[8] In other words, publication of a work (of whatever origin and language) in one of the union countries automatically activated the BC mechanism of protection and made the BC universally applicable, and moreover gave the union country precedence over all other non-union publishing locations. By these means, works were legally nationalized for BU purposes.

What is more, a practice that in earlier periods would probably have been classified as "illicit publishing," that is, the (re)publishing of a work in a country other than the country of (cultural, linguistic, national, printing) origin and its subsequent import back into the "country of origin" or its international distribution and trade—all practices that had vexed the core countries in the consolidation period

7 Ladas, *The International Protection*, 97.

8 For the treaty text, see "Rome Act," https://wipolex.wipo.int/en/text/278725.

of their own national printing industries—was now made legal by the simple act of allowing for simultaneous publishing in two or more locations, and moreover by legally giving precedence to the BU edition as "the" official one. Such a mode of regulation made sense only for locations that were international, industrialized publishing hubs like Paris or Leipzig, and not for small and insignificant publishing locations of limited local and/or national magnitude. In this regard, it is worth highlighting a few additional aspects. Firstly, what was legally codified here was not a neutral solution to a dilemma or a problem, which is the normative function of law. Rather, what was codified was a specific commercial practice that in a given moment fitted a particular group of international players. In a pattern already witnessed in the case of translations, a specific, customized commercial model was legitimized as a standard of international copyright and subsequently universalized. Secondly, it is worth observing the usefulness of the BU as a sanctioning mechanism for such "rites of passage," that is, for the promotion from concrete yet random commercial model to abstract, universal legal principle. Without the legal, sanctioning force of the BU, such practices could not have been vindicated or enforced internationally. Finally, it is worth observing how the principles of territoriality and nationality are applied flexibly here in order to contrive—as already observed in other places such as China—new zones of commerce and legitimacy.

As already analysed in an earlier chapter, France consciously kept its colonies outside subsequent revisions of the BC. Whereas with the union's foundation in 1886 it had initially confirmed that its own accession included its colonies and possessions, France ratified the revised Berlin Convention in 1910 without specifying whether the ratification also extended to its colonies, which, as was revealed in retrospect, it did not. She gave up this "ambiguous" regime only in 1930 when pressured by Great Britain.

Finally, an additional way of favoring certain countries was through omissions, that is, by turning a blind eye to issues and areas that would have otherwise deserved to be included within the sphere of BU supervision but which for expedient reasons were excluded.[9] Equivalently, the legal regulation of topics where no consensus could be reached because the vital interests of the respective national stakeholders and industries were too divergent, was usually left to the discretion of each nation state.

---

9 See, for example, the early exclusion of music boxes from copyright regulation. On this point, Monika Dommann, "Notieren, Aufzeichnen, Vervielfältigen: Medientechnische Umbrüche von Musik im Urheberrecht," in *Ökonomien des Medialen: Tausch, Wert und Zirkulation in den Medien- und Kulturwissenschaften*, eds. Ralf Adelmann et al. (Bielefeld: Transcript, 2006), 149–51.

Legacies of Empire in the Conception of Copyright Law

Regarding the legacy of the Habsburg and Ottoman Empires for their successor states, it can be broadly argued that the states and regions that emerged from the realm of the Habsburg Empire, such as Czechoslovakia and Croatia, were comparatively more familiar with copyright as a legal instrument than those that evolved from the Ottoman context. Apart from the generic observation that a concept of knowledge as property was novel in many parts of the world, several reasons go to explain differences between the two empires. On the formal level, copyright legislation was introduced earlier in the Habsburg (1846) than in the Ottoman Empire (1910). The Ottoman Civil Code, the *Mecelle*, created between 1869 and 1876, represented a first attempt to codify the regulation of proprietary issues pertaining to Islamic law, but did not include provisions on copyright. A series of socioeconomic and cultural factors account for additional variation between the two empires, such as the belated commercialization of knowledge and culture, different epistemologies regarding the nature and status of knowledge, deferred diffusion of print in the Ottoman Empire, and, conversely, the proximity to and dependence of the Habsburg Monarchy on the German Reich, as well as the organic inclusion of the former into the established German book trade networks. Under the monarchy, Czech authors' associations were already acquainted with the concept of copyright, and Czech publishers were integrated into the system of the Leipzig book fair, even if only as intermediaries for the Viennese publishers. Many ensuing publishers and booksellers in the Yugoslav lands had been apprenticed to German professionals. Since the second half of the nineteenth century, the doctrines and philosophy of industrial and intellectual property protection were well developed among German-speaking legal scholars and were consequently integrated into the teaching of civil/private law. It can be assumed that law graduates of German or German-speaking universities were acquainted with the legal notion of copyright. It therefore comes as no surprise that Yugoslavia's foremost copyright jurist, Janko Šuman, had studied law in Graz and Vienna and worked in the Austro-Hungarian Patent Office for 17 years before becoming head of the Bureau for the Protection of Industrial Property of the Ministry of Commerce and Industry in the Kingdom of SCS.

Bohemia's specific position at the intersection between the Holy Roman Empire and the Habsburg lands transformed it into a hub in the circulation of legal knowledge in the Central European context, creating a kind of "Habsburg" legal matrix with long-lasting legacies and lineages that went far beyond 1918.[10] Moreover, regardless of all (real or alleged) discontinuities, Czech jurists could contend a pedigree of legal studies, dating back to the fourteenth century. Prague University split in the late nineteenth century (1882) into a German and a Czech university, but the law schools of both institutions continued to share the same premises in Karolinum. Apparently, already by the beginning of the twentieth century, the university offered courses in copyright and trademark law, which were taught as part of private and commercial law respectively. Both Jan Löwenbach and Karel Hermann-Otavský, leading jurists in the institutionalization of the Czechoslovak interwar copyright regime, were graduates of that faculty. Löwenbach was also an energetic cultural mediator between the Czech- and German-speaking worlds and arts,[11] and in a certain way was almost predestined for such a role due to his own artistic inclinations (poetry, translations, cultural journalism, music).

As a matter of fact, this generation of lawyers active in the interwar period could build on the groundwork that had been laid by the previous generation of lawyers/intellectuals/statesmen. In the Czech case, it involved often graduates in law (or the broader social sciences) with a particular predisposition for the arts, often combining legal expertise in an artistic field like theatre with cultural and political activism in the revival movement: figures like Karel Kadlec (1865–1928), jurist, journalist and secretary of the National Theatre in Prague, or František Ladislav Rieger (1818–1903), economist, politician with a vivid interest in issues of intangible property. They participated at the turn of century in wider discussions about cultural rights (for example theatrical rights) that were debated within expert knowledge networks in the broader German-speaking world, and which included figures like Otto Opet (1866–1941), judge, scholar, specialist in law history, theatre and copyright law, and cofounder of the influential copyright journal *Archiv für Urheber-, Film- und Theaterrecht* (better known as *Ufita*). Finally, it should be remembered that despite fragmentation and the creation of distinct ethnic public spheres, nationalization and internationalization represented not only mutually exclusive but also entangled processes in the late Habsburg Empire with regard to both the arts and

10 See Franz L. Fillafer, "Böhmen Transimperial: Die böhmische Jurisprudenz als Drehscheibe der zentraleuropäischen Wissenszirkulation," *Beiträge zur Rechtsgeschichte Österreichs* 12, no. 2 (2022): 163–80.

11 For example, Löwenbach brought Max Brod and Leoš Janáček together and recommended the first as translator of Janáček's opera librettos into German. See Alena Wagnerová, "Max Brod als Übersetzer der Libretti der Opern Leoš Janáčeks," in *Max Brod (1884–1968): Die Erfindung des Prager Kreises*, eds. Steffen Höhne et al. (Cologne: Böhlau, 2016), 254.

sciences.[12] Without negating the role of other influences and looking at the bigger picture, it can be argued that the role of German legal science and doctrine was instrumental for the reception of copyright law in Central and Eastern Europe overall.

The Interwar Context and the Rise of New Media

East Central and Southeast Europe properly connected to the system of international copyright in the interwar period, that is, in the age of diffusion of broadcasting media and the rise of mass entertainment. This goes to explain why, in certain respects, these regions went through the heyday of print capitalism (late nineteenth and early twentieth centuries), that is, the period when written culture and the book prevailed as a major cultural commodity, almost unaffected by international copyright regulation. Additionally, the imperial frameworks functioned as hubs and networks regarding the transmission and multiplication of knowledge. This circumstance likely had a benevolent effect on the capacity of local cultures to import, absorb and amalgamate foreign knowledge. There are good reasons to assume here a correlation between the absence of a rigorous copyright regime and literacy. Along with, and in combination with, other factors, such as the educational policy of the state, the degree of diffusion of print and so on, weak copyright provisions contributed to the quickly improved literacy in certain territories, such as the Bulgarian principality. Therefore, when Bulgaria and Czechoslovakia officially connected to the system of international copyright after WWI, processes such as the nationalization of their literatures, the centralization of their publishing industry and a certain, satisfactory degree of literacy were well on their way and/or had reached a certain level of maturity. This was not the case with interwar Yugoslavia, which as well as being a young state, soon had to face the centrifugal forces of ethnic friction. Here, due to the lack of experience and weak reflexes of non-consolidated and immature national structures and institutions, copyright interventions on behalf of international actors had a distressing effect, deepened existing fissures and further disrupted countrywide professionalization processes.

12 For a comprehensive discussion on the correlation between nationalization, internationalization and science in East Central Europe, see Mitchell G. Ash and Jan Surman, eds., *The Nationalization of Scientific Knowledge in the Habsburg Empire, 1848–1918* (London: Palgrave Macmillan, 2012); also Philipp Ther, "Das Europa der Nationalkulturen: Die Nationalisierung und Europäisierung der Oper im 'langen' 19. Jahrhundert," *Journal of Modern European History* 5, no. 1 (2007) (Issue: "Demarcation and Exchange: 'National' Music in 19th Century Europe"): 39–66.

Assisted by the rise of new media, the interwar period represented a time of intense internationalization of the means and forms of cultural diffusion and expression. Interventions by international stakeholders (e.g. collecting societies) in the main targeted precisely those fields that were most internationalized, promised quick mass consumption and easy returns, that is, cinema, various forms of theatrical and musical performances, and first and foremost, various forms of performed and broadcast music. Foreign interventions targeting infringements of books and prints were comparatively limited. Overall, I have found little evidence regarding large-scale interventions in copyright issues related to publications. As observed for other world peripheries as well, copyright law emerged among the cutting-edge issues of the time, including copyright in recorded music, in talking movies and in broadcast matter, that is, it concerned "a world of sounds, where the focus was on performing music, rather than copying it."[13] The rise and expansion of new technologies of sound and image, requiring heavier investments, continuous R&D, technological equipment and know-how, recast the issue of symmetries in the content industries worldwide. The development of new technologies went along with efforts to dominate international markets with and through them. If, in the realm of print, a certain convergence was slowly taking place, the development of film, especially the advancement of talkies since the 1930s and the invention of audio appliances like the gramophone and the radio, enforced a new divergence between importers and exporters, and at the same time witnessed the rise of new players, such as the USA, in the global market of media industries.[14] In this new context, cultural commodities could be broadcast by the new media technologies, that is, they could be consumed but could not be reproduced/copied so easily. This circumstance recalibrated the focus of copyright from concerns regarding reproduction to concerns regarding distribution, diffusion and access. Along with the massification of society, this is the principal reason why issues like the private-public dichotomy, remuneration for music in films, and public performance of music (live or through mechanical instruments) dominated the copyright agenda. Peripheries had to initially content themselves with subordinate roles in the global media economy, such as organizing the distribution of foreign (American, French, German, British) cultural artefacts like films or records, before they could develop their own self-sustained industries in

13 Birnhack, *Colonial Copyright*, 164.

14 Discussing related issues from the perspective of the development of visual cultures in Southeast Europe, also emphasizing the asymmetrical relationship between importers and exporters, see Karl Kaser, *Hollywood auf dem Balkan: Die visuelle Moderne an der europäischen Peripherie (1900–1970)* (Vienna: Böhlau, 2018).

those genres. There were of course always exceptions to the rule, such as the development of cinematography in Hungary, which became herself a significant producer and regional exporter of films in the interwar period. The home production of new media advanced, on the one hand, under the auspices of programmatic state protectionism, as in the case of film, and on the other, in connection with international (multinational) companies and labels, which consequently established local, national branches of their enterprises in the relevant countries, as in the case of music.

In this early audiovisual phase, works could be consumed but not yet reproduced privately; nonetheless, grey zones still existed in the crossover between different media. Such was the case, for example, with theatrical plays, which next to performance also had a material component as written and printed texts. The resulting conundrum was resolved by keeping plays in a state of ontological legal "in-between." It was therefore possible to "release" (*herausgegeben*) a theatrical play in written form, and even have it printed, but "released" did not mean "published" (*erschienen*). Released plays could not be performed without permission and payment of fees, even if they circulated in a written version. Authors, agents and publishers simply indicated the appropriate status by placing the label "manuscript" on the book. By this token, the book was only a "release," not a "publication," and by this logic the unauthorized staging of a play (based on a written text) could be prosecuted as an infringement. Furthermore, a work could be released in one place but published in another, preferably the country whose nationality the work should officially carry. The case of theatrical plays offers an interesting example of how the tangible-intangible interface was managed practically. Moreover, it demonstrates how the law helped to invent a formula, and ultimately a legal status, which though not very intelligible or really credible (after all, an explicit criterion in order to qualify for copyright protection in the framework of the print paradigm had been to have a work appear in fixed form), provided a skilful way to control the access to and the process from written text to performance and vice versa.

Copyright in Southeast and East Central Europe

With some reservations, concerning the Czechoslovak case in particular, it could be argued that not only the introduction but also the activation of copyright law in the geographical space under examination was instigated largely by foreign players: a collecting society connected to a Viennese theatre agent looking into the repertory of the Sofia National Theater; an Italian music association demanding fees for the music performed during the screening of sound films in Bulgaria; local collecting agents in the service of international collective management organizations in the case of Yugoslavia, targeting mainly theatrical plays and performed music; the heirs of Guy de Maupassant in the case of Czechoslovakia. The players that set the law in motion, or respectively, those that realized first that the application of copyright contained a potential for profit, were initially foreign actors, acting on behalf of foreign authors. In contradistinction, local authors made much less use of copyright litigation as a primary means for settling their professional relations and disputes with publishers within the national context. Inclusion into the system of international copyright meant, in the first place, an ordering into the global division of labor in culture and the content industries; international copyright was a handy instrument that facilitated this global labor division and simultaneously obscured it under the guise of civilization. Given the fact that the countries under examination were neither pioneers of broadcasting technologies nor major exporters of the products of those industries, but rather importers and consumers, copyright regulations protecting local creators in those creative areas made little sense. The Bulgarian copyright law included articles on cinema with the indication that they would potentially be useful when the country eventually developed its own cinematographic industry, while Yugoslavia not only lacked a domestic cinematographic industry but authorities were primarily concerned with censorship and the equity of representation of languages and scripts rather than with film production as such. In such instances, the law did not reflect local needs but was more or less a takeover that ought to communicate—symbolically as well as literally—the contemporaneity of the local context with broader modernity. This was also true in the case of legal transplants, yet not with the intention of regulating actual labor conditions within the local cultural industries. In such cases, the law did not reflect or regulate reality but rather anticipated the future.

Contrary to the common belief that the introduction of copyright marked a significant turning point in the organization of culture, as well as in the professionalization and remuneration of creators in the countries and regions involved, this research on the interwar period cannot confirm such an overtly optimistic interpretation. Conversely, it appears that the introduction of copyright in fact effected very little change, if any, in the sphere of culture. Rather, it was usually a combination of several factors, ranging from the establishment and maturation of institutions of higher learning and academies to the degree of bourgeoisification and urbanization, the expansion of literacy and tastes, the availability of relevant infrastructure and the development of the press and other media in a given society that worked to strengthen cultural production. If copyright played any role, it was as one variable among many others, and often not the decisive one; nor can it be claimed that copyright was instrumental in helping to structure better, more productive or more equitable relationships between stakeholders in the field of culture.

In the case of Bulgaria, although authors were dissatisfied with their social position and modest incomes, there was no overt or vocal movement among intellectuals advocating either the introduction of copyright legislation as a means of ameliorating their professional position or the entry of the country into the BU. Copyright as a topic was thoroughly secondary among intellectuals. Quite importantly, there were no lawyers trained expressly in this field of law and aiming to make a living from litigation cases. Finally, there was a widespread conviction among political (and intellectual) elites that Bulgaria needed cheap access to knowledge, and that due to structural asymmetries this goal was impaired by the country's inclusion in the international system of IP protection. All these factors contributed to copyright remaining by and large a peripheral topic at the level of public discourse. In addition, until the sphere of culture was sufficiently commercialized, which did not happen before WWI, there was no perceptible need to employ copyright as a regulatory instrument, nor was such a claim raised by the relevant stakeholders in the field of culture. Contractual arrangements between authors and publishers had already developed a tradition by the early twentieth century, and the introduction of copyright legislation in the 1920s did not impact the balance of power between these two groups of actors.[15] In fact, the language of copyright never became the language of authors in Bulgaria. On the contrary, the actors who accommodated themselves more quickly with, and made sure to use the options offered by the legal framework, were the publishers and authors' heirs. By the 1930s, copyright terminology had become a habitual feature in contracts between authors and publishers but changed little in publishing practice. There was highly differential treatment of authors according to the publishers' expectations: generous contracts were offered to a tiny group of select, established writers, who on top of a one-time fee were usually offered remuneration at regular intervals on the basis of sales and/or the appearance of new volumes or editions, and a great majority of authors received a modest one-time remuneration (often in rates) with a couple of free exemplars. The content of contracts could vary substantially from case to case. The trend was for

[15] The insignificant impact of copyright legislation on the economy of Bulgarian publishing and the development of literary life in the interwar period has already been highlighted by Ani Gergova, "Sădbata na bălgarskija avtor," *Izdatel* 1 (1995): 14.

publishers to try to gain rights in perpetuity over works, to buy rights with no temporal limit, and thereby legally bind commercially promising authors and/or works to their publishing houses. Copyright changed nothing in this practice, which rather strengthened the position of the publishers. Recognizing these concrete problems in practice, the legislator intervened in the late 1930s forbidding the contractual acquisition of rights in perpetuity for both existing and future works, and cancelling contracts that stipulated perpetual rights. Last but not least, the legislator intervened correctively by amending regulations concerning the free use of works by Bulgarian authors in textbooks and supplementary educational materials destined for school education. The amendment prescribed the mandatory remuneration of Bulgarian authors (works by foreign authors could still be used for free) on the basis of fixed tariffs. Crafted in the corporatist spirit of the authoritarian regime of the interwar period, the legislator literally blackmailed Bulgarian publishers, whose textbooks the state refused to subsidize and publish if they had not provenly remunerated Bulgarian authors first. This last measure was a proper departure from a libertarian notion of copyright and literally anticipated the communist practice of fixed tariff remuneration. Paradoxical as it may seem, this prescribed (mandatory, if you like) copyright, which abrogated free contractual arrangements and imposed a practice of fixed, standardized remuneration, was actually beneficial to authors.

The payment of honoraria and fees was already an established practice before copyright legislation was introduced in Bulgaria in the mid-1920s, and there are no indications that copyright law and its application effected any significant change in that respect. The Bulgarian market for books was limited, as were its possibilities for expansion. Honoraria for both original texts and translations were particularly low.[16] Only a handful of authors (if any) could earn a living exclusively from writing; the majority practiced—as was common in many places—another intellectual profession, for example journalism, editorial work or teaching, while the most common employment option was that of civil servant. Intelligentsia networks connected to the state (e.g. the Ministry of Education) helped to position authors in civil servant posts; one popular and favored location for such placements was the National Library, but diverse ministries and public institutions (banks, theatres, museums etc.) were also chosen. Authors' syndicalist organizations came into being around the time of the Balkan Wars, and though respected, they had little leverage and were not particularly successful in promoting real solutions to important practical issues.

16 See here Todor Borov, *Bălgarskata kniga* (Sofia: Pridvorna pečatnica, 1935), 21–23.

Bulgarian publishing reached maturity and started centralizing seriously in the second decade of the twentieth century with the consolidation of a handful of well-developed and more stable publishing enterprises. Historiographically constructed as the pinnacle in the history of Bulgarian publishing—which, from a literary, intellectual, artistic and entrepreneurial viewpoint, interwar publishing undeniably was—it is often overlooked that publishers were able to develop and consolidate their businesses not only due to their entrepreneurial skills but also because the protective hand of the state (as in most other branches of Bulgarian industry) ensured the demand and circulation of printed matter in manifold ways. When the reels of the "real" market got stuck, the state kept "oiling" them at both ends of the line (i.e. production and circulation) and thereby helped to avoid impasses. Due to the narrowness of the market, competition among Bulgarian publishers was intense, and despite several efforts to promote binding rules of conduct and regulation, Bulgarian publishers did not really manage to form a consolidated and disciplined body of professional interests. There was a significant number of ephemeral, and only few solid, prosperous and lasting publishing enterprises. Individualism in business prevailed, often expressed in disloyal competition between them, vying for preferential treatment by the state and faced with an underdeveloped communications network, which hindered efficient and rational distribution, as well as a rationalized division of labor between publishers and retailers, particularly in the provinces. Professionalization processes in the publishing professions remained precarious and fluid.

With respect to international copyright, interwar Bulgaria is an interesting case study, as it represented a showpiece of a "pirate state" in the relevant period. It can serve therefore as a testing ground for several, overt or covert, assumptions regarding the benevolent or harmful effects of copyright and/or the lack thereof. After its compulsory accession to the BU, and fearful of repercussions, the Bulgarian state quickly complied with the obligation to release its own national copyright law soon after. In practice, however, Bulgarian publishers did not bother much about the rights of foreign authors. They rather ignored international obligations and continued to translate and publish foreign authors and their works at will. As a rule, they took things as they came, reacting only when foreign authors and/or agencies pressed charges against them, and obviously counted on the fact that such interventions would not happen on a regular basis. During my archival research, I found no indications that procuring the rights of foreign authors was a regular and/or normal practice; rather the contrary: free translation was the rule and the payment of royalties to foreign authors the exception.[17] A seemingly more widespread practice was to occasionally ask for permission

[17] Vasil Zagorov, who has also looked into archival evidence, has reached similar conclusions regarding the publishing of foreign works in translation. Even a respectable publishing house like Hemus,

to translate a work, which corresponded to the pre-copyright-age mode of conduct regarding translations. In the main, Bulgarian publishers resorted to such strategies only in order to restrict home competition by fellow publishers, and rarely out of a sense of obligation towards foreign authors; acquiring official permission legally fortified a local monopoly claim to a certain work. They also disposed of other means, however, such as "courtesy of the trade," in order to regulate the translation market. Moreover, the Bulgarian law, following as its blueprint the Russian copyright law of 1911, allowed for the free use of works by countries that were non-members of the BU. This window of opportunity was amply used, and many works by West European authors were translated into Bulgarian via the initial Russian translations of the same works. Finally, constituting a European periphery, speaking a fairly exotic Slavic idiom, not mastered by many, and in the absence of willing intermediaries, such as we witnessed in the Yugoslav case, eager to represent foreign collective management organizations, Bulgaria somehow remained on the periphery of the attention of copyright protagonists, except for issues such as film screenings or theatrical performances.

One common economic assumption regarding cultural industries is that cheap (i.e. free) translations impair the development of local literature. According to this school, publishers show a preference for established foreign authors and works that have already scored success in the market and are guaranteed commercial front-runners. As a result, local authors are put on the back burner and get the short end of the stick. Without wanting to formulate any kind of axiom, this assumption can apparently not be confirmed by the Bulgarian experience (which does not mean that it might not be valid for other contexts). Rather, publishing successful foreign authors usually brought Bulgarian publishing houses the necessary surplus for them to invest in the publication of local literature, which was somewhat riskier. The production of high-quality national literature depended on other factors, and there was apparently no conflict of interest between local and translated literature. Bulgarian literature in the interwar period (1920s and 1930s) reached a high level of maturity and expression, at the same time as the local market was inundated with translations of the sensationalist works of Eugène Sue and Ponson du Terrail. Instead of representing rival products, the latter category of works rather facilitated access to reading

which represented the most efficient and successful publishing house of duration in interwar Bulgaria, avoided paying fees to foreign authors for their translated works in Bulgarian. Zagorov, however, reaches exactly the contrary conclusion to mine. He interprets this practice as a calamity, a serious violation of IP law and the international copyright regime, which was perpetuated due to the inability or unwillingness to legally prosecute this kind of infringement. In other words, the problem consisted in the lack of appropriate penalization of such practices and the fact that legal enforcement was simply too lax. See here Vasil Zagorov, "'Prestăplenie i nakazanie': Reglementirane na otnošenijata avtor – prevodač – izdatel v Bălgarija za perioda 1921–1944 g.," *Izdatel* 12, no. 1–2–3 (2010): 87–89.

and contributed to the massification of reading practices. The low price of books perhaps also played its part in this respect. Translations were an important source of income for home intellectuals. As in other countries, translation in Bulgaria reached a saturation point around the mid-1930s, when for different reasons there was a reorientation towards native literature.[18] Though officially incorporated into the nexus of the BU and the BC, Bulgaria traversed the interwar period entertaining few points of contact with the international copyright regime, a circumstance that on the whole had a neutral to benevolent effect on the Bulgarian cultural economy, at least in the sphere of print.

Though the passing of the 1929 copyright law helped the newly created Kingdom of Serbs, Croats and Slovenes to overcome the legal pluralism of the former imperial era (i.e. different laws being valid for different regions), it did not manage to surmount a whole array of other significant social, economic, cultural and political discrepancies that ultimately destabilized the country in the course of the interwar period. Contrary to Bulgaria, copyright featured on the lists of demands of authors' organizations in the Kingdom of SCS, and informed the vocabulary of cultural elites in their efforts towards assertion, autonomization and professionalization. This was apparently for good reason, as publishers, for example in Serbia, were ostensibly more exploitative and unscrupulous[19] than their Bulgarian colleagues. However, similar to the Bulgarian case, the introduction of copyright hardly played a role in ameliorating the bargaining position and remuneration of local authors and creators. Apart from a few renowned authors such as Branislav Nušić and Miroslav Krleža, who were able to make a living from writing (literature and theatre), and a handful of local composers who could boast decent earnings from performed music, copyright did not affect the livelihood of the majority of Yugoslav creators in the interwar period. Other factors, such as the creation and expansion of educational institutions related to the arts (academies, musical and drawing secondary schools etc.), the development of infrastructure, the institutionalization of new professional bodies and ensembles (such as radio orchestras, choirs), the expansion of leisure opportunities, the development of amateur cultural organizations and societies (like Sokol), the evolution of cultural journalism and criticism, played a far greater role in expanding the options for professional integration and securing an income for

18 On foreign translations in Bulgaria in the interwar period, see Žak Eskenazi, "Prevodna hudožestvena literatura v Bălgarija (1878–1944): Izdateli, izdanija, klasifikacija," *Izvestija na narodnata biblioteka "Sv. Sv. Kiril i Metodii"* 21, no. XXVII (1993): 327–53.

19 According to M. J. Bogavac, disrespect for authors' rights was common, as their works were often reprinted without their knowledge and permission and, most significantly, without remuneration. See Milovan J. Bogavac, *Udruženje srpskih književnika*, 17.

educated cadres in culture and the arts. As in the case of Bulgaria, authors and creators were employed, in the great majority, in various civil service branches, as well as educational and cultural state institutions. Major art figures, like the sculptor Ivan Meštrović, earned a living by combining academic teaching with carrying out big, representative works commissioned by the state. With the expansion of entertainment options, musicians and other artists could also rely more on the private sector for remuneration, though even in that area processes remained fluid: the advance of talkies seriously threatened the existence of a significant number of musicians who up to that point had provided live accompaniment to the screening of silent films, and in Czechoslovakia the official disbanding of military orchestras created intense competition among other categories of professional musicians in the market of performed music.

Even though professionalization processes in the cultural professions advanced in interwar Yugoslavia, they remained in many ways labile and undecided. Judging by the publishing sector[20] (although similar observations could be applied to other professions as well), boundaries between the various specializations and tasks in the book trade remained persistently fluid[21] during the whole interwar period, a tendency that naturally intensified with the economic crisis of the late 1920s and early 1930s. No clear demarcation lines divided printers, binders, publishers, booksellers, retailers and antiquarian booksellers; in fact, they often tended to swap jobs and glide from one sphere of activity into another. A combination of factors affected the book trade and perpetuated a cycle of crisis. Access to books hinged on social parameters of education. Illiteracy rates (not including the semi-literate) averaged approximately 51.5% in the late 1920s, and significant discrepancies characterized the distribution of illiteracy between regions and genders.[22] The absence of an elaborate social

20 See here Augusta Dimou, "Blurred Boundaries Resulting from a Weak Market: The Professionalization of Publishing in Interwar Yugoslavia in a Comparative European Perspective," in *Professionen, Eigentum und Staat: Europäische Entwicklungen im Vergleich, 19. und 20. Jahrhundert*, eds. Dietmar Müller and Hannes Siegrist (Moderne Europäische Geschichte, vol. 8) (Göttingen: Wallstein, 2014), 272–97.

21 For a good general discussion of the development of professions in Southeast Europe, see Wolfgang Höpken, "Professionalisierung an der Peripherie: Juristen und Beamte in Bulgarien, 1878–1930," in *Professionen im modernen Osteuropa: Professions in Modern Eastern Europe*, eds. Charles McClelland, Stephan Merl and Hannes Siegrist (Berlin: Duncker & Humblot, 1995), 98–100.

22 City inhabitants made up approximately 15.8% of the population. In the 1930s, Yugoslavia's analphabetism rate amounted to 45%, and concerned 42% of the male and 60% of the female population. There were grave regional discrepancies in the illiteracy rates across the country, with the lowest registered in Slovenia at less than 9%, followed by Vojvodina (23%), Croatia, Slavonia and Istria (32%), Dalmatia (50%), North Serbia (65%), Montenegro (67%), Bosnia and Herzegovina (80%) and finally Kosovo (84%). See here Augusta Dimou, "'Wir verwandeln uns in eine Kolonie fremdsprachiger Bücher': Das Buch als Kulturproblem in Jugoslawien der Zwischenkriegszeit," in *Kultur und Beruf in Europa*, eds. Isabella Löhr, Matthias Middell and Hannes Siegrist (Europäische Geschichte in Quellen und Essays, vol. 2) (Stuttgart: Franz Steiner, 2012), 266.

structure was mirrored in an elementary client differentiation, which in turn impeded greater intra-professional differentiation and a proper division of labor among booksellers. The book market was underdeveloped, and the sale of books—except textbooks, which were the chief source of income for both publishers and booksellers—rather difficult. Book prices reflected the tight market conditions: compared to the pre-war period, the interwar costs of book production had increased by a factor of 10 to 20, whereas the prices of printed books rose only five- to sevenfold. Communication and postal networks were poorly developed; daily postal exchange with smaller and remote cities was deficient and postal tariffs disproportionately high. In addition, the interwar period witnessed the rise of new forms of mass entertainment and mass communication media like radio, film and sports, whose social character had a strong appeal to the youth and generated intense competition for the book.

Besides the abovementioned predominantly structural problems, the dearth of regulation in the commercial realm also caused exigencies. As in the case of Bulgaria, unfair competition, in its various and mutable forms, remained the bookseller's gravest predicament throughout the interwar period. The most common and recurrent form of unfair competition was the granting of arbitrary book discounts, which was practiced by all groups along the circulation chain.[23] It was, however, the lack of a dynamic market that is primarily to blame for the deficits in the division of labor, the muddied contours of the different occupations and the permeable professional borders between them. Fluidity also characterized the status and degree of professionalization, exemplified by the parallel existence of novices, latent and undecided entrants, and newcomers arriving in the book trade due to a change of employment.

Like most Balkan countries, interwar Yugoslavia had only a meagre reading public, a predicament resulting directly from the country's social composition, which put the book trade at a disadvantage from the start: approximately two-thirds of the population were automatically excluded from the categories of customer and author, and the absence of a broad middle class that valued reading and took time for it was painfully felt. The reading public was random and temporary, consisting mainly of civil servants and a small section of the free professions. The intelligentsia, civil servants and state employees were poorly paid, and their purchasing power was further reduced in conjunction with the economic crisis.[24]

As a rule, professions subdivide under certain kinds of pressure brought to bear by market demands, needs and changes in specialization, or interprofessional competition, but these conditions were largely absent in the Yugoslav interwar

23 Dimou, "Blurred Boundaries," 277–81.

24 Dimou, "Blurred Boundaries," 286.

book trade. Here, modest demand triggered interprofessional competition, which fostered instead all-round, conventional trade rather than extensive and exclusive specialization, and which furthermore supported tradesmen's constant encroachment on neighboring specializations. As was the experience with other professional unions as well, a countrywide association of publishers and booksellers was formed in 1921, disintegrated by the end of the 1920s, and was reconstituted with mandatory membership in 1933 but altogether fell short of becoming an operative national organization.[25] The book trade never really centralized, nor did it manage to coordinate its distinct parts into a joint and coherent system encompassing the whole state, but rather remained more or less entrenched in the production and distribution networks of the pre-WWI period. In addition, trade in foreign books continued unconstrained, either through official channels, as in the case of French books, or through unofficial conduits including unlicensed commercial firms and contraband activities by itinerant merchants, as was often the case with German books, which were distributed through both formal and informal circulation.[26] Yugoslavia remained in the orbit of the German book trade even after WWI. The publishers' and booksellers' association became a member of the "Börsenverein des deutschen Buchhandels" in 1933. German publishers joined in the game of disloyal competition. In order to promote their books, they offered super reductions, which they recanted in 1937, only to reintroduce them in 1938, by granting a full discount to all Yugoslav booksellers that were members of their association, and 5% less to non-members.[27]

Interestingly, publishers channeled enormous energies into finding legal, practical and commercial solutions to the above issues but made hardly any effort to regulate their legal relationship to authors. This circumstance probably indicates how little they felt threatened from that side and testifies to the ease with which they were able to dominate this relationship. It is also symptomatic of authors' negligible negotiating power, since a limited book market translated into limited bargaining power for writers. A bitter war of reciprocal recriminations broke out between authors and publishers, first in the 1920s and later in the early 1930s, with each side accusing the other of failing to live up to their vocation; authors accused publishers of professional ineptitude in the proper promotion of books, while publishers blamed authors for producing irrelevant and unmarketable works.[28] The polemic was fought

25 Dimou, "Blurred Boundaries," 273–74.

26 Dimou, "Blurred Boundaries," 181. See also Dimou, "Wir verwandeln uns in eine Kolonie fremdsprachiger Bücher."

27 Ljubomir Durković-Jakšić, *Jugoslovensko Knjižarstvo 1918–1941* (Belgrade: Narodna Knjiga, 1979), 131.

28 Durković-Jakšić, *Jugoslovensko Knjižarstvo*, 145–148.

as a public feud, and though it touched on practical issues, it was argued on purely intellectual grounds and induced no legal action or litigation, that is, it did not activate the machine of copyright as a means of claiming rights or justice. The disequilibrium climaxed in 1930 with the Zagreb booksellers demonstrating a negative balance sheet in the sale of Yugoslav authors, and publishers declining to publish Yugoslav authors due to their inability to recoup their investments. Publishers concentrated on the sale of textbooks and foreign, predominantly German literature. Authors' fee rates in the interwar period were five times lower than before the war, and translations were likewise badly remunerated, paid mostly in instalments over an indeterminate period of time.[29]

These practical problems were in part perpetuated, enforced by and refracted through the unresolved national question, and the presence of rivalrous identity concepts regarding the ideological foundations, the character and orientation, as well as the administrative organization of the state. Yugoslavia was far too young a state to have achieved a meaningful degree of cultural, economic, administrative or geographic consolidation. Its administrative set-up was reconfigured at least three times in its short lifespan from 1918 to 1943,[30] a period insufficient to allow the different territories and regions to organically grow together into a single entity. Moreover, despite the efforts of the nationalizing state and the promulgated ideology of integral Yugoslavism, the presence of multifarious ethnic and religious groups, with their different historical legacies and expectations, slowed the process of cultural homogenization. The political polarization that ensued by the end of the 1920s further decelerated and eventually stopped this process. These circumstances left national consolidation administratively, culturally and geographically incomplete, so it can be understood rather as a "contested and imperfect nationalization." The nationalizing state failed to assemble various ontologies and interests within a shared model of intertwined identities and nationalities. Upon the rejection of Yugoslavism, identity groups reverted to their particularisms and turned against the nationalizing state.[31]

29 Durković-Jakšić, *Jugoslovensko Knjižarstvo*, 151.

30 From its creation in 1918 up to 1922, the Kingdom of Serbs, Croats and Slovenes (Kingdom of SCS) was more or less subdivided into its pre-WWI divisions, which amounted roughly to the lands that had previously belonged to Austria-Hungary, plus the Kingdom of Serbia and Montenegro. The Vidovdan Constitution of 1921 established the Kingdom of SCS as a unitary state, and in 1922, 33 new centrally ruled administrative counties (*oblasti*) were institutionalized. Under the authoritarian rule of King Alexander in the period 1929–1941, the Kingdom of SCS was subdivided into nine wholly new administrative provinces called *banovinas*. In 1939, the Banovina of Croatia was declared autonomous and granted its own parliament.

31 Pieter Troch advances this argument in his article on the relationship between religion and statehood in the Kingdom of SCS. See Pieter Troch, "The Intertwining of Religion and Nationhood in

Timing was a crucial component in the Yugoslav case. It proved to be significant that Yugoslavia connected to the international copyright regime before it had had an opportunity to assemble and test its own, home-relevant copyright organization. Although claims supporting the introduction of copyright law had been periodically raised by Yugoslav creators, the law was ultimately a top-down rather than a bottom-up creation. The country connected to international copyright before it had managed to solidify and centralize its own syndicalist organizations in the realm of culture and the arts, and moreover in conditions of a very unstable and fragile national ideology and identity. Finally, it was inconvenient that the Yugoslav state was trying to consolidate all of these different levels at once in a period of intense transnationalization of cultural genres and commodities. Several factors are to be credited for the fact that the internationalization and juridification of authors' rights contributed nothing, or little, to the improvement of local conditions. Rather, the installation of the copyright regime turned to the advantage of foreign creators represented by local agents, commissioned by international collecting societies, which received their legitimacy via the BU's international copyright regime.

The specific application of the copyright regime was not a random calamity. Instead of creating a system that sensibly persuaded society to remunerate its creators for their services, achievements and the use of their works, it simply put into place an extracting machine, operated with the sole concern of extorting maximum profit, simply because it was possible to do so. This again was not some sort of "Balkanic" vice. Rather, it is the logical culmination of any copyright regime that regards copyright as an end in itself, and thereby fails to ask the central question: What is the purpose and scope of copyright? Furthermore, it is the consistent outcome of any copyright regime that is justified mainly through the prerogatives of a crude property ideology. Finally, the law was operationalized by the local collecting societies/agents in a purely instrumental manner, that is, it was applied principally as a legitimating façade in order to conduct business; its main purpose was to discipline local business owners and end users into compliance.

A series of factors contributed to the fact that the institutionalization of a copyright regime in the new-born state of Czechoslovakia took a different path. Both intellectual and legal elites had already had some experience and attained a certain degree of maturity in operating with the instrument of copyright during the

Interwar Yugoslavia: The School Celebrations of St. Sava's Day," *Slavonic and East European Review* 91, no. 2 (2013): 261; also Marie-Janine Calic, *Geschichte Jugoslawiens im 20. Jahrhundert* (Bonn: BpB, 2010), 113–17. On the concept and practice of Yugoslavism, see Dejan Djokić, ed., *Yugoslavism: Histories of a Failed Idea 1918–1922* (London: Hurst, 2003).

Habsburg era. The beginnings of professionalization and syndicalization of relevant professions (publishers, authors, musicians, lawyers etc.) had their roots in that period and advanced through inspiration and/or contradistinction with equivalent Austro-Hungarian and German examples. Bohemia was industrially the most significant and versatile region in the monarchy, and by the time of the creation of the First Czechoslovak Republic, processes of urbanization and the formation of urban middle classes were well advanced. The institutionalization of the copyright regime, at least at the level of legislation, was a joint Czech-German venture and both the Austro-Hungarian and German traditions and knowhow played into the Czechoslovak copyright design.

In contrast to Bulgaria and Yugoslavia, the introduction of copyright was not advanced as a purely legal-technical issue but received an important political streak from the start. It concerned, on the one hand, the intellectual (and legal) elite's consciousness of the geopolitics at stake in the newly created Czechoslovak state. The installation of a copyright regime was properly understood as a signal of the desire to affiliate with the "progressive" world, a view shared vertically from the chief copyright lawyer, Jan Löwenbach, to the foreign minister, Eduard Beneš. Indeed, the Czechoslovak state had come into being as a result of the interplay between national and international policy-making. Maintaining and perpetuating the balance of this correlation was of vital importance for the state. On the other hand, there were different political views on issues such as the scope, reach, form and purpose of copyright, which included at times properly radical designs; a pro-author attitude was shared horizontally, however, across the whole political spectrum. "Petka" politics ensured that although different opinions were aired, issues did not derail excessively. There was therefore a consciousness of the necessity to coordinate the internal and external orientation of the state, which in practice showed that Czechoslovakia connected consciously to the international copyright regime but with a clear perception of the priorities of the national context. This attitude translated concretely, internally, into an emphasis on the legal regulation of the labor relationships of cultural professions; and externally into a visible protectionist approach that structured relationships with foreign creators predominantly, if not exclusively, through the relevant state-supervised institutions (for example, OSA) and the creators' unions. The copyright system was therefore quickly centralized in regard to both its internal and external structure and orientation.

Although literary authors organized early on (Máj was founded in the mid-nineteenth century and the association was in favor of Austria-Hungary's accession to the BU), it could be argued that the catalyst for copyright development was rather music, a field far more advanced in the Czechoslovak case than in the other two cases under comparison. A significant number of creative associations (literary and music authors) closed ranks, forming one weighty union, the Syndicate of Czechoslovak Writers and Composers, a circumstance that helped them to emerge as a powerful and influential interest group with a coherent agenda. Instead of acting as singular associations, they opted for a corporate structure, that is, they formed an umbrella organization consisting of different specialized units and sections (on theatre, legal issues, social issues, relations to foreign societies etc.), which allowed them to keep an eye on the bigger picture in the management of the field of culture. The Czech model was organized on the basis of the autonomy and self-management of creators/artists through a state-sanctioned, -bestowed and -protected monopoly. It consisted of an intertwined system of close cooperation between creators' associations, legal expertise and the state, who collaborated together on a series of crucial issues such as the annual setting up of remuneration tariffs by the Ministry of Education. It was always the same circle of people, in fact a network, that moved between these levels and moreover connected them to different corners of society, including the educational sector, civil organizations, political parties and also the (expert) media. It was also the same network that represented Czechoslovakia in copyright-relevant international organizations (BU, ALAI etc.) and, inversely, processed instructions on international copyright locally by adapting them to home circumstances. Though such networking is not unusual in the sphere of action of interest groups, it is the degree of density and consolidation of such structures that stands out in the case of Czechoslovakia (certainly in comparison with the other two cases under analysis). As a last point, the observation that publishers were—to my knowledge—barely included in this network deserves some attention.

The copyright regime in interwar Czechoslovakia can be characterized as pro-author, an attitude shared across the whole political spectrum. Though creators had to stand their ground and fight their battles with publishers, in broad terms they enjoyed substantial support from the political and legal elites. The maturity of the relevant actors was demonstrated by the agenda followed in the setting up of institutions. Though drafting the copyright law was a protracted process that was finalized only in 1927, several important practical measures were given priority and swiftly legislated in advance, among them the institutionalization of OSA in 1919, and in 1923 the passing of the law on the publishing contract, both actions that demonstrate that the actors understood well what was at stake and how to go about it. The centrality of OSA's formal role in rights management was consolidated in the 1926 copyright law, and its monopoly right properly legislated in the 1936 amendment to the copyright law. The truly important law on the publishing contract included a whole series of author-friendly measures concerning the conclusion of contracts, and although it did not completely debilitate old contracts, it imposed the new framework of regulation on all new editions, regulated the size of an edition and intervened regarding price adjustments, and it also contained provisions that were governed by mandatory law and could not be circumvented by the contracting parties.

Most importantly, the regulation of the author–publisher relationship was not abandoned to copyright law but was largely tackled through instruments of labor regulation. The already mentioned law on the publishing contract was one dimension of this policy; the second and even weightier one was the direct negotiation of collective agreements between interest groups. This resulted in an agreement regarding minimum remuneration for authors, while fee rates, tariff categories and collective agreements were also negotiated between OSA, the Ministry of Education and interest groups. Altogether, the system of regulation relied heavily on institutionalized cooperation between the social partners involved. It could thus be argued that the interwar copyright regime circumscribed the propertization tendencies of the publishers/intermediate agents in favor of the authors/creators, perhaps also at the expense of the end users, though it would be necessary to include other parameters in this analysis, for example the institutionalization of an elaborate system of public libraries from 1919 onwards. As was demonstrated in the analysis of the law's drafting, authors were more or less able to frustrate a series of measures which they deemed unfavorable to their interests. The marked pro-author approach was revised to some extent in the second half of the 1930s, when state competences were altogether enhanced, particularly regarding the use of radio and the operationalization of compulsory licenses. The protectionist attitude was also manifested in the attuning of external and internal objectives, so that while Czechoslovakia in broad lines followed the main tenets of the BU and remained receptive and extroverted regarding international trends, at the same time, locally, it devised a legal-practical framework that channeled copyright relations with foreign creators almost exclusively through the formal institutions of the Czechoslovak state. Indirectly, it also put a ceiling on the profit margins of foreign creators, ensuring that their remuneration could not exceed fee rates for locals.

It can be argued therefore that the Czechoslovak copyright regime, though not indifferent to the market, in many ways departed from a traditional liberal conception of copyright. While, on the one hand, copyright was partially applied in its traditional function as an instrument for regulating competition, on the other, it was enforced in such a regulated and protectionist manner that it became more of a centralizing, state-building instrument. Though copyrights were presented as strong subjective rights, the individualistic tendencies of copyright were both theoretically and practically watered down; at the end of the day, it was always possible to discern the silhouette of the collectivity on the horizon. The fate of nationally significant works was put under the supervision of the national community, with the option of disregarding, and even circumventing entitled trustees (like heirs), if they failed to live up to the assignment of protecting the creator's and the work's reputation and integrity. The requirement that vital components such as remuneration rates had to be negotiated between copyright institutions, professional organizations, the state and creators, and moreover prescribed that creators' organizations could negotiate with OSA only in their capacity as branches (not individual associations) of specific cultural industries, essentially enforced the syndicalization of creators, encouraging them to act as a collectivity. Before 1936, it was theoretically possible to circumvent OSA, but it was not advisable. Although the copyright regime allowed for differentiated incomes according to marketability criteria, minimum remuneration arrangements ensured that nobody was left behind.

Actors

On the whole, it can be argued that in East and Southeast Europe, similar to the early West European experience, authors were not the grand protagonists, but rather the supporting actors in the introduction of copyright in their societies. In Western Europe (in the eighteenth and nineteenth centuries), publishers had been the most energetic promoters of copyright. Authors, and increasingly specialized lawyers, eventually jumped on the bandwagon of copyright as allies of the publishers, not the other way around.

As a result of the specific timing and the way in which the concept of copyright was introduced in East and Southeast Europe, there was a shift in the configuration and distribution of roles in the copyright game. Lawyers shifted from the status of supporting actors to the role of principal mouthpieces and advocates of copyright law. This change came about both as a result of the energetically promoted internationalization and globalization of copyright through transnational networks and organizations, and due to the increasing commercialization of culture through transnational trends and new transmission media that augmented the demand for specialized knowledge, intervention and/or international regulation. Through the codification of international copyright, the function of lawyers and legal expertise was significantly upgraded, and this new division of labor was also reflected in the peripheries. Due to both international and local circumstances, and often as a combination of the two, lawyers' local professionalization processes coalesced in East and Southeast Europe with a state commitment—for whatever reasons—to international copyright. Excellent preconditions corroborated to this end. Law was among the—if not the most—popular academic degree(s) in Southeast and East Central Europe in the nineteenth and twentieth centuries due mainly to its proximity to state affairs and public administration, and lawyers assumed a prominent role in both public and private life. Summing up, it could be argued that in the case of East and Southeast Europe, all actors (lawyers, authors and publishers) entered the stage almost simultaneously, with lawyers playing an enhanced and prominent role in this constellation. Publishers, in comparison to their leading role in Western Europe, played a somewhat different role, for several reasons. (1) In conditions of a limited market for books, they were conscious that they could dominate the relationship with authors without the help of copyright. However, they also used copyright in order to strengthen their position by buying up rights in perpetuity or by binding authors for longer periods, or even a lifetime. As long as the market was weak and authors failed to unite into strong pressure groups, publishers could retain the upper hand in the relationship. (2) In addition, due to the controllable and manageable size of the cultural sphere in the case of small nations, the publisher–author relationship in these milieus remained personalized for longer, and did not acquire the impersonal character typical of big enterprises. (3) Due to their preference for the freedom of translation, publishers in the peripheries were not eager to connect to the international copyright regime. (4) An additional reason could be, as witnessed in the case of Czechoslovakia, that the author–publisher relationship was subjected relatively early to some kind of regulation, which in one way or another restricted publishers' arbitrariness.

Similar to the West European experience (see la Société des Auteurs et Compositeurs Dramatiques, SACD, founded in 1829), the category of author most actively engaged in promoting the copyright cause in the regions under discussion was that of the theatrical author/composer, that is, authors whose works were staged/performed and thereby more quickly commercialized, and/or whose remuneration was directly linked to consumption of public performances. By contrast, there is little correspondence in East and Southeast Europe to the group of prominent prose authors of the nineteenth century (Hugo, Dickens, Zola, Balzac etc.), who were vocal advocates of international copyright protection, and who toured the world making flamboyant media campaigns in defense of the copyright cause.[32] There is no equivalent group of East European authors (to my knowledge, at least) that made the defence of either domestic or international copyright its prime issue of engagement in the public sphere.

Copyright protection claims were therefore taken up energetically in practice by unions like UJDA (Union of Jugoslav Dramatic Authors) in Yugoslavia, or ΕΕΘΣ (Greek Company of Theatrical Authors) in Greece, but not necessarily by authors engaged generically in the field of literature (prose, poetry etc.). This observation is confirmed by the experience of other East European countries. Playwrights were the first vocal advocates of copyright protection in pre-revolutionary Russia. Founded in 1874 by Aleksander Ostrovsky, the Society of Russian Dramatic Writers was broadened in 1885 to include composers, thus forming the Society of Russian Dramatic Writers and Opera Composers.[33] In Poland, it was the generation of authors active around the time of WWI and engaged predominantly in cabaret and similar theatrical performances that promoted the idea of copyright and pioneered the organization of ZAIKS, the Polish collecting society, in 1918.[34] Theatrical authors usually embraced copyright with a twofold perspective, firstly as a positive instrument, in order to assert, determine and secure their own remuneration conditions locally, and secondly as a defensive instrument, that is, they sought alignment with international copyright in order to limit and control the staging of foreign authors, expecting that the payment of expensive fees would have a deterrent effect upon the choices of theatre entrepreneurs. In other words, and as experienced in other world regions like the US, international copyright protection was eventually embraced by local actors in order to promote the nationalization of genres (the local novel, operetta in the local mother tongue etc.) and the preponderance of home production in the cultural sphere and economy. Contrary to the intentions of its initiators, international copyright was supported by actors in the peripheries not in order to guarantee stability and predictability in conditions of free exchange but rather the contrary, in order to directly or indirectly promote protectionism.

---

32 See here Albrecht Götz von Olenhusen, "Lobbyisten für ein internationales Copyright im 19/20 Jahrhundert: Charles Dickens und Mark Twain im Vergleich," *UFITA* 80, no. 2 (2010): 401–415; also Catherine Seville, "Authors as Copyright Campaigners: Mark Twain's Legacy," *Journal of the Copyright Society of the USA* 55 (2008): 283–359.

33 On their history, see the webpage of the Russian Authors' Society, "Rossijskoe avtorskoe obshhtestvo: Istorija," https://rao.ru/about-rao/history/.

34 Initially named "Union of Cabaret Authors," it was later renamed "ZAIKS," that is, Union of Stage Authors and Composers (Związek Autorów i Kompozytorów Scenicznych). On the history of ZAIKS, see its webpage "100 lat ZAIKS-u," https://zaiks.org.pl/100-lat-zaiks-u; also Walery Rudnicki, "La société polonaise des auteurs Zaiks," *Inter-Auteurs*, no. 126 (1957): 120–125.

Broader Social Trends of the Interwar Period

Naturally, the conceptualization of the author as a social and toiling subject, the preoccupation with authors' socioeconomic welfare and endeavours promoting the syndicalist organization of intellectuals were general tendencies in the interwar period.[35] They formed part of the considerations of international organizations associated with the League of Nations, such as the International Labor Organization (ILO), of which Czechoslovakia had been a founding member,[36] but also the International Committee on Intellectual Cooperation (ICIC) and the International Institute of Intellectual Cooperation (IIIC), as well as the International Confederation of Professional Intellectual Workers (Confédération internationale des travailleurs intellectuels). Whereas, broadly speaking, the discovery and conceptualization of the "social subject" was a major concern and developed into the mainstream "language" of the interwar period, there were also underlying concerns regarding the prospect of pauperized intellectuals succumbing massively to the radical left. The emphasis therefore on the social rights of authors and creators kept pace with general European and international trends in the interwar period. An extension of social rights, particularly health and pension benefits, to authors and creators was a general trend in the interwar period, but of all three cases, authors' social claims were conceived, organized and implemented earlier and more elaborately in the case of Czechoslovakia. Relevant legislation in Austria and Germany (the Austrian law of December 11, 1906 on pension insurance for private employees and the German law of December 1911) obviously served as a vanguard and model in large parts of East Central and Southeast Europe. They were followed by the Czechoslovak law of December 20, 1918 on social security, which was revised twice in the interwar period (February 21, 1929 and July 1, 1934), the 1937 Yugoslav social security law against work incapacity, age and death of workers and employees, and finally the Bulgarian law on the security of intellectual workers (*umstvenite rabotnici*), whose planification started in 1935 but which was officially promulgated only in January 1941. The designation "intellectual/mental workers" was generous; it included specialized administrative and technical personnel, office workers like bookkeepers, hosts and housekeepers,

35 See here Christophe Verbuggen, "'Intellectual Workers' and Their Search for a Place within the ILO during the Interwar Period," in *Essays on the International Labour Organization and Its Impact on the World during the Twentieth Century*, eds. Jasmien Van Daele et al. (Bern: Peter Lang, 2010), 271–92.

36 On the influence of the ILO and the Versailles settlement on the social systems of East Central Europe, see Natali Stegmann, "The ILO and East Central Europe: Insights into the Early Polish and Czechoslovak Interwar Years," *Acta Universitatis Carolinae*, Studia Territorialia 1 (2017): 11–34.

insurance agents, employees of commercial firms, teachers and educators as well as artists, musicians, painters and other artistic professions.[37]

The role of the interventionist state is another important transnational trend of the interwar period. In Western Europe, the state had kept out of most cultural industries but this attitude changed with the ascent of broadcasting media, including radio and cinema.[38] The involvement of the state in the management and diffusion of new media represented a common feature of Western and Eastern Europe in the interwar period. In fact, the private ownership of radio broadcasting as in the case of Yugoslavia was rather the exception than the rule. State intervention, as well as intervention in cultural markets, was heightened by the great depression, and the 1920s and 1930s were years of widespread protectionism. As maintained by Donald Sassoon, "cultural markets became at the same time more international and more state-controlled, the latter often in response to the former."[39] Though East and Southeast Europe kept pace with this common trend, specifically with respect to the development of copyright, which is the main concern of this study, the late 1930s witnessed a second wave of amendments of the existing copyright laws in the countries under discussion, a development that is somewhat specific and can be interpreted as a further "nationalization," that is, a deeper anchoring of the laws into local circumstances. In the cases of both Bulgaria and Yugoslavia, the amendments were clearly "correctives," that is, they were intended to rectify specific problems that had arisen through the application of the copyright law in the local context. In both cases, the enactment of the copyright law had been a top-down process. Both laws were modern, in the sense that they were drafted by taking up-to-date legal standards into consideration, but they were "outlandish" in the sense that they had not arisen from below, and in that sense did not address concrete local concerns or specificities. Both amendments aimed at strengthening the position of local creators internally and externally. In the Czechoslovak case, the 1936 amendment aimed at legally codifying the monopoly position of OSA, and also confirmed and strengthened the central role of the state and its institutions in the regulation of new media. Equivalent developments can be observed in the case of Bulgaria, where certain state-sensitive reproductions like maps and photographs were declared state property.

---

37 On the Bulgarian insurance of intellectual workers, see *Proektă za zakonă za osigurjavaneto na umstvenite rabotnici* (Sofia: Izdanie na profesionalnite săjuzi na službitelite vă častnite predprijatija vă Bălgarija, 1939) and *Zakonă za osigurjavane na umstvenite rabotnici* (utvărdenă că ukază Nt. 4 ot 17 Januarij 1941 godina i obnarodvană vă "Dăržavenă vestnikă, broj 17 ot 24 januarij 1941 god.) (Sofia: Dăržavna pečatnica, 1941).

38 Sassoon, *The Culture of the Europeans*, 601.

39 Sassoon, *The Culture of the Europeans*, 860–61.

Collecting Societies

New technologies, the massification and equalization of society, the juridification of new media and mechanisms of reproduction gave rise to new practices of valorization and utilization of cultural products, which brought the institution of collecting societies to the fore.[40] Via OSA's central position and centralizing policy, that is, through the creation of a single, national, state-endorsed collecting society, with a monopoly mandate in the handling of fees both within and outside of Czechoslovakia, the first republic was able to escape the fate of Yugoslavia. However, the build-up and expansion of collecting societies was not a story without frictions.[41] The institution of collecting societies was inaugurated in the region of East Central and Southeast Europe as a rule after WWI, parallel to the introduction of copyright law. Collective management organizations or collecting societies were introduced in the western part of the continent (France, Italy, Austria, Germany) already by the late nineteenth century, and had, by the time East and Southeast Europe joined the international copyright regime, accumulated significant experience in the management of rights. On the continent, the French collecting society SACEM (Société des Auteurs, Compositeurs et Editeurs de Musique, founded in 1851) played both a pioneering and dominating role, as has already been witnessed in the Yugoslav chapter. By the late nineteenth century, SACEM expanded territorially, founding branches according to its own model in a series of foreign countries; furthermore, it represented those foreign nationals and collected royalties on behalf of Belgium, the Netherlands, Switzerland, Spain, Greece, Monaco, Luxemburg, Portugal, Egypt, Romania, Morocco and Syria. Many foreign creators, lacking their own national collecting society, authorized SACEM with the representation of their rights and collection of fees. When foreign countries eventually constituted their own national collecting societies, SACEM concluded reciprocal treaties with them.[42] Building on its reputation as a "pioneer" of the international concept of authors' rights, SACEM continued well into the twentieth century to represent in certain foreign countries not only its own members, but also numerous other foreign

---

[40] On the structure, purpose and organization of Collective Management Organizations, see several WIPO publications, including: Ulrich Uchtenhagen, *Copyright Collective Management in Music* (Geneva: WIPO, 2011); Mihály Ficsor, *Collective Management of Copyright Related Rights* (Geneva: WIPO, 2002).

[41] For a good and concise critical historical account of CMOs, see Monika Dommann, *Autoren und Apparate: Die Geschichte des Copyrights in Medienwandel* (Frankfurt a.M: Fischer, 2014), 107–133.

[42] Jean-Jacques Lemoin, *La Société des Auteurs, Compositeurs et Editeurs de Musique 1850–1950* (Paris: Lebois, 1950), 19 and 156–57.

authors' societies that lacked local representation and authorized SACEM to represent them instead.[43] The organization's official title was "Société française," but the attribute "French" should not distract from the fact that SACEM was only nominally French; in reality, the society was a global player.

Collecting societies started operating in the German lands around the turn of the century. The pluralization of rights and rights owners in performed and broadcast music were the motors behind the creation of the German collecting society GEMA (Genossenschaft zur Verwertung musikalischer Aufführungsrechte) in 1913. It united composers, publishers and librettists and functioned as a non-state organization, in-between copyright owners and the market. Its legal status was that of a cooperative with limited liability. After a protracted period of strife with competing societies (such as the GDT–Genossenschaft Deutscher Tonträger, AfmA–Anstalt für musikalisches Aufführungsrecht, the Austrian AKM etc.), GEMA was able to "absorb" them and through the creation of a central association solidify a stern monopoly position in the German market. By that time, music rights had long transformed into a business resource. As observed by Louis Pahlow, "GEMA operated its royalty administration rigidly as a means to strengthen its negotiating position with music consumers (especially the film, radio and phonographic industries) and to drive the expansion of its rights to the use of music (to new adaptations, new locations and new media). This system was certainly market-oriented, but by no means market-transparent."[44] Both GEMA and SACEM functioned as models for the creation of OSA. The critical history of the various European collecting societies (both East and West) still waits to be written.[45] The local acceptance of collecting societies did not proceed without resistance, and end users had to become accustomed to both the notion of copyright and the practice of fee payments, as well as disciplined into compliance.[46] Although OSA was institutionally and financially independent, it owed a great deal of its authority and supremacy to the protective hand of the state. Initial resistance was slowly curbed and local acceptance began to grow when OSA completed its first contract with Czechoslovak radio, which

---

[43] Lemoin, *La Société des Auteurs*, 160.

[44] Louis S. Pahlow, "Industrialized Music Brokers as Competing Market Players: The Administration of Music Rights in Germany (ca. 1870–1930)," *Popular Entertainment Studies* 6 (2015): 67.

[45] Research on the history of national and international collecting societies is a real lacuna and is making headway on very slowly, see Georg Fischer, Stephan Klingner and Malte Zill, eds., *Monopole im medienindustriellen Komplex? Verwertungsgesellschaften gestern, heute, morgen* (Marburg: Büchner, 2023).

[46] Reports on the difficulties in enforcing and/or having the model of collecting societies accepted locally are also available in the case of the Polish ZAIKS. See Rudnicki, "La société polonaise des auteurs," 121–123.

amounted to a public recognition of its function and a confirmation of the practical application of copyright.[47] Above all, OSA's central functions (monopoly status, negotiating power with society and the state, disciplinarian competences) were all sanctioned by the state and the copyright law, which provided the organization with a unique and privileged position and fortified it legally.

Other Actors: Intermediaries

The late nineteenth and early twentieth century witnessed the expansion of the intermediary, who acted as an official/legal representative on behalf of foreign collecting societies and authors' associations. Involved were private individuals broadly related to the arts and/or entertainment, at times lawyers, owners of registered businesses, impresarios and other related professions that acted as local proxies for foreign clients, firms, associations, CMOs and agencies in faraway places. Their main function was to screen local markets for infringements that could interest and bring profit to their faraway clients: theatrical plays and musical stage works performed without previous authorization and royalty payments, works appearing under another title or slightly altered, music being performed in public places and so on, and most importantly the collection of royalties on their clients' behalf. Functionally, they occupied a particular space, constituting an intermediary level in-between international organizations, international associations of interest groups, state actors, society and the arts. Their main responsibility was to surveil local practice in the name and for the benefit of their foreign clients, although along the way some developed their own shady initiatives and parasitic businesses, extracting personal profit from their intermediary position, as witnessed here in the case of Yugoslavia but also in Bulgaria. They were among the agents that most energetically promoted notions of commodification and propertization in culture. As modern authors' rights have traditionally been associated overwhelmingly with affirmative attributes such as "protection," "creativity" and "morality," it is worth pointing out here by way of discussing these intermediary structures that the establishment of modern copyright regimes was also associated with practices of surveillance and/or misuse.[48] The Belle

47 See here OSA's official history, https://www.100letosa.cz/1920#obtizna.

48 Surveillance was not simply a defensive mechanism, a haphazard by-product of efforts to restrict "piracy." In the discussions revolving around the regulation of translation, for example, publishers encouraged the creation of the figure of the local monitoring/policing observer, who would not

Epoque and the interwar period likely represented the rise and peak of the figure of the "private" collecting agent. In most countries, such competences were passed over to self-managing authors' associations and collective management organizations, at least in the field of music. Collecting agents received their legitimacy from the existence of international organizations and structures, which they officially represented at the local level. The avarice of the local agents cannot be examined separately from the design and objectives of these global and transnational actors and structures, whose transnational story still remains to be told.

An equivalent intermediary role was played by the figure of the modern lobbyist, who played a not insignificant role in promoting international copyright. Often recruited from a similar pool of professionals (local intellectuals, journalists, lawyers, state/ministry officials), they were people with a good command of the local context and disposed of far-reaching networks. The objective was to engage individuals who exercised influence in order to mobilize public opinion, governments and local interest groups. The ALAI, for example, mastered this strategy by founding local branches of its association in the widest circle of countries. By these means, it also established a crucial transmission belt for the circulation of information from the various national contexts towards its own "coordinating" center and vice versa; it could ensure that its agenda was brought to the most remote places in the world and thereby also had the capacity to (try to) influence the "orientation" of national actors. Of the three cases under analysis here, Bulgaria represents the country with the weakest institutionalization of copyright structures. At the same time, it represents the case that lacked two crucial ingredients in the interwar period: (1) the central figure of an authoritative lawyer, who builds a career on the basis of copyright expertise; and (2) a local ALAI branch. The interconnection of these factors as a precondition for the effective promotion of international copyright should not be regarded as a coincidence.

only report copyright infringements but also suggest the most competent local translator for each national context. The intention was twofold: (1) to ensure that there was no more than one authorized translation circulating in foreign markets, and (2) to thereby extend their own monopoly in other markets and cultures as well. In a certain way, this system of individualized monopoly extension via surveillance is similar to Foucault's "panopticon."

Copyright, Creative Elites and Avant-Garde Practices in the Interwar Period

It can generally be argued that in the case of East and Southeast Europe, copyright was not perceived as an instrument, nor did it serve as an impulse for the emergence of national literatures, as was partially the case in North and South America and other world regions. This circumstance is to be explained predominantly by the fact that nation-building in Eastern Europe proceeded differently than in the case of nations emerging from within the same linguistic group, as was frequently the case with maritime empires and their colonies (the anglophone, hispanophone, francophone, lusophone etc. worlds). In East and Southeast Europe, the spoken idiom was the central diacritic mark distinguishing between "own" and "foreign," and national literatures were organized as a rule around the language principle. Although copyright was not conducive to an identity formation purporting distinction, it played indirectly into ways of building (imagining) community, as in the case of generous free uses (particularly for education), by limiting the individualizing aspects of copyright, by protecting works of national significance beyond the individual, but also by promoting protectionism, that is, as an instrument to curb the excessive number of foreign imported works (as experienced in the case of Yugoslavia as well as Greece).

In all three cases it is possible to observe in the interwar period a retreat from liberal copyright, that is, copyright understood as an instrument that is modelled on the individual creator, who singularly produces and sells his/her work in conditions governed by free market exchange in the arts. Rather, the copyright regimes that prevailed in the 1930s modelled and addressed creators as a professional corporation (standardized tariffs, administrative regulation of remuneration, interventions constraining contractual freedom etc.). If in the period of national movements, the full-fledged commercialization of culture was restrained initially by limited demand and subsequently by the need to improve literacy, that is, to nationalize the peasant masses, in the interwar period the market was restrained by the goal of fostering the welfare of national creators as a group.

Regarding the professional development of creative elites in the interwar period, the broad picture tends to confirm—naturally with certain variations and different gradations—that professionalization processes were driven largely from above rather than from below, that is, they developed rather in relation to and/or through the intervention of the state than through pressures exerted by the market. This trend is strongest in the case of the two Balkan countries with a declining tendency in the case of Czechoslovakia. This observable tendency of top-down professionalization can be variously explained: on the one hand, time constraints and the imperative to accelerate developments conditioned the state-driven nation-building projects in the regions discussed; on the other, on account of insufficient market pressure encouraging durable and stable professional differentiation, professional groups often looked to the state to enforce (administratively, legally etc.) such professionalization barriers on their behalf. In spite of all the differences, it is possible to observe a synchronization of parts of the creative elites with large state projects like state building, and efforts to further their professional interests and programme as a consequence of this alignment. In all cases there was a rapprochement between creative elites and the state that was mediated through the respective national agenda and translated into increased state patronage and state intervention on behalf of the creators' professionalization agenda. If in the case of the Bulgarian state it involved engagement with the state's irredentist policy, in the case of Yugoslavia it concerned the endorsement of the ideology and the state-building project of Yugoslavism, while in the case of Czechoslovakia it revolved around the state's geopolitical orientation, where state internal consolidation went hand-in-hand with a deliberately outward-facing and active international commitment. It was due to this social and political climate, as well as generous state patronage promoting the international entanglement of local arts, that the interwar avant-garde could ascend to such a dominant force in the case of Czechoslovakia.[49]

In all three cases it is possible to observe in the interwar period, in a more explicit or implicit manner, the presence of a discourse among creative elites regarding the value and social status of cultural creations, which was articulated as a competition between "high" and "low" culture, and which went together with demands for professional distinction and the institutionalization of selection criteria and exclusion mechanisms that could also enforce such professional barriers on a practical level. As witnessed in greater detail in the cases of both Yugoslavia and Czechoslovakia, such professionalization struggles were communicated as an essential dichotomy between serious/high/authoritative/state-sanctioned versus entertainment culture. These professionalization battles were fought over "distinction" in the Bourdieuian sense, as position-takings within the field of cultural production, whereby social actors used diverse strategies to differentiate and distance themselves from others in society, assigning themselves greater value in this process. Aesthetic merit, social/

49 Derek Sayer, "How We Remember and What We Forget: Art History and the Czech Avant-Garde," in *The Inhabited Ruins of Central Europe: Re-imagining Space, History and Memory*, eds. Dariusz Gafijczuk and Derek Sayer (London: Palgrave Macmillan, 2013), 148–77.

moral/national worth and formal education were criteria that were employed to draw the line between high and low, legitimate and "illegitimate" creativity.

Such professionalization conflicts were a Europe-wide phenomenon from the turn of the twentieth century and were related to the emergence of new media as well as to the transnational flows of cultural commodities that incited both new consumption tastes and opportunities but also protectionist reflexes. The ever-greater commercialization of cultural goods as a result of the disbanding of aristocratic patronage and society's growing bourgeoisification created a tension between aesthetic value and economic/market valuation on account of the fact that it put two things in relation to each other, which—strictly speaking—had little to do with one another.[50] A prime example of this tension was the distinction between "serious" and "light" music (or high- vs. lowbrow/E-Musik vs. U-Musik), which had its origins in the classifications applied by collecting societies. In the practices of societies like GEMA, and upon the insistence of composers like Richard Strauss, highbrow music was awarded higher royalties on account of the need to financially safeguard serious music; cultural rather than economic "value" was applied here as a criterion of differentiation.

However, the winds of change were blowing. From the 1900s, "light" music was growing in popularity, prevailing in cafes and restaurants, varietè theatres and entertainment venues as atmospheric background noise, provoking the concern of professional composers. The recording industry (gramophones, shellac records etc.), in search of appropriate repertoires, particularly of short duration (a five-minute play on average), equally coveted entertainment music. Contemporary technical facilities for recording and broadcasting (requiring a specific sound intensity and frequency) favored a particular kind of music, usually marches, waltzes, schlager, arias and overtures, which became the most commonly reproduced musical forms. With the advent of radio in the 1920s and talkie films in the 1930s, this tendency was strengthened even further. Demand for entertainment programmes focused on genres like schlager, overtures, suites and short virtuoso pieces, and due to their popularity, their composers were able to generate a substantial flow of royalty payments for collecting societies.[51] The tension between cultural and economic capital was solidified.

Similar discursive, aesthetic-ideological constructions of distinction and professional competition can be encountered in Southeast and East Central Europe in the

50 Susanne Binas-Preisendörfer, "Verteilungsplan, ideologische Konstruktion und sozialer Filter: Zur Geschichte der Kategorien von E-Musik und U-Musik," in *Jahrbuch für Kulturpolitik 2006*, vol. 6 (Thema: Diskurs Kulturpolitik), eds. Norbert Sievers and Bernd Wagner (Essen: Klartext, 2006), 271–72.

51 Binas-Preisendörfer, "Verteilungsplan," 172–73.

interwar period as well. Their framing, however, was assisted by dissimilar structural conditions, such as the absence of a lengthy and weighty past, the lack of a social middle-class foundation for intellectual professions and the absence of continuity with pre-modern forms of the same professions, as well as the lack of solidified upper middle-class audiences, at least in the cases of Yugoslavia and Bulgaria. Though native entertainment was vexing as well, it was mainly the fact that the newest trends for such genres came largely from abroad that exacerbated the situation, especially when the status of local creative professions (of the liberal tradition) was so labile and resources were scarce.

Common to all three cases and more broadly valid for the status of art and avant-gardes in the interwar period was their effort to become autonomous from the market (which might be an additional reason for their rapprochement with the state). The era between the two World Wars represents a period of intense transnationalization and internationalization of radical avant-gardes with an explicit claim to "originality," which is defined in contradistinction to the tastes and the institutions of the literary/artistic status quo and the marketability criteria of "philistine" creators and publishers. It therefore comes as no surprise that the interwar period was the period of avant-garde periodicals and group anthologies *par excellence*, and less that of individualistic genres such as the novel.[52] This new definition of "originality" focused not so much on uniqueness (as the quality of artistic genius) as on the *break with* (academic, national) *tradition*. Creators claimed the prerogative to define the content of "originality," which in a certain, indirect way constituted a challenge to the juridical milieu, which also had a stake in the privilege of sanctioning "originality." The avant-gardes repositioned themselves—to phrase it in Bourdieu's terms—within the "field" of cultural production, defining "original" neither in relation to the market nor through the purely internal semiotics of art (l'art pour l'art), but in relation to practical life, the new modes and means of production and the (political) organization of society.

It is in the context of the above developments, and as the result of a synergy of factors, that the international codification of moral rights took place in the interwar period (Rome revision of the BC in 1928). Although the quest for moral rights (the demand to respect the author's personality) had a long pedigree in intellectual/

52 On magazines as strategic publications of the transnational European avant-gardes in the interwar period, see Meghan L. Forbes, "Advertisement as Collaboration in the Central European Avant-Garde Magazines," *post: notes on art in a global context*, March 16, 2016, https://post.moma.org/advertisement-as-collaboration-in-the-central-european-avant-garde-magazines-2/; also idem, "In the Middle of It All: Prague, Brno, and the Avant-Garde Networks of Interwar Europe." PhD diss., University of Michigan, 2016.

literary/art history, and had been articulated—historically speaking—earlier than the quest for copyright, moral rights, until the early twentieth century, acquired nothing of the prominence reserved for pecuniary rights in international copyright codification. The specific timing in which moral rights became relevant was therefore significant. In the generic field of the arts, the dawn of the twentieth century bore witness to a series of transgressions and the creative blurring of all kinds of boundaries: (1) between genres, their academic disciplines and their forms of expression, for example the blending between applied arts, decorative arts and architecture; (2) between high and lowbrow culture, and between culture and entertainment as in melodrama, opera, operetta, musical; (3) between man-crafted reproductions (e.g. literary adaptations) and reproductions on a purely mechanical basis such as lithography and photography; (4) between private and public spaces of consumption of cultural goods; (5) between sound and image and their technical synchronization and so on. All these processes were coupled with the massification of society and ever-greater direct access of the masses to cultural artefacts, without the intermediation of expert skills or knowledge. Class, taste and cultural boundaries were equally being collapsed. The proliferation of moral rights in the first decades of the twentieth century aimed to reposition the figure of the author in the novel competitive environment that characterized the transition of copyright from the printing to the audiovisual paradigm.

The avant-gardes' "prises de position" and their explicit endorsement of a politics of art challenged, perhaps unintentionally, the epicenter of the copyright edifice, that is, the very notion of the "romantic" (ultimately bourgeois) author as a "genius" guarding his/her rightful and unique "property." In the period of the mechanical reproduction of art, the avant-gardes' self-positioning and copyright's liberal construction of the romantic author were on a clear collision course. Although theoreticians of art such as Walter Benjamin acknowledged that artistic reproduction had a long history throughout the ages, he underscored the revolutionary effect that the new means of mechanical reproduction, such as film and photography, had in collapsing the borders between the original and its copy.[53] Thereby, one of copyright's most existentialist dichotomies was being systematically eroded. Moral rights effected in the first place an "enlargement," an "amplification" of the notion of the author, and in the second, they stabilized and solidified anew—enhanced now with superior moral capital—the figure of the author as the supreme sanctioning authority of copyright.

[53] See Walter Benjamin, *The Work of Art in the Age of Mechanical Reproduction*. London: Penguin, 2008 (original 1936).

Finally, two more processes that culminated in the interwar period deserve attention and could potentially be analysed against the background of the developments discussed hitherto. On the one hand, in international forums, we witness the ultimate abandonment of theoretical discussions on the nature of copyright, which had been quite frequent in the early constituent period of the BU/BC. From approximately the first decades of the twentieth century, a pragmatic and technocratic approach to international codification and the management of copyright issues prevailed and became the customary way of going about legislating international copyright. On the other, the Rome revision cancelled the option of acceding to the BC with reservations, which undoubtedly streamlined the international copyright regime. Both issues deserve further contextualization.

Chapter 11

Communist Copyright

The current chapter offers a cursory overview of copyright law development under communism, focusing on the evolution of copyright legislation from the late 1940s to the late 1970s. Its purpose is twofold. First, to offer an elementary typologization of communist copyright through an analysis of some of its basic features and functions. This was deemed necessary in light of the fact that there are often implicit or explicit assumptions about the nature of communist copyright, including: the presumed uniformity of copyright law under real socialism, as well as the contention that copyright law in East Central and South East Europe was entirely predicated on the Soviet model; the supposition that copyright law after 1945 was a clear departure from what had preceded it, as well as the certainty that it represented a diversion from European developments, or again the conception of the sanctimonious character of authors' rights under communism due to the existence of censorship mechanisms and the absence of real market competition. The second purpose is to analyse the evolution of copyright legislation in Bulgaria, Yugoslavia and Czechoslovakia, to outline and characterize the evolution of their respective copyright laws with a view to their particular traits as well as continuities and discontinuities. It is outside the purview of this chapter to provide a detailed analysis of copyright practice in the mentioned countries; nonetheless, and to the extent possible, the analysis strives to embed the development of copyright legislation within the sociocultural and political context of the times.

Copyright in communist systems served partially familiar, and partially distinct, purposes. As in liberal political systems, it served the basic purpose of directing and distributing income flows, emanating from the use and consumption of cultural goods and activities, into the hands of cultural producers and rightsholders. Whereas in liberal systems copyright is basically a management mechanism arbitrating roles and revenue between individual stakeholders in a "market" of culture, in communist systems copyright was a constituent mechanism of the system of state-planned economy and culture. It is possible to elucidate this by way of a metaphor: whereas copyright habitually enables the slicing of the pie of culture into different and, according to the circumstances, varying sizes and shapes, the main purpose of communist copyright was to ensure the slicing of the pie according to set standards, where all stakeholders involved got a decent slice. Through the practice of mandatory and specialized model contracts, it formed an inexorable part of the system of planning, production and remuneration of culture and its creators. Copyright management was therefore intertwined with a series of institutions and organizations that made up the system of corporate culture under communism, which included ministries and committees of culture, production enterprises, cultural funds, collective management societies, propaganda agencies, creative unions and so on.

On account of the desire to retain the prerogative of interpretation over the role, significance and application of creativity, communist ideology regarded culture, information and scientific knowledge to be key areas in the engineering of future society, and by the same token, creators (and their active participation and/or compliance) occupied a pivotal position in the communist worldview and policy. Copyright in this universe was more than simply a system of rewards for creative labor; rather, it was conceived as a social instrument shaping the conditions of creativity and the modality of circulation of cultural goods to conform to communist conceptions of socioeconomic and political order. If liberal copyright followed the vagaries of the market, communist copyright aspired to shape holistically the conditions of production, the dissemination and use of works as well as the "market" of culture in accordance with ideological precepts.

For this reason, socialist copyright went beyond a conception of copyright as a mere distributing mechanism that simply had to be adjusted periodically in order to adapt to technological change. The socialist take on copyright was rather pragmatic and, above all, profoundly utilitarian; copyright was to serve the communist social order and help to materialize the cultural revolution. It fulfilled essentially a social mission, whose primary task was to guarantee the broadest possible dissemination of creative works within society and harmonize the traditionally antagonistic relationship between authors, intermediaries and end users. As a result, the protection of the author was a corollary of the abovementioned priorities.

Due to this worldview, but also due to the specific socioeconomic set-up of communist societies and the prevailing position of the state within them, which effectively diminished the number and role of commercial intermediaries, copyright law under communism experienced a kind of despecialization.[1] Copyright law was

[1] Legal scholars have often attributed the "despecialization" of these legal areas to the absence of a really dynamic innovation economy, which is, without doubt, an accurate observation. See for example Adolf Dietz, "Trends in the Field of Copyright Law in the Countries of Central and Eastern Europe," *Revue International du Droit d'Auteur (RIDA)* 162 (October 1994): 121–25. However, at the same time, scholars fail to ask the same question in the reverse, that is, whom and what purposes

not the only legal field that was restrained. In a related manner, competition law also proportionately lost significance. A great many issues were resolved through administrative measures, negotiations and adjustments. Generally speaking, communist copyright law was altogether not so rich in case law (there were exceptions of course), as problems could be settled administratively through arbitrations in the diverse levels of decision-making (i.e. within unions, organizations and institutions, party organs, production units, collective management organizations etc.). Moreover, there was little societal, political and economic interest in elaborate disputes and litigations. By contrast, copyright contract law, which formed the foundation of the copyright system, was particularly well developed.[2]

Broadly speaking, socialist copyright was rather disinterested in defining boundaries and limits of "property," and by default what constitutes transgressions thereof, an additional aspect that distinguishes it in practical and philosophical terms from a liberal conception of copyright. Indisputably, several practical reasons go to explain this stance: the system of culture was so state-regulated that the possibilities for misdemeanor by intermediaries/entrepreneurs were seriously restrained; though there was competition between institutions, there was no strong commercial competition between enterprises tasked with the production and dissemination of cultural goods; access to technical equipment that would permit uncontrolled copying was extremely restrained and controlled; laying excessive emphasis on the exclusive and absolute rights of authors made little sense practically, since works were monitored in various ways (institutional and self-censorship) and reproduction channels were predominantly official and controlled; and the economy was not geared towards the fast absorption and commercialization of innovation.

At the same time, disinterest in property boundaries constituted part of the communist cosmology. Communist copyright law was mainly focused on regulating the modality of uses, rather than on penalizing transgressions and trespassing. Socialist copyright was not preoccupied with sanctioning, or not, access to cultural goods as a mechanism to help the cultural market expand. On the contrary, the broadest possible participation and indiscriminate access to culture were consequently anticipated and promoted. The precise definition of uses served not so much to determine

are served by "hyperspecialization" (sometimes beyond comprehension), which such fields of law experience in conditions of capitalism? For example: which user takes the time to read 10–20 pages of legal regulations concerning "conditions of use" for different online services? Whose interests are protected via hyper-juridification?

2 Artur Wandtke, "Entwicklungstendenzen des Urheberrechts in Osteuropa (unter besonderer Berücksichtigung der Gesetze in Polen, Russland, Ungarn sowie in Tschechien und der Slowakei)," *GRURInt.* (1995): 566.

access (i.e. who can/should be left outside and when and why, or how to optimize the correlation between access and revenue) but rather to determine recompense (i.e. who receives remuneration, under which conditions and for what). Culture under communism was not wholly independent of market considerations (publishing houses knew the difference between bestsellers and unpopular works and often adjusted their print runs accordingly, save for the obligatory Marxist-Leninist classics; theatrical flops also had to be removed from the stage in communist systems etc.), but it was essentially more indifferent to market and financial pressures. In its turn, this circumstance had an impact on the way different forms of capital (cultural, social, economic, political) were rearranged and played out, and moreover on the way cultural actors repositioned themselves by validating—according to the circumstances—different types of capital as being more relevant or authentic than others, and therefore more conducive to creative autonomy.

Through a combination of diverse instruments, compulsory, voluntary and optional measures (statutory licenses, authorization by the author with and without remuneration, free or controlled uses, uses only after the compulsory notification of the author, restriction of the author's right to withdrawal, the right of the Ministry of Culture to override the author's permission in exceptional cases etc.), communist copyright sought to regulate relationships between various stakeholders. On the one hand, this handling of rights aimed at divesting the legal "fortification" going by the name of "author" of its exclusive prerogatives. Throughout copyright history, the author was modelled as an extra-robust proprietor figure in order to secure and justify diverse pretentions to monopoly. In communist copyright, the legal "author" was no longer a monolithic figure with absolute entitlements to a bundle of rights, but was rather broken down into its constituent parts; rights, needs and goals were weighted and hierarchized in alignment with the needs of the state, the ideological and practical precepts of the Communist Party, society and international relations. Paradoxically, the author came off better most of the time, as remuneration was usually guaranteed and standardized.

On the other hand, communist copyright management aimed at safeguarding the notion of culture as a public good from market distortions. Although the proliferation of compulsory licenses can be interpreted as an encroachment on the author's freedom, at the same time it also deprived copyright owners of the capacity to dictate exaggerated conditions for the use of their works. Analogous measures such as the restriction of the rights of heirs, prevalent in several communist copyright legislations, aimed at avoiding the deformation of copyright into rent-seeking behavior. A central balancing instrument of the cultural economy were fixed remuneration rates. By providing minimum and maximum remuneration rates for works, it was possible to diminish the likelihood that a work became the object of market speculation. In communist reasoning, creative labor entitled someone to remuneration, not to value extraction. In a certain way, communist copyright disrupted the "circularity of legal reasoning," whereby copyright offers legal protection to property as a value asset, when, in actual fact, the economic value of the asset "depends upon the extent to which it will be legally protected."[3]

Although achieving a balance of interests between stakeholders in society and economy belongs to the professed goals of liberal copyright, in practice its main focus is catered to the commercial sphere. Naturally, society is also a concern and certain forms of free uses (targeting predominantly educational purposes), personal uses (for purely private purposes) as well as the institution of the public domain are geared towards satisfying society's need for access to knowledge and culture by enfeebling strong exclusive rights. However, they form a small appendix in comparison to copyright's core business. In this respect, communist copyright engaged with different priorities. Its core mission was not commercialization, and for this reason the positioning of actors in the field of copyright was reversed. The prerogatives of intermediaries were restricted to the benefit of authors/creators, and the prerogatives of authors/creators restricted to the benefit of end users, who—as paradoxical as it may sound—benefited the most from this constellation.[4]

Although it may seem paradoxical, it was communist indifference towards value extraction in combination with variable degrees and periodical waves of political repression and publishing ostracism that triggered and nurtured phenomena such as *Samizdat* and *Tamizdat*, that is, alternative networks of cultural circulation that aimed at revitalizing economic or political or cultural capital, or combinations thereof. Often analyzed as diametrical opposites to communist culture, they represented phenomena that were more closely interrelated with the logic and function of the communist political economy, market and culture and cannot be thought independently of them,[5] in the same way that piracy cannot be thought independently

3 Felix S. Cohen, "Transcendental Nonsense and the Functional Approach," *Columbia Law Review* 35, no. 6 (June 1935): 814–17.

4 See here Andrew Baruch Wachtel, *Remaining Relevant after Communism: The Role of the Writer in Eastern Europe* (Chicago: Chicago University Press, 2006).

5 For a similar rationale, see Josephine von Zitzewitz, *The Culture of Samizdat: Literature and Underground Networks in the Late Soviet Union* (London: Bloomsbury, 2020). There exists an elaborate literature on *Samizdat* and *Tamizdat*; here, only exemplarily, see the special issue "Publish and Perish: Samizdat and Underground Cultural Production Practices in the Soviet Block," *Poetics Today* 29, no. 4 (Winter 2008); Ann Komaromi, "Samizdat and Soviet Dissident Publics," *Slavic Review* 71, no. 1 (Spring 2012): 70–90, idem, "The Material Existence of Soviet Samizdat," *Slavic Review* 63,

of industrial publishing or avant-gardes independently of time-honored, status-quo culture. *Samizdat* and *Tamizdat* represented complex and multilayered phenomena related to the shifting cartographies, significations and valuations of culture within communist states and between cultures in the global Cold War divide and cannot be reduced solely to resistance responses to political repression, which—without doubt—they were, but only partially.

Despite the common general characteristics that constituted the broad framework of communist copyright as described above, the legislation of the three countries under analysis differed, in alignment with the specific political trajectories they followed in the post-WWII period as well as the traditions they had inherited from the interwar period.

Copyright in Communist Bulgaria

The first Bulgarian copyright law to be released after the communist takeover was issued in 1951,[6] and was amended and supplemented twice, first in 1956[7] and again in 1972.[8] Until 1951, interwar legislation remained in place, though it was probably of minor significance given the gradual, yet radical, engineering that took place at the institutional level in the field of culture and the socioeconomic structure in general, and which affected the production and circulation of cultural goods in far more rigorous ways (nationalization of publishing and printing enterprises, progressive media monopoly, installation of censorship etc.). Many practices and institutions were founded and regulated by decree, which allowed ad hoc adjustments and interventions.[9]

---

no. 3 (Fall 2004): 597–618; Friederike Kind-Kovács and Jessie Labov, eds., *Samizdat, Tamizdat, and Beyond: Transnational Media during and after Socialism* (New York: Berghahn Books, 2013), etc.

6 "Zakon za avtorskoto pravo," *Izvestija*, no. 92, November 16, 1951, amended *Izvestija*, no. 10, February 1, 1952. Also: *Zakon za avtorskoto pravo i tarifa za honorarite na avtorite, prevodačite, redaktorite, hudožnicite, korektorite i na sătrudnicite na direkcijata na radioinformacijata* (Sofia: "Nauka i Izkustvo," 1952).

7 "Zakon za avtorskoto pravo," *Izvestija*, no. 55, August 10, 1956. Also: *Zakon za avtorskoto pravo, tarifa za avtorski i drugi văznagraždenijata i tarifa za văznagraždenijata na avtori, izpălniteli i dr.* (Sofia: "Nauka i Izkustvo," 1961).

8 "Zakon za avtorskoto pravo," *Dăržaven vestnik*, no. 35, May 5, 1972. Also: *Zakon za avtorskoto pravo, tarifi za avtorski, izpălnitelski i drugi văznagraždenija za tvorčeski trud* (Sofia: "Nauka i Izkustvo," 1975).

9 The installation of censorship in the postwar period has been well researched. See Ilko Penelov, "Censurata vărhu knigite v Bălgarija, 1944–1956" (PhD diss., Sofia, filosofski fakultet, University

As had also been the case in the interwar period, Bulgarian postwar copyright legislation turned largely to the Soviet model for inspiration and guidance and followed the Russian prototype: the 1928 Soviet copyright law and the provisions of the civil code of the Soviet Union (1947), as well as the broader theoretical framework of Soviet civil law, were mentioned as sources. Bulgarian civil law at the time thwarted the option of accommodating copyright and the publishing contract under one law, which would have required the installation of a new republican civil code.[10]

Copyright law was supplemented by the law on liabilities and contracts,[11] which regulated the practical implementation of the use of works, as well as responsibilities and rights, corresponding approximately to the law on the publishing contract. Whereas in the interwar period provisions regulating the contract had been partially integrated into the copyright law, in the communist period they were separated again and functioned as different pieces of legislation. Copyright management relied on a series of auxiliary measures: infringements were partially regulated by the penal code, tariffs and fee rates for uses by periodically updated decrees, the funds of the creative unions through the law on creative funds and so on. The socialist copyright regime included, next to the copyright law, a web of instruments that linked state institutions, organizations and functions, as well as the spheres of decision-making, production and consumption. Although decrees are prescriptive in character, they could also provide for flexibility, as they represented instruments of government below the legislature and could be revised, amended, proclaimed or ceased with greater ease than laws.

Comparative Overview of Copyright Law Development

A comparative juxtaposition of the three copyright laws of communist Bulgaria reveals a clear tendency. Whereas the laws and amendments of the 1950s were still

Sv. Kliment Ochridski, 2007), as well as several works by Vesela Čičovska: "Glavlit (1952–1956): Izgraždane na edinna censurna sistema v Bălgarija," *Istoričeski pregled* 47, no. 10 (1991): 38–69; "Kulturnata politika na narodnodemokratičnata vlast (1944–1948 g.)," *Istoričeski pregled* 35, no. 4 (1979): 114–137; "Dăržavni kulturni institucii v Bălgarija," in *Bălgarija 1300: Institucii i dăržavna tradicija*, vol. 1, (Sofia: Bălgarsko istoričesko družestvo, 1981), 459–82.

10 Stenografski dnevnici, 1 NS, IV RS, 1 3, 1/XI, 1951, 15.

11 "Zakon za zadălženijata i dogovori," *Dăržaven vestnik*, no. 275, November 22, 1950, amended *Izvestija*, no. 2, December 5, 1950 and no. 69, August 28, 1951.

very much within a framework of a revolutionary mindset, conforming more or less to the prototype described in the introductory section, the 1972 copyright law struck a decisively different note. This last legislation was characterized on the one hand by strong propertization tendencies, that is, many of the instruments and provisions that initially relativized exclusive copyright were revised with the intention of restricting free uses and strengthening individual entitlements; in a certain way, it could be argued that in the 1970s the "author proprietor" was reinstated. On the other, benchmarks were revised, aiming at a greater harmonization with BC international standards and norms. Thereby, the law relinquished a certain proportion of the characteristics that had set it apart as a specific model of rights management and began to resemble more closely the average BC legislation. Both national and international motives prompted this double metamorphosis.

Subsequent to a typically programmatic introduction, emphasizing copyright's vocation to serve the construction of communist society, the 1951 law reserved a prominent role for moral rights. The interwar legislation had already highlighted moral rights as an important building block of copyright, but now they were given even greater prominence as a foundational component in the constitution of the copyright regime. Articles 3 and 4 dealt with the right of attribution, the right to preserve the integrity of a work, the right to control its uses and the right of disclosure. An equally prominent place was reserved for the enumeration of free uses, without authorial permission or remuneration. These involved in particular transformations between genres (such as the possibility to use existing works in order to create new independent ones, e.g., to depict pictorial works by sculptural means and vice versa), and the right to quote different works or excerpts in other media. Concerning specific types of transformations, such as the modification of a literary work into a drama or screenplay and vice versa, or the reproduction of works of literature, science and special news correspondents, the consent of the author was mandatory.

Statutory licences (art. 7) formed a second group of free uses, which, though not requiring authorial consent, nevertheless necessitated the payment of authors' fees, for example the use of artistic and photographic works for industrial products or the use of foreign literary texts by (home) composers. Works of drama, music, pantomime, choreography and cinematography, once issued and/or performed, could be further used without the author's consent but against the payment of fees. By contrast, the 1972 copyright law amendment restricted free uses and narrowed down the size of permissible content; here, only fractions of already published musical, literary and small format works could be used against fee payment, save for use by amateur groups, youth organizations and reading rooms.

The laws of the 1950s leaned on the Soviet model concerning the use of works in audiovisual media. Works for radio (art. 9), once published or broadcast, could be subsequently used without the author's consent and without remuneration. Works specially commissioned for radio were remunerated once. Both radio and television were obliged to mention the author's name in every broadcast. Adaptations of works of literature, drama and musical drama for broadcasting required the author's consent. Authors had to be notified in advance when works of drama, musical drama, choreographies and pantomimes were scheduled to be performed in their entirety. The 1972 amendment confirmed radio and television's prerogative to broadcast in unchanged form already published works of literature, arts and science without the author's approval, but now stipulated, in contradistinction to the earlier version of the copyright law, the payment of fees.

With respect to the carriers of copyright, there was a rebalancing of the nationality and territoriality principles. Interwar legislation had combined both principles, but had laid greater emphasis on nationality. It had stipulated the protection of "Bulgarian subjects/nationals/citizens" (*bălgarski podanici*) for works published in Bulgaria and abroad, as well as works of foreigners published in Bulgaria. Communist legislations (art. 10), on the contrary and in line with the Soviet school of thought, shifted the emphasis from nationality to territory, and protected all works that were found or were published on the territory of the Bulgarian Republic. Bulgarian citizens and their heirs also enjoyed copyright in Bulgarian territory for their works created and published in foreign states, independent of whether there was a reciprocal arrangement with the foreign state or not.

Continuing the tradition of the interwar legislation was the modelling of popular and folk art as commons (art. 14), and their free use for the creation of new works and compilations. Works created in the workplace and their use were a central concern of all communist legislations as a great majority of authors produced works in employment conditions. The various national legislations often followed different paths. Though broadly speaking, in Bulgaria, the author held copyright to his/her work, the employer had the right to use the work without the author's consent. The employer could use the work for scientific and other formal business purposes without remunerating the author, and could additionally disseminate the work, free of charge, among different services and sectors of the same institution. The employer was entitled to large-scale publishing only by paying a relevant remuneration to the author and could retain this right for two years. The same work could be published by another state institution upon agreement with the author, but only with the written permission of the authority or institution in whose service it was initially published.

Carriers of copyright in films also underwent a transformation, triggered both by processes of increasing specialization and professionalization equivalent to international trends, and by local processes of liberalization of film production and propertization trends among creators. In the initial 1951 law, the General Directorate of Cinematography held total copyright to all films produced by the directorate. The screenplay author and the film's composer maintained copyright over their individual contributions, but were excluded from claims to supplementary payments save the contractually agreed remuneration with the producing enterprise. The 1972 amendment terminated the directorate's monopoly and ascribed copyright to cinematographic and television films to the respective producing enterprise. It also significantly enlarged the circle of creators, with copyright entitlements to include, next to the screenplay author and the composer, also the director-producer, the chief operator, the production designer as well as all authors whose works made up the film's constituent parts. No category could raise claims to additional, separate remuneration apart from the contractually agreed fees. The producing enterprise could reuse excerpts from its own films without consulting or remunerating the authors. Use by other organizations, enterprises and private persons required authorial permission and remuneration.

The area in which the changing character of the copyright regime was most pronounced was the regulation of the term of protection and the distribution of copyrights p.m.a. In its initial revolutionary fervour, the 1951 law aimed at limiting, wherever possible, pretentions to property. This philosophy was reflected in a series of measures: limited rights for heirs, augmented prerogatives for the state, limited possibilities to pass copyrights to third persons via testamentary dispositions. Copyrights for radio, television and cinematography were initially held by public institutions, and only later were individual copyrights acknowledged. This attitude was relaxed in 1956, and eventually reversed in 1972. With almost complete certainty, the comeback of the author in the 1970s is to be credited to the assertiveness of the creative unions and coincided with a period of relaxation in cultural politics, characterized by the strategic rapprochement between the CP's general secretary, Todor Živkov, and the creative intelligentsia.

The 1951 law (art. 18) confirmed copyright for the duration of the author's lifetime. Post-mortem, copyrights were transferred to the author's heirs and lasted throughout the spouse's lifetime and the offspring's coming of age. Testamentary dispositions to the benefit of third persons were valid for a maximum of 10 years. After the lapse of the term of protection, and in cases of heirless authors, works were transferred to the benefit of the state.

The 1956 amendment brought small adjustments. Copyrights were assigned post-mortem in cascading sequence: to the author's parents for the duration of their lifetime, to the surviving spouse during their lifetime or until a subsequent marriage, to all others until adulthood or until the completion of education (but not later than 24 years of age), and in cases of work disability, for the period of incapacitation. After heirs passed away, the inherited copyrights were terminated. Testamentary dispositions were activated in accordance with the law of inheritance; their duration could not exceed 10 years.

The 1972 amendment brought some significant changes to the modality of copyright transfer. The term of duration was harmonized with BU standards for the first time and lasted for the author's lifetime plus 50 p.m.a. (similar to the practice concerning the arts in the interwar period). After death, copyrights passed to the author's descendants, spouse and parents, according to the law of inheritance. In cases of heirless authors or when heirs died before the end of the term of protection, copyright passed to the state for the term's duration. Testamentary dispositions became active according to the law of inheritance (i.e. the 10-year limit was dropped). Film copyright lasted for 50 years (previous duration 10 years), while copyright to works of applied arts, art photography, sound recordings, works (compilations, encyclopedias, journals etc.) published by scientific institutes, public and other organizations, radio and television programmes, as well as the copyrights of compilers of collections, encyclopedias and so on, lasted for 25 years for every edition, recording or programme, starting from 1 January of the year succeeding publication. Radio and television held copyrights to their broadcast programmes; copyright to the individual works included in radio and television belonged to the authors. Previous terms for the above-mentioned categories had varied between 10 and 15 years. In the initial 1951 law, analogue images had been protected for five years and photographic collections for 10 years, respectively. An additional novelty of the 1971 amendment was the possibility to include legal entities into the category of copyright owners.

Article 20 regulated the mode of rights transfer via specialized standardized contracts (publishing contract, screenplay contract, commissioning contract etc.), and the contract's duration could not exceed five years. The 1972 amendment abandoned the strongly dirigiste provisions included in articles 22 and 23, which were dropped altogether. The first had permitted the transfer of copyrights on the basis of suggestions by the Science, Arts and Culture Committee (KNIK) and concomitant decision by the Ministerial Council. The second had authorized, in cases of works of particular social and cultural importance, circumvention of authorial permission and allowed state and social organizations, authorized via the KNIK's president, to publish and use already published or performed works in an altered form.

Justifying the 1972 amendment, the legislator evoked customary motivations such as changes in the socioeconomic organization of society and technological change, but also international relations. It was judged that several regulations of the Bulgarian copyright law were too particularistic and contradicted both the Rome Act of the BU (being the latest revision which Bulgaria had ratified) and changes adopted in the Stockholm revision of the BC (1967), which Bulgaria had also endorsed. Such contradictions harmed Bulgaria's political authority and prestige in international relations and restricted the country's capacity to participate actively in international fora deliberating copyright. Moreover, they hampered the possibility to broaden cultural exchange with foreign countries. All these reasons taken together directly affected the country's capacity to partake in the ideological struggles that were fought internationally.[12]

The legislator acknowledged the strengthening of pecuniary rights as a measure intended to create a stimulating system of remuneration and eradicate authors' apparent indifference in the dissemination and broadcasting of their works. Accordingly, overkills were removed; contents of free uses were shortened (art. 8) and radio and television broadcasting (art. 9) was harmonized with article 11 of the BC (already published works could be published in unchanged form without the author's authorization but against payment of fees). The monopoly of Bulgarian cinematography was indirectly terminated by acknowledging the contribution of other organizations and enterprises in film production. In the same direction as the new civil code of the Soviet Union, the circle of copyright holders in film was broadened. The group of rightsholders was extended altogether to include legal entities, thus pre-empting the needs of socialist organizations in their exchange with other countries.

Changes in the modality of inheritance of copyrights were justified by pointing at the Bulgarian law's idiosyncratic regulations, which rendered it incompatible with any other legal regime. Bulgarian copyright provisions were not compatible with the local laws of inheritance, with international conventions or with other countries' civil law regulations. Particulars regarding the clarification of heirs made it practically impossible to apply the law in the regulation of relationships with foreign authors. By the same token, the works of renowned Bulgarian authors remained unprotected abroad. In order to avoid precarities and remove incongruencies, the BC's 50-year term of protection was adopted.

12 *Motivi kăm zakonoproekta za izmenenie i dopălnenie na zakona za avtorskoto pravo*, VI NS, III. Sesija, II. Zasedanie, April 27, 1972.

JUSAUTOR: The Bulgarian Copyright Agency

The first copyright agency, institutionalized as the Copyright Bureau, was created in the early 1950s and was initially integrated into KNIK (the Science, Arts and Culture Committee). Its functions and services were regulated by rule book. Remuneration rates for various categories and uses of works were based on KNIK's suggestions to the Ministerial Council. The bureau's institutional name was changed in the early 1960s to *Direkcija za zaštita na avtorskoto pravo* (Office for Copyright Protection),[13] and again in the early 1970s to *Agencija za avtorsko pravo* (Copyright Agency). The agency was affixed to the Press Committee (*Komitet za pečata*) and it functioned as a public government body (*obštestveno-dăržaven organ*) of the creative unions and relevant departments. It formed a self-financed, non-profit organization and held a monitoring monopoly over copyright application in Bulgaria. Its duties[14] were to: monitor the application of copyright law and remuneration tariffs regarding authors, performers and other forms of creative labor; conclude contracts and protect the rights of Bulgarian and foreign authors in the Bulgarian Republic, as well as the rights of Bulgarian authors abroad according to existing legislation and international treaties; conclude contracts for the use of Bulgarian authors' works by publishing houses, theatres, radio and television, cinematography, enterprises, institutions and organizations, and to collect and pay remuneration fees; monitor the use of Bulgarian works abroad, collect and pay rightsholders; conclude agreements with relevant CMOs abroad; collect fees for public broadcasting, recordings and any kind of performance by Bulgarian and foreign authors and ensure their remuneration according to established tariffs; endorse and approve licences for publishing and public performances. The Agencija was a central knot in the collection and redistribution of copyright revenues and a single point of contact for the registration and monitoring of the works used. It also functioned almost as a national (propaganda) agency for the international promotion of Bulgarian culture and its coordinated presence in foreign countries. It promoted, with the help of the Committee for Culture (*Komitet za kultura*), Bulgarian authors, composers and performers abroad, translated or printed their works and note sheets, and planned and concluded with Bulgarian authors authorization contracts for the transfer of their rights abroad. The agency's intermediation was mandatory; contracts could be issued only by the agency

13 See "Pravilnik za zadačite i ustroistvoto na Direkcijata za zaštita na avrotskoto pravo," *Izvestija na Prezidiuma na Narodnoto săbranie*, no. 69, August 28, 1962.

14 See "Pravilnik za zadačite i ustroistvoto na Agencijata za avtorsko pravo," *Dăržaven vestnik*, no. 18, March 2, 1973, amended no. 23, 1987.

or by decision and on conditions endorsed by the agency. As can be observed from the above, the agency was much more than a traditional CMO. Apart from fulfilling financial tasks, it was also a meeting point for all associations and unions involved in the organization, creation and dissemination of arts and sciences, whose representatives sat in the agency's general assembly and on various committees and could air their views, suggest improvements or make requests. Although the agency also served the individual author/creator, it was strategically oriented towards the promotion of national culture as a whole.

Creative Funds

Next to creative unions, creative funds were the second most important institution for authors/creators/performers in the communist organization of culture. More than the unions, which were often politically streamlined, the funds were the type of organization that actually allowed for extended forms of self-government, financial and administrative autonomy in practice. The first three funds were created in the 1950s ("Creative support for authors," "Creative support for painters" and "Creative support for composers, musicologists and concert artists"),[15] and were later extended to all unions: writers, composers, painters, film makers, journalists, artists, musicians, scientific workers, architects, translators as well as the Committee for Culture. The funds served to warrant the necessary material conditions for the creative process, to help popularize the best works, to stimulate creators morally and materially so that they would engage with competitions, prizes and so on. The resources could be used to arrange homes and clubs of creative labor; to organize economic activities, ateliers, groups and so on related to the goals and tasks of the creative funds; to maintain the creative unions, including their administration, publications, infrastructure, construction of their own buildings, use of other premises, creative houses and recovery homes; to maintain relations with foreign countries and artists; and, finally, to support needy writers and creators, their families and progeny.

The funds' wealth was assembled from the following resources: (1) 2% deductions from the gross remuneration of writers, performers and others, paid to members of the creative unions, foreign authors and performers; (2) payments by publishing houses and other organizations involved in publishing, consisting of 3% for

15 "Zakon za tvorčeskite fondove," *Dăržaven vestnik*, no. 27, April 3, 1973, amended twice: *Dăržaven vestnik*, no. 101, December 27, 1977, and no. 29, March 9, 1979.

original and 4% for already published works, assembled from the retail price of all works of literature, arts and science by Bulgarian and foreign authors; (3) payments by publishing houses and other organizations involved in publishing, consisting of 5% from the retail price of all works of literature, arts and science by Bulgarian and foreign authors of unprotected works or works already in the public domain published in Bulgaria; (4) 2% of the retail price of all gramophone discs and sound recordings destined for commercial use; (5) 0.2% by the state organization "Bălgarska kinematografija" on the gross income from the ticket sales for the screening of films across the whole country; (6) 5% by the film producing studios on fees for all kinds of screenplays, librettos, scenario plans and film texts; (7) 4% from gross box office revenue from all public drama, opera, operetta and puppet theatre performances; (8) 0.15% from investments on the value of architectural projects for any type of construction created by the designing organization; (9) income from business organizations, publishing houses, printing authorities, ateliers, galleries, shops, concerts, spectacles and other events and manifestations of the creative unions; (10) income from the funds' own properties and deposits; (11) donations and wills and other kinds of income. Finally, the Committee for Culture could release, upon request, additional resources to the various creative funds of the unions for the materialization of special events.

Next to the publishing contract, an instrument that substantially shaped the copyright regime was the system of remuneration based on maximum and minimum tariff fees. Rates of remuneration were periodically announced and amended via Ministerial Council decree (*postanovlenie*). They encompassed and regulated in a minutely detailed manner all possible processes and steps in the realization of a cultural product, from the composition of an opera to the design of its posters and the language editing of its programme booklet. Works and processes were categorized according to *genres* (drama, opera, concert, ballet, puppet show etc.), *categories of works* (translations, dictionaries, monographs etc.), *tasks/professions* (composer, conductor, director, choreographer, pianist accompanying a whole programme/half a programme/a play, concert soloist, orchestra soloist, artistic decoration etc.), *duration* (one act, short recitation, ballet as independent show, as part of an opera or an operetta etc.), *procedures* (recordings, broadcasting etc.) as well as *effort*, *degree of participation* and *number of editions*, and in their combination covered pretty much all possible aspects of creative labor. Naturally, categories and fee rates were not always neutral, and as can be expected, often reflected the hierarchies of the communist conception of culture and its validation of the "new cultured socialist person" as well as the priorities of communist ideology. Certain forms and genres, such as classical music and opera, were more highly esteemed and better remunerated than Estrada (i.e. popular/hit songs) or jazz music; treatises on Marxism-Leninism were *a priori* categorized as valuable. Without disregarding the ideological bias of the system, what is noteworthy about this structured form of remuneration is the way it demystifies the creative process, proposing alternatively a conception of cultural creativity in terms of (measurable) labor. Overall, it can be argued that regulations were favorable and accommodating for authors/creators, particularly in material terms.

Contextualizing the Propertization Trend of the 1970s

Increasing political and economic stability in the 1970s and the accompanying "honeymoon" period between Todor Živkov and the creative unions formed the background for the final copyright law revision. The de-Stalinization process of the early 1960s not only brought Živkov to power, but also signaled a change of policy towards the intelligentsia. In his efforts to get rid of the vestiges of his predecessor, Vălko Červenkov, and win the allegiance of Bulgarian intellectuals, Živkov relinquished the practice of delivering straightforward dictates and showed tolerance towards the intelligentsia's free thinking and democratization tendencies. This change of policy signified a parting of ways with bureaucratic rule in culture. Creative unions were granted greater autonomy and self-management and were simultaneously called to relinquish repressive practices towards alternative and/or critical voices.[16] While preparing public opinion for the removal of his rivals and his own ascendance to state power, Živkov sought to normalize his relationship with the creative world. Naturally, the boundaries set by Marxism-Leninism remained but they were significantly extended.[17] Ascending to power in 1962, Živkov made his political version of liberalization, known as the "April line," the new government dogma and a criterion for the social mobility of intellectuals towards the state's top echelons.[18] His plan included significant reforms in the economic sphere, the structure of cultural institutions and the financing of culture, with the purpose of achieving greater financial independence and self-sustainability of institutions and greater

16 Evgenija Kalinova, *Bălgarskata kultura i političeskijat imperativ 1944–1989* (Sofia: Paradigma, 2011), 216.

17 Kalinova, *Bălgarskata kultura*, 220.

18 Kalinova, *Bălgarskata kultura,* 232.

participation of society; the goal was no longer a dictatorship of the proletariat but a popular state.

In spite of the fact that both Khrushchev's downfall and the Prague Spring posed serious challenges to his position, Živkov was able to maintain power and adjusted his style of rule accordingly: between 1965 and 1966 he reduced pressure on intellectuals and relaxed party control in the cultural sphere; after 1968 he kept talented writers in his entourage and sought to control losses. With the consolidation of his regime, his rapprochement with Brezhnev and sustainable economic development, the succeeding decade of the 1970s represented a period of stability and peace. Moreover, intellectuals appeared to have drawn their lessons from the events of 1968 and realized the price it entailed.[19]

In the 1970s, Bulgarian intellectuals rarely contested power openly. By optimizing the instruments for enticing creators, the ruling political elite stimulated and rewarded the loyalty of the intelligentsia, from awarding high posts and bestowing generous prizes and titles to reserving large financial resources for cultural initiatives. Under conditions of détente in the relations between East and West and the fading of ideological confrontation, the political elite gained greater self-confidence, broadened the margins of what was permissible in the cultural sphere and showed greater tolerance towards creative pursuits. Several factors contributed to the new climate: Živkov's personal charm offensive; his strategy to purposefully socialize with intellectuals, particularly writers; his efforts to build personal relationships with them; his reluctance to favor a single group and instead take an all-inclusive and open approach; the policy of attracting broader creative milieus into the governance of culture; and last but not least, the activity of his daughter, Ljudmila Živkova, whose political career was predicated on cultural politics.

The 1970s brought the adoption of a new constitution (1971) and a change of official party doctrine, which proclaimed Bulgaria's entry into the phase of a "developed socialist society," in which the intelligentsia was beckoned to play a significant participatory role. Reforms encompassed the restructuring of cultural institutions and witnessed the rise of new party cadres, active in the field of culture, who boasted both a professional background and a more modern way of thinking; they were also personally indebted to Živkov for their careers. Arts and culture received significant material support, and through the construction of new theatres, cinemas, museums and so on a considerable expansion of their infrastructure.[20] Through Živkov's

19 Kalinova, *Bălgarskata kultura*, 293.

20 Kalinova, *Bălgarskata kultura*, 301.

personal intervention and/or consent, intellectuals were endowed with positions and functions, rising in the party and state hierarchy; the best represented within state authorities were the Union of Composers (35.36%) and the Union of Writers (8.23%), while the Union of Musicians (2.64%) and the Union of Artists (3.39%) exhibited the lowest participation rates. Social ascendance was no longer linked to party membership or participation in the antifascist struggle, as had been the case in the early years of the republic.[21] The distribution of prizes and material privileges flattered creators. Given that censorship had been officially abolished by the end of the 1950s, intellectuals were expected to anticipate party expectations and practice self-censorship.[22] All these aspects combined in a "carrot and stick" policy, and Živkov's strategy of winning over creators through a stable economy and political relaxation in international relations created the particular recipe for the symbiosis of the intelligentsia and political power in the 1970s.

Copyright in Communist Yugoslavia

Two major political experiences influenced the development of post-WWII Yugoslavia.[23] The first was the political failure and disintegration of the first Yugoslav state (1918–1944), the second the dispute and subsequent break with Stalin and the Cominform, in 1948. These two experiences—particularly the break with Stalin, which had been completely unpredicted—laid the foundations for the long-term policy orientation of the Yugoslav communists in the postwar period and had a decisive impact on their approach to state building and on their notion and organization of culture, which in turn both directly and indirectly influenced the development of copyright.

The first Yugoslav state was constructed after the First World War on the basis of a unitary nation state model. The identity project of "integral Yugoslavism" proclaimed the existence of a single nation, made up of three tribes, two languages and

21 Kalinova, *Bălgarskata kultura,* 333.

22 Kalinova, *Bălgarskata kultura,* 336.

23 Federal People's Republic of Yugoslavia – FNRJ (1945–1963) / Socialist Federal Republic of Yugoslavia SFRJ (1963–1992). The text for this section has already been published in a more extensive and slightly modified form. See Augusta Dimou, "From State Governance to Self-Management: Culture and Intellectual Property Rights in Communist Yugoslavia," in *Expanding Intellectual Property: Copyrights and Patents in Twentieth-Century Europe and Beyond*, eds. Hannes Siegrist and Augusta Dimou (Budapest: CEU Press, 2017), 173–203.

three religions. This model was unsuccessful for several reasons, and even the establishment of the royal dictatorship in 1929 and its targeted efforts to implement the Yugoslav national idea from above, or at least to control the conflicting centrifugal dynamics of interethnic relations, failed to reinforce integral Yugoslavism as the state ideology. Several lessons were learned from this failure with respect to the form of political organization, the regulation of interethnic relations and the role and organization of culture. Due to their negative interwar experiences, the communists abandoned the idea of an amalgamation of all ethnicities into a supranational nation. The attitude of the Yugoslav communists towards the national question was neither linear nor unitary but it can be broadly argued that the second Yugoslav state was founded upon the recognition of existing differences. The new state was constructed on a federative basis and the communists even officially recognized ethnic groups and nationalities that had not enjoyed such status in the first Yugoslav state, such as the Macedonians, Albanians and Bosnian Muslims. All groups enjoyed equal rights and every group enjoyed the right to self-determination; the new federalism therefore allowed the potential institutionalization of multiple identities and loyalties. Admittedly, the interpretations of this concept varied widely and led to fluctuations in the path towards greater or lesser centralization and/or decentralization, a circumstance that recast political and socioeconomic problems with ethnic divisions. Moreover, according to socialist doctrine, there was little need to repress national identities, which were only a transient stage on the road to socialism. With time they would inevitably wither away, just as the state was expected to wither away as well. Ideology was therefore the fulcrum and impetus of identity construction in the second Yugoslavia.

The second formative experience in the postwar period was the break of the Yugoslav communists with Stalin and the Cominform in spring/summer 1948. With the expulsion of Yugoslavia from the international association of socialist states in 1948, the country became politically isolated. Initially, in an unsuccessful attempt to appease Moscow, the Yugoslav communists reinforced ideological orthodoxy but soon modified their course, opting for a comprehensive reorientation in all spheres of life, ranging from the contents of socialist doctrine and the social and economic model of the state to the country's cultural orientation and its broader geopolitical alignment. The break with the wider communist world led to a search for alternatives and the Yugoslav system understood itself explicitly to be a counter project to the Soviet Union. Yugoslavia drew its legitimacy and internal cohesion from the claim to be more democratic than the USSR, and moreover from its ability to withstand the latter's political pressure. In their search for alternatives, the Yugoslavs turned once more to the classics of Marxism and to their own indigenous revolutionary tradition: a popular revolution and war of liberation during WWII. Without doubt, Yugoslavia's reorientation was an attempt to turn calamity into virtue. The Yugoslav blueprint was therefore a fundamental critic of Soviet etatism and demanded that the means of production be controlled directly by the people, a concept that was to become the cornerstone of the Yugoslav brand of socialism, the system of *self-management*.[24] Socialist self-management thus developed gradually from the 1950s and reached its pinnacle in the late 1970s when it was legally codified and anchored in the Yugoslav constitution. The programme of self-management championed de-bureaucratization through the establishment of elective workers' councils, decentralization of the administration, politics, fiscal policy and culture, as well as the democratization of all spheres of life. Aimed at involving as great a percentage of the population in economic and social processes as possible, the intention of the new policy was to further legitimize the regime. As a result, the state claimed for itself the role of coordinator rather than that of the leading planner.[25]

Renegotiating Key Notions of Socialism

The above-mentioned developments and the broader ideological reorientation of the Yugoslavs away from Stalinism significantly affected two key concepts of socialist polity. The first was related to a particular understanding of the concept of "pluralism" and the representation of interests in socialist society; the second touched upon the very heart of socialist doctrine and was related to the notion of property.

24 The system of self-management was an issue of debate during the existence of the Yugoslav state and remains so in the scholarship dealing with ex-Yugoslavia. Several aspects are up for debate, from its efficiency to its impact and its actual function. There are several interesting treatises on the topic; see here exemplarily Susan L. Woodward, *Socialist Unemployment: The Political Economy of Yugoslavia, 1949–1990* (Princeton, NJ: Princeton University Press, 1995); Vladimir Unkovski-Korica, *The Economic Struggle for Power in Tito's Yugoslavia: From WWII to Non-Alignment* (London: I. B. Tauris, 2016); Milica Uvalić, *The Rise and Fall of Market Socialism in Yugoslavia*, Special Report (Berlin: Dialogue of Civilizations Research Institute, 2018). For an overview and discussion of the historiography on self-management, see Sabine Rutar, "Betriebliche Selbstverwaltung zwischen den Blöcken – und danach? Das Jugoslawische Modell in Rückschau und Perspektive," *Südost-Forschungen* 75 (2016): 118–35.

25 Marie-Janine Calic, *Geschichte Jugoslawiens im 20. Jahrhundert* (Bundeszentrale für politische Bildung, vol. 1093) (Munich: Beck, 2010), 192. For an overarching qualification of Yugoslav socialism with reference to existing hermeneutical models on the nature of communist rule, see Wolfgang Höpken, "'Durchherrschte Freiheit': Wie 'autoritär' (oder wie 'liberal') war Titos Jugoslawien?" in *Jugoslawien in den 1960er Jahren: Auf dem Weg zu einem (a)normalen Staat?*, eds. Hannes Grandits and Holm Sundhaussen (Wiesbaden: Harrassowitz, 2013), 39–65.

The development of "pluralist socialism" was the historical and theoretical negation of Stalinism.[26] In the case of Yugoslavia, this negation took place earlier (in 1948) than the general de-Stalinization wave that swept through the rest of communist Europe between 1953 and 1963/4. The initial point of reflection in the Yugoslav discussion on pluralism was the relationship between individual and societal interests in socialism. While initially fully espousing ideological orthodoxy regarding the automatic abolition of contradictions between capital and labor in socialism, after a series of external events such as the Cominform conflict and internal quandaries such as the failure of collectivization (it was revoked in 1952) and the first industrial strikes (in Trbovlje in 1958), Yugoslav communists were forced to rethink the representation of interests.

Self-management provided in fact an apposite platform through which to renegotiate the issue of interests; in contrast to Soviet socialism, where it was enforced through repressive state action, the harmonization of individual and societal interests in socialist self-management would ultimately materialize through the producers' self-managing interests. In addition, the Yugoslav communists were forced to accept that antagonistic interests were not only a "privilege" of capitalism but that they had their share in socialist society as well. At the same time, Yugoslav pluralism sought to distance itself from Western theories of pluralism. For this reason, it claimed distinction as much from the Western type of party pluralism as from the one-party system type. Instead of the pluralism of parties, Yugoslav doctrine promulgated the pluralism of political subjects.[27] The "pluralism of political subjects" was brought to bear in the existing societal organizations, unions and associations. In contrast to the methods practiced by pressure groups in bourgeois democracies, political subjects within socialism had no need to exercise pressure upon the state. Rather, they could express their interests through the existing participatory channels of the self-managing organizations in enterprises and society in general, which was an integral part of self-management.[28]

26 Wolfgang Höpken, *Sozialismus und Pluralismus in Jugoslawien* (Untersuchungen zur Gegenwartskunde Südosteuropas, vol. 22) (Munich: Oldenbourg, 1984), 42.

27 Höpken, *Sozialismus und Pluralismus*, 59.

28 Höpken, *Sozialismus und Pluralismus*, 63. On the representation of interest groups in communist Yugoslavia, see also Jovan Djordjevic, "Interest Groups and the Political System of Yugoslavia," in *Interest Groups in Four Continents*, ed. Henry W. Ehrmann (Ann Arbor: University of Pittsburgh Press, 1960), 197–228. Naturally in practice things were unquestionably more complicated. Without doubt, mass organizations were also partially instrumentalized by politics, and the newest research on the practice of self-management in factories has shown that managers had much greater authority and power than workers when it came to taking crucial decisions in enterprises.

The second notion particular to the Yugoslav interpretation of Marxism was the concept of "social property" (*društvena svojina*). The concept's most distinguishing feature was the fact that social property had no owner. As a concept, it eluded classification along traditional categories of ownership such as private, collective or state property; nobody—not the individual, the state or an institution—held the right of ownership. Rights to manage social property originated from labor and the social character of productive relations. The collective hence had the right to take decisions but possessed no ownership rights over the property. Society was consequently the "owner" of social property but not its legal proprietor. "Social property" was not a legal concept in the proper sense;[29] the fundamental right emanating from social property was the "right of use." It represented therefore a new civil law right, which was the legal expression of social property.[30]

Similar to the concept of "pluralism," social property was defined *ex negativo*; it was conceptualized as being profoundly different both from private property and from socialist state property. With respect to cultural production, the bourgeois concept of private property had only helped to commoditize works of literature. The author's exclusive right to determine the fate of his/her work had only a formal character, since in essence the author was transformed into the publisher's wage laborer. Yugoslav legal scholars like Svojslav Spaic negated the identification of copyright with private property and questioned its intellectual origins in the work of John Locke and his conceptual pooling of work and property. Though Locke's argument had been progressive at the time, due to the fact that it sought to emancipate the author, it became ineffectual thereafter. The Yugoslavs proposed rather a different conception, founded upon Proudhon's "Les majorats littéraires" (1868), which claimed from the start an essential incompatibility between material and immaterial property. While the material world was predestined for appropriation, the

29 Views differ among Yugoslav academics as to how to interpret "social property" and whether it represented a social convention or a legal category. See UN-Habitat, *Housing and Property Rights in Bosnia and Herzegovina, Croatia and Serbia and Montenegro* (Nairobi: UN-Habitat, 2005), 17. There, footnote 4 explains that most views regarding the nature of social property "were based on the premise that social ownership was a new socioeconomic category and tenure system, which would neither be fully explained nor grasped by traditional civil law criteria. Many academics agreed that social ownership is an ideological, philosophical, but also (pseudo-)legal category, which cannot be understood as entailing an unlimited right over real property." The definition and formal introduction of "social property" in the 1963 constitution is also abstruse; there it states that "nobody has the ownership right over social production means—nobody meaning neither social-political communities, associated labor organizations nor single workers—and nobody can under any legal ownership title claim the product of the 'social work,' nor operate, nor dispose of social production forces, nor arbitrarily determine the conditions of distribution." Höpken, *Sozialismus und Pluralismus*, 17.

30 Vojislav Spaić, *Društvena svojina i autorsko pravo* (Belgrade: Naučno delo, 1965), 10.

world of ideas was fundamentally dissimilar. Ideas were useful when they expanded and acquired universal validity. Such a condition of non-rivalry *a priori* disqualified the notion of property; the author had a right to remuneration. It was in fact the heretical character of Yugoslav communism that allowed references to heretical leftist, anarchist thinkers such as Proudhon. Nowhere else in Eastern Europe was an intellectual pedigree for the conception of copyright traced back to him, though he certainly prompted one of the most forceful debates on the nature of intellectual property in the late nineteenth century. He was simply too much of a provocation for orthodox Marxism.

The notion of social property permitted the balancing act and the merging of individual and social interests, as social property was considered the basis of copyright. Copyright in conditions where social property prevailed differed from that in conditions of state property (of the Soviet type), where the interests of the socialist state were given priority and the author was deprived of comprehensive protection. It was because social property precluded the possibility of exploitation that it guaranteed—in an ideational manner—the producers' direct control over the means of production.

Precarious Balancing between Market and Ideology

The introduction of self-management brought changes to the entire state structure, from the political system to the administration and particularly in the economic sphere. Pointedly labelled a "market-planned economy,"[31] the Yugoslav economic system combined elements of Marxist socialism with aspects of free enterprise. From the 1950s onwards, the Yugoslav communists progressively introduced a series of reforms aimed at the liberalization and decentralization of the economy and a greater reliance on market mechanisms, a process that was pursued more rigorously and in a more concerted manner towards the end of the 1960s. Although the Yugoslav system was not without its flaws and imbalances, it managed to successfully combine over a longer period of time such opposing elements as workers' self-management with the extensive use of market mechanisms and the monopoly power of the League of Communists.

---

31 Svetozar Pejovich, *The Market-Planned Economy of Yugoslavia* (Minneapolis: University of Minnesota Press, 1966).

Until the break with the Cominform, Yugoslav communists pursued a system of nationalization, rigorous economic planning and management. With the subsequent introduction of self-management, many political and economic decisions were decentralized from the federal government to the six individual republics, two autonomous provinces, and multiple communes and enterprises in order to accommodate the diverse needs and aspirations of the country's various nationalities. The concept of self-management became the cornerstone of the country's socioeconomic and political system and was later extended to other institutions, public and social areas. The Yugoslav communists questioned the central directing role of the state, and reinterpreted Marxist classics in such a way that the withering away of the state was not only possible but was to be encouraged in the course of constructing socialist modernity.[32]

The 1950s saw the creation of the communal system, which established the commune as the country's primary political unit and gave them the power to legislate on all matters other than those reserved for the federal and republican government levels. The reforms of the 1960s went a step further and aimed at bringing together an economic mechanism combining administrative and market instruments and a fully-fledged labor-managed economy. The constitution of 1963 strengthened self-management and the reforms introduced between 1966 and 1970 pursued long-term goals, such as an increase in economic efficiency by relying more on market mechanisms, a reform of the price system, a revision of growth and investment policies, the liberalization of foreign trade and the improvement of the international competitiveness of the country. Since the early 1970s, the relationship between the economic organizations of productive (factories etc.) and non-productive (culture, education etc.) spheres came to be governed by the principle of free exchange of work, according to which production units allocated part of their income to the respective units of non-productive sectors (like culture) in return for the latter's services. The last constitution of socialist Yugoslavia in 1974 gave the federal republics almost unlimited economic and political sovereignty.

As in the case of economic development, in the domain of culture the state also abandoned a unitary approach but was faced with a demanding dual task; while it saw the need to liberalize, it had at the same time to ensure that discrepancies and divisions in economic, social and cultural development between the different republics and regions were progressively bridged. Decentralization in Yugoslavia was conditioned by its multinational population structure, which was the touchstone for the

[32] See Dejan Jović, *Jugoslavia: A State that Withered Away* (West Lafayette: Purdue University Press, 2009).

survival of the Yugoslav experiment. As a consequence, the identity model adopted aimed at equality in representation and was implemented through administrative measures such as the implementation of a rota system, representation quotas and so on. The communists institutionalized a demanding model of cultural pluralism. Cultural and national diversity was mirrored in the federal constitution but also in the various constitutions of the republics and provinces, which guaranteed every nation and nationality[33] the right to free development and the protection of their particular national and cultural identities.

As a result, a thorough decentralization of culture took place parallel to the development of self-management. Every nation and nationality could set its own priorities and settle its own cultural issues within its political and administrative unit (republic, province or community). There existed no federal ministry of culture with the competence to override local decisions. The only authorities at federal level were those with a coordinating function.[34] Decentralization touched all aspects of cultural organization; for example, every republic had its own writers' union, which sent representatives to the countrywide/federal congresses of the national writers' association of Yugoslavia. The individual federal associations were largely autonomous in their policies. At the same time, the creative unions were organized at the federal level according to artistic fields (the union of composers, writers, painters, performers, interpreters etc.). The licensing agencies were also organized at the level of the republics and functioned as local, autonomous branches of the federal licensing agency. Their revenues were also administered locally. Every republic had its own, autonomous, academy of sciences, ministry of culture and education and so on. In other words, all federal-level institutions were mirrored at the political and administrative levels.

Culture was sponsored through a complex, mixed parity financing system, consisting of a contingent from the income of the labor organizations (enterprises, factories etc.), set aside for cultural activities, the revenue earned by the cultural institutions themselves (theatres, opera etc.) as well as subsidies from the communities. The financing system was based on pooling labor and the working funds of the labor and cultural organizations. The funding of cultural institutions and policy changed after 1951. Cultural institutions were expected to function as enterprises and all state

33 The Socialist Federal Republic of Yugoslavia consisted of "nations" (*narodi*) and "nationalities" (*narodnosti*). Officially, there were six nations (Serbs, Croats, Slovenes, Macedonians, Montenegrins and Muslims) and 18 nationalities (Bulgarians, Albanians, Slovaks etc.).

34 Stevan Majstorović, *Cultural Policy in Yugoslavia: Self-Management and Culture* (Studies and Documents on Cultural Policies) (Paris: UNESCO, 1980), 32–33.

financing was suspended (or was kept to a minimum). All personnel appointments in cultural institutions were financed by the institutions themselves and the salary system was replaced by an allotment system based on effectiveness and quality.

The Yugoslav system became partially caught up in the contradictions of its own different and intricate roles; on the one hand was the desire to integrate market mechanisms in the economy, and on the other the promise to guarantee comprehensive and uniform development for the whole country. National income, however, was allocated according to market mechanisms and they tended to favor the stronger and wealthier nationalities and republics in comparison to the weaker ones. Economic inequality constantly undermined and jeopardized the political project of Yugoslav communism (equality for all), which in turn represented a danger for Yugoslavia's continued existence as a multinational state. This circumstance created a tension between the objectives of culture (safeguarding individual identity and distinctness) and the market, since the appropriate representation of all cultural groups was not necessarily cost-effective (rather the contrary) but was politically indispensable.

The expenditure for publishing and translations provides a good example. It is important to note at this point that Yugoslavia had a provision ensuring the equality of all languages in the federation.[35] For multiethnic regions such as Vojvodina, where the administration was bilingual or even trilingual, and radio and television were broadcast in five languages, the issue of translations was crucial for maintaining equilibrium in cultural politics. In practice, it meant that all important literary and scholarly works had to be translated into at least one local language, which generally proved unprofitable as such insignificant numbers were involved in each edition in a regional or minority language. For example, the production of a book in Slovak (there were approximately 84,000 Slovaks in Vojvodina) was 20 times more expensive than the production of a book in Serbo-Croat (spoken by around 15 million people). The same applied for the production of books in Bulgarian, Romanian or Ruthenian. Editions in those languages were exceedingly small (approximately 500 copies). Even editions in Macedonian or Slovene (1.2 and 1.6 million respectively) were not necessarily profitable. The cost of book production in those languages was three to five times higher than for equivalent publications in Serbo-Croat.[36] The

[35] On the language policy and politics of the Yugoslav state, see Ksenija Cvetković-Sander, *Sprachpolitik und nationale Identität im sozialistischen Jugoslawien (1945–1991): Serbokroatisch, Albanisch, Makedonisch und Slowenisch* (Balkanologische Veröffentlichungen, vol. 50) (Wiesbaden: Harrassowitz, 2011).

[36] Majstorović, *Cultural Policy in Yugoslavia*, 59.

same asymmetries prevailed in the production of newspapers and journals in the various different languages.[37] These were some of the reasons that dictated the rationale that culture should not be left solely to the workings of the market and resulted in the institutionalization of a common fund to finance the cultural development of smaller nationalities.

In addition, in the field of culture the disparities between the goals of a socialist society and the aims of the market led to clashes during the implementation of the self-management system. The self-managing organizations contributed to a rapprochement between cultural institutions and society, which in turn transformed organizations and enabled the implementation of new, more developed and more successful working methods; yet this development resulted in institutions being motivated more by commercial than by ideological and cultural motives, which consequently jeopardized the political project of the communists.[38]

Finally, the break with the Soviet Union brought far-reaching changes in the realm of cultural policy: abandonment of socialist realism, freedom of creation, changes in the curricula and teaching content, availability of literature in a variety of foreign languages, pluralism in literary and art movements, cooperation and communication with the world and an openness to the West. The Communist Party had to acknowledge that it was not an uncontested authority in ideological and intellectual questions. It even changed its name from the Communist Party to the League of Communists of Yugoslavia, pointing at the democratization within its ranks but also at the political separation between party and state. It was a tightrope walk nevertheless; the party abandoned the cultural sector largely to the creative artists themselves but did not give up entirely the claim to be the ultimate authority in artistic and cultural life. On the one hand, it claimed the right to set the norms for artistic creation, and on the other, it provided space for artists themselves to participate in the standardization of the same norms. Liberalism in culture was accepted and restricted at the same time. Avant-garde movements and all Western schools of thought were tolerated, unless they touched a nerve within the regime, that is, if they questioned the superiority of the Yugoslav system and its leaders.[39] The Yugoslav Communist Party, in common with other communist parties, initiated modernization processes, which at the same time it felt compelled to control.

---

37 Majstorović, *Cultural Policy in Yugoslavia*, 78.

38 A good analysis of popular culture in Yugoslavia is offered by Zoran Janjetović, *Od "Internatiocionale" do komerciajale: Popularna kultura u Jugoslaviji, 1945–1991* (Belgrade: Altera, 2011).

39 Predrag Marković, *Beograd između istoka i zapada 1948–1965* (Belgrade: Novinsko-izdavačka ustanovka Službeni list SRJ, 1996), 524.

Yugoslav Copyright Legislation: From State Governance to Self-Management to Liberal Propertization

The subsequent copyright legislations passed in Yugoslavia at roughly 10-year intervals (1946, 1957, 1968, 1978)[40] reflect in many ways the socioeconomic, cultural and political developments in the country but also its broader hybrid geopolitical position in the world between East and West. A series of important internal developments such as the introduction and maturation of self-management and the greater federalization of the country were directly reflected in the change of roles and competences between different institutions, organizations and state levels. The Yugoslav copyright legislation also reflects its search for an intermediate path between East and West.

There were certain constant parameters in the diachronic development of copyright between the first and second Yugoslavia. The most salient feature concerned the mode and fate of translation rights. As had been the case with other multinational state formations such as the East European continental empires and later the Soviet Union, the right to translation proved to be one of, if not the most, significant testing grounds for the participation in, or opting out of, international organizations. The first Yugoslavia signed the Rome revision (1928) of the Berne Convention in 1931, albeit with reservations concerning the translation of foreign works (a book could be translated into the Yugoslav languages 10 years after its initial publication even without the author's authorization). The reservations were inscribed into Yugoslav copyright law (1929) and this tradition was taken over intact from the communist legislators; in fact, similar provisions were used to regulate inter-Yugoslav relationships and translation rights between the different Yugoslav languages.

Communist Yugoslav copyright legislation showed a clear tendency towards liberalization over the decades. Language pertaining to property was, by and large, initially absent; however, it picked up from the late 1960s onwards (laws of 1968 and 1978). Starting in the 1950s there was a steady weakening of state and federal competencies, while the author (propertization through devolution of competences) and decentralization (competencies at the level of the republics and regions) were overall significantly strengthened. There was a tendency (mirrored throughout society) to independently regulate labor relations and the distribution of duties and

40 See Slavica Krneta, "Zur Entwicklung des Urheberrechts in Jugoslawien," *GRURInt.* 11 (1981): 663–69.

competencies between the various levels and sectors of society (unions, labor organizations, cultural authorities, publishers etc.), through self-management agreements (e.g. the conditions and standards for remuneration of radio broadcasts). Finally, similar to other socialist countries, there was also an intention (laws of 1968 and 1978) to recognize the social usefulness of works and thus incorporate evaluation criteria concerning the same in the drafting of authors' agreements.

The new communist state that was created in 1943 stood for a new social and economic order and the copyright law passed on May 25, 1946 reflected precisely this intention.[41] The regime purposely stressed the discontinuity between the old and the new state, and for this reason, in the initial postwar years, Yugoslavia ceased being a member of the Berne Union, although there was no official rupture in international relations. The new copyright law was drafted in the midst of the nationalization process and naturally reflected this condition by reserving a prominent role for the state. The overall character of the 1946 law was prescriptive and through a series of restrictive measures incapacitated the author in several respects. It envisioned strengthening the state as the ultimate proprietor of all artistic works and therefore institutionalized a *domain public payant* in article 11, whereby at the end of the term of copyright all rights returned to the state. In essence, it eradicated the possibility of the public domain, ensuring that after the death of the author and his heirs all rights were recouped by the state. The use of artistic works already in the *domain public payant* was impossible without state authorization and the payment of fees; the law even failed to stipulate a maximum duration of protection p.m.a. (it was simply not mentioned, apart from provisions regarding heirs' rights, that is, until the death of the spouse or the youngest offspring's 25th birthday, whichever was sooner/later). In the case of folklore, the state was in fact the prime copyright owner. The law provided for a long list of free uses for the purposes of education, press use and so on. In cases where the state was the direct copyright owner, 50% of the revenue was used to finance the national arts and sciences and the remainder was allotted to the creative unions to support and compensate artists. A Yugoslav citizen could publish an original work for the first time abroad only if he had previously offered the work to a Yugoslav publisher and the manuscript had been rejected. In any other case, the author lost all rights and could potentially be prosecuted (art. 24). Generally speaking, the author's consent was necessary for the reproduction of his/her works. It was nevertheless possible to override the author and perform already published dramatic, musical and other works without the author's permission. Heirs could not

41 *Službeni list Federativne Narodne Republike Jugoslavije*, no. 45, June 4, 1946, 518–21.

prohibit the publication or performance of a literary, artistic or scientific oeuvre but retained, in the same vein as the author, the right to compensation.

The passage from state property to social property in the 1950s instigated a revision of the copyright law. The conception of a society where free-willed workers self-managed their labor relations did not fit well with the image of the disadvantaged author. In the sphere of production, changes had already been legislated through the 1950 law on the management of state enterprises, which transferred the administration of public enterprises to the workers' collectives. Moreover, on June 23, 1951, Yugoslavia ratified the Berne Convention and the country's existing copyright law now came into conflict with its international obligations. Fear of the application of *iure conventionis*,[42] and the fact that Yugoslavia might be overwhelmed by future developments, propelled the country into action. The copyright law of July 10, 1957[43] reversed several provisions made in the previous law. The *domain public payant* was dropped and the state abrogated its copyrights; the public domain was reinstalled. Popular art could be used freely against a contribution to the Fund for the Development of Artistic Activities. The term of protection was set at 50 years p.m.a. and the new law placed an emphasis on moral rights, which could now be passed on to heirs and appropriate artists' associations. The transfer of copyrights was free. In cases of heirless authors, copyrights were transformed into social property and the community in whose territory the author had died became the new rightsholder. The greatest influence of the self-managing philosophy and practice was reflected in the autonomy and self-administration accorded to the creative unions. Authors' associations became entitled to administer copyrights and royalty payments within their artistic field. They could exercise the same function concerning the rights of Yugoslav citizens living abroad and they were even entitled to create special institutions, which could function as licensing agencies. Authorial permission became mandatory for the reproduction of works, and the amount of works available for free use was reduced from one-third of the total to one-quarter. Authors were no longer penalized for organizing the inaugural publication of an original work abroad; in fact, under the new law the author was not even obliged to offer it to a Yugoslav publisher in the first place.

Developments within Yugoslavia and abroad in the 1960s prompted the next legal adjustment. The revision of the Berne Convention through the Stockholm diplomatic conference of 1967 was heavily supported by the Yugoslavs, who were

42 The application of *iure conventionis* refers to the possibility that the law stipulated by the Berne Convention (because it is more rigorous and/or comprehensive) might be able to override national legislation.

43 *Zakon o autorskom pravu* (Belgrade, 1957), 1–25.

active participants in its demanding negotiations. Furthermore, Yugoslavia ratified the UNESCO-sponsored Universal Copyright Convention (UCC) in 1966, which, due to less stringent admission standards than the Berne Convention, was more attractive for developing and socialist states. Yugoslavia then brought its legislation in line with the stipulations of this convention as well. Self-management was broadened to include additional spheres of administrative, social and cultural life. Finally, the moral and material protection of authors was inscribed in the new 1963 Yugoslav constitution (art. 45). The law of July 29, 1968[44] addressed, in particular, copyright for cinematographic works and the relationships between the various creative artists involved in film production; it dedicated for the first time a special section to publishing contracts and expounded in greater detail on works for hire and on commission. The 1968 law reinstalled—upon the insistence of the creative unions—the *domain public payant*, not in the conventional sense as a term of protection but as a special tax for the right to use works whose copyright had expired, the proceeds of which were for the benefit of the community. Concerning the publishing contract, the Yugoslav legislators found a solution that lay somewhere between the Anglo-Saxon and the East European models. Whereas in the case of the former, the author–publisher relationship was regulated by a free contract based on the general framework provided by contract law, in the case of the latter, the contracting parties used standard form contracts for different types and categories of works. The Yugoslav approach was a compromise between the two. The new law provided the binding framework for all author agreements, while all specific provisions in contracts were regulated by free agreements. Civil law regulations could be additionally applied to this arrangement.[45] Membership of the UCC added one more option to the existing translating alternatives; the use of statutory licenses on the basis of article 5 of the UCC.

Copyright law in socialist Yugoslavia was amended for the last time in 1978.[46] The new 1974 constitution had brought the greatest decentralization of competences from the federal level to the individual republics and regions and it proved necessary to adjust copyright law in line with the new realities. The 1978 copyright law can be rightfully regarded as the culmination of de-etatization, decentralization and author-centered propertization in the long modification processes of the Yugoslav copyright regimes ever since the mid-1940s. The new law brought into play for

44 *Službeni list Socialističke Federativne Republike Jugoslavije*, no. 30, July 24, 1968, 597–606.

45 Vojislav Spaić, "Savremena zaštita autorskog prava u svijetu i kod nas," in *Autorsko pravo i izdavači* (Belgrade: GRO Prosveta, 1984), 38.

46 *Zakon o autorskom pravu* (Zagreb, 1978), 1–51. See also Miodrag Janjić, "La nouvelle loi Yougoslav sur le droit d'auteur," *Yugoslav Law* 1 (1979): 49–57.

the first time the notion of "exclusive rights" and also introduced *droit de suite* as a distinctive property right, authorizing the author to demand supplementary payments when profits from resales of his work far exceeded the original payment received (art. 58). Remuneration rates for public broadcasting were decided through self-management agreements on equal terms between the authors' unions, the organizations of associated labor for radio and television, the Confederation of Trade Unions and the Socialist Alliance of Working People. A long list of provisions devolved authority from the federal level to the republics and regions. The federal state merely regulated copyright; all other competences were entrusted to intermediary levels. Licensing agreements for translation rights commensurate with the terms of the UCC were now also accorded to the regions and were further regulated by regional statutes (art. 45, 46). Remuneration for the staging and exhibition of literature, modern and folk art was regulated by republican and regional guidelines. The rights of heirs were regulated according to the respective republican and regional inheritance laws. The new law delegated the protection of portraits, photographs, diaries, letters and other personal belongings to the republican and regional levels. The legal regulation of publishing activities was relegated to the republics and regions. Although the federal copyright law functioned as the encompassing framework for copyright protection, specific competencies were still regulated by separate copyright rule books in the various republics. The republics determined how "free works were managed," whether and how dues were to be paid and for which purposes they would be used. Standards and benchmarks for fees and remuneration were settled though self-management agreements and the authors could act as advisors to the publishing houses' executive boards or belong to the publishers' self-management organizations or even participate in self-management meetings on an equal basis. Authors' fees were regulated on a sliding scale through the contract but their total remuneration was agreed freely between the author and the publisher. In practice, authors could communicate freely with foreign publishers and negotiate contracts on their own or through their unions; they did not need to go through the central licensing agency, barring the transfer of foreign currency.

As already mentioned, copyright development in Yugoslavia aimed to find an equilibrium between the Eastern and the Western experience. The features that brought it closer to a socialist conception of copyright were the greater flexibility conceded to various forms of free use as well as the retention of statutory licences, usually, but not always, including remuneration for artists and their heirs. Reproduction rights for radio, television and the press were often subsumed under forms of free use, a model that was most consequentially developed and followed by the

Soviet Union and was prevalent in one form or another in most communist countries of Eastern Europe. A second distinctive feature of socialist copyright were the short terms of contracts (on average four years); when a contract expired, a new one was usually drafted instead of the old one being renewed or extended. Quite distinct for socialist countries, and in contrast to Western copyright, was the particular attention paid to the regulation of works for hire and works resulting from an employment relationship. The law sought an accommodation between employer (labor organization) and the creator, particularly considering the interests of the creator. In Yugoslavia, the employer (organization) received an exclusive exploitation right of such works for a period of five years only, and even within that time span the creator/employee had a right to adequate remuneration according to the stipulations of the self-management agreement.

As experienced also in the case of Bulgaria in the 1970s, the trend towards greater liberalization of the home copyright regime, either for local reasons (i.e. giving in to pressure from local interest groups) or triggered through international motives (i.e. greater adjustment and harmonization with the BU regime), almost automatically resulted in a process encouraging propertization, which restricted the space of free uses and the public domain.

An additional development, starting from the 1980s, was the effort to regulate labor relations for the ever-growing number of freelancers in culture with the intention to equalize the socioeconomic standing of independent cultural workers with that of full-time cultural employees in socialist art institutions.[47] To this purpose, the Law on Independent Artistic Performance and Other Cultural Activities[48] was promulgated in 1982, which created a new category of cultural worker, the independent self-employed worker in the field of culture. The purpose of the law was to legalize and regulate the option for artists to function as "free enterprises" in the framework of the socialist market, whereby artists became contractors of the cultural community in exchange for providing services to cultural users. Nevertheless, artists remained integrated in the state welfare regime as their welfare provisions were financed and paid via social contract between independent cultural workers and the cultural community. One of the law's main objectives was to reduce

---

47 Katja Praznik, "Autonomy or Disavowal of Socioeconomic Context: The Case for Law on Independent Cultural Workers in Slovenia," *Historical Materialism* 26, no. 1 (2018): 103–135; see also idem, "Wages For and Against Art Work: On Economy, Autonomy, and the Future of Artistic Labour," *Reshape*, December 8, 2020, https://reshape.network/article/wages-for-and-against-art-work-on-economy-autonomy-and-the-future-of-artistic-labour; idem, *Art Work, Invisible Labour and the Legacy of Yugoslav Socialism* (Toronto: Toronto University Press, 2021).

48 *Zakon o samostalnom obavljanju umetničke ili druge delatnosti u oblasti kulture.*

financial pressure on the government to fund permanent full-time employment in public cultural institutions. Though initially well-received as a means of enhancing independence and autonomy, with time it created a two-tiered system buttressing socioeconomic precarization of cultural and intellectual labor, a process that was accelerated in the 1990s with the break-up of the Yugoslav state.

Yugoslavia in the Cold War

Yugoslavia profited like no other country of the Eastern Bloc from the global competition of the Cold War. Through its liminal and idiosyncratic global positioning after the mid-1950s (it should not be forgotten that Yugoslavia was also a founding member of the Non-Aligned Movement), it managed to sit on the fence and extract advantages from both sides by playing the superpowers against each other. Its particular brand of liberal cultural politics served both as an instrument of legitimization for domestic politics and as a showcase of open-mindedness in foreign affairs. The country's cultural policy and self-image fed each other reciprocally, underscoring the fact that Yugoslavia was to be reckoned as something particular, neither East nor West. Its particular brand of self-managed, humane socialism was more progressive than the East, and therefore a match for the West and deserving of its unconditional support. As a result, cultural openness became a trademark of Yugoslav socialism and concealed some of the less pleasant aspects of the system such as the prevalence of one-party rule.[49] The need to maintain this image also brought tangible results; it served as a "security blanket" for artists and intellectuals and, in the realm of popular culture, it offered common people a "decompression valve" in the form of virtually unhindered access to Western material culture.[50]

This interplay between the national and international context goes some way to explaining the embedded character of Yugoslav copyright. Against this backdrop it is possible to elucidate the mixed character of Yugoslav copyright and its more "liberal" provisions, such as the absolute freedom to publish abroad without

49 Dean Vuletic, "Sounds Like America – Yugoslavia's Soft Power in Eastern Europe," in *Divided Dreamworlds? The Cultural Cold War in East and West*, eds. Peter Romijn, Giles Scott-Smith and Joes Segal (Amsterdam: Amsterdam University Press, 2012), 116–17.

50 Predrag Marković, "Where Have All the Flowers Gone? Yugoslav Culture in the 1970s between Liberalization/Westernization and Dogmatization," in *The Crisis of Socialist Modernity: The Soviet Union and Yugoslavia in the 1970s*, eds. Marie-Janine Calic et al. (Schriftenreihe der FRIAS School of History, vol. 3) (Göttingen: Vanderhoeck und Ruprecht, 2011), 123.

previous approval or interference from state authorities, the negotiated character of the publishing contract, and the decentralized organization and flow of royalties, but also the more liberal character of the economy of culture in Yugoslavia through multilateral funding, the strong negotiating capacity of the creative unions and the self-management organizations, the existence of a greater percentage of freelancers in cultural production and so on. Yugoslavia adopted a copyright regime that best fitted both its own political constitution and its geopolitical positioning, that is, a regime that was compatible with the country's international obligations (a situation that the Soviet Union, for example, circumvented until the late 1970s by purposely avoiding being bound to international standards) and the specific socioeconomic and cultural model that the Yugoslav communists were trying to devise domestically.

Copyright in Communist Czechoslovakia

Two copyright laws were released during the 42-year lifespan of the Czechoslovak Socialist Republic (ČSR/ČSSR, 1948–1990), the first in 1953 and the second and final one in 1965. The initial 1926 law (amended in 1936) remained in place until 1953. New copyright laws were released following revisions of the civil code in 1950 (no. 141/1950 Sb.) and in 1964 (no. 40/1964 Sb.) respectively. In the early 1950s, Roman law's traditional dualism (private and public law) was regarded as incongruous with socialist society and the new social relations emerging from it. In addition, the 1950 civil code provided for the first time a unified legal framework for both Czech and Slovak territory. The issue of property rights, including the distinction between personal and private property, was also central to the 1964 civil code.[51]

Changes in the state's political and socioeconomic structure and the need to introduce new entitlements and institutions, such as the rights of performing artists and the creation of cultural funds, provided the impetus behind the release of the 1953 copyright law. Czechoslovak lawyers did not forget to underscore, nonetheless, the organic, home-grown impulses of those institutions, tracing them partially (and accurately) back to blueprints of the interwar period.[52]

51 Vilém Vinopal, "Analýza českého autorského práva v kontextu společenských změn: vývoj od poloviny 20. století do současnosti" (Diploma thesis, Právnická Fakulta Masarykovy Univerzity, Katedra občanského práva, 2010), 31.

52 Karel Knap, *Das neue Urheberrechtsgesetz der Tschechoslowakei* (Schriftenreihe der UFITA, no. 2) (Baden-Baden: Verlag für Angewandte Wissenschaften, 1956), 9.

Some Theoretical Innovations

In the realm of ideas and legal history, Czechoslovak jurists claimed continuity and clearly identified a Central European path of development, into which they classified their home copyright development correspondingly. Its trajectory constituted a third, complementary type to the initial Anglo-Saxon and French schools of copyright. While descending from the French continental tradition, the Central European (German) model differed from the latter in its emphasis on society. Whereas the French conception departed from the individuality of the creator, in Central Europe, although individuality was respected, it was society in its entirety that was copyright's major point of reference. Albeit acknowledging the creator's distinctive personal connection to his work, exclusive rights were restricted to the degree required in order to meet the needs of society and guarantee the fulfilment of a work's cultural mission. Representing the copyright tradition of states like Germany and Austria, it was this conception that historically had been at the heart of Czechoslovak copyright regulation. Communist legislation was considered the climax of this "social" conception of copyright; next to the protection of creators and the stimulation of creativity, its principal goal was the greatest possible dissemination of works within society with the purpose of raising the cultural level of the masses and helping to construct a socialist society.

While theorizing about copyright, Czechoslovak lawyers at times took original paths that diverged from mainstream BC doctrine. Copyright protected literary, scientific and artistic works, which were the result of creative labor. Adaptations of works likewise enjoyed independent protection, as long as they were the result of creative labor and resulted in the making of a new creation. In contrast to the legal codification of the BC, Czechoslovak lawyers considered translations into foreign languages to be adaptations, that is, reworkings (modifications) of an original rather than reproductions (as was the BU canon). The same goes for the application of the concepts of "published works" (*uveřejnění díla*) and "published/released works" (*vydání díla*) regulated by articles 12 and 13. Contrary to the Rome revision of the BC (art. 4, par. 4), in Czechoslovak law a work was considered "published" the day of the first performance, exhibition or any other form of public display or communication. A work was considered "released" when it was multiplied and publicly circulated.

Continuing the tradition of interwar legislation, communist copyright law(s) reserved a particularly prominent role for moral rights, which were inviolable, non-transferable and could not become subject to compulsory licenses, save for absolutely indispensable modifications in the case of theatrical productions. Moral rights were unlimited (i.e. did not expire with the author's death) and their protection could be assigned to any of the following: family heirs, creative unions and copyright organizations. Extending the already existing conception of the 1926 copyright law, moral rights protection was granted to nationally significant works but was now broadened to cover all works, independently of heirs' succession; similar provisions governed the rights of performing artists.

What is more, the concept of moral rights acquired much broader content and meaning as an absolute right. It involved not only the author's personal rights but the build-up of systematic protection of the immaterial rights to a work, which though stemming from the author were not limited to his person and heirs, but were immanent to a work without any limitation in time.[53] In fact, in the subsequent 1965 copyright law, this principle was articulated even more clearly as Czechoslovak copyright theory went beyond the moral–pecuniary rights dichotomy and clearly articulated a third category of rights predicated specifically on the work. By such means, the work acquired an independent ontology in its own right beyond the figure of the author.

Therefore, subjective authors' rights included the right to protection, the right to dispose of the work and the right to remuneration. The legislator distinguished three categories of authors' rights: (1) moral rights, (2) mixed rights (rights with respect to the work) and (3) pecuniary rights (rights to remuneration). This differentiation was supposed to emphasize the fact that the rights to the work were not merely pecuniary rights, although they undoubtedly contained an economic aspect. This tripartite conception was also reflected in the classifications of the 1965 law, which distinguished a moral right protecting the author (art. 12, par. 1a), the right to dispose of the work (1b) and the right to remuneration (1c). Moral rights protected the personality of the author and contained the right of paternity, the right to use a pseudonym or to publish anonymously (art. 8), the right to determine publication and decide first publication (art. 10 ff.) and the right to the integrity of the work (art. 12, par. 1a). Mixed rights comprising the prerogative to dispose of the work consisted of the right to publish a work and strive in every manner possible to provide consent for its utilization (art. 12, par. 1b), whereas pecuniary rights referred to the right to demand remuneration in exchange for the use of a work; this last point also included the right to a fair share from the resale of works. In contrast to earlier laws, the 1965 law applied the principle of *droit de suite* not

[53] Knap, *Das neue Urheberrechtsgesetz*, 17.

only to figurative arts but to all works with a material basis (it thus also applied to literary works). Finally, Czechoslovak copyright also diverged from BC norms. Authors' rights (moral, mixed and pecuniary) came into being at the moment when the creative idea that constituted the content of the work was expressed orally, in writing or by means of a draft, sketch or any other form allowing the perception of the work through the senses. Moreover, moral rights were protected even in cases not foreseen or covered by international treaties.[54]

The Evolution of Copyright Legislation

The 1953 law relied, on the one hand, on the nationality principle, protecting the works of Czechoslovak citizens, irrespective of if and where they were published, and on the other, on the territoriality principle, protecting works of nationals and foreigners that were first published in the ČSR; the principle of reciprocity applied where relevant treaties were available. In contrast to the interwar period, when the law on the publishing contract and copyright law had formed two separate pieces of legislation, communist copyright laws integrated provisions regarding the different types of standardized contracts into the main copyright law. Otherwise, numerous dimensions of copyright regulation were managed by different laws: the civil code regarding deadlines and statutes of limitations (law no. 141/1950 Slg.), the code of civil procedure on the enforceability of sentences regarding claims to compensation (law no. 142/1950 Slg.), the penal code in cases regarding copyright infringements (law no. 86/1950 Slg.) and so on.

Whereas pecuniary rights were guaranteed, authorial permission (notably concerning statutory licenses and certain copyright restrictions that affected only published works) could be overridden in certain select cases. The rights of radio and television enterprises were formulated anew, and in contrast to the old law (of the 1930s), they were now transformed into a pure statutory licence. A significant new addition was the regulation of works created during employment and their use (art. 19, 20). Academic institutions could use works produced by authors under employment or in the context of an employment relationship without their authorization, (1) freely and without time limit, when used for their own operations, and reproduce them to an extent required as long as the reproductions were distributed free of

[54] Stefan Luby, "La protection des droits des auteurs dans la république socialiste tchécoslovaque," *Bulletin de droit tchécoslovaque* 3 (1966): 178–80.

charge, and (2) they could reproduce the work against remuneration for a two-year period. In cases where the author wished to authorize a third organization with the use of the same work, he could do so only with the consent of the employer organization. In order to fulfil their tasks, authorities, institutions, organizations and enterprises could use a work created under employment conditions without authorial permission but against a fee payment. Theoretically, in cases where authorization could not be obtained or the author declined use without substantial reasoning, the Ministry of Culture could ordain the use of a work; remuneration was nevertheless mandatory. This extreme option was rarely applied.[55]

Authors' fees were regulated through collective agreements but could also be settled administratively through the Ministry of Culture. Pecuniary rights were transferable both *mortis cause* and *inter vivos*. Deceased authors' rights were transferred first to heirs, and if unavailable, then to the state. Authors could transfer their rights only via a copyright organization. Euphemistically phrased in the law text as a right, this circumstance obscured the fact that it was impossible to circumvent an official organization in the transfer of rights.

The written contract was the only valid form of contract and mandatorily included and regulated the following components of the work: mode and range of use, time frame (beginning) of distribution, author's fees and contract duration. The contents of contracts were also determined through collective agreements and the law's stipulations were *ius cogens* (compelling law), that is, they could not be altered or shortened through an arrangement between the parties involved. Individual contracts could not aberrate from the collective agreement endorsed by the Ministry of Culture, regardless of the type of contract concerned, be it a publishing contract (art. 35–40), filming contract (art. 41–45), film screening contract (art. 46–49), radio and television broadcasting contract (art. 50–52), transmission to a sound storage medium (art. 53, 54) or finally small rights contract (art. 55, 56).

Aspects of the previous (interwar) law on the publishing contract were retained and integrated into the 1953 copyright law. For example, article 40 stipulated that if a work was sold out before the contract's official termination, the author had the right to demand a new edition even if this had not been previously explicitly agreed upon. The author even had the right to conclude a contract with another publisher if the initial publisher failed to issue a contract for a new edition within six months of the author's petition. Favorable conditions also governed the staging of theatrical works; a contractual agreement to stage a play in one location did not hinder the

[55] Knap, *Das neue Urheberrechtsgesetz*, 18–20.

author from concluding a contract for the staging of the same play in a theatre of a different location.[56]

Interesting in the application of exclusive rights is the practice of a certain "gradation" (calibration, scaling). Exclusivity by itself was not necessarily considered a virtue; rather, it was meaningful when its application was reasonable. This becomes evident in the option that was given to authors to contract the same work simultaneously with different users, provided that certain conditions were met. Concerning films, authors could, for example, enter a contract for a work already contracted with another producer if the latter consented to such action (art. 47, par. 2). The same was valid for radio broadcasts and theatrical plays, as long as the broadcast/performance took place in a different location (art. 52, 42). In other words, in instances where simultaneous usage was non-rivalrous, that is, it did not affect the dissemination of the work and multiple usage was not damaging or conflicting, then it was permissible. It is possible to characterize this as a form of "negotiated" and/or "flexible" exclusivity, in view of the fact that it envisaged context-bound gradations of exclusivity rather than pre-empting a state of absolute monopoly.

Concerning contracts concluded before the entry into force of the new law, although the author could not rescind the contract, it was possible to recuperate his rights in cases where the work's user deceased before the end of protection and was heirless. If the contract had been settled on a tariff lower than deserved, the creator/author could demand in the future a remuneration settlement according to the fee regulations of the new law. Finally, if the stipulations of the contract contradicted the stipulations of copyright law, but served public interest, it was possible to evade legal consequences via decision of the Ministry of Culture.

Enforcement measures applied only to pecuniary rights. Sequestrations of fee payments could not exceed 1/5 of the claim, while an additional 1/5 could be seized only under very specific circumstances and only if the author's general financial condition allowed to.

Terms of protection for works were among the longest for East European countries; generically the 50-year term of protection was valid, while 10-year protection from the date of publication applied to works (collected volumes, journals) of authorities, institutions and organizations as well as to films, photographic works and works published posthumously. The institution of *domain public payant* regulated the use of expired works. After the end of the term of protection, works were free and could be used by everybody against payment to the cultural funds (art. 81).

56 Knap, *Das neue Urheberrechtsgesetz*, 23–25.

Through governmental ordinance that also specified their use, works possessing an extraordinary significance for the nation could be declared cultural property of the nation, an additional takeover from the interwar copyright law. The maintenance of the institution of *droit de suite* also exemplified continuity with the interwar period. Creators and their heirs were entitled to a share of the price of a work of art if, during the artist's lifetime, the work was resold with excessive profit. Whereas the interwar legislation had established a 20% upper limit to the amount of compensation, this ceiling was abandoned in the communist law.[57]

Belonging to the category of collective works, film rights represented one of the most complex issues of copyright regulation due to the existence of multiple stakeholders. The 1953 law attributed copyright to the film producer (art. 9), but simultaneously sustained the rights of additional creators such as the authors of the literary source, novel or screenplay, as well as the rights of the authors of the film's various (literary, musical, photographic, visual arts) components. Although the film producer clearly acted as a "hinge" helping to unify these diverse derivative rights, many competences and prerogatives remained imprecise. The film's director in particular was in a disadvantageous situation. The 1926 law (art. 7) had equalized the director to a kind of editor. Even if he had had a substantial influence on the film's making, being considered only an editor of the screenplay, he disposed of no moral rights to oppose mutilations of the film.

Films were regulated by two kinds of contract. Through the filming contract, various authors, including the camera operator, transferred their rights to the producer against payment, thus enabling him to use their works for the film's creation. This right, however, did not include the right to screen the film, which was subject to a different contract and provided a certain category of authors with the capacity to claim rights to royalties, which were settled through collective contracts. Concerning the terms of protection, the 1953 law contained several moments of collision. Whereas the film was protected for 10 years from the issuing year, all other authors enjoyed regular terms of protection (i.e. during their lifetime plus 50 years p.m.a.). The rights of the producer expired after 10 years, whereas the rights of the other creators remained intact.[58]

The handling of neighboring rights[59] was among the most interesting aspects of the law and reserved advantageous treatment for performing artists. The 1926

57 Knap, *Das neue Urheberrechtsgesetz*, 29–31.

58 Knap, *Das neue Urheberrechtsgesetz*, 32–36.

59 Neighboring rights included: the rights of performing artists (art. 83–91), rights of enterprises to produce recordings as well as to broadcast works through radio and television (art. 92–94) and the rights to one's own correspondence and portraits (art. 95 and 96).

law had already granted a rudimentary recognition to performing artists, who were regarded as processors/arrangers of the works they performed, provided their labor contained a creative element. Conductors were considered to be the arrangers of choirs and orchestra concerts. This early regulation systematically prepared the ground for the rights of performing artists. The 1953 law related to the 1951 Rome draft for an international convention for the protection of performers, producers of phonograms and broadcasting organizations (which actually materialized in October 1961), but it also took an independent path. In order to avoid an ever-growing list of rights claimants, the law protected only the rights of those artists who, during public performances of literary and artistic works, performed as soloists (art. 83). In the case of reproduction of musical works, members of a chamber ensemble or quartet also fell into this category, while in the case of orchestras, choirs and/or dancing ensembles, apart from the regular soloists, the conductor, choir and ballet masters were also subsumed under the soloist category.

Performing artists' rights were conceptualized quite broadly, almost creating the impression that they were better protected than authors. They disposed of both pecuniary and moral rights, the latter being non-transferable and unlimited. Moreover, performers were able to pass a regulation whereby their own creative union could not represent their moral rights during their lifetime, parallel and complementarily to the performers themselves, as was common practice with other categories of creators and unions (art. 63, par. 3); only after the death of the artist/performer could the union exercise such rights parallel to the spouse, progeny, and in the absence of the two previous groups, the parents of the deceased creator. Performing artists' pecuniary rights consisted of the right to dispose of their performance and the right to remuneration. Fees were determined by the Ministry of Culture but the government also had the right to make exceptions to the law. Performers' rights consisted of: (1) mechanical, electrical and visual recordings destined for public distribution/sales; (2) public performance of recordings and public screening of films; and (3) broadcasting through radio, television and similar devices, when the performance was materialized by a different party than the enterprises normally charged with those tasks. Use was permitted only with the artists' consent (art. 83), though it was also possible to apply statutory licenses (art. 84); remuneration was guaranteed in either case. Moreover, performing artists maintained a strong position and their authorization could not be replaced by governmental ruling as in the case of authors (art. 22). Artists' exclusive right to authorize use and collect fees could be potentially limited through a decision by the Ministry of Culture to confer such competences to a union of performing artists or a copyright organization.[60] Performing artists' pecuniary rights lasted for 20 years after the successful fixation of the performance. In this case also there was leeway for collisions between the various terms of protection; terms of protection for authors were longer, whereas those for films were shorter than the 20 years reserved for performing artists.

As in all communist systems, authors' unions and collective management organizations constituted a central pillar of copyright organization.[61] Creative unions (art. 70) were legally sanctioned and "voluntarily" constituted organizations, uniting authors according to different creative areas. They consisted of: (1) the Union of Czechoslovak Writers, (2) the Union of Czechoslovak Composers, and (3) the Central Union of Czechoslovak Visual Artists (consisting of three unions: painters; sculptors and graphic artists; architects and applied arts). Collective management organizations (art. 71, 72) were based on the cooperative principle and took care of the financial and legal support and supervision of their members. They were answerable to the Ministry of Culture, a circumstance that allowed them to act more independently and evade the traditional compulsory membership of the Central Council of Cooperatives. CMOs had the exclusive right (art. 72) to: (1) supply permissions for the use of works and conclude contracts for the diffusion of works, (2) collect authors' fees, and (3) collect dues destined for cultural funds. They were also responsible for copyright transfers abroad.

The following organizations were active in Czechoslovakia: the Czech theatre and literary agency in Prague (DILIA) and the Slovak theatre agency in Bratislava (LITA), whose area of competence was published literary and dramatic works.[62] Music works with or without text were represented by the collective management organizations in Prague (OSA) and Bratislava (SOZA).[63] Finally, there was the Czech Fund of Fine Arts in Prague and the Slovak Fund of Fine Arts in Bratislava, whose competence lay in fine and graphic arts, including architectural, applied arts and photographic works.[64]

---

60 Knap, *Das neue Urheberrechtsgesetz*, 36–38.

61 Knap, *Das neue Urheberrechtsgesetz*, 41–42.

62 These included: (1) literary works, i.e. publications in journals, public lectures, use of published works in films and the public screening of films, their broadcasting through radio and television, recording for the creation of sound carriers and their sales and distribution; (2) public performances of dramatic works.

63 These concerned: public, non-theatrical performances, use of works in films and their public screening, broadcasting through radio and television, recordings for the creation of sound carriers, their distribution and sales.

64 These included: publication of works, public shows, use of published works in order to produce films and their public screening, broadcasting of published works through television.

An additional, important pillar in the organization of culture was the elaborate set-up and institutionalization of cultural funds, whose task was to support creative labor in the fields of literature, music and the fine arts. The idea harked back to a 1920s draft of the copyright law, which contained a similar provision but was eventually dropped, whereby fees from the use of free works (i.e. works already in the public domain) would flow into a cultural fund to support the arts. The 1953 law provided for the creation of three funds for literature, music and fine arts. The funds were entrusted with the following tasks: granting of long-term loans, regular monthly monetary advances, stipends and travel allowances, support for creators and their families in case of illness, invalidity or age and through the creation of homes and organizations for creators. Means were recruited via contributions from remuneration fees, publishing houses and other users, the use of free works, earnings from real estate, surpluses from the funds' own enterprises, donations, inheritances, endowments and state support. Rates and exceptions were usually determined by the government. Rates for publishers and other users were fixed through the collaboration of the ministers of culture and finance. In the 1950s, authors' contributions amounted uniformly to a 2% reduction of authors' fees, and for users of free works, they varied according to the purpose of usage, but could not exceed 50% of the standard rate for authors' fees; for publishers and other users, contributions amounted to 1% of the unit that was used as the basis of calculation (for example, the same price as a written work). Funds were also recipients of the assets of literary, music and arts organizations and societies that ceased to exist or were for various reasons discontinued, as well as of different foundations, residual funds and so on. The funds were self-governed organizations and their administrating bodies and committees were elected by the unions.[65]

The installation of a new constitution in 1960 meant that important sectors of legislation were codified anew, among them authors' rights. In addition, it was necessary to ensure that local legislation was in harmony with the country's international obligations arising from membership of the BU, the UNESCO Universal Convention on Copyright, which the ČSSR joined in 1960, and finally the Rome Convention on the Rights of Performers, Producers of Phonograms, Radio and Television Organizations, which the country joined in 1964. Participation in international fora was sought not only for the sake of economic considerations but also for cultural-political reasons, that is, in order to be able to partake in decision-making processes concerning the regulation of international copyright and ensure the best

---

65 Knap, *Das neue Urheberrechtsgesetz*, 42–43.

possible representation of local creators abroad. The new copyright law of March 25, 1965 (no. 35/1965) entered into force on July 1, 1965.

A vivid and broad discussion, even polemic, preceded the voting of the law. A great number of stakeholders were involved, including cultural organizations, authors' and performing artists' unions, enterprises charged with the use of authors' works and artists' performances, as well as the public.[66] On the basis of this discussion, the government submitted a new project law to the national assembly on November 25, 1964. The draft was largely influenced by a conception of authors' rights predicated on labor rights and concerned largely the regulation of rights related to works created during employment, as well as resultant rights to remuneration; in addition, the question of appropriate remuneration for "freelancers" was raised. Apparently, copyright organizations perceived the framing of the discussion to be incongruent with legal scholarship standards, and the relevant committees of the national assembly, acknowledging those reservations, returned the project to the government in order to be reconsidered. The new draft law of February 10, 1965 adopted the conceptions of the legal experts and was fashioned more closely on the precepts of legal theory.

Remuneration, particularly concerning the use of works by Czechoslovak media (radio and television), was at the heart of the debate (which provoked lengthy written confrontations but is not treated here in detail). Creators demanded the right to authorize every single use of their works by state media, arguing that unauthorized use could lead to abuse and (involuntary) co-authoring of their works, as was the case with author/director Martin Frič, who protested against the montage of his earlier films by Czechoslovak television without his knowledge or consent. State media (and legal scholars) declined authors' claim to seek authorization for the use of any kind of creation (song, poem, small sketch etc.) indiscriminately, especially concerning already broadcast works, arguing that such conduct would make their work cumbersome and more bureaucratic, and delegated the issue to the negotiations of collective agreements between interest groups. Nevertheless, the responsibility of state media and organizations to respect moral rights (works should not be condensed or treated inappropriately) was stressed, and the obligation confirmed to inform the author in advance concerning broadcasts of larger (i.e. lengthier) works.[67] Authors were clearly pushing for greater returns for the use of their works, irrespective of the fact that the discourse was outwardly fought with a major emphasis on moral rights.

---

66 Luby, "La protection des droits des auteurs," 172.

67 NS RČS 1964–1968, 5. schůze, část 19/23 (March 25, 1965), https://www.psp.cz/eknih/1964ns/stenprot/005schuz/s005019.htm.

The second cause of perturbation and extensive debate was the exact nature of authors' remuneration, and whether it represented a reward for the labor invested in the work, or for the work/result produced, or for the use of the work. Legal scholars resolved the issue by arguing for the indelibility of all these aspects of labor: the work/oeuvre was the embodiment of the labor invested in the creation, and the use of the work depended on the social usefulness of the work. All three aspects were intertwined; however, it was the social usefulness of the work that was expressed in reward.[68]

The 1965 copyright law was intended to be simpler and handier and was for this reason downsized to half the number of paragraphs (from 113 paragraphs in the 1953 law to 55). Among the changes introduced were the new competence of heirs to become guardians of authors' moral rights, a prerogative that had been previously reserved only for family members. Also noteworthy was a new regulation concerning translations that obviously took advantage of the accession of Czechoslovakia into the Universal Convention. Article 18 (par. 2) specified that to the degree permitted by international treaties, the Ministry of National Education and Culture had the authority to sanction the translation of works by foreign authors (i.e. to override foreign authors' authorization for translations) into the languages of the peoples of the Czechoslovak Republic.

The new Constitutional Law adopted in 1968 (no. 143/1968 Sb.) resulted in the federalization of the state and also touched on powers in the field of copyright. Although legislative powers remained the responsibility of the federal assembly, executive powers were with the national republics. The practice of a unitary ministry of culture was abandoned, resulting in the creation of two independent ministries of culture, one for the Czech (ČSR) and one for the Slovak (SSR) Socialist Republics.[69]

68 Ibid.

69 The development trajectory of Czechoslovak copyright law in relation to international copyright codification, including a discussion of select case law studies regarding the local implementation of the law in Czechoslovakia from the perspective of the early 1980s, is treated comprehensively in Karel Knap and Jiři Kordač, "Letter from Czechoslovakia," *Copyright* 17, no. 9 (September 1981): 248–62.

Chapter 12

Conclusions: Copyright in East Central and Southeast Europe— A Long-Term Perspective

Is copyright a universal or a context-dependent institution? Is copyright's primary concern the protection of authors' rights or the streamlining and expansion of global markets? Does scale (size of the economy, expansion capacity of the cultural industries, global positionality etc.) influence the orientation and application of copyright? Has copyright been a consistent institution, merely supplemented and extended on a regular basis following the "natural" course of economic development and technological change or is copyright regulation the result of specific constellations of interests and power struggles? Is copyright a natural or a statutory right and what consequences do such philosophical substantiations and legal doctrines bring along? How have social actors (authors, publishers, various intermediaries, lawyers, consumers etc.) argued and legitimized their own positionality in the field of culture and the striving for copyright regulation? What is the dynamic between national and international exchange and how significant is their entanglement for the configuration of the global copyright regime?

The main objective of the current book was to analyse the function and significance of authors' rights in the societies of East Central and Southeast Europe in the period from the mid-nineteenth to the mid-twentieth century, broadly covering a time span from the late imperial to the late communist period. Its starting point was on the one hand the detection of a historiographic gap, whereby the regions of East and Southeast Europe were persistently absent from narratives of modern copyright history and were "resuscitated," broadly speaking and for obvious reasons, mainly in the post-1989 period in the process of legal harmonization as potential candidates for EU accession. On the other hand, this absence of historicity was accompanied by implicit assumptions regarding historical trajectories and influences, breaks and discontinuities, especially after 1945.

This concluding chapter brings together in condensed form some of the main strands of thought and conclusions regarding the development of modern copyright in East Central and Southeast Europe from a longue durée perspective.

1. Whereas the print revolution of the Renaissance ushered in a first era of "mass communication" that encompassed a large part of Europe (Germany, Italy, France, Spain, the Netherlands, Belgium, Switzerland, Britain, Bohemia, Poland),[1] the remarkable industrialization and commercialization of print in the late eighteenth and particularly the nineteenth century unmistakably changed this geographic configuration, shifting the epicenter of printing towards Western Europe. Industrialization transformed print, media, production, consumption and literacy on an unprecedented scale. Innovation of print was slow until approximately the 1800s but developed quickly thereafter. Through large-scale manufacture and functioning in an increasingly competitive environment, it transformed along the way all aspects of the production process and the printing industry.[2] Both the institution of modern copyright and the movement for international copyright protection were therefore initiated, and/or led, by a group of West and Central European countries (Britain, France, Germany) with variable self-interests. Having completed the passage from feudal to modern capitalistic society earlier, these countries developed a vested interest in the industrial organization and commercialized diffusion of their cultural industries and saw themselves confronted sooner with the need to regulate the roles of the various stakeholders in the knowledge economy and cultural production. It was usually their needs and norms that justified the set-up of global guidelines, which were naturalized and universalized over time. When legitimizing their positions, they developed a repertoire of arguments around propriety, equity, civilization and property able to substantiate different standpoints and claims.

---

1 In the early modern period, parts of Eastern Europe regulated knowledge production and the printing trade along the lines of the widely diffused system of privileges. Developments in the Polish-Lithuanian Commonwealth in the early modern period and until the eighteenth century followed European trends. Poland was, for example, very close to switching from a regime of privileges to a more modern copyright regime in the late eighteenth century, a development that was for different reasons frustrated. See Katarzyna Gracz, "Opposing the Expansion of Copyright Law," 289–93. On early printing see Benito Rial Costas, ed., *Print Culture and Peripheries in Early Modern Europe: A Contribution to the History of Printing and the Book Trade in Small European and Spanish Cities* (Leiden: Brill, 2013).

2 "Industrialization of Print: Automation, Mass Production, Changes in Literacy, and Aesthetic Responses," in *History of the Book*, ed. Johanna Drucker (ucla.edu), https://hob.gseis.ucla.edu/HoB-Coursebook_Ch_9.html.

2. The juridification of translation rights was an important consolidating moment in the establishment of the international copyright regime. The regulation of translation in the late nineteenth century represented the first act of intermediality and initiated a proper paradigm shift. The legal integration of translation into the logic of copyright expanded the notion of reproduction and extended the concept of multiplication.[3] This represented a reversal of previous regulatory practices, which usually consisted of rather short periods of protection for translations, whereby protection depended on the discretion of the author and regulation could vary greatly among jurisdictions. Moreover, non-use within a specific time period often resulted in the loss of translation rights for the author. The juridification of translation rights was one of the main, if not the main reason for the creation of the Berne Union in the late 1880s and a cornerstone of the international expansion of copyright law. International legalization resulted in the gradual extension of the term of protection for translations, until they were treated on an equal footing with original works. In retrospect, the juridification of translation led to a solidification of the "authorship paradigm" at a critical juncture in time, when translation was becoming a lucrative but also an uncontrollable business. The rapid internationalization and transnationalization of cultural commodities, genres and tastes on the one hand had resulted in the "industrialized" production of translations occasioning the banalization of works, while on the other, it became necessary for the publishing industry to secure stability and control over both the constitution and the "value" of those commodities in the process of their circulation. The price to be paid in order to obtain financial and legal predictability when dealing with a transformative process like translation was the "taming of difference" and the sacrifice of a notion of translation as an inventive and dialogical process of inter-, trans- and cross-cultural communication and exchange. Translation was imagined to be a perfect, mechanical and coherent replication of an original text, just as the nation was imagined to be a perfect, organic and coherent representation of an original people.

International attitudes towards translation began to change when a number of countries recognized it to be an instrument capable of assisting the expansion of their cultural and knowledge industries, in the context of the world's changing geopolitical and linguistic landscape. Political, economic, cultural and, more broadly,

3 Here I disagree with the otherwise wonderfully erudite work of Monika Dommann, who argues that the first paradigm shift in copyright took place with the introduction of audio technologies like the phonograph/gramophone around the 1900s. I deem that translation was quite seminal in broadening the contents and margins of the category of reproduction beyond the established framework of the print paradigm; cf. Monika Dommann, "Notieren, Aufzeichnen, Vervielfältigen," 151.

linguistic influences fed on and reinforced each other. This transformation process included the development of new vernacular languages, the nationalization, regionalization and internationalization of new knowledge markets, the reorganization of the roles and hierarchies of world, scholarly, mediating, regional, national and local languages, coupled with the increased potential in means of communication, the growth of literate and educated publics and an accompanying change in aesthetic and philosophical teachings. Their combined effects promoted engagement with the legal nature of translation, which had not been an issue in previous periods. In other words, print capitalism, the new geopolitical order and ensuing division of labor posed anew the question of access to knowledge and culture in commercial, legal, political and symbolic terms.

3. Though not indifferent to the protection and commercialization of their cultural industries, the East European empires (Habsburg, Ottoman, Romanov) had a different calculation to make regarding their alignment or not with the international copyright regime. The multi-ethnic empires of Southeast and East Central Europe abstained from membership in the BU for a variety of political but also economic reasons. Over the course of the nineteenth century, both the Habsburg and the Romanov empires developed elementary legal provisions in order to protect authors in one form or another. Instead of international copyright regulation, however, they remained largely focused on their own internal cultural relations and dynamics. The continental empires of Eastern Europe were not only multi-ethnic but also multilingual. As political spaces, they fluctuated between different, often contradictory legitimation projects whose boundaries were periodically renegotiated, such as legitimacy based on the traditional dynastic aura, but also on modern forms of political participation; the use of censorship and control coupled with phases of political liberalization and loosening of surveillance; the desire and necessity to provide mass education (in the spirit of the Enlightenment ideals, in order to modernize their states and meet the educational demands of rising ethnic groups) and the effort to hold the political project of empire together. These complex sociocultural and sociolinguistic conglomerates represented multicultural and pluricultural communication spaces in which language, social milieu and identity long remained in a fluid and dialectical relationship to one another at the level of everyday communication and exchange. At the same time, they were tense power fields, where the structural asymmetries between the use, reach and prestige of different languages sowed the seeds of future conflicts.

The multi-ethnic, pluri- and multilingual setting of the East European empires, the variable movements for national/linguistic emancipation among the empires' nationalities, their exigencies and priorities, ultimately constituted a different background setting for the reception and conceptualization of the institution of copyright in Eastern Europe that was altogether not conducive to the exclusivist proprietary paradigm. On the contrary, broad, cheap and unrestricted access to knowledge was deemed a precondition and a constituent part of the nation-building process, where the codification of languages and the constitution of literatures went hand in hand. As long as such processes were given primacy (as was the case throughout most of the nineteenth century), the commercial dimension of publishing was less prevalent. Though all three empires attempted at different times to establish their "national" languages as idioms of administration, education and social ascendance, they were ultimately unsuccessful in enforcing them as exclusive communication media. The explosive capacity and symbolic character of language use, and the demand for education in the mother tongue, forced concessions, most observable in the institutionalization of "porous" and/or "soft" (in contradistinction to rigid) translation regimes in all three empires, as a means of maintaining their fragile, state-internal equilibria (between different nationalities, between centers and peripheries, between urban and rural areas, between entangled social, ethnic, religious, professional, political identities etc.). Various practices and levels of translation, formal and informal, streamlined or spontaneous, constituted what could be called the "communicating space of empire," which otherwise was truncated in separate and sometimes antagonistic public spheres. Translation rights in this context were not treated as private interest rights (as was largely the case in Western Europe), but were elevated to an issue of national significance. The East European empires therefore opted to maintain their own "rhythm" in the regulation of culture and copyright relationships, and were predominantly concerned with issues of internal rather than external regulation, which also explains their predilection for time-limited bilateral rather than multilateral engagements.

Further reasons, such as differing technologies and epistemologies of knowledge, played an additional role in sustaining an indifferent attitude towards copyright as a regulatory instrument. Examples include the perseverance of (and veneration for) an elaborate calligraphic tradition (next to print culture) in the Ottoman Empire or conceptions about knowledge and the role of intellectuals such as the intelligentsia model, which regarded knowledge as materializing in the exchange (the giving and taking) rather than in an atomistic/individualistic process of knowledge production; or again, apprehensions about the injurious effects of an excessive privatization of intellectual goods and the resulting exclusion of the public from the benefits of modern knowledge and literature, as in the case of Russia.

Contextual conditions and needs determine the rise, acceptance and/or viability of institutions. A series of contextual parameters—including the already-mentioned imperial legacies, the more collectivistic concoction of the author figure, the degree of professionalization of the publishing business as well as the maturation and self-consciousness of creative elites, the degree of commercialization of the cultural sphere, the pace and reach of reading revolutions, an appreciation for copying and imitation practices as a constitutive part of modernity, the existence of alternative forms of regulation, etc.—all formed important framework conditions that influenced the reception of copyright in the regions of Eastern and Southeastern Europe and slowed the breakthrough of copyright as a central regulatory instrument of the cultural economy.

This initial phase of copyright development in Eastern Europe resulted in a first pattern of legal reception: it was predicated on a utilitarian understanding, where the cultural, social and political mission of copyright (access to knowledge, maintaining the balance between nationalities, smooth or facilitated transitions between languages, etc.) was given equal, if not superior status to the economic mission (regulation of the flow of assets within the cultural industry, commercialization of cultural goods). Distance from the system of international regulation promoted by the BU ultimately meant protected markets, which benefited primarily (small) nationalities and were also demanded by them. The main contours of this legal regime (albeit in a slightly modified form and adapted to new circumstances) were passed on in subsequent eras and became even more pronounced under communism.

Historically, IP is an institution that arose in modern industrial, mass capitalist societies, with a reasonably developed, consolidated, centralized and commercialized cultural sector and a certain division of labor in the creative industries. In societies where these socioeconomic benchmarks were weak or absent, or where culture was organized on different premises, IP remained irrelevant or superfluous and regulation relied on other social practices and/or arrangements. Historical reasons therefore go to explain regional variations in the development of copyright in Europe. For example, copyright law in parts of Western Europe was introduced as a measure to break the consolidated commercial monopolies of publishers like the Stationers' Company and the Parisian publishers' guild and established cultural institutions like the theatrical monopoly of the Comédie-Française. Such long-established professional groups and deep-rooted monopolies did not exist in the sphere of culture in East and Southeast Europe in the eighteenth and nineteenth centuries.

An interesting contrast emerged from the comparison with the colonial empires of Britain and France regarding the reasons why copyright claims in these imperial realms were often entangled with identity discourses of peoples seeking self-determination (as in the cases of Canada, USA, Australia, etc.). This was not the case with the Eastern European empires, where ethnic distinction centerd mainly around the issue of language. The architecture of the international copyright regime both complicated and facilitated the expansion of the cultural industries of the two empires. While Britain sought to assuage these contradictions and use them to its own advantage, France deliberately kept its colonies apart from the BU regime until 1930, aiming to avoid precisely such complications. The French position is explained with reference to the contracting French book trade and the crucial role that Francophone colonies had in the overall French publishing business around 1900.

4. In terms of legal transfer, German and eventually also Russian (pre-revolutionary as well as revolutionary) influences were vital for the codification of copyright laws. Though other legal traditions undeniably had an impact as well (for example French and Italian conceptions and influences, among others), it would not be an exaggeration to claim that copyright law in the regions of East and Southeast Europe was largely shaped in-between the two poles of German and Russian copyright conceptions. This doubtless represents a schematic picture, and transfers were of course more intricate and multidirectional, but it is nevertheless a useful simplification when seeking to understand the bigger picture. German laws (particularly the copyright laws of 1901 and 1907, as well as the regulation of the publishing contract—*der Verlagsvertrag*) had a model character and served as the blueprint for the creation of Russian copyright legislation.[4] The further east the copyright legislation and doctrine moved from their original French matrix, the weaker the notion of authors' rights as exclusive property rights became. German law was a kind of initial "processing" unit (or gestation machine) that adapted those conceptions in the Central European setting by advocating a concept of copyright law based on more practical and pragmatic aspects of regulation. Further, it is to be assumed that the German codification by idealistic philosophy (i.e. Kant, Fichte, Hegel) of the author as an intellectual, addressing the public with a particular "voice," had greater appeal for East European intellectual audiences than a codification of the author as a simple proprietor, endowed with the task of guarding access or as a solitary genius existing

[4] Concerning the German influence and formal exchanges between German and Russian stakeholders in the early twentieth century, with a particular emphasis on music, see Jana Ferran, "Die Regelung der Musikurheberrechtsfragen zwischen Deutschland und Russland in den Jahren 1900–1917," *Iskusstvo muzyki. Teorija i istorija* 21 (2019): 69–88.

for and by himself. The "practical" German model was then transferred further eastwards, "reprocessed" once more in Russia (in the legislation of 1911), and adjusted further to local conceptions, the major characteristic being the combination of an understanding of strong subjective authors' rights with a conception of broad access to culture. Authors and access to culture were therefore constructed not as antithetical or mutually exclusive (as in the property paradigm). To put it in contemporary terms, copyright in Eastern Europe was largely framed as "open" (not as free) access. Paragon conceptualizations can also be encountered in the Habsburg context. It is not surprising, therefore, that in both cases authors' rights were often framed as the right of the author to remuneration rather than to exclusive ownership. The public character/destination of culture is therefore inscribed into the conception of copyright/authors' rights long before it is officially and programmatically heralded by communist copyright. This does not mean to say that there were no other opinions (for example, opinions making the case for intellectual property), but rather that this specific conceptualization nicely demonstrates the necessities of the local contexts when adapting copyright law. It also does not mean to say that preoccupations of an economic nature (such as economizing on royalty payments or seeking cheap access to knowledge) did not play a (significant) role (at times) as well.

The departure from the property paradigm was predicated in the first place in the turning away from the philosophy of natural law. Both the Austrian and Russian conceptions showed a strong inclination towards a philosophical and legal justification of copyright as statutory law. In the Russian case, this became obvious when arguing against the exclusive right of translation. The distancing from natural law could also be accomplished through a predilection for the pandectic school of law (*Pandektistik*), whose emphasis on historical roots and the attachment of law to culture offered leeway for local understandings/interpretations (and away from universalistic conceptions) of law. The second major German influence was the taking over of the theory of moral rights (*Persönlichkeitsrechte*), which—it can be argued—constitutes the proper "trademark" of copyright law in Eastern Europe. Whether through Joseph Kohler's theory of *Immaterialgüterrecht* or the school of moral rights proper (von Gierke, Gareis etc.), moral rights played a key role in the codification of copyright law in East and Southeast Europe. They usually held a prominent position in the respective national copyright laws of East Central Europe, and in direct continuation, retained this prominence also in the subsequent communist legislation.

Timing certainly played a role in the transfer process. Natural law was declining by the late nineteenth century, and other schools of thought, such as justifications based on the uniqueness of the creator's personality (*Persönlichkeitsrecht*), had been gaining ground and recognition. I am, however, inclined to believe that the strong emphasis on moral rights served in the first place specific needs that in their turn determined the modality of transfer. They were handy as an ideational foundation in order to construct strong subjective rights, while at the same time circumventing the long tradition of civil law that defended strong subjective rights on the basis of sovereign property rights (*Herrschaftsrechte*). It involved a delicate, yet not insignificant shifting of emphasis, away from the complete individualization and absolute sovereignty of the author, and if read inversely, confirmed that (collective) culture was always "bigger" than the individual. At the same time, moral rights highlighted the particular connection of creators to their works and celebrated works as reflecting the unique personality of their creators, all images and attributes that underscored, both historically and symbolically, the important role played by the intelligentsia in culture and nation-building. Though also in the German case the doctrinal defense of moral rights had arisen out of a realization of the inadequacy of defending authors' rights singularly on the basis of pecuniary rights, the East European take on moral rights contained an extra level of intensification in relation to the German source. Moreover, it developed into a kind of proper doctrinal matrix that was taken over intact by the communist legislators.

As became evident by the analysis of the interwar legislations, significant Russian influences were prevalent long before 1945. The Bulgarian 1923 copyright law was predicated on the blueprint of the 1911 Russian law, which was also taken into consideration in the codification of Yugoslav copyright law, and finally, Czechoslovak interwar copyright discussions were constantly framed through references to the Soviet example. By contrast, before and after 1945, though the Soviet impact on the practical organization of culture (nationalization, centralization and monopolization of print media, singular representation of creative unions etc.) and literary paradigms (socialist realism) is indisputable, it is not evident that copyright development in Eastern Europe qualifies as a proper Sovietization of copyright law. More on this later.

5. At the end of the nineteenth and beginning of the twentieth centuries, the Eastern European empires were reluctant to join the newly created international structures for the protection of intellectual property. The end of the First World War radically changed this situation, when older and newly created nation states of Southeast and East Central Europe were mandated into the BU through clauses inserted in the postwar peace settlement. The Treaty of Versailles presented a window of opportunity

and the moment was expediently seized to advance the Union's agenda and expand its membership and territorial reach. The subsequent institutional linking of the Berne Union with the League of Nations and the resulting association with an emerging global player in international law meant a considerable upgrade of the Union and the institution of intellectual property.

The new member states, although differently predisposed to the BU, were aware of the political impact of the accession processes and made their own cost-benefit calculations. The period after the First World War also marked a new chapter in the history of communications with the breakthrough of the audiovisual revolution, the massification and internationalization of new media and cultural products. Commercialization and the wide diffusion into society of a series of media innovations from the previous century (cinema, phonograph, radio) signalled the rise of a new technology-oriented cultural industry, which multiplied intermediality and the number of actors interested in regulating copyright relations.

The extension of the BU into East Central and Southeast Europe has to be best understood as part of a global expansion strategy, which was grounded on a hierarchical perception of world regions and was indebted to the colonial mindset of the nineteenth and early twentieth centuries. It is argued that the triumphant multilateralism of the late nineteenth century did not necessarily signify (albeit often so portrayed in the relevant literature) the superseding of bilateralism, and that the global expansion of intellectual property was not based on one unified strategy, but remained flexible and was adapted to fit political circumstances, short- and long-term goals, historical legacies, the status of particular regions and countries, the positioning of competitors and/or allies, geopolitical arrangements and concerns, specific commercial plans and other factors contingent upon the possibilities at hand. Copyright could assemble diverse territories and ensure the territorialization and legal stability of commercial regimes by creating new geographies of alliances, expansion, dependency and extraction. This is best demonstrated through the example of China, where foreign countries applied a thick web of bilateral treaties over its territory in order to establish and legally legitimize newly imagined territorial-administrative units of intervention.

6. The end of the First World War represented a high point—the last one, however—in the attempts to dominate and shape global IP policy under French auspices. The post-WWI era was characterized by efforts to conceptualize and organize the field of knowledge holistically, by bringing areas and fields of erudition together. Efforts to coordinate the various branches of IP had already taken place in 1893,

when the two, until then independent, bureaus of the Paris and the Berne unions merged to form the United International Bureau for the Protection of Intellectual Property, better known by its acronym BIPRI (the forerunner of WIPO).

As a result of the war experience, a series of intertwined structures and institutions were created in the post-WWI period, including the Organization for Intellectual Cooperation (Organisation de la coopération intellectuelle; OCI), a subsidiary organ of the League of Nations. Initiated by the creation of the International Commission for Intellectual Cooperation (Commission internationale de la coopération intellectuelle; ICCI) in 1921 and completed by the International Institute for Intellectual Cooperation (Institut international de coopération intellectuelle; IICI) in 1924, their aim was to work towards the moral disarmament of minds and pacifism. Though not the only one, France was the main sponsor and supporter of this institutional network, which was largely predicated to serve the goals of French cultural imperialism, i.e., to help France recover its place and influence in the world and compensate for the loss of financial power with an increase in cultural influence.[5] IP was integrated into that larger complex, which covered the whole gamut of intellectual activity, including the cooperation of nations in education, science and culture.

Preoccupations with IP in the context of the peace settlement were related to strategic considerations regarding the postwar order, and France was eager to politically and economically exploit the vacuum left by Germany in order to secure the distribution of its own products (partly as a measure to limit the previous German counterfeiting of French products), but most crucially in order to have a good head-start economically in the new era and to occupy a propitious position with respect to ex-Austria-Hungary, and more generally the region of East Central Europe, previously a German stronghold.[6] Due to its ability to structure entangled politico-cultural as well politico-economic relations, IP was embroiled directly or indirectly in these much broader geostrategic and commercial considerations.

The interwar period provided an interesting laboratory, giving birth to many ideas and many more designs, few of which actually materialized. Nevertheless, revisiting them helps to shed light on the trends and intentions of the actors of the times.

5 Jean-Jacques Renoliet, *L'Unesco oubliée: La Société des Nations et la coopération intellectuelle (1919–1946)* (Paris: Éditions de la Sorbonne, 1999), particularly 323–33.

6 See Joseph Gaillard, "Rapport d'expansion économique de la France dans les pays d'ancienne monarchie Austro-Hongroise et particulièrement en Autriche," Archives diplomatiques (La Courneuve), Europe 1918–1929, Cote: 80CPCOM, Autriche/Commerce/146, 23–51; on French economic and commercial activity, see also 80CPCOM/147. On the postwar economic order, see Ministère des Affaires étrangères, Direction des Affaires politiques et commerciales/Conditions économiques de la Paix, P 1599, P 12909.

The interwar period continued the trend towards propertization of IP, and next to expansion, it now put greater emphasis on consolidating the international regime through disciplinary, legal enforcement and standardization provisions. Among the proposals were (1) cancelling the right of reservations to a treaty, (2) inserting a clause of binding jurisdiction in order to assure unanimity of interpretation of the union's acts, (3) plans for a universal convention that would harmonize and potentially draw the European and American IP systems closer together, (4) international codification of moral rights as an extension of authorial personality, and (5) institutionalization of a germane authority (e.g. a court) that would ensure the binding international resolution of conflicts.

Regarding IP's international institutional architecture, designs envisioned a greater entanglement of areas, fields and planes of activity, which went hand in hand with greater centralization. The interwar period witnessed discussions about whether it was necessary to introduce a "right of the scientist" as scientific property (*droit du savant, propriété scientifique*). It concerned the remuneration of scientists, and most importantly, how to regulate interests between the industry and scientific institutions. Next to the structures of intellectual cooperation and the BIPRI, the creation of a Central Bureau of Inventions (Bureau central des brevets d'invention) was envisioned. The internationalization of IP in the post-WWI period carried a decisively French flair, and it was both expedient and desirable that the multiple threads of the aforementioned networks crossed through Paris. For the first time since its institutionalization in the late nineteenth century, international IP was coherently and strategically conceived in the nexus between science, technology, culture, communications, industry and commerce.

The interwar period was one with an eminent focus on all things social. This trend also impacted IP and resulted in the temporary conjunction of the language of rights with the language of labor. Social issues and rights, their scope and regulation, were put on the table, a circumstance also testified by the closer cooperation between the International Labor Organization (ILO) and the BIPRI. A series of measures were deliberated that highlighted the laboring dimension of intellectual work and sought a certain degree of standardization and measurement of labor and remuneration. Among the debated options in the 1920s were the already-mentioned rights of scientists, plans to devise standardized (publishing) contracts, legal conditions of international non-profit associations and foundations, moral rights, resale rights (*droits de suite*), the legal deposit (*dépôt legal*), the paying public domain (*domaine publique payant*), obligatory licences and so on. Several were abandoned early on, either due to disagreements among the stakeholders (for example, disagreements between authors' and publishers' organizations or objections from publishers and heirs) or on the grounds that inordinate regulation strongly encroached on the principles of the free market.

It is worth mentioning that several of these measures, such as the standardized (publishing) contract, the application of obligatory licences or a greater dissemination of the paying public domain, were later integrated in several communist copyright legislations. They have often been mistakenly identified as particularistic traits of communist copyright, whereas our analysis has shown that these legal instruments informed international IP discussions at the turn of, and during the first decades of the twentieth century. Next to their utilitarian approach and treatment of copyrights as statutory rights, it was the communist regimes' state and power monopoly that allowed them to overpower the objections of stakeholders such as heirs. For pragmatic reasons, but also because they remained loyal to their discipline's historical pedigree (i.e. the tradition of civil law), copyright jurists in communist countries rarely professed or enforced theoretical interpretations that amalgamated copyrights with labor rights. De facto, however, the practical set-up of communist copyright regimes, which relied heavily on standardized contracts and measurable labor, was the closest the modern world ever got to an alignment between copyrights and labor rights, despite the fact that legal copyright doctrine under communism insisted on neatly keeping them apart.

7. The introduction of copyright in the three countries that inform this analysis (Bulgaria, Yugoslavia and Czechoslovakia) in the interwar period confirms the thesis of IP history as a history of asymmetries. It can be argued generically that the internationalization and expansion of IP in the aftermath of the First World War in East Central and Southeast Europe did not *a priori* bolster or improve conditions for the local stakeholders in culture. Analysis showed that the implementation of copyright could produce very different outcomes in local settings and that the degree of professionalization, commercialization and maturity of the local cultural, legal and economic spheres played an important role in determining this outcome. By contrast, inclusion into the international copyright regime benefited in the first place the forerunner exporting countries in the fields of entertainment and culture and provided the legal basis that enhanced their expansion and extracting capacities, as well as their capacities to withstand international competition. Local reactions to this form of asymmetrical internationalization included various forms of nationalization, the application of mercantilist policies or attempts to play international competitors off against each other.

In countries like interwar Bulgaria, where the commercialization of culture and the professional organization of artists were relatively weak, copyright barely influenced the configuration of relationships among stakeholders or the social and economic organization of local culture. To the degree possible and on the basis of a tacit consensus, international copyright obligations were eschewed or ignored, emphasizing the primacy of local cultural development. In the 1930s, libertarian copyright was replaced by more prescriptive measures (for example, fixed remuneration tariffs) that partially curtailed contractual freedom in copyright relations and fixed roles and responsibilities in the cultural sector. Yugoslavia, which initially connected to the international copyright regime by espousing the exact opposite policies to Bulgaria (i.e. it endorsed unregimented association in international copyright relations and permitted the installation of unsupervised local private collecting societies) had to learn the hard way. The Kingdom of Yugoslavia adopted protectionism out of the need to shield its cultural sector from the incursion and avarice of foreign collecting societies and their local proxies. Different again was the experience in interwar Czechoslovakia. Czech cultural and legal elites had had a longstanding symbiotic association with their German-speaking colleagues and thereby brought a more profound experience with copyright regulation into the newly created Czechoslovak state; in this case, there was an indisputable continuity with the Habsburg tradition. Closely networked cultural and legal elites well understood the significance of using copyright as a means to contribute to the broader state-building process of interwar Czechoslovakia, which was strongly predicated on international relations and internationalization strategies. The Czechoslovak copyright regime, therefore, was conceived as both open and protectionist at the same time; it relied, on the one hand, on a strong syndicalist organization of the arts and institutionalized bargaining arrangements among all stakeholders, while on the other, it partook in the international copyright regime by keeping a close eye on and deliberately structuring the institutional channels of international cultural exchange. In both instances the state played a nodal coordinating role, while the centralized organization of culture was a reality long before the communist takeover.

It can be broadly argued that the introduction of copyright did not significantly affect the development of the cultural field. It did not create greater incentives for cultural production, and only brought greater returns when the cultural market was sufficiently broad, commercialized and capable of expansion. The socioeconomic parameters of cultural production (availability and size of the market, degree and extent of alphabetization, maturity of the intellectual/literary elite, diversification of tastes and media, availability of infrastructure and educational institutions etc.)

affected, to a greater extent than copyright, the potential of the cultural establishment to expand and flourish.

In order to energize and/or protect domestic cultural industries, expand national cultural production and withstand competition from the culture-exporting nations, the majority of the nation states of Central and Eastern Europe intervened in the 1930s to amend existing legislation. They passed protectionist copyright laws, placing the category of "author" and his work directly or indirectly under state protection, and thereby promoted, in one way or another, a form of "nationalization." By placing authors' rights at the service of the new sociopolitical order and curtailing them to varying degrees, for example by introducing censorship mechanisms or by linking them to the *raison d'être* of the state in the sense of a corporatist policy, the authoritarian and occupational regimes at the end of the interwar period legally overhauled this nationalization. The communists molded the postwar order directly on this already existing framework, while at the same time adapting the institution of intellectual property to the ideological premises of the new socioeconomic system.

8. The systemic integration of copyright into the logic and priorities of the new power system—that is, the cultural revolution, the construction of the socialist social order and the creation of the "new man"—characterized the third phase in the development of copyright in Southeast and East Central Europe in the second half of the twentieth century.[7] Intellectuals were assigned a central role in this context. The socialization of the means of production and the concomitant principle of holistic social planning, including the area of culture, formed the basis of the socialist social system. Private cultural enterprises and institutions were gradually nationalized in the late 1940s and early 1950s. Mass media, collecting societies, publishing houses, theatres, record companies and other enterprises of creative labor were transferred into the hands of socialist organizations, and the distribution of works was possible only through socialist organizations. While in the Western European tradition the institution of copyright was founded on the basis of natural law and its claims of universalistic validity, socialist law, on the other hand, embedded copyright into a historicist and evolutionary scheme of development, predicated on the means of production and society's social priorities. Socialist jurisprudence regarded copyright not just as an institution that was periodically readjusted to new technologies, but ascribed to it a decidedly social function.

---

[7] I have expounded in more detail on the longue durée of copyright in Eastern Europe; see Augusta Dimou, "Urheberrecht und Kultur im kommunistischen Südost- und Ostmitteleuropa. Grundzüge und Thesen zur historischen Entwicklung einer rechtlichen Institution – eine Langzeitperspektive," in *Kulturpolitik in Ostmittel- und Südosteuropa (1945–2015)*, ed. Steffen Höhne (Wiesbaden: Harrassowitz, 2019), 141–77.

It is difficult to evoke the notion of Sovietization to describe copyright development in communist Southeast and East Central Europe; this stands in contrast to transfers of artistic and literary genres and institutions (including the original censorship mechanisms), where the claim of Sovietization can certainly be made (although here as well a differentiation of the respective national experiences as well as an appropriate periodization would be advisable for various reasons). The communist takeovers did not necessarily prompt the adoption of new copyright legislations in the countries of Southeastern and Central Eastern Europe. On the contrary, most of the interwar legislation remained intact for a long time (the only exception here was the Yugoslavia Copyright Act of 1946, which had more radical features and a clear tendency towards nationalization along Soviet lines, but this was very quickly reversed in the early 1950s). The majority of Eastern Bloc countries did not adopt new copyright laws until the 1950s, and in some cases, such as the GDR and Hungary, even later, in the 1960s. Usually, laws were supplemented by decrees and regulations that permitted swift and flexible adaptations of copyright standards, eschewing the need for proper legislative amendments.

Although the majority of communist copyright laws demonstrated some similar features, which typologically could be bundled into an independent category of "socialist copyright," this was due to leanings on, but by no means an absolute alignment with, the Soviet experience. The construction of Soviet copyright law was structurally and substantively intended to serve the specific political constellation of the USSR, especially with a view to the numerous nationalities in the multi-ethnic state, and as a result could not be easily replicated. The Soviet copyright regime did not have a copyright law per se; the copyright regulations were anchored in the foundations of the civil legislation of the USSR of 1961 (Articles 96–106), which were then largely adopted by the civil codes of the Union republics and supplemented according to local needs.[8] This flexible legal construction was only roughly imitated by countries with a similar multi-ethnic structure, such as Yugoslavia and Czechoslovakia. Although both countries had national copyright laws, in the post-war period—and this is in contrast to the experience of the interwar period—they organized the administration of copyright on a federal basis and also allowed leeway for local adaptations of copyright provisions.

Although a number of similar features (administrative fixation of royalties, the standardized publishing contract, copyright agencies with monopoly powers, etc.)

8 Artur-Axel Wandtke, "Entwicklungstendenzen des Urheberrechts in Osteuropa (unter besonderer Berücksichtigung der Gesetze in Polen, Russland, Ungarn sowie in Tschechien und der Slowakei)," *GRUR International* 7 (1995): 565.

formed the core of socialist copyright law, the national laws of the interwar period continued to serve as important templates and often determined the idiosyncratic features of individual national legislations.[9] This is also evident from the fact that it was not until the late 1970s that lawyers in socialist countries made the first transnational attempts to standardize and coordinate socialist copyright law.[10] It is noteworthy that the Soviet Union played no more than a secondary role in this expert exchange that was largely led by lawyers from Central and Eastern Europe (Poland, GDR, Hungary and Czechoslovakia).

The communist copyright legislation of Southeastern and East Central Europe can therefore only be understood to a limited extent as a true break with its predecessors of the interwar period. As can be deduced from their own analyses, copyright lawyers often referred to the legislation of the interwar period dispassionately and even positively, and interpreted their own activity under communism as an extension and perfection of previous traditions rather than a true turning point in the development of national copyright legislation. Without doubt, socialist copyright law served a new social order; the interwar legislation was considered "bourgeois" but was generally respected. Copyright lawyers did not shy away from building retrospective genealogies that included the interwar period.[11] This habitus certainly reflected the heightened consciousness of the legal profession; most likely it also displayed the awareness of a "kinship" between the two periods. Finally, there was also physical continuity of professional cohorts; a large number of the copyright lawyers active in the communist period had been trained in the interwar period (in the late 1930s) and this group of jurists reached its professional peak under communism.

Additional reasons go to explain the absence of systematic Sovietization or the somewhat more independent copyright development of the Southeast and East Central European countries. One of the most important was the almost uninterrupted membership of these countries in international copyright organizations and

9 Eugen Ulmer, "Urheberrechtsfragen in den Beziehungen zwischen Westen und Osten," *GRUR International* 12 (1968): 406f.

10 Heinz Püschel, "Zehn Jahre Tagungen von Expertengruppen der Urheberrechtsorganisationen sozialistischer Länder," *Zeitschrift für Urheber- und Medienrecht/Film und Recht* 33 (1989): 23–28.

11 See for example Janusz Barta and Ryszard Markiewicz, "Schutz der Urheberpersönlichkeitsrechte, Geschichte und Perspektiven," in *Centenaire de la Convention de Berne et 60 ans de la legislation sur le droit d'auteur en Pologne, Symposium International 18–21 Novembre 1986*, ed. Janusz Szwaja and Jerzy Serda (Zeszyty Naukowe Uniwersytetu Jagiellońskiego DCCCLXVI, Międzuczelniany Institut Wynalazczości i Ochrony Własności Intelektualnej, Prace z wynalazczości i ochrony własności intelektualnej, zeszyt 45) (Kraków: Nakładem Uniwersytetu Jagiellońskiego, 1988), 183–93. See also Jan Bleszyński, "Le droit d'auteur polonaise. Traditions et perspectives," in Szwaja and Serda, *Centenaire de la Convention de Berne*, 156–69.

structures like the Berne Union and the Universal Copyright Convention (UCC) later on. Overcoming their initial hesitation and uncertainty, the majority of Southeast and East Central European countries continued their membership in these organizations in the postwar period. Membership in international organizations meant firstly that the copyright laws of these countries continued to adhere to the basic framework and legal standards of international agreements (albeit with some deviations, for example the Polish law of 1952 broke with the BU standard of 50 years of protection p.m.a. and instead followed the Soviet example of 25 years). Secondly, it meant that East European lawyers continued to participate in international copyright fora and were informed about international developments and discussions. Some among them even achieved considerable international recognition (Heinz Püschel, György Boytha, Mihály Ficsor, Karel Knap, Árpád Bogsch and others) and held leading positions in international organizations such as the WIPO (for example Ficsor, Boytha and Bogsch). Here, too, the USSR and the countries of Southeastern and Central Eastern Europe went their separate ways, as the Soviet Union remained aloof from all international obligations until the 1970s and only joined the original (1952) version of the Universal Copyright Convention in 1975.

Communist copyright cannot therefore be made to comfortably fit ready-made categories. In the narrow symbiosis between creative elites and state power, communist copyright strikingly resembled the pre-modern system of privileges; in its distancing from the volatility of the market, however, communist copyright came the closest to fulfilling the fundamental pledge of modern copyright, i.e. serving the intellectual needs of society and protecting its creators. Moreover, as paradoxical as it may sound, copyright provisions sometimes actually came to the help of noncomformist authors that had fallen from grace with communist authorities. Though outcasted from the official literary establishment and the privileges it contained, ostracized authors could occasionally continue to produce, have their works published (provided they did not irritate excessively with their writings) and (due to copyright) demand remuneration for them, even though standing outside the sanctioned literary system. The case of the Bulgarian author Ivan Bogdanov et al. is a representative example of such a complicated biography.[12]

Communist regimes generally pursued a strategy of depropertization in the realm of culture, although as witnessed in this analysis, by the 1960s and 1970s the creative unions in several countries were able to reverse this trend and push an agenda of greater or smaller "repropertization" in copyright relations. In their

12 See Ivan Bogdanov's archive in the National Literary Museum, Sofia.

majority, authors became dependent full-time employees, resembling rather a "civil service" of the literary professions, while their professionalization was sanctioned almost exclusively "from above," i.e. by the state. Although this signaled a departure from the ideal type of the freelance writer, it needs to be remembered that this type of professional was poorly represented in Southeast Europe in the interwar period; the majority of intellectuals earned their living by engaging in other professions (often as teachers or civil servants), and only in a few cases such as interwar Czechoslovakia was the proportion of literary professions and other forms of employment roughly balanced. It is therefore important to underline that under communism the literary and artistic establishment was subjected to the primacy of politics. However, it should be mentioned likewise that the communist period represented one of the rare moments in the history of copyright law when authors were able to enforce their conditions over the will and power of publishers and intermediaries, and as a result, copyright became an instrument that served holistically the interests of authors as a professional class or status group.

9. Thinking of the longue durée of copyright history in East and Southeast Europe, it can be argued that changes after 1989 and the concomitant streamlining with the *acquis communautaire* likely signified a greater fissure than 1945 with a view to the broad parameters and the utilitarian philosophy of copyright as it had developed historically in the region since the nineteenth century. This is a thesis worth reflecting on; moreover, it should highlight how misleading it can be to conceptualize various eras and regions of the continent in terms of "departures" from and/or "returns" to Europe. Regrettable, moreover, is the fact that the East European copyright experience received so little attention, and its legacy was so easily pushed aside before it had been adequately processed and/or reflected on. What is more, the way it impacted international copyright (the treatment of which would far exceed the scope of this book) should be reviewed and evaluated anew, including the contribution of Yugoslav jurists in defending lower copyright standards for Third World countries, the insistence of Hungarian jurists on defending copyright exceptions for people with disabilities, or the attention paid by socialist countries to the protection of various forms of traditional knowledge. Many of these achievements, which appear so evident to us today, can partially trace their roots back to Eastern Europe.

10. Contrary to the theory that recommends copyright as an institution capable of structuring and guaranteeing more stable and predictable relations among stakeholders in the cultural economy and offering creators the long-wished-for

protection, autonomy, incentive and reward for their labor, the current work has shown the application of copyright to have varied outcomes, some of which are controversial and contradictory. Moreover, its effects have been shown to be contingent on a variety of parameters, such as genre (for example, the differences between literature and music), social and economic context (for example, the massification or not of culture) and/or cultural and political factors. It is apparent that the rhetorical and moral vigor that often accompany justifications of copyright do not automatically translate into vigorous and felicitous results in practice.

On the one hand, in contexts where culture was only barely commercialized, copyright is shown to have had little to no effect. Instead of market *cum* copyright, it was the veneration of culture, the stubborn and persistent commitment of intellectual creators, help from the state, civil society and/or self-help and other factors that aided the perseverance of culture. On the other hand, it is demonstrated that copyright could have a decisive and crucial impact in structuring (world) markets and determining royalty flows, but often in a very uneven and rather obscure (non-transparent) manner. The current work has shown copyright to also be a volatile instrument, often supporting and naturalizing inequalities in the cultural field; remuneration is predicated not on labor (as the property theory would like us to believe) but is whimsical and market(ing)-dependent. Discrepancies here can be considerable. The current analysis has shown that the way and the purposes for which copyright regimes are designed and applied do matter.

Far too often and more than necessary, our archival research brought misuses and embezzlements to light in connection with copyright application. Though the specific role of the human factor herein cannot be dismissed or ignored, the current analysis makes evident that there are also structural reasons that support such inequality. By favoring big players, copyright encourages and augments the rule of the strongest and perpetuates established structures through the philosophy of "the winner takes all," but also through its preference for economies of scale. These last require industrial, made-to-measure (i.e. guaranteed success) production, which in turn structures creative processes.

Our analysis has clearly shown that the application of copyright did not signify the same thing and did not have the same effect for all parties involved. Beyond the well-known and evident conflict of interests between "importers" and "exporters," copyright sanctions a specific attitude to cultural creation and validates specific models that sideline other approaches, attitudes, philosophies of knowledge and culture. One such typical example is the contrast between written/oral culture, and the way West European copyright obviously favored text-intensive cultural production and (mechanical) textual reproduction to the detriment of other forms of cultural expression. In the same vein, it promoted a concept of knowledge as an atomized occurrence or skill to the detriment of a notion of knowledge as interactive experience and/or exchange. Similarly, copyright is heralded as a generic mechanism for the regulation of intellectual labor, whereas in reality its historical trajectory has been predicated, in the main, upon highly commercialized genres and sectors of intellectual production. The aura of copyright is thereby inflated and extended indiscriminately to all intellectual creation, assuming the copyright model of regulation to be the only and real standard of knowledge production and circulation, instead of it being one possibility among others.

In several instances throughout this book, international solutions promoted via copyright legislation were revealed to be business models serving particularistic corporate interests, usually assisting the expansion of specific industries or branches instead of best-practice principles for regulatory policy. What is worse, in those long chains of stakeholders and intermediaries, it was often difficult to determine where money flowed to and who actually profited from royalties and revenues.

In the period examined in this book—the late nineteenth and a good part of the twentieth century—all these contradictions were often obscured through the civilizational rhetoric and the concomitant aura of correctness and prestige radiated by authors' rights. Without doubt, copyright was intellectually indebted to the nineteenth-century notion of progress, and its international charisma was largely grounded on faith in human and social evolution; empowering authors, acknowledging their labor and helping them become independent was indeed progressive. But there were also additional nuances attached to the coding of "civilization" that had the exact opposite effects, such as the affinity and reciprocity between the civilizational and the colonial project, but also the reciprocal legitimization and intertwinement of law and capitalism.

Sources and Bibliography

Periodicals/Newspapers

- *Le Droit d'auteur*. Organe officiel. Bureau de l'Union Internationale pour la protection des œuvres littéraires et artistiques, 1898–1920.
- *Soutěz a Tvorba*, 1926–1927.
- *Věstník Syndikátu českých spisovatelů*, 1926, 1929.
- *Knižarska Duma*, ratnik za knižarskija suŭz v Bălgarija, 1927–1928.
- *Knižarska Duma*, vestnik na struženieto na knižarite, knigoizdatelite i knižnite skladove v Bălgarija, 1934–1935.
- *Dăržaven Vestnik* (online), https://dv.parliament.bg/DVWeb/index.faces.
- *Knijižarski Glasnik*, 1922–1926.
- *Glasnik Knjižara*, 1929–1933.
- *International Institute of Intellectual Co-operation*, League of Nations, Bulletin 1931, 1934, 1936, 1938.
- *International Intellectual Cooperation*, League of Nations, 1932, 1938.
- *Informations sur la Coopération Intellectuelle*, no. 1–2 (1939).

Archival Fonds and Online Depositories

Bulgaria

- National Library, Historical Arhive, fond 260, 501, 560.
- Central State Archives (CDA) Sofia, fond 177, 284, 551, 904, 921.
- Stenographic Protocols of the Plenary Sessions of the National Assembly of the Republic of Bulgaria (online) https://www.parliamofficial literary establishmentent.bg/bg/plenaryst
- National Literary Museum, fond Ivan Bogdanov, Afera Vera Slovena Nr a 1067/97.

Czechoslovakia

- Stenographic Protocols of the National Assembly of the Czechoslovak Republic, Senate (online)
- National Archives, Ministry of Justice, karton 1813.
- Památník Národního Písemnictví

Yugoslavia

- Arhiv Jugoslavije, Belgrade, fond 66, 498.
- Historical Archive of the City of Belgrade, Belgrade, Fond "Knižarska organizacija u Beogradu" (unclassified collection), box 25.

France

- Ministère des Affaires étrangères, Archives diplomatiques – La Courneuve, Paris.
- Papiers Marcel Plaisant (1945–1950), PAAP 220 (220/166, 167, 168, 169).
- Affaires politiques et économiques de 1897–1940, Correspondance politique et commerciale Série A-Paix 1914–1918, 4CPCOM, MNESYS, 80 CPCOM (146, 147, 169).
- Service français de la Société de Nations 1917–1940, 242Q0.
- Ministère des Affaires étrangères, Direction des Affaires politiques et commerciales/Conditions économiques de la Paix, P 1599, P 12909.
- Serie SDN N 1879 (08.1930–08.1939) Coopération intellectuelle

Unesco Archives (Paris)

- IICI, Correspondance E III, 1–3.
- IICI, 1932–1939, Questions juridiques E/ 4–122.
- Archives 347.78 A55, part I and II.
- Archives 347.78 A102/064 (44) 47, 51.
- E /54–61/1930.
- E/69–79/1931.

Bibliography

Monographs and Edited Volumes

Abbott, Andrew. *The System of Professions: An Essay on the Division of Expert Labor*. Chicago: University of Chicago Press, 1988.

Adelmann, Ralf, Jan-Otmar Hesse, Judith Keilbach, Markus Stauff, and Matthias Thiele, eds. *Ökonomien des Medialen: Tausch, Wert und Zirkulation in den Medien und Kulturwissenschaften*. Bielefeld: Transcript, 2006.

Ágoston, Gábor, and Bruce Masters, eds. *Encyclopedia of the Ottoman Empire: Facts on File*. New York: Facts on File, 2009.

Alexander, Isabella, and H. Tomás Gómez-Arostegui, eds. *Research Handbook on the History of Copyright Law*. Cheltenham: Edward Elgar, 2016.

Anderson, Benedict. *Imagined Communities: Reflections on the Origin and Spread of Nationalism*. London: Verso, 1983.

Apel, Simon, Louis Pahlow, and Matthias Wiessner, eds. *Biographisches Handbuch des Geistigen Eigentums*. Tübingen: Mohr Siebeck, 2017.

Aplin, Tanya, and Jennifer Davis. *Intellectual Property Law: Text, Cases and Materials*. 3rd ed. Oxford: Oxford University Press, 2013.

Ash, Mitchell G., and Jan Surman, eds. *The Nationalization of Scientific Knowledge in the Habsburg Empire, 1848–1918*. Basingstoke: Palgrave Macmillan, 2012.

Association Littéraire et Artistique Internationale (ALAI). *Son histoire – ses travaux 1878–1889*. Paris: Bibliothèque Chacognac, 1889.

Atkinson, Benedict. *The True Story of Copyright: The Australian Experience 1905–2005*. Sydney: Sydney University Press, 2007.

Avramov, Ljusien, and Vitali Tadžer. *Avtorsko pravo na narodna republika Bălgarija*. Sofia: Nauka i izkustvo, 1965.

Babović, Jovana. "Entertaining the Yugoslav Capital: Culture, Urban Space, and Politics in Belgrade between the Two Wars." PhD diss., University of Illinois at Urbana-Champaign, 2014.

Babović, Jovana. *Metropolitan Belgrade: Culture and Class in Interwar Yugoslavia*. Pittsburg: University of Pittsburg Press, 2018.

Bappert, Walter. *Wege zum Urheberrecht: Die geschichtliche Entwicklung des Urheberrechtsgedankens*. Frankfurt a.M.: Vittorio Klostermann, 1962.

Barbier, Frédéric. *L'Empire du livre: Le livre imprimé et la construction de l'Allemagne contemporaine (1815–1914)*. Paris: Cerf (Bibliothèque franco-allemande), 1995.

Barbier, Frédéric, ed. *Est – Ouest: Transferts et réceptions dans le monde du livre en Europe (XVIIe–XXe siècles)*. Leipzig: Leipziger Universitätsverlag, 2005.

Barbier, Frédéric, and Catherine Bertho Lavenir. *Histoire des médias: De Diderot à Internet*. Paris: Armand Colin, 1996.

Barbier, Frédéric, Sabine Juratic, and Dominique Varry, eds. *L'Europe et le livre: Réseaux et practiques du négoce de librairie XVIe–XIXe siècles*. Langres: Dominique Guéniot, 1996.

Baric, Daniel. *Langue allemande, identité croate: Au fondement d'un particularisme culturel*. Paris: Armand Colin, 2013.

Basalamah, Salah. *Le droit de traduire: Une politique culturelle pour la mondialisation*. Ottawa: Les Presses de l'Université d'Ottawa, 2009.

Benjamin, Walter. *The Work of Art in the Age of Mechanical Reproduction*. London: Penguin, 2008.

Bently, Lionel, Jennifer Davis, and Jane C. Ginsburg, eds. *Copyright and Piracy: An Interdisciplinary Critique*. Cambridge: Cambridge University Press, 2010.

Bently, Lionel, Uma Suthersanen, and Paul Torremans, eds. *Global Copyright: Three Hundred Years since the Statute of Anne, from 1709 to Cyberspace*. Cheltenham: Edward Elgar, 2010.

Beránková, Hana. "Kolektivní správa autorských práv – slepá ulička v institucionálním vývoji?" PhD diss., Prague University of Economics and Business, Faculty of Economics, 2010–2011.

Berk, Özlem. "Translation and the Westernization of Turkey (from the 1840s to the 1890s)." PhD diss., Translation Studies, Centre for British and Comparative Cultural Studies, University of Warwick, June 1999.

Berne Convention Centenary 1886–1986: The Berne Convention for the Protection of Literary and Artistic Works from 1886–1986. Geneva: BIPRI, 1986.

Biagioli, Mario, Martha Woodmansee, and Peter Jaszi, eds. *Making and Unmaking Intellectual Property: Creative Production in Legal and Cultural Perspective*. Chicago: University of Chicago Press, 2011.

Birkhold, Matthew H. *Characters before Copyright: The Rise and Regulation of Fan Fiction in Eighteenth-Century Germany*. Oxford: Oxford University Press, 2019.

Birnhack, Michael D. *Colonial Copyright: Intellectual Property in Mandate Palestine*. Oxford: Oxford University Press, 2012.

Bogavac, Milovan J. *Udruženje srpskih književnika 1905–1945*. Belgrade: Mrlješ, 2007.

Boguslawski, Mark Moissejewitsch. *Urheberrecht in internationalen Beziehungen*. Berlin: Staatsverlag der DDR, 1977.

Booth, Marilyn, ed. *Migrating Texts: Circulating Translations around the Ottoman Mediterranean*. Edinburgh: Edinburgh University Press, 2019.

Börnstein, Heinrich. *Fünfundsiebzig Jahre in der Alten und Neuen Welt: Memoiren eines Unbedeutenden*, vols. 1–2. New York: Lang, 1986.

Borov, Todor. *Bălgarskata kniga*. Sofia: Pridvorna pečatnica, 1935.

Bouche, Nicolas. *Le principe de la territorialité de la propriété intellectuelle*. Paris: L'Harmattan, 2002.

Bourdieu, Pierre. *The Field of Cultural Production*. New York: Columbia University Press, 1994.

Bourdieu, Pierre. *The Rules of Art: Genesis and Structure of the Literary Field*. Stanford, CA: Stanford University Press, 1995.

Boutet, M., and R. Plaisant. *Le régime international du droit d'auteur: La convention de Berne, révise à Bruxelles*. Paris, 1959.

Boyle, James. *Shamans, Software and Spleens: Law and the Construction of Information Society*. Cambridge, MA: Harvard University Press, 1997.

Breň, Tomáš, and Pavel Janáček, eds. *"O slušnou odměnu bude počováno...": Ekonomické souvislosti spisovatelské profese v české kultuře 19. a 20. Století*. Prague: Ústav pro českou literature AN ČR, v.v.i., 2009.

Calic, Marie-Janine. *Geschichte Jugoslawiens im 20. Jahrhundert*. Bonn: Bundeszentrale für politische Bildung, 2010.

Calic, Marie-Janine, Dietmar Neutatz, and Julia Obertreis, eds. *The Crisis of Socialist Modernity: The Soviet Union and Yugoslavia in the 1970s* (Schriftenreihe der FRIAS School of History, vol. 3). Göttingen: Vanderhoeck und Ruprecht, 2011.

Casanova, Pascale. *La République mondiale des Lettres*. Paris: Editions du Seuil, 1999.

Cavalli, Jean. *La genèse de la Convention de Berne pour la protection des œuvres littéraires et artistiques du 9 novembre 1886*. Lucerne: Imprimeries réunies, 1986.

Cavallo, Guglielmo, and Roger Chartier, eds. *A History of Reading in the West*. Amherst: University of Massachusetts Press, 1999.

Chartier, Roger. *The Order of Books: Readers, Authors, and Libraries in Europe between the Fourteenth and Eighteenth Centuries*. Cambridge: Polity Press, 1994.

Chartier, Roger. *Won in Translation: Textual Mobility in Early Modern Europe*. Philadelphia: University of Pennsylvania Press, 2022.

Činkov, P.K. *Sega šte čuete našija komentator*. Sofia: Sineva, 2001.

Cohen, Gary B. *Education and Middle-Class Society in Imperial Austria 1848–1918*. West Lafayette, IN: Purdue University Press, 1996.

Cohen, Monica F. *Pirating Fictions: Ownership and Creativity in Nineteenth-Century Popular Culture*. Charlottesville: University of Virginia Press, 2017.

Coombe, Rosemary J. *The Cultural Life of Intellectual Properties: Authorship, Appropriation and the Law*. Durham, NC: Duke University Press, 1998.

Cornis-Pope, Marcel, and John Neubauer, eds. *History of the Literary Cultures of East Central Europe*, vols. 1–4. Amsterdam: John Benjamins, vol. 1 (2004), vol. 2 (2006), vol. 3 (2007), vol. 4 (2010).

Rial Costas, Benito, ed. *Print Culture and Peripheries in Early Modern Europe: A Contribution to the History of Printing and the Book Trade in Small European and Spanish Cities*. Leiden: Brill, 2013.

Cvetković-Sander, Ksenija. *Sprachpolitik und nationale Identität im sozialistischen Jugoslawien (1945–1991): Serbokroatisch, Albanisch, Makedonisch und Slowenisch* (Balkanologische Veröffentlichungen, vol. 50). Wiesbaden: Harrassowitz, 2011.

Daskalov, Roumen. *Bălgarskoto Obštestvo, 1878–1939*, vol. 1. Sofia: Gutenberg, 2005.

Daskalov, Roumen, and Diana Mishkova, eds. *Entangled Histories of the Balkans* (Transfers of Political Ideologies and Institutions, vol. II) (Balkan Studies Library, vol. 12). Leiden: Brill, 2014.

Daskalova, Krasimira. *Gramotnost, knižina, čitateli: Četene v Bălgarija na prehoda kăm modernoto vreme*. Sofia: Lik, 1999.

Daskalova, Krasimira, and Ilko Penelov, eds. *Ani Gergova: Život s knižovni pristrastija* (Sbornik v čest na 75-godišninata i). Sofia: Universitetsko izdatelstvo "Sv. Kliment Ochridski", 2012.

Davidova, Evgenia. *Balkan Transitions to Modernity and Nation-States: Through the Eyes of Three Generations of Merchants (1780s–1890s)*. Leiden: Brill, 2013.

Davies, Margaret. *Property: Meanings, Histories, Theories*. Abingdon: Routledge, 2007.

Deazley, Ronan, Martin Kretschmer, and Lionel Benthly, eds. *Privilege and Property: Essays on the History of Copyright*. Cambridge: Open Book Publishers, 2010.

Desbois, Henri, et al. *Les conventions internationales du droit d'auteur et les droits voisins*. Paris: Dalloz, 1976.

Dietz, Adolf. *Protection of Intellectual Property in Central and Eastern European Countries: The Legal Situation in Bulgaria, CSFR, Hungary, Poland and Romania*. Paris: OECD Documents, 1995.

Dietz, Adolf. *Urheberrecht und Entwicklungsländer: Urheberrechtliche Probleme bei der Errichtung einer neuen internationalen Weltordnung* (Urheberrechtliche Abhandlungen des Max-Planck-Instituts für ausländisches und internationales Patent-, Urheber- und Wettbewerbsrecht, 17). Munich: C.H. Beck, 1981.

Dillenz, Walter. *Materialien zur Geschichte des österreichischen Urheberrechts 1895–1936* (Österreichische Schriftenreihe zum gewerblichen Rechtschutz, Urheber- und Medienrecht – ÖSGRUM). Vienna: Manz Verlag, 1989.

Dimić, Ljubodrag. *Kulturna politika Kraljevine Jugoslavije 1918–1941*, vols. 1–3. Belgrade: Stubovi kulture, 1996.

Dittrich, Robert, ed. *Die Notwendigkeit des Urheberrechtsschutzes im Lichte seiner Geschichte*. Vienna: Manz'sche, 1991.

Dittrich, Robert, ed. *Woher kommt das Urheberrecht und wohin geht es? Wurzeln, geschichtlicher Ursprung, geistesgeschichtlicher Hintergrund und Zukunft des Urheberrechts* (Österreichische Schriftenreihe zum gewerblichen Rechtschutz, Urheber- und Medienrecht – ÖSGRUM). Vienna: Manz Verlag, 1998.

Dejan Djokić, ed. *Yugoslavism: Histories of a Failed Idea 1918–1922*. London: C. Hurst & Co., 2003.

Dommann, Monika. *Autoren und Apparate: Die Geschichte des Copyrights im Medienwandel*. Frankfurt a.M.: Fischer, 2014.

Dugast, Jacques. *La vie culturelle en Europe au tournant des XIXe et XXe siècles* (Greek translation). Athens: Gutenberg, 2020.

Durković-Jakšić, Ljubomir. *Jugoslovensko Knjižarstvo 1918–1941*. Belgrade: Narodna knjiga, 1979.

Dykmann, Klaas. *Internationale Organisationen und ihre Zivilisierungsbestrebungen: Die Geschichte der Weltgesundheitsorganisation*. Vienna: Lit, 2017.

Elenkov, Ivan. *Kulturnijat Front, Bălgarska kultura prez epohata na komunizma – političesko upravlenie, ideologičeski osnovanija, institutionalni režimi*. Sofia: Ciela, 2008.

Elst, Michiel. *Copyright, Freedom of Speech and Cultural Policy in the Russian Federation* (Law in Eastern Europe Series, no. 53). Leiden: Martinus Nijhoff, 2004.

Elst, Michiel, and K. Malfliet, eds. *Intellectual Property in the Russian Federation: A System in Transition*. Brussels: Bruylant, 1994.

Fischer, Ernst, and Stephan Füssel, eds. *Geschichte des deutschen Buchhandels im 19. und 20. Jahrhundert*, vol. 2: Die Weimarer Republik 1918–1933, part 1. Munich: K.G. Saur, 2007.

Fischer, Georg, Stephan Klingner, and Malte Zill, eds. *Monopole im medienindustriellen Komplex? Verwertungsgesellschaften gestern, heute, morgen*. Marburg: Büchner, 2023.

Fitzgerald, Brian, and Benedict Atkinson, eds. *Copyright Future: Copyright Freedom*. Sydney: Sydney University Press, 2011.

Forbes, Meghan L. "In the Middle of It All: Prague, Brno, and the Avant-Garde Networks of Interwar Europe." PhD diss., University of Michigan, 2016.

Gellner, Ernest. *Nations and Nationalism*. Ithaca, NY: Cornell University Press, 1983.

Georgiev, Lăčezar. *Teorija na knigoizdatelskija process: aspekti, problem, tendencii*. Veliko Tărnovo: Universitetsko izdatelstvo "Sv. sv. Kiril i Metodii", 2001.

Gergova, Ani. *Knižninata i Bălgarite: XIX – načaloto na XX vek*. Sofia: Izdatelstvo na Bălgarskata akademija na naukite, 1991.

Gerhartl, Sybille. "'Vogelfrei' – Die österreichische Lösung der Urheberrechtsfrage in der 2. Hälfte des 19. Jahrhunderts oder Warum es Österreich unterließ, seine Autoren zu schützen." Diploma Thesis, Faculty of Humanities Vienna, 1995.

Gieseke, Ludwig. *Vom Privileg zum deutschen Urheberrecht: Die Entwicklung des Urheberrechts in Deutschland bis 1845*. Baden-Baden: Nomos, 1995.

Gigova, Irina. "Writers of the Nation: Intellectual Identity in Bulgaria 1939–1953." PhD diss., University of Illinois at Urbana-Champaign, 2005.

Gooday, Graeme, and Steven Wilf, eds. *Patent Cultures: Diversity and Harmonization in Historical Perspective*. Cambridge: Cambridge University Press, 2020.

Göpfert, Herbert, Gerard Kozielek, and Reinhard Wittmann, eds. *Buch- und Verlagswesen im 18. und 19. Jahrhundert: Beiträge zur Geschichte der Kommunikation in Mittel- und Osteuropa*. Berlin: Camen, 1977.

Halbert, Debora J. *The State of Copyright: The Complex Relationships of Cultural Creation in a Globalized World*. Abingdon: Routledge, 2014.

Hall, Murray G. *Böhmische Verlagsgeschichte 1919–1945*. www.boehmischeverlagsgeschichte.at.

Hall, Murray G. *Österreichische Verlagsgeschichte 1918–1938*, vol. I: Geschichte des österreichischen Verlagswesens (Literatur und Leben, Neue Folge Bd. 28/I). Vienna: Böhlau Verlag, 1985.

Hemmungs Wirtén, Eva. *Cosmopolitan Copyright: Law and Language in the Translation Zone* (Meddelanden från Institutionen för ABM vid Uppsala universitet, 4). Uppsala: Universitetstryckeriet, 2011.

Herren, Madelein. *Internationale Organisationen seit 1865: Eine Globalgeschichte der internationalen Ordnung*. Darmstadt: Wissenschaftliche Buchgesellschaft, 2009.

Hesse, Carla. *Publishing and Cultural Politics in Revolutionary Paris 1789–1810*. Berkeley: University of California Press, 1991.

Hofmann, Jeanette, ed. *Wissen und Eigentum: Geschichte, Recht und Ökonomie stoffloser Güter* (Bundeszentrale für politische Bildung, vol. 552). Bonn: BpB, 2006.

Höhne, Steffen, Anna-Dorothea Ludewig, and Julius H. Schoeps, eds. *Max Brod (1884–1968): Die Erfindung des Prager Kreises*. Cologne: Böhlau, 2016.

Höpken, Wolfgang. *Sozialismus und Pluralismus in Jugoslawien: Entwicklung und Demokratiepotential im Selbstverwaltungssystem* (Untersuchungen zur Gegenwartskunde Südosteuropas, vol. 22). Munich: Oldenburg, 1984.

Hristova, Natalija. *Specifika na bălgarskoto "Disidentstvo": Vlast i inteligencija 1956–1989*. Sofia: Letera, 2005.

Iriye, Akira. *Global Community: The Role of International Organizations in the Making of the Contemporary World*. Berkeley: University of California Press, 2002.

Jäger, Georg, ed. *Geschichte des deutschen Buchhandels im 19. und 20. Jahrhundert: Das Kaiserreich 1871–1918*, vol. III. Berlin: De Gruyter, 2001.

Janićijević, Milosav. *Stvaralačka inteligencija međuratne Jugoslavije*. Belgrade: Institut društvenih nauka – Centar za sociološka istraživanja, 1984.

Janjetović, Zoran. *Od "Internatiocionale" do komerciajale: Popularna kultura u Jugoslaviji, 1945–1991*. Belgrade: Altera, 2011.

Jedlicki, Jerzy, ed. *Dzieje inteligencji polskiej do roku 1918*, vols. 1–3. Warsaw: Neriton, 2008.

Johns, Adrian. *Piracy: The Intellectual Property Wars from Gutenberg to Gates*. Chicago: University of Chicago Press, 2009.

Jović, Dejan. *Jugoslavia: A State that Withered Away*. West Lafayette: Purdue University Press, 2009.

Kalinova, Evgenija. *Bălgarskata kultura i političeskijat imperativ (1944–1989)*. Sofia: Paradigma, 2011.

Kaser, Karl. *Hollywood auf dem Balkan: Die visuelle Moderne an der europäischen Peripherie (1900–1970)*. Vienna: Böhlau, 2018.

Katsarov, Konstantin. *Gewerblicher Rechtsschutz und Urheberrecht der UdSSR und der Volksdemokratien Europas*. Weinheim: Chemie, 1960.

Keiderling, Thomas. *Die Modernisierung des Leipziger Kommissionsbuchhandels von 1830 bis 1888* (Schriften zur Wirtschafts- und Sozialgeschichte, vol. 58). Berlin: Ducker & Humblot, 2000.

Kessler, Wolfgang. *Buchproduktion und Lektüre in Zivilkroatien und Slawonien zwischen Aufklärung und "Nationaler Wiedergeburt" (1767–1848)*. (Sonderdruck aus dem Archiv für Geschichte des Buchwesens, vol. XVI). Frankfurt a.M.: Buchhändler Vereinigung, 1976.

Khan, Zorina B. *The Democratization of Invention: Patents and Copyrights in American Economic Development 1790–1920*. New York: Cambridge University Press, 2005.

Knap, Karel. *Das neue Urheberrechtsgesetz der Tschechoslowakei* (Schriftenreihe der UFITA, no. 2) Baden-Baden: Verlag für Angewandte Wissenschaften, 1956.

Köllner, Alena. *Buchwesen in Prag: von Václav Matej Kramerius bis Jan Otto*. Vienna: Praesens, 2000.

Kon, Geca. *Katalog izdanja 1901–1935 izdavačkog i knjižarskog preduzeća Geca Kon a.d.* Belgrade: Geca Kon, 1935.

Konrád, Gyorgy, and Ivan Szelényi. *The Intellectuals on the Road to Class Power*. Brighton: Harvester Press, 1979.

Koskenniemi, Martti. *The Gentle Civilizer of Nations: The Rise and Fall of International Law 1870–1960*. Cambridge: Cambridge University Press, 2001.

Koumanos, Giorgos. *Pnevmatiki idioktisia*. Athens: Sakoulas, 1995.

Krăstev, Hrăstjo. *Mladi i stari*. Sofia: Zaharii Stojanov, 2003.

Ladas, Stephen P. *The International Copyright Protection of Literary and Artistic Property in Two Volumes*. New York: Macmillan, 1938.

Lasic, Stanko. *Les intellectuels et la contrainte idéologique: Conflits internes de la gauche littéraire en Yougoslavie 1928–1952*. Paris: Editions Denoël, 1974.

Latour, Bruno. *Pandora's Hope: Essays on the Reality of Science Studies*. Cambridge, MA: Harvard University Press, 1999.

Leible, Stefan, Ansgar Ohly, and Herbert Zech, eds. *Wissen – Märkte – Geistiges Eigentum*. Tübingen: Mohr Siebeck, 2010.

Lemberg, Hans, et al., eds. *Bildungsgeschichte, Bevölkerungsgeschichte, Gesellschaftsgeschichte in den böhmischen Ländern und Europa, Festschrift für Jan Havranek zum 60. Geburtstag* (Schriftenreihe des Österreichischen Ost- und Südosteuropainstituts, 14). Vienna: Verlag für Geschichte und Politik, 1988.

Lemoine, Jean-Jacques. *La Société des Auteurs, Compositeurs et Editeurs de Musique SACEM 1850–1950*. Paris: Lebois, 1950.

Levitsky, Serge L. *Introduction to Soviet Copyright Law*. Leiden: Sijthoff, 1964.

Levitsky, Serge L., and W.B. Simmons, eds. *Urheberrecht Russlands und der UdSSR*. Vienna: Manz Verlag, 1985.

Loeber, D.A. *Urheberrecht in der Sowjetunion: Einführung und Quellen*. Frankfurt a.M.: Alfred Metzner, 1981.

Löhr, Isabella. *Die Globalisierung geistiger Eigentumsrechte: Neue Strukturen internationaler Zusammenarbeit 1886–1952* (Kritische Studien zur Geschichtswissenschaft, vol. 195). Göttingen: Vandenhoeck & Ruprecht, 2010.

Löhr, Isabella, Matthias Middell, and Hannes Siegrist, eds. *Kultur und Beruf in Europa* (Europäische Geschichte in Quellen und Essays, vol. 2). Stuttgart: Franz Steiner Verlag, 2012.

Löwenbach, Jan. *Autor a nakladatel: K chystanému zákonu a smlouvě nakladatelské*. Prague: Tiskem a nákladatelem pražké akciové tiskárny, 1921.

Löwenbach, Jan. *Právo autorské: komentované zákony československé republiky*. Prague: Československý kompas, 1927.

Ludžev, Dimităr. *Grad na dve epohi, istorija na obštestvenite grupi v bălgarskite gradove v sredata na XX vek*. Sofia: Sv. Kliment Ohridski, 2005.

Mächtel, Florian. *Das Patentrecht im Krieg* (Geistiges Eigentum und Wettbewerbsrecht, 25). Tübingen: Mohr Siebeck, 2009.

Majstorović, Stevan. *Cultural Policy in Yugoslavia: Self-Management and Culture* (Studies and Documents on Cultural Policies). Paris: UNESCO, 1980.

Malalpate, Léon. *Le Droit d'Auteur: Sa protection dans les rapports Franco-Étrangers*. Paris: Recueil Sirey, 1931.

Marek, Jaroslav. *Česka moderní kultura*. Prague: Mladá fronta, 1998.

Marković, Predrag. *Beograd između istoka i zapada 1948–1965*. Belgrade: Novinsko-izdavačka ustanovka Službeni list SRJ, 1996.

May, Christopher. *The Global Political Economy of Intellectual Property Rights: The New Enclosures?* London: Routledge, 2009.

May, Christopher, and Susan K. Sell. *Intellectual Property Rights: A Critical History*. Boulder, CO: Lynne Rienner Publishers, 2006.

Mazower, Mark. *Governing the World: The History of an Idea*. New York: Penguin, 2012.

McClelland, Charles, Stephan Merl, and Hannes Siegrist, eds. *Professionen im modernen Osteuropa: Professions in Modern Eastern Europe*. Berlin: Duncker und Humblot, 1995.

Michon, Jacques, and Jean-Yves Mollier, eds. *Les mutations du livre et de l'édition dans le monde, du XVIIIe siècle à l'an 2000*. Paris: L'Harmattan, 2001.

Milojković-Djurić, Jelena. *Tradition and Avant-Garde: The Arts in Serbian Culture between the Two World Wars* (East European Monographs, no. CLX). Boulder, CO: Columbia University Press, 1984.

Milojković-Djurić, Jelena. *Tradition and Avant-Garde: Literature and Art in Serbian Culture 1900–1918* (East European Monographs, no. CCXXXIV). Boulder, CO: Columbia University Press, 1988.

Mollier, Jean-Yves. *L'argent et les lettres: Histoire du capitalisme d'édition 1880–1920*. Paris: Fayard, 1988.

Mollier, Jean-Yves, ed. *La Commerce de la librairie en France au XIXe siècle*. Paris: IMEC/Éditions de la MSH, 1997.

Mollier, Jean-Yves, Jean-François Sirinelli, and François Vallotton, eds. *Culture de masse et culture médiatique en Europe et dans les Amériques 1860–1940*. Paris: Presses universitaires de France, 2006.

Moravcová, Hana. "Economic History of Authors' Rights and Creative Industries in Czechoslovakia." Dissertation, Charles University, Faculty of Social Sciences, Institute of Economic Studies, Prague, 2020.

Moretti, Franco. *Atlas of the European Novel: 1800–1900*. London: Verso, 1998.

Müller, Dietmar, and Hannes Siegrist, eds. *Professionen, Eigentum und Staat: Europäische Entwicklungen im Vergleich. 19. und 20. Jahrhundert* (Moderne europäische Geschichte, 8). Göttingen: Wallstein, 2014.

Müller, Tim B., and Adam Tooze, eds. *Normalität und Fragilität: Demokratie nach dem Ersten Weltkrieg*. Hamburg: Hamburger Edition, 2015.

Newcity, M.A. *Copyright Law in the Soviet Union*. New York: Praeger Publishers, 1978.

Okediji, Ruth L., ed. *Copyright Law in an Age of Limitations and Exceptions*. Cambridge: Cambridge University Press, 2017.

Ong, Walter J. *Orality and Literacy: The Technologizing of the Word*. London: Routledge, 2002.

Ort, Thomas. *Art and Life in Modernist Prague: Karel Čapek and His Generation 1911–1938*. New York: Palgrave Macmillan, 2013.

Orzoff, Andrea. *Battle for the Castle: The Myth of Czechoslovakia in Europe, 1914–1948*. Oxford: Oxford University Press, 2009.

Osterhammel, Jürgen. *Die Verwandlung der Welt: Eine Geschichte des 19. Jahrhunderts*. Munich: C.H. Beck, 2011.

Pejovich, Svetozar. *The Market-Planned Economy of Yugoslavia*. Minneapolis: University of Minnesota Press, 1966.

Penelov, Ilko. "Censurata vărhu knigite v Bălgarija, 1944–1956." PhD diss., Sofia, filosofski fakultet, University Sv. Kliment Ochridski, 2007.

Prasad, Pratima. *Colonialism, Race, and the French Romantic Imagination*. New York: Routledge, 2009.

Pravilova, Ekaterina. *A Public Empire: Property and the Quest for the Common Good in Imperial Russia*. Princeton, NJ: Princeton University Press, 2014.

Praznik, Katja. *Art Work, Invisible Labour and the Legacy of Yugoslav Socialism*. Toronto: Toronto University Press, 2021.

Püschel, Heinz. *100 Jahre Berner Union: Gedanken, Dokumente, Erinnerungen*. Leipzig: VEB Fachbuchverlag, 1986.

Püschel, Heinz. *Internationales Urheberrecht*. Berlin: Staatsverlag der DDR, 1982.

Rehbinder, Manfred. *Urheberrecht*. Munich: C.H. Beck, 2008.

Remnek, Miranda Beaven, ed. *Books in Russia and the Soviet Union, Past and Present* (Publishing, Bibliography, Libraries, and Archives in Russia and Eastern Europe, vol. III). Wiesbaden: Harrassowitz, 1991.

Renoliet, Jean-Jacques. *L'Unesco oubliée, La Société des Nations et la coopération intellectuelle (1919–1946)*. Paris: Éditions de la Sorbonne, 1999.

Requate, Jörg. *Journalismus als Beruf: Entstehung und Entwicklung des Journalistenberufs im 19. Jahrhundert; Deutschland im internationalen Vergleich* (Historische Studien zur Geschichtswissenschaft, 109). Göttingen: Vanderhoeck und Ruprecht, 1995.

Ricketson, Sam. *The Berne Convention for the Protection of Literary and Artistic Works: 1886–1986*. London: Kluwer, 1987.

Ricketson, Sam, and Jane Ginsburg. *International Copyright and Neighbouring Rights: The Berne Convention and Beyond*, vols. 1–2. New York: Oxford University Press, 2006.

Ringer, Monica M., and Etienne E. Charrière, eds. *Ottoman Culture and the Project of Modernity: Reform and Translation in the Tanzimat Novel*. London: I.B. Tauris, 2020.

Roeber, Georg, et al., eds. *Benvenuto Samson zum 90. Geburtstag*. Berlin: De Gruyter, 1978.

Roper, Geoffrey, ed. *The History of the Book in the Middle East* (The History of the Book in the East). Farnham: Ashgate, 2013.

Rose, Carol M. *Property and Persuasion: Essays on the History, Theory and Rhetoric of Ownership*. Boulder, CO: Westview Press, 1994.

Rose, Mark. *Authors and Owners: The Invention of Copyright*. Cambridge, MA: Harvard University Press, 1993.

Rothenberg, Stanley. *Copyright and Public Performance of Music*. The Hague: Martinus Nijhoff, 1954.

Ruppert, Wolfgang. *Der moderne Künstler: Zur Sozial- und Kulturgeschichte der kreativen Individualität in der Moderne im 19. und frühen 20. Jahrhundert*. Frankfurt a.M.: Surhkamp, 1998.

Sarakinov, Georgi. *Avtorsko pravo i srodnite mu prava v Republika Bălgarija*. Sofia: Sibi, 2005.

Sassoon, Donald. *The Culture of the Europeans: From 1800 to the Present*. London: HarperCollins, 2006.

Sayer, Derek. *The Coasts of Bohemia: A Czech History*. Princeton, NJ: Princeton University Press, 1998.

Scheideler, Britta. *Zwischen Beruf und Berufung: Zur Sozialgeschichte der deutschen Schriftsteller von 1880–1933*. Frankfurt a.M.: Buchhändler Vereinigung, 1997.

Schwanke, Inka. "Die Entwicklung des Urheberrechts auf dem Gebiet der heutigen Tschechischen Republik und seine Annäherung an den Schutzstandard der Europäischen Union." Masterarbeit, Charles University Prague, Faculty of Law, LL.M.-Programme The Czech Legal System in European Contexts, July 2002.

Seiragakis, Manolis. *To elafro mousiko theatro stin mesopolemiki Athina*. Athens: Kastaniotis, 2009.

Seville, Catherine. *The Internationalization of Copyright Law: Books, Buccaneers and the Black Flag in the Nineteenth Century*. Cambridge: Cambridge University Press, 2006.

Sherman, Brad, and Lionel Bently, eds. *The Making of Modern Intellectual Property Law: The British Experience, 1760–1911*. Cambridge: Cambridge University Press, 1999.

Sherman, Brad, and Alain Strowel, eds. *Of Authors and Origins: Essays on Copyright Law*. Oxford: Clarendon Press, 1994.

Siegrist, Hannes, ed. *Entgrenzung des Eigentums in modernen Gesellschaften und Rechtskulturen*, 16 Comparativ 5/6. Leipzig: Leipziger Universitätsverlag, 2006.

Siegrist, Hannes, and Augusta Dimou, eds. *Expanding Intellectual Property: Copyrights and Patents in Twentieth-Century Europe and Beyond*. Budapest: CEU Press, 2017.

Siegrist, Hannes, and Isabella Löhr, eds. *Intellectual Property Rights and Globalization*, 21 Comparativ 2, Leipzig: Leipziger Universitätsverlag, 2011.

Šimeček, Zdeněk. *Geschichte des Buchhandels in Tschechien und in der Slowakei*. Wiesbaden: Harrassowitz Verlag, 2002.

Sluga, Glenda. *Internationalism in the Age of Nationalism*. Philadelphia: University of Pennsylvania Press, 2013.

Spaić, Vojislav. *Društvena svojina i autorsko parvo*. Belgrade: Naučno delo, 1965.

Spoo, Robert. *Without Copyrights: Piracy, Publishing, and the Public Domain*. Oxford: Oxford University Press, 2013.

St. Clair, William. *The Reading Nation in the Romantic Period*. Cambridge: Cambridge University Press, 2004.

Starčević, Velimir. *Knjiga o Geći Konu*. Belgrade: Prosveta/Admiral Books, 2009.

Stehr, Nico. *Knowledge Societies*. London: Sage, 1994.

Stipčević, Aleksandar. *Socijalna povijest knjige u hrvata, od početka hrvatskoga narodnog preporoda (1835) do danas*, vol. iii. Zagreb: školska knjiga, 2008.

Strömholm, Stig. *Le droit moral de l'auteur en droit allemande, français et scandinave avec un aperçu de l'évolution internationale*. Stockholm: P.A. Norstedt & Söners Förlag, 1967.

Strowel, Alain. *Droit d'auteur et copyright. Divergences et convergence. Étude de droit comparé*. Paris: Bruylant, 1993.

Šuman, Janko. *Komentar zakona o zaštiti autorskog prava i međunarodnih propisa*. Belgrade: Geca Kon, 1935.

Sundara Rajan, Mira T. *The Cambridge Handbook of Intellectual Property in Central and Eastern Europe*. Cambridge: Cambridge University Press, 2019.

Sundara Rajan, Mira T. *Copyright and Creative Freedom: A Study of Post-socialist Law Reform*. London: Routledge, 2006.

Szwaja, Janusz and Jerzy Serda. *Centenaire de la Convention de Berne et 60 ans de la legislation sur le droit d'auteur en Pologne, Symposium International 18–21 Novembre 1986* (Zeszyty Naukowe Uniwersytetu Jagiellońskiego DCCCLXVI, Międzuczelniany Institut Wynalazczości i Ochrony Własności Intelektualnej, Prace z wynalazczości i ochrony własności intelektualnej, zeszyt 45). Kraków: nakłładem uniwersytetu jagiellońskiego, 1988.

Teilmann-Lock, Stina. *The Object of Copyright: A Conceptual History of Originals and Copies in Literature, Art and Design*. London: Routledge, 2016.

Thiesse, Anne-Marie. *La fabrique de l'ecrivain national: Entre littérature et politique*. Paris: Gallimard, 2009.

Tranfaglia, Nicola, and Albertina Vittoria. *Storia degli editori italiani: Dall' Unità alla fine degli anni sessanta*. Rome: Laterna, 2007.

Trgovčević, Ljubinka. *Istorija srpske književne zadruge*. Belgrade: Srpska književna zadruga, 1992.

Ulmer, Eugen, and Gerhard Schricker, eds. *International Encyclopaedia of Comparative Law*, vol. 14: Copyright and Industrial Property. Tübingen: Brill, 2007.

UNESCO. *Towards Knowledge Societies*. Paris: UNESCO, 2005.

Unkovski-Korica, Vladimir. *The Economic Struggle for Power in Tito's Yugoslavia: From WWII to Non-Alignment*. London: I.B. Tauris, 2016.

Uvalić, Milica. *The Rise and Fall of Market Socialism in Yugoslavia*. Special Report. Berlin: Dialogue of Civilizations Research Institute, 2018.

Venuti, Lawrence. *The Translator's Invisibility: A History of Translation*. London: Routledge, 1995.

Vesić, Ivana, and Vesna Peno. *Između umetnosti i života: O delatnosti udruženja muzičara u Kraljevini SHS/Jugoslaviji*. Belgrade: Musikološki institut SANU, 2017.

Viala, Alain. *Naissance de l'écrivain : Sociologie de la littérature à l'âge classique*. Paris: Editions de Minuit, 1985.

Vinopal, Vilém. "Analýza českého autorského práva v kontextu společenských změn: vývoj od poloviny 20. století do současnosti." PhD diss., Právnická Fakulta Masarykovy Univerzity, Katedra občanského práva, 2010.

Vodopija, Ivan Berislav, and Ivana Mandić Hekman, eds. *Iz povijesti hrvatskoga knjižarstva*. Zagreb: Exlibris, 2009.

Von Beyme, Klaus. *Das Zeitalter der Avantgarden: Kunst und Gesellschaft 1905–1955*. Munich: Beck, 2005.

Von Beyme, Klaus. *Die Kunst der Macht und die Gegenmacht der Kunst: Studien zum Spannungsverhältnis von Kunst und Politik*. Frankfurt a.M.: Suhrkamp, 1998.

Wadle, Elmar. *Beiträge zur Geschichte des Urheberrechts: Etappen auf einem langen Weg* (Schriften zum Bürgerlichen Recht, vol. 425). Berlin: Duncker and Humblot, 2012.

Wadle, Elmar, ed. *Historische Studien zum Urheberrecht in Europa: Entwicklungslinien und Grundfragen*. Berlin: Duncker und Humblot, 1993.

Wandtke, Artur-Axel, ed. *Urheberecht in Mittel- und Osteuropa. Handbuch mit Einführungen und Rechtstexten*, 2 vols. Berlin: Berliner Wissenschaftsverlag, 2002.

Wittmann, Reinhard, ed. *Buchmarkt und Lektüre im 18. und 19. Jahrhundert: Beiträge zum literarischen Leben 1750–1880*. Tübingen: Niemeyer, 1982.

Wolf, Michaela. *Die vielsprachige Seele Kakaniens, Übersetzen und Dolmetschen in der Habsburgermonarchie 1848 bis 1919*. Vienna: Böhlau, 2012.

Woodmansee, Martha. *The Author, Art and the Market: Rereading the History of Aesthetics*. New York: Columbia University Press, 1994.

Woodmansee, Martha, and Peter Jaszi, eds. *The Construction of Authorship: Textual Appropriation in Law and Literature*. Durham, NC: Duke University Press, 1994.

Woodmansee, Martha, and Mark Osteen, eds. *The New Economic Criticism: Studies at the Intersection of Literature and Economics*. London: Routledge, 1999.

Woodward, Susan L. *Socialist Unemployment: The Political Economy of Yugoslavia, 1949–1990.* Princeton, NJ: Princeton University Press, 1995.

Zagorov, Vasil. *Bălgarskata kniga (1878–1912): Ot văzroždenskija ideal do komersializacijata.* Sofia: "Za Bukvite – O pismeneh". 2014.

Articles and Chapters

Ayaydın Cebe, and Günil Özlem. "To Translate or Not to Translate? 19th Century Ottoman Communities and Fiction." *Die Welt des Islams* 56 (2016): 187–222.

Bachleitner, Norbert. "Tausch, Produktion und Übersetzung im österreichischen Buchhandel im 19. Jahrhundert." In *Est – Ouest: Transferts er réceptions dans le monde du livre en Europe (XVIIe–XXe siècles),* edited by Frédéric Barbier, 109–123. Leipzig: Leipziger Universitätsverlag, 2005.

Bachleitner, Norbert. "'Übersetzungsfabriken.' Das deutsche Übersetzungswesen in der ersten Hälfte des 19. Jahrhunderts." *Internationales Archiv für Sozialgeschichte der deutschen Literatur* 14, no. 1 (1989): 1–49.

Bannerman, Sara. "'We Are All Developing Countries': Canada and International Copyright History: Fault Lines in the Map of International Copyright." In *Copyright Future Copyright Freedom: Marking the 40th Anniversary of the Commencement of Australia's Copyright Act 1968,* edited by Brian Fitzgerald and Benedict Atkinson, 79–96. Sydney: Sydney University Press, 2011.

Barbier, Frédéric. "Le commerce international de la librairie française au XIXe siècle (1815–1913)." *Revue d'histoire moderne et contemporaine* 28 (Livre, Éducation, Savoirs XVIIe–XXe siècles) (January–March 1981): 94–117.

Barbier, Frédéric. "La librairie allemande comme modèle?" In *Les mutations du livre et l'édition dans le monde, du XVIIIe siècle à l'an 2000,* edited by Jacques Michon and Jean-Yves Mollier, 31–46. Paris: L'Harmattan, 2001.

Barbier, Frédéric. "Les marchés étrangers de la librairie française." In *Histoire de l'édition française,* edited by Roger Chartier and Henri-Jean Martin, vol. 3 (Le temps des éditeurs. Du romantisme à la Belle Époque), 268–281. Paris: Fayard, 1990.

Basalamah, Salah. "Translation Rights and the Philosophy of Translation: Remembering the Debts of the Original." In *In Translation: Reflections, Refractions, Transformations,* edited by Paul St-Pierre and Prafulla C. Kar, 117–132. Amsterdam: John Benjamins, 2007.

Bellido, Jose. "Colonial Copyright Extensions: Spain at the Berne Convention (1883–1899)." *Journal of the Copyright Society of the USA* 58 (2011): 501–522.

Bellido, Jose, "The Editorial Quest for International Copyright (1886–1896)." *Book History* 17 (2014): 380–405.

Bellido, Jose, "Latin American and Spanish Copyright Relations (1880–1904)." *The Journal of World Intellectual Property* 12, no. 1 (2009): 1–39.

Bellido, Jose. "Montevideo vs Berne: The Rise of an Interpretation in International Copyright (1888–1898)." *Revue internationale du droit d'auteur* 229 (2011): 4–155.

Bellido, Jose, and Fiona Macmillan. "Music Copyright after Collectivization." *Intellectual Property Quarterly,* no. 3 (2016): 231–246.

Bently, Lionel. "Copyright, Translations, and Relations between Britain and India in the Nineteenth and Early Twentieth Centuries." *Chicago-Kent Law Review* 82, no. 3 (2007): 1181–1240.

Bently, Lionel. "The 'Extraordinary Multiplicity' of Intellectual Property Laws in the British Colonies in the Nineteenth Century." *Theoretical Inquiries in Law* 12, no. 1 (2011): 161–200.

Beránková, Hana. "Interest Groups and Their Influence on the Czechoslovakian Author's Rights Act." In *Good Governance and Civil Society: Selected Issues on the Relations between State, Economy and Society*, edited by Adam Jarosz, 259–268. Newcastle upon Tyne: Cambridge Scholars Publishing, 2014.

Barta, Janusz, and Ryszard Markiewicz. "Schutz der Urheberpersönlichkeitsrechte, Geschichte und Perspektiven." In *Centenaire de la Convention de Berne et 60 ans de la legislation sur le droit d'auteur en Pologne, Symposium International 18–21 Novembre 1986*, edited by Janusz Szwaja and Jerzy Serda, 183–193 (Zeszyty Naukowe Uniwersytetu Jagiellońskiego DCCCLXVI, Międzuczelniany Instytut Wynalazczości i Ochrony Własności Intelektualnej, Prace z wynalazczości i ochrony własności intelektualnej, zeszyt 45). Kraków: naklładem uniwersytetu jagiellońskiego, 1988.

Binas-Preisendörfer, Susanne. "Verteilungsplan, ideologische Konstruktion und sozialer Filter: Zur Geschichte der Kategorien von E-Musik und U-Musik." In *Jahrbuch für Kulturpolitik 2006*, edited by Norbert Sievers and Bernd Wagner, 271– 277 (Institut für Kulturpolitik der Kulturpolitischen Gesellschaft e.V., vol. 6: Thema: Diskurs Kulturpolitik). Essen: Klartext, 2006.

Birnhack, Michael. "Hebrew Authors and English Copyright Law in Mandate Palestine." *Theoretical Inquiries in Law* 12, no. 1 (2011): 201–240.

Bleszyński, Jan. "Le droit d'auteur polonaise. Traditions et perspectives." In *Centenaire de la Convention de Berne et 60 ans de la legislation sur le droit d'auteur en Pologne, Symposium International 18–21 Novembre 1986*, edited by Janusz Szwaja and Jerzy Serda, 156–169 (Zeszyty Naukowe Uniwersytetu Jagiellońskiego DCCCLXVI, Międzuczelniany Institut Wynalazczości i Ochrony Własności Intelektualnej, Prace z wynalazczości i ochrony własności intelektualnej, zeszyt 45). Kraków: naklładem uniwersytetu jagiellońskiego, 1988.

Bond, Catherine. "'Cabined, Cribbed, Confined, Bound In': Copyright in the Australian Colonies." In *Research Handbook on the History of Copyright Law*, edited by Isabella Alexander and H. Tomás Gómez-Arostegui, 372–390. Cheltenham: Edward Elgar, 2016.

Botrel, Jean-François. "Entre imprimé et oralité: L'essor de la culture de masse en Espagne (1833–1936)." In *Culture de masse et culture médiatique en Europe et dans les Amériques 1860–1940*, edited by Jean-Yves Mollier, Jean-François Sirinelli, and François Vallotton, 143–156. Paris: Presses Universitaires de France, 2006.

Botrel, Jean-François. "L'exportation des livres et des modèles éditoriaux français en Espagne et en Amérique Latine (1814–1914)." In *Les mutations du livre et de l'édition dans le monde du XVIIIè siècle à l'an 2000*, edited by Jacques Michon and Jean-Yves Mollier, 219–240. Paris: L'Harmattan, 2001.

Boytha, György. "The Berne Convention and the Socialist Countries with Particular Reference to Hungary." *Columbia VLA Journal of Law and the Arts* 11 (1986): 57–72.

Boytha, György. "Der schillernde Schutz von Urheberpersönlichkeitsrechten in der Berner Übereinkunft." In *Recht im Wandel seines sozialen und technologischen Umfeldes: Festschrift für Manfred Rehbinder*, edited by Jürgen Becker et al., 199–214. Munich: C.H. Beck, 2002.

Boytha, György. "Urheber- und Verlegerinteressen im Entstehungsprozess des internationalen Urheberrechts." *UFITA* 85 (1979): 1–35.

Bugge, Peter. "Czech Democracy: Paragon or Parody?" *Bohemia, Jahrbuch des Collegium Carolinum* 47, no. 1 (2006–2007): 3–28.

Caglioti, Daniela L. "Property Rights in Time of Wars: Sequestration and Liquidation of Enemy Aliens' Assets in Western Europe during the First World War." *Journal of Modern European History* 12, no. 4 (Aliens and Internal Enemies during the First World War) (2014): 523–545.

Carroll, Michael W. "The Struggle for Music Copyright." *Florida Law Review* 57 (2005): 907–961.

Casanova, Pascale. "Consécration et accumulation de capital littéraire: La traduction comme échange inégal." *Actes de la recherche en sciences sociales* 144 (Traductions: les échanges littéraires internationaux) (September 2002): 7–20.

Chachereau, Nicolas, and Gabriel Galvez-Behar. "Patents, War and Peace: The Resilience of the International Patent Order through the First World War." *Journal of European Integration History* 29, no. 2 (2023): 205–226.

Charrière, Etienne E. "Translating Communities: Reading Foreign Fiction across Communal Boundaries in the Tanzimat Period." In *Ottoman Culture and the Project of Modernity: Reform and Translation in the Tanzimat Novel*, edited by Monica M. Ringer and Etienne E. Charrière, 177–192. London: I.B. Tauris, 2020.

Chaubet, François. "L'alliance française ou la diplomatie de la langue (1883–1914)." *Revue historique* 632, no. 4 (2004): 763–785.

Čičovska, Vesela. "Dăržavni kulturni institucii v Bălgarija." In *Bălgarija 1300: Institucii i dăržavna tradicija*, vol. 1, 459–482. Sofia: Bălgarsko istoričesko družestvo, 1981.

Čičovska, Vesela. "Glavlit (1952–1956): Izgraždane na edinna censurna sistema v Bălgarija." *Istoričeski pregled* 47, no. 10 (1991): 38–69.

Čičovska, Vesela. "Kulturnata politika na narodnodemokratičnata vlast (1944–1948 g.)." *Istoričeski pregled* 35, no. 4 (1979): 114–137.

Cohen, Gary B. "Cultural Crossing in Prague: 1900. Scenes from the Late Imperial Austria." *Austrian History Yearbook* 45 (April 2014): 1–30.

Darnton, Robert. "Histoire du livre. Geschichte des Buchwesens. An Agenda for Comparative History." *Publishing History* 22 (1987): 31–41.

Demirkol, Neslihan. "Ottoman Print Culture." *Lingua Franca, The History of Book in Translation* 5 (2019), http://www.sharpweb.org/linguafranca/issue-5-2019-ottoman-print-culture/.

Dietz, Adolf. "Intellectual Property and Desocialization in Eastern Europe." *International Review of Industrial Property and Copyright Law* 26, no. 6 (1995): 851–872.

Dietz, Adolf. "Transformation of Authors' Rights: Change of Paradigm." *Revue Internationale du Droit d'Auteur* 138 (1988): 38–42.

Dietz, Adolf. "Trends in the Development of Copyright Law in the Countries of Central and Eastern Europe." *Revue Internationale du Droit d'Auteur* 162 (1994): 121–226.

Dimou, Augusta. "The Expansion of Intellectual Property Rights in Southeast and East Central Europe in the Context of the First World War." *Südostforschungen* 75 (2016): 70–94 (*Erfahrungs- und Handlungsräume. Gesellschaftlicher Wandel in Südosteuropa seit dem 19. Jahrhundert zwischen dem Lokalen und dem Globalen*, Festschrift für Wolfgang Höpken, edited by Heike Karge, Ulf Brunnbauer und Claudia Weber).

Dimou, Augusta. "From State Governance to Self-Management: Culture and Intellectual Property Rights in Communist Yugoslavia." In *Expanding Intellectual Property: Copyrights and Patents in Twentieth-Century Europe and Beyond*, edited by Hannes Siegrist and Augusta Dimou, 173–203. Budapest: CEU Press, 2017.

Dimou, Augusta. "Das Recht am geistigen Eigentum im Jugoslawien der Zwischenkriegszeit. Internationaler Institutionentransfer zwischen rechtlicher Normierung und sozialer Praxis." *Zeitschrift für Ostmitteleuropaforschung* 61, no. 3 (2012): 356–378 (*Institutionenwandel und Rechtstransfer im 20. Jahrhundert*, edited by Hannes Siegrist und Stefan Troebst).

Dimou, Augusta. "Urheberrecht und Kultur im kommunistischen Südost- und Ostmitteleuropa. Grundzüge und Thesen zur historischen Entwicklung einer rechtlichen Institution – eine Langzeitperspektive." In *Kulturpolitik in Ostmittel- und Südosteuropa (1945–2015)*, edited by Steffen Höhne, 141–177. Wiesbaden: Harrassowitz, 2019.

Dimou, Augusta. "'Wir verwandeln uns in eine Kolonie fremdsprachiger Bücher': Das Buch als Kulturproblem im Jugoslawien der Zwischenkriegszeit." In *Kultur und Beruf in Europa* (Europäische Geschichte in Quellen und Essays, vol. 2), edited by Isabella Löhr, Matthias Middell, and Hannes Siegrist, 259–269. Stuttgart: Franz Steiner Verlag, 2012.

Djordjevic, Jovan. "Interest Groups and the Political System of Yugoslavia." In *Interest Groups in Four Continents*, ed. Henry W. Ehrmann, 197–228. Pittsburgh: University of Pittsburgh Press, 1960.

Dölemeyer, Barbara. "Urheber- und Verlagsrecht." In *Handbuch der Quellen und Literatur der neueren europäischen Privatgeschichte*, vol. 3/3, edited by Helmut Coing, 3955–4065. Munich: Beck, 1986.

Dölemeyer, Barbara, and Diethelm Klippel. "Der Beitrag der deutschen Rechtswissenschaft zur Theorie des gewerblichen Rechtsschutzes und des Urheberrechts." In *Gewerblicher Rechtschutz und Urheberrecht in Deutschland, Festschrift zum hundertjährigen Bestehen der Deutschen Vereinigung für gewerblichen Rechtschutz und Urheberrecht und ihrer Zeitschrift*, vol. 1, edited by Friedrich-Karl Beier, Alfons Kraft, Gerhard Schricker, and Elmar Wadle, 185–237. Weinheim: VCH, 1991.

Dommann, Monika. "Notieren, Aufzeichnen, Vervielfältigen: medientechnische Umbrüche von Musik im Urheberrecht." In *Ökonomien des Medialen: Tausch, Wert und Zirkulation in den Medien- und Kulturwissenschaften*, edited by Ralf Adelmann et al., 149–165. Bieledeld: Transcript, 2006.

Drucker, Johanna. "Industrialization of Print: Automation, Mass Production, Changes in Literacy, and Aesthetic Responses," in *History of the Book*, edited by Johanna Drucker et al., https://hob.gseis.ucla.edu/HoBCoursebook_Ch_9.html.

Ducreux, Marie-Elizabeth. "Langue et Histoire: L'Europe centrale entre l'érudition et la tradition, 1760–1810 (ou: quelques réflexions autour de Schlözer, Herder, Dobrovský et Dobner)." In *Est – Ouest: Transferts et réceptions dans le monde du livre en Europe (XVIIe–XXe siècles)*, edited by Frédéric Barbier, 263–282. Leipzig: Leipziger Universitätsverlag, 2005.

Durand, Pascal. "Éthos reproducteur et habitus techniciste: Naissance du 'modèle' éditorial belge francophone." In *Les mutations du livre et l'édition dans le monde du XVIIIe siècle à l'an 2000*, edited by Jacques Michon and Jean-Yves Mollier, 251–259. Paris: L'Harmattan, 2001.

Earle, Edward. "The Effect of Romanticism on the 19th Century Development of Copyright Law." *Intellectual Property Journal* 6 (1991): 269–290.

Eminescu, Yolanda. "Aktuelle Probleme des Urheberrechts der europäischen sozialistischen Länder." *Gewerblicher Rechtschutz und Urheberrecht*, Internationaler Teil 7 (1980): 387–396.

Erer, Nadine Güher. "A Short History of Copyright in the West, in the Ottoman Empire and in Turkey." *Türk Kütüphaneciliği* 28, no. 4 (2014): 638–644.

Eskenazi, Žak. "Prevodna hudožestvena literatura v Bălgarija (1878–1944): Izdateli, izdanija, klasifikacija." *Izvestija na narodnata biblioteka "Sv. Sv. Kiril i Metodii"* 21, no. XXVII (1993): 327–353.

Fernández, Pura. "El monopolio del mercado internacional de impresos en castellano nel siglo XIX: Francia, España y la 'luta' de Hispanoamérica." *Bulletin Hispanique* 100, no. 1 (1998):165–190.

Ferran, Jana. "Die Regelung der Musikurheberrechtsfragen zwischen Deutschland und Russland in den Jahren 1900–1917." *Iskusstvo muzyki. Teorija i istorija* 21 (2019): 69–88.

Ficsor, Mihály. "The Past, Present and Future of Copyright in the European Socialist Countries." *Revue Internationale du Droit d'Auteur* 118 (October 1983): 32–107.

Fillafer, Franz L. "Böhmen Transimperial: Die böhmische Jurisprudenz als Drehscheibe der zentraleuropäischen Wissenszirkulation." *Beiträge zur Rechtsgeschichte Österreichs* 12, no. 2 (2022): 163–180.

Forbes, Meghan L. "Advertisement as Collaboration in the Central European Avant-Garde Magazines." *Post: notes on art in a global context*, March 16, 2016. https://post.moma.org/advertisement-as-collaboration-in-the-central-european-avant-garde-magazines-2.

Foucault, Michel. *What Is An Author?* In *Aesthetics, Method, and Epistemology*, edited by James P. Faubion, 205–222. New York: The New Press, 1998.

Gergova, Ani. "Sădbata na bălgarskija avtor." *Izdatel*, no. 1 (1995): 12–15 and no. 2, 3, 4 (1995): 5–8.

Ghobrial, John-Paul. "Printing." In *Encyclopedia of the Ottoman Empire*, edited by Gábor Ágoston and Bruce Masters, 471–474. New York: Facts On File, 2009.

Gigova, Irina. "In Defense of Native Literature: Writers' Associations, State and the Cult of the Writer in Pre-1945 Bulgaria." *Slavic Review* 77, no. 2 (Summer 2018): 417–440.

Godechot, Olivier, and Jacques Marseille. "Les exportations de livres français au XIXe siècle." In *La Commerce de la librairie en France au XIXe siècle*, edited by Jean-Yves Mollier, 373–379. Paris: IMEC/Éditions de la MSH, 1997.

Götz von Olenhusen, Albrecht. "'Ewiges geistiges Eigentum' und 'Sozialbindung' des Urheberrechts in der Rechtsentwicklung und Diskussion im 19. Jh. in Frankreich und Deutschland." In *Festschrift für Georg Roeber zum 10. Dezember 1981*, edited by Wilhelm Herschel, Heinrich Hubmann, and Manfred Rehbinder, 83–111. Freiburg i. Br.: Hochschulverlag, 1982.

Götz von Olenhusen, Albrecht. "Lobbyisten für ein internationales Copyright im 19./20. Jahrhundert: Charles Dickens und Mark Twain im Vergleich." *UFITA* 80, no. 2 (2010): 401–415.

Gracz, Katarzyna. "Opposing the Expansion of Copyright Law: Social Norms in the Quest against ACTA and the 'Commodification of Knowledge and Culture Project'." In *Expanding Intellectual Property: Copyrights and Patents in Twentieth-Century Europe and Beyond*, edited by Hannes Siegrist and Augusta Dimou, 267–302. Budapest: CEU Press, 2017.

Granja, Lucia, and Valéria Bezerra, "Baptiste-Louis Garnier e Louis Hachette: contatos internacionais, direitos autorais e tradução." *Cadernos de Tradução* 43, no. 1 (2023): 1–26.

Haddad, Jonathan. "People Before Print: Gens de Lettres, the Ottoman Printing Press, and the Search for Turkish Literature." *Mediterranean Studies* 25, no. 2 (2017): 189–228.

Hartmann, Maj Antonie. "Towards a Global Copyright Law: Japan's Involvement in the Prewar International Copyright Negotiations." *Japan Forum* 34, no. 5 (2022): 601–623.

Heilbron, Johan. "Towards a Sociology of Translation: Book Translations as a Cultural World-System." *European Journal of Social Theory* 4, no. 2 (1999): 429–444.

Helfer, Laurence R. "Regime Shifting: The TRIPs Agreement and New Dynamics of International Property Lawmaking." *Yale Journal of International Law* 29 (2004): 1–83.

Hemmungs Wirtén, Eva. "A Diplomatic Salto Mortale: Translation Trouble in Berne 1884–1886." *Book History* 14, no. 1 (2011): 88–109.

Hesse, Carla. "The Rise of Intellectual Property, 700 B.C–A.D. 2000: An Idea in the Balance." *Daedalus* 131, no. 2 (2002): 26–45.

Hofmeister, Herbert. "Der österreichisch-sardinische Urheberrechtsvertrag von 1840." In *Die Notwendigkeit des Urheberrechtsschutzes im Lichte seiner Geschichte*, edited by Robert Dittrich, 239–251. Vienna: Manzsche Verlags- und Universitätsbuchhandlung, 1991.

Hoftijzer, Paul G. "The Dutch Republic, Centre of the European Book Trade in the 17th Century." *European History Online* (EGO), published by the Leibniz Institute of European History (IEG), Mainz, 2015. http://www.ieg-ego.eu/hoftijzerp-2015-en.

Höpken, Wolfgang. "'Durchherrschte Freiheit': Wie 'autoritär' (oder wie 'liberal') war Titos Jugoslawien?" In *Jugoslawien in den 1960er Jahren: Auf dem Weg zu einem (a)normalen Staat?*, edited by Hannes Grandits and Holm Sundhaussen, 39–65. Wiesbaden: Harrassowitz, 2013.

Höpken, Wolfgang. "Professionalisierung an der Peripherie: Juristen und Beamte in Bulgarien, 1878–1930." In *Professionen im modernen Osteuropa: Professions in Modern Eastern Europe*, edited by Charles McClelland, Stephan Merl, and Hannes Siegrist, 90–124. Berlin: Duncker & Humblot, 1995.

Horne, Janet. "'To Spread the French Language Is to Extend the *Patrie*': The Cultural Mission of the Alliance Française." *French Historical Studies* 40, no. 1 (2017): 95–127.

Jareš, Michal. "Autorské honoráře ve světle vzpomínek nakladatelů." In *"O slušnou odměnu bude počováno…". Ekonomické souvislosti spisovatelské profese v české kultuře 19. a 20. století*, edited by Tomáš Breň and Pavel Janáček, 145–150. Prague: Ústav pro českou literature AN ČR, v.v.i., 2009.

Kadir Yilmaztekin, Hasan. "The Legislative Evolution of Copyright in the Late Ottoman Empire." *Journal of Intellectual Law and Practice* 17, no. 1 (2022): 45–53.

Khan, Zorina B. "An Economic History of Copyright in Europe and the United States." https://eh.net/encyclopedia/an-economic-history-of-copyright-in-europe-and-the-united-states/.

Kiossev, Alexander. "Lists of the Missing." In *National Heritage – National Canon*, edited by Mihály Szegedy-Maszák, 23–36 (Collegium Budapest Workshop Series, no. 11). Budapest: Collegium Budapest, 2001.

Klippel, Diethelm. "Geistiges Eigentum: Privileg und Naturrecht in rechtshistorischer Perspektive." *Zeitschrift für Geistiges Eigentum* 7 (2015): 49–76.

Knap, Karel. "Grundzüge der persönlichkeitsrechtlichen Theorie im sozialistischen Urheberrecht." In *Benvenuto Samson zum 90. Geburtstag*, edited by Georg Roeber, Ernst Windisch, and Hans-Heinrich Schmieder, 99–122. Berlin: De Gruyter, 1978.

Knap, Karel, and Jiři Kordač. "Letter from Czechoslovakia." *Copyright* 17, no. 9 (September 1981): 248–262.

Kopeček, Michal. "Czechoslovak Interwar Democracy and Its Critical Introspections" (Forum: Demokratieverachtung / Contempt of Democracy in Europe). *Journal of Modern European History* 17, no. 1 (2019): 7–15.

Krejčí, Marek. "Stát coby patron umění? K státní kulturní politice v první polovině 20. století." In *"O slušnou odměnu bude počováno…". Ekonomické souvislosti spisovatelské profese v české kultuře 19. a 20. století*, edited by Tomáš Breň and Pavel Janáček, 130–144. Prague: Ústav pro českou literature AN ČR, v.v.i., 2009.

Krieger, Albrecht. "100 Jahre Revidierte Berner Übereinkunft: Eine rechtspolitische Zwischenbilanz." *Zeitschrift für Urheber- und Medienrecht* 10 (1986): 508–517.

Krneta, Slavica. "Zur Entwicklung des Urheberrechts in Jugoslawien." *GRUR International* 11 (1981): 663–669.

Kuhn, Annett. "Die Internationalen Verlegerkongresse von 1896 bis 1938: Arbeitsweise, Diskussionsschwerpunkte, Beschlüsse." *Leipziger Jahrbuch zur Buchgeschichte* 12 (2003): 285–299.

Lehmstedt, Mark. "Die Herausbildung des Kommissionsbuchhandels in Deutschland im 18. Jahrhundert." In *L'Europe et le livre: Réseaux et pratiques du négoce de librairie XVIe–XIX siècles*, edited by Frédéric Barbier, Sabine Juratic, and Dominique Varry, 451–483. Paris: Klincksieck, 1996.

Levitsky, Serge L. "Soviet Copyright Law at the Crossroads." *Review of Socialist Law* 9, no. 1 (1983): 5–33.

Lillova, Anna. "Bulgarian Tradition." In *Encyclopaedia of Translation Studies*, 2nd edition, edited by Mona Baker and Gabriela Saldanha, 354–361. London: Routledge, 1998.

Löhr, Isabella. "Geistiges Eigentum in Kriegszeiten: Der Schutz von Urheberrechten und die Berner Übereinkunft im Ersten und Zweiten Weltkrieg." *Comparativ* 16, no 5/6 (2006): 234–248.

Loué, Thomas. "Le Congrès international des éditeurs 1896–1938: Autour d'une forme de sociabilité professionnelle internationale." In *Les mutations du livre et l'édition dans le monde du XVIIIe siècle à l'an 2000*, edited by Jacques Michon and Jean-Yves Mollier, 531–543. Paris: L'Harmattan, 2001.

Luby, Stefan. "La protection des droits des auteurs dans la république socialiste tchécoslovaque." *Bulletin de droit tchécoslovaque* 3 (1966): 178–180.

Madl, Claire. "Pour une étude des choix de langue en milieu plurilingue: représentations et pratiques en Bohême á l'époque des Lumières." *Revue Historique* 667, no. 3 (2013): 637–659.

Marković, Predrag. "Where Have All the Flowers Gone? Yugoslav Culture in the 1970s between Liberalization/Westernization and Dogmatization." in *The Crisis of Socialist Modernity: The Soviet Union and Yugoslavia in the 1970s* (Schriftenreihe der FRIAS School of History, vol. 3), edited by Marie-Janine Calic et al., 118–133. Göttingen: Vanderhoeck und Ruprecht, 2011.

McGill, Meredith L. "Copyright and Intellectual Property: The State of the Discipline." *Book History* 16 (2013): 387–427.

Mollier, Jean-Yves. "La construction du system éditorial français et son expansion dans le monde du XVIIIe au XXe siècle." In *Les mutations du livre et de l'édition dans le monde du XVIIIe siècle a l'an 2000*, edited by Jaques Michon and Jean-Yves Mollier, 31–45. Québec: Presses de l'Université Laval/Paris: L'Harmattan, 2001.

Ochoa, Tyler T., and Mark Rose. "The Antimonopoly Origins of the Patent and Copyright Clause." *Journal of Patent and Trademark Office Society* 84 (2002): 909–940.

Orzoff, Andrea. "Das Personal und das Vokabular der Demokratie: Die Erste Tschechoslowakische Republik." In *Normalität und Fragilität: Demokratie nach dem Ersten Weltkrieg*, edited by Tim B. Müller and Adam Tooze, 436–462. Hamburg: Hamburger Edition, 2015.

Pahlow, Louis S. "Geistiges Eigentum." In *Enzyklopädie der Neuzeit*, edited by Friedrich Jaeger, vol. 4, 291–296. Stuttgart: J. B. Metzler, 2006.

Pahlow, Louis S. "Industrialized Music Brokers as Competing Market Players: The Administration of Music Rights in Germany (ca. 1870–1930)." *Popular Entertainment Studies* 6, no. 2 (2015): 56–70.

Pahlow, Louis S. "'Intellectual Property', 'Propriete intellectuelle' und kein 'Geistiges Eigentum'? Historisch-kritische Anmerkungen zu einem umstrittenen Rechtsbegriff." *Archiv fur Urheber- und Medienrecht* (UFITA), no. 3 (2006): 705–726.

Paker, Saliha. "Ottoman Conceptions of Translation and Its Practice: The 1897 'Classics Debate' as a Focus for Examining Change." In *Translating Others*, vol. 2, edited by Theo Hermans, 325–348. London: Routledge, 2012.

Paker, Saliha. "Ottoman Interculture: A Short Interview with Saliha Paker on Her Studies in Ottoman Translation History." In *Borders and the Changing Boundaries of Knowledge*, edited by Inga Brandell, Marie Carlson, and Onver A. Cetrez (Transactions, vol. 22), 209–218. Stockholm: Swedish Research Institute in Istanbul, 2015.

Pelanda, Brian. "Declarations of Cultural Independence: The Nationalistic Imperative behind the Passage of Early American Copyright Laws 1783–1787." *Journal of the Copyright Society of the USA* 58 (2011): 431–454.

Praznik, Katja. "Autonomy or Disavowal of Socioeconomic Context: The Case for Law on Independent Cultural Workers in Slovenia." *Historical Materialism* 26, no. 1 (2018): 103–135.

Praznik, Katja. "Wages For and Against Art Work: On Economy, Autonomy, and the Future of Artistic Labour." *Reshape*, December 8, 2020. https://reshape.network/article/wages-for-and-against-art-work-on-economy-autonomy-and-the-future-of-artistic-labour.

Püschel, Heinz. "Zehn Jahre Tagungen von Expertengruppen der Urheberrechtsorganisationen sozialistischer Länder." *Zeitschrift für Urheber- und Medienrecht/Film und Recht* 33 (1989): 23–28.

Raven, James. "British Publishing and Bookselling: Constraints and Developments." In *Les mutations du livre et l'édition dans le monde du XVIIIe siècle à l'an 2000*, edited by Jacques Michon and Jean-Yves Mollier, 19–30. Paris: L'Harmattan, 2001.

Ricketson, Sam. "Rights on the Border: The Berne Convention and Neighboring Rights." In *Copyright Law in an Age of Limitations and Exceptions*, edited by Ruth L. Okediji, 341–374. Cambridge: Cambridge University Press, 2017.

Rose, Mark. "Copyright and Its Metaphors." *UCLA Law Review* 50 (2002): 1–16.

Roueff, Olivier, and Séverine Sofio. "Intermédiaires culturels, territoires professionnels et mobilisations collectives dans les mondes de l'art." *Le Mouvement Social* 243, no. 1 (2013): 3–7.

Rudnicki, Walery. "La société polonaise des auteurs Zaiks." *Inter-Auteurs* 126 (1957): 120–125.

Rutar, Sabine. "Betriebliche Selbstverwaltung zwischen den Blöcken – und danach? Das Jugoslawische Modell in Rückschau und Perspektive." *Südost-Forschungen* 75 (2016): 118–135.

Sabev, Orlin. "A Virgin Deserving Paradise or a Whore Deserving Poison: Manuscript Tradition and Printed Books in Ottoman Turkish Society." In *The History of the Book in the Middle East*, edited by Geoffrey Roper, 143–164 (The History of the Book in the East). Farnham: Ashgate, 2013.

Sagot-Duvauroux, Dominique. "La propriété intellectuelle, c'est le vol! Le débat sur le droit d'auteur au milieu du XIXe siècle." *L'économie politique* 22, no. 2 (2004): 34–52.

Sajdi, Dana. "Print and Its Discontents: A Case for Pre-Print Journalism and Other Sundry Print Matters." *The Translator* 15, no. 1 (2009): 105–138.

Sapiro, Gisèle. "Propriétaires ou travailleurs intellectuels? Les écrivains français en quête de statut." *Mouvement Social* 214 (2006): 119–145.

Sayer, Derek. "How We Remember and What We Forget: Art History and the Czech Avant-garde." In *The Inhabited Ruins of Central Europe: Re-imagining Space, History and Memory*, edited by Dariusz Gafijczuk and Derek Sayer, 148–177. London: Palgrave Macmillan, 2013.

Scaglia, Evelina. "The 'Invincible Dualism' of the Italian School System: History of a 'Controversial' Relationship from the Casati Law Debate to Gaetano Salvemini's Interventions in the Early 20th Century." *Formazione, lavoro, persona* 38, no. XII (2022): 9–26.

Schwarz, Kathryn A. "Did Ottoman Sultans Ban Print?" *Book History* 20 (2017): 1–39.

Seckelmann, Margrit. "Schutz oder Monopolisierung von Ideen? Die Anfänge der deutschen Diskussion um das 'geistige Eigentum'." In *Ökonomien des Medialen*, edited by Ralf Adelmann et al., 127–148. Bielefeld: Transcript, 2006.

Sell, Susan. "Intellectual Property and Public Policy in Historical Perspective: Contestation and Settlement." *Loyola Los Angeles Law Review* 38 (2004): 267–321.

Sène, Henri. "Le dépôt légal et la législation sur le droit d'auteur au Sénégal: évolution historique et situation actuelle." *Les cahiers de propriété intellectuelle* 23, no. 1 (January 2011): 333–362.

Seville, Catherine. "Authors as Copyright Campaigners: Mark Twain's Legacy." *Journal of the Copyright Society of the USA* 55 (2008): 283–359.

Seville, Catherine. "British Colonial and Imperial Copyright." In *Research Handbook on the History of Copyright Law*, edited by Isabella Alexander and Tomás Gómez-Arostegui, 268–287. Cheltenham: Edward Elgar, 2016.

Siegrist, Hannes. "Professionalization/Professions in History." In *International Encyclopedia of the Social and Behavioral Sciences*, edited by Neil J. Smelser and Paul B. Baltes, 12154–12160. Oxford: Elsevier, 2001.

Siegrist, Hannes. "Professionelle Autonomie in der modernen Gesellschaft, Wissenschaft und Kultur." In *Professionen, Eigentum und Staat. Europäische Entwicklungen im Vergleich. 19. und 20. Jahrhundert*, edited by Dietmar Müller and Hannes Siegrist (Moderne europäische Geschichte, 8), 15–38. Göttingen: Wallstein, 2014.

Siegrist, Hannes. "Die Propertisierung von Gesellschaft und Kultur: Konstruktion und Institutionalisierung des Eigentums in der Moderne." *Comparativ* 16, no. 5/6 (2006): 9–52.

Siegrist, Hannes. "Strategien und Prozesse der 'Propretisierung' kultureller Beziehungen – Die Rolle von Urheber- und geistigen Eigentumsrechten in der Institutionalisierung moderner europäischer Kulturen (18.–20. Jh.)." In *Wissen – Märkte – geistiges Eigentum*, edited by Stefan Leible, Ausgar Ohly, and Herbert Zech, 3–11. Tübingen: Mohr Siebeck, 2010.

Şişmanoğlu Şimşek, Şehnaz. "The Yeniceriler of Ioannis Gavriilidis: A Palimpsest in Karamanlidika." In *Turkish-Speaking Christians, Jews and Greek-Speaking Muslims and Catholics in the Ottoman Empire*, edited by Evangelia Balta and Mehmet Ölmez, 245–275. Istanbul: Eren, 2011.

Spoo, Robert. "Courtesy Paratexts: Informal Publishing Norms and the Copyright Vacuum in Nineteenth-Century America." *Stanford Law Review* 69 (March 2017): 637–710.

St. Clair, William. "Metaphors of Intellectual Property." *In Privilege and Property: Essays on the History of Copyright*, edited by Ronan Deazley, Martin Kretschmer, and Lionel Bentley, 369–395. Cambridge: Open Book Publishers, 2010.

Stegmann, Natali. "The ILO and East Central Europe: Insights into the Early Polish and Czechoslovak Interwar Years." *Acta Universitatis Carolinae*, Studia Territorialia 1 (2017): 11–34.

Stern, Simon. "Copyright, Originality, and the Public Domain in Eighteenth-Century England." In *Originality and Intellectual Property in the French and English Enlightenment*, edited by Reginald McGinnis, 69–101. New York: Routledge, 2008.

Strauss, Johann. "Les livres et l'imprimerie à Istanbul (1800–1908)." In *Turquie, livres d'hier, livres d'aujourd'hui* (Etudes turques – USHS, 1), vol. 1, edited by Paul Dumont, 5–24. Strasbourg: Centre de Recherche sur la Civilisation Ottomane et le Domaine Turc Contemporain, Université des Sciences Humaines Strasbourg, 1992.

Strauss, Johann. "Who Read What in the Ottoman Empire (19th–20th Centuries)." In *The History of the Book in the Middle East*, edited by Geoffrey Roper (The History of the Book in the East), 471–492. Farnham: Ashgate, 2013.

Szyliowicz, J.S. "Functional Perspectives on Technology: The Case of the Printing Press in the Ottoman Empire." In *The History of the Book in the Middle East*, edited by Geoffrey Roper (The History of the Book in the East), 333–344. Farnham: Ashgate, 2013.

Ther, Philipp. "Das Europa der Nationalkulturen: Die Nationalisierung und Europäisierung der Oper im 'langen' 19. Jahrhundert." *Journal of Modern European History* 5, no. 1 (2007): 39–66.

Troch, Pieter. "The Intertwining of Religion and Nationhood in Interwar Yugoslavia: The School Celebrations of St. Sava's Day." *Slavonic and East European Review* 91, no. 2 (2013): 235–261.

Tziovas, Dimitris. "Residual Orality and Belated Textuality in Greek Literature and Culture." *Journal of Modern Greek Studies* 7, no. 2 (1989): 321–335.

Uchtenhagen, Ulrich. "Zur Geschichte der amerikanische Urheberrechts-Konventionen." In *Die Notwendigkeit des Urheberrechtsschutzes im Lichte seiner Geschichte*, edited by Robert Dittrich (ÖSGRUM, vol. 9), 252–275. Vienna: MANZ'sche, 1991.

Ulmer, Eugen. "Urheberrechtsfragen in den Beziehungen zwischen Westen und Osten." *GRUR International* 12 (1968): 406–413.

Vasilev, Ljuben. "Kritični beležki vărhu reformata na bălgarskoto avtorsko pravo." *Yuridičeski arhiv* 11 (1940): 247–270.

Verbuggen, Christophe. "'Intellectual Workers' and Their Search for a Place within the ILO during the Interwar Period." In *Essays on the International Labour Organization and Its Impact on the World during the Twentieth Century*, edited by Jasmien Van Daele, Magaly Rodríguez García, Geert Van Goethem et al., 271–292. Bern: Peter Lang, 2010.

Verdery, Katherine. "Konrád and Szelényi's Model of Socialism: Twenty-Five Years Later" (Symposium: Rereading the Intellectuals on the Road to Class Power). *Theory and Society* 34 (2005): 1–36.

Vesić, Ivana. "Radio Belgrade in the Process of Creating Symbolic Boundaries: The Example of the Folk Music Program between the Two World Wars (1929–1940)." *Muzikologija* 14 (2013): 31–55.

Vogel, Martin. "Die Entfaltung des Übersetzungsrechts im deutschen Urheberrecht des 19. Jahrhunderts." In *Die Notwendigkeit des Urheberrechtsschutzes im Lichte seiner Geschichte*, edited by Robert Dittrich (ÖSGRUM, vol. 9), 202–221. Viena: Manzsche Verlags- und Universitätsbuchhandlung, 1991.

Vogel, Martin. "Geschichte des Urheberrechts." In *Urheberrecht: Kommentar*, edited by Gerhard Schricker, 73–84. Munich: Beck, 1987.

Von Lewinski, Silke. "Copyright in Central and Eastern Europe: An Intellectual Property Metamorphosis." *Fordham Intellectual Property, Media and Entertainment Law Journal* 8, no. 1 (1997): 39–61.

Vuletic, Dean. "Sounds Like America: Yugoslavia's Soft Power in Eastern Europe." In *Divided Dreamworlds? The Cultural Cold War in East and West*, edited by Peter Romijn, Giles Scott-Smith, and Joes Segal, 115–131. Amsterdam: Amsterdam University Press, 2012.

Wadle, Elmar. "Entwicklungsschritte des geistigen Eigentums in Frankreich und Deutschland: Eine vergleichende Studie." In *Eigentum im internationalen Vergleich (18.–20. Jahrhundert)*, edited by Hannes Siegrist and David Sugarman, 243–261. Göttingen: Vandenhoeck & Ruprecht, 1999.

Wagnerová, Alena. "Max Brod als Übersetzer der Libretti der Opern Leoš Janáčeks." In *Max Brod (1884–1968): Die Erfindung des Prager Kreises*, edited by Steffen Höhne, Anna-Dorothea Ludewig, and Julius H. Schoeps, 251–264. Cologne: Böhlau, 2016.

Wandtke, Artur-Axel. "Entwicklungstendenzen des Urheberrechts in Osteuropa (unter besonderer Berücksichtigung der Gesetze in Polen, Russland, Ungarn sowie in Tschechien und der Slowakei)." *GRUR International* 7 (1995): 564–572.

Westren, Herceg Michael. "The Development and Debate over Copyright in Imperial Russia, 1828–1917." *Russian History* 30, no. 1–2 (Spring–Summer 2003): 145–223.

Wilfert-Portal, Blaise. "Traduction Littéraire: Approche Bibliométrique." In *Histoire des traductions en langue française, XIXe siècle 1815–1914*, edited by Yves Chevrel, Lieven D'Hulst, and Christine Lombez, 255–344. Lagrasse: Verdier, 2012.

Wittmann, Reinhard. "Was There a Reading Revolution at the End of the Eighteenth Century?" In *A History of Reading in the West*, edited by Guglielmo Cavallo and Roger Chartier, 284–312. Amherst, MA: University of Massachusetts Press, 1999.

Woodmansee, Martha. "The Genius and the Copyright: Economic and Legal Conditions of the Emergence of the 'Author'." *Eighteenth-Century Studies* 17, no. 4 (1984): 425–448.

Yosmaoğlu, İpek K. "Chasing the Printed Word: Press Censorship in the Ottoman Empire 1876–1913." *The Turkish Studies Association Journal* 27, no. 1–2 (2003): 15–49.

Yu, Peter K. "Currents and Crosscurrents in the International Intellectual Property Regime." *Loyola of Los Angeles Law Review* 38 (2004): 323–443.

Zagorov, Vasil. "Iz istorijata na avtorskoto pravo v Bălgarija (1878–1948)." *Biblioteka* 1 (2013): 25–34.

Zagorov, Vasil. "Knigoizdanie russkogo zarubežija v Bolgarii do 1944 g.: periodizacija – organizacija – problemii." *Izvestija viisših učebnih zavedenii*, no. 2 (2014): 65–78.

Zagorov, Vasil. "Lost in Translation or Lost in Publishing: Introduction of World Literature in Early Modern Bulgarian Publishing via Russian Language Editions." *Publishing Research Quarterly* 33, no. 2 (June 2017): 160–172.

Zagorov, Vasil. "'Prestăplenie i nakazanie' Reglementirane na otnošenijata avtor – prevodač – izdatel v Bălgarija za perioda 1921–1944 g." *Izdatel* 12, no. 1-2-3 (2010): 87–89.

Index

Abdülhamid II 108
Academy of Sciences 119, 124, 200, 215, 237
acquis communautaire 441
Act on Publication of a Book (alias, Literary Creation Act, Ottoman Empire, 1857) 109
adaptation(s) 9, 25, 41, 64-65, 99, 11, 129, 134, 195, 210, 253, 255, 258, 285, 367, 374, 385, 412, 438
Additional Protocol, Berne (March 20, 1914) 191, 339
AfmA (Anstalt für musikalisches Aufführungsrecht) 367
Africa 7, 143-144, 160
Agency-Author for the Protection of Author's Rights in the Kingdom of Yugoslavia (Agencija-Autor za zaštitu autorskog prava u kraljevini Jugoslaviji) 271
AKM (Gesellschaft der Autoren, Komponisten und Musikverleger) 329, 367
Albanians 106, 395, 401
Albini, Srećko 270-271, 275, 277-278
Alexander I (of Russia) 276
Algeria 144
All Slavic Choral Union (Sveslovenski pevački savez) 249
Alliance Française 168
American-Japanese treaty (November 10, 1905) 53
Americas 132, 147, 152, 167, 186, 338
Amsterdam 49, 106, 310
anglophone 144, 370
Anglo-Saxon 167, 407, 412
Annenkof 94
anticolonial 143
Apra (private copyright agency, Bulgaria) 223-224, 260
Arabic 104-107
Argentina 151
Armenian 106-107
Armenian Mekhitarist order 107
Armeno-Turkish 106
Asia xix, 14, 85, 104, 144, 154
Association of Authors of the Kingdom of Yugoslavia (Udruženje autora kraljevine Jugoslavije) 233
Association for the Protection of Literary and Artistic Property (Udruženje za zaštitu književne i umetnicke svojine) 232, 270
Association of Czechoslovak Publishers and Booksellers 309, 311
Association of Friends of Fine Arts "Cvijeta Zuzorić" 236
Association of Yugoslav Theatrical Authors (Udruženje jugoslovenskih dramskih autora, UJDA) 231, 275
Association of Yugoslav Music Authors (Udruženje jugoslovenskih musičkih autora, UJMA) 243, 271
Atanasov, Stojan (Bulgarian publisher) 43, 68, 205
audiovisual 15, 60, 220, 258, 260, 262, 346, 374, 385, 432

Ausgleich 77-78
Australia 40, 141, 183, 220, 258-259, 270, 429
Austria-Hungary 13, 70-71, 73-74, 80, 84, 87, 92, 155, 173, 176, 253, 356, 358, 433
Austrian civil code of 1811 (Kaiserliches Patent) 298
Austrian patent of 1846 77
Author-Central for Copyrights (Autor-Centrala za autorska prava) 271
authorial paradigm 12, 26, 62, 126
author-function 60
authorship/ co-authorship xiv, 25, 60, 101, 112, 126-128, 174, 187, 190, 213, 314, 326, 425
autonomy xiii, 138-140, 143, 231-232, 242, 244, 335, 336, 359, 380, 390, 392, 406, 409-410, 442
avant-garde(s) 61, 64, 169, 236, 337, 370-371, 373-374, 382, 403
avtorskoe pravo 100

Babović, Jovana 239-241
Bălgarski knižarski suiuz (Bulgarian booksellers association, 1897) 202-203
Balkan(s) 116, 120, 122, 129, 249, 349, 354, 357, 370
Baltics 170
Barbier, Frédéric 160, 166, 170
Bavaria 71
Beaumarchais, Pierre-Augustin Caron de 44
Bakarčić, Silvestar 271-273, 279-281
Belgium 28, 43, 83-84, 152, 156, 161, 163, 171, 312, 366, 424
Belle Époque 15, 161
belles lettres 63, 80, 93
Bellido, Jose 149, 151-152, 174, 263
Beneš, Edvard 297, 322, 358
Beneš, K.J. 333
Benjamin, Walter 374
Berlin Act (of the Berne Convention) / Berlin conference (1908) 6, 39, 53, 72, 142, 191, 258, 339-341
Berne Bureau 5, 163, 174, 181
Berne Convention for the Protection of Literary and Artistic Works (BC, 1886) 5, 6, 43, 55, 84, 136, 191
Bibliographie de la France 163
BIEM (Bureau international de l'édition musicomécanique) 282, 285
BIPRI (United International Bureau for the Protection of Intellectual Property) 433-434
Birnhack, Michael 11, 110, 126, 128, 141, 214, 262, 286
Bogdanov, Ivan 440
Bogdanović, Milan 233
Bogsch, Árpád 440
Bohemia 116-117, 119, 170, 289, 308, 325, 332, 342, 358, 424
Böhr, Josef 309
book market 12, 31, 80, 108, 124, 132, 168, 201-205, 318, 354-355
Booksellers' Union (1923, Bulgaria) 200, 203-204
Börsenblatt für den deutschen Buchhandel 163
Börsenverein des deutschen Buchhandels 80, 355
Booth, Marilyn 67
Bordeaux 167
Boytha, György 440
Braila 107, 200
Braunschweig 71
Brazil 86, 150-152, 168, 176

Bucharest xvii, 107, 118, 249
Buda / Budapest 107, 170, 268, 271
Bulaq (district of) 103
BUMA (Het Bureau Voor Muziek-Auteursrecht) 282
Bureau for the Protection of Industrial Property 254, 342

cabaret 181, 363
Cairo 103
calligraphy/ calligraphers 104-105, 427
Canada 40, 139-140, 429
canon (literary) 21, 97, 120, 182, 237, 412
canonization 8, 31, 83, 100, 120
Čapek generation 322
Čapek, Josef 317, 326
Čapek, Karel 317, 326
Čapek-Chod, K.M. 317, 324
Castilian (Spanish) 165, 167
Castle (Hrad) politics 322
Catherine II (of Russia) 322
Central Powers 172
Cervantes 68
Červinka, Adolf 318-320, 323
Cesta (weekly magazine, interwar Czechoslovakia) 296
Chase Act (1891) 91, 339
Chartier, Roger 338
Chateaubriand, François-René de 44
choreography 384-385
Činkov, P.K. 209-210
Circle de la Librairie 34
CISAC (Confédération International des Sociétés d'Auteurs et Compositeurs) 221, 246, 267, 271-272, 324
Cisleithania 78, 298
Claudel, Paul 44
Clemenceau, Georges 43
Club of Czechoslovak Composers, Publishers and Librettists (Klub československých skladatelů, nakladatelů a textařů) 330
Cold War 8, 382, 410
collective management organization (CMO) 16, 260, 329, 347, 351, 366, 369, 379, 419
collective rights administration 260
Collegium Musicum 236
Comédie-Française 135, 428
Cominform 394-395, 397, 400
commodity (exchange) 2, 60, 88, 279, 344
commodification 21, 33, 64, 119, 222, 279, 368
commons 30, 97, 198, 385
communism 334, 377-378, 380, 399, 402, 428, 435, 439, 441
compulsory license(s) 16, 258, 268, 292, 298, 310, 312-313, 328, 360, 380, 412
Concordia (journalists' and writers' union, Austria) 73
cordon sanitaire 148
cosmopolitan 22, 31, 47, 49-50, 67, 107, 116-117, 181, 202
Council of Science Act (Ottoman Empire, 1850) 109
counterfeit/ counterfeiting 7, 28-29, 37, 95, 153-155, 433
Cracow 74, 78
creative intelligentsia 228, 238-239, 386
creative funds 383, 390
creative labor xiii, 1, 30, 128, 203, 212, 239, 251, 378, 381, 389-391, 412, 420, 437
Criminal Code of 1858 (Ottoman empire) 110
Croatia/ Croatian 68, 117-119, 123, 170, 228, 231, 234, 247, 255, 342, 353, 356, 398

cross-cultural 179, 425
ČSR (Československá republika) 325, 411, 414, 422
ČSSR (Československá socialistická republika, Czechoslovak Socialist Republic) 411, 420
cultural small Entente 247
cultural world system 50-52
Cyrillic 107, 251
Czech Association of Booksellers and Publishers 300
Çuhaciyan, Dikran 110

Danov, Hristo G. 205
Danubian principalities 106
Danzig 176
Decembrist uprising (1825) 82
decolonization 147
de Maupassant, Guy 290-291, 347
de Silva Leal, Jose 41
Defoe, Daniel 68
Denmark / Danish 29-30
derivative work(s) / copies 26, 31, 45, 68, 417
Deutsch-österreichische Schriftstellergenossenschaft digitalization xv,
DILIA (Czech theatre and literary agency) 419
Directorate of Public Education (Ottoman empire) 112
Direkcija za zaštita na avtorskoto pravo (Office for Copyright Protection, Bulgaria) 389
disaster of 1898 152
Divan (literature) 65-66
domaine public payant 215, 306
drawing(s) 61, 98, 111-112, 154, 299, 328
droit de suite 316, 408, 413, 417
droit du savant / propriété scientifique 434
Droz, Numa 37-38, 155
Društvo Sv. Jeronima (Croatia) 234
Društvo za potporu iznemoglih srpskih umetnika i njihovih porodica 228
Dyk, Victor 309, 312, 323

East and Southeast Asia 154
EDIFO (Édition phonographique et cinématographique) 285
ΕΕΘΣ (Greek Company of Theatrical Authors) 363
Egypt 103, 107, 220, 366
Eirich, Theaterverlag (Viennese publishing house) 222-223, 275
encyclopedia(s) 164, 387
England 6, 166-167, 185, 310, 318
Engliš, Karel 294
engraving(s) 46, 111-112
Enlightenment/ enlighteners 40, 69, 86, 101, 103, 109, 113, 121-122, 125-126, 144, 147, 165, 195, 211, 240, 308-309, 315, 328, 331-333, 426
Entente 172, 178, 180
Estonians 93
extraterritorial 155

Far East 156
fascist 137
Fénelon, François 68
feuilleton 77, 316
fine arts 128, 236-238, 257, 314, 324, 419-420
Finland 129, 172, 176, 220
Fischer (Verlag) 78
folk (art, poetry) 65-66, 97-98, 125, 127, 198, 385, 408
folklore 95-97, 125, 128, 405

francophone 14, 144-145, 161, 166, 370, 429
Frankfurt Entwurf 72
Frankl, Otto 323
Franz I (of Austria) 79
free use(s) 212, 349, 351, 385, 406, 408
French-Japanese treaty (September 14, 1909) 154
French Revolution 44, 82, 136
French West Africa 143
Frič, Martin 421

Galicia 74, 170
Garnier, Baptiste-Louis 167-168
GATT (General Agreement on Tariffs and Trade) 7
Gautier, Théophile 61
GDT (Genossenschaft Deutscher Tonträger) 367
Gellner, Ernest 55
Gellner, Otto 320, 324
GEMA (Gesellschaft für musikalische Aufführungs- und mechanische Vervielfältigungsrechte) 329, 336, 367, 372
General Directorate of Cinematography (Bulgaria) 386
German Bund (Deutscher Bund) 43, 72
German Christian Social People's Party (Czechoslovakia) 309, 312
German Reich 13, 78, 81, 142, 342
Gesamtkunstwerk 61
Gesellschaft der Autoren, Komponisten und Musikverleger (Habsburg Monarchy) 73
Gewerbeordnung 80
Ghent system 294
Ghobrial, J. P. 102, 104
Glasunov 124
gramophone 15, 160, 181, 220, 259, 261-264, 345, 391, 425
graphic (arts) 61, 137, 216, 231, 253, 297, 301, 313, 315, 419
Great Britain 18, 97, 142, 153, 163, 339, 341
Greek Orthodox 107
großdeutsche Lösung 81
Guadeloupe 145
guild(s) 105, 135, 201, 293, 326-327, 335, 428
Gutenberg 1, 104

Hachette, Louis 33-35, 138, 168
Haiti 143, 171, 317
Hauptmann, Gerhart 127
Hebrew 106, 110, 126, 128
Helleno-Ottomanism 117
Hemmungs Wirten, Eva 19, 53, 62
Hemus (Bulgarian publishing house) 205-208, 210, 350
heritage 40, 96, 100
Hermann-Otavský, Karel 323-324, 343
Herrschaftsrechte 431
Hispanic 167
Hispanic America(s) / (Hispano)Americas 148, 167
Hoca, Nasreddin 107
Holland 161, 163, 220, 256
Homesteads 91
Hospodářská Politika 316
Hugo, Victor 44, 61, 362
Hundred Years' War 165
Hungarian copyright law of 1884 77, 252-253

Ianjoul, M. J. (Russia) 85
Ibero-America 167, 175
Ibsen, Henrik 127

ICCI (International Commission of Intellectual Cooperation) 433
ICIC (International Committee on Intellectual Cooperation) 364
ideology 4, 54, 128, 241-242, 244-246, 248-250, 252, 356-357, 371, 378, 391, 395, 399
Ignjatov (Bulgarian publisher) 204, 210
Ihrenew 88
IIIC (International Institute of Intellectual Cooperation) 364
ILO (International Labor Organization) 267, 364, 434
Immaterialgüterrecht 254, 292, 430
Imperial Society for the Encouragement of the Arts (Russia) 92
India 7, 40, 140-141, 145
Indochina 144
Indochinese Union 145
industrialization 20, 33, 48-49, 127, 137, 160, 169, 171, 325, 424
industrial (revolution) 5, 17, 33, 125
industrial property 137, 155, 172-173, 176, 191, 254, 342
information xv, 2, 5, 11, 17, 30, 63, 69, 99, 104, 112, 116, 123, 159, 163, 221, 273, 296, 302, 329, 331, 333, 369, 378
infringement 45, 68, 77, 96-97, 153, 194, 197-198, 207, 209, 213, 257, 261, 309, 314, 323, 330, 346, 351
Institute for National and Cultural Action (Yugoslavia) 251
intangible (goods, property) xv, 2, 62, 133, 146, 185, 261, 267, 343, 346
intellectual property rights/ IPRs xv, 1, 3-5, 7, 17, 159, 179, 185-186, 229, 270, 285, 337, 394
intelligentsia 13, 84, 95, 100, 125-126, 128, 199, 228, 238-239, 349, 354, 386, 392-394, 427, 431
intercultural 59, 62, 67-68, 134
intergovernmental 18, 151, 218
intermediality 15, 64, 425, 432
International Bureau of Weights and Measures (1875) 17
International Bureau (alias BIPRI) 433
International Confederation of Professional Intellectual Workers (Confédération internationale des travailleurs intellectuels) 364
International Congress of Publishers 163
international organization(s) 171, 182
International Telegraph Union (1865) 17
invention(s) 34-35, 127, 134, 139, 155, 219
Irish 161
Islamic 104-105, 109, 342
Istanbul 106-108, 110, 112, 118, 249
Italy/ Italian 28, 40, 79, 118, 163-164, 219, 256, 366, 424
iure conventionis 6, 177, 406

Janićijević, Milosav 231, 238,
Japan/ Japanese 39, 53-54, 142, 153-154, 156, 256
Jäger, Georg 121
Jewish 102, 107, 122
Joseph II (Austria) 79
July Monarchy 43
Jugoslovenska akademija znanosti i umjetnosti 119
jurisdiction 11, 14, 19, 86, 153-155, 242, 252, 268, 434
Jusautor 389

Kadlec, Karel 324, 343
Kaiserliches Patent (16.10.1846) 71, 298
Karadjordje dynasty 245

Kazanlăška Dolina (Bulgarian publisher) 205, 224
King Alexander (Yugoslavia) 242, 254, 276, 356
Kingdom of Sardinia 71
Kingdom of Serbs, Croats and Slovenes 225, 352, 356
Kingdom of Yugoslavia 225-226, 233-234, 239, 244, 255, 271, 436
Knap, Karel 440
KNIK (Science, Arts and Culture Committee, Bulgaria) 387, 389
Knižarska Duma 204
Knižarski suiuz v Bălgarija (Booksellers' Union of Bulgaria, 1923) 202, 203-204
Kohler, Josef 292
Komitet za kultura (Committee for Culture) 389
Kommissionsbuchhandel/Zwischenbuchhandel 169
Kon, Geca 121, 122, 287
Konrád, György 128
Konzessionspflicht 79
Koran 104-105
Korea/ Korean 142, 153, 155
Krleža, Miroslav 244, 352

Lamartine, Alphonse de 44
Langer, Stanislav 317
lateral cosmopolitanisms 67
Latin 19, 31, 49, 165, 167, 251
Latin America(n) 151-152, 166-167, 175
Latvians 93
Lausanne Treaty 176
Lebanon 143
League of Nations 15, 148, 152, 173-175, 268, 322, 364, 432-433
legal deposit (dépôt legal) 188, 434
Leipzig xvii, 80, 106, 118, 138, 161, 163, 169-170, 341-342
Lemberg 74, 78
Leopold II (Austria) 79
Lermina, Jules 32
Lex Herriot 320
library(ies) xvii-xviii, 34, 41, 44, 108, 119, 124, 130, 188, 205, 216, 295, 325, 332, 329, 349, 360
lingua franca 165
linotype 160
LITA (Slovak theatre agency) 419
literary-artistic councils (književno-umetnički odbori) 246-247
Literary Creation and Translation Act (Ottoman Empire,1870) 110
literary (and artistic) property 26, 37, 41, 43, 47, 153, 173-174, 191-192, 228, 232, 252, 270, 290, 339
lithography 45-46, 105, 160, 374
Lithuanian 424
Little Entente 322
Ljubljana 230, 234-235, 246, 270
lobbyism 293
Locke, John 398
London 28, 38, 40-41, 144, 161, 274
Loué, Thomas 163
Löwenbach, Jan 183, 303-307, 317, 320-321, 323-324, 327, 343, 358
Lykochine, Aleksander Ivanovich 90-92

Macedonian 402
Madagascar 144-145
magazine(s) 66, 77, 123, 164, 177, 190, 198, 201, 233, 296, 316, 328, 373
Máj (Czech writers' association) 74, 294, 297, 325, 358
manuscript xvii, xviii, 45, 99, 101, 104-105, 111, 133, 191, 209-210, 223,

239, 287, 298, 302, 304, 332, 346, 405
Marek, Rudolf 323
Mareš, František 311
Maria Theresia 79
Masaryk, Tomáš Garrigue 291, 295, 321
Matica 119, 228
Mayr-Harting, Robert 312, 335
Mauritius 145
Maximilian I (emperor of Mexico) 167
Mecelle (Ottoman Civil Code, 1869–1876) 342
mechanical reproduction (right) 259, 264, 285, 316, 374
Mehmed Ali of Egypt 103
Meiji Japan 171
mercantilism/ mercantilist 1, 43, 95, 144, 267, 338, 435
Meštrović, Ivan 245
metropolitan 7, 140, 143, 145, 235, 240
Mexico / Mexican 29, 167-168
Mickiewicz, M. 41, 120
Middle East 104
minimum protection 6
Miřička, August 323
Mitteleuropa 180
model contract 295, 378
modernity/ modernization 9, 12-13, 41, 47, 64, 66, 68, 81, 102-104, 109, 116, 129-130, 138, 171, 199, 202, 242, 347, 400, 403, 428
monotype 160
Monroe Doctrine 147
Montevideo treaty/convention 151
Moravec, Emanuel 332
Moravia 289, 325, 332
Morel, Henri 163
Moretti, Franco 165
Morris, William 61
Moscow University Press 124
movable type 46, 105
Mühendisyan, Ohannes 107
multicultural 69, 176, 426
multilateral/ multilateralism 5, 9, 14, 18-19, 52, 71, 84, 149-151, 156, 162, 172, 175, 335, 427, 432
Muslim 67, 103, 106-108, 395, 401
Müteferrika, Ibrahim 102

Nagy, Josip 270
national (domestic) treatment 5, 18, 21-22, 148, 339
nation-building 97, 125-126, 131, 135, 370-371, 427, 431
National Chamber of Culture (Bulgaria) 212
National Democratic Party (Czechoslovakia) 308-309
natural right(s) 27, 95
Naturalism 127
Netherlands 49, 155-156, 282-283, 366, 424
Neuilly conference/ Neuilly-sur-Seine 43, 176, 191, 210, 217
Neumann, Christoph 105
news/ newspaper(s) xx, 77, 89, 99, 103-104, 111-112, 123, 130-131, 164, 174, 198, 204, 209, 214, 257, 316, 328, 384, 403
non-francophone 144
non-governmental 163
non-Muslim 106-107
non-unionist 153, 173, 179
North and South America 147, 164, 186, 370
North German Confederation (Norddeutscher Bund) 43
Norway 29, 39, 129, 267, 306

notes (musical) 111
novel(s) 15, 34-35, 63, 65-66, 77, 108, 120, 132, 164, 316, 318, 328, 363, 373, 414
Nušić, Branislav 236, 287, 352

Old World 147, 253
Oceania 144, 160, 164
open access 97, 118
opera (comic) 82, 110, 130, 181, 200, 223, 236-239, 246, 259, 278, 281, 291, 343, 363, 374, 391-392, 401
operetta 73, 178, 181, 235, 247, 363, 374, 391
Opet, Otto 343
oral (culture, tradition)/ orality 66, 95-96, 97-98, 121-123, 130, 193, 198, 442
Ordnung für die Buchhändler in den kaiserl. Königl. Erblanden vom 28 März 1772 79
Original-Copy paradigm 45, 47
OSA – Ochranný svaz autorský (Association for the protection of composers, writers and publishers of musical works) 298, 323-324, 328-332, 336, 358-361, 365, 367, 419
Association for the Protection of Composers, Writers and Publishers of Musical Works (Ochranné sdružení skladatelů, spisovatelů a nakladatelů hudebních děl) 323, 329
Österreichisch-ungarischer Buch-, Kunst- und Musikalienhändler 73
Ostrovsky, Aleksander 363
Ottoman copyright law (1910) 110

Pahlow, Louis xviii, 292, 367
painting(s) 46, 61, 96, 236, 239
Paker, Saliha 67
Palestine 110
Pandektistik 430
pan-Slavic 117, 119
pan-American 147, 186
pantomime 384-385
paradigm shift 19, 36, 133, 425
Paris Book Guild 135
Paris Convention for the Protection of Industrial Property (1883) 176, 191
Paris Act of the Berne Convention (1896) 72
Paris Peace Conference 15, 176, 337
penny magazine 164
perpetual rights 349
Persian 65, 106
personal rights 4, 413
Persönlichkeitsrechte 430
Pest (Hungary) 118
Peter the Great (of Russia) 42
Pětka 322, 358
phonographic industry 258-259, 310
photography/ photograph(s) 45, 72, 128, 153, 199, 254, 374, 387
Pichl, Jiří 309
piracy/ pirates 8, 40-41, 47, 88, 95, 108, 131, 161-162, 167, 183-184, 213, 260-261, 317, 381
plagiarise/ plagiarism 112, 131
Platt-Simonds Act (alias, Chase Act, 1891) 91
plurilingual 13, 55, 70, 72, 116
p.m.a. (post mortem auctoris) 36
pocket book 33, 120, 164
Poland/ Polish 41, 74, 118, 148, 176, 247, 249, 363, 424, 439
polysystem 50, 66
Portugal 28, 41, 366
positive right 11, 89

post-war 173, 180-181, 184
post-World War I 43, 147-148, 159, 172, 225, 303, 335, 432-434
post-World War II xix, 8, 54, 147, 382, 394
Pouillet, Eugène 37, 42, 46,56
Pramen 296
primitive art 97
print-induced modernity 104
print revolution 104, 424
printing paradigm 45-46, 48
printing press 102-104, 107, 188
prisoner's dilemma 59
private-public dichotomy 261-262, 268, 345
private use 262
propriété intellectuelle 100, 179
propertization 221, 267, 279, 292, 298, 313, 335, 360, 368, 384, 386, 392, 404, 407, 409, 434, 440
prose 65-66, 98, 212, 296, 318, 362-363
protectionism 44, 58, 199, 230, 232, 241, 244, 284, 310, 324, 335, 346, 363, 365, 370, 436
Protectorate of Bohemia and Moravia 332
Protestant 169, 308
Proudhon, Pierre-Joseph 38, 398-399
Prussia 71, 169
public domain 2, 29-31, 43-44, 57, 83, 89, 131, 194, 290, 310, 381, 391, 405-406, 409, 420, 434-435
public performance (right) 99, 219-220, 257-261, 263-265, 282, 345, 418
Publishers' Circular 163
publishing contract 94, 99, 190, 295-300, 304-305, 315, 322, 326, 333, 359-360, 383, 387, 391, 407, 411, 414-415, 429, 435, 438
publishing industry 14, 82, 145, 169, 302, 304, 344, 425
Pushkin, Alexander Sergeyevich 100, 120
Pyrenees 167

race 42, 56, 167,
reading revolution(s) 48, 120-123
Realism 127, 321
record(s) 160, 264, 266, 285, 437
reciprocal treatment 31, 153
Reclam, Philipp 44
reform 78, 103, 119, 308, 400
regime shifting 148
Reichskulturkammer 212
reprint / reprinting 28, 31, 47-49, 77, 98, 109, 112, 161, 193-194, 198, 207, 260
reservation(s) 29-30, 38, 72, 77, 86, 143, 176-177, 179, 193-194, 253, 255, 270
res publica literaria 48-49
revision (treaties, conference) 6, 25, 39, 40, 60, 137, 142, 177, 217, 254-255, 258-259, 267, 327-328, 339-340, 373, 375, 388, 404, 406, 412
Revision Conference in Rome (1928) 142, 177, 255, 267, 327-328, 340, 373, 375, 404
revue 181, 274
Revue des deux mondes 138
Rieger, František Ladislav 343
Rikker 124
Rome Act of the Berne Convention (1928) 5, 137, 142, 254-255, 258-260, 267, 327, 340,
Romania/ Romanian 68, 106, 170, 176, 247, 255, 366, 402
Romanov 13, 69, 101, 426
Rosa y Bouret 168

Russian copyright law (1911) 95-96, 100-101, 193, 255, 351
Russian Geographical Society 92
Russian Publishers' and Booksellers' Union 101
Ruthenian 402

Sabev, Orlin 105
SACD (Société des Auteurs et Compositeurs Dramatiques) 282, 362
SACEM (Société des Auteurs, Compositeurs et Éditeurs de Music) 219-220, 271, 274, 282-283, 366-367
Saint-Germain-en-Laye (treaty of) 176, 253, 289-290
Salonika 102, 107
Samizdat 381-382
Sarajevo 246
Sassoon, Donald 161, 365
Saxony 71, 169
Scandinavia / Scandinavian 7, 18, 29, 31, 54, 129, 161, 163, 169
Scherschenevich (Russia) 94
script 104-106, 183, 251
Scottish 161
sculpture 96
Şişmanoğlu Şimşek, Şehnaz 67
self-management 335, 359, 392, 396-397, 399-401, 403-405, 407-409, 411
Semenoff, E. (Russia) 95
Senegal 144-145
seventeenth century 49, 52, 81
Seville, Catherine 138, 140
Sèvres, Treaty of (10.8.1920) 178
Silesia 170, 289
sixteenth century 81, 165, 169
Slavs / Slavic 78, 80, 96, 100, 119-120, 124, 155, 170, 180, 192, 200, 227-229, 249-250, 317, 324, 340, 351, 381
Slavonia 119, 123, 170, 353
Slovak 124, 308-309, 312, 402, 411, 419, 422
Slovenia 170, 353, 409,
Smrikarov, Mirčo (Bulgarian publisher) 209
social property 398-399, 406,
social rights 337, 364,
socialist copyright 128-129, 378-379, 383, 409, 438-439
Society of Art and Literature (Russia) 92
Society of Publishers, Music Publishers and Printers (Russia) 92
Sortimentsbuchhändler 80
source and target culture 64
Soutěž a tvorba 316, 323, 330
South America 144, 147, 151, 155, 160, 163-164, 176, 186, 340, 370
South Slavic Choral Union (Južnoslovenski pevački savez) 249
South Slavs 227
Soviet Russia 157, 292, 306
Soviet Union 8, 70, 292, 388, 395, 403-404, 409-411, 439-440
SOZA (Slovak collecting society) 419
Spaic, Svojslav 398, 407
Spassovich (Russia) 94
St. Clair, William 10, 97
STAGMA (German collecting society) 331
State Film Centre (Državna filmska zentrala, Yugoslavia) 252
state governance 404
Stationers' Company 135, 428
Statute of Anne 128, 137, 261
statutory right(s) / license(s) 88, 110, 269, 423, 435
stereotype 46, 160
St. Petersburg Society of Jurisconsults 88, 92

St. Petersburg Photographic Society 92
Strafrecht 91
Stražnicki, Milorad 254
Strindberg, August 61
substantive protection 76
Šuman, Janko 254, 342
Suvorin 124
Svatobor 294, 311
Switzerland 28, 38-39, 161, 163, 310, 366, 424
syndicalism 293
Syndicate for the Protection of Intellectual Property 154, 337
Syndicate of Czech Writers and Composers (Syndikát českých spisovatelů a hudebních skladatelů) 294-295, 318, 320, 323, 359
Syndicate of Czech and Slovak Authors 312
Synod 124
supranational xiv, 18, 22, 32, 62, 163, 185, 218, 283, 395
Sytin 124
Szelényi, Iván 128
talkies (talking pictures, sound films) 219-221, 252, 270, 274, 329, 345, 347, 353, 372

Tamizdat 381-382
Tanzimat 66, 102, 107, 109
Tărnovo Constitution (1879) 187, 190
technology/ technological xiii, xiv, 1, 14-15, 17, 23, 48, 93, 102, 105, 124, 137, 141, 146, 170, 181, 183, 199, 240, 251, 259, 266-267, 378, 388, 423, 432, 434
territorial rights 2, 20, 180
territorialization 2, 49, 180, 432
text-based culture 48
Tille, Vàclav 304-306, 324
Tolstoy, Leo 100, 127
trademark(s) 154-155, 172, 343, 410, 430
translation studies 12, 50, 59
transport 1, 30, 48, 159-160
Transylvania / Transylvanian 102, 170
Trialism 78, 117
Trianon (treaty) 176, 253
tribunaux territoreaux 153
TRIPS 7, 148
Tunis 143, 171
Tunisia 42, 145
Turgenev, Ivan 42
Turkey / Turkish xx, 65-66, 103, 105-109, 111-112, 116, 176, 175-178
Turkish-speaking Orthodox 107

Übersetzungsfabriken 63
USSR 438, 440
UFA (Universum-Film AG, German Film Society) 222
Ujakow 91
UK 141, 144
Umělecka Beseda 294, 297
Unesco 1, 147, 185, 407, 420
Union of Bulgarian Writers (UBW) 200-201
Union of Russian Authors 87
Union of Viennese applied crafts 73
Union of Writers of Yugoslavia (Savez književnika Jugoslavije) 234
unitarian 102
Universal Copyright Convention (UCC) 147, 152, 407, 440
Universal Postal Union (1874) 17, 149
universalism / universalistic xiv, 42, 44, 53, 163, 430, 437
Urheberrecht xv, 72, 100, 192

Uruguay 151
US / USA 73, 91-92, 103, 137, 139, 15, 156, 162, 167, 179, 181, 185, 291, 339, 363,
ustav o tsenzure 82
utilitarian 38, 91, 93, 128, 242, 264, 292, 378, 428, 435, 441

varieté 181, 372
Venice 49-50, 106-107
Verein der österreichischen Buchhändler 80
Verlagsbuchhändler 80
Verlagsrecht 95, 191, 298, 300
Versailles (settlement) 43, 148, 159, 171-172, 175, 177, 179, 184, 186, 337, 364, 431
Vertovyan, Agop 110
Vienna 50, 79, 106-107, 118, 170, 223, 230, 236, 249, 342
Viennese Operetta 73
visual (arts) 45-46, 61, 104, 237, 316, 417
Vojnović, Ivan 246
Vojvodina 170, 353, 402
von Gareis, Karl 292, 430
von Gierke, Otto 292, 430

Washington Act of the 1883 Paris Convention (1911) 191
westernization 66, 170
Western Europe 3, 48, 64, 67, 81, 88, 97, 107, 117, 121, 125-127, 133, 135-138, 160, 170, 180, 183, 326, 361-362, 365, 424, 427-428
Whitman, Walt 42
WIPO 7, 267, 433, 440
World War I 11, 13-15, 70, 81, 115, 120-121, 125, 168, 171-172, 174-175, 177, 179-181, 325, 394, 431-432, 435
World War II 211, 234
works (made) for hire 214, 299, 407, 409
Württemberg 71

Yilmaztekin, Hasan Kadir 109, 112-113
Yugoslav Joint-Stock Company for the Use of Authors' Rights (Jugoslovensko dioničko društvo za izkoriščivanje autorskih prava 271, 285-286

Zagorov, Vasil 197, 205, 213, 350-351
Zagreb 170, 228, 230, 233-236, 245-246, 254, 270-271, 275-276, 281, 356
ZAIKS (Związek Autorów i Kompozytorów Scenicznych)
Zapolska, Gabriela 363, 367,
Zensurpatent of 11 June 1781 79
Živkov, Todor 386, 392-393
Zola, Émile 85, 127, 362
Zurich 170
Zvon 394